A GUIDE TO FEDERAL AGENCY ADJUDICATION

THIRD EDITION

JEREMY S. GRABOYES
EDITOR

Section of Administrative Law
and Regulatory Practice
American Bar Association

AMERICAN BAR ASSOCIATION
Administrative Law and
Regulatory Practice Section

Cover design by ABA Design

Printed in the United States of America.

27 26 25 24 23   5 4 3 2 1

A catalog record for this book is available from the Library of Congress.

CONTENTS

CONTRIBUTORS

Michael Asimow is a Professor of Law Emeritus at University of California–Los Angeles Law School and the Dean's Executive Professor of Law at Santa Clara University School of Law. He edited the first edition of the *Guide to Federal Agency Adjudication* (2002) and contributed to the second edition in 2012.

George M. Cohen is the Brokaw Professor of Corporate Law at the University of Virginia School of Law.

Stefanie K. Davis is Deputy General Counsel and Ethics Officer at the Legal Services Corporation.

Matthew A. Gluth is an Attorney Advisor at the Administrative Conference of the United States. The views expressed in Chapter 16 are those of the author and do not necessarily represent the Administrative Conference or the federal government.

Jeremy S. Graboyes is the Research Director at the Administrative Conference of the United States. He serves as Vice Chair of the Adjudication Committee of the American Bar Association's (ABA's) Section of Administrative Law and Regulatory Practice. The views expressed in the Preface and Chapters 1, 12, 18, 21, 26, 27, and 28 are those of the author and do not necessarily represent the Administrative Conference or the federal government.

Daniel E. Ho is the William Benjamin Scott and Luna M. Scott Professor of Law and Director of the Regulation, Evaluation, and Governance Lab (RegLab) at Stanford Law School; Professor of Political Science at Stanford University; Senior Fellow at the Stanford Institute for Economic and Policy Research; and Associate Director of the Stanford Institute for Human-Centered Artificial Intelligence.

Jeffrey S. Lubbers is a Professor of Practice in Administrative Law at American University Washington College of Law.

David Marcus is the Vice Dean for Curricular and Academic Affairs and a Professor of Law at the University of California–Los Angeles School of Law.

Jerry L. Mashaw is the Sterling Professor Emeritus of Law and Professorial Lecturer in Law at Yale Law School.

Austin Peters is a graduate of Stanford Law School and a Ph.D. Candidate in Political Science at Stanford University.

Richard J. Pierce, Jr. is the Lyle T. Alverson Professor of Law at the George Washington University School of Law.

Gerald K. Ray was previously Deputy Executive Director of the Social Security Administration's Office of Appellate Operations.

Michael Sant'Ambrogio is a Professor of Law and Senior Associate Dean for Faculty and Academic Affairs at Michigan State University College of Law.

Bijal Shah is an Associate Professor and Provost Faculty Fellow at Boston College Law School.

Judith R. Starr is the Principal at Starr ADR, LLC and Director and Secretary of Suncoast Community Mediation, Inc. She was previously General Counsel of the Pension Benefit Guaranty Corporation.

Louis J. Virelli III is a Professor of Law at Stetson University College of Law.

Christopher J. Walker is a Professor of Law at the University of Michigan Law School. He previously served as Chair of the ABA's Section of Administrative Law and Regulatory Practice.

Matthew L. Wiener is a Lecturer in Law at the University of Pennsylvania Carey Law School. He was previously Vice Chairman, Acting Chairman, and Executive Director of the Administrative Conference of the United States. He is the Co-Chair of the Adjudication Committee of the ABA's Section of Administrative Law and Regulatory Practice.

FOREWORD

It is an honor to introduce readers to this essential guide to agency adjudication published by the American Bar Association (ABA). While labeled a third edition, it is really much more than that—a rethinking and expansion of the former editions into a comprehensive analysis of the field of administrative adjudication. As such, it has meaning not only for law students and practitioners but also for agency officials who must understand and comply with demands stemming from judicial and executive branch requirements in many new areas.

Before highlighting those areas, I want to acknowledge the authors themselves. This is an all-star lineup by any measure, with almost half of the contributors having produced textbooks and treatises in the field. They are acknowledged experts, and they show why throughout these pages. It is inevitable in these kinds of presentations that there will be overlap, which can be distracting. But in some ways repetition is beneficial to students learning the field. Several commentators, for example, discuss *Crowell v. Benson*, and in doing so, add new perspectives on that foundational case.

The most important new contributions revolve around questions of adjudicator integrity, constitutional challenges, and internal agency management. When the Administrative Procedure Act was passed in 1946, Congress's biggest concern was to make agency deciders (then hearing examiners, now administrative law judges (ALJs)) independent of agency control or interference. The act separates and restricts access to ALJs accordingly. For many years, this status was assumed. But challenges to decider integrity have now arisen thanks to recent U.S. Supreme Court and executive decisions. Professors Jeffrey Lubbers and Richard Pierce explain how the independence, if not the integrity, of ALJ hiring has been jeopardized by *Lucia v. Securities & Exchange Commission*, in which the Court found that Securities and Exchange Commission ALJs were constitutional "officers" for Appointments Clause purposes, and by President Trump's subsequent Executive Order No. 13,843, which moved the power to select and appoint ALJs from the Office of Personnel Management to agency heads directly. As they explain, neither the Court nor the president nor Congress has yet had the final word on this development, and there are still issues to be resolved.

When the appointment lens is broadened to include not just ALJs but all administrative judges (AJs, who are five times larger in number than the 2,000 ALJs), the independence problem grows dramatically. Professor Lubbers calls AJs "at-will" administrative judges, by which he means they can be removed as judges by their superiors, certainly not what one would call independence. It is true AJs would still have civil service protections more generally, but even that is not a guarantee in these times.[1]

This divergence in protections for decisional independence between ALJs (so far) and AJs has too long gone unaddressed as our authors suggest. Readers would do well also to read Professor Louis Virelli's contribution on administrative integrity and ponder upon what is at stake. ALJs are hired on politically neutral criteria (in that sense they are more objectively selected than federal judges). Agencies and the president now have the opportunity to honor that insulation—or not.

The other major innovation of this guide is its expanded focus on internal agency management. Subjects like management productivity, decisional quality, and institutional design have for too long been ignored by administrative lawyers, who see those subjects as the territory of business schools, not law schools. But the truth is that schools of public administration have always merged these fields, which are at the heart of administrative law and process. The instinct of lawyers is to turn first to the judiciary even when considering questions of administrative management, but the courts come in late and have never been good at the management game. Such matters are usually left to the agencies, which has created a vast administrative process world that the courts rarely see. Indeed, many administrative lawyers ignore such matters as well. Thankfully, the authors have done the opposite and opened up these important subjects for us to consider. Gerald Ray's contribution is especially relevant, as he explains from the perspective of the Social Security Disability Insurance program just how indispensable decisional quality is to administrative decisionmaking. Jeremy Graboyes's chapter on formats for participation in oral hearings provides additional insights into the importance of innovative administrative management.

1. *See* Max Stier, *The Patronage System Was Corrupt. It's Threatening a Comeback.*, Politico (Aug. 8, 2022), https://www.politico.com/news/magazine/2022/08/02/trump-civil-service-public-safety-00048796.

One of the unexpected benefits of the COVID-19 crisis has been the need for the administrative system to adjust its decisional formats, by using technology (including artificial intelligence) to decide cases and deliver services. Video and telephone hearings have replaced face-to-face ones, and big data analysis has empowered agencies to newly refined techniques of oversight. The pandemic having forced innovations on the administrative state, the crucial thing is not to backslide into old habits now that things are "normal." Video hearings, for example, have been shown to be more efficient than face-to-face hearings in many circumstances and just as reliable. Resistance to their continued use often stems more from lawyer shibboleths about the need for in-person deciding than logical thinking. The authors explore many of these subjects and offer up many good practice ideas for agency officials to digest.

I am sorry not to comment on all the fine submissions, but I can't end without mentioning one. Professor Jerry Mashaw has taught so much to those of us who study the administrative state. His typology of the goals that should motivate deciders in this sphere—professional treatment, moral judgment, and bureaucratic rationality—remains the best way to understand what inspires those who adjudicate administrative cases.

Finally, as the former chairman of the Administrative Conference of the United States (ACUS), I can't resist putting in a plug for my former agency. The ABA Section and ACUS have had a long and deep connection, including the creation of ACUS itself. Virtually all of the topics raised here have been the subject of ACUS recommendations that should be also considered by those in and out of government who want to understand the nuances of this complex world we inhabit. Fully 100 of the roughly 300 recommendations ACUS promulgated since its inception have dealt with adjudication.[2]

For a time, administrative adjudication was subordinated to interest in administrative rulemaking after the Supreme Court freed up the informal rulemaking process in the 1970s. But given the current critiques of the administrative state and the matters raised in this essential guide, administrative adjudication is once again assuming center stage. Welcome back.

Paul R. Verkuil
Chair, Administrative Conference of the United States (2010–2015)

---

2. *Recommendations*, ACUS, https://www.acus.gov/recommendations (last visited June 27, 2023).

PREFACE

Two decades ago, the American Bar Association (ABA) Section of Administrative Law and Regulatory Practice adopted a blackletter statement of federal administrative law.[1] That statement led to a series of guidebooks covering major topics of federal administrative law: *A Guide to Federal Judicial and Political Review of Federal Agencies*, *A Guide to Federal Agency Rulemaking*, and this *Guide to Federal Agency Adjudication.*

The first two editions of this guide—published in 2003 and 2012 and edited by Michael Asimow and Jeffrey B. Litwak, respectively—were intended as "handbook[s] to assist government and private counsel engaged in administrative adjudication under the federal Administrative Procedure Act (APA)." [2]

Since 2012, there have been significant changes in the law, policy, and practice of federal agency adjudication. Greater scholarly attention has also been given to the expanse of federal agency adjudication that takes place "outside the APA." And more than a decade of activity by the Administrative Conference of the United States (ACUS), an independent federal agency charged with improving administrative procedure, has resulted in a flurry of recommended best practices and new studies. These developments necessitated a new approach to the guide, and so this project was born.

This third edition covers nearly all of the topics addressed in the first and second editions, but it considerably expands the scope of the inquiry. New topics that this edition covers include:

- Constitutional challenges to federal agency adjudication, which have proliferated in the past decade or so and resulted in several important U.S. Supreme Court opinions

---

1. The Section Council approved the blackletter statement on November 3, 2001, and approved it as amended on February 5, 2012. The original blackletter statement was published in 54 ADMIN. L. REV. 1 (2002) and subsequently made available in two printed editions in 2004 and 2013.

2. A GUIDE TO FEDERAL AGENCY ADJUDICATION vii (Jeffrey B. Litwak, ed., 2d ed. 2012.)

- The wide world of "informal" adjudication—that is, adjudicative processes that are not governed by the formal-adjudication provisions of the APA
- The internal management and external oversight of federal agency adjudication programs, which have been the subject of numerous ACUS recommendations
- Developments in the use of technology to support and manage federal agency adjudication (e.g., video hearings, electronic case management, artificial intelligence)

While government and private counsel engaged in administrative adjudication under the APA will still find this guide practically useful, its focus on questions of institutional design will serve an expanded audience of executive and legislative branch policymakers, federal judges, academic researchers, nongovernmental organizations, advocates, and others who interact with federal adjudicative systems outside the adjudication of individual cases.

The first and second editions noted that errors and omissions are inevitable in a work of this scope with multiple authors. That remains true here. We also acknowledge, as the first two editions did, that readers may disagree with some of the propositions discussed here. While virtually every statement of law or fact in this book finds support in some authority, the topics addressed here cannot be fully examined without including at least some normative views and individual perspectives and opinions. The views, perspectives, and opinions expressed in each chapter are ultimately those of its author(s). Authors are identified at the top of each chapter.

We continue to welcome your suggestions to improve the next editions, especially as the law and practice of federal agency adjudication continue to evolve. Please send any input to the author of the chapter in question with a copy to Jeremy Graboyes.

Part I

Foundations of Federal Agency Adjudication

Chapter 1

What Is Federal Agency Adjudication?

Jeremy S. Graboyes

1.1 CHAPTER OVERVIEW

This guide provides an overview of "federal agency adjudication"—that is, a broad category of decision-making processes (adjudication) used within a specific institutional setting (federal agencies). This first chapter begins by defining "adjudication" and examining what it means for a federal agency to adjudicate (section 1.2). Next, it asks:

why does it matter? (section 1.3). That is, why is it important to discuss adjudication as a category of federal agency decision processes distinct from other processes for agency decision-making? It posits three key reasons why federal agency adjudication matters as a conceptual matter: (1) constitutional due process applies more readily in adjudication than in other federal agency decision-making processes; (2) adjudication is a statutorily significant form of federal agency decision-making; and (3) study of adjudicative systems reveals common basic elements of institutional design. As discussed in this chapter, those basic elements of institutional design form the skeleton for this guide (section 1.4).

1.2 WHAT IS ADJUDICATION?

1.21 Defining Adjudication as an Exercise of the Federal Executive Power

Black's Law Dictionary defines "adjudication" as the "legal process of resolving a dispute." This definition is overinclusive and underinclusive, because not all disputes are adjudicative and not all adjudications involve a dispute. A better definition is *a process for arriving at a decision that involves the application of generally applicable principles to particular facts.*[1]

Lots of institutions perform adjudication. Governments adjudicate. Nongovernmental entities like insurance companies, financial institutions, religious bodies, homeowners' associations, sports organizations, and philanthropic foundations do too. Within the federal government, the courts adjudicate "cases" and "controversies" through their exercise of "the judicial Power." But adjudication is not the sole dominion of the judiciary. Although Congress is most closely associated with lawmaking, it adjudicates cases involving "high Crimes and Misdemeanors" by public officials, and legislative branch agencies adjudicate copyright claims and government contract bid protests. And to "take Care that the Laws be faithfully executed," executive branch agencies adjudicate matters (and issue rules with legal effect). These functions have always been fundamental to what agencies do. As Justice Scalia explained:

> Agencies make rules ("Private cattle may be grazed on public lands *X*, *Y*, and *Z* subject to certain conditions") and conduct

1. *Cf.* Freytag v. Comm'r of Internal Revenue, 501 U.S. 868, 909 (1991) (Scalia, J., dissenting) ("It is no doubt true that all such bodies 'adjudicate,' *i.e.*, they determine facts, apply a rule of law to those facts, and thus arrive at a decision.").

> adjudications ("This rancher's grazing permit is revoked for violation of the conditions") and have done so since the beginning of the Republic. These activities take "legislative" and "judicial" forms, but they are exercises of—indeed, under our constitutional structure they *must be* exercises of—the "executive Power."[2]

Some federal agency adjudication can indeed look distinctly judicial, complete with agency subunits called "courts" (e.g., immigration courts), decision-makers in black robes called "judges" (e.g., administrative law judges (ALJs)), and "quasi-judicial" practices modeled on the Federal Rules of Civil Procedure and Federal Rules of Evidence. But an executive branch entity is not a court merely because it looks like one.[3] What primarily distinguishes executive branch adjudication from judicial branch decision-making (and executive branch lawmaking from legislative branch lawmaking) is (1) the institutional context in which it takes place, and (2) constitutional and customary constraints on its exercise.[4] Chapter 6 discusses that context and those constraints in greater detail.

Readers should be aware that what constitutes a "federal agency" can be a complicated question, at least at the margins.[5] For present purposes, the term encompasses most units of the federal executive branch, including the executive departments and independent agencies. This guide generally sidesteps discussion of certain authorities that, though probably within the executive branch, are often considered separately. These include military tribunals and certain "Article I courts" such as the Court of Appeals for Veterans Claims, Court of Appeals for the Armed Forces, and Tax Court. In addition, this guide largely overlooks the vital role that state and local governments, contractors, and nongovernmental entities play in adjudicating matters

---

2. City of Arlington v. Fed. Commc'ns Comm'n, 569 U.S. 290, 304 n.4 (2013); *see also* Oil States Energy Servs., LLC v. Greene's Energy Grp., LLC, 138 S. Ct. 1365, 1378 (2018); *Freytag*, 501 U.S. at 909–11 (Scalia, J., dissenting).

3. *See Oil States Energy Servs.*, 138 S. Ct. at 1378.

4. *See Freytag*, 501 U.S. at 909–11 (Scalia, J., dissenting); *see also* Paul M. Bator, *The Constitution as Architecture: Legislative and Administrative Courts under Article III*, 65 Ind. L.J. 233, 264–65 (1990).

5. *See, e.g.*, Dep't of Transp. v. Ass'n of Am. R.Rs., 135 S. Ct. 1225 (2015); *see also* Jennifer L. Selin & David E. Lewis, Admin. Conf. of the U.S., Sourcebook of United States Executive Agencies 8–16 (2d ed. 2018); Anne Joseph O'Connell, *Bureaucracy at the Boundary*, 162 U. Pa. L. Rev. 841 (2014).

under federal programs. These are all important topics worthy of a guide of their own.

1.22 Defining Adjudication under the Due Process Clause

Executive actions can be roughly divided into actions that involve the development of general legal principles and those that involve the application of those principles to particular facts. This division between what we now call "rulemaking" and "adjudication" is central to understanding how federal agencies exercise "the executive Power."

Administrative law casebooks typically begin by offering a pair of early 20th century U.S. Supreme Court cases to illustrate this division between rulemaking and adjudication and its constitutional significance: *Londoner v. City & County of Denver* and *Bi-Metallic Investment Co. v. State Board of Equalization. Londoner* involved an action by a local government body that levied a special assessment on a property to pay for improvements to an adjoining road. The Court held that the 14th Amendment's Due Process Clause required that the government provide the property owner notice of the action, an opportunity for a hearing, and an opportunity to present evidence.[6] *Bi-Metallic* concerned an action by a state government body that uniformly increased the tax rate for all properties in a jurisdiction. The Court held that such action did not implicate due process and that a property owner therefore had no constitutional right to notice or a hearing.[7]

The Court reasoned that due process required notice and a hearing in *Londoner* because the action at issue affected a small number of people and required individualized fact-finding. Due process did not require the same in *Bi-Metallic* because the action at issue affected a large number of people equally without consideration of individual circumstances. These cases teach us that due process generally requires notice and some kind of hearing for "quasi-judicial" action (i.e., adjudication)—at least where a protected life, liberty, or property interest is at issue—but generally does not require such protections for "quasi-legislative" action (i.e., rulemaking).

1.23 Defining Adjudication under the Administrative Procedure Act

Our modern understanding of adjudication derives from the foundational statute of federal administrative law: the Administrative

6. Londoner v. City & County of Denver, 210 U.S. 373 (1908).
7. Bi-Metallic Inv. Co. v. State Bd. of Equalization of Colo., 239 U.S. 441 (1915).

Procedure Act (APA). The APA is a blunt instrument. Like the Supreme Court in *Londoner* and *Bi-Metallic*, it cleaves the universe of administrative actions in two. There are "rules," formulated through a process called "rulemaking," and there are "orders," formulated through "adjudication." Under 5 U.S.C. § 551, a rule is "the whole or a part of an agency statement of general or particular applicability and future effect." An order is anything else,[8] at least anything that "contain[s] the element of final disposition."[9]

These definitions pose at least two practical problems. The first is that the APA's text does not clearly distinguish between orders and rules.[10] As a general matter, actions that have general applicability and future effect are rules, and actions that have particular applicability and involve fact-finding related to past circumstances are orders. But the APA treats certain agency actions with particular applicability, like ratemaking, as rules. And it treats certain actions with future effect, like licenses and cease and desist orders, as orders.[11] Even actions that are obviously particularized and backward-looking, and therefore clearly adjudicative, can be given prospective, rule-like effect when they are treated as precedential (see Chapter 5).[12] In most cases, there is no question whether an action is an order or a rule; either it is clear, or it does not matter. But when a question does arise and the APA's text supplies no clear answer, courts typically analyze the specific action to see whether it more closely resembles an order or a rule.[13]

---

8. 5 U.S.C. § 551.

9. Int'l Tel. & Tel. Corp. v. Loc. 134, Int'l Bhd. of Elec. Workers, 419 U.S. 428, 442–43 (1975) (quoting Attorney General's Manual on the Administrative Procedure Act 40 (1947) [hereinafter Attorney General's Manual]).

10. *See* Ronald M. Levin, *The Case for (Finally) Fixing the APA's Definition of "Rule,"* 56 Admin. L. Rev. 1077 (2004); A.B.A. Resolution 106B (2016); 106 A.B.A. Ann. Rep. 549, 783 (1981); Statement of the Administrative Conference on ABA Resolution No. 1 Proposing to Amend the Definition of "Rule" in the Administrative Procedure Act, 39 Fed. Reg. 4,849 (Feb. 7, 1974); 95 A.B.A. Ann. Rep. 548, 1025 (1970).

11. 5 U.S.C. § 551; *see also* Attorney General's Manual, *supra* note 9, at 42.

12. *See* Nat'l Lab. Rels. Bd. v. Bell Aerospace Co., 416 U.S. 267 (1974); Sec. & Exch. Comm'n v. Chenery Corp., 332 U.S. 194 (1947); *see also* Administrative Conference Recommendation 2022-4, Precedential Decision Making in Agency Adjudication, 88 Fed. Reg. 2,312 (Jan. 13, 2023).

13. *See, e.g.*, MacLean v. Dep't of Homeland Sec., 543 F.3d 1145, 1151–52 (9th Cir. 2008); Coal. for Common Sense in Gov't Procurement v. Sec'y of Veterans Affs., 464 F.3d 1306, 1316–18 (Fed. Cir. 2006); Nat'l Ass'n of Home Builders v. U.S. Army Corps of Eng'rs, 417 F.3d 1272, 1284 (D.C. Cir. 2005); DIA Navigation Co. v. Pomeroy, 34 F.3d 1255 (3d Cir. 1994); Shell Offshore, Inc. v. Babbitt,

The second problem is that adjudication under the APA is a behemoth, encompassing not only the judicialized processes that are universally considered adjudicative but also innumerable processes used, for example, to process initial applications for benefits, permits, grants, and loans; to allocate agency resources; to site government facilities; to investigate suspected regulatory violations; to perform inspections; to prepare environmental assessments; to manage federal lands; to auction spectrum rights and energy leases; to process records requests; to hire and fire federal employees; and to procure contractor services. Now *that* is an unwieldy category that probably includes the vast bulk of federal agency actions, which leads us to the next section.

1.24 Defining Adjudication as a Practical Matter

The term "adjudication" can be an amorphous one, simultaneously encompassing recognizably trial-like processes, mundane transactions like charging national park admission fees, and decisions with broadly dispersed effects such as the decision to route an interstate through a city park.[14] As a practical matter, people usually mean something narrower than the APA's vast definition when they talk about adjudication. A Congressional Research Service report offers one definition: "an agency action with the force of law that resolves a claim or dispute between specific individuals in a specific case."[15] Michael Asimow offers a similar definition: "a decision by government officials made through an administrative process to resolve a claim or dispute between a private party and the government or between two private parties arising out of a government program."[16] Notice the emphasis on a specific claim or dispute involving specific private parties. This definition, or something like it, is what most authors in this guide and others have in mind when they describe agency adjudication.

This definition excludes, most notably, processes for deciding matters of "policy implementation," to borrow a term from Professor Asimow. Policy implementation includes

---

238 F.3d 622, 629–30 (5th Cir. 2001); Phillips Petroleum Co. v. Johnson, 22 F.3d 1255 (3d Cir. 1994); U.S. Dep't of Lab. v. Kast Metals Corp., 744 F.2d 1145 (5th Cir. 1984).

14. *See* Citizens to Pres. Overton Park v. Volpe, 401 U.S. 402 (1971).

15. Ben Harrington & Daniel J. Sheffner, Cong. Rsch. Serv., R46930, Informal Administrative Adjudication: An Overview (2021).

16. Michael Asimow, Admin. Conf. of the U.S., Federal Administrative Adjudication outside the Administrative Procedure Act 8–9 (2019).

> priority setting, maintaining databases, allocating funds between programs, closing a post office, approving state Medicaid rate adjustments, administering grant-in-aid programs managed by states, managing public institutions such as hospitals or prisons, conducting environmental impact assessments, making decisions involving multiple uses of public lands, designating . . . public lands as national monuments or prohibiting mineral extraction, siting airports or power plants, and protecting habitats of endangered species.[17]

Because these types of decisions do not establish a legal principle with future effect, they are not "rules" for purposes of the APA. They are therefore "adjudications," at least for APA purposes, even though their outcomes do not have the same kind of particularized effect as decisions regarding whether a specific individual qualifies for benefits or violated the law. Most authors in this guide exclude such decisions in their analyses of federal agency adjudication.

Even excluding policy implementation, "adjudication" means different things to different people in different contexts. Some scholars, for example, draw a distinction between judicialized "adjudicative" processes, such as those presided over by ALJs, and less trial-like processes that they call "executive" or "frontline."[18] Examples of the latter type might include examining patent applications (subject to de novo review by the Patent Trial and Appeal Board), processing initial applications for veterans' benefits (subject to de novo review by the Board of Veterans' Appeals), processing Freedom of Information Act requests (subject to de novo review in the federal courts), administering citizenship or civil service examinations, making supervisory determinations regarding regulated financial institutions, and deciding to pursue regulatory enforcement actions in an administrative or judicial tribunal (or settling them).

Sometimes it makes sense to draw this distinction, for example when comparing comparatively judicialized and nonjudicialized procedures; at other times, it may not. As a statutory matter, though, there is no such distinction.[19] And Congress, agencies, and practitioners

---

17. *Id.* at 9–10 (internal citations omitted).

18. *See, e.g.*, Emily S. Bremer, *The Rediscovered Stages of Agency Adjudication*, 99 WASH. U. L. REV. 377, 382–83 (2021); ASIMOW, *supra* note 16, at 8–9; Edward Rubin, *It's Time to Make the Administrative Procedure Act Administrative*, 89 CORNELL L. REV. 95, 108–09 (2003).

19. *See* ATTORNEY GENERAL'S MANUAL, *supra* note 9, at 40–41.

often consider such processes adjudicative and may even refer to them as such. (The State Department "adjudicates" passport applications, for example, and the Veterans Benefits Administration "adjudicates" initial benefits claims.) As a practical matter, judicialized processes are inextricable from frontline decision-making; case intakes at the Board of Veterans' Appeals, for example, are the direct outcome of decisions made by veterans service representatives.

Another possible distinction concerns whether adjudication is a form of dispute resolution, involving definitive fact-finding and a legally binding decision rendered by a quasi-judicial officer, or whether it encompasses all individualized decision-making under a given administrative program. Consider the fact that alternative dispute resolution (ADR) modalities, such as mediation and arbitration, are often described as alternatives to, and therefore separate from, adjudication. Unlike traditional adjudication, ADR modalities typically leave it to parties to consensually resolve a dispute with the aid of a "neutral," who may or may not be a federal employee. But the Administrative Dispute Resolution Act (ADRA) makes clear that federal agency dispute resolution proceedings are part of "administrative programs," including programs that "involve[] protection of the public interest and the determination of rights, privileges, and obligations of private persons through . . . adjudication."[20] Although ADR modalities can be considered alternatives to traditional, often adversarial, adjudication, it is clear that ADR plays an important role in the overall administration of federal adjudicative programs (see Chapter 20).

1.3 WHY DOES ADJUDICATION MATTER?

"Adjudication" clearly means different things to different people in different contexts. But why does it matter? That is, why is it important to define "adjudication" and examine it as a distinct category of processes for federal agency decision-making? There are at least three responses. First, adjudication is a constitutionally significant form of decision-making. The procedural requirements of the Due Process Clause frequently turn on whether a government action is "quasi-legislative" or adjudicative (section 1.31). Second, adjudication is a statutorily significant form of decision-making. The requirements of the APA, in particular, turn on whether an action is a rule, formulated through rulemaking, or an order, formulated through adjudication

20. *See* 5 U.S.C. § 571(2).

(section 1.32). More generally, agency adjudicative systems are, as a class, characterized by distinct legal, managerial, political, and social features. As a result, we can meaningfully discuss the institutional design of systems of agency adjudication (section 1.33).

1.31 Adjudication Is a Constitutionally Significant Form of Decision-Making

The Due Process Clause of the Fifth Amendment specifies that no person shall "be deprived of life, liberty, or property, without due process of law." The application of this provision typically depends on two factors. First, it matters whether a government action is directed at a particular person rather than a class of persons. If an action is particularized, due process may require notice to the affected person, an opportunity for a hearing, and an opportunity to submit evidence. If an action is generalized, no such process is typically due under the Fifth Amendment. That is the lesson of *Londoner* and *Bi-Metallic.*

It also matters whether particularized action implicates "life, liberty, or property." As a practical matter, courts have treated all sorts of legal entitlements as property for purposes of the Due Process Clause, including rights to public benefits, public employment, public education, and basic utilities.[21] But courts have also found that certain interests do not constitute a "life, liberty, or property" interest protected by the Due Process Clause. Congress and agencies can still provide protections that mirror due process in such contexts, and they have often done so.

1.32 Adjudication Is a Statutorily Significant Form of Decision-Making

A second reason why adjudication matters is that the APA imposes different procedural requirements on rules and adjudicative orders. Here, it is important to note that, in addition to distinguishing between adjudication and rulemaking, the APA also sets forth formal and informal modes for each. With some exceptions, the formal mode applies when a statute requires a matter to be determined "on the record after opportunity for an agency hearing."[22] These are called the "magic

21. *See, e.g.*, Cleveland Bd. of Educ. v. Loudermill, 470 U.S. 532 (1985); Memphis Light, Gas & Water Div. v. Craft, 436 U.S. 1 (1978); Mathews v. Eldridge, 424 U.S. 319 (1976); Goss v. Lopez, 419 U.S. 565 (1975); Goldberg v. Kelly, 397 U.S. 254 (1970).

22. 5 U.S.C. §§ 553(c), 554(a).

words," because courts will usually only require formal adjudication or formal rulemaking when a statute employs this specific incantation or something like it. Mere reference to a "public hearing" is typically insufficient.[23]

For formal adjudication and formal rulemaking, which has all but disappeared, the APA requires a trial-like process, including the opportunity for an evidentiary hearing before an agency head or a special kind of adjudicator called an ALJ.[24] Informal rulemaking requires notice and an opportunity for submission of written comments.[25] For informal adjudication, the APA prescribes only minimal requirements applicable to all agency actions, such as the right to be represented, the right to procure copies and transcripts of data and evidence, and the right to receive prompt notice that an application or other request has been denied accompanied by a brief statement of the grounds for denial (see Chapter 17).[26] There are also differences in how courts review the orders and rules that result from these different formal and informal processes (see Chapter 27).

Formal adjudication is the paradigmatic form of agency adjudication. It is certainly the simplest to describe because a single statute, the APA, neatly sketches out its contours across programs administered by more than two dozen agencies. But formal adjudication is far from representative of the majority of adjudicative processes used by federal agencies. More common are "informal" processes that are not subject to the APA's formal adjudication provisions.

That an adjudicative process is "informal" for APA purposes does not mean that it is, in fact, informal. Some "informal" processes, such as those used by the immigration courts and the Patent Trial and Appeal Board, can be quite formal. The APA itself anticipates that other statutes might provide different procedures and that agencies might adopt additional procedures by rule.[27] This has led to the development of a three-part taxonomy for adjudicative processes:

- **Type A.** Type A adjudications include an opportunity for an evidentiary hearing that is governed by the APA's formal

---

23. John F. Stanley, Note, *The "Magic Words" of § 554: A New Test for Formal Adjudication under the Administrative Procedure Act*, 56 Hastings L.J. 1067 (2005).

24. 5 U.S.C. §§ 553, 554, 556–557.

25. *Id.* § 553.

26. *Id.* § 555.

27. *Id.* § 559.

adjudication provisions (5 U.S.C. §§ 554, 556–557) and usually presided over by an ALJ.

- **Type B.** Type B adjudications include an opportunity for an evidentiary hearing that, while required by statute, executive order, or regulation, is not governed by the APA's formal adjudication provisions and is often presided over by an adjudicator other than an ALJ (e.g., immigration judge, veterans law judge, administrative patent judge).
- **Type C.** Type C adjudications include no legally required opportunity for a hearing.

This division, proposed by Professor Asimow,[28] has become common in the literature. The American Bar Association used it in a resolution and draft legislation, and the Administrative Conference of the United States (ACUS) has used it in several recommendations.[29]

1.33 There Are Common Principles of Institutional Design for Adjudication

Federal agencies adjudicate an extraordinary range of matters, and the processes they use to do so are fantastically varied. That makes sense. There is no reason why an immigration court proceeding to determine whether an immigrant is eligible for asylum should be identical to the Fish and Wildlife Service's procedure for processing applications to import sport-hunted trophies. Nevertheless, all such processes take place within a common constitutional and institutional framework and share a common objective, in Professor Asimow's words again, to "resolve a claim or dispute between a private party and the government or between two private parties arising out of a government program."[30] Given these commonalities, we can meaningfully identify and discuss principles of institutional design for federal agency adjudicative systems.

This is no academic exercise. At some level, the most significant contemporary debates over federal agency adjudication are fundamentally design-oriented. Consider a few examples:

---

28. Michael Asimow, *The Spreading Umbrella: Extending the APA's Adjudication Provisions to All Evidentiary Hearings Required by Statute*, 56 Admin. L. Rev. 1003 (2004).

29. *See* A.B.A. Resolution 114 (2005); Administrative Conference Recommendation 2016-4, Evidentiary Hearings Not Required by the Administrative Procedure Act, 81 Fed. Reg. 94,314 (Dec. 23, 2016).

30. Asimow, *supra* note 16, at 8–9.

- Consistent with the Constitution, how should Congress and agencies insulate career adjudicators from political control and promote decisional independence?
- What role should political appointees play in adjudication, particularly in reviewing decisions rendered by career adjudicators?
- Should adjudication under a certain federal program be moved to another administrative agency, to an Article I court, or to an Article III court?
- What combination of procedures achieve the optimal balance of fairness, efficiency, and accuracy in a given program?
- Should there be more procedural uniformity across adjudicative programs?
- What impact do managerial tools, such as production goals and performance incentives, have on procedural fairness and decisional accuracy?
- How should agencies respond to systemic issues of decisional accuracy and interdecisional consistency in some high-volume adjudicative programs?
- What managerial tools can agencies use to address case backlogs and delays?
- What steps can agencies take to identify and correct burdens that may adversely affect individuals' ability to access benefits and services to which they are entitled?
- How do technological developments, such as the use of artificial intelligence and video hearings, affect the accuracy, fairness, and efficiency of agency adjudication?

These and other design-oriented questions are discussed throughout this guide.

1.4 HOW IS ADJUDICATION STRUCTURED?

Previous editions of this guide were "intended as a handbook to assist government and private counsel engaged in administrative adjudication under the [APA]."[31] While the practice of adjudicating individual cases remains an important subject, this third edition shifts its focus in light of the growing attention paid to constitutional questions and

31. A GUIDE TO FEDERAL AGENCY ADJUDICATION vii (Jeffrey B. Litwak ed., 2d ed. 2012).

the operation of widely varying processes that are not subject to the uniform principles of the APA's formal adjudication provisions. It tackles these subjects by focusing on six broad topics of institutional design, described in this section, which are common across federal agency adjudicative systems. Each topic receives its own part of the guide, which in turn are divided into chapters. I use the term "system" purposefully. Although individual adjudications take the form of discrete, linear processes, they take place within, and are influenced by, complex systems made up of an interconnected web of legal, political, policy, administrative, and social considerations.

1.41 Foundations of Federal Agency Adjudication

Part I introduces the legal, social, and administrative framework against which federal agency adjudication takes place. After Chapter 1, which you are currently reading, Chapter 2 provides an overview of the sources of legal authority governing federal agency adjudication. Chapter 3 delves deeper into constitutional questions, given their increasing prevalence and prominence in litigation. Chapter 4 explains how goals and values of agency adjudication—like fairness, accuracy, consistency, timeliness, and efficiency—can affect institutional design. Chapter 5 situates adjudication within agency programs more broadly, describing how individualized decision-making intersects with policymaking.

1.42 Delegation of Adjudicative Authority

Part II examines how Congress and agencies decide where to situate decisional authority. Chapter 6 focuses on Congress, asking why it vests adjudicative authority within the executive branch, within a particular agency, or with a particular agency official. Chapter 7 focuses on how agencies allocate adjudicative authority internally, focusing in particular on delegations of authority and the development of multistage processes for decision-making.

1.43 Adjudicators

Part III examines the agency personnel who preside over adjudications and resolve claims and disputes arising under federal programs. Chapter 8 introduces the role and authority of different types of adjudicators. Chapter 9 explores how agencies select, supervise, and oversee adjudicators. Chapter 10 addresses issues of adjudicator impartiality and integrity.

1.44 Parties, Other Interested Persons, and Representatives

Part IV examines the people, besides adjudicators, who participate in adjudications. Chapter 11 focuses on parties and other interested persons. Chapter 12 focuses on how the costs incurred in adjudication are allocated among participants. Chapter 13 addresses how agencies regulate the conduct of representatives. Chapter 14 examines important issues surrounding access to justice in federal agency adjudication.

1.45 Procedures

Every decision-making process employs some procedure. Naturally, those rules vary significantly across and sometimes within agencies. Part V begins with an overview of the constitutional and statutory foundations of adjudicative procedures (Chapter 15). The next several chapters address procedures used in frontline decision-making (Chapter 16), legal requirements for proceedings that do not involve a legally required evidentiary hearing (Chapter 17), proceedings that do involve a legally required evidentiary hearing (Chapter 18), appellate review (Chapter 19), and ADR (Chapter 20). The last two chapters of this part focus on the format for adjudicative proceedings, which can be conducted orally (Chapter 21) or in writing (Chapter 22).

1.46 Management, Oversight, and Coordination

Part VI examines how individual agencies manage their adjudicative programs, especially high-volume programs, and how outside entities oversee and coordinate them. Chapter 23 explores how agencies operate and manage adjudicative programs, and Chapter 24 focuses on an increasingly prominent approach to oversight called "quality assurance." Chapter 25 explains broader executive branch oversight of agency adjudication, focusing in particular on the role of the president. Chapter 26 addresses congressional oversight of federal agency adjudication. Chapter 27 addresses how the courts oversee agency adjudication, through review of individual cases and systemically. Recognizing that transparent government is foundational to effective external oversight, Part VI concludes by examining public access to adjudication-related records, information, and proceedings (Chapter 28).

Chapter 2

Agency Authority to Adjudicate and Sources of Law in Agency Adjudication

Matthew L. Wiener

2.1 CHAPTER OVERVIEW

This chapter begins with a threshold question (section 2.2): what is the source of an agency's authority to adjudicate? It then turns to its main subject: the sources of law that govern federal agency adjudications. It first addresses the main sources of substantive law (section 2.3) and then, drawing on other chapters, the main sources of procedural law (section 2.4). (Of course, the line between substance and procedure here, as in other areas of law, can be notoriously difficult to draw at the margins.[1]) Sections 2.3 and 2.4 for the most part order the presentation of each source by reference to where it sits in the hierarchy of authorities. Section 2.5 concludes by noting the statutory publication requirements for certain administrative sources of law discussed here. The legal status of these sources can depend on whether the agency has published them. A full discussion of disclosure is left for Chapter 28. As for constitutional provisions involving structural features of adjudication with which agencies must sometimes reckon, they are addressed in Chapter 3.

2.2 AGENCY AUTHORITY TO ADJUDICATE

Just as agencies must have statutory authority to issue rules with the force of law (legislative rules), they must have statutory authority to adjudicate cases (and, for that matter, do just about anything else). The question of statutory authority, however, is seldom at issue in adjudications. It is usually clear enough that the agency has authority to adjudicate. A statutory delegation to an agency to administer a program alone, even if it says nothing explicitly about adjudication, often carries with it implicit authority to adjudicate—and, as a matter of constitutional due process, the obligation to do so using certain procedures. Oftentimes a statute will explicitly authorize an agency to adjudicate, by providing, for example, that an agency may impose a civil penalty for some violation after providing a hearing.

The important statutory question in the adjudication context is usually not whether the agency has statutory authority to adjudicate but what procedures it must use when adjudicating. A central question that arises in several chapters of this guide is what language a statute must use to require an agency to comply with the Administrative Procedure Act's (APA's) formal hearing provisions.

One question of authority, though, does sometimes arise and will likely arise with increasing frequency in coming years: whether an agency has constitutional authority to adjudicate a case. Article III of the Constitution imposes some limits on Congress's power to assign cases to agencies rather than Article III-constituted federal courts for

1. The issue comes up most often when the issue is whether an agency rule fails within the exemption from required notice-and-comment rulemaking procedures for procedural rules under 5 U.S.C. § 553(b)(A). *See, e.g.*, Elec. Priv. Info. Ctr. v. U.S. Dep't of Homeland Sec., 653 F.3d 1 (D.C. Cir. 2011).

adjudication. What those limits are is not so clear. Chapters 3 and 6 address that issue.

2.3 SOURCES OF SUBSTANTIVE LAW

There are four main sources of law that provide the substantive rule of decision in most agency adjudications: (1) the Constitution, (2) statutes, (3) agency rules (legislative and nonlegislative), and (4) agency adjudicative precedents. Sources of law in various specialized adjudications, including those relating to international and foreign affairs matters, are not covered here.

2.31 The Constitution

Substantive constitutional law may not figure prominently in most agency adjudications, but it is an important source of law that must be noted. Agencies no less than courts and Congress are bound by the Constitution. An adjudication might require, for example, an agency to interpret a regulatory statute or legislative rule that regulates speech in some manner. Any interpretation must comport with the First Amendment and the fair-notice component of the Fifth Amendment's Due Process Clause. A notable example reflected in recent U.S. Supreme Court case law concerns the Federal Communications Commission's decisions applying federal law's prohibition on the broadcast of "indecent" speech.[2] Another notable example concerns the National Labor Relations Board's interpretation of statutory restrictions on employer statements involving employees' collective bargaining rights.[3]

2.32 Federal Statutes

Needless to say, the most common and usually the most important source of authority is a federal statute. Sometimes a statute directly provides the rule of decision in an adjudication. More often, the statute does so indirectly: the agency adjudicator directly applies a legislative rule that the agency has adopted through the rulemaking process, typically after notice and comment, on the basis of a statutory delegation of authority.

---

2. Fed. Commc'ns Comm'n v. Fox Television Stations, Inc., 567 U.S. 239 (2012).
3. *See*, *e.g.*, Int'l Union of Operating Eng'rs Loc. 150, 371 N.L.R.B. No. 8 (2021).

2.33 Rules—Legislative and Nonlegislative

As suggested, legislative rules often supply the direct rule of decision. Perhaps the most important point to note here is that, like statutes, legislative rules have the force of law. They impose obligations or confer rights on the agency and the private party alike.[4] Those obligations or rights will be enforced—against the private party or the agency—on judicial review (assuming review is available). It is sometimes said that, for this reason, legislative rules are "externally" enforceable.[5]

Next down in the hierarchy of authorities, but at many agencies of enormous importance, are nonlegislative rules and agency adjudicative precedents, which share similar attributes. Nonlegislative rules consist of agency statements of policy and interpretive rules—together often known as "guidance documents"—promulgated outside the APA's notice-and-comment process. Under the standard formulation, a policy statement announces how the agency will exercise its discretion in administering a statute or legislative rule; an interpretive rule announces how the agency will interpret a statute or legislative rule.[6] (Distinguishing between the two types of guidance can be difficult—especially when a single document partakes of both elements—and many agency officials do not even try to do so when naming or using guidance documents.[7]) Guidance documents can bear many different names and vary in their level of formality.

---

4. *See, e.g.*, Perez v. Mortg. Bankers Ass'n, 575 U.S. 92, 97 (2015); *see generally* Kristine E. Hickman & Richard J. Pierce, Jr., Administrative Law Treatise § 4.3 (6th ed. 2019).

5. *See, e.g.*, Gillian E. Metzger & Kevin M. Stack, *Internal Administrative Law*, 115 Mich. L. Rev. 1239, 1281 (2017).

6. *See, e.g.*, Administrative Conference Recommendation 2019-1, Agency Guidance through Interpretive Rules, 84 Fed. Reg. 38,927 (Aug. 8, 2019); Administrative Conference Recommendation 2017-5, Agency Guidance through Policy Statements, 82 Fed. Reg. 61,734 (Dec. 29, 2017); Nat'l Mining Ass'n v. McCarthy, 758 F.3d 243, 252 (D.C. Cir. 2014). *See generally* John F. Manning, *Nonlegislative Rules*, 72 Geo. Wash. L. Rev. 893, 917–18 n.129 (2004).

7. *See, e.g.*, Blake Emerson & Ronald M. Levin, Admin. Conf. of the U.S., Agency Guidance through Interpretive Rules 1, 9–12 (2019); Ronald M. Levin, *Rulemaking and the Guidance Exemption*, 70 Admin. L. Rev. 263, 266 (2018); *see also* Nicholas R. Parillo, *Should the Public Get to Participate before Federal Agencies Issue Guidance? An Empirical Study*, 71 Admin. L. Rev. 57, 60 n.6 (2019).

Guidance documents, unlike legislative rules, do not have the force of law.[8] They do not in and of themselves establish rights or duties for the agency or the private party to an adjudication. The agency decision must find its authority in a statute or legislative rule.[9] To illustrate: A complaint in an administrative enforcement action would not properly allege that the respondent violated a guidance document, and the agency's final adjudicative decision would not properly impose liability based on the respondent's violation of the document. Both the complaint and decision would identify the violation of a statute or legislative rule as the only basis of liability.

One important caveat, though, is necessary. Occasionally a (private) party to an agency adjudication will seek to invalidate a decision on judicial review based on the agency's failure to follow a guidance document. The question then usually becomes whether and when administrative law's *Accardi* doctrine,[10] which requires an agency to follow its own rules, applies to guidance documents. The predominant (and probably correct) answer appears to be "no," but the case law is shot through with inconsistency.[11]

---

8. *See, e.g.*, Hickman & Pierce, *supra* note 4, §§ 4.3.2, 4.4.1. Some commentators and judges contend, however, that a guidance document interpreting an ambiguous legislative rule in effect enjoys the force of law when it receives deference on judicial review. *See, e.g.*, *Perez*, 575 U.S. at 108–12 (Scalia, J., concurring); *see also* Kisor v. Wilkie, 139 S. Ct. 2400, 2443 (2019) (Gorsuch, J., dissenting).

9. *See, e.g.*, Administrative Conference Recommendation 2017-5, *supra* note 6; Administrative Conference Recommendation 2019-1, *supra* note 6. On the legislative-rule/nonlegislative-rule distinction, see, for example, Richard J. Pierce, Jr., *Distinguishing Legislative Rules from Interpretive Rules*, 52 Admin. L. Rev. 547 (2000); Thomas W. Merrill, *The* Accardi *Principle*, 74 Geo. Wash. L. Rev. 569, 602 (2007).

10. *See* Accardi v. Shaughnessy, 347 U.S. 260 (1954); *see also* Ariz. Grocery Co. v. Atchison, Topeka & Santa Fe Ry. Co., 284 U.S. 370 (1932). *See generally* Merrill, *supra* note 9; Elizabeth Magill, *Agency Self-Regulation*, 77 Geo. Wash. L. Rev. 859, 873–81 (2009).

11. *See, e.g.*, Merrill, *supra* note 9, at 592, 598; Magill, *supra* note 10, at 878; *see also* Metzger & Stack, *supra* note 5, at 1284. (One complication here is that much of the case law citing *Accardi* involves procedural rules. *See* Merrill, *supra* note 9, at 589.) A guidance document that gives rise to frequent litigation in this context (though mostly with respect to procedural issues) is the Social Security Administration's (SSA's) *Hearings, Appeals, and Litigation Law Manual* (HALLEX), https://www.ssa.gov/OP_Home/hallex, which provides guidance to SSA's hearing-level and appellate adjudicators—on both procedural and substantive matters—when deciding social security disability cases. *See id.* § I-1-0-1. The circuits have split on whether HALLEX can be enforced against SSA and, if so, on what grounds. *See* Timothy H. Gray, Note, *Manual Override?* Accardi, Skidmore, *and*

Although they do not have the force of law, guidance documents (especially interpretive rules) can play an important role in agency adjudication. They will bind, but only through internal administrative mechanisms (e.g., discipline), agency officials below the agency head (or the head's delegate), including prosecutorial staff (when deciding whether to initiate an adjudication) and adjudicators (when deciding cases).[12]

On administrative appeal, a guidance document does not bind the agency head.[13] But a party can certainly cite it, and an agency head can rely on it. An agency might be justified in relying on the reasoning of a guidance document (if it is adequately reasoned) in writing its decision;[14] the agency need not necessarily repeat its reasoning in an adjudicative decision. In this respect, the guidance document might be said to have some precedential effect, much like an adjudicative decision.[15] An agency cannot, however, deny a party a meaningful opportunity to urge the adoption of an interpretation at variance with the guidance document.[16] At the same time, an agency might need to explain its departure from the interpretation in a guidance document (at least one that represents the agency's authoritative position) to satisfy administrative law's reasoned decision-making requirement.[17]

2.34 Precedential Decisions

The fourth main source of authority is adjudicative precedents. These are adjudicative decisions issued by the agency (usually by its head or the head's delegate) whose holdings, unless and until overruled, bind

---

the Legal Effects of the Social Security Administration's HALLEX Manual, 114 COLUM. L. REV. 949 (2014); Frederick W. Watson, Comment, *Disability Claims, Guidance Documents, and the Problem of Nonlegislative Rules*, 80 U. CHI. L. REV. 2037 (2013).

12. *See* A.B.A. Resolution 100B (2019) (providing that agencies may require compliance with "official and authoritative agency guidance of general applicability"). *But cf.* Chapter 9, section 9.43 (discussing administrative law judges (ALJs)).

13. *See, e.g.*, Administrative Conference Recommendation 2019-1, *supra* note 6, § 3.

14. *See, e.g.*, Manning, *supra* note 6, at 929–37; Ronald M. Levin, *Nonlegislative Rules and the Administrative Open Mind*, 41 DUKE L.J. 1497, 1501–02, 1506–07 (1992).

15. *See* Peter Strauss, *Publication Rules in the Rulemaking Spectrum: Assuring Proper Respect for an Essential Element*, 53 ADMIN. L. REV. 803, 823–24 (2001); *see also* Manning, *supra* note 6, at 934.

16. *See, e.g.*, Levin, *supra* note 14, at 1502, 1504.

17. *See, e.g.*, Manning, *supra* note 6, at 935–36.

lower level adjudicators, much like the holdings of Supreme Court decisions bind lower federal courts.[18] They interpret—and, in some cases, can be said to establish policy under—statutes, agency rules, or agency precedents (see Chapter 5). They supply the rule of decision for the adjudicator. While binding on lower level adjudicators, they do not bind the agency itself, at least not in the same way as a legislative rule. A party to an adjudication may always ask the agency to overrule or modify a precedent on appeal, and the agency may do so freely, subject to administrative law's requirement of reasoned decision-making.[19] (An unexplained or inadequately explained departure from precedent will usually condemn an agency's decision on judicial review.[20]) In this respect, adjudicative precedents differ importantly from legislative rules. An agency must follow its legislative rules in an adjudication. Only through a procedurally valid rulemaking proceeding may an agency rescind or modify a legislative rule.

Whether an agency's adjudicative decisions are precedential depends on how the agency decides to treat them, whether by rule or decisional law. Some agencies treat all their adjudicative decisions as precedential. Others treat some decisions as precedential and others as non-precedential. A few agencies of note, such as the Social Security Administration and the Board of Veterans' Appeals, do not treat any of their decisions as precedential. The adjudicative rules of decision at agencies in this third category are supplied by statutes and detailed legislative rules, often as interpreted by guidance documents.[21]

2.4 SOURCES OF PROCEDURAL LAW

The main sources of procedural law are (1) the Constitution; (2) the APA and other statutes; (3) agency procedural rules; (4) agency adjudicative precedents; (5) adjudicators' orders; and (6) agency custom.[22]

---

18. Appellate review is addressed in Chapter 5.

19. *See* CHRISTOPHER J. WALKER ET AL., ADMIN. CONF. OF THE U.S., PRECEDENTIAL DECISION MAKING IN ADMINISTRATIVE ADJUDICATION 27 (2022).

20. *See, e.g.*, Fed. Commc'ns Comm'n v. Fox Television Stations, Inc., 556 U.S. 502 (2009); Allentown Mack Sales & Serv., Inc. v. Nat'l Lab. Rels. Bd., 522 U.S. 359, 374 (1998).

21. *See* Administrative Conference Recommendation 2022-4, Precedential Decision Making in Agency Adjudication, 88 Fed. Reg. 2,312 (Jan. 13, 2023); WALKER ET AL., *supra* note 19, at 26–31.

22. For a similar taxonomy, see Administrative Conference Recommendation 2017-1, Adjudication Materials on Agency Websites, 82 Fed. Reg. 31,039 (July 5, 2017).

Judicial decisions might be identified as another source of procedural law. This is especially true when an agency must decide what procedures to adopt to satisfy constitutional due process. As noted in section 2.41, courts give content to the meaning of "due process" under a case-by-case, policy-laden utility-calculus test (see Chapter 15). Even here, though, the role of judicial decisions can be overstated. Procedural design decisions implicating due process lie, in the first instance at least, with the agencies, and courts review their choices with more deference than the conventional account allows.[23]

Judicial decisions are otherwise a limited source of procedural law in agency adjudication. An important reason why is that, under the *Vermont Yankee* principle,[24] federal courts may not modify or add to the procedural protections of the APA, and those protections are minimal in most adjudications.[25] The judicial role is largely confined to interpreting an agency's own procedural rules, which often entails deferring to the agency's own interpretation of them.[26] Litigation is relatively uncommon here.

Brief mention should also be made of the president and presidential offices as sources of law (see Chapter 25). Whereas they have been an important source of (nonjudicially enforceable) law in the rulemaking context, they have not been in the adjudication context. A recent notable exception were several executive orders issued by President Trump. The most centrally concerned with agency adjudication was Executive Order No. 13,924, which directed agencies to "consider" certain broadly stated principles of "fairness" in enforcement and adjudication and to "revise their procedures and practices in light of them, consistent with applicable law and as they deem appropriate in the context of particular statutory and regulatory programs."[27] An implementing memorandum from the Office of Information and Regulatory Affairs in the Office of Management and Budget identified specific

---

23. *See* Adrian Vermeule, *Deference and Due Process*, 129 HARV. L. REV. 1890 (2016).

24. Vt. Yankee Nuclear Power Corp. v. Nat. Res. Def. Council, Inc., 435 U.S. 519 (1978).

25. *See* Pension Benefit Guar. Corp. v. LTV Corp., 496 U.S. 633, 653–56 (1990).

26. *See* Kisor v. Wilkie, 139 S. Ct. 2400 (2019).

27. 85 Fed. Reg. 31,353, 31,356 (May 20, 2020), *revoked by* Exec. Order No. 14,018, 86 Fed. Reg. 11,855 (Mar. 1, 2021); *see also* Exec. Order No. 13,892, 84 Fed. Reg. 55,239 (Oct. 9, 2019), *revoked by* Exec. Order No. 13,992, 86 Fed. Reg. 7,049 (Jan. 1, 2021); Exec. Order No. 13,891, 84 Fed. Reg. 55,235 (Oct. 15, 2019), *revoked by* Exec. Order No. 13,992, 86 Fed. Reg. 7,049 (Jan. 1, 2021).

procedures agency should consider adopting—all designed to enhance the fairness of adjudications for regulated businesses.[28] As the quoted language suggests, though, these directives were largely hortatory. They also resulted in few, if any, changes to agency procedures. In any case, President Biden rescinded Executive Order No. 13,924 (among others), and has not since addressed adjudication in a similar manner.

2.41 Constitutional Due Process

Nearly all federal agency proceedings that fall within the common understanding of an adjudication reflected in this guide (as opposed to the sweepingly broad definition in the APA itself) are subject to the procedural requirements of the Fifth Amendment's Due Process Clause. What particular requirements apply—that is, what process is due—in any particular case will depend, as Chapter 15 explains, on application of the balancing test of *Mathews v. Eldridge*,[29] which considers the precise nature of the interest affected by the agency action, the risk that it will be erroneously deprived by that action, the probable value of "additional or substitute procedural safeguards," and the government's interest. Application of this test, needless to say, is usually context-specific. Some cases call for a hearing resembling a judicial trial on the model of the formal hearing provided for in the APA; other cases call for a hearing of much less formality, even a paper-only hearing (see Chapter 22). (One common due process requirement identified in this guide is the provision of an impartial decision-maker, although, as discussed in Chapter 10, that requirement is limited and is seldom litigated.) When an agency follows the formal hearing provisions of the APA,[30] or a close approximation of them (as in many Type B adjudications), its adjudication will almost invariably satisfy due process requirements (see Chapter 15).

2.42 The Administrative Procedure Act and Other Statutes

As for statutory law, the APA supplies an important source of procedural law if an adjudication must be "determined on the record after opportunity for an agency hearing" and is therefore subject to the

28. Memorandum for the Deputy Secretaries of Executive Departments and Agencies from Paul J. Ray, Adm'r, Off. of Info. & Regul. Affs., M-20-31, Implementation of Section 6 of Executive Order 13924 (Aug. 31, 2020), https://www.whitehouse.gov/wp-content/uploads/2020/08/M-20-31.pdf.

29. 424 U.S. 319 (1976).

30. *See* 5 U.S.C. §§ 554, 556–557.

APA's formal hearing requirements. They provide for, among other things, a hearing before an administrative law judge (in most cases), an oral hearing at which parties may submits facts (through documents and testimony) and arguments, the separation of adjudicative and prosecutorial agency staff, cross-examination when necessary to develop the facts, the exclusion of irrelevant evidence, and a decision based on the exclusive record consisting only of evidence introduced at the hearing and hearing-related filings (see Chapter 18). The APA's formal hearing provisions also govern agency appellate review of a hearing-level adjudicator's decision, including the scope and standard of review (see Chapter 19). If an adjudication is not subject to the APA's formal hearing provisions, the APA supplies only a limited source of procedural law (see Chapter 17).[31]

Agency-specific (or organic) statutes can also supply procedural law in adjudications, whether by supplementing or modifying APA procedures or providing alternative ones. With a few notable exceptions, however, relatively few such statutes govern agency procedures in any significant detail.[32] They often say nothing on even such important matters as the nature of the required hearing or the availability and structure of internal appellate review. Perhaps their most important function is to dictate whether an adjudication is subject to the APA's formal hearing provisions (see Chapter 3, section 3.4; Chapter 15, section 15.33; and Chapter 22, section 22.2). Those that provide for formal hearings often include provisions that are largely redundant of the APA's and hence unnecessary.

Other statutes, while they may not provide a source of procedural rights or duties in individual adjudications, do affect how adjudications are conducted in ways often important to litigants. Examples include the Paperwork Reduction Act, which regulates the use of standard forms (common in many adjudication programs); the civil service laws, which may confer tenure protection, and thereby some limited decisional independence, on adjudicators;[33] the Freedom of Information Act (FOIA), which dictates what legal materials (e.g., rules, adjudicative decisions) must be made available to the public (see section

---

31. *Id.* § 555.

32. For exceptions, see 35 U.S.C. §§ 311–319 (Patent and Trademark Office inter partes review proceedings); 8 U.S.C. § 1229a (Department of Justice immigration removal proceedings); and the Veterans Appeals Improvement and Modernization Act of 2017, Pub L. No. 115-55, 131 Stat. 1105 (veterans' benefits).

33. *See* 5 U.S.C. § 7521 (for-cause protection for ALJs).

2.5);[34] and the Government in the Sunshine Act, which requires that certain adjudicative proceedings of multimember agencies be open to the public.[35]

2.43 Agency Procedural Rules

Most procedural law in administrative adjudication is provided administratively by the adjudicating agencies themselves. That is true even in adjudications governed by the APA's formal hearing provisions. The APA imposes important baseline fairness requirements for such adjudications (as previously noted), but it otherwise leaves to agencies the discretion to design their adjudicative procedures.[36] Agencies whose adjudications are not governed by the APA's formal hearing provisions are often left entirely free to do so, subject only to the important but limited constraint of due process (see Chapter 3, section 3.4).[37]

Most agencies set forth their public-facing procedures in formal rules—often called "rules of practice"—published first in the *Federal Register* and then in the *Code of Federal Regulations* (CFR). They resemble the Federal Rules of Civil Procedure and Federal Rules of Appellate Procedure in the subjects they address, though they tend to be considerably shorter.[38] (Rules of evidence, among other things, may also be found in such rules, although evidentiary rules are always less detailed than the Federal Rules of Evidence's.) The Administrative Conference of the United States has recommended that agencies "set

---

34. *See id.* § 551(a).

35. *See id.* § 552(b); Administrative Conference Recommendation 2021-6, Public Access to Agency Adjudicative Proceedings, 87 Fed. Reg. 1,715 (Jan. 12, 2022).

36. *See generally* Emily S. Bremer, *Reckoning with Adjudication's Exceptionalism Norm*, 69 Duke L.J. 1749 (2020).

37. Agencies that conduct what this guide calls "Type B" adjudications often use procedures that align with the APA's, except that they usually do not use ALJs to preside over hearings. *See* Michael Asimow, Admin. Conf. of the U.S., Federal Administrative Procedure outside the Administrative Procedure Act ch. 4 (2019). *But cf.* Bremer, *supra* note 36, at 1754.

38. *See, e.g.*, CFPB Rules of Practice for Adjudicative Proceedings, 12 C.F.R. pt. 1081 (2022); FCC Rules of Practice for Adjudicative Proceedings, 16 C.F.R. §§ 3.18–.83 (2022); NLRB Statement of Procedures, 29 C.F.R. pt. 101 (2022). See also Admin. Conf. of the U.S., Model Adjudication Rules (rev. ed. 2018), which provides model procedural rules through all stages of an adjudication, explains the alternatives available to agencies on specific subjects, and cites examples of agency rules.

forth all important procedures and practices that affect persons outside the agency" in CFR-codified regulations.[39]

Agency procedures often reside in less formal pronouncements than such CFR-codified regulations. These pronouncements can take many forms and bear many different names—practice manuals, handbooks, guides, freestanding website statements and explainers, model and compulsory forms, and so forth. Most of these pronouncements, however titled, will probably meet the APA's definition of a "rule."[40]

Not all rules have the same legal status. Some will bind the agency (as well as a private party when an adverse order is issued against it based on noncompliance with a procedural requirement) on judicial review of an adjudicative order. Others will not.

Distinguishing between the two can be difficult, in no small part due to widespread, long-standing inconsistency and confusion in the case law.[41] The case law is inconsistent even with respect to the doctrinal frameworks under which the issue should be addressed. The predominant approach is to apply the *Accardi* doctrine (discussed in section 2.33). But confusion and inconsistency still remain. One question that courts have not answered consistently (as suggested in section 2.33) is whether *Accardi* binds agencies only to legislative procedural rules or instead also to nonlegislative rules as well (sometimes lumped together, perhaps too imprecisely in the procedural context, under the label "guidance").[42] Assuming that the *Accardi* principle covers only legislative rules, another question obviously arises: what procedural rules count as legislative? One reason it can be difficult to answer the question is that an important marker of a substantive rule—namely, promulgation through the APA's notice-and-comment process—is not present in the case of procedural rules, because the latter need not be

39. Administrative Conference Recommendation 2016-4, Evidentiary Hearings Not Required by the Administrative Procedure Act, § 28, 81 Fed. Reg. 94,314 (Dec. 23, 2016); *see also* Administrative Conference Recommendation 2020-3, Agency Appellate Systems, § 2, 86 Fed. Reg. 6,618 (Jan. 22, 2021).

40. *See* 5 U.S.C. § 551(4).

41. *See generally* Hickman & Pierce, *supra* note 4, § 4.3; *see also id.* § 4.6 (distinction between substantive and procedural rules).

42. Some reserve the term "legislative rules" for legally binding substantive rules. The term here is used to cover both legally binding substantive and procedural rules. For examples of the more inclusive usage here, see, for example, Administrative Conference Recommendation 2019-6, Independent Research by Agency Adjudicators in the Internet Age, 84 Fed. Reg. 71,350 (Dec. 27, 2019); Merrill, *supra* note 9, at 602.

promulgated (or usually are not) using that process.[43] The prevailing test asks whether the rule evinces the agency's intent to bind itself. Most CFR-codified rules will usually do so.[44] Others rules may present more difficult calls.

There is, however, one important exception to the *Accardi* principle in the context of procedural rules that courts have recognized: an agency will be bound on judicial review only by those rules that confer important benefits on private parties to an adjudication—as opposed to rules governing internal agency affairs and the like—and even then only if the agency's departure from the rule substantially prejudices a party.[45]

2.44 Agency Adjudicative Precedents

Rules are not the only important source of agency procedural law. Another are precedential adjudicative decisions. An agency's "rule" on the standard of review governing an internal appeal of a hearing-level adjudicator's factual determinations, an agency's criteria for hearing appeals when appeals are discretionary, and any number of other procedural matters will sometimes reside only in (precedential) adjudicative decisions. Decisions can also provide evidentiary rules. The generally more important function of decisions here, though, is to interpret, and thereby give meaning to, sometimes vague or ambiguous rules of practice. If a rule is ambiguous, an agency's reasonable interpretation of it may well receive deference on judicial review (see Chapter 27).[46]

2.45 Adjudicators' Orders

Another source of procedural law are case-management orders. These orders, usually issued at the outset of the case, establish filing requirements, set deadlines, and the like. Some agencies issue standing case-management and similar orders that apply to all cases within a category. At least the latter type of order may qualify as a "rule" under the APA, but the terminology is unimportant.

---

43. *See* 5 U.S.C. § 553(b)(A).

44. *See, e.g.*, Merrill, *supra* note 9, at 592, 599–603; *see also* Hickman & Pierce, *supra* note 4, § 4.3.2.

45. *See* Hickman & Pierce, *supra* note 4, § 4.3.2; Magill, *supra* note 10, at 879. The foundational Supreme Court cases are *American Farm Lines v. Black Ball Freight Service*, 397 U.S. 532, 538–39 (1970), and *United States v. Caceres*, 440 U.S. 741, 754–55 (1979).

46. *See* Kisor v. Wilkie, 139 S. Ct. 2400 (2019).

2.46 Agency Custom

A final source of procedural law that cannot be ignored is agency custom. Procedural requirements or the interpretation of procedural requirements may be reflected only in a well-settled agency practice or custom rather than in any authoritative written pronouncement. This nonpositive customary law, as it might be called, is not binding in a strictly legal sense. But an agency might rely on it, if only impliedly, when interpreting positive law procedural authorities and, if it is sufficiently well entrenched, might need to explain departures from it to avoid acting arbitrarily and capriciously.[47] Whatever the exact legal status of agency conventions, practitioners new to an adjudication system would do well to familiarize themselves with them. Useful sources of information include internal (but usually publicly available) explanatory materials on agency websites, manuals and benchbooks prepared by and for hearing-level adjudicators and enforcement staff, and especially treatises and other reference materials prepared by private authors and professional associations like the American Bar Association.

2.5 PUBLICATION REQUIREMENTS

Chapter 28 notes what legal materials must be published, where, and under what statutory authority. For purposes of this chapter, it is important to recognize that the legal effect of the materials described previously may well depend on the agency's compliance with publication requirements, especially those in FOIA.[48]

FOIA requires that some documents be published in the *Federal Register.* They include, as relevant here, generally applicable substantive legislative rules, nonlegislative rules (i.e., policy statements and interpretive rules) of "general applicability formulated and adopted by the agency," and procedural rules. (None of the terms are defined.) Non-publication may have legal consequences. FOIA provides that a "person may not in any manner be required to resort to, or be adversely affected by," any such document unless it is published in the *Federal Register* (or unless the person has "actual and timely notice" of it).[49]

FOIA requires that an agency index and make certain documents available electronically, which means, as a practical matter, on their

47. *Cf.* Immigr. & Naturalization Serv. v. Yang, 519 U.S. 26, 32 (1996).
48. *See* Strauss, *supra* note 15.
49. 5 U.S.C. § 552(a)(1).

websites. These include "final" adjudicative "opinions," policy statements and interpretive rules that have been "adopted by the agency" but not published in the *Federal Register*, and "staff manuals and instructions to staff that affect a member of the public." None of these documents "may be relied on, used, or cited as precedents by an agency against a party other than the agency" unless it was indexed and electronically "published" (or unless the party had actual and timely notice of it).[50] One important result of this provision is that precedential adjudicative decisions regularly appear on agency websites (see Chapter 28, section 28.31).

50. *Id.* § 552(a)(2).

Chapter 3

Constitutional Foundations

Richard J. Pierce, Jr.

3.1 INTRODUCTION

There have been many controversies about the constitutionality of practices related to agency adjudication. As discussed in this chapter, the most prominent have been:

1. Can an agency, consistent with constitutional principles, adjudicate a particular dispute or class of disputes (section 3.2)?
2. Does a process for adjudicating a class of disputes comply with due process (section 3.3)?
3. Is the adjudicator neutral or unbiased, consistent with the requirements of due process (section 3.4)?
4. Does a congressional limitation on appointment, removal, or oversight of adjudicators by executive branch officials comply with the Constitution (section 3.5)?

The provisions that have been primarily implicated in those controversies include the Vesting Clauses, the Appointments Clause, the Take Care Clause, the Fifth Amendment right to due process, and the Seventh Amendment right to a jury trial in civil cases. Controversies sometimes also arise under other constitutional provisions, such as the First Amendment right of public access to certain government records and proceedings (see Chapter 28). This chapter provides a brief overview of especially notable constitutional questions.

3.2 AGENCY JURISDICTION TO ADJUDICATE

Because the Constitution does not confer any power on an agency, an agency only has the power to adjudicate classes of disputes that Congress has delegated to it. The Constitution limits the authority of Congress to authorize an agency to adjudicate a class of disputes in two ways.

First, the Seventh Amendment provides a right to a jury trial in "suits at common law." Types of disputes that were subject to jury trial in 1789 must be decided by a jury today in the context of a judicial proceeding. (The scope of the jury trial in 1789 was limited by the existence of a category of disputes that were considered to be equitable in nature.) This limits the power of Congress to authorize an executive branch agency to adjudicate disputes in which parties are guaranteed the right to a jury trial.

More significantly, the Constitution vests the "judicial Power" in Article III courts.[1] This limits the authority of Congress to authorize an agency to adjudicate disputes involving the exercise of the judicial power. Traditionally, the starting point in deciding whether Congress can authorize an agency to adjudicate a class of disputes that arguably involves the judicial power is to decide whether the disputes involve "private rights" or "public rights."[2] Generally, the U.S. Supreme Court has characterized a class of disputes as involving the adjudication of private rights if the rights at stake existed in 1789 and were adjudicated by Article III courts at that time. If so, Article III generally prohibits Congress from reallocating the power to adjudicate that class of disputes to agencies. By contrast, if the rights at stake in the disputes did not exist in 1789, the Court characterizes them as public-rights disputes that can be assigned to agencies to adjudicate.

The Court has, however, on three occasions upheld congressional decisions to authorize agencies to adjudicate classes of disputes that seem to involve private rights. The first, *Crowell v. Benson*, involved the reallocation of disputes involving longshore and harbor workers' tort actions against their employers to an agency. Since that class of disputes existed and was adjudicated by Article III courts in 1789, the Court concluded that the disputes involved private rights. The Court

1. U.S. Const. art. III, § 1.
2. Murray's Lessee v. Hoboken Land & Improvement Co., 59 U.S. 272 (1856).

held that it was nevertheless permissible for Congress to reallocate that class of disputes to an agency.[3]

The Court's holding in *Crowell* rested on the nature of judicial review of agency actions at the time. In 1932, a court could engage in plenary de novo review of all agency findings of "constitutional facts" and "jurisdictional facts." Since clever lawyers were able to persuade courts that many of the findings of fact made by agencies in adjudications fell in one of those two categories, courts were often free to conduct a whole new trial. Agencies therefore seemed to be performing limited tasks similar to those that special masters had long performed. The agency seemed to merely conduct a preliminary hearing and make tentative findings of fact, thereby leaving Article III judges with the ultimate power to adjudicate the dispute.

But this form of judicial review did not survive much longer after *Crowell* was decided. It was inefficient to have two evidentiary hearings to adjudicate disputes, and so the Court abandoned the "constitutional fact" and "jurisdictional fact" doctrines just a few years later. The Court acquiesced enthusiastically in the limited appellate review model that Congress incorporated in the Administrative Procedure Act (APA) in 1946 (see Chapter 27). As a result, the Court can no longer use the reasoning it used in *Crowell* to justify a decision to reallocate a class of adjudications of private disputes from courts to agencies.

Two more recent cases reflect the current state of the law. The first, *Commodity Futures Trading Commission v. Schor*, asked whether the Commodity Futures Trading Commission (CFTC) could adjudicate the common-law counterclaims that are often raised by parties who are accused of violating the statute that the CFTC is responsible for implementing. It made a lot of sense from an efficiency perspective to allow the CFTC to resolve those disputes since they are usually based on the same set of disputed facts as the statutory enforcement disputes. On the other hand, doing so seemed to involve reallocation of authority to adjudicate a class of private-rights disputes from Article III courts to an agency. The Court upheld the power of CFTC to adjudicate the common-law counterclaims.[4]

The second case, *Thomas v. Union Carbide Agricultural Products*, also involved a class of private-rights disputes that arose out of a regulatory regime that the agency was assigned to implement. For reasons of efficiency, applicants for licenses often want to rely on studies that a

3. Crowell v. Benson, 285 U.S. 22 (1932).
4. Commodity Futures Trading Comm'n v. Schor, 478 U.S. 833 (1986).

prior successful applicant conducted and submitted to an agency. But if the agency allows the second applicant to rely on the first applicant's studies, it has taken the first applicant's property. The government must provide some means through which the first applicant can receive just compensation for the use of its property. In *Union Carbide*, the Environmental Protection Agency used agency-supervised arbitration to determine the amount of compensation the second applicant must pay the first applicant. Again, the Court upheld this exercise of adjudicative power by an agency even though the right involved seemed to be a private right.[5]

Constitutional law scholars were perplexed by the contrast between these two cases and several other cases in which the Court held that seemingly similar congressional decisions to reallocate adjudication of private-rights disputes from Article III courts to bankruptcy courts were unconstitutional.[6] The Court finally explained that although Congress cannot reallocate the power to adjudicate a class of private-rights disputes from Article III courts to any other tribunal, it can, through a narrow exception, permit agencies to adjudicate private-rights disputes "in which the claim at issue derives from a federal regulatory scheme, or in which resolution of the claim by an expert government agency is deemed essential to a limited regulatory objective within the agency's authority."[7] The Court explained that what makes a right "public" is that the right is integrally related to a particular federal government action.[8]

The Court today often finds rights that are subject to agency adjudication and integral to a regulatory regime to be "public" and thereby upholds the decision of Congress to allocate power to adjudicate such rights to agencies.[9]

3.3 FAIR PROCEDURE

The Fifth Amendment requires that the government must provide someone with due process of law before it can deprive the person of "life, liberty, or property." Due process can require an agency to

5. Thomas v. Union Carbide Agric. Prods., 473 U.S. 568 (1985).

6. *E.g.*, Granfinanciera, S.A. v. Nordberg, 492 U.S. 33 (1989); N. Pipeline Constr. Co. v. Marathon Pipe Line Co., 458 U.S. 50 (1982).

7. Stern v. Marshall, 564 U.S. 462, 490–91 (2011).

8. *Id.*

9. *See, e.g.*, Oil States Energy Servs., LLC v. Greene's Energy Grp., LLC, 138 S. Ct. 1365 (2018).

use a wide range of decision-making procedures, depending on the outcome of a balancing test in which a court considers three factors: (1) the importance of the interest at stake; (2) the risk of an error in fact-finding using the procedures the agency provides and the increase in accuracy that would result from changing those procedures; and (3) the cost to the government of changing the procedures used by the agency.[10]

Sections 554, 556, and 557 of the APA require an agency to use procedures that include most of the procedural safeguards, including an opportunity for an evidentiary hearing, that are available in a bench trial in a federal court. Adjudications to which those procedures apply are often referred to as "formal." Those sections only apply, however, when an agency conducts an adjudication under a statute that requires it to conduct a hearing "on the record." When an agency adjudicates disputes under a statute that just requires it to provide a "hearing," the agency has much greater discretion to choose its own procedures. Adjudications of that type are often referred to as "informal."

In the early 1950s, the Supreme Court held that all agencies were required to use the procedures required by sections 554, 556, and 557.[11] The Court based those decisions on its belief that Congress included those sections in the APA in an attempt to codify the requirements of due process. Congress signaled its disagreement with the Court by amending the Immigration and Nationality Act in ways that allowed the agency that adjudicates certain immigration disputes to use procedures that fall short of the procedures required by sections 554, 556, and 557. The Supreme Court retreated from its prior position and upheld those amendments over a claim that they violated due process.[12]

At present, the Court uses the three-part balancing test described in this section to determine the procedures that are required to satisfy due process. That test can produce a wide variety of results, but it never requires procedures that are as protective of due process interests as those required by APA sections 554, 556, and 557.

---

10. Mathews v. Eldridge, 424 U.S. 319, 335 (1976).

11. Cates v. Haderlein, 342 U.S. 804 (1952); Riss & Co. v. United States, 341 U.S. 907 (1951); Sung v. McGrath, 339 U.S. 33 (1950).

12. Marcello v. Bonds, 349 U.S. 302 (1955).

3.4 NEUTRAL AND UNBIASED ADJUDICATOR

Many of the cases in which the Supreme Court has addressed the relationship between due process and agency decision-making procedures have focused on one important requirement of due process: the government must provide a neutral or unbiased decision-maker when it adjudicates a dispute.

In some cases, parties who lost in agency adjudications have argued that the decision-makers were unconstitutionally biased against the petitioner because they had a conflict of interest in their capacity as competitors of the petitioner. Thus, for instance, the Supreme Court has held that a state board that consisted entirely of optometrists who are in private practice was impermissibly biased when it concluded that optometrists who work for commercial firms cannot practice optometry in the state.[13] Cases of that type rarely, if ever, arise in the context of federal agency adjudication because federal agencies operate at a scale that justifies the use of full-time decision-makers and the adoption of elaborate conflict-of-interest rules (see Chapter 10). By contrast, many states and localities must rely on part-time government employees who also have private-sector jobs that are relevant to their area of decision-making to adjudicate disputes.

The Supreme Court's famous opinion in *Withrow v. Larkin* addresses two potential sources of bias that are equally applicable to state and federal agencies: (1) bias attributable to an agency's performance of multiple functions in an adjudication (i.e., investigator, prosecutor, and adjudicator), and (2) bias attributable to a decision-maker's position within an agency. The petitioner argued that a state agency's decision in an adjudication was impermissibly biased because the agency performed investigative and prosecutorial functions and the arguably inconsistent function of deciding the case that it investigated and prosecuted. The Court held that the combination of functions within an agency does not violate due process as long as the functions are divided among different people at the agency.[14]

The Court included dicta in its opinion in *Withrow* that indicated its approval of the way in which Congress had addressed the separation-of-functions issue when it enacted the APA in 1946. Congress authorized agencies to perform all three functions—investigation, prosecution, and adjudication—but it included statutory provisions

13. Gibson v. Berryhill, 411 U.S. 564 (1973).
14. Withrow v. Larkin, 421 U.S. 35 (1975).

that require agencies, with some exceptions, to maintain strict separation of those functions within the agency. Thus, for instance, employees who engage in investigation or prosecution of a case cannot have any role in the process of formally adjudicating the case and are prohibited from engaging in ex parte communications with administrative law judges (ALJs).

But the strict statutory separation of functions required by the sections of the APA, which the Supreme Court referred to approvingly in *Withrow*, applies only when an agency is required to conduct a hearing "on the record."[15] Most statutes that authorize agencies to adjudicate disputes do not use language that triggers those provisions. When an agency adjudicates disputes through authority granted in a statute that does not require an "on-the-record" hearing, the APA does not specify the procedures that the agency must use and does not require separation of functions within the agency. The procedures the agency uses and the degree of separation of functions within the agency are determined by a combination of the statute that authorizes the agency to conduct the adjudication, the agency's rules of procedure, and, in some circumstances, the Due Process Clause of the Constitution.

In a few contexts, including occupational and mine health and safety, Congress has decided to create what is called a "split-enforcement" model. One agency—the Occupational Safety and Health Administration or the Mine Safety and Health Administration—makes the rules that regulated firms must follow, conducts investigations to determine whether firms have violated the rules, and then brings enforcement actions before a separate agency—either the Occupational Safety and Health Review Commission or the Federal Mine Safety and Health Review Commission. That agency adjudicates the dispute. The split-enforcement model furthers the goals of due process at some sacrifice in efficiency. No court has ever held that due process requires the split-enforcement model, and the Supreme Court in *Withrow* rejected the argument that due process requires such a structure.

As discussed in Part III, the APA also provides many sources of decisional independence for the ALJs who preside in formal adjudications. Congress created those statutory sources of the decisional independence of ALJs in 1946 in response to widespread complaints that the hearing examiners who previously presided in agency adjudications

15. *See* United States v. Fla. E. Coast Ry. Co., 410 U.S. 224 (1973); Pension Benefit Guar. Corp. v. LTV Corp., 496 U.S. 633 (1990); Dominion Energy Brayton Point LLC v. Johnson, 443 F.3d 12 (1st Cir. 2006).

were systemically biased in favor of the agencies where they presided and to studies that supported those complaints.[16]

But Congress has required only a few agencies to use formal adjudication to adjudicate a few classes of disputes. As a result, only a minority of agency adjudications are conducted by ALJs.[17] In most of the statutes in which Congress has authorized an agency to adjudicate a class of disputes, Congress has permitted the agency to rely on presiding officers that have a wide variety of titles such as immigration judge, administrative patent judge (APJ), or contract appeals board member. These adjudicators, sometimes collectively referred to as administrative judges (AJs), have one characteristic in common that distinguishes them from ALJs: most have no statutory safeguards of their decisional independence. As a result, they are more vulnerable to potential pressure from agency officials to perform their duties in ways that favor the views of the agency. Nonetheless, courts generally have not found the use of AJs to violate parties' due process right to a neutral and unbiased adjudicator.

3.5 APPOINTMENT, REMOVAL, AND OVERSIGHT OF ADJUDICATORS

In recent years, the Supreme Court has decided many cases that have effects on agency adjudication through application of the Appointments Clause, the Executive Vesting Clause, and the Take Care Clause. The reasoning, results, and effects of those decisions overlap and interrelate for a good reason. All three clauses are designed to ensure the president has adequate control of, and responsibility for, all significant actions that are taken by the executive branch of government, including those executive branch agencies that have the power to adjudicate.[18]

The Appointments Clause permits only the president, the head of a department, or a court of law to appoint an inferior officer, and then only if Congress has authorized such a method of appointment.[19] In its 2018 decision in *Lucia v. Securities & Exchange Commission*,

16. Ramspeck v. Fed. Trial Exam'rs Conf., 345 U.S. 128, 131–32 (1953).

17. Kent Barnett et al., Admin. Conf. of the U.S., Non-ALJ Adjudicators in Federal Agencies: Status, Oversight, and Safeguards (2018); Michael Asimow, Admin. Conf. of the U.S., Adjudication outside the Administrative Procedure Act (2016).

18. In *Bowsher v. Synar*, 478 U.S. 714 (1986), the Court held that Congress cannot control an agency.

19. U.S. Const. art. II, § 2.

the Supreme Court held that ALJs who preside in adjudications at the Securities and Exchange Commission are officers (presumably inferior officers) rather than employees.[20] The Court's reasoning and holding undoubtedly apply to all ALJs and AJs who preside in adjudications at regulatory agencies. A good argument can be made that the reasoning and holding in *Lucia* do not apply to ALJs and AJs who preside at agencies like the Social Security Administration (SSA) that conduct adjudications to decide whether to provide government benefits to individuals. It is not clear that the courts will ever have occasion to make that decision, however. In a Supreme Court proceeding in 2020 to address a related issue, the solicitor general "conceded" that ALJs at SSA are "inferior officers."[21] Unless the government changes its position on that issue, it is unlikely to come before a court.

The *Lucia* decision had several immediate direct effects. First, most agency heads immediately ratified the decisions of other agency personnel to appoint the roughly 2,000 ALJs who were already serving at various agencies. Congress had empowered agencies to appoint ALJs in the APA and various other statutes. Most agencies chose to delegate that authority to personnel other than the head of the agency (e.g., the agency's chief ALJ or the head of the agency's human resources division) to appoint ALJs. The Court's decision in *Lucia* made it clear that no one except the head of an agency has the power to appoint an ALJ. By ratifying the past appointments of lower level personnel, the heads of agencies rendered those appointments lawful and consistent with the Constitution beginning with the date of the ratification.

Second, the *Lucia* decision also strongly suggested that the process long used to appoint ALJs was unconstitutional. For decades, the Office of Personnel Management (OPM) had implemented a complicated, meritocratic system for determining whether applicants for ALJ positions were qualified to be ALJs. Based on many criteria, including each applicant's performance on a test, OPM ranked each of the typically hundreds of applicants. An agency that wanted to appoint a new ALJ could then choose among the top three applicants on the OPM list. Congress almost certainly has some power to condition the appointment power by, for instance, providing that an ALJ must be a member of the bar of some state. However, the Court's decision in *Lucia* suggested that Congress cannot limit the discretion of the

---

20. 138 S. Ct. 2044 (2018).

21. Brief of Solicitor General of the United States, Carr v. Saul, 141 S. Ct. 1352 (2021) (No. 19-1442).

appointing officer to the extent that the traditional system of appointment of ALJs limited it.

Immediately after the Court issued its decision in *Lucia*, the president issued an executive order that stripped OPM of its power to implement its traditional method of selecting ALJs for potential appointment.[22] Going forward, unless the executive order is rescinded, the criteria for appointment and the method of applying those criteria will be in the discretion of the president and agency heads. A 2019 study conducted by the Administrative Conference of the United States found that most agencies have been exercising that discretion in a responsible manner.[23]

The *Lucia* decision also has the potential to have another important effect on agency adjudications conducted by ALJs. In its earlier decision in *Free Enterprise Fund v. Public Co. Accounting & Oversight Board*, the Supreme Court held that the Executive Vesting Clause (which requires that the "executive Power" be vested in the president[24]) and the Take Care Clause (which requires that the president "take Care that the Laws be faithfully executed"[25]) make it unconstitutional for Congress to limit the president's power to remove an officer by providing more than one level of "for-cause" protection from removal.[26]

Under the APA, an ALJ can only be removed "for cause" as determined by the Merit Systems Protection Board (MSPB).[27] The members of the MSPB can only be removed "for cause." Thus, ALJs are subject to two layers of for-cause protection from removal. The Court included a footnote in its opinion in *Free Enterprise Fund* in which it stated that its holding did not necessarily apply to ALJs.[28] However, there are cases now pending in which courts may decide whether the for-cause limit on the power to remove ALJs is constitutional.

The results of those pending cases are difficult to predict. Those who challenge the for-cause limit on ALJ removal argue that because ALJs are officers, double for-cause protections violate the Executive Vesting Clause and the Take Care Clause. Defenders of the for-cause limit argue that it is important to protect the due process rights of

---

22. Exec. Order No. 13,843, 83 Fed. Reg. 32,755 (July 13, 2018).

23. Administrative Conference Recommendation 2019-2, Agency Recruitment and Selection of Administrative Law Judges, 84 Fed. Reg. 38,930 (Aug. 8, 2019).

24. U.S. CONST. art. II, § 1.

25. *Id.* § 3.

26. 561 U.S. 477 (2010).

27. 5 U.S.C. § 7521.

28. *Free Enter. Fund*, 561 U.S. at 507 n.10.

parties that adjudicate cases at agencies by reducing the risk that agency heads will pressure ALJs into acting in ways that exhibit systemic bias in favor of the agencies at which they preside. They also argue that agency heads, and derivatively the president, retain complete power to faithfully execute the laws because the APA allows an agency to review every initial decision that is made by an ALJ and to replace it with a final decision written by the agency.

In some statutes, however, Congress did not provide any right for an agency to review a decision issued by an adjudicator. That feature of a statute can convert an adjudicator from an inferior officer to a principal officer. A principal officer can only be appointed through the process of nomination by the president followed by confirmation by the Senate.

In cases involving special trial judges on the Tax Court[29] and civilian members of the Coast Guard Court of Criminal Appeals,[30] the Court announced and applied a three-part test for deciding whether someone is an inferior officer or a principal officer. One part of that test asks the question whether the officer's decisions are reviewable by a principal officer. The Court implied that any officer whose decisions are not reviewable by a principal officer must be a principal officer.

APJs at the Patent Trial and Appeal Board make decisions about the validity of patents. APJs are appointed by the Secretary of Commerce. By statute, APJs' decisions are not reviewable by any executive branch official. In *United States v. Arthrex*, the Supreme Court held that APJs were unconstitutionally appointed principal officers because their decisions were not reviewable by a principal officer. The Supreme Court decided that the appropriate remedy was to authorize the Senate-confirmed director of the Patent and Trademark Office to review all decisions made by APJs. Subjecting their decisions to review by the director, a principal officer, rendered APJs constitutionally appointed inferior officers.[31] It will be interesting to see whether the Supreme Court uses this approach when it is presented with another case in which an ALJ or AJ is arguably a principal officer because the judge's decisions are not reviewable by a principal officer.

The only thing that is certain in this area of law is that the Supreme Court will have to decide many more cases in which there is an arguable conflict between an agency adjudication system and the Constitution.

---

29. Freytag v. Comm'r of Internal Revenue, 501 U.S. 868 (1991).
30. Edmond v. United States, 520 U.S. 651 (1997).
31. United States v. Arthrex, 141 S. Ct. 1970 (2021).

Chapter 4

Goals, Values, and Institutional Design of Federal Agency Adjudication

Jerry L. Mashaw

4.1 CHAPTER OVERVIEW

Administrative adjudication is often said to serve or have as its objective certain goals and values—ideals like fairness, accuracy, consistency, efficiency, timeliness, customer service, and participant satisfaction. Realistically, designing the institutions that administer these systems requires trade-offs among these different and often competing ideals. The nature of those trade-offs will necessarily vary according to the needs of and resources available to specific programs. As a result, Congress and agencies have adopted widely varying structures and processes for adjudication in different contexts.

This chapter begins with a discussion of the goals and values that animate administrative adjudication and describes how the design of adjudicative systems often requires trade-offs among these different and often competing objectives (section 4.2). Acknowledging the need for such trade-offs, the next section introduces three models of administrative justice, each of which emphasizes different values and goals for decision-making and therefore suggests the utilization of different structures, organizations, and cognitive techniques for decision-making (section 4.3). The chapter concludes with a case study of the system for adjudicating Social Security Disability Insurance (DI) claims to illustrate how different trade-offs and competing visions of administrative justice have determined one system's institutional design (section 4.4).

4.2 GOALS AND VALUES OF ADMINISTRATIVE ADJUDICATION

American systems of administrative adjudication are heterogeneous. The process for deciding whether an applicant is eligible for Medicaid is not likely to mirror the process by which the Securities and Exchange Commission determines whether a trader has violated the securities laws and should be barred from the securities industry. Neither is likely to have much in common with a border patrol agent's determination that an immigrant has just crossed the border illegally and should be returned to Canada or Mexico or a social service worker's judgment of whether a child requires protective services or placement in foster care.

Notwithstanding this heterogeneity, society has expectations concerning the quality of administrative justice meted out by all systems of agency adjudication. In some general sense, we expect all of these systems to be fair. We expect that adjudicators will act on an accurate assessment of the facts of the case; that they will consistently apply appropriate legal standards to the cases presented to them; that persons affected will have a reasonable opportunity to present evidence and argument; that decisions will be made with reasonable promptness; that reasons for those decisions will be provided to the extent possible; and that persons disappointed by administrators' decisions will have some opportunity to appeal to higher authority. This listing hardly exhausts our expectations. The crucial thing to note about this list is the constant use of modifiers like "reasonable," "appropriate," "to the extent possible," and "some opportunity."

The concrete meaning of these terms can be supplied only in the context of the administrative adjudication system under discussion. And here a whole host of considerations will influence system design: How many cases will this system be expected to process in a particular time period? How important is the decision to affected parties? What are the resources available to process this caseload? How complex is the factual development necessary to make an accurate decision? How likely is relevant evidence available? What training is necessary for adjudicators to be capable of making appropriate decisions? What are the capacities of affected parties to participate in the proceedings? To what extent does the development of facts impinge on personal privacy, trade secrets, or even national security? Once again, this list is only partial.

These considerations suggest the sorts of trade-offs that must be made in the design of any system of administrative adjudication. Where cases are simple and facts easily found, we are unlikely to think that a system should devote extensive resources and highly trained personnel to decision-making. On the other hand, where otherwise straightforward cases involve extremely important interests of individuals or firms, we might believe that a system should provide extensive opportunity for party participation and elaborate opportunities for appeal. Yet should these cases also involve state secrets or urgent public interests in quick resolution, we are likely to feel the need for summary process and be willing to place relatively severe restrictions on the giving of transparent reasons for decisions.

Trade-offs in institutional design are ubiquitous, as is recognized in the U.S. Supreme Court's due process jurisprudence. The Court's famous balancing test in *Mathews v. Eldridge* tells us that we must balance the private parties' interests against the government's interest while also considering the risk of an erroneous determination and the prospects that some procedural change will make a significant contribution to avoiding error.[1] This is a test of wonderful generality, but its content can only be supplied case by case.

From the standpoint of institutional design, the Supreme Court's approach has two weaknesses. The first is its indeterminacy. What counts as a legitimate private or governmental interest? How are legitimate values to be weighed against each other when, as is often the case, the values are incommensurate? Personal freedoms and national security can hardly be measured in the same currency. How are we to know what the value of some additional process characteristic might be in avoiding erroneous determinations? The questions go on and on. The second is that satisfying due process at the constitutional level is much too low a standard by which to measure the goodness or badness of a particular institutional design. At the level of judicial review for constitutionality, the Supreme Court puts a heavy, separation-of-powers thumb on the scale—a presumption in favor of the government's design.

Designers of systems of administrative adjudication, or critics of existing designs, need better metrics for assessing whether an

1. 424 U.S. 319 (1976).

adjudicatory system is successful. Judging success is, of course, a straightforward, even banal, approach to assessing the quality of any implementing activity. And administrative adjudication is, like all administrative activity, aimed at implementing some program or policy. The simple question then is whether the system of administrative adjudication is good at promoting the aims of the administrative program whose purposes it serves. But alas, this simple question is not so simple. Administrative programs have multiple and complex purposes. Moreover, it is often controversial what exactly those purposes are or should be. And these programs operate in an environment laden with political, social, and economic constraints related to yet additional public values.

4.3 THREE MODELS OF ADMINISTRATIVE JUSTICE

Research suggests that there are at least three distinct conceptual models of administrative justice: (1) "bureaucratic rationality," (2) "professional treatment," and (3) "moral judgment." Each emphasizes different values and goals and therefore suggests the use of different structures, organizations, and cognitive techniques for decision-making.

Features of the Three Justice Models

Dimension/ Model	Legitimating Values	Primary Goal	Structure or Organization	Cognitive Technique
Bureaucratic Rationality	Accuracy & efficiency	Program implementation	Hierarchical	Information processing
Professional Treatment	Service	Client satisfaction	Interpersonal	Clinical application of knowledge
Moral Judgment	Fairness	Conflict resolution	Independent	Contextual interpretation

The basic goal of the bureaucratic-rationality model is to create a decision-making system for accurately and consistently distinguishing between true and false claims. The system's task is conceived in essentially factual and technocratic terms. The general decisional technique is information retrieval and processing, and the managerial task is to see that this is done both with thoroughness and consistency. The latter demands the usual bureaucratic, organizational routines of detailed specification of administrative tasks and decisional norms, specialization and division of labor, and hierarchical review of accuracy and consistency of decision-making. The legitimating force of this conception flows from its claim to correct implementation of democratically determined social purposes while minimizing costs.

A system based on professional judgment, by contrast, is oriented toward individualized client service. Professional judgment about what clients need and how they might be helped relies on information collection that must be manipulated in accordance with standardized professional procedures. But professional treatment also demands recognition that facts may be incomplete, that individual contexts may be unique, and that decision-making may ultimately be intuitive (i.e., based on professional judgments that cannot be fully rationalized). At the managerial level, the task would not be oversight and routinization of professional actions but making sure that claimant-clients were routed to an appropriate professional who could make judgments about their needs for income support, rehabilitative services, and the like. The legitimating appeal of a professional-judgment model lies in its commitment to client service—the trusteeship relationship implicit in professional-client relationships.

A system based on a commitment to moral judgment is one likely to be similar to traditional common-law legal processes. The idea is to resolve disputes about rights, all things considered. Once again, like a process based on bureaucratic rationality, the moral-judgment approach demands fact-finding. But judgments are not mere applications of objective legal rules to established facts. The moral-judgment model views decision-making as value-defining. The question is not just who did what, but who is to be preferred, all things considered, when different values, goals, and interests collide. This model's claim to legitimacy is that judgment will be made by an independent decider after all parties have been given an open and fair opportunity to present their positions.

Each model of administrative justice is, or may be in appropriate contexts, coherent and attractive. For example, an adjudicative system premised on the moral-judgment model may be well suited for decision-making that ordinarily involves competing interests, high stakes, and complex legal and factual questions (e.g., the process by which the Federal Energy Regulatory Commission licenses interstate pipeline projects). A system premised largely on the bureaucratic-rationality model might be sufficient for low-stakes decision-making, such as issuing permits to camp in national parks, or decision-making in which questions of law and fact are easily resolved by frontline workers, such as entitlement to social security retirement benefits. And a system premised largely on the professional-treatment model might be well suited for determining access to medical and vocational services administered by the Department of Veterans Affairs.

These are, of course, ideal types that can be to some degree blended, or perhaps applied in serial fashion at different levels of the administrative process (see Chapter 7). As explained in the case study that follows this section, the process for adjudicating claims for Social Security DI emphasizes the bureaucratic-rationality model but provides a review process modeled on the moral-judgment model and retains vestiges of the professional-treatment model in the use of medical and vocational professionals to provide relevant evidence.

This blending of models produces an uneasy compromise because, while not mutually exclusive, these models of administrative justice seem to be highly competitive. For example, a bureaucratically rational system—one that relies on formal rules, objective standards, and strict hierarchical control—is hardly consistent with a system, premised on the professional-treatment model, that aims to provide individualized services to claimants based on the clinical judgment of medical, vocational, or other professionals. Nor is it consistent with a moral-judgment-type system that features independent, neutral, and passive adjudicators, determinations based on broad standards rather than well-defined rules, and party control of the collection and testing of evidence in trial-type proceedings.

These reflections seem to lead to a somewhat ironic conclusion: a system of administrative justice that seeks to pursue one conception of administrative justice will seem unjust from the vantage point of competing conceptions. More poignantly, a system that attempts some compromise—that is, that seeks to preserve bonds to the values and insights of all of these conceptions—will, from the perspective of each separate conception, appear incoherent and unjust.

In the study that the next section summarizes, I hypothesized that virtually every adjudicatory system will contain compromises among antagonistic visions or models of administrative justice. I concluded that realism counsels modesty about the degree to which our competing values can all be realized in any system of administrative adjudication.

4.4 CASE STUDY: DESIGNING THE DISABILITY INSURANCE ADJUDICATION SYSTEM

Because the answers to institutional-design questions depend on the system under discussion, let me give an example based on my own experience in studying the process for adjudicating claims for DI under the Social Security Act.[2]

DI claims are adjudicated through a multistage process. State Disability Determination Services (DDSs), working on contract with the Social Security Administration (SSA), decide all initial and reconsideration claims to disability benefits. Claimants dissatisfied with a DDS decision can request a hearing before an SSA administrative law judge (ALJ). ALJ decisions are subject to agency appellate review and ultimately judicial review in the federal courts.

Having been engaged in a project to study the processes of hearings and appeals before ALJs and federal courts concerning the denial of DI benefits,[3] I was struck first by the degree to which these processes dealt with a miniscule proportion of the DI claims actually adjudicated. Second, appellate personnel, particularly ALJs, routinely laid the blame for various faults in the system on the underlying bureaucratic process at the state-agency level. While the claims that reached ALJs or federal courts numbered in the hundreds or tens of thousands, respectively, these state-agency adjudicators decided millions of claims every year. And while ALJ, district court, and circuit court opinions provided written reasons and the judicial decisions were sometimes published, the underlying state-agency process, where all cases began and most cases ended, were essentially invisible. It struck me that if one was concerned about the quality of administrative justice, one should be concerned more with the levels at which most claimants' claims were decided than with those levels of appeal that encountered a small proportion of claims—claims whose characteristics might or might not reflect the mine-run of claims at the earlier stages of the administrative process.

---

2. JERRY L. MASHAW, BUREAUCRATIC JUSTICE: MANAGING SOCIAL SECURITY DISABILITY CLAIMS (1983) [hereinafter BUREAUCRATIC JUSTICE]; Jerry L. Mashaw, *Conflict and Compromise among Ideals of Administrative Justice*, 1981 DUKE L.J. 181 (1981) [hereinafter *Conflict and Compromise*]; JERRY L. MASHAW ET AL., SOCIAL SECURITY HEARINGS AND APPEALS (1978) [hereinafter SOCIAL SECURITY HEARINGS AND APPEALS]; Jerry L. Mashaw, *The Management Side of Due Process: Some Theoretical and Litigation Notes on the Assurance of Accuracy, Fairness, and Timeliness in the Adjudication of Social Welfare Claims*, 59 CORNELL L. REV. 772 (1974); JERRY L. MASHAW, ADMIN. CONF. OF THE U.S., QUALITY ASSURANCE SYSTEMS IN THE ADJUDICATION OF CLAIMS OF ENTITLEMENT TO BENEFITS OR COMPENSATION (1973).

3. SOCIAL SECURITY HEARINGS AND APPEALS, *supra* note 2.

This led me to begin a study of the initial and reconsideration decision-making processes for DI claims and of the state and federal efforts to manage that process.[4] When burrowing into the literature on this program and its administration, I discovered something interesting: much of the literature was critical, but the critics had quite different criticisms.

One strand of the critical commentary was concerned that the disability program fails to provide adequate services to claimants and beneficiaries. This view implicitly characterizes the program's purposes as paternalistic and therapeutic, purposes that would seem to require a major role for health care, vocational, social service, and other professionals in program administration. Failure of the program to emphasize the role of professional judgment and to adopt a service orientation is seen as a major defect in the administrative process.

The second, more legalistic perspective lamented the incapacity of claimants to adequately assert and defend their rights to benefits. These critics were concerned with standard administrative law issues such as the adequacy of notice, the opportunity for adversarial testing of evidence, and the substantial reversal rate of cases heard orally by independent ALJs. This was a concern essentially with the failure of the DI process to provide the standard ingredients of a judicial trial.

Finally, a third set of critics chided SSA for failing to manage the adjudication process in ways that would produce timely, predictable, and consistent outcomes. Critics in this camp suggested reforms that were essentially managerial: SSA should provide more objective criteria for the exercise of bureaucratic discretion; greater control should be exerted over the internal routines of the DDSs; and the system of management oversight and statistical quality assurance should be strengthened. From this perspective, the system is viewed in standard bureaucratic terms and criticized for its inadequate hierarchical controls.

To evaluate the goodness of the system of administrative justice for DI claims, I needed to develop the implications of these different conceptions of administrative justice. This led me to identify the models of administrative justice described in the previous section: (1) *professional treatment*, which aims for a service-oriented system that emphasizes client satisfaction through decision-making rooted in the clinical application of knowledge; (2) *moral judgment*, which relies on independent decision-makers to fairly resolve conflicts through contextual

4. Bureaucratic Justice, *supra* note 2.

interpretation; and (3) *bureaucratic rationality*, which aims for accurate and efficient implementation of a public policy program through hierarchical organization and technocratic information processing.

I also needed to pursue four questions empirically: How did the social security disability adjudication system actually work at the lower levels? What model or models of administrative justice actually inhered in the system? Why had the system taken the form it did? And how should one evaluate the quality of the administrative justice provided?

Choosing a model of administrative justice for the DI program was not a simple matter. Each has attractive features that respond to some aspect of the statutory mandate. Exploring the choices SSA made when constructing an adjudicatory system for DI benefits provides a useful case study in the difficult compromises that must be made given the competing values at stake.

DI benefits are a legal entitlement, which suggests that the adjudicatory system might be modeled on the formal adjudicatory processes of civil courts. But the experience of private disability insurance in the 1920s suggested that adversarial adjudication pursuant to a moral-judgment model would not achieve one of Congress's important purposes: ensuring that the program did not turn into a residual unemployment program. Judicial reinterpretation of the meaning of "disability" in private disability insurance ultimately made the risk actuarially unpredictable, and all private disability carriers abandoned the field. Intense pressure from applicants to expand the beneficiary class during cyclical economic downturns suggested that the program required forms of tight administrative oversight that would be impossible if decision-making were allocated to independent ALJs operating in the absence of objective criteria.

Farming out disability determinations to the medical profession operating on a professional-judgment model was equally unattractive from the standpoint of controlling program costs. Medical professionals are notoriously conservative in their advice. Their primary concern is maintaining their patients' health, which often involves advising them that they should not be working. The disability program was the legislative statement of a complicated, new social goal—call it cautious benevolence. Only an organization tailored specifically to that legislative purpose was likely to realize congressional goals. An adjudicatory system burdened by the historic perspectives of service-oriented professionals or the dominant legal culture was not likely to realize those goals. Only the bureaucratic-rationality model seemed promising.

That choice did not, however, mean that professional judgment could not be factored into the decision process. For example, the statutory definition of "disability" in the DI program requires professional input. The disease or trauma that is the underlying cause of an applicant's disability must be "medically determinable," a standard that contemplates delegating authority to the medical profession to establish the basic condition underlying eligibility. Moreover, for purposes of determining vocational capacities, Congress delegated decisional authority to state vocational rehabilitation services, which were presumably staffed by professional therapists and counselors. The presumption was that these professional rehabilitation specialists would view their job as getting people back to work, not as facilitating their access to disability benefits.

Moreover, the all-things-considered approach of the moral-judgment model retained appeal for disability determinations. The question for decision was not just what the claimants' skills, impairments, and work experience are, but whether persons with that particular set of characteristics ought to have public support. Many claims will be resolved informally by the state-agency examiners who decide initial claims on contract with SSA. But given the complexity of the criteria to be considered and the critical interests at stake in these decisions, an acceptable resolution of the benefits question requires an opportunity for an individualized hearing and for appeal outside the agency to a court of general jurisdiction. Indeed, these traditional legal forms of administration are elaborately provided for in the Social Security Act.

The hybrid nature of the DI adjudicatory process—combining aspects of bureaucratic, professional, and moral decision-making—should not mislead us. The fundamental mode of disability administration was to be bureaucratic rationality. Congress was concerned about program expansion, and SSA had a strong sense of mission arising from the administration of the old-age- and survivors-insurance programs. That mission was accurate, speedy, and inexpensive disposition of claims—a mission that was no less important in the new disability program. Responsible discharge of that mission included preserving the DI fund for future beneficiaries. That responsibility made necessary a controllable, and therefore hierarchical, decision structure.

Historically, a program based on a model of professional treatment or moral judgment had several drawbacks. Delegation of broad decisional authority to medical professionals had two plausible variants, both politically unattractive. The first abandoned budgetary control. If SSA were to take a physician's judgment that the patient was disabled, it would necessarily forgo control over the level of generosity of the program, as previously mentioned. The second, which had the prospect of maintaining budgetary control, would be the creation of government-run treatment and diagnostic centers that would also make disability determinations subject to agency oversight. That approach ran headlong into the objection that it created a system of socialized medicine. Congress has never been willing to create such a system save for veterans.

It was also the obvious problem that medicine's professional concerns—diagnosis and treatment of disease or trauma—did not exhaust the facts to be considered in disability decision-making. Some official had to discover, in light of the claimant's impairments, what that person's residual functional capacity was and then relate that capacity to the demands of various occupations. This seemed to be a job for some kind of vocational specialist or job counselor. As previously noted, these sorts of professionals existed in state agencies, but their set of professional skills, scientific methods, and cultural norms were not nearly as unified as that of the medical profession. Outside some matrix of bureaucratic standards and objective criteria, vocational professionals' decisional behavior might be unpredictable and inconsistent. Delegation to medical and vocational professionals was simply not a responsible strategy.

Nor was individualized adjudication by independent hearing officers pursuant to a moral-judgment model a politically appropriate alternative for disability determinations. SSA was not merely a neutral decider of disability claims. It had a positive program of income security to administer and was responsible for active pursuit of information sufficient to perform that decisional task. In the words of a judge who chastised a different agency for its investigative passivity, SSA was not "an umpire blandly calling balls and strikes."[5] This responsibility did not necessarily exclude some traditional form of adjudication, but the dynamics of such a system would be awkward. SSA could retain control over factual development, for example, by adopting an approach similar to that of the Internal Revenue Service. SSA investigators could decide whether to honor claims or to refer claimants to a hearing. At the hearing, an SSA investigator would then present the case for denial. But this would mean that disability adjudications would be adversarial, a peculiar posture for a social welfare agency. SSA could

5. Scenic Hudson Pres. Conf. v. Fed. Power Comm'n, 354 F.2d 608, 620 (2d Cir. 1965).

hardly be charged with the duty to defeat the claims of the sick and the developmentally challenged.

The disability program has thus adhered primarily to a bureaucratic-rationality model but has made concessions to other models. Initial disability determinations were delegated to state rehabilitation agencies—an obvious but limited concession to the professional-treatment model. This concession has steadily eroded over time. The increasingly elaborate and objective criteria on the basis of which state-agency personnel make initial and reconsideration decisions in the DI program have convinced most states that disability examiners do not need to have the specialized training of those who staff state rehabilitation programs. Professional treatment, in the form of decisions by vocational rehabilitation specialists, remains a part of the program largely in the form of referring denied applicants to state vocational rehabilitation agencies and providing testimony as expert witnesses during ALJ hearings.

The program has also obviously made concessions to the traditional moral-judgment model in the form of nonadversarial hearings and judicial review. The disability program cannot be structured otherwise and still maintain the insurance-entitlement conception of social security benefits. The compromise between bureaucratic rationality and moral judgment was thus struck in the form of a temporal separation: bureaucracy first, followed by individualized hearings for the dissatisfied. The statutory mandate to provide support for disabled persons has, of course, influenced the structure of this hearing process. No one represents the government and attempts to defend the denial of benefits at the state-agency level. The hearing officer operates, therefore, in an investigatory mode. The hearing is a de novo proceeding in which the ALJ is charged with developing the record, conducting an oral hearing, and deciding the case.[6]

The hybrid and multilayered design of the disability adjudication system is, in many ways, a sensible and reasonable response to the objectives of the DI program and the complex constraints that surround its implementation. But as the persistent criticisms of DI adjudicatory performance illustrate, the synthesis or compromise among models of administrative justice built into the program predictably create systemic stress. At an abstract level, it is easy to see that the bureaucratic-rationality model's demands for accuracy and efficiency are undermined by professional insistence on a treatment modality or

---

6. *See* Richardson v. Perales, 402 U.S. 389 (1971).

by a search for moral deservedness inherent in traditional adjudication. The just-allocation goal of the moral-judgment model is similarly lost in a system of objective rules and expertly determined facts. Likewise, professional judgment constrained by objective criteria and harnessed to the efficiency imperatives of programmatic rationality ceases to be professional judgment. Hence, more concretely, the story of DI administration has been a story of systemic stress in which the supporting roles allocated to professional treatment and moral judgment place judges, doctors, and vocational experts in the role of subversives who threaten to undermine the predominant bureaucratic model.[7]

Consider first ALJs and the hearing process. The history of stress and conflict resulting from the provision of a de novo hearing for disappointed disability applicants is much too long to be recounted here in detail. The historic position of ALJs has been that they are independent of SSA management and that their function is to provide handcrafted justice as close as possible to the traditional judicial trial. Some ALJs believe that their only adjudicatory guides should be the all-things-considered statutory definition of "disability" in the Social Security Act. And their view of a proper hearing is modeled on the exquisite evidentiary processes of civil trials. This view presents clear challenges in a system that must reasonably promptly process three million new claims and complete more than 500,000 hearings per year. Backlogs in processing DI claims are notorious,[8] and Congress has brought intense pressure on SSA to speed up DI decision-making. The major cause of delay is the hearing process. Moreover, ALJs are, as a group, much more likely to grant claims than are state disability examiners. Claimants who request de novo hearings before ALJs are given awards in more than half of the cases. Because requesting and obtaining a hearing is virtually costless, there is little to prevent an ultimate shift of control to ALJs through a nearly 100 percent appeal rate of DDS denials.

This systemic stress has prompted SSA to experiment with a number of managerial controls designed to tame the hearing process, making it both more efficient and more consistent with the underlying disability criteria that guide judgment at the state-agency level. These efforts have included increasingly detailed objective criteria for decision-making, enhanced training of ALJs, quality assurance

---

7. *Conflict and Compromise*, *supra* note 2.

8. *See, e.g.*, Adam S. Zimmerman, *Surges and Delays in Mass Adjudication*, 53 Ga. L. Rev. 1335 (2019).

programs designed to identify errors in hearing decisions, and the provision of additional staff to expedite ALJ decision-making. Some of these managerial efforts are discussed in greater detail in Chapters 23 and 24.

These efforts have been only partially successful. But they have prompted intense resentment among ALJs and persistent litigation attempting to reinforce ALJ independence and to free them from regulatory constraints that make ALJ decision-making more objective and consistent across deciders.[9] Suffice it to say that the disconnect between the bureaucratic processes for decision-making at the state-agency level and the legalistic approach taken in ALJ hearings, which are themselves subject to federal court review, remains a serious issue as does the significant inconsistency in award rates from one ALJ to another.[10]

Controlling the professional-treatment culture of vocational rehabilitation specialists presents a similar but more tractable problem for SSA system designers. While the original idea seemed to be to harness the expertise of state vocational rehabilitation agencies to disability determination, the adjudicatory system moved rapidly away from that model. State vocational rehabilitation specialists have a professional culture that might easily produce enormous expansions in the number of persons deemed eligible for DI benefits. State vocational rehabilitation agencies provide assistance to persons with physical or mental impairments, but only after determining that the services that they can provide are likely to make their clients employable. And agency performance tends to be judged by the success rate of client placements in jobs. Were these professionals given the job of determining whether a particular client was to receive vocational rehabilitation services or be placed on disability benefits, they would surely find a substantial number of claimants eligible for DI who are currently denied benefits. The test under the Social Security DI program is whether the claimant can do *some* job that provides reasonable income anywhere in the national economy, not whether the claimant would in fact be employed. Indeed, many rejected claimants for DI benefits are referred to state vocational

9. Ass'n of Admin. L. Judges v. Colvin, 777 F.3d 402 (7th Cir. 2015); Nash v. Califano, 613 F.2d 10 (2d Cir. 1980); Ass'n of Admin. L. Judges v. Heckler, 594 F. Supp. 1132 (D.D.C. 1984); *see also* Jennifer Nou, *Dismissing Decisional Independence Suits*, 86 U. Chi. L. Rev. 1187 (2019).

10. Administrative Conference Recommendation 2013-1, Improving Consistency in Social Security Disability Adjudication, 78 Fed. Reg. 41,352 (July 10, 2013).

rehabilitation services only to be rejected there as well, based on a finding that they are too disabled to benefit from vocational rehabilitation.

Hence, while SSA contracts with state agencies to make initial and reconsideration decisions with respect to the DI program, it does not require that state agencies employ vocational rehabilitation specialists to make these decisions, and it provides the state disability examiners with elaborate objective criteria for decision-making. How DI adjudication became separated from the professional-treatment approach built into vocational rehabilitation is, again, a long story that cannot be recounted here. Suffice it to say that the current state-agency process is so nearly divorced from the line activity of state rehabilitation services that a visit to a DDS reveals little about the historic association of disability adjudication and vocational rehabilitation.

The federal courts have been unwilling to grant this divorce in all circumstances. When claimants are denied benefits at the hearing level on the ground that they can engage in some employment other than their prior employment, the courts have insisted that the finding of capacity to do other work be supported by evidence in the hearing record. The only way SSA can produce such evidence is to call a vocational expert witness, usually a vocational rehabilitation counselor. In relying on a vocational expert as a witness, however, SSA again confronts the problem of the delegation of decision-making to a therapeutically oriented professional. How is the ALJ to ask whether the claimant can perform a new job without conceding the decisional role to the expert witness, who presumably acts out of his or her professional, therapeutic culture? The system's answer has been to try to avoid vocational expert witnesses by regulation. SSA's so-called grid regulations now specify for every combination of age, education, work experience, and residual functional capacity a simple answer: disabled or not disabled.[11] The ALJ makes factual findings with respect to the regulatory criteria and, in many cases, the regulatory grid supplies the requisite answer to whether the claimant should be awarded benefits. This routinization by rule led claimants to object that they were not being accorded the individualized hearings that the statute promised—a claim rejected by the Supreme Court.[12] The grid applies, however, only to cases in which claimants have only exertional limitations. Where mental health issues or environmental limitations are present, vocational expert testimony may still be required.

11. 20 C.F.R. pt. 404, subpt. P, app. 2 (2022).
12. *See* Heckler v. Campbell, 460 U.S. 458 (1983).

The moral of this tale is straightforward: like virtually every adjudicatory system, the DI system has required compromises among antagonistic visions or models of administrative justice. While this was a study of only one specific adjudicatory system, realism counsels modesty about the degree to which our competing values can all be realized in any system of administrative adjudication. In my study, I concluded:

> [T]he best system of administrative adjudication may be the one most open to criticism. A compromise that seeks to preserve the values and to respond at once to the insights of all of these conceptions of justice will, from the perspective of each separate conception, appear incoherent and unjust. The best system of administrative adjudication that can be devised may fall tragically short of our inconsistent ideals.[13]

13. Bureaucratic Justice, *supra* note 2, at 21–23.

Chapter 5
Adjudication and Policymaking

Matthew L. Wiener

5.1 CHAPTER OVERVIEW

An agency-administered statute will often require the agency to make policy decisions when particularizing its commands in legal form. The statute might, for example, leave an operative term undefined, thereby requiring the agency to supply a definition. This chapter will call this activity "policymaking." (It can also be called, depending on the context, interpretation or lawmaking. The terminology does not much matter here.[1]) A recurring question in administrative law will often arise: how must or should the agency establish the policy it will apply

1. *See generally* Thomas W. Merrill, The Chevron Doctrine 28 (2022); *cf.* Martin v. Occupational Safety & Health Rev. Comm'n, 499 U.S. 144, 154 (1991) (using apt term "[delegated] lawmaking by interpretation").

when, in administering the statute, adjudication of some matter may be required? Or, put another way, what policymaking form or procedure must or should it use?

Conventional administrative law identifies two possibilities. First, the agency might establish policy by promulgating, before an adjudication arises, a substantive legislative rule, which this chapter calls a "regulation." The regulation will provide the rule of decision in any adjudication that may arise. Second, the agency might do so, common-law style, through case-by-case adjudication.[2] It will establish and announce a rule—though not a "rule" in the Administrative Procedure Act (APA) sense, since it will have been the product of an adjudication rather than a rulemaking[3]—in the context of or incident to adjudicating a particular case.[4] The agency's decision will then supply a precedential decisional rule in subsequent cases involving the same issue.

These two policymaking forms are not mutually exclusive. They may be combined, and often are. An agency may promulgate a regulation that, when applied to a particular matter in an adjudication, must itself be particularized to varying degrees by a decisional rule in the adjudication. (Agency adjudicators will often prefer to characterize this activity as interpretation rather than policymaking.[5])

Sometimes a statute will require an agency to establish policy by regulation.[6] More commonly, though, it will not dictate the policymaking form of regulatory action, even if it authorizes the agency to adopt regulations with the force of law or to issue legally binding orders through adjudication (as the statute must if the agency is to do either).

This chapter addresses four main questions that arise when a statute does not require legislative rulemaking:

1. May an agency choose between rulemaking and adjudication when establishing policy?
2. When an agency may do so, what policy and strategic considerations attend the choice?
3. What do agencies do in practice?

2. *See, e.g.*, Shalala v. Guernsey Mem'l Hosp., 514 U.S. 87 (1995).

3. *See* 5 U.S.C. §§ 551(4) (definition of "rule"), 551(6) (definition of "order"). *But see* Matthew C. Stephenson, *Embedded Rules*, 39 Yale J. on Regul. Bull. 59 (2021).

4. Stephenson, *supra* note 3.

5. Christopher J. Walker et al., Admin. Conf. of the U.S., Precedential Decision Making in Agency Adjudication (2022).

6. *See, e.g.*, *Guernsey Mem'l Hosp.*, 514 U.S. 87.

4. What processes and procedures do agencies use in adjudication to make policy?

This chapter is limited to the choice between legislative rulemaking and adjudication as policymaking forms. It is important to recognize, though, two other ways familiar to administrative lawyers by which agencies make policy. One is to issue a nonlegislative rule (or guidance document)—that is, either an interpretive rule or policy statement, neither of which has the force of law—and the other is to bring (if authorized by statute) a federal court action to enforce a statute it administers. It is also important to recognize that agencies make policy in numerous ways largely outside the ken of administrative law.

5.2 RULEMAKING VERSUS ADJUDICATION: LEGAL CONSIDERATIONS

5.21 The Chenery II Principle

The starting point for addressing whether and when an agency must establish policy by rulemaking remains the U.S. Supreme Court's 1947 decision in *Securities & Exchange Commission v. Chenery Corp.*,[7] known as *Chenery II*.[8] At issue was a Securities and Exchange Commission (SEC) adjudicative decision refusing to approve a corporate reorganization plan because the transactions it provided for were inconsistent with a vague statutory provision the SEC was charged with administering. The decision was challenged mainly on the ground that the SEC had established its policy implementing the statute for the first time—and then applied it retroactively—in the very adjudicative decision reviewed by the Court rather than, as the statute would have allowed, in a pre-adjudicative regulation of general applicability. A seven-justice majority of the Court rejected this argument over the objection of Justices Jackson and Frankfurter in dissent.

The Court acknowledged that the SEC had "less reason to rely upon ad hoc adjudication to formulate new standards of conduct" because, unlike a court, it "had the ability to make new law prospectively through the exercise of its rule-making powers." The Court also acknowledged that when "filling the interstices" of the statute it

---

7. 332 U.S. 194 (1947).

8. *See generally* Ronald A. Cass & Matthew Lee Wiener, *Securities and Exchange Commission v. Chenery Corp. (Chenery II)*, *in* LEADING CASES IN ADMINISTRATIVE LAW (Anna Shavers et al. eds., forthcoming); Gary S. Lawson & Joseph Postell, *Against the* Chenery II *"Doctrine,"* NOTRE DAME L. REV. (forthcoming 2024).

was implementing, the SEC "should" do so "as much as possible . . . through" the "quasi-legislative promulgation of rules to be applied in the future." But the Court was unwilling to impose "any rigid" requirement that the SEC proceed by "general rule." To do so, the Court explained, would render "the administrative process inflexible and incapable of dealing with many of the specialized problems" that it must address. Sometimes the agency will not have foreseen the problem. Sometimes the agency "may not have had sufficient experience with a particular problem to warrant rigidifying its tentative judgment into a hard and fast rule." And sometimes the agency could not have "capture[d]" a "specialized" and "var[ied]" problem "within the boundaries of a general rule." As a result, the Court concluded in an oft-cited sentence: "[T]he choice made between proceeding by general rule or by individual, ad hoc litigation is one that lies primarily in the informed discretion of the administrative agency."[9]

There matters stood until the Court's 1969 decision in *National Labor Relations Board v. Wyman-Gordon Co.*[10] What, exactly, the Court decided in that fractured decision is not altogether clear. The plurality opinion and the dissent together might well have been read to require rulemaking for certain (not well-specified) rules. Some lower courts justifiably read it exactly that way.[11] But, in any case, the Court foreclosed that interpretation just five years later in *National Labor Relations Board v. Bell Aerospace*,[12] where it reaffirmed the *Chenery II* principle that the choice between rulemaking and adjudication lies within the agency's "informed discretion."[13] The Court has never revisited the issue.[14]

Bell Aerospace followed *Chenery II* in seemingly recognizing the possibility that a court might find an agency to have abused its discretion

9. *Chenery Corp.*, 332 U.S. at 202–03.

10. 394 U.S. 759 (1969).

11. *See, e.g.*, 1 Kristin E. Hickman & Richard J. Pierce, Jr., Administrative Law Treatise § 4.9 (6th ed. 2019); M. Elizabeth Magill, *Agency Choice of Policymaking Form*, 71 Chi. L. Rev. 1383, 1407 & n.80 (2004); *see also* Ronald A. Cass, *Models of Administrative Action*, 72 Va. L. Rev. 363, 382–83 (1986).

12. 416 U.S. 267 (1974).

13. The Court ignored its decision, issued just a few months earlier, in *Morton v. Ruiz*, 415 U.S. 199 (1974), where it had concluded with little analysis and in an anomalous context that an agency's rule was "ineffective" because it was established by adjudication rather than by legislative rule. Lower courts have also generally ignored *Morton*.

14. The Court has nodded to the *Chenery II* principle. *See, e.g.*, Martin v. Occupational Safety & Health Rev. Comm'n, 299 U.S. 144, 154 (1991).

by foregoing rulemaking. But only in a few outlier decisions have lower courts actually done so,[15] and usually only because the agency unduly burdened a regulated party by changing a policy residing in precedent.[16] (As noted in section 5.22, most courts address this fair-notice/reliance problem not by invalidating the choice of form but by denying the new policy retroactive effect.) Most courts have not even required agencies to explain their choice of form despite the reason-giving requirement that ordinarily attends arbitrary-and-capricious review of discretionary agency decisions.[17] As one contemporary critic of *Chenery II* notes, the principle that agencies can choose to establish policy by adjudication long ago assumed the status of "black-letter administrative law."[18]

5.22 The Retroactivity Limitation

One important limitation on an agency's choice must be recognized: when an agency adopts a new decisional rule in an adjudication, the agency may not always be allowed to apply it retroactively—that is, so as to proscribe and remediate past conduct. This limitation can be traced to *Chenery II*, where the Court faced the objection that the SEC had impermissibly applied retroactively a "new standard of conduct" that the regulated party could not reasonably have anticipated given the open-ended statutory language. The Court answered that retroactivity, which after all inheres in most adjudication, is not "fatal" to the "validity" of an agency decision but instead must be balanced against the "mischief of producing a result which is contrary to a statutory design or to legal and equitable principles." "If that mischief is greater than the ill effect of the retroactive application of the new standard," the Court added, "it is not the type of retroactivity which is condemned by law."[19] The Court has never elaborated on this standard.

---

15. *See* 1 Hickman & Pierce, *supra* note 11, § 4.9; Magill, *supra* note 11, at 1408; Richard K. Berg, *Re-Examining Policy Procedures: The Choice between Adjudication and Rulemaking*, 38 Admin. L. Rev. 149, 155 (1986). A leading case is *Ford Motor Co. v. Federal Trade Commission*, 673 F.2d 1008 (9th Cir. 1981). Dissenting from the denial of rehearing en banc, Judge Reinhardt noted that the decision conflicted both with Ninth Circuit precedent and *Bell Aerospace*.

16. *See* Magill, *supra* note 11, at 1408.

17. *See id.* at 1414–15. *But cf.* Lisa Schultz Bressman, *Beyond Accountability: Arbitrariness and Legitimacy in the Administrative State*, 78 N.Y.U. L. Rev. 461, 535–36 (2003).

18. Aaron L. Nielson, *Three Wrong Turns in Agency Adjudication*, 28 Geo. Mason L. Rev. 657, 667 (2021).

19. Sec. & Exch. Comm'n v. Chenery Corp., 332 U.S. 194, 203 (1947).

This retroactivity limitation, though, is infrequently imposed. Post-*Chenery II* lower court decisions have given agencies wide latitude to apply—and sometimes required them to apply—new policies established in adjudicative decisions retroactively.[20] Courts have allowed agencies to do so even when giving content to vague, ambiguous, or open-ended statutory provisions in what might be called the *Chevron* Step 2 context[21] and thereby exercising delegated lawmaking authority in discretionary ways that could not have been reliably predicated from those provisions. Most courts have not attempted to identify a point along the "adjudicative spectrum from pure application of law . . . to pure law creation"[22] at which to demarcate permissible from impermissible retroactivity in adjudication.[23] (Whether courts might establish justiciable standards to draw that line is a debated question.[24]) One result is that whereas the law disfavors retroactive application of legislative rules (presuming them to be prospective only),[25] it favors (indeed often compels) the retroactive application of decisional rules in agency adjudications; and (again) it does so even when, in the *Chevron* Step 2 situation, the agency is exercising discretionary policymaking/lawmaking authority within the permissible bounds of a legislative delegation of authority. Now-Justice Gorsuch, while a judge on the Tenth Circuit, has objected to this asymmetry. The presumption against retroactivity, he contends, should apply to adjudicative decisions when the agency is acting within the *Chevron* Step 2 space, for it is there that the agency is making new rather than applying existing law, just as it often is doing in a rulemaking.[26]

---

20. *See, e.g.*, Sanitary Truck Drivers & Helpers Loc. 350 v. Nat'l Lab. Rels. Bd., 45 F.4th 38 (D.C. Cir. 2022).

21. *See* Chevron U.S.A., Inc. v. Nat. Res. Def. Council, Inc., 467 U.S. 837 (1984). On the *Chevron* doctrine, see Chapter 27.

22. Abner S. Greene, *Adjudicative Retroactivity in Administrative Law*, 1991 Sup. Ct. Rev. 261, 265 (1992).

23. *But cf.* De Niz Robles v. Lynch, 803 F.3d 1165, 1173 (10th Cir. 2015) (Gorsuch, J.).

24. *Compare* 1 Hickman & Pierce, *supra* note 11, § 4.9 (noting that courts "are poorly situated to determine when rulemaking is appropriate"), *and* Russell L. Weaver & Linda D. Jellum, Chenery II *and the Development of Federal Administrative Law*, 58 Admin. L. Rev. 815, 824–26 (2006) (same), *with* Magill, *supra* note 11, at 1424 (noting existence of criteria that courts could use to review agency choice of policymaking form).

25. *See* Bowen v. Georgetown Univ. Hosp., 488 U.S. 204 (1988).

26. *See De Niz Robles*, 803 F.3d at 1172.

The predominant approach, reflected in numerous decisions of the U.S. Court of Appeals for the D.C. Circuit, is to disallow retroactive application only when two (often accompanying conditions) are met: (1) an agency has actually "substitute[ed] new law for old law that was reasonably clear"—as opposed to applying existing law to new circumstances[27]—and (2) the affected litigant has established detrimental reliance on the old law.[28] (Varying multifactor tests—all flung in the same direction with their emphasis on reliance—appear in the case law.[29]) Most courts have grounded this limitation in "notions of fairness and equity" without identifying any specific positive law, statutory or constitutional, that compels it.[30] As for agency decisions on retroactivity, they align with the courts' in their focus on reliance. Courts usually give such decisions some limited deference.[31]

5.23 The Prospectivity of Adjudicative Decisional Rules

When an agency decides not to apply, or is foreclosed on judicial review from applying, a new policy established in an adjudication retroactively, it will usually apply the decision prospectively. The agency will treat the decision announcing the policy as a precedent that will control the outcome of future cases involving the same issue but unrelated parties. (Of course, a party in a future case may always ask the agency to overrule the precedent or hold it inapplicable.) Sometimes the agency will say explicitly, in the precedential decision itself, that it will apply the policy only prospectively.[32] More often, though, the

---

27. Am. Tel. & Tel. v. Fed. Commc'ns Comm'n, 454 F.3d 329, 332 (D.C. Cir. 2006) (modification in original; citations omitted).

28. *See, e.g.*, Sanitary Truck Drivers & Helpers Loc. 350 v. Nat'l Lab. Rels. Bd., 45 F.4th 38, 45 (D.C. Cir. 2022). *See generally* 2 Charles H. Koch & Richard Murphy, Administrative Law and Practice § 5.67 (3d ed. 2022); Greene, *supra* note 21, at 265 n.13.

29. *See* Williams Nat. Gas Co. v. Fed. Energy Regul. Comm'n, 3 F.3d 1544, 1554 (D.C. Cir. 1993). The seminal case in the D.C. Circuit is *Retail, Wholesale & Department Store Union v. National Labor Relations Board*, 466 F.2d 380 (1972). *See Williams*, 3 F.3d at 1553.

30. Cassell v. Fed. Commc'ns Comm'n, 154 F.3d 478, 486 (D.C. Cir. 1988). *But cf. De Niz Robles*, 803 F.3d at 1177 (Gorsuch, J.) (grounding limitation in, among other things, the "due process concern" of fair notice that lies "at the heart of retroactivity analysis"); *see also* Greene, *supra* note 21, at 266–67 (identifying as potential sources of the limitation due process and the APA's definitions of "rule" and "order").

31. *See, e.g.*, *Sanitary Truck Drivers*, 45 F.4th at 45–46.

32. *See, e.g.*, Total Sec. Mgmt. Ill. 1, LLC, 364 N.L.R.B. 1532 (2016).

agency will announce instead simply that it will not apply the decision retroactively—without mentioning prospectivity—and then apply it as precedent in later cases. An agency's decision not to apply a decision retroactively appears to carry the (arguably necessary) implication that it will apply the decision prospectively.

But is prospective-only application permissible? The plurality opinion and the dissenting opinions in *National Labor Relations Board v. Wyman-Gordon Co.* together might have been read to say "no," at least when the agency can be said to have used prospective-only decision-making to evade the APA's rulemaking requirements.[33] But it appears that no such limitation has taken hold in subsequent case law, and there is ample precedent for prospective-only decision-making.[34] As suggested earlier, moreover, decisions holding that an agency may not apply a decisional rule retroactively might well imply the corollary that the agency may apply it prospectively only. It is difficult to read the case law to provide otherwise. On this understanding, prospective-only application might be deemed permissible when—and perhaps only when—retroactive application is impermissible.

5.24 Legal Regularity and Other Requirements in Adjudicative Decision-Making

A final, if obvious, point should be emphasized. Although agencies can generally establish policy by adjudication free of judicial scrutiny, the manner in which they do so is subject to judicial scrutiny. Agencies must, among other things, support their adjudicative decisions with adequate factual findings, provide reasoned explanations for their decisions, consider arguments that policy established in an adjudicative precedent (unlike one established by regulation) should be overturned, allow parties to challenge a decisional rule "predicated on facts" that may not exist in subsequent cases,[35] apply precedents con-

---

33. 394 U.S. 759 (1969); *see also* Bowen v. Georgetown Univ. Hosp., 488 U.S. 204, 221 (1988) (Scalia, J., concurring).

34. *See, e.g.*, *De Niz Robles*, 803 F.3d at 1177 n.8; Greene, *supra* note 21, at 300 n.125. *But see* Berg, *supra* note 15, at 164 (questioning practice under *Wyman-Gordan*). Courts themselves sometimes apply their decisions prospectively despite the objection from some judges and commentators that Article III's case-and-controversy requirement always requires retroactive adjudication. (Of course, Article III does not limit agency action.) If courts can make rules prospectively, agencies should have discretion to engage in analogous rulemaking through adjudication. Greene, *supra* note 21, at 294 n.97.

35. 1 Hickman & Pierce, *supra* note 11, § 4.9.

sistently, decide cases according to announced decisional rules,[36] and adequately explain changes in decisional rules.[37] Professor Elizabeth Magill has noted that, by employing these and other principles, courts can and do "respond to whatever concerns they might have about an agency's choice of procedure."[38]

5.3 RULEMAKING VERSUS ADJUDICATION: POLICY AND STRATEGIC CONSIDERATIONS

5.31 General Preference for Rulemaking

Even as the Court in *Chenery II* left to agencies the choice between rulemaking and adjudication to establish policy, it expressed its general preference for rulemaking as agencies' predominant policymaking form. "The function of filling in the interstices" of a statute, the Court emphasized in *Chenery II*, "should be performed, as much as possible, through" the "quasi-legislative promulgation of rules to be applied in the future."[39] This preference runs throughout the Court's—and especially the lower courts'—post-*Chenery II* case law.[40] It is still more pronounced in the academic literature, much of if written during the 1960s and 1970s when rulemaking activity increased significantly and the post-*Chenery II* case law developed.[41] It is also reflected in a 1985 resolution adopted by the American Bar Association's House of Delegates.[42] In recent years, libertarian-oriented critics of the administrative state have staked out an especially strong position in favor of policymaking by rulemaking. One of their concerns is that the

36. Allentown Mack Sales & Serv., Inc. v. Nat'l Lab. Rels. Bd., 522 U.S. 359, 373–75 (1998).

37. *See* Atchison, Topeka & Santa Fe Ry. Co. v. Wichita Bd. of Trade, 412 U.S. 800, 808–09 (1973); Walker et al., *supra* note 5, at 27.

38. Magill, *supra* note 11, at 1437.

39. Sec. & Exch. Comm'n v. Chenery Corp., 332 U.S. 194, 202 (1947).

40. *See, e.g., Allentown Mack*, 522 U.S. 359; Richard J. Pierce, *Two Problems in Administrative Law: Political Polarity on the District of Columbia Circuit and Judicial Deference to Agency Rulemaking*, 1988 Duke L.J. 300, 308 (1988).

41. *See infra* note 45; *see also* Henry J. Friendly, *The Federal Administrative Agencies: The Need for Better Definition of Standards* (Pt. 1), 75 Harv. L. Rev. 863 (1962); Henry J. Friendly, *The Federal Administrative Agencies: The Need for Better Definition of Standards* (Pt. 3), 75 Harv. L. Rev. 1263, 1298 n.449 (1962). For a rare and questionable contemporary defense of adjudication as the superior policymaking form, see Todd Phillips, *A Change of Policymaking by Adjudication*, 73 Admin. L. Rev. 495 (2021).

42. Berg, *supra* note 15, at 177 (reproducing resolution).

retroactive application of policies not fairly inferable from the text of statutes and regulations deprives regulated parties of fair notice of their legal obligations.[43]

Whatever the overall advantages of rulemaking, it is difficult to establish overarching criteria that should guide the choice. The answer will depend in "each case," as Professor Donald Elliot has emphasized, on a

> variety of factors, including how sure the agency is about what policy it wishes to adopt, how frequently the agency anticipates the question will come up, whether the issue is inherently entangled with other issues that can best be addressed comprehensively, and what other issues are currently pressing for the agency's attention.[44]

The rulemaking-adjudication choice, moreover, is not always mutually exclusive. Sometimes an agency will want to use—in fact must use—both rulemaking and adjudication in complementary ways. Even a strong proponent of policymaking by regulation must concede that not all policy questions can always be addressed by regulation. Sometimes regulations will leave gaps that must be filled or incorporate general standards that must be particularized in application.[45] The choice-of-form debate usually concerns significant policy matters of widespread applicability.

5.32 Advantages of Rulemaking

There is a voluminous literature, little of it recent, addressing the potential advantages of rulemaking over adjudication as a vehicle for policymaking.[46] The main arguments courts and commentators usu-

---

43. Nielson, *supra* note 18, at 667–70; *see also* Aaron L. Nielson, *D.C. Circuit Review—Reviewed: "I Vote for Chenery I, Not Chenery II,"* YALE J. ON REGUL.: NOTICE & COMMENT (Nov. 24, 2017), https://www.yalejreg.com/nc/d-c-circuit-review-reviewed-i-vote-for-chenery-i-not-chenery-ii/.

44. E. Donald Elliott, *Re-Inventing Rulemaking*, 41 DUKE L.J. 1490, 1492 (1992); *see also* Robert L. Glicksman et al., *An Empirical Assessment of Agency Mechanism Choice*, 71 ALA. L. REV. 1039 (2020).

45. *Cf.* Antonin Scalia, *Back to Basics: Making Law without Making Rules*, REGULATION, July/Aug. 1981, at 25, 28.

46. Especially notable and oft-cited sources from which the discussion below is partly drawn include Michael Asimow, *Nonlegislative Rulemaking and Regulatory Reform*, 1985 DUKE L.J. 381, 402–03 (1985); Berg, *supra* note 15, at 163–64; Frank E. Cross, *Pragmatic Pathologies of Judicial Review of Administrative Rulemaking*, 78 N.C. L. REV. 1013, 1026 (2000); Ralph F. Fuchs, *Development*

ally advance for choosing policymaking rulemaking can be summarized as follows:[47]

(1) **Instrumental justifications.** Rulemaking allows agencies to make more rational, informed, and coherent policy than adjudication. The most important reason why, perhaps, is that the APA's notice-and-comment requirements require participation from the public. Participation in adjudication often is narrowly limited to parties (often a single person), who may or may not represent similarly situated interests well and who, in in any event, will do so only from a narrowly self-interested perspective. In a rulemaking, any interested person can file a comment, and because rulemaking procedures are simpler and less legalistic (and hence lawyer-driven), can do so at generally a lower cost than participating in an adjudication by intervention or as an amicus curiae would require.[48] The result is that agencies will often receive

---

and Diversification in Administrative Rulemaking, 72 NW. U. L. REV. 83 (1977); 1 HICKMAN & PIERCE, *supra* note 11, § 4.8; Alan B. Morrison, *The Administrative Procedure Act: A Living and Responsive Law*, 72 VA. L. REV. 253 (1986); Pierce, *supra* note 39, at 308–09; Glen O. Robinson, *The Making of Administrative Policy: Another Look at Rulemaking and Adjudication and Administrative Procedure Reform*, 118 U. PA. L. REV. 485 (1970); David L. Shapiro, *The Choice of Rulemaking or Adjudication in the Development of Administrative Policy*, 78 HARV. L. REV. 921 (1965); *see also, e.g.*, KENNETH CULP DAVIS, ADMINISTRATIVE LAW TREATISE 283 (1970); Jeffrey J. Rachlinski, *Rulemaking versus Adjudication: A Psychological Perspective*, 32 FLA. STATE U. L. REV. 529 (2005); Peter L. Strauss, *Rules, Adjudications, and Other Sources of Law in an Executive Department: Reflections on the Interior Department's Administration of the Mining Law*, 74 COLUM. L. REV. 1231 (1974). The National Labor Relations Board (NLRB) has always occupied center stage in the literature as a result of its near-exclusive reliance on adjudication despite widespread criticism. *See, e.g.*, Mark H. Grunwald, *The NLRB's First Rulemaking: An Exercise in Pragmatism*, 41 DUKE L.J. 274 (1991); Merton C. Bernstein, *The NLRB's Adjudication-Rulemaking Dilemma under the National Labor Relations Act*, 79 YALE L.J. 571 (1969); Cornelius J. Peck, *The Atrophied Rulemaking Powers of the National Labor Relations Board*, 70 YALE L.J. 729 (1961).

47. The discussion that follows largely ignores an important consideration about which it is difficult to generalize acontextually and without normative commitments: whether and when each policymaking forum favors regulation or deregulation. *Cf.* Scalia, *supra* note 44, at 27. It also ignores the perennial jurisprudential question whether rules or standards should be preferred in adjudication. *See generally, e.g.*, Cass R. Sunstein, *Problems with Rules*, 83 CAL. L. REV. 953 (1995); Kathleen M. Sullivan, *Foreword: The Justices of Rules and Standards*, 106 HARV. L. REV. 22 (1992). For discussion of the latter issue in the particular context of agency adjudication, see Colin S. Diver, *The Optimal Precision of Administrative Rules*, 93 YALE L.J. 65 (1983); Shapiro, *supra* note 45, at 926.

48. *But see* Phillips, *supra* note 40, at 521.

much more information—including especially data and studies—and a broader, though not necessarily anything near a comprehensive, range of perspectives than adjudications allow.

Public participation aside, rulemaking allows agencies to plan and set their agendas and thereby optimize the use of their scarce resources in administering a statute, to focus on policy questions undistracted by the particular circumstances of and parties to an individual case,[49] and to devise regulatory responses appropriate in scope given the problem they are addressing. Adjudication may allow agencies to accomplish some of these things but not nearly to the extent as rulemaking does. As for agenda setting, agencies to at least some extent must take cases as they come, even if they exercise discretion when initiating enforcement actions. As for scope, agencies have some flexibility in adjudications. They can cast rules, for example, at different levels of generality. But if agencies are to use adjudication properly with due regard for the rights of the parties rather than a subterfuge to issue broadly framed general rules, the formulation of decisional rules will necessarily be limited (in an enforcement action) by the wrongdoing alleged and remedies sought.[50]

(2) **Rule-of-law and utility justifications.** The rule of law has always loomed large in the debates over the choice between rulemaking and adjudication in establishing policy. Rulemaking serves, first and foremost, the law's notice-giving function. When an agency establishes policy by rulemaking, affected persons know their legal obligations and rights in advance and can plan their affairs accordingly. They need not predict how an adjudicator will interpret a vague, ambiguous, or open-ended statutory provision. Uncertainty will still often exist to some degree—in the interstices of rules, which may be vague, standard-like, and so forth—but often not nearly to the same degree as in the adjudication context.

Relatedly, policymaking by rule allows affected persons to ascertain their rights from a single or a small number of codified regulations rather than from a large body of sometimes messy case law. It can be notoriously difficult to extract a rule from even a single decision. Doing so from a body of decisions can be still more difficult. Inconsistency in decisional law can be more pronounced in agency adjudication

---

49. *See, e.g.*, Pierce, *supra* note 39, at 308 (noting that rulemaking "encourages the agency to focus on the broad effects of its policy rather than the often idiosyncratic adjudicative facts of a specific dispute").

50. *But cf.* Rachlinski, *supra* note 45, at 546.

than judicial adjudication as a result of, among other things, frequent changes in politically appointed adjudicators and partisan selection criteria that aligns an adjudicator's preferences with those of the appointing president on particular issues.

Another rule-of-law argument sounds in equality. A rule governs the conduct and rights of all members of the class it covers. Generality is often considered the defining feature of a legislative rule (notwithstanding the possibility of rules of particular applicability under the APA[51]). An adjudicative decision governs only the parties to the adjudication. Of course, consistent adjudicative application of a stable decisional rule in favor of or against all similarly situated persons over time may, in some contexts, achieve much the same effect as a regulation. But it may be difficult to achieve in some contexts. Some adjudication programs have come under criticism for deciding similarly situated parties inconsistently.

A final, related consideration sometimes cited here is basic fairness. The formulation of policy (at least in the regulatory enforcement context) necessarily requires selective enforcement against regulated entities. Enforcement activity will not be distributed evenly across them. The result is that only some regulated entities may bear the cost of the agency's formulation of a policy.

Often closely associated with these rule-of-law justifications for proponents of rulemaking are utility-based justifications. At least if they are sufficiently determinate, regulations enhance social welfare by allowing firms to plan their affairs knowing what the law allows and disallows with reasonable certainty. The generality of rules, moreover, may ensure that a regulatory system does not competitively advantage or disadvantage similarly situated firms in the market.

(3) **Efficiency and stability justifications.** At one point, many commentators considered rulemaking to be a more efficient way to make policy than adjudication. The APA's rulemaking provisions are not, on their face, as procedurally demanding as the APA's provisions for formal adjudication. This efficiency-related rationale lost much of its force in the 1970s and beyond as courts interpreted the APA to require procedures not explicit in its provisions and ratcheted up their scrutiny of rules through hard-look review, Congress and presidents imposed new procedural and analytical requirements on agencies, and presidents subjected significant regulations at least to White House oversight and review—all leading to what is often referred to as the

51. *See* 5 U.S.C. § 551(4).

"ossification" of rulemaking.[52] Yet efficiencies associated with rulemaking do remain, at least taking the long-term view, for several reasons. First, once a rule is in place, the agency often need not engage in successive and resource- and time-intensive, piecemeal adjudications to establish policy, especially policy dependent on complex legislative facts. Second, a party to an adjudication might challenge the factual predicate of a precedential decisional rule in a particular adjudication to which it is a party. Where a valid legislative rule is in place, its factual predicates will often be conclusive in an adjudication. Third, a legislative rule can resolve definitely and categorically frequently arising factual issues that would otherwise have to be resolved on a case-by-case, individualized basis in an adjudication.[53] Fourth, regulations of adequate specificity and clarity may even obviate or lessen the need for enforcement adjudications in the first place. Regulated parties will align their conduct with the rule.

In any case, the inefficiency of rulemaking may suggest a countervailing consideration: rules may be more perdurable and hence a regulatory regime more stable, with attendant rule-of-law and economic benefits, precisely because they can be more difficult to change. The frequent policy oscillations sometimes associated with adjudication—especially pronounced at the National Labor Relations Board (NLRB)—might diminish if the agency were to make policy by rulemaking.

(4) **Democratic justifications.** A notice-and-comment rulemaking is not a plebiscite, but it does offer the public an opportunity to participate in policymaking. This form of what might be called participatory democracy may have intrinsic benefits—even if they mostly boil down to legitimating agency decision-making—apart from whatever it may contribute to rational policymaking. The democratic features of notice-and-comment rulemaking may be especially important when Congress broadly delegates lawmaking to agencies—what Congress would otherwise decide through its democratic process are now decided by agencies—and when a policy decision requires value judgments rather than technical agency expertise.[54]

---

52. *See, e.g.*, Richard J. Pierce, Jr., *Seven Ways to Deossify Agency Rulemaking*, 47 ADMIN. L. REV. 59 (1995); Connor Raso, *Agency Avoidance of Rulemaking Procedures*, 67 ADMIN. L. REV. 65, 109–10 (2015); Thomas O. McGarrity, *Some Thoughts on "Deossifying" the Rulemaking Process*, 41 DUKE L.J. 1449 (1992).

53. Heckler v. Campbell, 461 U.S. 458 (1983).

54. *See, e.g.*, Nina A. Mendelson, *Democracy, Rulemaking, and Outpourings of Comments*, REGUL. REV. (Dec. 20, 2021), https://www.theregreview.org

(5) **Transparency justifications.** Policymaking by rulemaking is, by its nature, more visible to the public, White House officials, and Congress.[55] Policymaking by adjudication is more likely to go unnoticed, especially when it is undertaken over time and incrementally in multiple decisions rather than in a single, high-profile decision. The visibility of rulemaking is enhanced by formal legal requirements—on the presidential side, by the executive-order requirement that agencies announce anticipated rulemaking activity and then submit certain planned regulatory activities to the Office of Management and Budget's Office of Information and Regulatory Affairs (OIRA) for review;[56] and on the congressional side, the Congressional Review Act's (CRA's) requirement that agencies notify Congress of rules before they take effect.[57] No such notice requirements apply in adjudications.

(6) **Political control justifications.** Proposed rules of particular significance are subject to the above-noted OIRA review process, and all rules are subject to the CRA's disapproval process. (CRA-designated "major rules" may not go into effect until the expiration of a 60-day period during which Congress may disapprove them.[58]) Policy residing in rules is subject to presidential oversight and directive authority through the review mechanism established by executive orders and congressional oversight through the CRA. Policy adopted incidental to adjudication is not subject to such oversight.[59] Whether this an advantage of rulemaking depends on one's views of political controls and the policy-related benefits of presidential review.

(7) **Judicial review justifications.** Policymaking by rulemaking can facilitate orderly judicial review of regulatory review in several respects. One reason why is that anyone sufficiently affected by a regulation to have standing to sue may often challenge it without awaiting an agency enforcement proceeding.[60] Only the party to an adjudication, by contrast, ordinarily can challenge an adjudicative order, even though it may establish a general policy affecting others similarly situated.

/2021/12/20/mendelson-democracy-rulemaking-and-comments; Nina A. Mendelson, *Should Mass Comments Count?*, 2 MICH. J. ENV'T & ADMIN. L. 173 (2012); Mariano-Florentino Cuéllar, *Rethinking Regulatory Democracy*, 57 ADMIN. L. REV. 411 (2005).

55. Morrison, *supra* note 45, at 255–56.

56. Exec. Order No. 12,866, §§ 4, 6, 58 Fed. Reg. 51,735 (Sept. 30, 1993).

57. 5 U.S.C. § 801(a).

58. *See id.* § 801(a)(3).

59. *See, e.g.*, Stephenson, *supra* note 3.

60. *See* Abbott Laby's v. Gardner, 387 U.S. 136 (1967).

5.33 Advantages of Adjudication

The most commonly cited "advantage of adjudication as a form of lawmaking," as then-Professor Scalia explained it well, is that adjudication allows an agency to "proceed[] gradually in an inductive fashion from one specific case to another, in the context of concrete circumstances and on the basis of accumulated experience." An agency's engagement with a "concrete, detailed situation," moreover, "may serve to clarify both the facts and equities relevant to decision."[61] This may be especially desirable—indeed, sometimes necessary—when information is scarce and predictions about the effects of regulatory interventions difficult to make.

The other commonly cited advantage of policymaking by adjudication is its comparative efficiency. It allows agencies to avoid the judicially, congressionally, and presidentially imposed procedural and analytic requirements that encumber modern rulemaking. Whether that is in fact an advantage depends on contested views about the regulatory process and regulatory policy.[62]

5.34 Strategic Considerations for Agencies

Brief mention should also be made of what might be called strategic rather than policy considerations that might bear on an agency's choice between rulemaking and adjudication. One has already been noted: the use of adjudication to avoid rulemaking procedures. Others include the following:

(1) **Political oversight and congressional disapproval.** As already suggested, adjudication may allow agencies to make policy less visibly and thereby lessen the potential for (especially) congressional scrutiny. One reason is that adjudicative decisions are not as visible or easily obtained. Unlike rules, decisions are usually not published in the *Federal Register*, though at least precedential ones must be posted on an agency's website.[63] (They also may appear in private databases like Westlaw or Lexis or privately published (and expensive) reporters.) Another reason is that a rule of decision may be ascertainable only after reading a whole line of decisions rather than a single decision. Even then, something approaching a rule may be difficult to extract from a pattern of fact-specific decisions over a period of many years,

61. Scalia, *supra* note 44, at 26, 28.

62. *Compare, e.g.*, Stephenson, *supra* note 3, *with, e.g.*, Phillips, *supra* note 40; *see also* Scalia, *supra* note 44.

63. 5 U.S.C. § 552(a)(2).

and there may be a difficult-to-perceive disjuncture between a rule as stated and a rule as applied.[64]

Congress does not, moreover, have the same legislative tools available to override an adjudicative decision as it does a regulation. The CRA provides for the disapproval of an APA-qualifying rule, and provides for expedited procedures for consideration resolutions of disapproval. The CRA does not apply to decisional rules.[65] Any override must be accomplished by ordinary legislation (see Chapter 26).

(2) **Allocation of power within agencies.** Final adjudicative and rulemaking authority usually resides with the agency head. But below the agency head, the identity of the decision-maker will often be different in a rulemaking than an adjudication. This may be an especially important consideration at Cabinet departments, whose heads often delegate adjudicative decision-making authority to a relatively insulated (career-staffed) adjudicative body. While the heads often retain final decision-making authority, they may exercise it infrequently.[66] No doubt the allocation of internal decision-making authority will sometimes dictate the choice of policymaking form.[67]

(3) **Deference to agency interpretations of statutes.** The scope and extent of judicial deference to agency interpretations of ambiguous statutes they administer under the *Chevron* doctrine (see Chapter 27) may depend on whether the agency has proceeded by notice-and-comment rulemaking or adjudication. Although an interpretation of an ambiguous statute that resides in a decision resulting from a formal adjudication under the APA may receive deference, it is not always clear whether an interpretation of an ambiguous statute that resides in a decision resulting from an informal adjudication should receive deference.[68]

(4) **Perdurability and bindingness of rules.** Policy that resides in a legislative rule will often be more perdurable than a policy that resides

64. *See* Allentown Mack Sales & Serv., Inc. v. Nat'l Lab. Rels. Bd., 522 U.S. 359, 373–74 (1998).

65. 5 U.S.C. §§ 801–808.

66. *See, e.g.*, Christopher J. Walker & Melissa F. Wasserman, *The New World of Agency Adjudication*, 107 CAL. L. REV. 141 (2019); *see also* CHRISTOPHER J. WALKER & MATTHEW LEE WIENER, ADMIN. CONF. OF THE U.S. AGENCY APPELLATE SYSTEMS 9 (2020).

67. *See* Berg, *supra* note 15, at 168. *See generally* Elizabeth Magill & Adrian Vermeule, *Allocating Power within Agencies*, 120 YALE L.J. 1032, 1081 (2011).

68. *See, e.g.*, Kristin E. Hickman & Aaron L. Nielson, *Narrowing* Chevron's *Domain*, 70 DUKE L.J. 931, 937 (2021).

in an adjudicative decisional rule. One practical reason, already suggested, is that legislative rulemaking can be slow and cumbersome.[69] An agency that wishes to modify or rescind a regulation must observe the same procedures required to promulgate a rule in the first place.

There is also a legal reason as well: a party may always, as of right, argue for the overruling of a decisional rule embodied in a precedent from an earlier adjudication to which it was not a party. (How seriously the agency will take the argument is another matter. An adjudicative rule hardened in many precedents over time can be difficult to dislodge.) A regulation, of course, is not subject to overruling in an adjudication; the agency must apply it until it is changed through legally prescribed (usually notice-and-comment) procedures. (That is not to say that the validity of a regulation will be unchallengeable in an enforcement adjudication. It may be if the statute of limitations has not run.)

A related difference between adjudicative/decisional rules and regulations occasionally arises when the former are predicated on factual findings. When an unrelated party to a later adjudication in which the agency seeks to apply a "fact-dependent" decisional rule of general applicability claims that the rule's predicate facts do not exist in its particular circumstances, the party must be given the opportunity to challenge the applicability of the rule.[70] Such a rule can sometimes be thought of as establishing only a rebuttable presumption on some point.[71] A regulation, by contrast, can establish a rule of law whose factual predicates cannot be questioned.

5.35 Generalizations about Agency Practices

There is no question that, by the 1970s, rulemaking had become the predominant mode of agency decision-making for significant policy matters.[72] When creating new regulatory agencies in the 1960s and 1970s, Congress usually conferred rulemaking authority on them. It

---

69. *See* Aaron L. Nielson, *Sticky Regulations*, 85 U. CHI. L. REV. 85, 91 (2018).

70. 1 HICKMAN & PIERCE, *supra* note 11, § 4.9 (citing the leading case of *Shell Oil Co. v. Federal Energy Regulatory Commission*, 707 F.2d 230 (5th Cir. 1983)); *see also* Berg, *supra* note 15, at 170–71.

71. *See, e.g.*, Nat'l Lab. Rels. Bd. v. St. Francis Hosp., 601 F.2d 404 (9th Cir. 1979).

72. As then-Professor Scalia observed in 1978, "perhaps the most notable development in federal government administration during the last two decades is the constant and accelerating flight away from individualized adjudicatory proceedings to generalized disposition through rulemaking." Antonin Scalia, Vermont

also conferred rulemaking authority on some agencies, like the Federal Trade Commission, that did not previously have it (or arguably did not). Most agencies deemed rulemaking to be superior to adjudication as a policymaking form on significant matters. Rulemaking allowed agencies with significant new regulatory mandates, in particular, to make policy more efficiently and comprehensively than adjudication could possibly have allowed. It is difficult to imagine agencies implementing certain far-reaching and complex regulatory statutes effectively, let alone with the necessary speed, through adjudication.

In the early 1980s, then-Professor Scalia predicated that many agencies would return to adjudication for policymaking—on the model of the NLRB, which has always established nearly all its policy by adjudication—to avoid the increasingly burdensome processes for rulemaking already noted.[73] That has not happened to any substantial degree, if at all. ("Rulemaking avoidance" may be an important phenomenon, but it occurs mainly through APA exceptions to notice-and-comment rulemaking.) The NLRB remains an outlier in establishing nearly all of its substantive policy in case-by-case adjudications.[74]

That said, adjudication continues to play an important role in policymaking. All adjudicating agencies make at least some policy by adjudication, if only in modest and sometimes seemingly imperceptible ways. Most agency policymaking in adjudication probably consists of filling the interstices of regulations rather than statutes. Even the most detailed, rule-like regulation may require such interstitial policymaking at the point of application.

5.4 STRUCTURES AND PROCESSES FOR ADJUDICATIVE POLICYMAKING

Certain institutional structures and decision-making processes are associated with adjudication systems that establish agency policy. Some may be critical depending on the scope and scale of an agency's policymaking by adjudication. The following stand out.

Yankee: *The APA, the D.C. Circuit, and the Supreme Court*, 1978 SUP. CT. REV. 345 (1978).

73. *See* Scalia, *supra* note 44; *see also* McGarrity, *supra* note 51.

74. *See, e.g.*, Catherine L. Fisk & Deborah C. Malamud, *The NLRB in Administrative Exile: Problems with Its Structure and Function and Suggestions for Reform*, 58 DUKE L.J. 2013 (2009).

(1) **Fact-finding and nonparty perspectives.** Good policy decisions often depend on the agency's receipt and analysis of so-called general or legislative facts—facts independent and outside the knowledge of the parties to an adjudication—and consideration of a range of sometimes competing perspectives from different sources. As suggested earlier, notice-and-comment rulemaking has an obvious advantage over adjudication in this respect: agencies more effectively can receive information and perspectives from a diverse range of sources beyond the parties.

Amicus briefs are perhaps the most common substitute for the notice-and-comment process in adjudications. Many agency rules or practices liberally permit amicus briefs. Some appellate systems even solicit briefs in significant cases by public notice on their websites.[75] That said, amicus briefs can be considered, at best, an imperfect substitute for the notice-and-comment process.[76] The costs of and incentives for filing them limits their numbers and the diversity of perspectives they offer. They are often, moreover, inadequate mechanisms for offering rich empirical data and analysis as a result of page limits, the lawyerly argumentative forms they take, and other factors.[77]

At least a few agency programs actually incorporate rulemaking's comment process into adjudicative decision-making. Examples include the Environmental Protection Agency (EPA) when considering certain permit applications[78] and the Federal Trade Commission when it considers applications for waivers.[79] (The EPA process allows also for public participation in hearings on permit applications.) The Administrative Conference of the United States is now studying how agencies might enhance public participation in adjudications.[80]

Intervention should also be noted. When an adjudication is likely to affect a nonparty's interests in a sufficiently direct way, the nonparty may be allowed to intervene in the proceedings and thereby bring to bear important information and perspectives. Intervention is certainly more liberally granted in some agency adjudications than it is in federal court cases. But intervention on any extensive scale occurs

75. *See* Walker & Wiener, *supra* note 65, at 23–40.
76. *But cf.* Shapiro, *supra* note 45, at 931.
77. *See, e.g.*, Bernstein, *supra* note 45, at 44.
78. 40 C.F.R. §§ 124.10–.12 2022.
79. 15 U.S.C. § 2302(c).
80. *Public Participation in Agency Adjudication*, Admin. Conf. of the U.S., https://www.acus.gov/research-projects/public-participation-agency-adjudication (last visited June 27, 2023).

at relatively few agencies. One agency at which it does is the Federal Energy Regulatory Commission, which maintains an Office of Public Participation whose mission includes facilitating broad-based intervention in adjudicative proceedings.

(2) **Appellate structures and procedures.** Significant adjudicative policymaking at agencies usually resides at the appellate, rather than the hearing-level, stages of adjudications. Any number of structural arrangements and procedures may facilitate appellate review of significant policy and legal questions, or focus appellate review away from simple error correction and toward policymaking. They include the provision in many procedural rules for interlocutory appeals, standards and scopes of review that limit appellate review to important questions with implications beyond a particular case, and allowance for discretionary rather than mandatory appellate review.[81] As for discretionary review, it is invariably the only review that Cabinet department heads exercise, when they exercise their final decision-making authority themselves at all rather than delegating it to other officials. Such discretionary review allows an agency head to intervene only in selected cases—invariably few in number—that present policy questions suitable for resolution by politically accountable officials. The Supreme Court's recent decision in *United States v. Arthrex*,[82] if read broadly, may encourage more agencies to provide for discretionary agency head review in their rules.

(3) **Precedential decision-making.** Agencies that make policy by adjudication nearly always do so in precedential decisions—that is, decisions binding on all agency adjudicators (and sometimes other officials) unless overruled by the final agency decision-maker. Some agencies, especially boards and commissions, treat all their decisions as precedential. Other agencies, like the federal courts of appeals, designate some decisions as precedential and others as non-precedential. Their criteria for designating decisions as precedential often include whether a decision establishes new or modifies existing policies. Some agencies have formal procedures, which may provide for public input, for deciding which decisions should be deemed precedential.[83]

---

81. *See* Walker & Wiener, *supra* note 65, at 23–40; Admin. Conf. of the U.S., Model Adjudication Rules 75–85 (rev. ed. 2018).

82. 114 S. Ct. 1970 (2021). *Arthrex* is discussed in Chapter 19. Some agency rules make no such provision, but rather delegate final review authority to a lower level official without contemplating further review.

83. *See* Walker et al., *supra* note 5, at 31–36.

(4) **Notice to the public of policymaking by adjudicative decisions.** Identifying agency policy that resides in adjudicative decisions can be difficult and time-consuming. Policies must often be extracted from a voluminous body of decisions. Even identifying them often requires access to subscription-only electronic databases and expensive secondary materials that only specialized lawyers possess. Search engines on agency websites tend to be of limited value.

Agencies have taken modest steps to address this problem (see Chapter 28). Some agencies post on their websites current decisions of note, digests or summaries of significant decisions, and the like.[84] Some also post explanatory materials. No agency, though, has adopted anything approaching a comprehensive statement of its decisional rules.[85]

---

84. *See id.* at 43; Walker & Wiener, *supra* note 65, at 46–51.

85. *Cf.* Scalia, *supra* note 44, at 28 (discussing possibility of post-decision codification).

Part II

Structure of Adjudicative Authority

Chapter 6

Congressional Delegation of Adjudicative Authority

Jeffrey S. Lubbers

6.1 CHAPTER OVERVIEW

Although Article III of the Constitution vests the judicial power of the United States in courts made of judges with life tenure, whom we refer to as Article III judges, most adjudication of federal cases today occurs within administrative agencies and so-called Article I courts. In those instances, Congress has delegated a form of judicial power to executive branch adjudicators. Over time, the U.S. Supreme Court has allowed such delegation, and Congress enacted the Administrative Procedure Act (APA) in part to provide a set of procedures for agency adjudications that, in time, would also be recognized as meeting the requirements of the Due Process Clause (at least for the formal adjudications to which they apply).

This chapter details the history of this delegation, largely founded on a court-made distinction between public-rights and private-rights types of cases (section 6.2). It also sketches out the advent of the APA and how it helped cement the model of internal agency adjudication within agencies by administrative law judges (ALJs) whose decisional independence is protected (section 6.3). It then turns to the post-APA case law that has raised some constitutional law concerns about the delegation of adjudicative power (section 6.4) before closing with a discussion of proposals to make the ALJs more independent by removing them from the agencies (section 6.5).

6.2 HISTORY OF DELEGATION OF ADJUDICATIVE AUTHORITY OUTSIDE THE ARTICLE III COURTS

When discussing congressional delegation of adjudicative authority to executive branch agencies, the starting point is Article III, section 1, of the Constitution: "The judicial power of the United States, shall be vested in one Supreme Court, and in such inferior courts as the Congress may from time to time ordain and establish." Article III also bestows lifetime tenure on these so-called Article III judges. But Article I, section 8, gives Congress a series of enumerated powers authorizing it to regulate interstate and foreign commerce, to collect taxes and customs duties, to protect intellectual property, to regulate immigration and bankruptcies, and most importantly to "make all laws which shall be necessary and proper for carrying into execution" the enumerated powers.

Thus, the separation of powers among the three branches pertaining to adjudication is not absolute, and Congress, from the earliest days of our country, has allowed agencies to conduct adjudications.[1] In more modern times, despite the growth in our Article III judiciary, and the increasing number of "Article I" specialized courts—such as the Tax Court, Court of Appeals for Veterans Claims, bankruptcy courts, and so on—the number of cases adjudicated by federal agencies far exceeds the numbers in the federal courts. Compared to our 870 Article III judges, we have close to 2,000 ALJs and more than 10,000 other non-ALJ adjudicators, often called administrative judges (AJs), in federal government agencies. How did we get to this point?

Before discussing the developments in the Supreme Court, it should be noted that there are many policy reasons for Congress to assign some federal cases to agencies or Article I courts rather than to Article III courts. One major impetus is to avoid overloading the Article III courts. If all disputes that arise out of regulatory and benefits programs were assigned to be heard in the Article III courts, there would be a need for many more district court judges and correspondingly more appeals court judges (or circuits) as well. Such growth might also require creation of an intermediate appeals court to screen the

1. *See* Jerry L. Mashaw, *Recovering American Administrative Law: Federalist Foundations, 1787–1801*, 115 YALE L.J. 1256, 1260 (2006).

additional appeals and circuit splits that would otherwise go to the Supreme Court. This would be expensive, given Article III judges' high salaries and life tenure, and would also lead to a more disordered development of the law.

In addition, there are some affirmative reasons for such delegation. Administrative adjudication is generally more informal and efficient than cases heard under the Federal Rules of Civil Procedure and Federal Rules of Evidence, and there is no need to empanel a jury. It allows the use of specialized presiders and deciders, and the concomitant buildup of expertise in the adjudicatory arm of the agency that also helps to inform agency rulemaking, thus promoting more uniform development of policy.

To be sure, cases involving "private rights," which involve two private parties rather than the government and a private party, and "suits at common law" normally must, as discussed in this chapter, be assigned to the federal courts. Congress obviously may want to assign other cases of special significance to the courts as well. But otherwise, there are often good reasons for assigning cases to an agency or a specialized Article I court.

The practical distinction between adjudication by agencies as compared to adjudication by Article I courts is somewhat unclear. Each involves adjudicators who are "officers" under the Appointments Clause of the Constitution.[2] Decisions of both ordinarily are reviewable by the Article III courts, and each can bring the benefit of specialized expertise. Article I courts are considered more court-like, though, and Congress has often provided Article I judges with higher salaries and long, defined terms of office.

The first break from Article III adjudication that was accepted by the Supreme Court occurred when the Court, in a decision by Chief Justice Marshall, authorized the creation of territorial courts in *American Insurance Co. v. Canter.*[3] In that case, the Court allowed a Florida territorial court, staffed with judges who had four-year terms, to decide a case that would have been within the admiralty jurisdiction of federal district courts sitting in one of the states. Although these courts could also be deemed Article IV courts because of that Article's conferral to Congress the power to regulate federal territories, other

2. U.S. Const. art. II, § 2, cl. 2; Freytag v. Comm'r of Internal Revenue, 501 U.S. 868 (1991) (Tax Court); Lucia v. Sec. & Exch. Comm'n, 138 S. Ct. 2044 (Securities and Exchange Commission ALJs).

3. 26 U.S. 511 (1828).

non-Article III courts were also soon created, the first one being the Court of Claims, established in 1855, which heard—and still hears today—money claims against the federal government.[4]

Meanwhile, from the earliest days of our country, executive officers were given adjudicative responsibilities. As Professor Jerry Mashaw describes it:

> [L]arge classes of private claims—for remission of taxes, payments on contracts with the Post Office, veterans' disability pensions, and disaster relief—were subject to individualized administrative adjudication and administrative appeal. But save for those claims that used courts as commissioners, and therefore borrowed judicial procedures for finding facts, there seems to have been little legislative, and no judicial, attention to the processes by which rules were promulgated or cases decided. The proceduralism that dominates post-APA legal thinking in administrative law is almost wholly absent, except in the internal rules and practices adopted by the various departments or ad hoc commissions, and perhaps in the use of merchant arbitrators to value goods and to report on the seaworthiness of vessels.[5]

He goes on to explain:

> [J]udicial review in the Federalist period was quite unlike our contemporary practice, which emphasizes access to prohibitory and mandatory injunctions and declaratory judgment. Federalist Congresses relied instead on criminal penalties, bonds, qui tam enforcement, and the preexisting broad opportunities for common law damage actions. Where we see judicial review as a relatively unified and statutorily prescribed practice of holding government accountable to law, Federalist Congresses, administrators, and courts accepted and constructed a variegated set of highly particularized common law remedies against individuals. Appellate review within departments may have been more

4. Harold H. Bruff, *Specialized Courts in Administrative Law*, 43 ADMIN. L. REV. 329, 333 (1991); Floyd D. Shimomura, *The History of Claims against the United States: The Evolution from a Legislative toward a Judicial Model of Payment*, 45 LA. L. REV. 625 (1985).

5. Mashaw, *supra* note 1, at 1341.

like modern judicial review than were the available remedies against federal officials in court.[6]

During these early years, two of the major issues confronting Congress were how to handle money claims against the government and public-land claims. While it took until 1855 for Congress to create the Court of Claims, Congress, in 1812, created the General Land Office in the Department of the Treasury with a commissioner to oversee disputes over land claims.[7] The courts generally treated decisions by the commissioner as unreviewable.[8] More importantly for future jurisprudence on the constitutionality of administrative adjudication, in *Murray's Lessee v. Hoboken Land & Improvement Co.*, the Supreme Court treated public-land adjudication as a "public-rights" dispute that could be conclusively adjudicated by either Congress or, if Congress so delegated, to an executive officer or agency. In that case the Court said:

> [T]here are matters, involving public rights, which may be presented in such form that the judicial power is capable of acting on them, and which are susceptible of judicial determination, but which [C]ongress may or may not bring within the cognizance of the courts of the United States, as it may deem proper. Equitable claims to land by the inhabitants of ceded territories form a striking instance of such a class of cases . . . .[9]

The 19th century saw the creation of the first regulatory agencies, the first being the Board of Supervising Inspectors, which, in 1852, was tasked with regulating the safety of steamboats,[10] followed by the creation of the Interstate Commerce Commission to regulate railroads in 1887. But while these agencies conducted adjudications, their decisions were not self-enforcing and could be challenged in

---

6. *Id.*

7. Jerry L. Mashaw, *Reluctant Nationalists: Federal Administration and Administrative Law in the Republican Era*, 1801–1829, 116 Yale L.J. 1636, 1696–734 (2007).

8. Joseph D. Kearney & Thomas W. Merrill, *Contested Shore: Property Rights in Reclaimed Land and the Battle for Streeterville*, 107 Nw. U. L. Rev. 1057, 1092 (2013).

9. Murray's Lessee v. Hoboken Land & Improvement Co., 59 U.S. 272, 284 (1856).

10. Jerry L. Mashaw, *Administration and "The Democracy": Administrative Law from Jackson to Lincoln, 1829–1861*, 117 Yale L.J. 1568, 1628–66 (2008).

courts, which tended to review their decisions de novo. As Professor Thomas Merrill explains:

> Either courts would review administrators' actions under one of the prerogative writs such as mandamus or habeas corpus, or there was no judicial review at all, with aggrieved claimants relegated either to filing internal complaints with the agency or petitioning Congress for relief. Not until the early decades of the twentieth century did courts embrace the salient features of the appellate review model, which allowed decisional authority to be shared between agencies and courts. Insofar as federal courts are concerned, the appellate review model first emerged in full blown form in the context of judicial review of orders of the Interstate Commerce Commission around 1910. The model spread from there to other contexts, including review of orders of the Federal Trade Commission.[11]

This helps to explain why the Supreme Court, without much difficulty, decided that Congress could assign the adjudication of disputes arising out of federal laws to an administrative agency in *Crowell v. Benson*.[12] The case arose out of a piece of social legislation enacted in 1916 that created the U.S. Employees' Compensation Commission (USEC) to administer workers' compensation benefits for civil employees of the United States suffering personal injuries while in the performance of official duties. The USEC's jurisdiction was broadened in 1927 to include administration of the Longshore and Harbor Workers' Compensation Act, which provided similar benefits to employees in private enterprise engaged in maritime work on navigable waters of the United States.

In *Crowell*, the Court upheld Congress's ability to delegate adjudicative power to the USEC. An employer sought to enjoin the enforcement of a USEC award to a dockworker, arguing in part that the act violated Article III of the Constitution by assigning a case within the jurisdiction of the federal district courts' admiralty jurisdiction to an executive agency with judicial review (but no trial or jury) in the federal courts. But the Court, in rebuffing this argument, cited *Murray's Lessee* and distinguished cases involving matters of "public rights" in

11. Thomas W. Merrill, *Article III, Agency Adjudication, and the Origins of the Appellate Review Model of Administrative Law*, 111 COLUM. L. REV. 939, 942 (2011).

12. 285 U.S. 22 (1932).

which the government and private persons were opposing parties, and matters of "private rights" where two private parties were opposed. The Court reasoned that because Congress could assign public-rights disputes to itself or to executive officers, it could also assign them to administrative tribunals like the USEC. Even though, in this particular case, the USEC essentially was a referee between the private employer and employee in the longshoremen and harbor workers context so that distinction did not apply, the Court nevertheless upheld the delegation because it found that Article III courts had the power to independently review all issues of law and "questions of constitutional and jurisdictional fact." The Court still pays heed to this public rights/private rights distinction in cases challenging non-Article III adjudication programs.

6.3 THE ADMINISTRATIVE PROCEDURE ACT

Crowell v. Benson served to usher in the debates leading up to the enactment of the APA in 1946. That decision established the constitutionality of assigning adjudicative duties to administrative agencies, but the appropriateness of doing so continued to be a major issue in the run-up to the enactment of the APA. Indeed, one of the leading accounts of the APA's legislative history highlighted the anti-New Deal American Bar Association Special Committee on Administrative Law's goal in these legislative negotiations as "amputat[ing] agencies' adjudicatory functions" because "the Supreme Court would not" do so.[13] But since agencies were already adjudicating to some degree, most of the ultimate reform efforts strove to reach a compromise on how it should be done.

The foundational document was provided by the *Final Report of the Attorney General's Committee on Administrative Procedure*.[14] One of the main reasons for the formation of the committee was the concern about the lack of uniformity among agency hearing officers and the perceived procedural unfairness of agency adjudication. As the committee report stated, "Most of the controversy over administrative

---

13. *See* George B. Shepherd, *Fierce Compromise: The Administrative Procedure Act Emerges from New Deal Politics*, 90 Nw. L. Rev. 1557, 1577 (1996).

14. Final Report of the Attorney General's Committee on Administrative Procedure, S. Doc. No. 8 (1941) [hereinafter Attorney General's Committee Report]. Author note: This and the following two paragraphs of the text are adapted from my earlier account, Jeffrey S. Lubbers, *APA Adjudication: Is the Quest for Uniformity Faltering?*, 10 Admin. L.J. Am. U. 65, 65–67 (1996).

procedure has centered around formal adjudication." The report went on to describe the lack of uniformity that existed in 1941:

> The methods of hearing and initial decision and the internal procedural structure vary from agency to agency. In general, it has been customary to designate hearing officers before whom evidence may be adduced—whether they be a board of three or more individuals, or, as is more common, a single hearing officer, variously known as a trial examiner, a referee, a presiding officer, a district engineer, a deputy commissioner, or a register. These hearing officers have been selected in various ways. . . .
>
> * * *
>
> No less varied is the weight attached by the several agencies to the judgments of those who conduct the hearings. In most of the agencies the person who presides is an adviser with no real power to decide.[15]

This led the committee to conclude that where

> agencies have recognized the importance of hearing officers in the salaries paid, in the independence of view encouraged and accorded, and in the importance given to their decisions, the positions have attracted and held men whose ability and fairness have been recognized by the bar and the public. Where the opposite has happened, progressive decline has occurred. . . .
>
> * * *
>
> This is the heart of formal administrative adjudication. It cannot succeed without competent and well-paid men exercising functions of responsibility and interest.[16]

The committee then went on to recommend a highly structured system of "hearing commissioners," to be appointed by a proposed Office of Federal Administrative Procedure (OFAP), for seven-year terms (subject to a one-year "provisional appointment"), with "substantial" but tiered salaries. Agencies that "deal with many small cases" could request permission from the OFAP to pay the lower salary.

It is striking that the committee's report, recommendation, and proposed bill focused almost exclusively on the need to establish a

---

15. Attorney General's Committee Report, *supra* note 14.
16. *Id.*

system of "hearing commissioners" to handle all on-the-record adjudications. The committee's recommendations on the hearing *procedures* were much less prescriptive. Title III ("Administrative Adjudication") of the proposed bill almost completely revolved around the hearing commissioners' status, powers, and duties. In the interest of maintaining flexibility, the majority of the committee eschewed a proposed code of administrative procedures, preferring instead to rely on the creation of the hearing commissioner system and on the proposed new OFAP to provide additional uniformity. However, three (ultimately influential) committee members felt strongly enough about the need for more prescriptive and uniform procedures that they departed from the majority and went so far as to draft a "code of standards of fair procedure."[17]

The enacted APA, which passed unanimously, ultimately reflected both points of view—a heavy reliance on a system of "hearing examiners" and a rather prescriptive, albeit not inflexible, set of formal hearing procedures, reflected in sections 5, 7, and 8 of the APA (now 5 U.S.C. §§ 554, 556, and 557).[18]

Note, however, that § 554(a) requires that these formal-hearing provisions must be triggered by a requirement of a hearing "on the record" in the program statute. This means that agencies are not required to follow the formal-adjudication provisions for other hearing programs, which allows them to use non-ALJ adjudicators (now commonly called "administrative judges," or AJs). The APA does not contain specific procedural requirements for such "informal" or "nonformal" hearings, although, of course, they must conform to due process.[19] This has led to

17. Carl McFarland, E. Blythe Stason, and Arthur T. Vanderbilt urged the adoption of "legislative standards of fair procedure" and proposed text as well. The differences among committee members are described in Walter Gellhorn, *The Administrative Procedure Act: The Beginnings*, 72 VA. L. REV. 219, 227–30 (1986). *See also Present at the Creation: Regulatory Reform before 1946*, 38 ADMIN. L. REV. 511 (1986).

18. Daniel J. Gifford, *Adjudication in Independent Tribunals: The Role of an Alternative Agency Structure*, 66 NOTRE DAME L. REV. 965, 979 (1991). The OFAP was not created. Instead, the functions of overseeing the hearing examiner program fell to the Civil Service Commission, now the Office of Personnel Management.

19. Paul R. Verkuil, *Study of Informal Adjudication Procedures*, 43 U. CHI. L. REV. 739 (1976). Section 555 does provide for some general rights (e.g., right to representation) that are applicable to all proceedings. *But see* Emily S. Bremer, *The Rediscovered Stages of Agency Adjudication*, 99 WASH. U. L. REV. 377 (2021) (arguing that the conventional wisdom that the APA establishes two types of adjudication—formal and informal—is wrong and that the APA's foundational history shows it instead codified informal and formal stages—not modes—of adjudication).

a large number of AJs used by agencies.[20] This chapter concentrates on formal adjudication conducted by ALJs. The dichotomy between ALJs and AJs is explored more in Chapters 8–10.

6.4 DEVELOPMENTS SINCE THE ADMINISTRATIVE PROCEDURE ACT

In the early years after the enactment of the APA, there were relatively few hearing examiners. In 1947, there were 196, of whom 125 (64 percent) were employed in agencies generally considered to be economic regulatory agencies.[21] This number grew steadily, fueled by the large increases in number at the Social Security Administration to the point that, by 1971, there were more than 1,000. In 1972 their name was changed to "administrative law judge" by the Civil Service Commission (CSC), and the APA was amended to reflect that name change in 1978. Today there are approximately 1,700 ALJs, but only about 2 percent of them are employed in economic regulatory agencies.

The status of ALJs was also enhanced by the Supreme Court soon after the enactment of the APA, when, in *Universal Camera Corp. v. National Labor Relations Board*, the Court ruled that when courts review agency adjudications under the substantial evidence test, they had to review "the whole record" including the decision of the hearing examiner.[22] That means that when an agency head reverses the decision of the ALJ, the reviewing court will likely look more closely at the final decision.

How hearing examiners were to be selected was a controversial issue. The APA was not specific on this point but did provide that they should be selected by the agencies, subject to the civil service laws. The act, and its legislative history, made clear that general authority over the hearing examiner program should be exercised by the CSC, later succeeded by the Office of Personnel Management (OPM) in 1978. The CSC, after navigating a lot of controversy about what to do about

20. Kent Barnett et al., Admin. Conf. of the U.S., Non-ALJ Adjudicators in Federal Agencies: Status, Selection, Oversight, and Removal (2018).

21. Thomas C. Mans, *Selecting the Hidden Judiciary: How the Merit Process Works in Choosing Administrative Law Judges* (Pt. I), 63 Judicature 60, 64 (1979).

22. 340 U.S. 474 (1951).

incumbent hearing examiners,[23] developed a competitive process for ranking eligible applicants that lasted until 2018, when President Trump removed OPM from the process (see Chapter 9).[24]

Meanwhile, despite the apparent entrenchment of administrative adjudication and the recognition of the importance of ALJs in several Supreme Court decisions,[25] disputes continued to arise concerning the delegation of adjudicative authority to non-Article III adjudicators.

Several of these cases concerned the creation and powers of the Article I bankruptcy courts. In *Northern Pipeline Construction Co. v. Marathon Pipe Line Co.*, the Supreme Court invalidated a statute that created these courts and had assigned to them the trial of all issues involved in such cases including breach of contract cases—the classic example of private-rights cases.[26] The Court, in a 4–3 decision, found this to be an improper delegation, which raised new questions about the assignment of adjudication to agencies or, put another way, whether the broad reading of *Crowell v. Benson* was no longer appropriate.

Just four years later, the Court put that question to bed again in its ruling in *Commodity Futures Trading Commission v. Shor.*[27] Under the Commodity Exchange Act, the Commodity Futures Trading Commission (CFTC) could award reparations (money damages) to customers from brokers who were adjudged (in an agency adjudication conducted by ALJs) to have violated the act. Under the act, the brokers could file counterclaims against customers in court, but the CFTC issued a regulation allowing it to decide broker counterclaims if the broker preferred the agency forum over the court. In this case, the CFTC ALJ ruled against the customer's reparations claim and also in favor of the broker's counterclaim for breach of contract. The customer sought judicial review of both rulings. The D.C. Circuit affirmed the reparations decision, but, citing *Northern Pipeline*, found that the

---

23. For two detailed historical accounts, see LLOYD D. MUSOLF, FEDERAL EXAMINERS AND THE CONFLICT OF LAW AND ADMINISTRATION 139–72 (1953), and John W. Macy, Jr., *The APA and the Hearing Examiner: Products of a Viable Political Society*, 27 FED. BAR J. 351 (1967). Macy was the CSC's executive director during this formative period.

24. Exec. Order No. 13,843, Excepting Administrative Law Judges from the Competitive Service, 83 Fed. Reg. 32,755 (July 10, 2018).

25. *See, e.g.*, Ramspeck v. Fed. Trial Exam'rs Conf., 345 U.S. 128, 142 (1953); Butz v. Economou, 438 U.S. 478, 513 (1978); Fed. Mar. Comm'n v. S.C. State Ports Auth., 535 U.S. 743, 758 (2002).

26. 458 U.S. 50 (1982).

27. 478 U.S. 833 (1986).

CFTC's claim of jurisdiction over the counterclaim violated Article III. The Supreme Court disagreed and allowed the CFTC to decide both claims. In so doing, the Court said that the Commodity Exchange Act's scheme "hews closely to the model approved by the Court in *Crowell v. Benson*." The Court used a four-prong balancing test:

> [I]n reviewing Article III challenges, we have weighed a number of factors, none of which has been deemed determinative, with an eye to the practical effect that the congressional action will have on the constitutionally assigned role of the federal judiciary. Among the factors upon which we have focused are the extent to which the "essential attributes of judicial power" are reserved to Article III courts, and, conversely, the extent to which the non-Article III forum exercises the range of jurisdiction and powers normally vested only in Article III courts, the origins and importance of the right to be adjudicated, and the concerns that drove Congress to depart from the requirements of Article III.[28]

The Court emphasized the inefficiency of requiring "a bifurcated examination of the single dispute," as well as the availability of judicial review in the Article III courts. As for the fact that the counterclaim in this case was a classic private-rights case, the Court acknowledged that it is "a claim of the kind assumed to be at the 'core' of matters normally reserved to Article III courts." But the Court said this factor was not determinative: "there is no reason inherent in separation of powers principles to accord the state law character of a claim talismanic power in Article III inquiries."[29]

Since *Schor*, the Court has reiterated its *Northern Pipeline* holding in the context of another bankruptcy court case,[30] but has upheld the creation of an administrative adjudication program administered by the Patent Trial and Appeal Board (PTAB) (within the U.S. Patent and Trademark Office (USPTO) in the Department of Commerce) to decide private parties' challenges to patents previously granted by the

28. *Id.* at 851.

29. *Id.* at 853.

30. Stern v. Marshall, 564 U.S. 462 (2011) (bankruptcy judges cannot hear and decide private-rights counterclaims). *But see* Exec. Benefits Ins. Agency v. Arkison, 573 U.S. 25 (2014) (upholding the use of bankruptcy judges to hear and propose decisions in private-rights disputes to district court judges); Wellness Int'l Network, Ltd. v. Sharif, 575 U.S. 665 (2015) (bankruptcy judges can decide private-rights issues if both parties voluntarily consent).

USPTO.[31] Congress created this program in 2011 as an alternative to requiring objectors to challenge patents in federal district court. While it looks like this could be considered a private-rights type of case, because it involves a dispute between two private parties, the Supreme Court held that the initial decision to grant a patent is a public-rights issue since it is the government that must decide whether to do so. The dispute before the PTAB "is simply a reconsideration of that grant," and therefore remains a public-rights case.

This issue is related to the question of when the Seventh Amendment's right to a jury trial for "suits at common law" might limit Congress's assignment of disputes to an administrative agency or Article I court. When Congress assigned the adjudication of Occupational Safety and Health Act violations to an agency, a respondent challenged this procedure, claiming it violated his right to a jury trial, but the Supreme Court rejected that claim because this statutory program involved "public rights" not "private rights."[32] Later, however, the Court clarified that a jury trial right still obtains when Congress required the agency to seek any civil money penalty via a traditional court-collection lawsuit as is required by the Clean Water Act.[33]

But this issue does not simply depend on congressional assignment. The Supreme Court, in *Granfinanciera, S.A. v. Nordberg*, has also made clear, albeit in a private-rights case, that "the Seventh Amendment also applies to actions brought to enforce statutory rights that are analogous to common-law causes of action ordinarily decided in English law courts in the late eighteenth century, as opposed to those customarily heard by courts of equity or admiralty."[34] This has led the Fifth Circuit to overturn a Securities and Exchange Commission securities fraud enforcement action on the ground that Congress could not assign such an action to agency adjudication because fraud actions have been heard by common-law courts for centuries.[35] A dissenting judge said that the majority was flouting *Atlas Roofing*, misreading *Granfinanciera*, and that "our sister circuits routinely hold that an enforcement action by the Government for violations of a federal

31. Oil States Energy Servs., LLC v. Greene's Energy Grp., LLC, 138 S. Ct. 1365 (2018).

32. Atlas Roofing v. Occupational Safety & Health Rev. Comm'n, 430 U.S. 442 (1977).

33. Tull v. United States, 481 U.S. 412 (1987).

34. 492 U.S. 33, 41 (1989); *see also* Feltner v. Columbia Pictures Television, Inc., 523 U.S. 340 (1998).

35. Jarkesy v. Sec. & Exch. Comm'n, 34 F.4th 446, 455 (5th Cir. 2022).

statute or regulation is a 'public right' that Congress may assign to an agency for adjudication without offending the Seventh Amendment."[36] Obviously if such a decision were to stand, the validity of much agency enforcement adjudication would be called into question.

6.5 PROPOSALS TO CREATE MORE INDEPENDENCE FOR ADMINISTRATIVE LAW JUDGES

The U.S. model of an administrative adjudication system relies heavily on "internal" as opposed to "external" administrative adjudication, the model used in most other countries, which relies on separate administrative courts or tribunals to conduct evidentiary hearings in such cases.[37] However, despite the APA provisions that promote ALJ independence, the fact that ALJs do remain employees of the agency has created hard-to-eliminate perceptions of unfairness among the private bar.

In several situations, Congress has responded to these concerns by creating a "split-enforcement" structure, whereby the regulatory agency does not conduct enforcement hearings before its own ALJs but rather must allow respondents to defend themselves before the ALJs of a separate agency. The two main examples of this are cases brought by the Occupational Safety and Health Administration (OSHA) and the Mine Safety and Health Administration (MSHA), both of which are within the Department of Labor. These agencies investigate violations of their statutes and regulations and issue notices of violations. But respondents can request a hearing in the Occupational Safety and Health Review Commission (OSHRC) and the Federal Mine Safety and Health Review Commission (FMSHRC), respectively. Each of the two commissions is an independent agency headed by multimember boards and have their own fleets of ALJs to decide these cases. If OSHA or MSHA loses their case, they can petition for review of OSHRC's or FMSHRC's decision in federal court. A similar split-enforcement structure was created in the area of enforcement against federally licensed pilots, whereby pilots can contest Federal Aviation Administration citations before ALJs of the independent National

36. *Id.* at 468.

37. Michael Asimow, *Five Models of Administrative Adjudication*, 63 Am. J. Compar. L. 3 (2015); Jeffrey S. Lubbers, *Administrative Adjudication—the U.S. Is the Outlier*, *in* The Oxford Handbook of Administrative Justice 45 (Marc Hertogh et al. eds., 2022).

Transportation Safety Board. While this type of system does augment the independence of the adjudication, it creates additional costs, complexities in judicial review, and the potential for discord among agencies.[38]

Others have suggested removing ALJs from the agencies entirely, and housing them in their own separate agency. This structure is used in about 30 states, where it is known as the "central-panel" approach.[39] Bills have been introduced in Congress to create such a system (often called the "independent corps" approach) for many years, but they have been opposed by the agencies and the Department of Justice on the grounds that it would erode the subject-matter expertise that ALJs currently acquire while working in their agencies.[40] Recently, these proposals have reemerged as a possible fix to constitutional challenges to the so-called "double for-cause" removal protection enjoyed by ALJs.[41] See Chapter 9 for a discussion of these challenges.

---

38. George R. Johnson, Jr., *The Split-Enforcement Model: Some Conclusions from the OSHA and MSHA Experiences*, 39 ADMIN. L. REV. 315 (1987).

39. Malcolm C. Rich & Alison Goldstein, *The Need for a Central Panel Approach to Administrative Adjudication: Pros, Cons, and Selected Practices*, 39 J. NAT'L ASS'N ADMIN. L. JUDICIARY 1 (2019).

40. Jeffrey S. Lubbers, *A Unified Corps of ALJs: A Proposal to Test the Idea at the Federal Level*, 65 JUDICATURE 266 (1981).

41. Richard E. Levy & Robert L. Glicksman, *Restoring ALJ Independence*, 105 MINN. L. REV. 39 (2020); *see also* Richard J. Pierce, Jr., *Agency Adjudication: It Is Time to Hit the Reset Button*, 28 GEO. MASON L. REV. 643 (2021).

Chapter 7
Stages of Agency Adjudication Processes

Christopher J. Walker

7.1 CHAPTER OVERVIEW

Although there is great variation throughout the federal administrative state, the standard model for the federal agency adjudication can be sequentially divided into four stages: (1) hearing-less informal agency adjudication (Chapters 16 and 17); (2) hearing-level review (Chapter 18); (3) agency appellate review, including agency-head review (Chapter 19); and (4) judicial review (Chapter 27). This chapter provides an overview of the stages of the adjudication process to help situate the remaining chapters.[1]

7.2 INFORMAL AGENCY ADJUDICATION WITHOUT A LEGALLY REQUIRED EVIDENTIARY HEARING

As further detailed in Chapters 16 and 17, the federal adjudicatory process often begins with some informal adjudicative decision from a

1. This chapter incorporates material, where appropriate, from the second edition of *A Guidebook to Federal Agency Adjudication* as well as from the subsequent, more-detailed chapters on each stage from this edition.

frontline agency official. These agency decisions are diverse and wide-ranging and include those relating to grants, benefits, loans, and subsidies; licensing and accrediting; inspections, grading, and auditing; planning, policymaking, economic development, and public works; penalties for nontenured government employees or prison inmates; labor relations; and violations of statutes or agency rules by regulated entities—just to name a few. As discussed in Chapter 16, agencies usually engage in numerous activities before this first, frontline informal adjudication decision, such as engaging in consultations and investigations and then exercising enforcement and settlement discretion. In many administrative programs, it is much more efficient to begin with an informal process and decision that allows the agency and the regulated party to first attempt to resolve the matter through less formal and less costly procedures.

These frontline agency decisions fit within the "informal adjudication" category of the Administrative Procedure Act (APA) for issuing orders when the formal-adjudication provisions of the APA are not applicable. Except for a few provisions set forth in the APA (5 U.S.C. §§ 555 and 558), the APA does not spell out the procedures that an agency must follow when engaging in informal adjudication. Instead, by agency organic statute and implementing regulations, informal adjudication comprises a wide variety of agency procedures, some resembling what may be traditionally thought of as adjudication and others not resembling adjudication at all.[2] In the Types A-B-C adjudication framework introduced in Chapter 1, these agency actions would be categorized as Type C informal adjudications in which no evidentiary hearing is required by statute or regulation.

The vast majority of agency adjudications each year fall into this Type C informal adjudication category. To provide one example, the Internal Revenue Service (IRS) routinely makes tax deficiency determinations following an audit without a legally required evidentiary hearing.[3] Although the number of IRS deficiency determinations is not publicly available, we know that the IRS audits or reviews around 5 percent of the tax returns filed each year, totaling more than five

---

2. *See, e.g.*, Izaak Walton League of Am. v. Marsh, 655 F.2d 346, 361 n.37 (D.C. Cir. 1981) (observing that "informal adjudication is a residual category including all agency actions that are not rulemaking and that need not be conducted through on the record hearings").

3. *See, e.g.*, Stephanie Hoffer & Christopher J. Walker, *The Death of Tax Court Exceptionalism*, 99 MINN. L. REV. 221, 235–37 (2014).

million audits and reviews. And in fiscal year 2016, for instance, the IRS imposed civil penalties on nearly 40,000 filers.[4]

Generally speaking, these informal agency adjudications are subject to further review within the agency and then judicial review, though some decisions are formally nonreviewable by statute and most others as a practical matter never receive further review (either because the regulated party prevails or lacks the wherewithal to seek further review).[5] This review could include additional Type C adjudications before reaching a more formal hearing-level adjudication.[6]

7.3 HEARING-LEVEL ADJUDICATION

The next stage in the federal adjudication process is typically a hearing before an agency adjudicator. This stage can be triggered when a party is dissatisfied with the agency's frontline decision, such as a denial of a benefit or application or an order providing for a coercive remedy such as a sanction. But some agency adjudications start at this hearing stage, such as an enforcement action that has been brought in agency adjudication by a financial regulator or a removal proceeding brought against a noncitizen by the Department of Homeland Security in the Justice Department's immigration court system.

The hearing-level adjudication stage can be grouped into two categories: (1) APA-governed formal adjudication, where the statute requires a hearing on the record (Type A adjudication), and (2) formal-like adjudication where the agency's organic statute, implementing regulations, or an executive order requires an evidentiary hearing (Type B adjudication). Both will be addressed in turn, and are further explored in Chapter 18.

---

4. 1 NATIONAL TAXPAYER ADVOCATE, 2016 ANNUAL REPORT TO CONGRESS 28 fig.S.6, 42 tbl.7 (2016), https://www.taxpayeradvocate.irs.gov/wp-content/uploads/2020/08/ARC16_Volume1.pdf.

5. *See, e.g.*, Christopher J. Walker, *Constraining Bureaucracy beyond Judicial Review*, DÆDALUS, Summer 2021, at 150, 159–61 (discussing statutory nonreviewability provisions as well as the practical reasons why agency adjudication decisions never make it to federal court).

6. *See generally* Emily S. Bremer, *The Rediscovered Stages of Agency Adjudication*, 99 WASH. U. L. REV. 377, 402–10 (2021) (exploring as a historical matter how APA formal and informal adjudications were viewed, and should be viewed, as stages—not modes—of regulatory action).

7.31 Type A, Administrative Procedure Act-Governed Formal Adjudication

Paradigmatic APA-governed formal adjudication requires an evidentiary hearing (usually) held before an administrative law judge (ALJ) in which parties are entitled to present oral or documentary evidence, submit rebuttal evidence, and cross-examine witnesses (if required for a full disclosure of the facts).[7] ALJs presiding over this formal adjudicatory hearing are functionally equivalent to a trial judge in a bench trial. The ALJ is the principal fact finder and initial decision-maker in an agency adjudication, and the APA generally empowers ALJs to "regulate the course of the hearing."[8] In such circumstances, the APA requires a number of trial-like procedures similar to a bench trial in federal court, subject to modification in the agency's governing statute.[9] Moreover, Congress has sought to limit agency control over the selection, retention, and removal of ALJs, such that ALJs enjoy strong decisional independence.[10]

The ALJ's decision must be based exclusively on the record created at the hearing and supported by "reliable, probative, and substantial evidence."[11] Accordingly, the APA requires the agency to provide the parties with an "exclusive record" of "[t]he transcript of

---

7. 5 U.S.C. § 556(d).

8. *Id.* § 556(c)(5).

9. *See generally* 1 RICHARD J. PIERCE & KRISTIN E. HICKMAN, ADMINISTRATIVE LAW TREATISE ch. 6 (6th ed. 2019) (discussing formal adjudication procedures set forth in the APA, 5 U.S.C. §§ 554–557).

10. While agencies may "appoint as many administrative law judges as are necessary" to handle their caseload, 5 U.S.C. § 3105, agencies have historically been limited in selecting ALJs from a list of candidates selected by the Office of Personnel Management (OPM). *But see* Exec. Order No. 13,843, 83 Fed. Reg. 32,755 (July 13, 2018) (directing, in light of *Lucia v. Securities & Exchange Commission*, 138 S. Ct. 2044 (2018), and for policy reasons that ALJs be exempted from OPM's competitive hiring rules and examinations and that federal agencies establish their own processes for hiring ALJs). Once appointed, ALJs are not subject to performance reviews, and their compensation is set by statute and OPM regulations. 5 U.S.C. §§ 4301(2)(D), 5372. ALJs can only be removed for "good cause," as determined by an independent agency, the Merit Systems Protection Board, after a formal adjudicative hearing. *Id.* § 7521(a). Because ALJs do not serve a fixed term, they in essence have life tenure. *See generally* Harold H. Bruff, *Specialized Courts in Administrative Law*, 43 ADMIN. L. REV. 329, 346 (1991); Jeffrey S. Lubbers, *Federal Administrative Law Judges: A Focus on Our Invisible Judiciary*, 33 ADMIN. L. REV. 109, 112–20 (1981); Paul R. Verkuil, *Reflections upon the Federal Administrative Judiciary*, 39 UCLA L. REV. 1341, 1344 (1992).

11. 5 U.S.C. § 556(d).

testimony and exhibits, together with all papers and requests filed in the proceeding."[12] Not only must the agency's decision be based solely on the exclusive record created at the hearing, but it must also include a statement of "findings and conclusions, and the reasons or basis therefor, on all the material issues of fact, law, or discretion presented on the record."[13]

7.32 Type B, Formal-Like Adjudication

Despite administrative law's fixation on APA-governed formal adjudication, most formal-like adjudications (i.e., those in which a statute, regulation, or executive order requires an evidentiary hearing before an agency adjudicator) do not involve APA-governed formal adjudications before an ALJ or the agency itself.[14] Instead, they are adjudicated by non-ALJ agency personnel that have diverse titles, such as administrative judge, immigration judge, hearing officer, and presiding official—just to name a few. As Michael Asimow has observed, the APA "fails to regulate in any significant way the vast and rapidly increasing number of more or less formal evidentiary adjudicatory hearings required by federal statutes that are not conducted by ALJs and yet are functionally indistinguishable from the hearings that are conducted by ALJs."[15]

Type B adjudication vastly outnumbers Type A adjudication. For instance, in 2002, agencies reported that they conducted more than 550,000 adjudications annually outside of the APA-governed formal adjudication process, a 41 percent increase from a 1992 survey. In 2002, there were 3,370 non-ALJ adjudicators, a 25 percent increase from 2,692 non-ALJ adjudicators in 1992. By comparison, there were only 1,351 ALJs in 2002 and 1,167 ALJs in 1992.[16] By 2017, there were more than 10,831 non-ALJ adjudicators in the surveyed agencies.[17] In

---

12. *Id.* § 556(e).

13. *Id.* § 557(c)(3)(A).

14. *See* Christopher J. Walker & Melissa F. Wasserman, *The New World of Agency Adjudication*, 107 CAL. L. REV. 141, 153–57 (2019).

15. Michael Asimow, *The Spreading Umbrella: Extending the APA's Adjudication Provisions to All Evidentiary Hearings Required by Statute*, 56 ADMIN. L. REV. 1003, 1020 (2004).

16. RAYMOND LIMON, OFF. OF ADMIN. L. JUDGES, THE FEDERAL JUDICIARY THEN AND NOW—A DECADE OF CHANGE 1992–2002, at 3 (2002) (comparing 2002 survey data with findings from John H. Frye III, *Survey of Non-ALJ Hearing Programs in the Federal Government*, 44 ADMIN. L. REV. 261 (1992)).

17. Kent Barnett & Russell Wheeler, *Non-ALJ Adjudicators in Federal Agencies: Status, Selection, Oversight, and Removal*, 53 GA. L. REV. 1, 8 (2019). This number includes 7,856 patent examiners at the U.S. Patent and Trademark Office,

contrast, the Office of Personnel Management reports that there were 1,931 ALJs across the federal administrative state as of March 2017, 85 percent of whom work at the Social Security Administration.[18] In other words, the non-ALJ adjudicator workforce is five times as large as the ALJ workforce.

Moreover, there is great breadth and diversity in Type B adjudications. The Administrative Conference of the United States has exhaustively documented that diversity, observing that these adjudications

> involve types of matters spanning many substantive areas, including immigration, veterans' benefits, environmental issues, government contracts, and intellectual property. Some involve disputes between the federal government and private parties; others involve disputes between two private parties. Some involve trial-type proceedings that are at least as formal as [APA-governed formal] adjudication. Others are quite informal and can be decided based only on written submissions. Some proceedings are highly adversarial; others are inquisitorial. Caseloads vary. Some have huge backlogs and long delays; others seem relatively current. The structures for internal appeal also vary.[19]

As such, it is difficult to generalize the adjudicative process or form of agency decision when it comes to Type B adjudication. But perhaps unsurprisingly, many agencies have adopted procedures and decision-writing approaches similar to those in the Type A, APA-governed formal adjudication discussed in section 7.31.[20]

---

compared to a reported 1,000 patent examiners in the 2002 Limon study. If patent examiners are excluded from both surveys, we see a more modest increase in non-ALJ adjudicators from 2,370 in the 2002 survey to 2,976 in the 2017 survey—a 26 percent increase in 15 years.

18. *Administrative Law Judges—ALJs by Agency*, U.S. OFF. PERS. MGMT., https://www.opm.gov/services-for-agencies/administrative-law-judges/ #url=By-Agency (last visited June 27, 2023).

19. Administrative Conference Recommendation 2016-4, Evidentiary Hearings Not Required by the Administrative Procedure Act, 81 Fed. Reg. 94,312, 94,315 (Dec. 23, 2016).

20. *See generally* MICHAEL ASIMOW, ADMIN. CONF. OF THE U.S., FEDERAL ADMINISTRATIVE ADJUDICATION OUTSIDE THE ADMINISTRATIVE PROCEDURE ACT (2019).

7.4 AGENCY APPELLATE REVIEW

The critical difference between agency adjudication and a civil bench trial is that the agency head (or agency appellate review body) typically has de novo review authority as to both facts and law, while an appellate court defers to the trial court's factual findings.[21] Indeed, federal courts scholars have long distinguished Article III federal courts and Article I legislative courts from agency adjudicatory tribunals on the ground that the agency head has final policymaking authority.[22]

When it comes to Type A, APA-governed formal adjudication, agency-head review is set as the default—or "standard federal model"—for agency adjudication.[23] The APA provides that, in cases where "the agency did not preside at the reception of the evidence, the presiding employee . . . shall initially decide the case," and that initial "decision then becomes the decision of the agency without further proceedings unless there is an appeal to, or review on motion of, the agency within time provided by rule."[24] When the agency decides to review an initial decision—either on appeal or via sua sponte review—the agency head has final decision-making authority.[25] Furthermore, the U.S. Supreme Court has interpreted the APA to provide that an ALJ's initial decision is not entitled to deferential administrative review.[26] An agency has complete freedom, as though it had heard the initial evidence itself, when reviewing the decision of the ALJ. Nevertheless, the agency is

---

21. *See generally* Thomas W. Merrill, *Article III, Agency Adjudication, and the Origins of the Appellate Review Model of Administrative Law*, 111 COLUM. L. REV. 939, 940 (2011) (detailing how "[m]odern administrative law is built on the appellate review model of the relationship between reviewing courts and agencies," which "borrow[s] from the understandings that govern the relationship between appeals courts and trial courts in civil litigation").

22. *See, e.g.*, RICHARD H. FALLON, JR. ET AL., HART & WESCHLER'S THE FEDERAL COURTS AND THE FEDERAL SYSTEM 379–80 (7th ed. 2015); *accord* Richard H. Fallon, Jr., *Of Legislative Courts, Administrative Agencies, and Article III*, 101 HARV. L. REV. 915, 923–24 (1988).

23. Ronald M. Levin, *Administrative Judges and Agency Policy Development: The Koch Way*, 22 WM. & MARY BILL RTS. J. 407, 412 (2013).

24. 5 U.S.C. § 557(b).

25. *See, e.g.*, Russell L. Weaver, *Appellate Review in Executive Departments and Agencies*, 48 ADMIN. L. REV. 251, 252 (1996) (noting that while the APA "imposed strict divisions between those who prosecute and those who adjudicate," it "imposed far fewer restraints on the appellate process; under the APA, ALJ decisions were fully reviewable within the agency").

26. Fed. Commc'ns Comm'n v. Allentown Broad. Corp., 349 U.S. 358, 364–65 (1955).

typically required to explain why it has rejected an ALJ's findings, and courts examine the evidence more critically when an agency's reversal of an ALJ ruling turns on the credibility of the witnesses who testified at the hearing.[27]

Perhaps unsurprisingly, agency-head final decision-making authority is also a common feature of Type B formal-like adjudications outside of the APA.[28] Indeed, in the context of certain Type B patent adjudications at the U.S. Patent and Trademark Office (USPTO), the Supreme Court in *United States v. Arthrex* in 2021 observed that "'higher-level agency reconsideration' by the agency head is the standard way to maintain political accountability and effective oversight for adjudication that takes place outside the confines of [APA-governed formal adjudication]." In that context, the Court concluded "that the unreviewable authority wielded by [administrative patent judges] during inter partes review is incompatible with their appointment by the Secretary to an inferior office."[29]

To be sure, agency-head review is not available in all agency adjudication systems. As further discussed in Chapter 19, some agency heads by statute are precluded from further review, leaving the final decision to an appellate tribunal within the agency.[30] Notable examples include the Department of Veterans Affairs' Board of Veterans' Appeals and the Department of Labor's Benefits Review Board. The Patent Trial and Appeal Board at the USPTO was another example—that is, until the Supreme Court in *Arthrex* invalidated as unconstitutional the prohibition on agency-head review. At other agencies, the agency head has subdelegated by regulation final decision-making authority to an internal appellate review tribunal. Prominent examples include the Social Security Administration's Appeals Council and, subject to narrow exceptions, the Environmental Appeals Board at the Environmental Protection Agency. In those situations, the agency head likely still has the authority to review decisions by, for example, rescinding the relevant rule subdelegating final decision-making authority or by making

27. Universal Camera Corp. v. Nat'l Lab. Rels. Bd., 340 U.S. 474, 496 (1951). When the agency reverses for factual disputes, the Court has stated that "evidence supporting a conclusion may be less substantial when an impartial, experienced [ALJ] who has observed the witnesses and lived with the case has drawn conclusions different from the [agency's]."

28. *See* Walker & Wasserman, *supra* note 14, at 157.

29. United States v. Arthrex, 141 S. Ct. 1970, 1984–85 (2021).

30. *See generally* Christopher J. Walker et al., Admin. Conf. of the U.S., Precedential Decision Making in Agency Adjudication (2022).

a case-specific exception. That distinction may well make a constitutional difference under *Arthrex*.

The final two models of appellate review are direct agency-head review, such as at the National Labor Relations Board, Securities and Exchange Commission, and Merit Systems Protection Board, and intermediate review by an appellate board with final decision-making still vested in the agency head, such as at the Justice Department's Board of Immigration Appeals and the Department of Labor's Administrative Review Board.

Within these four distinct models of agency appellate review, the procedures and standards differ dramatically. Some provide for discretionary appellate review, others mandatory. Some appellate review is de novo; others are for abuse of discretion or some other deferential standard. Some agencies allow for the introduction of new evidence (or claims) on appeal, while others review only the administrative record compiled at the hearing. Some agencies require the party to seek agency appellate review before there is a final agency action reviewable in federal court, while others provide that agency appellate review is optional and can be bypassed to get judicial review.

7.5 JUDICIAL REVIEW

Unless Congress has precluded judicial review in federal court, the final stage of the federal agency adjudication process is judicial review. The APA sets the default procedures and standards for judicial review, which can and often are modified in agency-specific statutes.[31] Judicial review in the agency adjudication context is further explored in Chapter 27.

31. 5 U.S.C. §§ 701–706.

Part III

Adjudicators

Chapter 8

The Role and Authority of Adjudicators

Louis J. Virelli III

8.1 CHAPTER OVERVIEW

"Agency adjudication" is a broad and somewhat amorphous term. It includes proceedings that are clearly quasi-judicial, such as enforcement proceedings, and decisions that appear more administrative, like granting permits or deciding where to build a highway.[1] Yet despite variations in form and function, a common thread connects all adjudicatory proceedings. They involve an individual or group of individuals ("adjudicators") presiding over a process designed to help them reach a conclusion in "cases" where context-specific information controls. That conclusion will manifest in an administrative order.

Agency adjudicators have a broad collection of responsibilities. Most obviously, adjudicators are responsible for issuing administrative orders that reflect their findings of fact and law in individual cases. To arrive at an order, adjudicators can have responsibilities related to managing proceedings (section 8.2) and developing the record (section

1. *See* Citizens to Pres. Overton Park v. Volpe, 401 U.S. 402 (1971).

8.3). Adjudicators may also have a duty to assist self-represented parties (section 8.4). As representatives of the administrative state, adjudicators also have a responsibility to exercise judgment impartially and competently (section 8.5).

8.2 MANAGING PROCEEDINGS

Adjudicators' authority to manage proceedings is assigned by statute—typically the agency's enabling act, the Administrative Procedure Act (APA),[2] or both—and may be augmented by agency regulations. Adjudicators may also be bound by the requirements of due process (see Chapter 15).[3] Adjudicators presiding over hearings in formal adjudications—typically administrative law judges (ALJs) or agency heads—garner authority directly from the APA's adjudication provisions. By contrast, the authority of adjudicators presiding over hearings in informal adjudication is far less predictable and far more varied (see Chapter 18). In some instances, the role and authority of informal adjudicators is virtually indistinguishable from that of formal adjudicators, while in others it is quite distinct. In addition to formal and informal adjudicators who preside over hearings, there are adjudicators—sometimes agency heads, sometimes not—who review decisions issued after a hearing (see Chapter 19). There may also be frontline decision-makers who make preliminary decisions prior to any hearing and, in some programs, there is no constitutional or statutory right to a hearing at all (see Chapters 15 and 16).

8.21 Authority of Adjudicators in Formal Adjudication

The powers of adjudicators presiding over hearings in formal adjudications are stated relatively clearly in the APA. Unless otherwise specified by statute, hearings can be presided over by the agency head, one or more members of the multimember body that comprises the agency, or one or more ALJs.[4] The adjudicator presiding over the initial hearing has power to:

- Administer oaths
- Issue subpoenas
- Rule on offers of proof and procedural requests
- Receive relevant evidence

2. 5 U.S.C. § 556(c)
3. *See* Goldberg v. Kelly, 397 U.S. 254 (1970).
4. 5 U.S.C. § 556(b).

- Require depositions
- Regulate the course of the hearing
- Encourage alternative dispute resolution
- Make initial decisions or recommend decisions
- Take other action authorized by agency rule[5]

In some cases, the agency head will preside over the hearing and development of the record in the first instance and decide the case without further administrative review.[6] But in most instances, an ALJ initially presides over the hearing and development of the exclusive administrative record in the case.[7] The ALJ then issues an "initial decision," which becomes the decision of the agency unless there is a timely request for review by one of the parties or the agency head chooses to review the decision sua sponte.[8] In some cases, intermediate or final review authority is delegated to an appellate body.

The agency reviewer (often the agency head) may adopt the ALJ's initial decision without additional reasoning or explanation, or it may perform an independent review of that decision. The agency reviewer has authority to review all aspects of the ALJ's initial decision de novo, including findings of fact, policy determinations, and conclusions of law.[9] The procedures for agency review of an ALJ's initial decision are governed primarily by the agency's enabling act and the agency's own regulations.

If the agency chooses, it can require that the ALJ hold a hearing to develop a record and then certify that record to the agency reviewer for an initial decision. In that instance, except in cases of applications for initial licenses, the ALJ generally provides a "recommended" decision to the agency heads for their consideration. The recommended decision will then be followed by an initial decision from the agency.[10]

8.22 Authority of Adjudicators in Informal Adjudication

The authority of adjudicators in informal adjudication is difficult to summarize because informal adjudication includes an extremely wide range of proceedings with a correspondingly wide array of procedures

---

5. *Id.* § 556(c)(1)–(11).
6. *Id.* § 556(b)(1).
7. *Id.* § 556(b)(3).
8. *Id.* § 557(b).
9. *Id.*
10. *Id.*; *see also* ATTORNEY GENERAL'S MANUAL ON THE ADMINISTRATIVE PROCEDURE ACT 82 (1947).

and responsibilities for adjudicators. The APA says little about an adjudicator's authority in informal adjudication. It specifies only that an adjudicator may determine whether an interested person may appear in the proceeding, issue subpoenas authorized by law, and hold people in contempt for failure to comply with orders in an enforcement proceeding.[11] Most of the interagency continuity in informal adjudication derives from the requirements of due process and judicial review. Otherwise, the specifics of adjudicative authority in informal adjudication are governed primarily by the agency's enabling act and its own rules.

This variability in informal adjudication is evidenced by two examples at opposite ends of the spectrum of adjudicator authority. Deportation hearings under the Immigration and Nationality Act are not subject to the formal-adjudication provisions of the APA, yet the authority granted to the immigration judges (IJs) that preside over those hearings is nearly identical to that of ALJs in formal adjudication. Hearings before IJs are generally conducted in person, and the IJ has authority to "administer oaths, receive evidence, and interrogate, examine, and cross-examine the alien and any witnesses," as well as issue sanctions for contempt.[12]

By contrast, the U.S. Army Corps of Engineers (USACE) engages in informal adjudication when it approves construction projects in navigable waters. USACE adjudicators are subject to very few, if any, procedural requirements. A USACE regulation was interpreted to require that at least one public meeting be held by the agency as part of its preconstruction planning and authorization of a lock and dam project on the Mississippi River, but there were few official requirements governing the conduct of those meetings or adjudicators' authority.[13]

8.3 DEVELOPING THE RECORD

8.31 Adversarial and Nonadversarial (Inquisitorial) Proceedings

Agency adjudication involving evidentiary hearings can be divided into two broad categories: (1) adversarial proceedings, in which opposing parties develop the record by presenting their own evidence, and (2) nonadversarial (or inquisitorial) proceedings, in which the adjudicator is

11. 5 U.S.C. § 555.
12. 8 U.S.C. § 1229a(b)(1).
13. Izaak Walton League of Am. v. Marsh, 655 F.2d 346, 361–65 (D.C. Cir. 1981).

responsible for record development.[14] The adversarial process resembles a traditional judicial proceeding, while inquisitorial proceedings are more distinctly administrative. Agency enforcement proceedings typically follow the adversarial model, while benefits determinations are more likely to be inquisitorial.[15]

Formal adjudication under the APA is ordinarily adversarial.[16] The parties are given notice and file pleadings, and record development is managed by an adjudicator but is ultimately the responsibility of the parties. The exclusive record in the case consists of "[t]he transcript of testimony and exhibits, together with all papers and requests filed in the proceeding."[17] In developing the record, the parties may submit "oral or documentary evidence . . . [as well as] rebuttal evidence."[18] Oral hearings are not necessarily transcribed, but transcripts must be made available to a party upon request and payment of a fee.[19] Interested parties may be permitted to submit, when time and public interest allows, "facts, arguments, offers of settlement or proposals for adjustment."[20] The record is further shaped by the adjudicator's discretion in controlling the proceeding. Cross-examination is available when needed for a "full and true disclosure of the facts."[21] The adjudicator may take depositions or permit the parties to take them when doing so would serve "the ends of justice."[22] The agency decision is part of the record and must include an explanation of the agency's conclusions and a statement of the action taken.[23]

Some informal adjudications also qualify as adversarial. Immigration court proceedings conducted by the Department of Justice's Executive Office for Immigration Review (EOIR) and discrimination claims before the Equal Employment Opportunity Commission (EEOC) are

---

14. Carr v. Saul, 141 S. Ct. 1352, 1358 (2021).

15. Jon C. Dubin, *Torquemada Meets Kafka: The Misapplication of the Issue Exhaustion Doctrine to Inquisitorial Administrative Proceedings*, 97 Colum. L. Rev. 1289, 1301 (1997).

16. Christopher J. Walker & Melissa F. Wasserman, *The New World of Agency Adjudication*, 107 Cal. L. Rev. 141, 151 (2019).

17. 5 U.S.C. § 556(e).

18. *Id.* § 556(d).

19. *Id.* § 556(e); *see also* Attorney General's Manual on the Administrative Procedure Act, *supra* note 10, at 79.

20. 5 U.S.C. § 554(c)(1).

21. *Id.* § 556(d).

22. *Id.* § 556(c)(4).

23. *Id.* § 557(c)(3).

adversarial adjudications that resemble bench trials, despite not being governed by the formal-adjudication provisions of the APA.[24]

Inquisitorial proceedings are distinct from informal adjudication at agencies like EOIR and EEOC because they do not involve interactions between opposing parties. Inquisitorial proceedings generally include only the private claimant and an adjudicator who is responsible for developing the record, raising arguments for and against the private party, and making an ultimate determination. Counsel for the government may not be present. It is therefore imperative for the adjudicator in an inquisitorial case to ensure that a full and fair record is developed upon which to evaluate the party's claims. Inquisitorial cases most commonly involve claims for benefits. The two most prominent examples of agency benefit adjudications are social security and veterans' benefits. Despite the fact that the courts have held such benefits to be protected property interests within the meaning of the Constitution,[25] inquisitorial proceedings in general do not run afoul of due process.[26]

8.32 Exclusive Record, Official Notice, and Independent Research

Adjudication that involves an evidentiary hearing, whether adversarial or inquisitorial, is generally subject to the "exclusive-record" requirement.[27] The exclusive-record requirement means that the record developed in the adjudication is the only information upon which an agency may rely in reaching its decision and is the sole background for judicial review of the agency's factual and policy conclusions.[28]

In formal adjudication, the APA describes the exclusive record as "the transcript of testimony and exhibits, together with all papers and requests filed in the proceeding."[29] The exclusive-record concept also generally applies in informal adjudication that involves an evidentiary hearing but is not statutorily mandated by the APA. As a result, agency-specific statutes and regulations govern how the record

24. 8 U.S.C. § 1229a (EOIR); 29 C.F.R. § 1614.109 (2022) (EEOC).

25. Cushman v. Shinseki, 576 F.3d 1290 (Fed. Cir. 2009); Gonzalez v. Sullivan, 914 F.2d 1197, 1203 (9th Cir. 1990).

26. Richardson v. Perales, 402 U.S. 389, 410 (1971).

27. 5 U.S.C. § 556(e).

28. *Id.* § 706.

29. *Id.* § 556(e).

is developed and who is responsible for developing it.[30] In the absence of statutory or regulatory standards, courts may be required to take a functional approach to defining the "record" relied on in informal adjudication.[31] At minimum, information that the agency actually relied on in reaching its decision and that is necessary to support its decision on judicial review should be part of the administrative record (see Chapter 27).[32] The APA's judicial review provisions, which implicitly require that agencies base their decisions on the exclusive record in the adjudication, apply to informal as well as formal adjudication.[33]

The official-notice doctrine functions as an exception to the exclusive-record doctrine. Whereas the record is typically developed through the presentation of evidence by the participants in the hearing, official notice is the mechanism by which an adjudicator can accept legislative or adjudicative facts into the record on his or her own.[34] Official notice is derived from the ancient common-law doctrine of judicial notice, which permits courts to accept into the record facts that are "not ordinarily capable of dispute."[35] In the administrative context, official notice is designed to promote efficiency in adjudication by "avoid[ing] 'laborious proof of what is obvious and notorious.'"[36] Due to the fact that agencies often possess greater experience and expertise in the subject matter of their proceedings than generalist courts, agencies may take notice of a wider range of factual information than is available through judicial notice.[37]

The APA explicitly provides for official notice in formal adjudication. Adjudicators do not, however, have unfettered discretion to add information to the record through official notice. The ALJ must notify the parties when taking official notice of factual information and must

---

30. Christopher J. Walker, *The Lost World of the Administrative Procedure Act: A Literature Review*, 28 Geo. Mason L. Rev. 733, 749 (2021); Paul R. Verkuil, *A Study of Informal Adjudication Procedures*, 43 U. Chi. L. Rev. 739, 796 (1976).

31. Pinnacle Armor, Inc. v. United States, 923 F. Supp. 2d 1226, 1237 (E.D. Cal. 2013).

32. *See, e.g.*, Doe v. Univ. of Cincinnati, 872 F.3d 393, 399–400 (6th Cir. 2017); Yount v. Barnhart, 416 F.3d 1233, 1236 (10th Cir. 2005). *But see* Kerry v. Din, 576 U.S. 86, 105 (2015) (Kennedy, J., concurring).

33. Citizens to Pres. Overton Park v. Volpe, 401 U.S. 402 (1971).

34. 5 U.S.C. § 556(e).

35. John Henry Wigmore, The Pocket Code of the Rules of Evidence in Trials at Law § 2120 (1910).

36. Attorney General's Manual on the Administrative Procedure Act, *supra* note 10, at 79.

37. Banks v. Schweiker, 654 F.2d 637, 641 (9th Cir. 1981).

disclose that information or specify which information is being noticed from publicly available sources. The APA then guarantees parties the opportunity to rebut the noticed information.[38]

The APA does not explicitly provide for official notice in informal adjudication, but to the extent it comports with due process principles requiring adjudicators to resolve disputes on the record, the arguments for official notice in formal adjudication should obtain similarly for informal adjudication.[39]

A distinct, yet related, issue pertaining to administrative record development is the use of independent research by agency adjudicators. In the judicial context, independent research is strongly discouraged. The American Bar Association's Model Code of Judicial Conduct states that "[a] judge shall not investigate facts in a matter independently, and shall consider only the evidence presented and any facts that may properly be judicially noticed."[40]

Agency adjudicators have broader authority to consider information gathered independently. Official notice is the most common example of independent research contributing to an administrative hearing, but it is not the only one. Adjudicators may engage in their own research in order to obtain background materials about a hearing, to evaluate a witness's credibility, or for other reasons.[41] When adjudicators seek to supplement their knowledge with independent research, especially on matters that are contested or outside the experience and expertise of the agency, it can raise several potential problems, such as surprise for the parties when they discover new facts in the record and questions about the source and validity of the facts presented by the adjudicator. Internet research potentially compounds these problems due to the breadth of information available and its potential for misinformation.[42]

In light of these concerns, adjudicators seeking to rely on independent research, including internet research, have generally been required

38. 5 U.S.C. § 556(e); Air Prods. & Chems., Inc. v. Fed. Energy Regul. Comm'n, 650 F.2d 687 (5th Cir. 1981).

39. Doe v. Univ. of Cincinnati, 872 F.3d 393, 399–400 (6th Cir. 2017); *Judicial Notice by Administrative Tribunals*, 44 YALE L.J. 355, 355–56 (1934).

40. MODEL CODE OF JUD. CONDUCT r. 2.9(C) (AM. BAR ASS'N 2007).

41. *See* Administrative Conference Recommendation 2019-6, Independent Research by Agency Adjudicators in the Internet Age, 84 Fed. Reg. 71,350, 71,351 (Dec. 27, 2019).

42. Davis v. Berryhill, No. 16-81872-Civ-Brannon, 2017 WL 7796054, at *2 (S.D. Fla. Aug. 3, 2017).

to include the resultant information in the administrative record.[43] In some instances, adjudicators may rely on independently gathered information outside of the record as long as there is no "substantial prejudice" to the parties.[44]

It is unclear whether concern over independent research by adjudicators is impacted by the nature of the adjudicator's role in the proceeding. Adversarial proceedings may be less vulnerable to the dangers of independent research because the very nature of the adversarial system empowers parties and their representatives to take control of the record. At the same time, the parties' active role in record development may lessen the need for independent research in the first instance.[45]

By contrast, the adjudicator's responsibility to develop the record in an inquisitorial proceeding effectively exempts such proceedings from a presumption against independent research by an adjudicator. Agencies must still be careful, however, to protect parties' access to, and awareness of, the record, both as a source of confidence in the integrity of the decision and to prevent mistakes.[46] Judicial review also depends on a fully developed record, which may be less likely when adjudicators take it upon themselves to engage in independent research.[47] The Administrative Conference of the United States has encouraged agencies that permit independent research by adjudicators to fashion agency-specific policies taking these concerns into account.[48]

8.4 ASSISTING SELF-REPRESENTED PARTIES

As with pro se litigants in judicial proceedings, self-represented (or "pro se") parties in agency adjudications have a due process right to a fair hearing that may require additional attention from an agency

43. Ohio Bell Tel. Co. v. Pub. Utils. Comm'n, 301 U.S. 292, 300–06 (1937); Ellison v. Barnhart, 355 F.3d 1272, 1276 (11th Cir. 2003); *Davis*, 2017 WL 7796054, at *2; *Ostborg v. Comm'r of Soc. Sec.*, 610 F. App'x 907, 912, 917 (11th Cir. 2015); Henry J. Friendly, *"Some Kind of Hearing,"* 123 U. Pa. L. Rev. 1267 (1975); *see also* Administrative Conference Recommendation 2019-6, *supra* note 41, ¶¶ 2, 6.

44. Air Prods. & Chems., Inc. v. Fed. Energy Regul. Comm'n, 650 F.2d 687, 697 (5th Cir. 1981); Administrative Conference Recommendation 2019-6, *supra* note 41, ¶ 6.

45. *See* Allison Orr Larsen, *Confronting Supreme Court Fact Finding*, 98 Va. L. Rev. 1255, 1257 (2012); Verkuil, *supra* note 30, at 743.

46. *See, e.g.*, *Ohio Bell Tel. Co.*, 301 U.S. at 300–06; *Davis*, 2017 WL 7796054, at *2.

47. *See, e.g.*, *Davis*, 2017 WL 7796054, at *2.

48. Administrative Conference Recommendation 2019-6, *supra* note 41.

adjudicator (see Chapter 11). In conjunction with their obligation under the APA to develop the administrative record, adjudicators in formal adjudication must protect the rights of a pro se party by ensuring that "all the relevant facts [were] sufficiently developed and considered" prior to a decision.[49] Pro se parties are not necessarily entitled to the same quality of representation an attorney could provide, but ALJs are under a heightened duty "'to scrupulously and conscientiously probe into, inquire of, and explore for all the relevant facts.'"[50] Special attention is not necessarily required simply because a party is represented by a nonlawyer, especially when the party is not contesting the quality of representation.[51]

The same due process requirements apply to informal adjudication. Some agencies that engage in informal adjudication have rules or standards regarding how adjudicators must treat pro se parties, but as with most issues in informal adjudication, the standards are agency-specific. For example, the Merit Systems Protection Board instructs its administrative judges to "make special efforts to accommodate pro se appellants," including scheduling status conferences, refraining from rejecting filings for technical deficiencies or issuing sanctions without fair warning, providing pro se parties greater latitude in presenting evidence, and interpreting their arguments "in the most favorable light."[52] Many other agencies, however, have no specific provisions governing self-represented parties.[53] The due process concerns associated with parties representing themselves in agency adjudication should be powerful incentives for agencies to create more specific standards for accommodating pro se parties.

8.5 REPRESENTING THE ADMINISTRATIVE STATE

In addition to making determinations in individual cases, adjudicators serve as public-facing representatives of the administrative state. The legitimacy of agency action is premised, at least in part, on public

---

49. Hankerson v. Harris, 636 F.2d 893, 895 (2d Cir. 1980); *see also* Moran v. Astrue, 569 F.3d 108, 113 (2d Cir. 2009).

50. Cruz v. Sullivan, 912 F.2d 8, 11 (2d Cir. 1990) (citations omitted).

51. Ellison v. Barnhart, 355 F.3d 1272, 1276 (11th Cir. 2003).

52. *See, e.g.*, U.S. Merit Sys. Prot. Bd., Judges' Handbook 10 (2017); EOIR, Dep't of Just., Ethics and Professionalism Guide for Immigration Judges (2011).

53. Michael Asimow, Admin. Conf. of the U.S., Evidentiary Hearings outside the Administrative Procedure Act 25 (2016).

confidence in, and acceptance of, unelected administrators' exercise of (often significant) governmental authority.[54] While actual competence and impartiality (Chapter 10) in individual cases can promote public confidence simply through a track record of sound decisions, it is also the role of agency adjudicators to actively create an appearance of competence and fairness.

54. *See, e.g.*, Louis J. Virelli III, *An Ethical Gap in Agency Adjudication*, 69 Buff. L. Rev. 1329, 1335 (2022).

Chapter 9

Selection, Supervision, and Oversight of Adjudicators

Jeffrey S. Lubbers

9.1 CHAPTER OVERVIEW

This chapter addresses the processes by which agencies select, manage, organize, and oversee adjudicators—both administrative law judges (ALJs) and administrative judges (AJs). As a general matter, it does not address the selection, supervision, or oversight of agency heads and members of multimember agencies who perform adjudicative functions, nor does it address frontline decision-makers, such as examiners in many benefits adjudication schemes, who are typically selected, supervised, and overseen in the same manner as other agency employees (see Chapter 18).

As explained in Chapter 1, federal agencies conduct two types of evidentiary hearings, cases heard "on the record" under sections 554 and 556–57 of the Administrative Procedure Act (APA), often called "formal" or "Type A" adjudications, and hearings involving other cases where the relevant statute does not contain the "on the record" language, often called "informal" or "Type B" adjudications. Agencies also issue adjudicative orders in many other cases that do not involve evidentiary hearings at all; these comprise another type of "informal" adjudication sometimes called "Type C" adjudications.

Both Type A and Type B adjudications ordinarily involve the use of presiding officers—usually career officials who serve across presidential administrations—who typically make first-level decisions subject to review by the agency head or an agency appellate body and then to judicial review in the courts. The main difference is that, under the APA, agencies must use ALJs when they decide to delegate their authority to hear Type A cases. For Type B cases, agencies are free to use other types of hearing officers, whom we typically refer to as AJs.

ALJs are a special class of federal officers, created originally in the APA, who are typically employed by the agencies whose cases they decide but have special statutory protections under the APA that are designed to preserve their decisional independence. AJs, on the other hand, who are now far more numerous, generally lack those same statutory protections and are therefore more susceptible to control by the agencies that employ them.

This chapter discusses various attributes of ALJs' and AJs' selection, supervision, and oversight, specifically (1) how Congress and agencies define the nature of ALJ and AJ positions, including their titles, duties, and compensation (section 9.2); (2) how agencies recruit, select, and appoint ALJs and ALJs (section 9.3); (3) how agencies supervise and oversee ALJs' and AJs' work through, among other things, training, binding rules and policies, case assignment, performance management, review of decisions, and discipline (section 9.4); and (4) how ALJs and AJs organize and collectively bargain with the agencies that employ them (section 9.5). Most sections first address the attributes of ALJs, followed by a discussion of the attributes of AJs.

An important thing to keep in mind while reading this chapter is that, in many respects, the distinction between ALJs and AJs is narrowing. As discussed, this is especially true after the U.S. Supreme Court's 2018 decision in *Lucia v. Securities & Exchange Commission*,[1] which impliedly treats ALJs and many AJs the same for Appointments Clause purposes, and President Trump's 2018 executive order, reaffirmed by President Biden, which ended the Office of Personnel Management's (OPM's) involvement in the "merit selection" of ALJs and gave agencies great discretion to select ALJs.[2]

Aside from selection and appointment, the APA contains specific provisions regarding ALJs—including their powers and duties, separation of functions between them and other staff, a ban on ex parte communications to and from them, case assignments, and agency-head review authority over their decisions—which do not apply to AJs. In practice, however, considerations of due process and agency accountability tend to lead agencies to follow similar practices in these regards. Only with respect to the statutory stipulations for salaries, and, most importantly, the statutory bar on performance appraisals and the provision for good-cause protection from removal, are ALJs in a much different place than most AJs. However, as detailed in this chapter, ALJ removal protections are now subject to serious constitutional challenge.

9.2 NATURE OF THE POSITION

9.21 Title

9.211 Administrative Law Judge

Although the origins of the position go back to the enactment of the APA, the title "administrative law judge" was not the original one in the act. It was changed, first administratively and then by amendment to the APA. However, even before the APA's passage, the idea for the

1. 138 S. Ct. 2044 (2018).

2. Exec. Order No. 13,843, 83 Fed. Reg. 37,255 (July 13, 2018) (Trump); Exec. Order No. 14,029, 86 Fed. Reg. 27,025 (May 19, 2021) (Biden).

position was described in the *Final Report of the Attorney General's Committee on Administrative Procedure.*[3] One of the main reasons for the formation of the committee was the concern about the lack of uniformity among agency hearing officers and the perceived procedural unfairness of agency adjudication. As the report stated, "Most of the controversy over administrative procedure has centered around formal adjudication." The report went on to describe the lack of uniformity that existed in 1941:

> The methods of hearing and initial decision and the internal procedural structure vary from agency to agency. In general, it has been customary to designate hearing officers before whom evidence may be adduced—whether they be a board of three or more individuals, or, as is more common, a single hearing officer, variously known as a trial examiner, a referee, a presiding officer, a district engineer, a deputy commissioner, or a register. These hearing officers have been selected in various ways.
>
> * * *
>
> No less varied is the weight attached by the several agencies to the judgments of those who conduct the hearings. In most of the agencies the person who presides is an adviser with no real power to decide.[4]

This led the committee to conclude that where

> agencies have recognized the importance of hearing officers in the salaries paid, in the independence of view encouraged and accorded, and in the importance given to their decisions, the positions have attracted and held men whose ability and fairness have been recognized by the bar and the public. Where the opposite has happened, progressive decline has occurred.
>
> * * *

---

3. Final Report of the Attorney General's Committee on Administrative Procedure, S. Doc. No. 8 (1941) [hereinafter Attorney General's Committee Report]. Author note: This, and the following material, is derived from Jeffrey S. Lubbers, *APA-Adjudication: Is the Quest for Uniformity Faltering?*, 10 Admin. L.J. 65, 65–66 (1996).

4. Attorney General's Committee Report, *supra* note 3.

> This is the heart of formal administrative adjudication. It cannot succeed without competent and well-paid men exercising functions of responsibility and interest.[5]

The committee went on to recommend a highly structured system of "hearing commissioners," to be appointed by a proposed Office of Federal Administrative Procedure for seven-year terms (subject to a one-year "provisional appointment") with "substantial" but tiered salaries. Agencies that "deal with many small cases" could request permission from the office to pay the lower salary.

Ultimately, the drafters of the APA eschewed the title of "hearing commissioner," and settled on the term "examiner." The APA, prior to its codification in 1966, simply provided: "Subject to the civil-service and other laws to the extent not inconsistent with this Act, there shall be appointed by and for each agency as many qualified and competent examiners as may be necessary for proceedings pursuant to sections 7 and 8 [now 5 U.S.C. §§ 556–557] . . . ."[6]

The title of examiner gradually morphed into "administrative law judge," largely due to a campaign by the examiners who sought a title more befitting the administrative judiciary. As then-Professor Scalia explained:

> The original statutory title [in the APA for ALJs] was "examiner," 60 Stat. 237, 244 (1946). This was changed to "hearing examiner" in the 1966 codification, 80 Stat. 386, 415. In 1972, pursuant to its authority to establish official class titles "for personnel, budget, and fiscal purposes," 5 U.S.C. § 5105(c) (1976), the Civil Service Commission adopted use of the title "Administrative Law Judge," 37 Fed. Reg. 16,787 (1972)—an appellation which the hearing examiners themselves much preferred, and which had been happily accorded by the lawyers appearing before them for some years. In 1978, the United States Code was amended by replacing "hearing examiner" with "administrative law judge" wherever it appeared. Act of Mar. 27, 1978, Pub. L. No. 95-251, 92 Stat. 183.[7]

---

5. *Id.*

6. Pub. L. No 79-404, § 11, 60 Stat. 237, 244 (1946).

7. Antonin Scalia, *The ALJ Fiasco—A Reprise*, 47 U. Chi. L. Rev. 57, 57 n.2 (1979).

Now the title "administrative law judge" is firmly ensconced in statute and common usage.[8]

Today, there are around 1,700 ALJs across the executive branch. The vast majority, about 85 percent, are employed by the Social Security Administration (SSA). Other agencies that employ ALJs include the Office of Medicare Hearings and Appeals, Department of Labor (DOL), National Labor Relations Board (NLRB), and about 25 other departments and agencies.[9]

9.212 Administrative Judge

"Administrative judge" is an informal name given by scholars to the many non-ALJ adjudicators used by agencies to preside over and initially decide Type B adjudications. While some agencies use that name to refer to their hearing officers,[10] agencies use a wide variety of titles for AJs, including administrative appeals judge, administrative patent judge, appeals board member, appeals officer, attorney-examiner, Board of Immigration Appeals member, board of contract appeals judge, copyright royalty judge, decision review officer, hearing officer, hearing panelist, immigration judge (IJ), judgment officer, labor arbitrator, ombudsman, patent examiner, presiding officer, regional director (RD), regional judicial officer, settlement officer, small claims officer, and veterans law judge. A recent survey for the Administrative Conference of the United States (ACUS) found that agencies reported 37 types of AJs, totaling at least 10,831 officials across the executive branch, almost six times the number of ALJs.[11]

9.22 Job Duties

Job duties for ALJs are specifically provided for by the APA, but for AJs are governed by agency- and program-specific statutes, agency policies, and due process requirements. In addition, the APA has a specific provision preventing agencies from assigning ALJs "duties inconsistent

---

8. *See, e.g.*, 5 U.S.C. §§ 1305, 3105, 3344, 5372, 7521.

9. OPM maintains a list of agencies that employ ALJs at https://www.opm.gov/services-for-agencies/administrative-law-judges/ #url=By-Agency (last visited June 27, 2023).

10. *See, e.g.*, 5 C.F.R. § 1200.3 (2022) (Merit Systems Protection Board (MSPB)); 29 C.F.R. § 1614.109 (2022) (Equal Employment Opportunity Commission).

11. Kent Barnett et al., Admin. Conf. of the U.S., Non-ALJ Adjudicators in Federal Agencies: Status, Selection, Oversight, and Removal 22 (2018).

with their duties and responsibilities as administrative law judges."[12] There is no such statutory protection for AJs—at least as a class.

For Type A adjudications, the APA provides generally that unless the agency head or one or more members of a multimember agency want to "preside at the taking of evidence," the agency must use "one or more" ALJs to do so.[13] The ALJ must then, at the agency's direction, make an "initial" decision (which can be final if there is no internal appeal or review) or a "recommended" decision (which must be reviewed before becoming final). The agency can also require the ALJ to simply certify the record to it for decision, without a first-level decision,[14] though this happens rarely. The APA also prescribes the duties and powers that ALJs may exercise as presiding officers, which are discussed in Chapter 8.

The APA does not describe any powers or duties of non-ALJ adjudicators, so their powers and duties are regulated by agency- or program-specific statutes, in the first instance, and by agency policies and practices.[15]

9.23 Compensation

9.231 Administrative Law Judges

ALJ salaries are set by statute. Since 1990, 5 U.S.C. § 5372 has set the parameters for ALJ salaries. It provides for three levels of basic pay (designated as AL-1, 2, and 3, respectively). The basic level is AL-3, with AL-1 and AL-2 reserved for ALJs with "significant administrative and managerial responsibilities" such as chief ALJs. Within level AL-3, there are six rates of basic pay, designated as rates A through F, respectively. Rate A is the beginning salary, after which ALJs "shall be advanced successively" to rates B, C, and D each year following and to rates E and F after two years of service in the next lower rate. This basically ties ALJ salaries to seniority and eliminates agency control

---

12. 5 U.S.C. § 3105.

13. *Id.* § 556(b). The APA allows Congress to "specially provide for" or "designate" the use of boards or employees other than ALJs to hear "specified classes of proceedings in whole or in part." Congress has done this occasionally, such as allowing the Nuclear Regulatory Commission to use atomic safety and licensing boards to hear licensing cases. 42 U.S.C. § 2241.

14. 5 U.S.C. § 557(b).

15. *See, e.g.*, 8 U.S.C. § 1229a(b) (describing the authority and listing the powers of IJs).

over their pay.[16] The statute also provides a floor and ceiling for ALJs tied to the Executive Schedule (ES) of pay for top officials, and, like the General Schedule (GS) for regular civil service employees, is revised every year by presidential executive order. Rates for 2022 were announced as follows: AL-3/A $117,600, AL-3/B $126,600, AL-3/C $135,700, AL-3/D $144,900, AL-3/E $154,100, AL-3/F $162,900, AL-2 $171,900, and AL-1 $176,300.[17] But, because of pay compression and the availability of locality pay adjustments, the average salary across all ALJs in 2020 was $178,852,[18] making it one of the highest paid positions in the U.S. government.

9.232 Administrative Judges

AJ salaries vary across the government. In some instances, Congress has provided for the salaries of particular types of AJs. For example, the pay for members of contract appeal boards is specified to be (1) chairman of an appeals board—the rate of basic pay payable for level IV of the ES; (2) vice chairman of an appeals board—97 percent of the rate under paragraph (1); and (3) other members of an appeals board—94 percent of the rate under paragraph (1).[19] This is a higher rate than authorized for ALJs. Similarly, another provision allows agencies to pay "administrative appeals judges" (defined as those whose duties "primarily involve reviewing decisions of administrative law judges") no more but no less than the rate of pay available for ALJs at the level of AL-3.[20] Statutes also set forth salary requirements for members of the Board of Veterans' Appeals[21] and IJs.[22]

But these provisions are unusual. Agencies retain a lot of discretion over the salary levels of their AJs. As the ACUS report on non-ALJ adjudicators showed, agencies assigned their AJs a wide range of salary levels geared to the GS pay grades, which has 15 grades (starting

16. 5 C.F.R. § 930.205(c) (2022). For an overview of ALJ pay, see *Fact Sheet: Administrative Law Judge Pay System*, OPM, https://www.opm.gov/policy-data-oversight/pay-leave/pay-administration/fact-sheets/administrative-law-judge-pay-system (last visited June 27, 2023).

17. Exec. Order No. 14,061, sched. 10, 86 Fed. Reg. 73,601, 73,613 (Dec. 28, 2021).

18. See statistics at *Pay Rates for "Administrative Law Judge,"* FEDERALPAY.ORG, https://www.federalpay.org/employees/occupations/administrative-law-judge (last visited June 27, 2023).

19. 5 U.S.C. § 5372a(b).

20. *Id.* § 5372b.

21. 38 U.S.C. § 7101A.

22. 8 U.S.C. § 1103 (note).

with the lowest salaries at GS-1 and the highest at GS-15). Each grade has ten steps within it. The report noted that 90 percent were paid under this schedule, with the rest paid under special pay scales. Of that 90 percent, 354 were GS-9, 507 were GS-11, 1,192 were GS-12, 2,039 were GS-13, 4,516 were GS-14, and 189 were GS-15.[23] In 2022, the ranges of pay for these grades are as follows: GS-9 ($47,097–$61,227), GS-11 ($56,983–$74,074), GS-12 ($68,299–$88,792), GS-13 ($81,216–$105,579), GS-14 ($95,973–$124,764), and GS-15 ($112,890–$146,757).[24] Thus, the average pay for AJs is, with some exceptions,[25] significantly lower than that of ALJs.

9.3 RECRUITMENT, SELECTION, AND APPOINTMENT

9.31 Administrative Law Judges

The process for selecting ALJs has been a controversial issue since the enactment of the APA, but only recently has the constitutionality of the process come into question. As discussed in Chapter 3, in 2018, the Supreme Court, in *Lucia v. Securities & Exchange Commission*, held that ALJs who preside in adjudications at the Securities and Exchange Commission (SEC) are officers (presumably inferior officers) rather than employees.[26] That meant that under the Appointments Clause,[27] only the president, the head of a department, or a court of law may appoint an ALJ—and, even then, only if Congress has authorized such a method of appointment.

Since the APA contained a provision, now codified in 5 U.S.C. § 3105, that authorized "each agency" to appoint as many ALJs as are necessary to hold APA hearings, that was understood as authorizing agency heads, constitutionally, to appoint ALJs. But, after *Lucia*, it was clear that *only* agency heads—like the commission itself in that case rather than lower level SEC officials—could do the appointing.

Lucia arguably also called into question the then-role of OPM to administer an examination to select those eligible to be chosen by agencies to be ALJs, and OPM's role was shortly eliminated by an

23. Barnett et al., *supra* note 11, at 23, 25.

24. Exec. Order No. 14,061, 86 Fed. Reg. 73,601, 73,603 (Dec. 28, 2021).

25. Some AJs make at least as much as ALJs, including contract appeals board members, administrative patent judges (who earned between $164,500 and $176,00 in 2019), and members of the Environmental Appeals Board (who are members of the Senior Executive Service).

26. 138 S. Ct. 2044 (2018).

27. U.S. Const. art. II, § 2, cl. 2.

executive order in 2018.[28] Before the issuance of that order, OPM's role—and before 1978, the role of its predecessor, the Civil Service Commission (CSC)—had been central to the appointment of ALJs. Immediately after the enactment of the APA, the issue arose as to the qualifications of the 197 incumbent hearing officers to serve in the newly created "examiner" positions. The CSC established a special board for that purpose, which found many of the incumbent hearing officers unqualified. The CSC overrode the board and ended up accepting nearly all of the incumbents.[29]

The APA was not clear on the CSC's role. As then-Professor Scalia later explained: "The House and Senate committee reports [on the APA] provided that 'the Civil Service Commission [should] fix appropriate qualifications and the agencies [should] seek fit persons.'" From that, he concluded, "it was evidently contemplated that the Civil Service Commission would establish qualifying requirements by general rule, and that the agencies would then select from among all individuals who met those requirements." But this is not what happened. He explained further:

> The regulations issued by the Commission in September of 1947 adopt the principle that has been uniformly followed since: not merely the establishment of qualifying requirements, but also the ranking of individual applicants, would be the responsibility of the Commission, and the agency role would be limited to selecting among the three applicants certified by the Commission as best qualified.[30]

Thus, for 71 years, the CSC and its successor, OPM, administered a complex rating system that was intended to produce a merit-selection process.[31] Basically, OPM provided applicants, who had to meet the threshold requirement of being a lawyer for at least seven years with

---

28. Exec. Order No. 13,843, 83 Fed. Reg. 37,255 (July 13, 2018).

29. This story was told in Ralph F. Fuchs, *The Hearing Examiner Fiasco under the Administrative Procedure Act*, 63 HARV. L. REV. 737 (1950), and recounted again in Scalia, *supra* note 7, at 57–58.

30. Scalia, *supra* note 7, at 59–60.

31. *See* Jeffrey S. Lubbers, *Federal Administrative Law Judges: A Focus on Our Invisible Judiciary*, 33 ADMIN. L. REV. 109, 112–16 (1981). This and the following paragraphs are derived from Jeffrey S. Lubbers, *The Regulatory Accountability Act Loses Steam but the Trump Executive Order on ALJ Selection Upturned 71 Years of Practice*, 94 CHI.-KENT L. REV. 741, 744–46 (2019) [hereinafter Lubbers, *The Regulatory Accountability Act Loses Steam*].

two years of litigating or administrative law experience, with a score on a 100-point scale after rating their experience, references, and conducting a written exam and panel interview. After that, any veterans' preference points (5, or 10 for disabled vets) were added, thus giving veterans quite a large advantage, since agencies had to select from those with the top three scores on the register. For a time, OPM allowed agencies to hire from the top three applicants on the list who were selectively certified as experts in the agency's field, but OPM ended that program after the American Bar Association (ABA) complained that agencies were hiring too many of their own employees as judges.[32]

The end of this so-called selective-certification approach exacerbated what became an increasing problem with this selection process: agencies chafed at having to hire applicants based solely on their OPM scores since many of those at the top of the register had little background in the agency's area of law. Washington-based agencies began to maneuver to avoid ALJ adjudication as much as possible, and, when they could not, to circumvent the register by hiring laterally ALJs who had already been hired around the country by SSA. (SSA was—and remains—by far the largest employer of ALJs.) Because women were less likely to be veterans, the scoring system was also a handicap for women in rising to the top of the register. Thus, the system, despite its merit-selection intentions, had begun to break down.[33]

In 1992, ACUS launched a study at OPM's request of the "federal administrative judiciary."[34] The report was the basis for an ACUS recommendation for a revised selection process that would (1) remove veterans' preference from this program; (2) leave with OPM the responsibility for preparing the register of eligibles (i.e., for determining the basic qualifications for the position and rating the applicants); and (3) allow agencies to select any eligible applicant from the top 50 percent of the register.[35]

---

32. John T. Miller, Jr., *Some Reflections on OPM's Administration of Its APA ALJ Functions*, ADMIN. & REGUL. L. NEWS, Winter 2005, at 6 (describing the ABA's, and Mr. Miller's, successful opposition to selective certification).

33. *See* Paul Verkuil et al., *The Federal Administrative Judiciary*, *in* 2 RECOMMENDATIONS AND REPORTS OF THE ADMINISTRATIVE CONFERENCE OF THE UNITED STATES 942–49 (1992).

34. *See generally id.* at 771–1139. Author note: I was one of the co-authors of that report.

35. Administrative Conference Recommendation 92-7, The Federal Administrative Judiciary, 57 Fed. Reg. 61,759, 61,760 (Dec. 29, 1992).

Congress did not act on the ACUS recommendation, but after *Lucia*, President Trump saw the decision as an opportunity to drastically change the process for hiring ALJs. On July 10, 2018, he issued Executive Order No. 13,483. In it, he said: "*Lucia* may . . . raise questions about the method of appointing ALJs, including whether competitive examination and competitive service selection procedures are compatible with the discretion an agency head must possess under the Appointments Clause in selecting ALJs."[36] President Trump exercised his statutory authority over what positions are in the competitive civil service by removing newly hired ALJs from it and placing them in a new "Schedule E" in the excepted service.[37] (Incumbent ALJs who stayed in the same position continued to serve in the competitive service.) The order went on to say that, starting immediately, the only minimum qualification for the position was that newly appointed ALJs "must possess a professional license to practice law and be authorized to practice law under the laws" of a state or U.S. territory. Significantly, however, the order allowed agencies to use additional criteria if they wish.

Several influential lawyer and ALJ associations criticized the president for going too far and for opening up the ALJ program to potential cronyism or political favoritism in the hiring of new ALJs.[38] This fear was somewhat ameliorated by the fact that many of the key ALJ-employing agencies did create and publicly disclose their own hiring criteria.[39]

For example, DOL established a set of qualifications, including being a member of a bar in good standing "for at least ten years total in at least one jurisdiction in which the applicant is admitted; seven years of relevant litigation or administrative law experience; and knowledge of statutes enforced by the Department of Labor." It also assigned an

---

36. Exec. Order No. 13,843, 83 Fed. Reg. 32,755 (July 10, 2018).

37. 5 U.S.C. § 3302(1).

38. Statement of the Fed. Bar Ass'n on Exec. Order No. 13,843 Regarding the Hiring of Federal Administrative Law Judges (Aug. 10, 2018); Marilyn Zahm, *Do You Have a Social Security Card? Then Take This Executive Order Personally.*, Wash. Post (July 18, 2018), https://www.washingtonpost.com/opinions/do-you-have-a-social-security-card-then-take-this-executive-order-personally/2018/07/18/4d66339c-89d6-11e8-85ae-511bc1146b0b_story.html.

39. Jack M. Beermann & Jennifer L. Mascott, Admin. Conf. of the U.S., Federal Agency ALJ Hiring after Lucia and Executive Order 13,843 (2019); Administrative Conference Recommendation 2019-2, Agency Recruitment and Selection of Administrative Law Judges, 84 Fed. Reg. 38,930 (Aug. 8, 2019).

office to screen candidates' applications and set up a panel made up of the department's chief ALJ, chief human capital officer, assistant secretary for policy, and a member of the Employees' Compensation Appeals Board. This panel is tasked with reviewing and ranking the qualified applications, interviewing the top-ranked candidates, and forwarding their recommended candidates to the deputy secretary. The deputy secretary, in consultation with a career ethics attorney from the Office of the Solicitor, is supposed to provide the secretary with the names of recommended candidates for appointment as well as résumés of the other top-ranked candidates interviewed but not recommended. The secretary makes the final decision and appointment but may also order that another candidate search be completed.[40]

Perhaps because of these agency actions, or perhaps because of the problems with the OPM selection process in the past, President Biden in his own executive order reaffirmed the changes made by President Trump, stating:

> Conditions of good administration warrant placing the position of administrative law judge in the excepted service and exempting appointment to this position from the requirements of 5 CFR, part 302, including examination and rating requirements, though each agency shall follow the principle of veterans preference as far as administratively feasible.[41]

The drafters of the APA anticipated that agencies would sometimes need to borrow ALJs from other agencies. The act permits agencies to use ALJs "selected by [OPM] from and with the consent of other agencies," and OPM has issued a regulation detailing how this is to be carried out.[42] After *Lucia*, OPM issued guidance requiring the lending agency to certify that the appointment of the ALJ being loaned was originally made or ratified by the agency head and requiring the borrowing agency to ratify the loan and approve the appointment as properly made under the Constitution.[43]

---

40. 83 Fed. Reg. 44,307, 44,307–08 (Aug. 30, 2018).

41. Exec. Order No. 14,029, § 3(a), 86 Fed. Reg. 27,025, 27,026 (May 19, 2021).

42. 5 U.S.C. § 3344; 5 C.F.R. § 930.208 (2022).

43. *See* OPM Memorandum to Chief Administrative Law Judge/Designee, Guidance on the ALJ Loan Program (Aug. 1, 2018), https://www.opm.gov/services-for-agencies/administrative-law-judges/opm-guidance-alj-loan-program-dated-august-1-2018.pdf.

Lastly, in 1984, Congress amended the general statutes allowing agencies to reemploy retired former employees receiving an annuity to provide specifically for the reappointment of a retired ALJ "for a specified period or for such period as may be necessary for such [ALJ] to conduct and complete the hearing and disposition of one or more specified cases."[44] After *Lucia*, this may require approval by the agency head.

9.32 Administrative Judges

The Supreme Court's *Lucia* decision, discussed previously, made clear that most ALJs are officers of the United States because they "hold a continuing office established by law" and exercise "significant discretion" when carrying out "important functions." But this could certainly apply to many AJs as well, which could create a potential problem. Under the Appointments Clause, Congress not only may, but also must, authorize the agency head to make the appointment; otherwise, the officer would have to be nominated by the president and confirmed by the Senate. Some AJs, however, are created by agency regulation, not by statute, so their appointment by the agency head may not be constitutional.[45]

A few statutes govern the hiring of certain types of AJs. One example is the statutory requirement that members of the Board of Veterans' Appeals be appointed by the Secretary of Veterans Affairs with the approval of the president and based on the recommendation of the presidentially appointed, Senate-confirmed chairman of the board. Members must also be members of a bar in good standing.[46] Another example is the requirement that administrative patent judges be "persons of competent legal knowledge and scientific ability who

---

44. Pub. L. No. 98-224, 98 Stat. 47 (1984) (adding subsection (b)(1) to 5 U.S.C. § 3323); *see also* 5 C.F.R. § 930.209 (2022).

45. William Funk, *Is the Environmental Appeals Board Unconstitutional or Unlawful*, 49 ENV'T L. 737 (2019). Another potential problem arises when a multimember board or commission lacks a quorum and therefore cannot review decisions of their AJs (or for that matter their ALJs), thus arguably rendering them unsupervised by a presidential appointee and therefore improperly appointed under *United States v. Arthrex*, 141 S. Ct. 1970 (2021). That issue arose with MSPB AJs, but the court rejected the constitutional challenge in *McIntosh v. Department of Defense*, 53 F.4th 630 (Fed. Cir. 2022).

46. 38 U.S.C. § 7101A.

are appointed by the Secretary, in consultation with the Director [of the U.S. Patent and Trademark Office]."[47]

There have been reports of political hiring in some AJ programs.[48] However, many agencies have established their own qualification requirements. The ACUS study of non-ALJ adjudicators reported that "applicants for 31 of the 37 identified types of non-ALJs must meet minimum qualifications." More specifically, the report found that agencies require that nearly two-thirds of the 27 initially hired non-ALJ types have a law degree, and some impose related requirements, such as expertise in general administrative law, bar membership, a mix of litigation and/or subject-matter expertise, or dispute-resolution experience. Applicants could meet agencies' years-of-legal-practice requirements with between five and ten years' experience. Only two other qualifications were common to more than one-third of the types: consideration of demeanor and references. Agencies reported "other" qualifications, such as scientific degrees and certain military rank. About half the agencies subjected their newly hired non-ALJs to a probationary period, and four agencies hired them for a term of years.[49] Both practices are prohibited for ALJs under the APA.[50]

ACUS has recommended that agencies design their guidelines and procedures for hiring attorneys who will act as non-ALJ adjudicators "to ensure that those hired will act impartially and maintain the appearance of impartiality."[51]

There is no specific statute or regulation concerning the detailing or reemployment of AJs, but they would generally be covered by general provisions allowing such actions for most employees.[52]

9.4 SUPERVISION AND OVERSIGHT

This section addresses a number of mechanisms by which agencies can supervise and oversee the work of the adjudicators they employ, including training, the issuance of rules and policies governing their job

---

47. 35 U.S.C. § 6(a).

48. Lubbers, *The Regulatory Accountability Act Loses Steam*, *supra* note 31, at 749–50 (describing episodes of political hiring of IJs and of nonhiring of veterans law judges).

49. Barnett et al., *supra* note 11, at 38–40.

50. 5 C.F.R. § 930.204(a) (2022).

51. Administrative Conference Recommendation 2019-9, Recruiting and Hiring Agency Attorneys, ¶ 22, 84 Fed. Reg. 71,355, 71,358 (Dec. 27, 2019).

52. 5 C.F.R. pt. 837 (2022).

functions, the assignment of cases to adjudicators and overall caseload management, performance appraisal (including the use of bonuses and other performance incentives), review of adjudicators' decisions, and discipline and removal.

9.41 Improper Supervision and Communication

9.411 Administrative Law Judges

As discussed in Chapter 10, the APA contains several provisions that attempt to protect ALJs from improper supervision and to protect parties from an unfair combination of adjudicative with prosecutorial or investigative functions. ALJs may not "be responsible to or subject to the supervision or direction of an employee or agent engaged in the performance of investigative or prosecuting functions for an agency."[53] ALJs are also barred from "consult[ing] a person or party on a fact in issue, unless on notice and opportunity for all parties to participate."[54] This strict provision has not been read to disallow an ALJ from discussing matters with a law clerk, since the clerk is part of the judges' "chambers."

The APA also specifies that an

> employee or agent engaged in the performance of investigative or prosecuting functions for an agency in a case may not, in that or a factually related case, participate or advise in the decision, recommended decision, or agency review pursuant to section 557 of this title, except as witness or counsel in public proceedings.[55]

Essentially, this requires agencies to wall off ALJs and appellate adjudicators, including agency heads, from prosecutors and investigators (sometimes lumped together as "adversaries") involved in a case or factually related case. This would seem to allow ALJs to talk to non-adversarial employees or other adjudicators about a case, but, aside from law clerks and paralegals in their offices, ALJs generally do not do so.[56] It should be noted, though, that section 554(d), which contains all these safeguards, does not apply to initial licensing or rate-making cases. The legislative history for this exception explains that

---

53. 5 U.S.C. § 554(d)(2).
54. *Id.* § 554(d)(1).
55. *Id.* § 554(d)(2).
56. *See* Michael Asimow, *When the Curtain Falls: Separation of Functions in the Federal Administrative Agencies*, 81 COLUM. L. REV. 759, 764 (1981).

the drafters thought such matters were not adversarial and more like rulemaking.[57]

Despite these safeguards in the APA, Congress has occasionally used another approach to adding fairness by creating a "split-enforcement" model by which the regulatory agency must bring its enforcement cases before an independent, purely adjudicative agency to be heard by that agency's ALJs. Congress has used that model in occupational safety and health, mine safety, and airline pilot sanction cases.[58] Some commentators have suggested that ALJs be removed entirely from the program agencies and placed in a "central-panel" agency of ALJs that would serve agencies as needed. Those advocates point to the fact that this type of structure is currently employed in "more than thirty" state governments.[59] Bills to create such a system on the federal level have not passed, however, largely because of concerns about loss of subject-matter expertise.[60]

Finally, section 557(d) of the APA, added in 1976 as part of the Government in the Sunshine Act, prohibits ex parte (off-the-record) communications "relevant to the merits of the proceeding" between "interested persons" outside the agency and any employee who "is or may be involved in the decisional process of the proceeding."

9.412 Administrative Judges

Because the separation-of-functions provisions in section 554(d) and the ex parte communications bar in section 557(d) only apply to formal adjudications, they typically do not apply specifically to informal, "Type B" adjudications that are usually presided over by AJs. However, principles of due process do apply when a protected life, liberty, or property interest is at stake, and the Supreme Court has made clear that one such principle is that the government must provide a neutral or unbiased decision-maker when it adjudicates a dispute (see Chapter 3). Thus, violations of separation-of-functions principles or instances of ex parte communications, if prejudicial, could trigger

---

57. Attorney General's Manual on the Administrative Procedure Act 50–53 (1947).

58. George R. Johnson, Jr., *The Split-Enforcement Model: Some Conclusions from the OSHA and MSHA Experiences*, 39 Admin. L. Rev. 315 (1987).

59. Malcolm C. Rich & Alison Goldstein, *The Need for a Central Panel Approach to Administrative Adjudication: Pros, Cons, and Selected Practices*, 39 J. Nat'l Ass'n Admin. L. Judiciary 1 (2019).

60. *See* Jeffrey S. Lubbers, *A Unified Corps of ALJs: A Proposal to Test the Idea at the Federal Level*, 65 Judicature 266, 273–75 (1981).

due process violations even in cases not subject to the APA hearing provisions.

Congress has occasionally required some separation of functions for certain types of AJs, and many agencies have adopted policies or use practices that, at least as a practical matter, impose some separation of functions. ACUS has urged agencies to make such policies public.[61]

9.42 Training

There are no government-wide requirements for training of new adjudicators—either ALJs or AJs—so it is up to each agency to have its own policy. To a great extent, this is a question of resources. SSA, by far the largest employer of ALJs, has had a training program for its ALJs for many years. The Office of the Inspector General (OIG) for SSA examined the program in 2011 and described it as a three-phase program: (1) on-the-job and video training; (2) four-week traditional classroom training; and (3) mentoring from experienced ALJs. Nearly all of the new ALJs surveyed said the training was helpful.[62]

In 2017, the OIG updated its report, mentioning that, after serving for a year, ALJs return for a mandatory week of in-person supplemental training. The training is in a seminar setting, with discussion of topics related to policy and judicial duties, including conducting hearings. Topics include dismissals, vocational issues, file review, note-taking, efficient hearing techniques, post-hearing development, and drafting decision-writer instructions.[63]

It should be noted that in the 1970s, SSA had a program that required ALJs who had what the agency considered to be overly high allowance rates to undergo special "training." Faced with a litigation

61. Administrative Conference Recommendation 2020-5, Publication of Policies Governing Agency Adjudicators, 86 Fed. Reg. 6,622 (Jan. 22, 2021).

62. SSA OIG, A-12-11-11126, Training of New Administrative Law Judges at the Office of Disability Adjudication and Review 2, 4–5 (2011).

63. SSA OIG, A-12-17-50247, Administrative Law Judge Allowance Rates, Quality, and Length of Service D-1 n.1 (2017). That same year, the Government Accountability Office (GAO) favorably reviewed SSA's training, tools, and policy guidance for its ALJs. GAO, GAO-18-37, Social Security Disability: Additional Measures and Evaluation Needed to Enhance Accuracy and Consistency of Hearings Decisions 32 (2017).

by ALJs, and a district court sympathetic to the ALJs claims, the agency withdrew most of that program.[64]

SSA also provides training to its non-ALJ "administrative appeals judges," who make up its Appeals Council. In a congressional hearing in 2016, a senior SSA official testified:

> [W]e are working right now on a pretty significant training plan that mirrors and tracks closely the plan in terms of ALJ training. One big difference between administrative appeals judges currently is they do not conduct face-to-face hearings. Part of the training that we do for a new ALJ who has never done a hearing in our process, we teach them sequential evaluation. We teach our [administrative appeals judges] the same thing. We teach a class on how to conduct and do fair and impartial hearings.[65]

Outside SSA, the Department of Justice's (DOJ's) Executive Office for Immigration Review (EOIR) conducts a six-week training course for its new IJs, combining classroom training and mentorship within their "home court."[66] The Patent Trial and Appeal Board (PTAB) also uses mentorship training and other ongoing training for its administrative patent judges. It released a video describing its training program in 2015.[67]

9.43 Binding Effect of Agency Rules and Policies

ALJs are supposed to follow properly issued agency policies.[68] The 1992 ACUS study of the federal administrative judiciary pointed out some of the issues concerning the need for ALJs to be subordinate to agency-head policy control while also having decisional independence:

---

64. Ass'n of Admin. L. Judges v. Heckler, 594 F. Supp. 1132, 1141–42 (D.D.C. 1984).

65. *Examining Due Process in Administrative Hearings, Hearing before the Subcomm. on Regul. Affs. & Fed. Mgmt. of the Sen. Comm. on Homeland Sec. & Gov't Affs.*, 114th Cong. (2016) (testimony of Theresa Gruber, Deputy Comm'r for Disability Adjudication & Rev., SSA).

66. EOIR, DOJ, Fact Sheet: Executive Office for Immigration Review Immigration Judge Training (2022), https://www.justice.gov/eoir/page/file/1513996/download.

67. *See* U.S. Patent & Trademark Off., *Training and Resources for Administrative Patent Judges at the Patent Trial and Appeal Board (PTAB)*, YouTube (Feb. 13, 2015), https://www.youtube.com/watch?v=I_BD-Hl12tQ.

68. *See Ass'n of Admin. L. Judges*, 594 F. Supp. at 1141 (citing D'Amico v. Schweiker, 698 F.2d 903, 907 (7th Cir. 1983)); Scalia, *supra* note 7, at 62.

> The real questions about the relationship between the agency hierarchy and the adjudicators focus on policy control. The policy relationship raises questions of special complexity. Various fairness values, including uniformity of results, require that the agency have dominance over policy questions. The adjudicators themselves recognize the need for policy guidance. The problem lies at the margin between mechanisms for ensuring application of the agency's policy and overreaching interference in the adjudicators' independent judgment.[69]

Of course, agency policy is expressed in different ways. Agency regulations ("legislative rules" issued after notice and comment, or procedural rules that are exempted from notice and comment) are binding on the public as well as on the agency, including adjudicators. Agency adjudicative opinions issued by agency heads (or delegated reviewing officials or boards) may be considered precedential and, although policies announced in such adjudications can be changed by them if properly explained, ALJs would normally be expected to follow precedent. But some agencies treat only selected decisions as precedential, and other decisions, or those that were never reviewed by the agency heads, may not be binding on ALJs.[70]

Finally, agencies issue many different types of guidance documents without going through notice and comment. Such policy statements and interpretive rules are not supposed to be binding on the public. As an ACUS recommendation explained, "policy guidance does not constitute a standard where noncompliance may form an independent basis for action in matters that determine the rights and obligations of any person outside the agency."[71] The recommendation suggested that while it was appropriate for agencies "to provide guidance to staff in the form of manuals and other management directives as a means to regularize employee action that directly affects the public," "affected persons should be afforded a fair opportunity to challenge the legality or wisdom of the document and to suggest alternative choices in an agency forum that assures adequate consideration by responsible agency officials."[72] Such officials would presumably include ALJs, so

69. Verkuil et al., *supra* note 33, at 918.

70. *See* Administrative Conference Recommendation 2022-4, Precedential Decision Making in Agency Adjudication, 88 Fed. Reg. 2,312 (Jan. 13, 2023).

71. Administrative Conference Recommendation 92-2, Agency Policy Statements, 53 Fed. Reg. 30,103 (July 8, 1992).

72. *Id.*

in such instances it would be appropriate for ALJs not to feel bound by guidance documents. The Federal Circuit and Merit Systems Protection Board (MSPB) have found, however, that ALJs may be disciplined for failing to follow agency case-processing directives, including policies set forth in guidance documents, that are unrelated to their decisional independence.[73]

If ALJs fail to follow agency regulations or agency precedent, they of course can be, and would likely be, reversed on review. That is to be expected and is one of the purposes of having internal appellate review. It follows, then, that these occurrences should not normally be a basis for discipline of an ALJ. But if an ALJ persisted in ignoring established policy or did so with great frequency, that would clearly create inefficiencies that might amount to "good cause" for discipline (see section 9.48).

The abovementioned considerations are similar for non-ALJ adjudicators, although they typically have less protection from discipline or removal and so may feel more bound to follow agency policy announced in guidance documents.

9.44 Case Assignment

The APA simply provides: "Administrative law judges shall be assigned to cases in rotation so far as practicable."[74] This requirement was intended to avoid situations in which an agency might strategically assign cases to sideline disfavored adjudicators, improperly influence adjudicators, or achieve preferred case outcomes. One example of this that has recently come to light in the world of Type B adjudication involves alleged "panel stacking" at the PTAB.[75]

Of course, where an agency only has a single ALJ, rotation is not possible. And even when there are multiple ALJs, the "so far as practicable" language does not require "mechanical rotation" without regard to practicality.[76] Courts have interpreted the APA to permit agencies to assign cases out of rotation to further the interests of administrative efficiency so long as the assignment is not made with

---

73. Abrams v. Soc. Sec. Admin., 703 F.3d 538, 545 (Fed. Cir. 2012); Soc. Sec. Admin. v. Manion, 19 M.S.P.R. 298, 303 (1984).

74. 5 U.S.C. § 3105.

75. Gene Quinn, *USPTO Admits to Stacking PTAB Panels to Achieve Desired Outcomes*, IPWatchdog (Aug. 23, 2017), https://www.ipwatchdog.com/2017/08/23/uspto-admits-stacking-ptab-panels-achieve-desired-outcomes/id=87206/.

76. Ramspeck v. Fed. Trial Exam'rs Conf., 345 U.S. 128, 139 (1953).

the "intent or effect of interfering with the independence of the ALJ or otherwise depriving a party of a fair hearing."[77] They have upheld agencies' consideration of factors such as case complexity, ALJs' experience and ability, scheduling conflicts, geographical convenience, and previous involvement in a particular case.[78]

9.45 Case Management

As for supervision of case management, especially in agencies with a high volume of cases, the techniques to be applied are similar to those used in federal and state courts around the country. In 1986, ACUS recognized the need for "Case Management as a Tool for Improving Agency Adjudication."[79] ACUS urged agencies involved in both formal and informal adjudication to consider implementing a series of case management methods, including:

- **Personnel management devices.** Agencies possess and should exercise the authority, consistent with the ALJ's or other presiding officer's decisional independence, to formulate written criteria for measuring case handling efficiency, prescribe procedures, and develop techniques for the expeditious and accurate disposition of cases. The experiences and opinions of presiding officers should play a large part in shaping these criteria and procedures. The criteria should take into account differences in categories of cases assigned to judges and in types of disposition (e.g., dismissals, dispositions with and without hearing). Where feasible, regular, computerized case status reports and supervision by higher level personnel should be used in furthering the systematic application of the criteria once they have been formulated.
- **Step-by-step time goals.** Case management by presiding officers and their supervisors should be combined with procedures designed to move cases promptly through each step in the proceeding. These include (1) a program of step-by-step time

77. Aaacon Auto Transp., Inc. v. Interstate Com. Comm'n, 792 F.2d 1156, 1163 (D.C. Cir. 1986).

78. *Id.*; Sykes v. Bowen, 854 F.2d 284, 287–88 (8th Cir. 1988); Nat'l Nutritional Foods Ass'n v. Food & Drug Admin., 504 F.2d 761 (2d Cir. 1974); Tractor Training Serv. v. Fed. Trade Comm'n, 227 F.2d 420 (9th Cir. 1955).

79. Administrative Conference Recommendation 86-7, Case Management as a Tool for Improving Agency Adjudication, 51 Fed. Reg. 46,989 (Dec. 30, 1986). The text has been edited slightly for brevity.

> goals for the main stages of a proceeding; (2) a monitoring system that pinpoints problem cases; and (3) a management committed to expeditious processing. Time guidelines should be fixed in all cases for all decisional levels within the agency, largely with the input of presiding officers and others affected. While the guidelines should be flexible enough to accommodate exceptional cases and should maintain their nonobligatory nature, they should be sufficiently fixed to keep routine items moving and ensure that any delays are justified. Agencies should encourage a management commitment by including specific goals or duties of timely case processing in pertinent job descriptions.

ACUS also recommended that agencies develop special expedited procedures, implement a case file system, and adopt policies that provide adjudicators sufficient flexibility to efficiently manage their cases (e.g., use of alternative dispute resolution, aggregation of similar cases, use of telephone hearings).

Despite its age, this recommendation remains quite relevant today. ACUS has updated it in several respects, for example by urging agencies to consider the benefits of electronic case management systems (see Chapter 23) and video hearings (see Chapter 21).

9.46 Performance Management and Appraisal

9.461 Administrative Law Judges

ALJs, unlike almost all other federal executive branch employees, are excluded by statute from the civil-service performance-appraisal system.[80] In addition, OPM has a long-standing rule that prohibits an agency from rating the job performance of, or granting "any monetary or honorary award or incentive" to, an ALJ.[81] When combined with the high threshold of proof demanded by the MSPB for charges brought against ALJs on productivity grounds (see section 9.48), these requirements have made it very difficult for agencies (even through chief ALJs) to exert managerial control over their ALJs. Such restrictions, however, have not prevented agencies from establishing time and, in some cases, quality goals, which ACUS recommended in its 1986 recommendation discussed in the previous section.[82]

80. 5 U.S.C. § 4301(2)(D).
81. 5 C.F.R. § 930.206 (2022).
82. Administrative Conference Recommendation 86-7, *supra* note 79.

Nevertheless, the statutory restriction on performance appraisal of ALJs has been controversial, especially given the prevalence of programs for evaluation of judges' performance on the state and local level.[83] Indeed, in its recommendation stemming from its study of the federal administrative judiciary in 1992, ACUS recommended that

> a system of review of ALJ performance be developed. Chief ALJs would be given the responsibility to coordinate development of case processing guidelines, with the participation of other agency ALJs, agency managers and others. These guidelines, which would address issues such as ALJ productivity and step-by-step time goals, would be one of the bases upon which Chief ALJs would conduct regular (e.g., annual) performance reviews. Judicial comportment and demeanor would be another basis for review.[84]

In a more recent recommendation, however, ACUS emphasized that agencies should not use certain information about decisional quality "in ways that could improperly influence decision-making or personnel matters."[85]

9.462 Administrative Judges

Federal AJs, unlike ALJs, are not exempt from performance appraisal, and in its 1992 report, ACUS found that several important groups of AJs, such as those at the MSPB, the Department of Defense Directorate for Industrial Security Clearance Review, the Trademark Trial and Appeal Board, and the Department of Health and Human Services Departmental Appeals Board, were subject to performance ratings.[86] More recently, the 2018 report for ACUS found:

> A large proportion of non-ALJs by type and by number are subject to performance appraisals. Of the 37 types of non-ALJs, 28 (76%) are subject to performance appraisals. Of the 10,831 total non-ALJs, all but 68 of them are subject to performance

83. *See* Jeffrey S. Lubbers, *The Federal Administrative Judiciary: Establishing an Appropriate System of Performance Evaluation for ALJs*, 7 ADMIN. L.J. AM. U. 589, 607–11 (1994). For a contrary view, see James P. Timony, *Performance Evaluation of Federal Administrative Law Judges*, 7 ADMIN. L.J. AM. U. 629 (1993).

84. Administrative Conference Recommendation 92-7, *supra* note 35.

85. Administrative Conference Recommendation 2021-10, Quality Assurance Systems in Agency Adjudication, 87 Fed. Reg. 1,722 (Jan. 12, 2022).

86. Verkuil et al., *supra* note 33, at 1031.

> appraisals. In other words, an overwhelming 99% of all non-ALJs are subject to performance appraisals.[87]

Similarly, the report found that 90 percent of all AJs were eligible for bonuses, and that in numerous AJ programs, the large majority of AJs did receive bonuses.[88] In 2021, the Court of Appeals for the Federal Circuit found that provision of bonuses to administrative patent judges, conditioned on performance appraisals, did not violate due process.[89]

9.47 Reviewability

Given the statutory prohibition against conducting performance appraisals of ALJs, "[t]he APA and agencies' enabling statutes authorize agencies to review ALJs' decisions, sometimes even de novo, as the primary means of ensuring ALJs' accountability."[90] The APA provides: "On appeal from or review of the initial decision, the agency has all the powers which it would have in making the initial decision except as it may limit the issues on notice or by rule."[91] This means that the agency head (or delegated reviewing official or board) has a great deal of discretion to reverse the initial decision of the ALJ on legal or policy grounds or even based on a different reading of the facts.

The one caveat is that, in 1951, the Supreme Court required reviewing courts in determining whether there was substantial evidence to support the agency's decision, to review "the whole record" of the decision, including both the initial or recommended decision of the ALJ and the final decision of the agency head.[92] That decision enhanced the importance of ALJs' decisions, and later cases have found that where the decision turned on the credibility of witnesses, especially their demeanor, agency-head reversals should be viewed with "heightened scrutiny" since the ALJ was the decision-maker that actually saw the testimony.[93]

---

87. Barnett et al., *supra* note 11, at 51, 54–57.

88. *Id.*

89. Mobility Workx, LLC v. Unified Pats., LLC, 15 F.4th 1146, 1155–56 (Fed. Cir. 2021).

90. L. Hope O'Keeffe, Note, *Administrative Law Judges, Performance Evaluation, and Production Standards: Judicial Independence versus Employee Accountability*, 54 Geo. Wash. L. Rev. 591, 602 (1986).

91. 5 U.S.C. § 556(b).

92. Universal Camera Corp. v. Nat'l Lab. Rels. Bd., 340 U.S. 474 (1951).

93. *See, e.g.*, Aylett v. Sec'y of Hous. & Urb. Dev., 54 F.3d 1560 (10th Cir. 2007).

The APA also contains a provision that essentially allows agencies to channel appeals from ALJ initial decisions to the agency head before the losing party can seek judicial review. It states: "Except as otherwise expressly required by statute, agency action otherwise final is final for the purposes of this section . . . unless the agency otherwise requires by rule and provides that the action meanwhile is inoperative, for an appeal to superior agency authority."[94] In effect, it provides agencies can, by rule, require exhaustion of administrative remedies, including internal appellate review, before seeking relief in federal court.

The considerations for agency-head oversight and review of informal, Type B adjudications would be similar except that the APA provisions in section 556 would not apply. But those provisions are quite permissive anyway. The exhaustion-of-remedies provision in section 704 would also seem to apply to such adjudications, since it applies to "agency action" that covers agency orders generally, whether issued after a formal or informal hearing.

For both ALJs and AJs, there is a constitutional dimension to the issue of reviewability. If a particular agency's ALJs or AJs only issued recommended decisions, which could never become final without agency review, those ALJs or AJs might not be considered "officers" at all under the Appointments Clause.[95] On the other hand, if an agency's ALJs or AJs were not subject to any review at all, that would likely make them "principal" officers who would have to be nominated by the president and confirmed by the Senate. That, at least, is the implication of the Supreme Court's opinion in *United States v. Arthrex*.[96]

9.48 Discipline and Removal

9.481 Administrative Law Judges

The disciplinary and removal provisions in section 11 of the APA, which survive today as 5 U.S.C. § 7521, required that an agency could discipline or remove an ALJ only after demonstrating to a separate agency—originally the CSC and, since 1978, the MSPB—that there is "good cause" for doing so. That proceeding entails providing the charged ALJ with an opportunity for a hearing on the record before another ALJ employed by the MSPB and an opportunity for review by the board. The APA does not define what constitutes "good cause."

94. 5 U.S.C. § 704.

95. Landry v. Fed. Deposit Ins. Co., 204 F.3d 1125 (D.C. Cir. 2000).

96. 141 S. Ct. 1970 (2021). *But see* McIntosh v. Dep't of Def., 53 F.4th 630 (Fed. Cir. 2022), discussed *supra* note 45.

Instead, the term has been defined by the MSPB, and the CSC before it, through case-by-case precedent.

The 1992 ACUS study reported that, since 1946, there had been fewer than two dozen cases brought by agencies to discipline or remove ALJs, and only five of them had led to removal. It went on to explain: "Most of the cases resulting in removals or suspensions of ALJs have been based on past misconduct, on-the-bench actions, or most frequently, other behavior. Cases involving 'insubordination' also have led to disciplinary actions."[97]

A more recent search of MSPB precedential decisions—excluding nonprecedential board decisions and cases not appealed to the board—showed only four cases involving such charges decided between 2010 and June 30, 2022. One such case involved a charge of "conduct unbecoming an ALJ." The charge involved a physical altercation between the ALJ and his domestic partner at home that resulted in a charge of domestic violence that ultimately was not prosecuted after the couple reconciled. After a hearing, an ALJ that the MSPB borrowed from the NLRB issued a decision reducing the removal to a 45-day suspension. But SSA appealed, and the board decided in favor of removal. The SSA ALJ sought judicial review, and the Court of Appeals for the Federal Circuit affirmed, concluding "that the Board's interpretation of 'good cause' to encompass conduct that 'undermines public confidence in the administrative adjudicatory process,' as informed by the ABA Model Code [of Judicial Conduct], is a permissible construction of the statutory language."[98] However, one judge wrote a concurring opinion suggesting that the result was "disquieting" because "neither the Office of Personnel Management nor the Board has articulated any consistent or comprehensive standard for when private, off-duty actions may . . . constitute 'good cause.'"[99]

The 1992 ACUS study also recounted the lack of success agencies had had in bringing actions against ALJs involving low productivity rather than misconduct.[100] It described the "trilogy of SSA-ALJ productivity cases decided by the MSPB in 1984,"[101] in which the agency

97. Verkuil et al., *supra* note 33, at 1018–19. The footnotes therein detail the types of actions brought.

98. Long v. Soc. Sec. Admin., 635 F.3d 526, 528, 535 (Fed. Cir. 2011).

99. *Id.* at 539 (Dyk, J., concurring).

100. The following is taken from Verkuil et al., *supra* note 33, at 1019–20.

101. Soc. Sec. Admin. v. Goodman, 19 M.S.P.R. 321 (1984); Soc. Sec. Admin. v. Brennan, 19 M.S.P.R. 335 (1984), *opinion clarified*, 20 M.S.P.R. 35 (1984); Soc. Sec. Admin. v. Balaban, 20 M.S.P.R. 675 (1984).

charged three ALJs with unacceptably low productivity. SSA had produced evidence in the lead *Goodman* case that the judge's disposition rate for the years 1980–1981 was 15 to 16 cases per month, compared to an average of 30 to 32 for all SSA ALJs. In addition, his average monthly "pending" caseload for 1981 was 64, compared with 178 for all SSA ALJs. After a hearing, the MSPB ALJ rejected the ALJ's legal defenses and recommended removal. The full MSPB heard oral arguments on the case and unanimously ruled that although "there is no generic prohibition to the filing of this charge," SSA's evidence that the ALJ's case dispositions were half the national average was not enough to show unacceptably low productivity "[i]n the absence of evidence demonstrating the validity of using its statistics to measure comparative productivity."[102] The board opined that SSA cases were not fungible and that SSA's comparative statistics did not take into sufficient account the differences among these types of cases. The same reasoning was later applied to two other cases against SSA ALJs with similar productivity records.

The ACUS study concluded that the result amounted to a pyrrhic victory for SSA: the agency won the right to bring charges against low-producing ALJs but was handed a virtually insurmountable burden of proof. Despite the fact that social security disability cases, because of their high volume and relative fungibility, lend themselves to statistical comparison (at least when compared to other types of agency adjudication), the MSPB found that several years' worth of half-of-average production did not meet its burden of proof without greater analysis of the particular cases heard by the cited ALJ. In the end, two of the ALJs involved in these cases later recovered attorneys' fees of almost $250,000 from the government.

It was thus not surprising that SSA essentially stopped bringing productivity-based charges to the MSPB until 2010, when it successfully brought a similar case against one of its ALJs. This time the agency meticulously documented the low productivity of the ALJ, and the extensive notice and opportunity for training it had afforded him for three years to improve his performance. The MSPB ALJ sustained the agency's charge, and the board affirmed, finding that the *Goodman* test had been met.[103] On appeal, the Court of Appeals for the Federal Circuit affirmed the board. In doing so, it stated:

---

102. *Goodman*, 19 M.S.P.R. at 330–31.

103. Soc. Sec. Admin. v. Shapiro, MSPB Docket No. CB-7521-11-0024-T-1 (Mar. 4, 2014).

> We agree that there must be a showing that the proffered production statistics are relevant to the determination—i.e., that they reflect the average disposition rate for a particular region across the same time period. But in extreme cases like this, where Mr. Shapiro's production is, at best, roughly a quarter of that performed by the rest of the ALJs in his region, that standing alone is highly relevant and potentially preponderant evidence that he failed to manage his cases acceptably.[104]

The task of determining "good cause" is a difficult one, but the entire APA framework of protecting ALJs from discipline absent good cause has been complicated and perhaps threatened by a series of decisions by the Supreme Court concerning the constitutionality, more generally, of statutory "for-cause" protections given to other officers in the executive branch. As discussed in Chapter 3, these cases have primarily involved the degree to which Congress can limit the president's power to remove an officer. As Professor Richard Pierce recounted in that chapter:

> [I]n *Free Enterprise Fund v. Public Co. Accounting & Oversight Board*,[105] the Supreme Court held that the Executive Vesting Clause (which requires that the "executive Power" be vested in the president[106]) and the Take Care Clause (which requires that the president "take Care that the Laws be faithfully executed"[107]) make it unconstitutional for Congress to limit the president's power to remove an officer by providing more than one level of "for-cause" protection from removal.

In that case, the Court ruled that an especially strong statutory protection given to members of the Public Company Accounting Oversight Board (PCAOB) from removal by the SEC (in which it was lodged) was unconstitutional because the SEC members themselves had for-cause protection from removal by the president. To remedy this newly found constitutional violation, the Court excised the PCAOB members' for-cause removal protection. The dissenting justices criticized this ruling, pointing out that it could also affect ALJs, many of whom worked in independent agencies whose heads also had for-cause removal protection. The majority responded in a footnote that said: "[O]ur holding . . .

104. Shapiro v. Soc. Sec. Admin., 800 F.3d 1332, 1339 (Fed. Cir. 2015).
105. 561 U.S. 477 (2010).
106. U.S. Const. art. II, § 1.
107. *Id.* § 3.

does not address that subset of independent agency employees who serve as administrative law judges. . . . [U]nlike members of the Board, many administrative law judges of course perform adjudicative rather than enforcement or policymaking functions, or possess purely recommendatory powers."[108]

That would seem to adequately protect ALJ removal protections from being governed by the *Free Enterprise Fund* line of cases, even where ALJs are working in independent agencies. However, this did not stop the Trump Administration from urging the Supreme Court to take up this issue in the *Lucia* case. The Court declined to do so, both at the certiorari stage and the merits stage, suggesting that it would wait until lower courts had opined on the issue.[109] Not surprisingly, that issue has since been raised by litigants in lower courts, in one case successfully, and will likely reach the Supreme Court in the near future.[110]

Moreover, the solicitor general in the Trump Administration also suggested that the involvement of the MSPB, an independent agency itself, in deciding removal cases is problematic because it creates another layer of for-cause protection in contravention of *Free Enterprise Fund*. The solicitor general intimated that DOJ would only defend section 7521 if the MSPB deferred to the agency's charge and stopped deciding these cases de novo.[111] Subsequently a judge on the D.C. Circuit wrote an opinion, concurring in part and dissenting in part, in a case that was dismissed on jurisdictional grounds by the panel, arguing that the MSPB's role in the process was unconstitutional.[112] That issue is sure to recur as well. As Professor Pierce wrote in Chapter 3, "[t]he results of those pending cases are difficult to predict." Will the Supreme Court overturn 70 years of upholding the role of ALJs? Would the Court really want to undermine the independence of ALJs and the loss of due process for litigants against the government that would be the result? Or will the Court take a more formalistic view of the Executive Vesting Clause and the Take Care Clause? Footnote 10

108. *Free Enter. Fund*, 561 U.S. at 507 n.10 (internal citations omitted).

109. Lucia v. Sec. & Exch. Comm'n, 138 S. Ct. 2044, 2050 n.1 (2018).

110. *See* Jarkesy v. Sec. & Exch. Comm'n, 34 F.4th 446 (5th Cir. 2022) (finding SEC ALJ's removal protection to be unconstitutional).

111. Memorandum from the Solic. Gen., DOJ, to Agency Gen. Counsels, Guidance on Administrative Law Judges after *Lucia v. SEC* (S. Ct.) (July 2018), https://perma.cc/Y2TW-BUD9.

112. Fleming v. U.S. Dep't of Agric., 987 F.3d 1093, 1113–24 (D.C. Cir. 2021) (Rao, J., concurring in part and dissenting in part).

of *Free Enterprise Fund* seems to provide the answer, but the makeup of the Supreme Court has changed in important ways since 2010.

9.482 Administrative Judges

Most AJs lack the for-cause removal protection afforded to ALJs by the APA. One rare exception is the members of the General Services Administration's Civilian Board of Contract Appeals. Its statute specifies that its members are "subject to removal in the same manner as administrative law judges."[113] Another is the Government Accountability Office's Personnel Appeals Board, whose members may be removed by a majority of the board (except the member subject to removal) only for inefficiency, neglect of duty, or malfeasance in office after an opportunity for a hearing before the board.[114] Otherwise, according to the ACUS study of AJs, most of them served in their positions at the will of the agency. Of the 36 non-ALJ types for which ACUS received responses, only two others reported protections from at-will removal. Equal Employment Opportunity Commission administrative judges and NLRB hearing officers have protection from removal under their collective-bargaining agreements.[115]

That said, AJs would normally have the usual civil-service protection afforded to career civil servants, namely that they can only be removed "for such cause as will promote the efficiency of the service" after notice and an opportunity for a hearing before the MSPB.[116]

The D.C. Circuit has made clear that there is no constitutional requirement that members of agency appeal boards be protected from at-will removal, at least from that position. In *Kalaris v. Donovan*, members of the DOL's Benefits Review Board challenged their removal from the board. The court held that, "in the face of congressional silence, the power of removal is incident to the power of appointment." The decision does reveal that members "were, however, only transferred to other positions in the Department of Labor, at like grade and pay."[117]

---

113. 41 U.S.C. § 7105(b)(3).

114. 31 U.S.C. § 751(d).

115. Barnett et al., *supra* note 11, at 60.

116. 5 U.S.C. §§ 7513(a), 7701. Unlike disciplinary cases involving ALJs, where the MSPB must afford a hearing before an ALJ, cases involving regular civil servants may be heard by AJs. *Id.* § 7701(b)(1).

117. Kalaris v. Donovan, 697 F.2d 376, 383 n.23 (D.C. Cir. 1983).

9.5 LABOR RELATIONS

Title VII of the Civil Service Reform Act of 1978 allows most agency employees to organize, bargain collectively, and participate through labor organizations of their choice in decisions affecting their working lives.[118] Unlike their private counterparts, however, federal employees do not have the right to strike.

"Employee" is defined in the act to exclude "a supervisor or a management official." "Management official" is defined as "an individual employed by an agency in a position the duties and responsibilities of which require or authorize the individual to formulate, determine or influence the policies of the agency."[119] This would imply that at least rank-and-file ALJs would be eligible to unionize.

Many of SSA's more than 1,500 ALJs have joined a union called the Association of Administrative Law Judges (AALJ). The AALJ was founded as a professional association in 1971 and, in 1999, chose to affiliate with the International Federation of Professional and Technical Engineers (IFPTE), AFL-CIO. It claims that "[t]oday, more than two-thirds of Social Security Administration (SSA) bargaining unit judges are active members of AALJ. There are also a number of associate members who serve as management administrative law judges."[120]

Rank-and-file AJs are also presumably eligible to unionize. One of the largest groups of AJs, the 500-plus IJs employed by EOIR, have formed the National Association of Immigration Judges (NAIJ). The NAIJ was founded in 1971 as a voluntary association but in 1979 was designated as the recognized representative for collective bargaining for all IJs. In 2000, it affiliated with the IFPTE. One of the reasons given for why IJs unionized was that, as DOJ employees, they were prohibited from speaking out publicly or lobbying Congress or DOJ. "Only as an Association, legally constituted as a labor organization, have we been able to speak independently of the DOJ and advocate for our members' interests."[121]

DOJ has twice brought actions before the Federal Labor Relations Authority (FLRA) seeking to exclude IJs from the bargaining unit because they were "management officials." In 2000, the FLRA rejected

---

118. 5 U.S.C. §§ 7101–7151.

119. *Id.* § 7103(a)(2)(iii), (a)(11).

120. *About AALJ*, AALJ, https://www.aalj.org/aalj-about (last visited June 27, 2023).

121. *About the NAIJ*, NAIJ, https://www.naij-usa.org/about (last visited June 27, 2023).

such a challenge. The FLRA accepted its RD's reasoning that IJs have to apply immigration laws and regulations, and their decisions are not published and do not constitute precedent. She also observed that IJ decisions are binding only on the parties to the case, are "routinely" appealed, and are subject to de novo review. Nor did the fact that some IJs participated on advisory committees to the Office of the Chief IJ, commented on internal operating memoranda, or participated in the court evaluation system make them management officials.[122]

Despite this ruling, in August 2019, DOJ filed a new decertification petition suggesting changed circumstances, the main ones being an increased caseload and a change from de novo review to "clear error" review. In a lengthy decision after a hearing, on November 2, 2020, the FLRA RD denied the petition, but the FLRA reversed her 2–1, finding simply that IJs "influence the policy of the Agency by interpreting immigration laws when they apply the law and existing precedent to the unique facts of each case."[123] In December 2021, the Biden Administration withdrew DOJ's support for the decertification,[124] but on January 21, 2022, the FLRA, which had retained the same membership, reaffirmed its decision after a motion for reconsideration.[125] As of February 2023, the situation has not changed, although the NAIJ has petitions outstanding in both in the FLRA and the D.C. Circuit.[126]

---

122. DOJ, EOIR, Off. of the Chief IJ & NAIJ, 56 F.L.R.A. No. 616 (2000).

123. DOJ, EOIR & NAIJ, 71 F.L.R.A. No. 207 (2020).

124. Settlement Agreement between the DOJ, EOIR, and the NAIJ (Dec. 7, 2021), https://www.aila.org/File/Related/19081303l.pdf.

125. DOJ, EOIR & NAIJ, 72 F.L.R.A. No. 622 (2022).

126. For a short period, from May 2021 to January 2023, the FLRA had a 2–1 majority of Democratic appointees so the NAIJ filed a second motion for reconsideration, but the FLRA did not act on it before one of those members' terms expired and created a new deadlock. Meanwhile, on November 17, 2022, the D.C. Circuit conducted an oral argument on NAIJ's petition for review of the FLRA's November 2020 and January 2022 decisions, but several of the judges suggested that they might be interested in waiting to see what the FLRA did with the pending petition for reconsideration. The case is *National Association of Immigration Judges v. Federal Labor Relations Authority*, No. 22-1028 (filed 2022).

Chapter 10

Integrity in Agency Adjudication

Louis J. Virelli III

10.1 CHAPTER OVERVIEW

Integrity in agency adjudication has two purposes: to ensure the fairness of a proceeding for the parties involved and to ensure that the parties and the public perceive the proceeding to be fair. While these two concepts often overlap, they are not synonymous. It is entirely possible that an adjudicator with a financial or personal relationship to a party in a case might act wholly impartially when adjudicating the case. As a professional who understands the importance of impartial adjudication, the adjudicator may be fully capable of putting aside any personal benefits that may accrue from their participation and render a truly impartial and rational decision. Nevertheless, the adjudicator's participation may create an integrity problem by diluting the observing public's confidence in the adjudicator's decision. A decision lacking in the appearance of impartiality and fairness threatens to create a public confidence gap that can draw even the most evenhanded decisions into question.

Concerns about integrity in agency adjudication and the corresponding remedies for those concerns thus seek to target both actual and apparent shortcomings in adjudicative integrity. This chapter addresses three main concerns about integrity in federal agency adjudication—bias (section 10.2), combination of adjudicative and adversarial functions (section 10.3), and ex parte contacts (section 10.4)—and their corresponding remedies.

10.2 BIAS

Bias in agency adjudication refers to the inability of an adjudicator to render an impartial decision. Bias may exist when any of the following threats to an adjudicator's impartiality is present: (1) a financial or personal interest in the case (a "conflict of interest"); (2) personal animus toward a party to the proceeding or an organization that party belongs to; or (3) prejudgment of the facts at issue in the adjudication.[1]

Various legal authorities govern adjudicator bias, including the Due Process Clause (section 10.21), the Administrative Procedure Act (APA) (section 10.22), government ethics laws (section 10.23), and individual agency rules and policies (section 10.24). Additional guidance is found in model rules, model codes of conduct, and recommended best practices (section 10.25). The usual remedy for bias is recusal. Procedures for recusal are discussed in section 10.26.

10.21 Due Process Clause

The Due Process Clause of the Fifth Amendment protects against bias in federal government proceedings, including administrative adjudications, that involve a deprivation of "life, liberty, or property."[2] At its core, due process is premised on the notion that all parties to an adjudication are entitled to a neutral, unbiased arbiter.[3] This includes principles such as ensuring that "no man shall be a judge in his own case,"[4]

---

1. Michael Asimow, Admin. Conf. of the U.S., Evidentiary Hearings outside the Administrative Procedure Act 23 (2016).
2. U.S. Const. amend. V.
3. Caperton v. A.T. Massey Coal Co., 556 U.S. 868, 877 (2009).
4. *Id.* at 886.

guaranteeing "an absence of actual bias" on the part of a decision-maker,[5] and requiring that adjudicators keep an open mind.[6]

The Due Process Clause applies to both formal and informal adjudication. This is in contrast with the APA, which only addresses bias in formal adjudication. The Due Process Clause's broader reach is tempered, however, by its narrower prohibitions. The U.S. Supreme Court has made clear that "most matters relating to judicial disqualification [do] not rise to a constitutional level," and that "matters of kinship, personal bias, state policy, [and] remoteness of interest, would seem generally to be matters merely of legislative discretion."[7]

In general, a violation of due process occurs when there is a "probability of actual bias" on behalf of the adjudicator.[8] There may be a probability of actual bias on the part of a government decision-maker in cases of financial conflicts, personal bias, or prejudgment of facts. In rare cases, the appearance of partiality may be strong enough to rise to the level of a due process violation, even if none of the other categories of bias are clearly present.[9]

The Supreme Court has applied the Due Process Clause most readily in cases of financial conflicts or personal bias.[10] The Due Process Clause forbids government decision-makers, including federal agency adjudicators, from presiding over a case in which they have a financial interest. This concept dates back to Blackstone's account of the English common law and was the standard for American judicial recusal at the Founding.[11] The Supreme Court has decided several cases in which a government decision-maker's financial interest in a proceeding has amounted to a due process violation.[12] Even in those cases, however, the Court has emphasized that due process violations generally require "extreme" circumstances.[13]

---

5. Williams v. Pennsylvania, 136 S. Ct. 1899, 1905 (2016) (quoting *In re* Murchison, 349 U.S. 133, 136 (1955)).

6. *Murchison*, 349 U.S. at 136 (quoting Tumey v. Ohio, 273 U.S. 510, 532 (1927)).

7. *Caperton*, 556 U.S. at 876.

8. Withrow v. Larkin, 421 U.S. 35, 47 (1975).

9. *Caperton*, 556 U.S. at 884–90.

10. *Murchison*, 349 U.S. at 133; *Tumey*, 273 U.S. at 310.

11. 3 William Blackstone, Commentaries 361 (1836); Louis J. Virelli III, Disqualifying the High Court: Supreme Court Recusal and the Constitution 5 (2016).

12. *Caperton*, 556 U.S. at 887; Aetna Life Ins. Co. v. Lavoie, 475 U.S. 813, 824 (1986); *Murchison*, 349 U.S. at 136.

13. *Caperton*, 556 U.S. at 887.

Personal bias under the Due Process Clause reflects personal animus on the behalf of the adjudicator toward a party or their representative. At common law, judges were presumed to be nearly immune to personal animosity toward a party such that establishing personal bias was extremely difficult.[14] The Supreme Court has on occasion found sufficient evidence of personal bias to warrant disqualifying a government decision-maker under the Due Process Clause.[15]

Prejudgment of facts by an adjudicator is prohibited by due process because it deprives the parties of a neutral arbiter and thus a fair hearing. Courts have applied the due process prohibition against prejudgment to administrative adjudicators. Prejudgment exists when "a disinterested observer may conclude that [the agency] has in some measure adjudged the facts as well as the law of a particular case in advance of hearing it." Evidence of prejudgment is most frequently found in extrajudicial statements by an adjudicator.[16]

Although the Supreme Court has noted that "justice must satisfy the appearance of justice" under the Due Process Clause,[17] it has consistently reaffirmed that the appearance of partiality, without more, ordinarily does not rise to the level of a constitutional violation.[18] The Court's references to the "appearance of justice" in due process cases can be read in conjunction with the "probability of actual bias" standard to show how an adjudicator's actions can serve as evidence of potential bias. A more probing look at the impact of an adjudicator's conduct on public perception of the agency is reserved for statutory and other legal protections against adjudicator bias, such as those discussed in the following sections.

There are several situations in which the Court has found that apparent bias does not rise to the level of a due process violation. In general, the animating principle in these examples is the well-established notion from English common law that "the law will not suppose a possibility of bias or favour in a judge, who is already sworn to administer

---

14. 3 Blackstone, *supra* note 11, at 361.

15. Williams v. Pennsylvania, 136 S. Ct. 1899 (2016); Mayberry v. Pennsylvania, 400 U.S. 455, 466 (1971); *Murchison*, 349 U.S. at 133.

16. Cinderella Career & Finishing Schs., Inc. v. Fed. Trade Comm'n, 425 F.2d 583, 591 (D.C. Cir. 1970) (quoting Gilligan, Will & Co. v. Sec. & Exch. Comm'n, 267 F.2d 461, 469 (2d Cir. 1959)); *see also* McClure v. Indep. Sch. Dist. No. 16, 228 F.3d 1205, 1215–16 (10th Cir. 2000); Bakalis v. Golembeski, 35 F.3d 318, 326 (7th Cir. 1994).

17. *Lavoie*, 475 U.S. at 825 (quoting *Murchison*, 349 U.S. at 136).

18. *Caperton*, 556 U.S. at 876.

impartial justice."[19] For instance, an adjudicator's previous resolution of a legal issue or ideological position is not disqualifying under the Due Process Clause. On the contrary, alleged bias toward a legal conclusion, as opposed to the parties, has been treated as a sign of professional competence.[20] Agency adjudicators likewise do not violate due process when they have established views on the relevant facts or law of a case that are unrelated to the specific parties,[21] or when they preside over a rehearing of a case they have already decided.[22] Like judges, agency adjudicators are expected to be able to retry cases and otherwise resolve cases on remand impartially.

10.22 Administrative Procedure Act

The APA requires that adjudicators in formal adjudications be "impartial."[23] A 2016 study for the Administrative Conference of the United States (ACUS) concluded that this impartiality requirement is synonymous with protections against the same three sources of bias discussed in section 10.2 in connection with the Due Process Clause: (1) financial interests, (2) personal animus, and (3) prejudgment of adjudicative facts.[24]

Prior rulings against a party are not sufficient evidence of bias under the APA to merit an adjudicator's disqualification, nor is conduct by the adjudicator associated with maintaining an orderly hearing, such as questioning witnesses.[25] Expressions of impatience or frustration by an adjudicator do not necessarily constitute impermissible bias,[26] nor does copying a party's proposed findings into a decision, provided the decision is the product of the adjudicator's independent consideration of the record.[27]

---

19. 3 Blackstone, *supra* note 11, at 361.

20. *See* Republican Party of Minn. v. White, 536 U.S. 765, 777–78 (2002); *see also* Kermit Roosevelt, *Ways a Judge Should, and Should Not, Be Impartial*, N.Y. Times (May 17, 2016), http://www.nytimes.com/roomfordebate/2013/11/03/judges-appearance-of-impartiality/ways-a-judge-should-and-should-not-be-impartial.

21. Fed. Trade Comm'n v. Cement Inst., 333 U.S. 683 (1948).

22. Nat'l Lab. Rels. Bd. v. Donnelly Garment Co., 330 U.S. 219, 236–37 (1947).

23. 5 U.S.C. § 556(b).

24. *See* Asimow, *supra* note 1, at 23.

25. Holly Hill Farms v. United States, 447 F.3d 258, 270 (4th Cir. 2006); McLaughlin v. Union Oil, 869 F.2d 1039, 1047 (7th Cir. 1989).

26. Rollins v. Massanari, 261 F.3d 853, 858 (9th Cir. 2001).

27. Casino Ready Mix v. Nat'l Lab. Rels. Bd., 321 F.3d 1190, 1201–02 (D.C. Cir. 2003).

Unlike the Due Process Clause, the APA's impartiality provision does not apply in informal adjudications. ACUS has recommended, however, that agencies adopt their own regulations prohibiting these three sources of bias in informal adjudications that include a legally required evidentiary hearing.[28] Many agencies have done so, as discussed in section 10.24.

10.23 Government Ethics Laws

As federal employees, all agency adjudicators are governed by federal ethics laws. The primary statute relating to the recusal of agency adjudicators "prohibits an employee from participating personally and substantially in any particular matter in which he has a financial interest, or in which certain others with whom he is associated have a financial interest."[29] It requires that the employee have knowledge of the disqualifying financial interest but does not require that the financial interest be substantial.[30]

The most significant federal ethics laws are enforced by the Office of Government Ethics (OGE), which is an independent agency within the executive branch. OGE regulations protect against financial and specific personal conflicts. The OGE regulation that most directly applies to agency adjudicators states that an employee "should not participate" in a matter when the employee knows that they have either a financial interest in the proceeding or a personal relationship with a party and the circumstances could reasonably draw the employee's impartiality into question.[31] An employee may take it upon themselves to seek ethics advice if a situation not otherwise covered by the regulation could cause a reasonable observer to question the employee's impartiality.[32]

OGE has also promulgated a list of "14 General Principles" that serve as the foundation for its regulations.[33] Principle 14 states that

---

28. *See* Administrative Conference Recommendation 2016-4, *Evidentiary Hearings Not Required by the Administrative Procedure Act*, ¶ 5, 81 Fed. Reg. 94,314, 94,315 (Dec. 23, 2016).

29. 18 U.S.C. § 208; Off. of Gov't Ethics, Report to the President and to Congressional Committees on the Conflict of Interest Laws Relating to Executive Branch Employment 28 (2006) [hereinafter OGE Report].

30. OGE Report, *supra* note 29, at 29.

31. 5 C.F.R. § 2635.502 (2022).

32. *Id.* § 2635.502(a)(1).

33. OGE, 14 General Principles, https://oge.gov/Web/OGE.nsf/0/CF823CA93BF7562A85258711006D29E4/$FILE/14%20General%20Principles.pdf.

"employees shall *endeavor* to avoid . . . creating the appearance that they are violating the law or ethical standards *set forth in this part.*" Although the principle's focus on appearances may be a bit broader than the OGE regulation, it is too closely tethered to the substantive provision of the regulation to add any further limitations on agency adjudicators.

OGE can also work with agencies to promulgate supplementary ethics regulations for the agency.[34] Supplemental regulations can serve as a useful vehicle for adopting agency-specific ethics standards, but there are few, if any, supplemental regulations pertaining specifically to the integrity of agency adjudication.[35]

OGE regulations are enforceable by individual agencies rather than the parties to the case. Violations of OGE rules can result in disciplinary action against an adjudicator.[36]

10.24 Agency Rules and Policies

Individual agencies have also adopted their own standards to protect against biased adjudicators. These various standards appear in published regulations, policy and practice manuals, and guidance documents. As explained in a 2020 ACUS report surveying agency recusal provisions, agencies' substantive approach to bias fits into one of several categories.[37] Some agencies have chosen to mirror the APA by simply requiring that adjudicators be impartial.[38] Others focus on conflicts of interest, for example prohibiting participation by an adjudicator who has a pecuniary interest in the outcome of the case or is related to a party.[39] A third group is concerned with adjudicators who had some

---

34. *See* 5 C.F.R. § 2635.105 (2022).

35. Louis J. Virelli III, Admin. Conf. of the U.S., Recusal Rules for Administrative Adjudicators 13 (2018) [hereinafter Virelli, Recusal Rules].

36. 5 C.F.R. §§ 2635.106(a), 102(g) (2022); *see also* Louis J. Virelli III, *An Ethical Gap in Agency Adjudication*, 69 Buff. L. Rev. 1329, 1369 (2022).

37. Louis J. Virelli III, Admin. Conf. of the U.S., Administrative Recusal Rules: A Taxonomy and Study of Existing Recusal Standards for Agency Adjudicators (2020) [hereinafter Virelli, Administrative Recusal Rules].

38. *See, e.g.*, 15 C.F.R. § 766.13 (2022) ("Hearings will be conducted in a fair and impartial manner by the administrative law judge . . . ."); Off. of Gen. Couns., Nat'l Lab. Rels. Bd., Guide for Hearing Officers in NLRB Representation and Section 10(k) Proceedings 1, 141 (2003) ("The hearing officer is not an advocate of any position but must be impartial in his/her rulings . . . .").

39. *See, e.g.*, 7 C.F.R. § 47.11 (2022) (precluding participation of Agricultural Marketing Service adjudicators if they have a pecuniary interest in the proceeding or are related to any person involved in that proceeding).

prior involvement with the case.[40] The fourth category, which is the most common, prohibits personal bias by the adjudicator.[41] The fifth focuses on the appearance of bias,[42] and the last mirrors the judicial recusal standard by combining all of the above.[43] In addition to those incorporating the judicial standard, many agencies have adopted some combination of these categories.[44] An agency's specific choice may be influenced by multiple factors, including whether its adjudicators are politically independent, preside over primarily adversarial or inquisitorial proceedings, are reviewable by another agency official, conduct high-profile adjudications, or are part of a multimember adjudicative body.[45]

10.25 Model Codes of Conduct, Model Rules, and Recommended Best Practices

Several model codes address potential bias problems for administrative adjudicators, but none are legally binding or universally accepted. The American Bar Association's (ABA's) National Conference of the Administrative Law Judiciary adopted the Model Code of Judicial Conduct for Federal Administrative Law Judges in 1989. It prohibited administrative law judges (ALJs) from participating in any proceeding in which their "impartiality might reasonably be questioned" but

---

40. *See, e.g.*, 20 C.F.R. § 260.3(e) (2022) ("The reconsideration of the initial [benefits determination] shall be conducted by a person who shall not have . . . directly participated in the initial decision which has been requested to be reconsidered . . . .")

41. *See, e.g.*, 42 C.F.R. § 405.1817 (2022) ("[N]o hearing officer (or officers) shall conduct a hearing in a case in which he is prejudiced or partial with respect to any party . . . ."); Merit Sys. Prot. Bd., Judges Handbook 13 (2017).

42. *See, e.g.*, Soc. Sec. Admin., Hearings, Appeals, and Litigation Law (HALLEX) Manual § I-3-1-40 (prohibiting an adjudicator from participating if his or her involvement in the case "would create an appearance of impropriety"); Ctrs. for Medicare and Medicaid Servs., Provider Reimbursement Review Board Rules 58 (2018) ("Board member may recuse him or herself if there are reasons that might give the appearance of an inability to render a fair and impartial decision.").

43. *See, e.g.*, 43 C.F.R. § 4.27(c) (2022) (excluding an adjudicator if "circumstances exist that would disqualify a judge in such circumstances under the recognized canons of judicial ethics"); 50 C.F.R. § 18.76 (2022) (same).

44. *See, e.g.*, 42 C.F.R. § 405.1817 (2022) (incorporating prior involvement, personal bias, and conflict standards).

45. *See* Virelli, *supra* note 36, at 1378–82.

has not been updated since and has not been codified by Congress.[46] In 2007, the ABA expanded the Model Code of Judicial Conduct to explicitly include ALJs but only to the extent that individual jurisdictions deemed it desirable.[47] At least some jurisdictions have resisted.[48] Although neither code has proven particularly influential in terms of federal ALJs' practices, the fact that both seek to explicitly protect not only actual impartiality but also the appearance of impartiality among ALJs serves as a useful reminder for agencies and legislators of the dual function of bias protections for agency adjudications.

In 2010, the National Conference of Commissioners on Uniform State Laws adopted the Revised Model State Administrative Procedure Act. It was followed in 2018 by the ABA's Model Code of Judicial Conduct for State Administrative Law Judges. Both of these codes govern only state adjudicators and prohibit participation in a wider range of proceedings than their federal counterparts.[49] Like their federal counterparts, the state model codes emphasize the importance of the appearance of impartiality.[50] Even though the state model codes are not legally binding on federal agencies, they can be useful guides for agencies and legislators seeking to update bias protections in federal administrative proceedings.[51]

As noted, the APA's impartiality requirement applies only in cases of formal adjudication. To ensure similar protections in informal adjudications, ACUS Recommendation 2016-4 encourages agencies to adopt their own regulations prohibiting bias in non-ALJ proceedings.[52] ACUS Recommendation 2018-4 expanded on that recommendation

---

46. Model Code of Jud. Conduct for Fed. Admin. L. Judges Canon 3(C) (Am. Bar Ass'n 1989); *see also* Steven A. Glazer, *Toward a Model Code of Judicial Conduct for Federal Administrative Law Judges*, 64 Admin. L. Rev. 337 (2012).

47. Model Code of Jud. Conduct r. I(B) (Am. Bar. Ass'n 2007).

48. *See* Lowry v. Barnhart, 329 F.3d 1019, 1024 (9th Cir. 2003).

49. Revised Model State Admin. Procedure Act § 402(c), (d) (Nat'l Conf. on Comm'rs of Unif. State Laws 2010); Model Code of Jud. Conduct for State Admin. L. Judges Canon 2, r. 2.11(A) (Am. Bar Ass'n 2018).

50. *See, e.g.*, Model Code of Jud. Conduct for State Admin. L. Judges, *supra* note 49, Canon 1, r. 1.2; Model Code of Jud. Conduct, *supra* note 47, Canon 1, r. 1.2; Model Code of Jud. Conduct for Fed. Admin. L. Judges, *supra* note 46, Canon 2.A.

51. Revised Model State Admin. Procedure Act, *supra* note 49, § 402(c), (d); Model Code of Jud. Conduct for State Admin. L. Judges, *supra* note 49, Canon 2, r. 2.11(A).

52. Administrative Conference Recommendation 2016-4, *supra* note 28, ¶ 5.

by encouraging agencies to issue procedural rules governing recusal of adjudicators (see section 10.26).[53]

ACUS also revised its Model Adjudication Rules (MARs) in 2018 to require that agency adjudicators in most adversarial proceedings (formal or informal) "conduct her/his functions in an impartial manner."[54] The MARs also require recusal on the grounds of personal bias.[55] Although the MARs are purely advisory, they highlight best practices for agencies seeking to revise their own adjudication rules.

10.26 Recusal Procedures

Recusal, or disqualification, is the process of removing an adjudicator from a specific case and is the predominant means of remedying adjudicator bias. Recusal has two goals. It ensures that adjudicators are impartial, and it promotes public confidence in agency adjudications by signaling to the observing public that adjudicators who either are not, or do not appear to be, impartial will not participate in agency proceedings.

An adjudicator in a formal adjudication under the APA may be disqualified for personal bias either by his or her own action or by motion from a party accompanied by an affidavit "of personal bias or other disqualification."[56] Motions to disqualify may be brought against an ALJ or an agency head,[57] and must be filed in a "timely" manner to prevent being waived.[58] Many agencies have also adopted their own recusal procedures, including in proceedings not subject to the APA's formal-adjudication provisions. These procedures may include opportunities for parties to file recusal motions, affidavit requirements, adjudicator reporting requirements, and administrative review of recusal decisions.[59]

ACUS Recommendation 2018-4 encouraged agencies to adopt standards and procedures for recusal by adjudicators who preside

53. Administrative Conference Recommendation 2018-4, Recusal Rules for Administrative Adjudicators, 84 Fed. Reg. 2,139 (Feb. 6, 2019).

54. Model Adjudication Rules § 112 (Admin. Conf. of the U.S. 2018).

55. *Id.*

56. 5 U.S.C. § 556(b).

57. Keating v. Off. of Thrift Supervision, 45 F.3d 322, 327 (9th Cir. 1995).

58. Marcus v. Dir., Off. of Workers' Comp. Programs, 548 F.2d 1044, 1051 (D.C. Cir. 1976).

59. Virelli, Administrative Recusal Rules, *supra* note 37, at 24–34.

over evidentiary hearings, including in informal adjudication.[60] Many agencies have adopted rules and policies on recusal, which reflect their own views of what constitutes impermissible bias (or the appearance thereof). A 2020 study for ACUS revealed a wide range of agency views on recusal and how to address potential bias among agency adjudicators.[61] Policymakers, adjudicators, practitioners, and potential parties should consider these agency-specific standards when participating in, or thinking of ways to improve, adjudications within individual agencies.

Recusal of agency heads, including an individual member of a multimember agency, creates additional challenges for the efficacy and integrity of agency adjudications. Agency heads typically cannot be replaced once recused, potentially leaving the agency without its designated final decision-maker. The rule of necessity is an ancient common-law rule targeted at precisely this concern.[62] The rule of necessity suggests that adjudicators should participate in cases that they would have otherwise been removed from "where disqualification would result in an absence of judicial machinery capable of dealing with a matter."[63] It is generally not applicable to recusal of lower level adjudicators because they are typically replaceable, either within the agency or through designating replacement adjudicators from other agencies.[64] But when unreplaceable agency heads are subject to recusal, the rule of necessity becomes relevant. Agency heads and reviewing courts must balance the agency's ability to fulfill its statutory mission with the ethical consequences of allowing the adjudicator to preside over the case.[65]

Recusal rules for multimember agency heads vary widely. Some treat agency members the same as lower level adjudicators, while

---

60. Administrative Conference Recommendation 2018-4, *supra* note 53, at 2,140.

61. *See* Virelli, Administrative Recusal Rules, *supra* note 37.

62. Frederick Pollock, A First Book of Jurisprudence: For Students of the Common Law 269 (5th ed. 1923); United States v. Will, 449 U.S. 200, 213–14 (1980).

63. Richard E. Flamm, Judicial Disqualification: Recusal and Disqualification of Judges 20.2, at 589–90 (2d ed. 2007).

64. *See, e.g.*, 5 C.F.R. § 930.208 (2022) (outlining the ALJ Loan Program, under which the Office of Personnel Management "coordinates the loan/detail of an administrative law judge from one agency to another"); *cf. Will*, 449 U.S. at 213.

65. Louis J. Virelli III, *Recusal in Administrative Adjudication*, 64 Ariz. L. Rev. 135 (2022).

others have adopted recusal provisions that exclude agency heads altogether.[66] For multimember agencies with recusal requirements for agency heads, recusal of one or more members changes the makeup of the panel for that adjudication. Excluding a member or members can lead to a series of problems, such as deadlocks, ideologically unbalanced bodies, or lack of a quorum, all of which must be taken into account by administrators and courts when evaluating whether recusal is justified in a given case.[67]

If a recusal decision is challenged, the issue of remedy arises. In general, a decision to recuse will neither be challenged nor require a remedy. The question of remedy arises far more readily when an adjudicator should have recused and did not. Improper failure to recuse may result in the adjudicator's decision being vacated and revisited. When the adjudicator's improper failure to recuse was determined in an interlocutory or collateral review of the recusal decision, vacation generally is not necessary. The adjudicator can simply be replaced, and the proceeding can continue with another adjudicator. If the failure to recuse was reviewed after a final order from the original adjudicator, the appropriate remedy depends on the legal basis for the recusal. Recusal failures that violate due process, whether by a single adjudicator or an individual member of a multimember body, must be vacated and remanded for rehearing by either a different adjudicator or the nonrecused members of the multimember body.[68] A recusal violation that does not amount to a due process violation requires balancing the problem of a potentially biased adjudicator with the costs of repeating the proceeding with a new adjudicator. Courts generally rely on the harmless error standard to determine if litigation before a recused judge must begin anew with a different judge.[69]

Agencies rely on their own rules and standards to govern appeals of recusal decisions. Not surprisingly, the results are varied. Some agencies allow for immediate appeal of a decision not to recuse, while others allow for review of recusal decisions only after a decision on

---

66. *Compare* 17 C.F.R. § 201.112 (2022) (treating Securities and Exchange Commission ALJ recusal differently from recusal of commissioners), *with* 16 C.F.R. § 3.42(g) (2022) (treating Federal Trade Commission members the same as ALJs for recusal purposes).

67. *See* Virelli, Recusal Rules, *supra* note 35, at 20.

68. Stivers v. Pierce, 71 F.3d 732, 748 (9th Cir. 1995); Cinderella Career & Fishing Schs., Inc. v. Fed. Trade Comm'n, 425 F.2d 583, 592 (D.C. Cir. 1970).

69. Cassandra Burke Robertson & Gregory Hilbert, *Judicial Disqualification on Appeal*, 53 Akron L. Rev. 573, 602–03 (2019).

the merits.[70] For agencies that address recusal questions after a merits decision, the general rule is that a failure to recuse is grounds to invalidate a decision when a party has been prejudiced by the adjudicator's participation in the proceeding.[71]

10.3 COMBINATION OF ADJUDICATIVE AND ADVERSARIAL FUNCTIONS

The concept of separation of functions is critical to the integrity of agency proceedings. Although some agencies are only responsible for adjudicating, many perform multiple functions, such as investigating and prosecuting, in addition to adjudicating claims involving private parties. When an agency adjudicator plays multiple roles in a single proceeding, or when agency staff responsible for investigating or prosecuting a case (called "adversaries") exercise potential influence over the adjudicator in the same case, it draws the impartiality of the adjudicator into question. Although having an adversary serve as, or work too closely with, an adjudicator could raise concerns about due process in certain circumstances, the combination of adversarial and adjudicative functions is not per se unconstitutional.[72] The most powerful restrictions on the combination of agency functions are statutory.

This section addresses three circumstances in which the failure to separate adjudicative from adversarial functions can raise integrity concerns: (1) an adversary's participating or advising in deciding a case (section 10.31); (2) supervision or control of an adjudicator by an adversary ("command influence") (section 10.32); and (3) communications between an adjudicator and an adversary ("nonconsultation rule") (section 10.33).

10.31 Adversary's Participating or Advising in Decision-Making

In formal adjudications, the APA prohibits an adversary in a given case from participating or advising in the agency's decision-making in that

---

70. *Compare* 12 C.F.R. § 1081.105(c)(2) (2021) ("If the hearing officer does not disqualify himself or herself within ten days, he or she shall certify the motion to the Director . . . ."), *with* 45 C.F.R. § 1149.31(c) (2022) ("if the ALJ denies a motion to disqualify, the matter will be determined by the authority head only during his/her review of the initial decision on appeal").

71. Attorney General's Manual on the Administrative Procedure Act 73 (1947).

72. Withrow v. Larkin, 421 U.S. 35 (1975).

case.[73] It also precludes adversaries from offering the decision-maker any off-the-record advice related to a case, regardless of whether that advice pertains to issues of fact, policy, or law.[74]

In general, the prohibition is designed to prevent individuals with previous exposure to information that would not otherwise be part of the exclusive record of the case from serving as adjudicators. The prohibition protects all levels of agency adjudicator decisions, from initial or recommended decisions by ALJs to decisions on review by agency heads, and excludes involvement by adversaries in factually related cases.[75]

When determining if an adjudicator's prior involvement with a case or a related case violated the APA's separation of functions, courts do not focus simply on whether the adversary held the title of investigator or prosecutor in the case, or even whether his or her prior involvement with the case gave the adversary access to ex parte information. Courts focus instead on the adversary's actual involvement in the case, and whether that involvement was in reality investigative or prosecutorial. For example, an ALJ who previously served as an attorney-advisor to an agency head in a related case did not necessarily have a sufficiently investigative or prosecutorial role to render him unable to participate.[76]

The APA's prohibition on combination of functions does not apply to advice from nonadversarial staff members or to initial decisions such as launching an investigation or issuing a complaint, even though participation in initial decisions may expose decision-makers to communication with agency adversaries.[77] The prohibition on combining functions also does not apply to initial licensing proceedings or to certain ratemaking proceedings on the theory that both of these categories of proceedings are heavily dependent on policy concerns and thus are more akin to rulemaking than adjudication.[78] The APA also permits agency heads to serve adversarial and adjudicative roles in a single case or in factually related cases provided the agency head occupied that position atop the agency while engaging in both functions.

---

73. 5 U.S.C. § 554(d). *See also* Kent H. Barnett, *Some Kind of Hearing Officer*, 94 Wash. L. Rev. 515, 533 (2019).

74. Greene v. Babbitt, 943 F. Supp. 1278, 1285–86 (W.D. Wash. 1996).

75. 5 U.S.C. § 554(d).

76. Grolier, Inc. v. Fed. Trade Comm'n, 615 F.2d 1215, 1220 (9th Cir. 1980).

77. RSR Corp. v. Fed. Trade Comm'n, 656 F.2d 718, 723 (D.C. Cir. 1981).

78. 5 U.S.C. § 554(d)(A), (B).

Agency heads may not, however, receive off-the-record advice from an agency adversary while the case is on agency-head review.[79]

Agency practices are more varied in cases of informal adjudication. In 2016, an ACUS study reported that more than 40 percent of the 37 agencies that responded to a survey reported no separation-of-functions requirements for adjudicators. Among agencies that reported some separation-of-functions requirement, several reported multiple separation-of-functions provisions, while six reported that their separation-of-functions requirements were solely a matter of agency custom.[80] For informal adjudications that consist of a legally required evidentiary hearing, ACUS Recommendation 2016-4 encourages agencies to adopt procedural regulations prohibiting "staff who took an active part in investigating, prosecuting, or advocating in a case from serving as a decision maker or staff advising or assisting the decision maker in that same case."[81]

10.32 Command Influence

Command influence refers to the challenge created when adjudicators are subject to the supervision or control of nonadjudicators. The APA includes a command-influence provision for formal adjudication, which prohibits an adjudicator from being responsible to or supervised by an adversary.[82] The prohibition does not depend on whether the adversary is involved with the same or a related case; it is a blanket prohibition on supervisory or control relationships between adjudicators and adversaries. Staff members who were but are no longer adversaries are permitted to supervise or direct adjudicators. Agency heads are also permitted to supervise or direct adjudicators.[83] But although some nonadjudicators, including agency heads, are permitted to supervise or direct adjudicators, the APA includes several important provisions intended to insulate ALJ decision-making from improper influence (see Chapter 9).

Informal adjudications are not subject to similarly broad guidance regarding command influence over agency adjudicators. In the 2016

---

79. Attorney General's Manual on the Administrative Procedure Act, *supra* note 71, at 56.

80. Kent Barnett et al., Admin. Conf. of the U.S., Non-ALJ Adjudicators in Federal Agencies: Status, Selection, Oversight, and Removal 40–42 (2018).

81. Administrative Conference Recommendation 2016-4, *supra* note 28, ¶ 3.

82. 5 U.S.C. § 554(d)(2).

83. *Id.* § 554(d)(2)(C) ("This subsection does not apply . . . to the agency or a member or members of the body comprising the agency.").

ACUS study on informal adjudication, nearly half of the responding agencies reported "no limitations" as to who may supervise or control agency adjudicators. The remaining agencies' responses ranged from prohibitions closely resembling the APA to requirements that supervisors have certain qualifications.[84] For informal adjudications that consist of a legally required evidentiary hearing, ACUS Recommendation 2016-4 encourages agencies to adopt procedural regulations that "require internal separation of decisional and adversarial personnel."[85]

10.33 Nonconsultation Rule

Adjudicators in formal adjudications under the APA may not "consult a person or party on a fact in issue" in the proceeding without providing notice and an opportunity for all parties to participate in the consultation.[86] This nonconsultation provision applies to all communications between adjudicators and anyone else regarding a fact in issue in the case, including agency staff members who are not adversaries.[87] Unlike the ex parte contacts provision discussed in the next section, the nonconsultation rule only prohibits discussions of "facts in issue" in the proceeding rather than all matters "relevant to the merits," and includes consultations with all people regardless of their connection to the agency, not just "interested person[s] outside the agency."[88]

The "fact-in-issue" prohibition does not include discussions by the adjudicator of issues of law or policy that may be relevant to the case at hand. It also does not preclude agencies from adopting their own, stricter consultation prohibitions for agency adjudicators. The facts in issue in an adjudication represent a narrower category of information than that which is "relevant to the merits" of the proceeding, as prohibited by the APA's ex parte contact provision.[89]

For informal adjudications that consist of a legally required evidentiary hearing, ACUS Recommendation 2016-4 encourages agencies to adopt procedural regulations that prohibit adversaries "from furnishing ex parte advice or factual materials to a decisionmaker or staff who advise or assist decisionmakers."[90]

---

84. BARNETT ET AL., *supra* note 80, at 46.
85. Administrative Conference Recommendation 2016-4, *supra* note 28, ¶ 3.
86. 5 U.S.C. § 554(d)(1).
87. *See, e.g.*, Butz v. Economou, 438 U.S. 478, 513–14 (1978).
88. *Compare* 5 U.S.C. § 554(d) (nonconsultation), *with* 5 U.S.C. § 557(d) (ex parte contacts).
89. *Id.* § 557(d)(1).
90. Administrative Conference Recommendation 2016-4, *supra* note 28, ¶ 3.

10.4 EX PARTE CONTACTS

Ex parte contacts are communications between an adjudicator and some, but not all, of the parties to a case. Because ex parte contacts are a secret to at least one of the parties, they can create an unfair situation for excluded parties. Allowing an adjudicator to engage in private conversations about a case can create an appearance of favoritism and invite corruption that threatens the integrity of the proceeding.

The APA responded to concerns about ex parte contacts in formal adjudication by prohibiting all "ex parte communications" between agency actors who may reasonably be involved in the decision and "interested person[s] outside the agency" on matters "relevant to the merits" of the case.[91] The APA defines "ex parte communications" as oral or written communications that are not on the public record and about which prior notice is not given to all parties. The statutory provision does not extend to "disposition of ex parte matters authorized by law," such as requests by a single party to a proceeding for subpoenas, adjournments, and continuances.[92] Nor is it meant to include requests for a status report or routine inquiries on the status of a case by members of Congress.[93]

The APA's ex parte provision covers all agency actors who may reasonably be involved in the decision. This includes ALJs, agency heads, and anyone else who may serve as an adviser in the decision—even permanent or temporary agency employees who are not adversarial and might be useful to the decision-maker. Because it mentions communications that an interested person may "cause to be made," the ex parte provision also prohibits indirect contact, for example from an interested party outside the agency to someone inside the agency who is not involved in the decision, to the ALJ.

The phrase "interested person" is meant to be read broadly. It includes any individual with a greater interest than a member of the general public might have, as well as staff at other agencies and members of the legislative and executive branches. It does not include "a member of the public at large who makes a casual or general expression of opinion about a pending proceeding."[94]

---

91. 5 U.S.C. § 557(d).

92. H.R. Rep. No. 94-880, pt. 1, at 19 (1976), *reprinted in* 1976 U.S.C.C.A.N. 2183.

93. 5 U.S.C. §§ 551(14), 557(d)(2).

94. H.R. Rep. No. 94-880, pt. 1, at 19–20 (1976), *reprinted in* 1976 U.S.C.C.A.N. 2183.

"Outside the agency" can be read literally, but also includes the president, despite his being the head of the executive branch.[95] It does not include organizations that agencies require regulated entities to join.[96]

Information "relevant to the merits" of a proceeding is broader than the "fact-in-issue" category discussed in connection with the nonconsultation rule. It includes communication about a specific issue in a pending case that is meant to influence the resolution of that issue. It includes legal and discretionary issues as well as factual ones but does not include procedural inquiries or settlement discussions.

The prohibition on ex parte contacts takes effect at the earliest of three events: when the agency so designates that it shall apply, when "the proceeding is noticed for hearing," or when the person responsible for the communication knows when the hearing will be noticed.[97]

The remedies for violations of the ex parte contact prohibition are disclosure of the communications on the record of the proceeding and potential dismissal of the violator's interest in the proceeding or,[98] in the case of a party being the violator, a decision against that party.[99] Agency proceedings that involve ex parte contacts are not per se invalid, but they may be vacated by the agency head or a reviewing court. The appropriate remedy is determined through the court's equitable discretion.[100]

Many agencies, including those not governed by the APA's formal-adjudication provisions, have adopted rules on ex parte contacts. For informal adjudications that consist of a legally required evidentiary hearing, ACUS Recommendation 2016-4 encourages agencies to adopt procedural regulations that "prohibit ex parte communications relevant to the merits of the case between persons outside the agency and agency decisionmakers or staff who are advising or assisting the decisionmaker."[101]

---

95. Portland Audubon Soc'y v. Endangered Species Comm., 984 F.2d 1534, 1545–46 (9th Cir. 1993).

96. Elec. Power Supply Ass'n v. Fed. Energy Regul. Comm'n, 391 F.3d 1255, 1265 (D.C. Cir. 2004).

97. 5 U.S.C. § 557(d)(1)(E).

98. *Id.* § 557(d)(1)(D).

99. *Id.* § 556(d).

100. Pro. Air Traffic Controllers Org. v. Fed. Lab. Rels. Auth., 685 F.2d 547, 564 (D.C. Cir. 1982).

101. Administrative Conference Recommendation 2016-4, *supra* note 28, ¶ 3.

Part IV

Parties and Representatives

Chapter 11

Parties and Interested Persons

Michael D. Sant'Ambrogio

11.1 CHAPTER OVERVIEW

This chapter examines the identity, roles, and procedural rights of parties (section 11.2) and other interested persons (section 11.3) who participate in federal agency adjudications. After introducing these concepts, it addresses disputes regarding which private individuals can intervene in agency adjudications to which they would otherwise not be parties (section 11.4). The chapter then discusses the ways in which self-representation can shape the role and procedural rights of parties and other interested persons and introduces various mechanisms that agencies have put in place to accommodate them (section 11.5). That subject is examined in greater detail in Chapter 14, Access to Justice. The chapter concludes by noting some agencies that allow for representative adjudication in which parties may be bound by the agency's decision even if they do not fully participate in the proceeding (section 11.6).

11.2 PARTIES

11.21 Who Is a Party?

Section 551(3) of the Administrative Procedure Act (APA) defines a "party" to include "a person or agency named or admitted as a party, or properly seeking and entitled as of right to be admitted as a party, in an agency proceeding, and a person or agency admitted by an agency as a party for limited purposes[.]" Consequently, parties in an agency adjudication are those who either are admitted by the agency as a party or have some right to party status derived from either the agency's organic statute or its rules. Moreover, the agency may admit some parties for limited purposes, without granting them all of the same rights as other parties to the proceeding.[1]

Agency statutes and regulations vary in how specifically they define the persons or entities who will be admitted as parties and for what purpose. Some designate specific persons or entities, including agencies themselves, that may be admitted as parties for certain types of proceedings. For example, a Department of Education rule governing student borrower defense and recovery proceedings specifies that the parties are the department and the "institution(s) against which the Department seeks to recover losses caused to the Department as a result of borrower defense relief." Student borrowers are not permitted to participate "except as witnesses put forth by either party."[2]

Other statutes and agency rules use general terms to describe who may participate as a party. For example, a Commodity Futures Trading Commission rule defines a "party" in reparations proceedings before the agency to mean "a complainant, respondent or any other person or agency named or admitted as a party in a reparation matter."[3]

To understand who participates as a party, it is helpful to think of several different categories of federal agency adjudication. Federal agency adjudication typically resolves disputes between private parties and the government, even when the government does not appear as a represented party in an adversarial proceeding (e.g., nonadversarial social security disability hearings). Disputes between the government and private parties generally fall into one or more of the following three categories: (1) disputes involving entitlement to traditional public benefits, such as social security or veterans' benefits; (2) disputes involving other kinds of relationships between the government and private parties, such as contracts, grants, employment, and licenses or permits; and (3) agency enforcement actions involving regulatory violations. Private parties may play an important role on both sides of these disputes. Agencies also occasionally adjudicate cases primarily

1. 5 U.S.C. § 551(3).
2. 34 C.F.R. § 668.87 (2022).
3. 17 C.F.R. § 12.2 (2022).

involving complaints by private parties against other private parties. Such complaints generally arise out of an overarching regulatory scheme administered by the adjudicating agency.[4]

Generally, there is little disagreement over who qualifies as a party in federal agency adjudication involving the administration of public benefits. Persons seeking social security,[5] Medicare,[6] or veterans' benefits,[7] just to name a few, are admitted as parties when they seek to challenge an agency decision concerning their entitlement to the benefits. The agency that administers the benefits may also be a party in these proceedings, although large swaths of adjudication involving public benefits are considered nonadversarial in the sense that the agency is not represented by counsel in the proceeding. Certain persons other than the beneficiary who are affected by a claim may also be able to obtain party status under the agency's statute or regulations.[8]

Similarly, there is little disagreement over who qualifies as a party in adjudication involving disputes between the federal government and private parties over a host of other government programs, including taxes, immigration, government contracts, and federal employment. Taxpayers who challenge the taxes they owe, immigrants who challenge their removal from the United States, and federal employees who challenge their termination or other adverse employment actions are all admitted as parties. But these same programs often allow other individuals or entities whose interests may be impacted by the outcome of the proceeding to participate in the proceeding, often as an intervenor (see section 11.4).

Finally, agency enforcement actions typically pit a government agency—such as the Securities and Exchange Commission, Federal Trade Commission, or Federal Communications Commission—against an entity the agency accuses of violating the law. In such cases, the agency and the subject of the enforcement action are parties. Other private parties often also participate in these cases on the side of the agency bringing the enforcement action, as an intervenor or in some other, more limited capacity.[9]

---

4. *See generally* Michael Sant'Ambrogio, *Private Enforcement in Administrative Courts*, 72 VAND. L. REV. 425 (2018).
5. 20 C.F.R. §§ 404.932(b), 416.1432(b) (2022).
6. 42 C.F.R. § 405.906(a), (b) (2022).
7. 38 C.F.R. § 20.3(f), (g) (2022).
8. *See, e.g.*, 20 C.F.R. § 404.932(b) (2022).
9. Sant'Ambrogio, *supra* note 4, at 45–52.

11.22 What Rights Do Parties Have?

Due process always requires a minimum level of procedural protections when the agency deprives a party of a property or liberty interest,[10] and statutes and agency rules often define the rights of parties with greater specificity.

Section 555 of the APA provides parties with certain baseline rights if not modified by another statute. The most important of these are:

1. The right to appear before the agency in an administrative proceeding
2. The right to be represented by counsel when compelled to appear before an agency
3. The right to have matters concluded by the agency in a reasonable time
4. The right to receive prompt notice from the agency of its decision in a matter, including, in most cases, a brief statement of the grounds for any denial of an application, petition, or other request

Parties are frequently guaranteed additional procedural rights under other applicable statutes or agency rules. Where they apply, for example, sections 554 and 556–557 of the APA require agencies to give parties an opportunity for "the submission and consideration of facts, arguments, offers of settlement, or proposals of adjustment when time, the nature of the proceeding, and the public interest permit."[11] Moreover, "[a] party is entitled to present his case or defense by oral or documentary evidence, to submit rebuttal evidence, and to conduct such cross-examination as may be required for a full and true disclosure of the facts."[12] In addition, the APA generally entitles parties to an opportunity to examine and respond to all information relevant to their cases by prohibiting certain ex parte communications and communications between adjudicators and agency staff involved in "investigative or prosecuting functions."[13] Finally, before an agency decision, parties are entitled to a reasonable opportunity to submit proposed findings and conclusions, including reasons for proposed findings or conclusions and any proposed exceptions.[14]

10. Goldberg v. Kelly, 397 U.S. 254 (1970).
11. 5 U.S.C. § 554(c).
12. *Id.* § 556(d).
13. *Id.* § 554(d)(2).
14. *Id.* § 557(c).

Parties' procedural rights under due process, statutes, and agency rules are discussed in greater detail in Chapters 15–22. It is worth noting, however, that section 551(3) states that parties may be admitted to a proceeding for "limited purposes." The implication is that not all parties are created equal and that different parties might have different procedural rights depending on the applicable law.

11.3 OTHER INTERESTED PERSONS

11.31 Who Is an Interested Person?

In addition to "parties," the APA refers to "interested persons." Section 555(b) gives interested persons the right to "appear" in agency proceedings so long as their appearance does not interfere with the "orderly conduct of public business."[15] Section 555(d) entitles them to "[p]rompt notice . . . of the denial in whole or in part of a written application, petition, or other request of an interested person made in connection with any agency proceeding."[16]

The APA's reference to "interested persons" implies yet another level of participation short of full party status. This reflects a realization that administrative adjudications may impact not just individuals whose rights and interests are directly at issue in a particular proceeding but also others who, for any number of reasons, have an interest in its outcome. By granting limited rights to "interested persons," the APA is designed to facilitate broad participation in administrative proceedings.

Unlike "parties," the APA does not define the term "interested persons." According to the *Attorney General's Manual on the Administrative Procedure Act* (1947), the term as used in section 555(b) means "one whose interests are or will be affected by the agency action which may result from the proceeding."[17] Certainly, a person with a financial interest implicated by the proceeding will generally qualify as "interested."[18] Similarly, other government officials or agencies with overlapping jurisdiction or whose jurisdictional responsibilities may be

15. *Id.* § 555(b).

16. *Id.* § 555(d).

17. Attorney General's Manual on the Administrative Procedure Act 70 (1947).

18. Nichols v. Bd. of Trs. of Asbestos Workers Loc. 24 Pension Plan, 835 F.2d 881, 896 (D.C. Cir. 1987) ("Beneficiaries in a plan qualifying under ERISA [the Employee Retirement Income Security Act] unquestionably possess an 'interest' in agency deliberations that might reduce their retirement benefits.").

impacted by the proceeding are likely interested.[19] Finally, organizations with mission-related interests in the outcome of an adjudication have been recognized as interested persons.[20]

For purposes of section 557(d), which prohibits certain ex parte communications between adjudicators and "interested persons outside the agency," the term has been defined to include

> any individual or other person with an interest in the agency proceeding that is greater than the general interest the public as a whole may have. The interest need not be monetary, nor need a person [] be a party to, or intervenor in, the agency proceeding to come under this section[.][21]

"The term includes, but is not limited to, parties, competitors, public officials, and nonprofit or public interest organizations and associations with a special interest in the matter[.]"[22] But it may not include "someone who has a curiosity or concern about a matter, although . . . neutral with respect to the outcome[,]" or someone with "a preference or a bias regarding a matter's outcome but no direct stake in the proceedings," although such individuals are "interested" in some sense.[23]

Although 557(d) serves a different function than 555(b), the two provisions are related: 555(b) allows "interested persons" to be heard

---

19. *See, e.g.*, Portland Audubon Soc'y v. Endangered Species Comm., 984 F.2d 1534, 1546 (9th Cir. 1993) (determining the president and White House staff are interested persons for purposes of section 557's prohibition on ex parte communications in agency adjudications); *see also* Elec. Power Supply Ass'n v. Fed. Energy Regul. Comm'n, 391 F.3d 1255, 1265 (D.C. Cir. 2004) (concluding that private "market monitors, who are charged with 'ensuring that markets within [their assigned regional transmission organizations] do not result in wholesale transactions or operations that are unduly discriminatory or preferential or provide opportunity for the exercise of market power,' qualify as interested persons under 557(d)").

20. *See, e.g.*, Animal Legal Def. Fund, Inc. v. Vilsack, 237 F. Supp. 3d 15, 23 (D.D.C. 2017) (recognizing the Animal Legal Defense Fund as an "interested person" in an agency enforcement action against a zoo due to its "interest in animal welfare and a specific interest in the health and treatment of the animals at the Cricket Hollow Zoo. . . . They would be impaired if [the agency] failed to prove the alleged violations or negotiated a settlement that did not provide for the adequate care of the zoo's animals, or if the ALJ [administrative law judge] imposed a penalty that did not sufficiently sanction the zoo's conduct.").

21. Pro. Air Traffic Controllers Org. v. Fed. Lab. Rels. Auth., 685 F.2d 547, 562 (D.C. Cir. 1982).

22. *Portland Audubon Soc'y*, 984 F.2d at 1544 (emphasis omitted).

23. *Id.*

in agency proceedings while 557(d) prohibits them from communicating with agency decision-makers ex parte. Nevertheless, 555(b) is likely to be construed more narrowly than 557(d) given the latter's broad purpose of ensuring "open decision-making and the appearance thereof, to preserve the opportunity for effective response, and to prevent improper influences upon agency decision makers."[24] By contrast, as discussed in the next section, there are a host of factors that may weigh against allowing persons to participate in a proceeding even if their ex parte communications would be prohibited by the APA to preserve the appearance of fair and open decision-making.

11.32 What Rights Do Interested Persons Have?

As with "parties," statutes and regulations often name the "interested persons" who may appear in agency proceedings and for what purpose.[25] The level of participation permitted to interested persons will vary depending on the nature of the interests at issue involved in a particular proceeding and the need for efficient and orderly administrative hearings in a particular program.

It is quite common, for example, for interested persons to file amicus briefs in agency adjudication without any formal party status.[26] Such persons are typically granted amicus status when they have "unique information or perspective that can help the court beyond the help that the lawyers for the parties are able to provide."[27] Moreover,

---

24. *Id.*

25. *See, e.g.*, 14 C.F.R. § 302.19 (2022) ("Any person, including any State, subdivision thereof, State aviation commission, or other public body, may appear at any hearing, other than in an enforcement proceeding, and present any evidence that is relevant to the issues. With the consent of the administrative law judge or the DOT [Department of Transportation] decisionmaker, such person may also cross-examine witnesses directly. Such persons may also present to the administrative law judge a written statement on the issues involved in the proceeding. Such written statements shall be filed and served on all parties prior to the close of the hearing.").

26. Thomas W. Merrill & Kristin E. Hickman, Chevron*'s Domain*, 89 Geo. L.J. 833, 886 (2001) (noting how interested persons can "voice their concerns through permissive intervention or by filing amicus briefs"). *See, e.g.*, 8 C.F.R. § 1292.1(d) (2022) ("The Board may grant permission to appear, on a case-by-case basis, as amicus curiae, to an attorney or to an organization represented by an attorney, if the public interest will be served thereby."); 46 C.F.R. § 502.73(b) (2022) ("A motion for leave to file an amicus brief must identify the interest of the applicant and must state the reasons why such a brief is desirable.").

27. Ryan v. Commodity Futures Trading Comm'n, 125 F.3d 1062, 1063 (7th Cir. 1997).

when agencies hold public hearings they may allow all interested persons to "express their views on the matter without cross examination or formal consideration of evidence."[28] In addition, interested persons are frequently permitted to submit evidence and arguments in an adjudicatory proceeding; sometimes they are even given their own hearing for such purpose.[29] These opportunities can improve the quality of adjudicatory decision-making because interested persons often have evidence and insights unavailable to the agency.[30] Their contributions may help the agency understand the nature of the case and its broader context or assist the agency with crafting a remedy.[31] Finally, sometimes interested persons are permitted to intervene for purposes of appealing an administrative decision.[32]

Another role interested persons might play in regulatory enforcement actions is that of complainant. In many programs, private parties can file a complaint concerning a regulatory violation. Private complaints generally trigger some kind of investigation by the agency, which might result in agency enforcement staff filing an action against a target in an administrative tribunal.[33] But in some cases the complainant can prosecute its own complaint as a formal party, triggering a process that may lead to an evidentiary hearing and agency decision in a manner very similar to a private enforcement action in court. For example, private parties take the laboring oar in prosecuting unfair competition and importation actions before the International Trade Commission, enforcement actions under the Shipping Act of 1984 before the Federal Maritime Commission, and claims by miners arising from black lung disease before the Department of Labor. The

---

28. Ronald M. Levin, *Preface*, 54 ADMIN. L. REV. 1, 30 (2002).

29. *See, e.g.*, 33 U.S.C. § 1319 (providing interested persons with "a reasonable opportunity to be heard and to present evidence" concerning proposed orders assessing a civil penalty); 40 C.F.R. § 71.27 (2022) ("All permit proceedings . . . shall provide adequate procedures for public participation, including notice, opportunity for comment, a hearing if requested, and administrative appeal.").

30. *See, e.g.*, Animal Legal Def. Fund, Inc. v. Vilsack, 237 F. Supp. 3d 15, 24 (D.D.C. 2017); Sant'Ambrogio, *supra* note 4, at 465 ("information derived from private complaints can be used by the agency not only in its own enforcement actions but also in rulemaking and other regulatory activities").

31. Sant'Ambrogio, *supra* note 4, at 465.

32. 40 C.F.R. § 124.19 ("Any person who filed comments on the draft permit or participated in a public hearing on the draft permit may file a petition for review as provided in this section.").

33. Sant'Ambrogio, *supra* note 4, at 450.

specific rights of complainants are generally set forth in the agency's rules of practice and procedure.[34]

11.4 DISPUTES OVER INTERVENTION

Disputes over who is a party or an interested person typically arise in the context of third-party intervenors whose interests may be affected by the outcome of an agency proceeding involving another party. For example, when the government grants a permit, license, or contract to one private party, other parties may be affected by the decision. The classic case involves a party who seeks to prevent the issuance of such a benefit to a competitor.[35] Decisions about granting a license or permit might also affect a broader public, however, such as consumers who might be affected by a proposed hydropower project or local communities who might be affected by emissions from a proposed source of air or water pollution.[36] Similarly, the beneficiaries of plans administered by a third party and regulated by an agency typically may intervene as interested persons in proceedings that might affect their benefits.[37]

The APA does not establish standards for intervention or define the rights of intervenors. Intervenors may rely on the APA's broad language to seek admission as parties or "interested persons" in an attempt, for example, to block a competitor from obtaining an advantageous license or to block a regulated entity from obtaining a permit that might adversely affect their interests.

An agency's organic statute or rules of practice and procedure usually address who may intervene in the agency's proceedings.[38] The

---

34. *Id.*

35. *See, e.g.*, Global Van Lines, Inc. v. Interstate Com. Comm'n, 804 F.2d 1293 (D.C. Cir. 1986); Am. Trucking Ass'ns, Inc. v. United States, 627 F.2d 1313, 1320 (D.C. Cir. 1980); Elm City Broad. Corp. v. United States, 235 F.2d 811, 814 (D.C. Cir. 1956).

36. *See, e.g.*, 40 C.F.R. § 124.19 (2022) (allowing parties affected by issuance of water permits under several environmental programs to appeal the Environmental Protection Agency's permitting decisions).

37. Nichols v. Bd. of Trs. of Asbestos Workers Loc. 24 Pension Plan, 835 F.2d 881, 896 (D.C. Cir. 1987) ("Beneficiaries in a plan qualifying under ERISA unquestionably possess an 'interest' in agency deliberations that might reduce their retirement benefits.").

38. *See, e.g.*, 17 C.F.R. § 10.33 (2022) ("Any person whose interests may be affected substantially by the matters to be considered in a proceeding [conducted by the Commodity Futures Trading Commission] may petition the Administrative Law Judge for leave to intervene as a party in the proceeding any time after the

agency may distinguish between persons admitted as parties and persons not admitted as parties but who may still have certain rights as interested persons, such as the right to be heard.[39] The agency can define the purposes for which a party or interested person may intervene.

The standards for intervention vary greatly across agencies and programs. Some statutes and agency rules provide little guidance.[40] Others include a detailed list of factors for the agency to consider.[41] Absent a clear statutory right to intervention, agencies generally enjoy broad discretion in deciding whether to allow a party to intervene and for what purpose.[42]

When deciding whether to grant a petition to intervene, agencies usually consider some combination of the following factors:

1. The nature of the petitioner's right under the statute to be made a party to the proceeding
2. The nature and extent of the property, financial, or other interest of the petitioner
3. The effect of the order that may be entered in the proceeding on the petitioner's interest
4. The availability of other means whereby the petitioner's interest may be protected
5. The extent to which the petitioner's interest will be represented by existing parties
6. The extent to which the petitioner's participation may reasonably be expected to assist in the development of a sound record
7. The extent to which participation of the petitioner will broaden the issues or delay the proceeding[43]

When courts are called upon to review whether a person is "interested" for purposes of intervention, they often look to whether a party

institution of a proceeding and before such proceeding has been submitted for final consideration.").

39. *Compare id. with* 17 C.F.R. § 10.34 (2022) ("Any person may, in the discretion of the Administrative Law Judge, be given leave to be heard in any proceeding as to any matter affecting his interests.").

40. *See, e.g.*, 15 U.S.C. § 45 (Federal Trade Commission); 29 U.S.C. § 160, 29 C.F.R. § 102.29 (National Labor Relations Board); 49 C.F.R. § 1113.7 (2022) (Surface Transportation Board).

41. *See, e.g.*, 14 C.F.R. § 302.20 (2022) (DOT).

42. *See* Fed. Commc'ns Comm'n v. Pottsville Broad. Co., 309 U.S. 134, 143 (1940).

43. *See* Am. Trucking Ass'ns, Inc. v. United States, 627 F.2d 1313, 1322 (D.C. Cir. 1980).

would have Article III standing to seek review of the agency decision in the proceeding.[44] "Because agencies are not constrained by Article III, they may sometimes permit persons to intervene in the agency proceedings who would not have constitutional standing to seek judicial review of the agency action."[45] But courts generally defer to reasonable agency rules for participation by interested persons, including those that limit intervention to those persons who will most effectively assist the agency in pursuit of its mission and avoid the "multiplicity of parties and duplication of effort."[46]

11.5 SELF-REPRESENTED PARTIES AND INTERESTED PERSONS

One factor that can affect the role of a party or interested person in an agency adjudication is whether he or she is represented. Self-represented parties challenge the ability of agencies to adjudicate claims efficiently, accurately, and equitably. Self-represented parties often do not understand the nature of the legal issues or the procedural requirements for advancing their cases. Poor presentation of a party's case, lacking in reasoned arguments or supported by substantial evidence, can lead to unsound adjudicatory decisions by the agencies. Because self-represented parties typically have fewer resources than represented parties, this can lead to inequitable outcomes in both individual cases and in the aggregate. Moreover, because many administrative schemes are designed to serve those in need, this inequity can undermine the agency's mission.

Although private participants are generally entitled to be represented, there is generally no requirement that agencies provide them with counsel. Consequently, many parties and other interested persons who participate in administrative proceedings are unrepresented and

44. *See, e.g.*, Nichols v. Bd. of Trs. of Asbestos Workers Loc. 24 Pension Plan, 835 F.2d 881, 896 & n.107 (D.C. Cir. 1987); Glob. Van Lines, Inc. v. Interstate Com. Comm'n, 804 F.2d 1293 (D.C. Cir. 1986); Elm City Broad. Corp. v. United States, 235 F.2d 811, 816–17 (D.C. Cir. 1956).

45. *See* Fund Democracy, LLC v. Sec. & Exch. Comm'n, 278 F.3d 21, 27 (D.C. Cir. 2002); *Nichols*, 835 F.2d at 896 n.108.

46. Off. of Commc'n of the United Church of Christ v. Fed. Commc'ns Comm'n, 359 F.2d 994, 1005–06 (D.C. Cir. 1966).

must "learn to navigate hearing procedures, which can be quite complex, without expert assistance."[47]

As discussed in greater detail in Chapter 14, some federal agencies have developed tools to help unrepresented parties navigate their proceedings. In some cases, these efforts are mandated by statutory design or other congressional directives. In other cases, they are the product of concerted efforts within the agencies to improve the experience of unrepresented parties. The tools and resources available to assist unrepresented parties (as well as represented parties) vary greatly by administrative scheme, making generalizations difficult. Nevertheless, it is worth noting a few of the ways in which different agencies have attempted to assist self-represented parties.

First, some government benefits programs in which parties are frequently unrepresented, such as those administered by the Board of Veterans' Appeals (BVA) and the Social Security Administration (SSA), are designed to be nonadversarial and claimant-friendly. Veteran law judges are charged with assisting claimants seeking veteran benefits by explaining the legal issues involved and suggesting "the submission of evidence which the claimant may have overlooked and which would be advantageous to the claimant's position."[48] Moreover, "[w]hen there is an approximate balance of positive and negative evidence regarding any issue material to the determination of a matter, the Secretary shall give the benefit of the doubt to the claimant."[49]

SSA administrative law judges (ALJs) have "an affirmative duty to develop the record irrespective of whether the claimant has representation, and many courts have found that ALJs have a heightened duty in cases with self-represented claimants."[50]

Similarly, the U.S. Department of Agriculture's (USDA's) National Appeals Division (NAD), which hears cases involving adverse program decisions by several agencies within USDA, "encourages its Administrative Judges (AJs) to actively question self-represented parties to ensure all relevant evidence has been identified," even though the proceedings are not nonadversarial. Moreover, NAD trains its AJs on "how to interact with self-represented parties," and uses prehearing

47. Connie Vogelmann, Admin. Conf. of the U.S., Self-Represented Parties in Administrative Hearings 1 (2016).

48. 38 C.F.R. § 3.103 (2022).

49. 38 U.S.C. § 5107(b).

50. Vogelmann, *supra* note 47, at 42.

conferences for the AJs to explain the administrative hearing process in terms understandable to unrepresented parties.[51]

Second, many agencies develop plain-language guides and resources on their websites that are particularly helpful to self-represented parties. The BVA, SSA, the Executive Office for Immigration Review (EOIR), and NAD, for example, have all developed online guides that explain their claims and appeals process, published FAQs, and provide private parties with contact numbers and hotlines for various types of questions or to obtain case-specific information.[52] Agency websites may also include direct links to the forms that the parties need to prosecute their cases.

Third, agencies may provide unrepresented parties with lists of pro bono service providers or even partner with nongovernmental organizations to provide representation. Immigration courts, for example, give unrepresented parties lists of pro bono service providers and additional time to obtain counsel when necessary.[53] Indeed, the EOIR goes even further in some locations, contracting with nonprofits to provide orientation and self-help workshops for individuals in removal proceedings and adult custodians of unaccompanied children in removal proceedings.[54]

Some agencies are also required or authorized to pay costs associated with representation in certain circumstances. The Equal Access to Justice Act, most notably, authorizes the award of attorneys' fees and other expenses to certain parties in some proceedings (see Chapter 12).[55] The Federal Power Act authorizes the Federal Energy Regulatory Commission to provide compensation for "reasonable attorneys' fees, expert witness fees, and other costs" incurred by some intervenors or other participants in agency proceedings.[56] And the EOIR funds direct representation of unaccompanied children who are under the age of 16 and whose cases are not joined with an adult's.[57]

---

51. *Id.* at 47, 49.
52. *Id.* at 33.
53. *Id.* at 37.
54. *Id.*; EOIR, U.S. Dep't of Just., Fact Sheet: EOIR's Office of Legal Access Programs (2016) [hereinafter EOIR Fact Sheet], https://www.justice.gov/sites/default/files/pages/attachments/2016/08/08/olapfactsheet082016.pdf.
55. 5 U.S.C. § 504.
56. 16 U.S.C. § 825q-1(b).
57. EOIR Fact Sheet, *supra* note 54.

Given that one goal of agency adjudication is to provide a less costly alternative to adjudication in court,[58] agencies should continue to explore ways in which they can help parties pursue their claims without lawyers or with pro bono representation.

11.6 AGGREGATION AND REPRESENTATIVE ADJUDICATION

A number of administrative agencies have rules permitting aggregation of cases or claims by multiple parties involving common questions of law or fact.[59] Most of these rules merely permit consolidation of similar cases, in which each party retains all the attributes and rights of a full party.[60] They engage their own lawyers; control decisions about how to prosecute the case, what evidence to submit, and which arguments to make; and receive an individualized decision at the end of the proceeding.[61] Nevertheless, consolidation can enhance the efficiency of adjudicating large groups of similar cases by allowing the parties to coordinate and streamline discovery, motion practice, and evidentiary hearings, while permitting the same decision-makers to resolve common questions of law and fact that repeatedly come before the agency.[62]

In addition, a few agencies that hear large numbers of similar claims have adopted more formal aggregation rules that permit representative adjudication akin to Federal Rule of Civil Procedure 23 class actions in federal court.[63] In representative adjudication, a single party may bind other parties who do not participate in the proceedings.[64] For example, federal employees may petition the AJs of the Equal Employment Opportunity Commission (EEOC) to certify "pattern and practice"

---

58. Sant'Ambrogio, *supra* note 4, at 432.

59. Michael Sant'Ambrogio & Adam S. Zimmerman, *Inside the Agency Class Action*, 126 Yale L.J. 1634, 1657 (2017) (identifying "more than forty administrative agencies and Article I courts with rules permitting some form of aggregation").

60. *Id.*

61. Michael Sant'Ambrogio & Adam Zimmerman, *Collective Decision-Making and Administrative Justice*, *in* The Oxford Handbook of Administrative Justice 591 (Marc Hertogh et al. eds., 2022).

62. *Id.*; Michael D. Sant'Ambrogio & Adam S. Zimmerman, *The Agency Class Action*, 112 Colum. L. Rev. 1992, 2042 (2012).

63. Sant'Ambrogio & Zimmerman, *supra* note 59, at 1658–59.

64. Sant'Ambrogio & Zimmerman, *supra* note 61, at 597–98.

class actions against federal employers in administrative proceedings.[65] The EEOC AJs ensure that class counsel is competent to represent the class, may certify subclasses to ensure adequate representation of parties with distinct interests, oversee class-wide discovery, and issue class-wide decisions that bind all members of the class except with respect to individualized determinations of damages.[66]

Similarly, the National Vaccine Injury Compensation Program (NVICP) has used "Omnibus Proceedings" to resolve common questions raised by numerous claimants regarding whether a particular vaccine causes a particular set of health problems.[67] In addition, the Office of Medicare Hearings and Appeals has offered hospitals, doctors, and other medical providers with large numbers of similar claims to try a small sampling of those claims and extrapolate the results to the rest.[68]

Although not without its challenges, well-designed aggregate adjudication can enhance the efficiency and consistency of decision-making by agencies that hear large numbers of cases involving similar legal and factual issues. Moreover, representative litigation can improve access to justice by parties who may not be able to pursue their claims on their own or access the same quality of legal representation or expert assistance due to limited resources.[69] Thus, representative adjudication may be most useful in large benefits programs supporting those most in need.

---

65. *See* 29 C.F.R. § 1614.204 (2016); Federal Sector Equal Employment Opportunity, 57 Fed. Reg. 12,634 (Apr. 10, 1992).

66. Sant'Ambrogio & Zimmerman, *supra* note 59, at 1667–69.

67. *Id.* at 1672 (describing how the NVICP used an omnibus proceeding to resolve whether a rubella vaccine could cause chronic arthritis and related problems).

68. *Id.* at 1679–80.

69. *Id.* at 1682 (discussing the benefits and challenges of aggregate agency adjudication).

Chapter 12
Costs, Fees, and Expenses

Jeremy S. Graboyes

12.1 CHAPTER OVERVIEW

Costs associated with conducting an individual adjudication (e.g., attorneys' fees, expert witness fees, travel) and operating a program of federal agency adjudication (e.g., salaries, technology, office space) are allocated among parties, other interested persons, and the government. This chapter addresses how costs are allocated in different programs. It first examines whether and when participants in different programs are eligible for financial or other assistance from other participants or the government (section 12.2). Next, it addresses how the government provides funding to nongovernmental service providers that assist participants in agency adjudications (section 12.3). It ends by discussing user fees that participants must pay to the government in certain programs (section 12.4). Several themes introduced in this chapter are addressed further in Chapter 14, Access to Justice.

12.2 PROVIDING FINANCIAL OR OTHER ASSISTANCE TO PARTICIPANTS

12.21 Fee-Shifting Statutes

The default rule when it comes to federal judicial and administrative practice alike is that each party pays its own legal fees. This is called the "American rule." It stands in contrast with the "English rule," under which the losing party pays the prevailing party's fees.

There are two common-law exceptions to the American rule. First, courts may order a party who acts in bad faith to pay another party's attorneys' fees. Courts may also, in some instances, order payment of attorneys' fees out of a common fund, such as in a class action. But these exceptions derive from courts' equitable authority. Because administrative agencies lack such authority, these exceptions are unavailable to them. Therefore, absent statutory authorization, agencies generally may not order one private party to a proceeding to pay another party's attorneys' fees.[1] At least two appeals courts have held that, absent statutory authorization, agencies may not themselves compensate parties for costs incurred in agency proceedings.[2]

Congress has enacted many fee-shifting statutes that authorize or require payment of attorneys' fees or other expenses to prevailing parties in certain circumstances. Most apply only in specific circumstances, for example in proceedings involving certain civil-rights protections, civil-service benefits and protections, whistleblower protections, agricultural commodities, unfair immigration-related employment practices, mine health and safety, workers' compensation, government contracts, flood insurance, and environmental protection.[3]

The best-known, generally applicable fee-shifting statute is the Equal Access to Justice Act (EAJA). EAJA entitles private parties to recover attorneys' fees and other expenses from federal agencies against which they prevail in certain agency adjudications (5 U.S.C.

---

1. *See* Unbelievable v. Nat'l Lab. Rels. Bd., 118 F.3d 795 (D.C. Cir. 1997); Turner v. Fed. Commc'ns Comm'n, 514 F.2d 1354 (D.C. Cir. 1975). *Cf.* Summit Valley Indus., Inc. v. Carpenters, 456 U.S. 717 (1982); Alyeska Pipeline Serv. Co. v. Wilderness Soc'y, 421 U.S. 240 (1975).

2. Pac. Legal Found. v. Goyan, 664 F.2d 121 (4th Cir. 1981); Greene Cnty. Plan. Bd. v. Fed. Power Comm'n, 559 F.2d 1227 (2d Cir. 1976).

3. A 2008 Congressional Research Service report catalogs federal statutes that authorize awards of attorneys' fees by federal courts and federal agencies. HENRY COHEN, CONG. RSCH. SERV., AWARDS OF ATTORNEYS' FEES BY FEDERAL COURTS AND FEDERAL AGENCIES 64–114 (2008).

§ 504) and in judicial proceedings (28 U.S.C. § 2142). Other expenses include "the reasonable expenses of expert witnesses" and "the reasonable cost of any study, analysis, engineering report, test, or project which is found by the agency to be necessary for the preparation of the party's case."[4]

In reality, EAJA benefits private parties far more often in judicial rather than administrative proceedings. In fiscal year 2021, for example, there were 15,683 awards in judicial proceedings compared with only eight in agency adjudications.[5] This is because, as described below, EAJA only applies in a limited number of agency adjudications.

In the administrative context, EAJA provides:

> An agency that conducts an adversary adjudication shall award, to a prevailing party other than the United States, fees and other expenses incurred by that party in connection with the party, unless the adjudicative officer of the agency finds that the position of the agency was substantially justified or that special circumstances make an award unjust.[6]

As discussed in the following paragraphs, this general rule contains several specially defined terms that significantly limit its scope.

First, EAJA is limited to "adversary adjudications." Four types of agency proceedings are "adversary adjudications" for purposes of the act:

1. Proceedings conducted according to the formal-adjudication provisions of the Administrative Procedure Act (APA), except for proceedings in which the government's position is not represented (e.g., nonadversarial hearings before the Social Security Administration (SSA) in which no government counsel is present[7]) and proceedings conducted for purposes of ratemaking or granting or renewing a license
2. Appeals before agency contract appeals boards

---

4. 5 U.S.C. § 504(b)(1).

5. The Administrative Conference of the United States, by statute, maintains a database of EAJA awards at https://www.acus.gov/eaja/statistics (last visited June 27, 2023).

6. 5 U.S.C. § 504(a) (emphasis added).

7. Sullivan v. Hudson, 490 U.S. 877, 891–92 (1989). There is a narrow exception to this rule. When a reviewing court retains jurisdiction over a case remanded to SSA, the court can award fees for the cost of post-remand proceedings before SSA. *Id.* at 883–93.

3. Hearings conducted under the Program Fraud Civil Remedies Act
4. Hearings involving the Religious Freedom Restoration Act[8]

EAJA does not apply in other agency adjudications, including in trial-like proceedings that, though similar in form and function to those conducted under the APA's formal-adjudication provisions, are not governed by those provisions. Parties in immigration court proceedings, for example, are not entitled to recovery under EAJA.[9]

Second, only a private "party" may recover under EAJA. To be considered a party, individuals must have a net worth not exceeding $2 million, and businesses, organizations, and local government units must have a net worth not exceeding $7 million. Tax-exempt charitable organizations and agricultural cooperatives can be parties regardless of their net worth. "Small entities," as defined in the Regulatory Flexibility Act (5 U.S.C. § 601), may also recover when an agency makes an excessive monetary demand in a regulatory enforcement proceeding.[10]

Third, the party ordinarily must have "prevailed" against the federal government. A party "prevails" when "actual relief on the merits of his claim materially alters the legal relationship between the parties by modifying the defendant's behavior in a way that directly benefits the plaintiff."[11] A party must prevail on the merits of at least some of its claims through a binding judgment or consent decree. A settlement or some other voluntary change in a party's behavior, even as a result of the litigation, is insufficient for recovery under EAJA.[12]

In enforcement adjudications, however, a private party that is the subject of an agency enforcement action may be able to recover attorneys' fees and other expenses, even if it did not prevail, if the agency's demand was "substantially in excess of the decision of the adjudication

8. 5 U.S.C. § 504(b)(1)(C).

9. Ardestani v. Immigr. & Naturalization Serv., 502 U.S. 129, 132–39 (1991); *see also* 2-Bar Ranch Ltd. P'ship v. U.S. Forest Serv., 996 F.3d 984, 994–95 (9th Cir. 2021) (discussing Collord v. Dep't of the Interior, 154 F.3d 933, 935–37 (9th Cir. 1998)).

10. 5 U.S.C. § 504(b)(1)(B).

11. Farrar v. Hobby, 506 U.S. 103, 111–12 (1992).

12. Perez-Arellano v. Smith, 279 F.3d 791 (9th Cir. 2002) (applying Buckhannon Bd. & Care Home, Inc. v. W. Va. Dep't of Health & Hum. Res., 532 U.S. 598, 603–10 (2001), to EAJA); Aronov v. Napolitano, 562 F.3d 84 (1st Cir. 2009); Goldstein v. Moatz, 445 F.3d 747 (4th Cir. 2006); Carbonell v. Immigr. & Naturalization Serv., 429 F.3d 894 (9th Cir. 2005).

officer" and "unreasonable when compared with such decision, under the facts and circumstances of the case."[13]

Finally, a party can only recover fees and expenses if the government's position was not "substantially justified." "Substantially justified" means that the government's position had a "reasonable basis in both law and fact." The government has the burden of showing that its position was substantially justified.[14]

EAJA also sets forth basic procedures for its administration. A party seeking an award of fees and other expenses must, within 30 days of a final disposition in the adjudication, submit an application containing an itemized statement of fees and expenses and other information. If the government appeals the underlying merits of the adjudication, the agency may not render a decision on the party's application "until a final and unreviewable decision is rendered by the court on the appeal or until the underlying merits of the case have been finally determined pursuant to the appeal."[15] Otherwise, an "adjudicative officer," usually an administrative law judge, determines the application's merits and the amount, if any, to be awarded to the party.

The adjudicative officer has some leeway to reduce the amount to be awarded, or even deny an award, when a party "engaged in conduct which unduly and unreasonably protracted the final resolution of the matter in controversy."[16] The U.S. Supreme Court's decision in *Pierce v. Underwood* sets forth general principles for calculating costs.[17]

EAJA requires each agency to "by rule establish uniform procedures for the submission and consideration of applications for an award of fees and other expenses" after consultation with the chairman of the Administrative Conference of the United States (ACUS). ACUS has carried out this charge by publishing model rules. Many agencies have relied on these model rules, including several financial and banking regulatory agencies, the Federal Trade Commission (FTC), the National Labor Relations Board, and the Occupational Safety and Health Review Commission. ACUS revised its model rules in 2019.[18]

---

13. 5 U.S.C. § 504(a)(4).
14. Pierce v. Underwood, 487 U.S. 552, 565–66 (1988).
15. 5 U.S.C. § 504(a)(2).
16. *Id.* § 504(a)(2), (3).
17. 487 U.S. 552.
18. Administrative Conference Recommendation 2019-4, Revised Model Rules for Implementation of the Equal Access to Justice Act, 84 Fed. Reg. 38,933 (Aug. 8, 2019).

12.22 Government-Funded Counsel

EAJA seeks to promote access to representation by allowing prevailing parties to recover attorneys' fees and expenses. An alternative method for defraying the costs associated with representation is for the government to provide parties with publicly funded counsel.

As a constitutional matter, the Sixth Amendment, which guarantees the accused in a criminal prosecution "the Assistance of Counsel for his defence,"[19] is inapplicable in civil administrative adjudications. The Fifth Amendment's Due Process Clause is another potential source of a constitutional right to publicly funded counsel. At least one agency, the FTC, once came close to finding a due process right to assistance by counsel, asserting in a 1969 opinion:

> We have no doubt that in a proper case where an adequate showing of financial inability is made out, a respondent is entitled to counsel. We can think of nothing less conductive to fairness and due process in administrative procedures than to pit the power of the State, armed with all of the panoply of the legal machinery (funds, investigatory resources, staff or skilled attorneys, etc.), against a single individual and then deny that individual the right to counsel when he denies the allegations and specifically asserts that he cannot afford counsel.[20]

But there has been no judicial recognition of a civil or administrative *Gideon*.[21] Courts have only in rare instances found that due process requires appointment of counsel in civil or administrative proceedings.[22]

Although statutes guaranteeing parties the right to representation have generally not been interpreted to confer a right to publicly funded counsel, at least one statutory program does provide certain parties with access to some sort of representation. Case advocates within the Taxpayer Advocate Service "work directly with taxpayers

---

19. *See* Johnson v. Zerbst, 304 U.S. 458 (1938).

20. Am. Chinchilla Corp., 76 F.T.C. 1016, 1037 (1969).

21. *See* Gideon v. Wainwright, 372 U.S. 335 (1963).

22. *See, e.g.*, Lassiter v. Dep't of Soc. Servs., 452 U.S. 18 (1981); Goldberg v. Kelly, 397 U.S. 254, 271 (1970) ("We do not say that counsel must be provided at the pre-termination hearing, but only that the recipient must be allowed to retain an attorney if he so desires.").

on identifying issues, researching solutions, and advocating on behalf of taxpayers within the IRS [Internal Revenue Service]."[23]

There have been calls for the government to provide counsel to certain parties in other administrative programs. These calls have been especially strong in the immigration context, where individuals often face detention and removal from the United States.[24] Although parties are entitled to representation under the Immigration and Nationality Act (INA), the INA specifically states that representation must be "at no expense to the Government."[25] The American Bar Association (ABA) supports eliminating this language and providing for "the appointment of counsel at federal government expense to represent all indigent persons in removal proceedings before EOIR [the Executive Office for Immigration Review]."[26] At least 20 senators and around 50 members of the House of Representatives have, in recent years, voiced support for providing additional funding for EOIR to expand legal representation programs to other populations,[27] and legislation

---

23. NAT'L TAXPAYER ADVOC., IRS, OBJECTIVES REPORT TO CONGRESS—FISCAL YEAR 2023 (2022), https://www.taxpayeradvocate.irs.gov/reports/2023-objectives-report-to-congress/full-report/.

24. *See, e.g.*, Ingrid V. Eagly, Gideon*'s Migration*, 122 YALE L.J. 2282 (2013); Ingrid V. Eagly & Steven Shafer, *A National Study of Access to Counsel in Immigration Court*, 164 U. PA. L. REV. 1 (2015); Andrew Leon Hanna, *A Constitutional Right to Appointed Counsel for the Children of America's Refugee Crisis*, 54 HARV. C.R.-C.L. L. REV. 257 (2019); Linda Kelly Hill, *The Right to Be Heard: Voicing the Due Process Right to Counsel for Unaccompanied Alien Children*, 31 B.C. THIRD WORLD L.J. 41 (2011); Robert A. Katzmann, *Study Group on Immigration Representation: The First Decade*, 87 FORDHAM L. REV. 485 (2018); Kevin R. Johnson, *An Immigration* Gideon *for Lawful Permanent Residents*, 122 YALE L.J. 2394 (2013); Mark Noferi, *Cascading Constitutional Deprivation: The Right to Appointed Counsel for Mandatorily Detained Immigrants Pending Removal Proceedings*, 18 MICH. J. RACE & L. 63 (2012); Margaret H. Taylor, *Promoting Legal Representation for Detained Aliens: Litigation and Administrative Reform*, 29 CONN. L. REV. 1647 (1997).

25. 8 U.S.C. § 1362.

26. *See* 2019 UPDATE REPORT: REFORMING THE IMMIGRATION SYSTEM: PROPOSALS TO PROMOTE INDEPENDENCE, FAIRNESS, EFFICIENCY, AND PROFESSIONALISM IN THE ADJUDICATION OF REMOVAL CASES 5–17 (2019) (prepared by Arnold & Porter for the ABA Commission on Immigration).

27. *See, e.g.*, Letter from Rep. Norma Torres et al. to Rep. Hal Rogers & Rep. Matt Cartwright (Mar. 31, 2023), https://torres.house.gov/sites/torres.house.gov/files/FY24%20Funding%20for%20Legal%20Representation%20in%20CJS%20Appropriations_FINAL.pdf; Letter from Sen. Kirsten Gillibrand et al. to Sen. Jeanne Shaheen & Sen. Jerry Moran (May 6, 2022), https://www.aila.org/infonet/senators-request-funding-for-legal-services; *see also* AM. IMMIGR.

was introduced in April 2023 that would entitle individuals in removal proceedings to legal representation at government expense.[28] Some state and local governments have also provided or proposed providing funding for legal representation for people facing removal.[29]

A district court judge found in 2013 that section 504 of the Rehabilitation Act requires EOIR to provide qualified representatives to unrepresented and detained individuals whom EOIR finds to be mentally incompetent to represent themselves in immigration proceedings.[30] EOIR established the National Qualified Representative Program for that purpose.[31] EOIR also established the Counsel for Children Initiative, which provides representation for certain unaccompanied children in eight immigration courts.[32]

There have been occasional calls for the government to provide counsel to parties in other administrative programs, primarily in adjudications involving public benefits and income support.[33] The ABA, for instance, adopted a resolution in 2006 calling on federal, state, and

---

LAW.'S ASS'N, AILA DOC. NO. 21050438, ENSURING LEGAL REPRESENTATION FOR PEOPLE FACING REMOVAL (2023), https://www.aila.org/advo-media/issues/all/featured-issue-ensuring-legal-representation.

28. Fairness to Freedom Act of 2023, S. 1187, 118th Cong. (2023); Fairness to Freedom Act of 2023, H.R. 2697, 118th Cong. (2023).

29. *See, e.g.*, *Advancing Universal Representation Initiative*, VERA INST. JUST., https://www.vera.org/ending-mass-incarceration/reducing-incarceration/detention-of-immigrants/advancing-universal-representation-initiative (last visited June 27, 2023); Press Release, Off. of N.Y. State Sen. Brad Hoylman-Sigal, First-in-Nation Legislation Would Create State Right for Legal Representation to Support Newly Arrived Asylum Seekers & Immigrant New Yorkers (Nov. 30, 2022), https://www.nysenate.gov/newsroom/press-releases/2022/brad-hoylman-sigal/first-nation-legislation-would-create-state-right.

30. Franco-Gonzalez v. Holder, No. CV 10-02211 DMG (DTBx), 2013 WL 3674492 (C.D. Cal. Apr. 23, 2013); *see also* Leslie Wolf, *After* Franco-Gonzales v. Holder*: The Implications of Locating a Right to Counsel under the Rehabilitation Act*, 23 REV. L. & SOC. JUST. 329 (2014).

31. *National Qualified Representative Program (NQRP)*, U.S. DEP'T OF JUST., EOIR, https://www.justice.gov/eoir/national-qualified-representative-program-nqrp (last updated Feb. 18, 2020).

32. Press Release, U.S. Dep't of Just., EOIR, EOIR Announces "Access EOIR Initiative" (Sept. 28, 2021), https://www.justice.gov/eoir/pr/eoir-announces-access-eoir-initiative.

33. *See, e.g.*, Russell Engler, *Connecting Self-Representation to Civil Gideon: What Existing Data Reveal about When Counsel Is Most Needed*, 37 FORDHAM URB. L.J. 37 (2010); Stephen Loffredo & Don Friedman, Gideon *Meets* Goldberg*: The Case for a Qualified Right to Counsel in Welfare Hearings*, 25 TOURO L. REV. 273 (2009).

territorial governments to "provide legal counsel as a matter of right at public expense to low income persons in those categories of adversarial proceedings [including administrative proceedings] where basic human needs are at stake, such as those involving shelter, sustenance, safety, health or child custody, as determined by each jurisdiction."[34]

12.23 Evidence

Parties can incur significant costs in obtaining evidence necessary to meet their burden of proof. Although parties are often responsible for their own costs, parties in some programs may be eligible for an award of fees or compensation or financial or other assistance from the agency.

The Social Security Act, for example, authorizes SSA to pay medical providers for evidence needed to adjudicate claimants' entitlement to disability benefits. SSA is authorized to compensate "all reasonably necessary witnesses" for adjudication-related travel expenses.[35] The Black Lung Benefits Act similarly requires the Department of Labor to offer miners a free pulmonary evaluation, which is used to adjudicate their claims. It also directs the agency to reimburse claimants "for reasonable medical expenses incurred by them in establishing their claims."[36] Claimants may also be entitled to expert witness fees.[37]

Beyond benefits programs, EAJA, discussed above, provides for compensation of witness and other evidence-related expenses in certain circumstances.[38] Another model: a bill introduced in 2022 would have directed the U.S. Patent and Trademark Office (USPTO) to compensate small and micro entities, no matter their prevailing status, for reasonable expenses, including expert witness fees, incurred in defending patent grants before the Patent Trial and Appeal Board (PTAB).[39]

12.24 Travel

Another source of expenses incurred in adjudication is travel, for example to an in-person or video hearing site. The Social Security Act authorizes SSA to compensate claimants, representatives, and

34. A.B.A. Resolution 112A (2006).

35. 42 U.S.C. §§ 401(j), 423(d)(5)(A), 1383(h).

36. 30 U.S.C. § 923(b).

37. Off. of Admin. L. Judges, U.S. Dep't of Lab., Judges' Black Lung Benchbook 27.27 (2013).

38. 5 U.S.C. § 504(b)(1).

39. Patent Trial and Appeal Board Reform Act of 2022, S. 4417, 117th Cong. (2022).

"all reasonably necessary witnesses" for adjudication-related travel expenses.[40] A bill pending in Congress at the time of this writing would direct the Secretary of Veterans Affairs to make recommendations on the feasibility and advisability of reimbursing veterans for expenses incurred for travel to video hearing sites.[41]

12.25 Intervenor Funding

As discussed in Chapter 11, many administrative adjudications involve interests beyond those of the parties directly involved. Regulatory agencies, for example, frequently consider applications for licenses that, if granted, would impact a broader universe of consumers, local communities, or others.

Beginning in the 1960s, there was a push to broaden public participation in federal agency decision-making by compensating non-regulated entities, especially organizations representing regulatory beneficiaries and other public interest groups, for costs incurred in participating in agency decision-making processes. In 1971, ACUS even considered, but ultimately rejected, a proposed recommendation that would have encouraged agencies to fund public participants in administrative hearings, including those conducted in the adjudication of cases.[42]

Several agencies, including the FTC and Nuclear Regulatory Commission (NRC), considered funding or actively funded public participants during this period. The comptroller general approved this practice, finding that even without explicit statutory authorization, funding intervenors "would constitute a proper exercise of administrative discretion."[43] But many agencies without explicit statutory authorization ceased funding intervenors following appeals court decisions

---

40. 42 U.S.C. §§ 401(j), 423(d)(5)(A), 1383(h); *see also* 20 C.F.R. §§ 404.999a–.999d, 416.1495–.1499 (2022); SSA, Hearings, Appeals, and Litigation Law (HALLEX) Manual § I-2-3-13 [hereinafter HALLEX].

41. Veterans' Appeals Backlog Improvement Act, H.R. 1378, 118th Cong. § 4 (2023).

42. Administrative Conference Recommendation 71-6, Public Participation in Administrative Hearings, 38 Fed. Reg. 19,789 (July 23, 1973); *see also* Ernest Gellhorn, *Public Participation in Administrative Proceedings*, 81 Yale L.J. 359, 394–97 (1972); Roger C. Cramton, *The Why, Where, and How of Broadened Public Participation in the Administrative Process*, 60 Geo. L.J. 525, 541, 546 (1972).

43. Carl Tobias, *Great Expectations and Mismatched Compensation: Government Sponsored Public Participation in Proceedings of the Consumer Product Safety Commission*, 64 Wash. U. L.Q. 1101, 1102–05 (1986).

in the late 1970s and early 1980s,[44] and Congress prohibited—and continues to prohibit—the practice at several agencies through appropriations riders.[45]

Congress in 1978 explicitly authorized the new Federal Energy Regulatory Commission (FERC) to fund intervenors in administrative proceedings, including adjudications. An amendment to the Federal Power Act directed FERC to establish an Office of Public Participation (OPP) to "coordinate assistance available to persons intervening or participating or proposing to intervene or participate in proceedings before the Commission." The statute also authorized FERC to compensate certain intervenors and other participants in agency proceedings for "reasonable attorneys' fees, expert witness fees, and other costs."[46]

As early as 1979, however, appropriations statutes prohibited FERC from compensating intervenors in regulatory or adjudicatory proceedings,[47] and OPP was never established. In 2016, 31 public interest groups, led by Public Citizen, petitioned FERC to establish and fund OPP.[48] Following action by Congress in 2020, FERC solicited input from stakeholders on establishing OPP. OPP became operational in 2021.[49]

This model has been suggested elsewhere. A 2022 report prepared by the NRC's Environmental Justice Review Team, for instance, notes that stakeholders "requested the agency assist with the costs associated with participating in litigation before the NRC." Intervenor funding would, in the agency's assessment, require congressional action.[50]

---

44. *See* Pac. Legal Found. v. Goyan, 664 F.2d 121 (4th Cir. 1981); Greene Cnty. Plan. Bd. v. Fed. Power Comm'n, 559 F.2d 1227 (2d Cir. 1976).

45. *See* Cohen, *supra* note 3, at 59–61; Carl W. Tobias, *Of Public Funds and Public Participation: Resolving the Issue of Agency Authority to Reimburse Public Participants in Administrative Proceedings*, 82 Colum. L. Rev. 906 (1982).

46. 16 U.S.C. § 825q-1.

47. Luther Caulkins, *Funding and Facilitating Public Participation at FERC*, 51 Env't. L. Rep. 10605, 10606–07 (2021).

48. Tyson Slocum, Energy Program Dir., Pub. Citizen et al., Petition to Initiate a Rulemaking to Establish the Office of Public Participation as Established by Congress and to Fund Its Work (Mar. 7, 2016), https://www.citizen.org/wp-content/uploads/public-citizen-ferc-public-participation-petition.pdf.

49. FERC, The Office of Public Participation (2021), https://www.ferc.gov/media/ferc-report-office-public-participation. For more information about OPP, see *Office of Public Participation (OPP)*, FERC, https://www.ferc.gov/OPP (last updated June 26, 2023).

50. *See* NRC, Environmental Justice Assessment, Enclosure 6, at 3–4 (2022), https://www.nrc.gov/about-nrc/regulatory/licensing/nepa/environmental-justice/assessment.html.

12.3 SUPPORTING NONGOVERNMENTAL SERVICE PROVIDERS

Another model by which the government can allocate costs incurred in adjudication is through grants or subsidies to entities that provide legal or other services to parties in agency adjudications.[51] The government does this in at least two ways, through the Legal Services Corporation (LSC) and through grant programs administered by individual agencies.

12.31 Legal Services Corporation

A congressionally chartered nonprofit, LSC provides "financial support for legal assistance in noncriminal proceedings or matters to persons financially unable to afford legal assistance."[52] Funded through appropriations, LSC awards grants to legal services providers that assist low-income individuals with many kinds of matters, including in proceedings before agencies such as SSA and the Department of Veterans Affairs (VA).

There are legal and practical limitations to this model, to be sure. People without lawful status in the United States are typically ineligible for representation by LSC grantees. Many individuals who cannot afford representation have assets that disqualify them from assistance by grantees. And legal service organizations often face significant resource limitations, with the effect that assistance may be unavailable to parties in adjudications who would benefit from it.[53]

12.32 Agency Grant Programs

Some agencies are authorized to provide grants to entities that provide legal or other services to individuals who participate in agency proceedings. Low-income taxpayer clinics, for example, receive partial funding from the IRS.[54] And the VA provides grants to private nonprofit organizations and consumer cooperatives through the Supportive Services for Veterans Families (SSVF) program. SSVF grantees

---

51. *See* Cramton, *supra* note 42, at 541–42.

52. 42 U.S.C. § 2996b.

53. Michael D. Sant'Ambrogio & Adam S. Zimmerman, *The Agency Class Action*, 112 Colum. L. Rev. 1992, 2026 (2012) (internal citations omitted).

54. 26 U.S.C. § 7626; *see also* Keith Fogg, *Taxation with Representation: The Creation and Development of Low-Income Taxpayer Clinics*, Tax Law., Fall 2013, at 3.

help veterans locate accredited representatives and in some cases may themselves be accredited to represent veterans in VA adjudications.[55]

Grantmaking has been proposed in other programs. The Senate Appropriations Committee has encouraged SSA to provide "grants to community-based organizations familiar with SSA programs for the purpose of assisting individuals with disabilities apply for benefits, including supporting them throughout the process."[56] A bill introduced in 2021 would have directed the VA to award grants to medical residency and fellowship programs to fund programs that assist veterans in substantiating claims for veterans' benefits through independent medical examinations and opinions.[57] One law professor has proposed an "Immigrant Representation Grants" program that would provide funding to local nonprofits that represent parties in EOIR adjudications.[58]

12.33 Supporting Pro Bono and Low-Cost Representation

Some parties in federal agency adjudications are able to access representation through pro bono service providers. While pro bono programs are privately run, many federal agencies routinely provide parties with information about available pro bono representation and expend resources to maintain information clearinghouses to help connect parties with pro bono service providers. The America Invents Act, for example, directed the USPTO to "work with and support intellectual property law associations across the country in the establishment of pro bono programs designed to assist financially under-resourced independent inventors and small businesses."[59] Today, the USPTO administers the Patent Pro Bono Program, as well as the PTAB Pro Bono Program and Trademark Trial and Appeal Board Pro Bono Clearinghouse Program.[60] By law, immigrants who apply for asylum or

---

55. 38 U.S.C. § 2044(b)(1)(C); 38 C.F.R. § 62.32 (2022); VA, Department of Veterans Affairs Supportive Services for Veteran Families (SSVF) Program: Program Guide (2021).

56. Explanatory Statement for Departments of Labor, Health and Human Services, and Education, and Related Agencies Appropriations Bill, 2023, at 310 (2022).

57. Veterans Pro Bono Corps Act of 2021, S. 3047, 117th Cong. (2021).

58. Erin B. Corocran, *Bypassing Civil* Gideon*: A Legislative Proposal to Address the Rising Costs and Unmet Legal Needs of Unrepresented Immigrants*, 115 W. Va. L. Rev. 643, 677–78 (2012).

59. Leahy-Smith America Invents Act, Pub. L. No. 112-29, § 32(a), 125 Stat. 284, 340 (2011).

60. *Patent Pro Bono Program for Independent Inventors and Small Businesses*, USPTO, https://www.uspto.gov/patents/basics/using-legal-services/pro-bono/pat

face deportation must be provided "a list of persons (updated not less often than quarterly) who have indicated their availability to represent [parties] on a pro bono basis."[61] EOIR also maintains a list of pro bono legal service providers on its website.[62] The Social Security Act similarly requires SSA to "notify each claimant in writing . . . of the options for obtaining attorneys to represent individuals in presenting their cases" before the agency. The notification must advise claimants "of the availability to qualifying claimants of legal services organizations which provide legal services free of charge."[63] Agency guidance requires administrative law judges and hearing office staff, in some circumstances, to provide claimants information about organizations that provide free legal services.[64]

12.4 CHARGING USER FEES

Agencies incur administrative costs (e.g., adjudicator and staff salaries, information technology, real estate) to operate adjudicative programs. Consistent with the Constitution's Appropriations Clause,[65] many agencies cover these costs using congressionally appropriated funds. Questions sometimes arise as to whether a particular, arguably administrative cost should be borne by the government or by private parties. Congress provided in the Federal Advisory Committee Act, for example, that agencies can charge parties for copies of transcripts of proceedings (including adjudicative proceedings) at no more than the "actual cost of duplication."[66] This provision, possibly inspired by a 1971 ACUS recommendation,[67] effectively ended the practice by which agencies could recoup transcription costs through fees charged to parties in adjudications.[68]

---

ent-pro-bono-program (last modified June 23, 2023).

61. 8 U.S.C. §§ 1158(d)(4), 1229(b)(2).

62. *List of Pro Bono Legal Service Providers*, U.S. Dep't of Just., EOIR, https://www.justice.gov/eoir/list-pro-bono-legal-service-providers (last updated May 26, 2023).

63. 42 U.S.C. § 406(c).

64. HALLEX, *supra* note 40, § I-2-1-80.B.2.

65. U.S. Const. art. I, § 9, cl. 7.

66. 5 U.S.C. app. § 11(a).

67. Administrative Conference Recommendation 71-6, *supra* note 42 ("The cost of recording formal proceedings should be borne by the agency, not by the parties or other participants to the proceeding (except to the extent that a person requests expedited delivery).").

68. Gellhorn, *supra* note 42, at 392–93.

Many programs, however, are funded, in whole or in large part, through fees charged to individuals who take advantage of them. User fees have a long history in American government. People regularly pay federal agencies to send mail, obtain passports, and access national parks, for example, and proposals for self-funding agencies have especially proliferated since the Reagan Administration.[69]

Federal law grants agencies broad authority to assess fair and reasonable user fees.[70] Many regulatory agencies—including FERC, the FTC, the Environmental Protection Agency, and the Food and Drug Administration—rely on filing fees to varying degrees. The USPTO collects fees used to cover its expenses in processing applications for patents and trademarks.[71] Another notable example of an agency that "self-funds" adjudication is the U.S. Citizenship and Immigration Service (USCIS), which decides applications for immigration benefits, immigration petitions, naturalization petitions, and asylum applications. The INA permits USCIS to set and collect fees for providing adjudication and naturalization services at a level that "will ensure recovery of the full costs of providing adjudication and naturalization services, including the costs of providing similar services without charge to asylum applicants and certain other immigrants."[72] USCIS and USPTO both charge additional fees for expedited adjudication, and both have processes in place to reduce or waive fees for those who might not be able to afford them.[73]

Funding an agency through user fees is often justified as a means to "allocate the cost of government services and products to the beneficiaries of those services and products, representing a normative concern."[74] User fees can also be used for economic reasons (to efficiently allocate public goods) or political reasons (to fund a program

---

69. Clayton P. Gillette & Thomas D. Hopkins, *Federal User Fees: A Legal and Economic Analysis*, 67 B.U. L. Rev. 795, 797 (1987); *see also* Administrative Conference Recommendation 87-4, User Fees, 52 Fed. Reg. 23,634 (June 24, 1987).

70. 31 U.S.C. § 9701; *see also* Off. of Mgmt. & Budget, Exec. Off. of the President, Circular No. A-25, User Charges (1993); U.S. Gov't Accountability Off., GAO-08-386SP, Federal User Fees: A Design Guide (2008).

71. 15 U.S.C. § 1113; 35 U.S.C. §§ 41, 42.

72. 8 U.S.C. § 1356(m); *see also* William A. Kandel, Cong. Rsch. Serv., R44038, U.S. Citizenship and Immigration Services (USCIS) Functions and Funding (2015).

73. *See* 8 C.F.R. § 106.3 (USCIS) (2022); 37 C.F.R. § 1.27 (2022) (USPTO rule providing reduced fees for "small entities").

74. Daimeon Shanks, *Entrance Fees: Self-Funded Agencies and the Economization of Immigration*, 93 U. Colo. L. Rev. 405, 409 (2022).

without raising taxes).[75] The imposition of adjudication-related fees may also deter litigation and encourage settlement, if that is desirable.[76]

On the other hand, concerns have been raised that funding agencies through user fees may distort agency decision-making, have regressive or inequitable effects on low-income individuals, or reduce democratic accountability. Michael Frakes and Melissa Wasserman, for example, have argued that USPTO's fee structure biases examiners toward granting patents.[77] Jill Family has argued that recent fee increases at USCIS are likely to "prohibit lower-income applicants from applying for legal status," "deter employers from applying for legal status for employees," and "add to the already increased cost and effort of applying" for legal status.[78] And Daimeon Shanks has argued that self-funding reduces democratic accountability because it "frustrates one of Congress's principal tools: the power of the purse, as exercised through regularized budgetary oversight."[79]

Whether the administrative costs of a particular adjudicative program should be funded primarily through appropriations or user fees is ultimately a normative, policy question. Its resolution depends heavily on factors including the nature and purpose of the program and how one conceptualizes the matter being adjudicated. Policymakers have reached different conclusions for different programs. And, of course, the success of a particular user-fee system depends heavily on its design and its suitability for a particular program.

---

75. *Id.*

76. Gillette & Hopkins, *supra* note 69, at 858–59.

77. Michael D. Frakes & Melissa F. Wasserman, *Does Agency Funding Affect Decisionmaking?: An Empirical Assessment of the PTO's Granting Patterns*, 66 VAND. L. REV. 67 (2013).

78. Jill Family, *An Invisible Border Wall and the Dangers of Internal Agency Control*, 25 LEWIS & CLARK L. REV. 71, 100 (2021); *see also* Nw. Immigr. Rts. Project v. U.S. Citizenship & Immigr. Serv., 496 F. Supp. 3d 31 (D.D.C. 2020).

79. Shanks, *supra* note 74, at 450–53; *cf.* Consumer Fin. Prot. Bureau v. All Am. Check Cashing, Inc., 33 F.4th 218, 225–241 (5th Cir. 2022) (finding the self-funding structure of the Consumer Financial Protection Bureau to violate the constitutional separation of powers).

Chapter 13

Rules of Conduct for Representatives

George M. Cohen

13.1 CHAPTER OVERVIEW

Many federal agencies permit parties or other interested persons to their adjudicative proceedings to be represented by attorney or nonattorney practitioners. Almost 50 agencies have one or more rules specifically regulating the conduct of representatives.[1] The number of agencies with such rules has steadily increased since the mid-20th century, with more than a dozen agencies adopting new rules or modifying existing ones in the past two decades.

Agency rules governing representatives vary greatly, and agencies have largely adopted them independently of each other. The rules have not been without controversy.[2] In 1982, some American Bar Association (ABA) committees proposed a set of Model Rules of Agency Conduct, but that proposal was rejected. Instead, the ABA adopted a resolution endorsing the enactment of federal legislation that would preclude federal agencies from adopting "standards of practice to govern the professional conduct of attorneys who represent clients" other than those "affecting such attorney's participation in a particular proceeding before it, as immediately necessary to maintain order in or assure the integrity of such proceeding."[3] Congress, however, did not adopt the proposed legislation. More recently, the Administrative Conference of the United States (ACUS) recommended that agencies "consider adopting rules governing the participation and conduct of representatives in adjudicative proceedings to promote the accessibility, fairness, integrity, and efficiency of adjudicative proceedings."[4]

This chapter discusses rules, including rules of conduct, regulating representatives in agency adjudicative proceedings. It begins by describing the statutory authority by which agencies issue such rules (section 13.2). Subsequent sections address the qualifications for attorney and nonattorney representatives under statutes and agency rules (section 13.3), the structure of agency rules regulating representatives (section 13.4), the conduct addressed by such rules (section 13.5), and the implementation and enforcement of agency rules of representative conduct (section 13.6).

---

1. George M. Cohen, *The Laws of Agency Lawyering*, 84 FORDHAM L. REV. 1963, 1991 (2016).

2. For a general discussion of the issue, see Michael P. Cox, *Regulation of Attorneys Practicing before Federal Agencies*, 45 CASE W. RSRV. L. REV. 173 (1984).

3. ABA Annual Meeting 1982, Joint Resolution of Section of Administrative Law, Section of Natural Resources Law, Section of Public Utility Law, and Federal Communications Bar Association.

4. Administrative Conference Recommendation 2021-9, Regulation of Representatives in Agency Adjudicative Proceedings, ¶ 1, 87 Fed. Reg. 1,721, 1,722 (Jan. 12, 2022).

13.2 STATUTORY AUTHORITY FOR RULES

The Agency Practice Act (5 U.S.C. § 500) and the Administrative Procedure Act (APA) are the two most important, generally applicable statutes governing representatives in agency proceedings. Neither expressly authorizes agencies to adopt, nor prohibits them from adopting, rules regulating representatives in agency adjudicative proceedings. The Agency Practice Act states that it does not "authorize or limit the discipline, including disbarment" of representatives.[5] The APA speaks only in vague terms. As a general matter, the act grants each agency "authority necessary to comply with the requirements of this subchapter through the issuance of rules or otherwise."[6] With respect to agency adjudication, the act's formal-hearing provisions ambiguously specify that, "[s]ubject to published rules of the agency and within its powers," presiding officials may, among other things, "regulate the course of the hearing" and "take other action authorized by agency rule consistent with this subchapter."[7]

In some cases, Congress has expressly authorized or directed individual agencies to regulate the conduct of representatives who practice before them. The language used, and the nature of the authority granted, varies significantly across authorizing statutes.[8]

Even where Congress has not specifically authorized agencies to regulate representatives, courts have consistently found that the authority to regulate the conduct of representatives is inherent in agencies' general rulemaking authority or their power to protect the integrity of their processes.[9] Courts have sometimes imposed limitations on these rules. For example, one court has held that before an agency

---

5. 5 U.S.C. § 500(d)(2).

6. *Id.* § 559.

7. *Id.* § 556(c)(5), (11).

8. *See, e.g.*, 7 U.S.C. § 2356 (U.S. Department of Agriculture (USDA) Plant Variety Protection Office); 8 U.S.C. § 1229a(b)(6)(A) (immigration courts); 15 U.S.C. § 7245 (Securities and Exchange Commission (SEC)); 31 U.S.C. § 330(a)(1) (Treasury); 35 U.S.C. § 2(b)(2)(D) (U.S. Patent and Trademark Office (USPTO)); 38 U.S.C. § 5904(a)(2) (Department of Veterans Affairs (VA)); 42 U.S.C. § 401(a)(1) (Social Security Administration (SSA)); 43 U.S.C. § 1464 (Department of the Interior (DOI)); 49 U.S.C. § 1303(c) (Surface Transportation Board (STB)).

9. *See, e.g.*, Checkosky v. Sec. & Exch. Comm'n, 23 F.3d 452, 455–56, 468–72, 493–94 (D.C. Cir. 1994); Davy v. Sec. & Exch. Comm'n, 792 F.2d 1418, 1421 (9th Cir. 1986); Touche Ross & Co. v. Sec. & Exch. Comm'n, 609 F.2d 570, 582 (2d Cir. 1979); Koden v. U.S. Dep't of Just., 564 F.2d 228, 233 (7th Cir. 1977); *see also* Goldsmith v. Bd. of Tax Appeals, 270 U.S. 117, 122 (1926).

may exclude an attorney from its proceedings, it must provide "concrete evidence" that the attorney's presence, when desired by the client, would "obstruct and impede" the proceeding.[10]

13.3 QUALIFICATIONS FOR REPRESENTATIVES

The APA entitles parties in administrative proceedings to be represented by an attorney or, if permitted by the agency, by a "qualified representative" who is not an attorney.[11] This right exists whether or not a party is compelled to appear before an agency.[12] This section discusses the qualifications for attorney and nonattorney representatives in agency proceedings.

13.31 Attorney Representatives

The Agency Practice Act states:

> An individual who is a member in good standing of the bar of the highest court of a State may represent a person before an agency on filing with the agency a written declaration that he is currently qualified as provided by this subsection and is authorized to represent the particular person on whose behalf he acts.[13]

Thus, the statute "prohibits agencies from erecting their own supplemental admission requirements for duly admitted members of a state bar."[14] (Agencies may, however, choose to permit attorneys to serve as representatives even if they are not in good standing.[15])

By permitting lawyers to practice before an agency so long as they are licensed in *some* state, the Agency Practice Act provides an important exception to restrictions on multijurisdictional practice, both under unauthorized practice of law rules and state ethics rules, that would otherwise restrict lawyer practice outside jurisdictions in

10. Sec. & Exch. Comm'n v. Csapo, 533 F.2d 7, 10–11 (D.C. Cir. 1976).

11. 5 U.S.C. § 555(b).

12. *See*, *e.g.*, Smiley v. Dir., Off. of Workers' Comp. Programs, 984 F.2d 278, 282 (9th Cir. 1993); Salem v. Pompeo, 432 F. Supp. 3d. 222, 231–32 (E.D.N.Y. 2020).

13. 5 U.S.C. § 500(b).

14. Polydoroff v. Interstate Com. Comm'n, 773 F.2d 372, 374 (D.C. Cir. 1985); Levine v. Saul, No. 19-569WES, 2020 WL 5258690, at *6 (D.R.I. Sept. 3, 2020).

15. *See*, *e.g.*, 20 C.F.R. §§ 404.1705(c), 416.1505(c) (2022) (SSA); 29 C.F.R. § 18.22(b)(1) (2022) (Department of Labor (DOL)).

which they are licensed. Lawyers who seek to practice in courts outside jurisdictions where they are licensed must generally be admitted pro hac vice for a particular proceeding, which includes associating with local counsel. The Agency Practice Act provision makes such a process unnecessary for lawyers practicing before federal agencies.

Congress has granted several agencies permission to impose additional qualification rules for attorneys. The Agency Practice Act specifically excludes the U.S. Patent and Trademark Office (USPTO) from its requirement that agencies recognize attorneys in good standing in any U.S. jurisdiction.[16] A separate statute authorizes the USPTO to "establish regulations, not inconsistent with the law, which . . . may govern the recognition and conduct of agents, attorneys, or other persons representing applicants or other parties before the Office."[17]

In addition, the Department of Veterans Affairs (VA) statute authorizes the Secretary of Veterans Affairs to "prescribe in regulations . . . qualifications . . . for" attorneys and other representatives.[18] Pursuant to that statute, the VA has adopted an "accreditation" process required of attorneys and nonattorneys, including achieving a passing score on a written exam and satisfying a continuing education requirement. However, an attorney's character and fitness is presumed "based on State bar membership in good standing unless the General Counsel receives credible information to the contrary."[19]

13.32 Nonattorney Representatives

The APA does not "grant or deny a person who is not a lawyer the right to appear for or represent others before an agency in an agency proceeding."[20] Similarly, the Agency Practice Act "does not . . . grant or deny" to nonattorneys "the right to appear for or represent a person before an agency or in an agency proceeding," other than to certified public accountants, who may represent persons before the Internal Revenue Service (IRS).[21] Thus, neither general statute prohibits agencies from permitting nonattorney representatives nor sets any requirements for such representatives. Many agencies have permitted

16. 5 U.S.C. § 500(e).
17. 35 U.S.C. § 2(b)(2)(D).
18. 38 U.S.C. § 5904(a)(2).
19. *Id.* § 14.629(b).
20. 5 U.S.C. § 555(b).
21. *Id.* § 500(c), (d).

nonattorney representatives to appear in agency proceedings, using a range of qualifications.[22]

Some agencies impose no express restrictions on who may serve as a representative.[23] Other agencies articulate standards of competence and character that nonattorney representatives must meet, but do not impose limitations on who may serve as representatives or identify specific requirements that nonattorney representatives must meet. For example, the regulations of the Social Security Administration (SSA) state that a nonattorney representative must be "capable of giving valuable help to [a claimant] in connection with [a] claim"; "not disqualified or suspended from acting as a representative in dealings with [the agency]"; "not prohibited by any law from acting as a representative"; and "generally known to have a good character and reputation."[24] The Department of Labor's (DOL's) rule states that, for a nonattorney representative, an administrative law judge (ALJ) "may require that the representative establish that he or she is subject to the laws of the United States and possesses communication skills, knowledge, character, thoroughness and preparation reasonably necessary to render appropriate assistance."[25]

Other agencies allow only certain types of nonattorneys to serve as representatives. For example, the Securities and Exchange Commission (SEC) and the Federal Energy Regulatory Commission (FERC) limit nonattorney representation to agents who are permitted to represent various types of entities.[26] The Department of Homeland Security (DHS) identifies five categories of permissible nonattorney representatives.[27]

13.4 STRUCTURE OF THE RULES

Agencies that have rules governing the conduct of representatives in adjudicatory proceedings generally publish those rules in the *Code of*

---

22. Zona Fairbanks Hostetler, *Nonlawyer Assistance to Individuals in Federal Mass Justice Agencies: The Need for Improved Guidelines*, 2 ADMIN. L.J. 85 (1988).

23. *See, e.g.*, 7 C.F.R. § 1.26(a) (2022) (USDA); 29 C.F.R. § 102.177(a) (2022) (National Labor Relations Board (NLRB)).

24. 20 C.F.R. §§ 404.1705(b), 416.1505(b) (2022).

25. 29 C.F.R. § 18.22(b)(2) (2022).

26. 15 C.F.R. § 201.102(b) (2022) (SEC); 18 C.F.R. § 385.2101(a) (2022) (FERC).

27. 8 C.F.R. § 292.1 (2022).

Federal Regulations (CFR). For attorney representatives, these rules serve as a parallel regulatory regime to the rules of professional conduct adopted and enforced by all states and the District of Columbia. Unlike those rules, which are typically based on the ABA's Model Rules of Professional Conduct, the agency rules do not follow any general pattern.

This section considers how agencies structure their rules of conduct for representatives. It addresses how agencies label such rules and make them publicly available (section 13.41), the degree to which agencies and offices within agencies coordinate on their representative conduct rules (section 13.42), and whether agencies incorporate other state or federal ethics rules or rules of professional conduct in their own rules (section 13.43).

13.41 Labeling and Location

Agencies do not use uniform terminology to label their rules of conduct for representatives. Some refer to their rules using a variant of the ABA's "Rules of Professional Conduct" terminology.[28] A greater number of agencies include their rules of conduct as part of their general "rules of practice and procedure" or some variant thereof.[29]

Agencies also vary in whether they choose to cast their professional conduct rules as a single rule[30] or a series of rules,[31] and, if the latter, whether the agencies locate their professional conduct rules in a single

---

28. *See, e.g.*, 7 C.F.R. § 97.157 (2022) (USDA); 8 C.F.R. § 292.3 (2022) (DHS); 12 C.F.R. §§ 1209.73–.74 (2022) (Federal Housing Finance Authority (FHFA)); 14 C.F.R. pt. 300 (2022) (Department of Transportation (DOT)); 17 C.F.R. pt. 205 (2022) (SEC); 20 C.F.R. § 404.1740 (2022) (SSA); 37 C.F.R. §§11.101–.901 (2022) (USPTO); 38 C.F.R. § 14.632 (2022) (VA); 49 C.F.R. pt. 511 (2022) (National Highway Traffic Safety Administration).

29. *See, e.g.*, 10 C.F.R. ch. 1, pt. 2, subpt. C (2022) (Nuclear Regulatory Commission); 12 C.F.R. pt. 19 (2022) (Office of the Comptroller of the Currency (OCC)), pt. 263 (2022) (Federal Reserve Board (FRB)), pt. 308 (2022) (Federal Deposit Insurance Corporation (FDIC)), pt. 747 (2022) (National Credit Union Administration (NCUA)); 18 C.F.R. pt. 18 (2022) (DOL); 28 C.F.R. pt. 68 (2022) (Department of Justice (DOJ)); 47 C.F.R. ch. I, subch. A, pt. 1, subpt. A (2022) (Federal Communications Commission (FCC)).

30. *See* 29 C.F.R. § 102.177 (2022) (NLRB); 31 C.F.R. § 1316.51(b) (2022) (Drug Enforcement Administration (DEA)).

31. 8 C.F.R. §§ 292.3(b) (2022) (DHS), 1003.102 (2022); 20 C.F.R. §§ 404.1740, 416.1540 (2022) (SSA); 29 C.F.R. pt. 300 (2022) (DOT); 31 C.F.R. pt. 8, subpt. D (2022) (Bureau of Alcohol, Tobacco, Firearms, and Explosives (BATFE)); 31 C.F.R. pt. 10 (2022) (IRS); 37 C.F.R. pt. 11 (2022) (USPTO); 38 C.F.R. § 14.632 (2022) (VA); 49 C.F.R. pt. 1103 (2022) (STB).

location or scatter them in different locations. Agencies may put these rules in multiple locations for several reasons. The rules may apply to different types of claims or to adjudications under different statutory regimes.[32] Alternatively, agencies may have different rules for different stages of an adjudication (e.g., hearings versus appeal),[33] or may apply different rules to different categories of people (e.g., representatives and/or parties, attorney and/or nonattorney representatives).[34] Agencies may also place rules covering different types of representative conduct in different locations.[35] To make the representative conduct rules more accessible, ACUS has recently recommended that agencies publish their rules governing representatives' conduct on a single web page or in a single document on their websites.[36]

13.42 Interagency Coordination

Most agencies do not coordinate their representative conduct rules with the rules of other agencies, even though representatives might practice before multiple agencies. Even when multiple agencies appear in the same title of the CFR, and therefore have at least some overlap in general subject matter, their rules generally differ in some way, such as topics covered, substance, or style. Some, but not all, of these differences are likely the result of the different functions the agencies serve (such as primarily investigative, primarily adjudicative, or a combination) or the distinct programs they administer. For example, the National Labor Relations Board (NLRB) and DOL have very different rules even though they appear in the same CFR title. That may reflect the fact that the NLRB focuses on union activity, whereas DOL oversees benefit programs under various employment statutes as well as employment visas related to immigration.

There are two notable exceptions to this general lack of interagency coordination. DHS and the Executive Office for Immigration

---

32. See USDA's rules, for example. *See, e.g.*, 7 C.F.R. §§ 1.26(b), 1.141(c)–(d)(1), 1.328, 97.157, 110.8(h)(3)–(4) (2022).

33. *See, e.g.*, 38 C.F.R. § 20.6 (2022) (VA, applicable only to appellate practice before the Board of Veterans' Appeals).

34. See SEC rules, for example. *Compare* 17 C.F.R. § 201.102(e) (2022) (attorney and nonattorney representatives) *with id.* pt. 205 (2022) (attorneys).

35. See FERC rules, for example. *See, e.g.*, 18 C.F.R. §§ 1b.16 (2022) (investigations), 385.411 (2022) (discovery abuse), 385.2102 (2022) (disruptive conduct and other unethical behavior).

36. Administrative Conference Recommendation 2021-9, *supra* note 4, ¶ 11.

Review (EOIR) both use the same rules of conduct.[37] And several financial regulatory agencies have adopted Uniform Rules of Practice and Procedure.[38]

13.43 Incorporation of Other Rules

Agencies may incorporate state or federal ethics rules as part of their own rules of conduct for representatives, either in addition to or instead of the agencies' own promulgated rules. Not all agencies with rules governing representatives have an incorporation rule,[39] but most do. Indeed, some agencies have no rules governing representative conduct other than an incorporation rule.[40] The vast majority of agencies that have an incorporation rule, however, supplement that rule with their own rules.

Agencies with incorporation rules differ in which rules they incorporate. A few agencies incorporate the ABA Model Rules of Professional Conduct[41] or the District of Columbia Rules of Professional Conduct.[42] A second approach, applicable only to lawyer representatives, that some agencies take is to incorporate the ethics rules of the jurisdiction or jurisdictions in which an attorney is licensed to practice.[43] A final approach that many agencies take is to incorporate the ethics rules generally applicable in federal courts or otherwise without specifying a particular jurisdiction.[44] This approach raises potential

---

37. *See* 7 C.F.R. § 292.3(a)(1) (2022) (DHS); 8 C.F.R. § 1003.102 (2022) (EOIR).

38. *See* 12 C.F.R. §§ 19.1–.41 (2022) (OCC), 263.1–.41 (2022) (FRB), 308.1–.41 (2022) (FDIC), 747.1–.41 (2022) (NCUA).

39. *See, e.g.*, 8 C.F.R. § 1003.102 (2022) (EOIR); 20 C.F.R. § 404.1740 (2022) (SSA); 31 C.F.R. pt. 10 (2022) (IRS); 37 C.F.R. pt. 11 (2022) (USPTO).

40. *See* 21 C.F.R. § 1316.51 (2022) (DEA); 29 C.F.R. § 102.177(a) (2022) (NLRB); 39 C.F.R. § 3010.143(d) (2022) (Postal Regulatory Commission (PRC)).

41. *See, e.g.*, 29 C.F.R. § 2200.104(a) (2022); 31 C.F.R. § 8.41(b)(2)(i) (2022) (BATFE).

42. *See, e.g.*, 39 C.F.R. § 3010.143(d) (2022) (PRC).

43. *See, e.g.*, 12 C.F.R. § 1081.107(c)(1) (2022) (Consumer Financial Protection Bureau (CFPB)); 16 C.F.R. § 4.1(e)(1)(i)(B) (2022) (Federal Trade Commission (FTC)); 29 C.F.R. § 18.22(c) (2022) (DOL); 38 C.F.R. § 14.632(d) (2022) (VA); 39 C.F.R. § 955.34(a) (2022) (U.S. Postal Service); 47 C.F.R. § 1.24(a)(2) (2022) (FCC).

44. *See, e.g.*, 7 C.F.R. §§ 1.141(c), 97.155, 110(h)(3) (2022) (USDA); 10 C.F.R. § 1708.112(a) (2022) (Defense Nuclear Facilities Safety Board); 12 C.F.R. § 308.109(a)(1)(ii) (2022) (FDIC); 14 C.F.R. §§ 300.1, 300.6(a), 300.12(a) (2022) (DOT); 17 C.F.R. § 14.8(c) (2022) (Commodity Futures Trading Commission (CFTC)); 17 C.F.R. § 201.102(e)(1)(ii) (2022) (SEC); 18 C.F.R. § 385.2101(c)

choice-of-law problems to the extent that the rules of different jurisdictions conflict.

The fact that some federal agencies incorporate state professional conduct rules does not mean that these agencies attempt to preempt discipline by states or other jurisdictions under their own professional conduct rules.[45] Moreover, except in cases of reciprocal discipline (see section 13.64), agencies have neither used, nor claimed the authority to use, incorporation rules to discipline lawyers for conduct outside an agency adjudicative proceeding or otherwise not involving practice before the agency. Rather, incorporating other professional conduct rules simply means that the agency can impose discipline on lawyers or other representatives who engage in conduct before the agency that the agency finds violates those other rules, whether or not the state disciplinary authority acts to discipline that conduct. Thus, attorney representatives remain subject to discipline by state authorities for violating applicable ethics rules.

13.5 CONDUCT ADDRESSED BY THE RULES

Agency rules governing representatives cover a wide range of topics. Many of these rules parallel, and are consistent with, rules in the ABA Model Rules of Professional Conduct. But most agencies do not adopt rules corresponding to all, or even most, ABA rules. (The USPTO is one notable exception.[46]) Almost no agencies, for example, have adopted rules covering the representation of an organizational client, or the duties owed to prospective clients, or rules that would be irrelevant in administrative proceedings (e.g., conduct relevant to jury trials).

The most common substantive rules adopted by agencies address conduct that would undermine or interfere with efficient and fair agency adjudication. These rules correspond to the "Advocate" rules in the ABA Model Rules of Professional Conduct.[47] The topics covered by the greatest number of agency rules are ex parte communications (section 13.51), disruptive conduct (section 13.52), frivolous claims (section 13.53), obstruction of justice (section 13.54), and delay (section 13.55). Rules governing these topics are the only ones adopted by

---

(2022) (FERC); 28 C.F.R. § 68.33(c)(3)(iii) (2022) (DOJ); 29 C.F.R. § 102.177(a) (2022) (NLRB); 45 C.F.R. § 500.4(a)(2) (2022) (Foreign Claims Settlement Commission); 49 C.F.R. § 1103.11 (2022) (STB).

45. *See* Gadda v. Ashcroft, 377 F.3d 934, 939 (9th Cir. 2004).

46. *See* 37 C.F.R. §§ 11.101–.804 (2022).

47. Model Rules of Pro. Conduct rr. 3.1–3.9 (Am. Bar Ass'n 2020).

more than 15 agencies. Many agencies have also adopted catchall-type rules requiring representatives to comply with agency rules.[48]

13.51 Ex Parte Communication

A fundamental tenet of due process in many adjudications is that advocates should present their arguments before an impartial tribunal in an open proceeding. Ex parte communication with a judge or other official outside of that process undermines this tenet. Thus, the APA's formal-hearing provisions prohibit any "interested person outside the agency" from making an "ex parte communication relevant to the merits of the proceeding" with an ALJ or other employee "involved in the decisional process of the proceeding."[49] The prohibition applies (though is not limited) to representatives but does not provide for any sanctions on representatives. The only remedy the statute specifies is dismissal or denial of a claim.[50]

Nevertheless, 27 federal agencies have adopted a rule that applies the prohibition on ex parte communication to representatives. The rules of many of those agencies expressly provide for sanctions against representatives who violate the rule.[51] Other agencies have adopted rules that, like the APA, apply to both parties and representatives but expressly state consequences only for parties.[52] Some of these agencies could, however, potentially use their rules requiring representatives to adhere to agency rules to sanction ex parte communication.

13.52 Disruptive Conduct

Like ex parte communication, conduct intended to disrupt a proceeding before a tribunal also undermines due process in adjudication. The duty to avoid disruptive conduct is captured in ABA Model Rule 3.5(d), which states that a lawyer shall not "engage in conduct intended to disrupt a tribunal." Although the APA does not expressly address disruptive conduct, the rules of many agencies do, often referring to

---

48. *See, e.g.*, 17 C.F.R. § 201.102(e)(1)(iii) (2022) (SEC); 20 C.F.R. §§ 404.1740(a)(2), 416.1470(c)(9) (2022) (SSA); 29 C.F.R. § 18.23(a)(1)(iii) (2022) (DOL).

49. 5 U.S.C. § 557(d)(1)(A).

50. *Id.* § 557(d)(1)(D).

51. *See, e.g.*, 17 C.F.R. § 201.114(a) (2022) (SEC); 20 C.F.R. §§ 404.1740(c)(7)(ii)(C), 416.1540(c)(7)(ii)(C) (2022) (SSA); 29 C.F.R. § 18.87(b) (2022) (DOL).

52. *See, e.g.*, 7 C.F.R. §§ 1.151(b), 1.316, 15.68, 110.8(n) (2022) (USDA); 38 C.F.R. § 18b.92 (2022) (VA).

the prohibited conduct using such colorful terms as "contumacious" or "contumelious."[53] In fact, rules prohibiting disruptive conduct by representatives are, along with rules prohibiting ex parte communication, the most common professional conduct rules in federal agencies, with an equal number of agencies (27) having these rules. Some of these agencies have both rules, while others have only one or the other.

13.53 Frivolous Claims

Related to the problem of disruptive conduct is the problem of frivolous claims, which waste the time and effort of agencies and cause delay for those with meritorious claims. For lawyers practicing in federal courts, the main rule governing frivolous claims is Rule 11 of the Federal Rules of Civil Procedure. ABA Model Rule 3.1 contains a similar prohibition. Twenty-one federal agencies have rules prohibiting the filing of frivolous claims.[54]

13.54 Obstruction of Justice

The next most common topic addressed by federal agency representative rules concerns obstruction of justice. Obstruction of justice covers a broad array of conduct that interferes with the due administration of justice, including disruptive conduct (see section 13.52), and is not limited to conduct in adjudication. In fact, ABA Model Rule 8.4(d), which states that "[i]t is professional misconduct for a lawyer to . . . engage in conduct that is prejudicial to the administration of justice," appears not with the other adjudication rules, but in a group of rules on "Maintaining the Integrity of the Profession" more broadly. Nineteen agencies have rules prohibiting similar conduct in adjudications[55] or in related contexts such as investigations.[56]

---

53. *See, e.g.*, 7 C.F.R. §§ 1.141(d)(1), 1.328(a)(3), 110.8(h)(4) (2022) (USDA); 8 C.F.R. § 1003.102(g) (2022) (DHS); 18 C.F.R. § 385.2012(b) (2022) (FERC); 20 C.F.R. §§ 404.1740(c)(7)(ii), 416.1540(c)(7)(ii) (2022); 29 C.F.R. §§ 18.22(d)(4), 18.87(b) (2022) (DOL); 38 C.F.R. §§ 18b.15, 18b.90 (2022) (VA).

54. *See, e.g.*, 7 C.F.R. § 1.303(a)(1) (2022) (USDA); 8 C.F.R. § 1003.102(j), (u) (2022) (DHS); 29 C.F.R. § 18.35 (2022) (DOL); 38 C.F.R. § 14.633(c)(4) (2022) (VA).

55. *See, e.g.*, 8 C.F.R. § 1003.102(n) (2022) (DHS); 20 C.F.R. § 404.1740(c)(7) (2022) (SSA); 29 C.F.R. § 18.22(d)(4) (2022) (DOL); 38 C.F.R. § 14.632(c)(9) (2022) (VA).

56. *See, e.g.*, 18 C.F.R. § 1b.16(c)(4) (2022) (FERC).

13.55 Delay

Another related form of adjudicative misconduct is delay, which is inconsistent with the general adjudicative goals of speedy, efficient, and just resolution of proceedings. ABA Model Rule 3.2 captures this concern by requiring a lawyer to "make reasonable efforts to expedite litigation consistent with the interests of the client." Seventeen agencies have rules prohibiting delay, though they are more likely to define an unreasonable delay as one lacking a "good cause" rather than as one that is inconsistent with the interests of the representative's client.[57]

13.56 Other Topics

Agency rules applicable to representatives cover a variety of other topics, but most of these topics are included in the rules of fewer than ten agencies. The most common additional topics dealing specifically with adjudication are candor toward the tribunal (false statements and false evidence),[58] covered in rules adopted by 15 agencies, and improper influence of a judge or other official,[59] covered in rules adopted by ten agencies. Additional topics covered by rules of at least ten agencies, but not specifically directed at representative conduct in adjudication, include communication,[60] conflicts of interest,[61] and truthfulness in statements to third parties (often limited to false statements to agency representatives).[62]

---

57. *See, e.g.*, 7 C.F.R. § 1.328(a)(2) (2022) (USDA); 8 C.F.R. § 1003.102(l) (2022) (DHS); 20 C.F.R. §§ 404.1740(c)(4), 416.1540(c)(4) (2022) (SSA); 29 C.F.R. §§ 18.22(d)(3), 18.87(b) (2022) (DOL); 38 C.F.R. § 14.632(c)(7) (2022) (VA).

58. *See, e.g.*, 8 C.F.R. § 1003.102(c) (2022) (DHS); 20 C.F.R. § 404.1740(c)(3) (2022) (SSA); 29 C.F.R. § 18.22(d)(2) (2022) (DOL); 38 C.F.R. § 14.632(a)(2) (2022) (VA).

59. *See, e.g.*, 8 C.F.R. § 1003.102(b) (2022) (DHS); 20 C.F.R. § 404.1740(c)(6) (2022) (SSA); 29 C.F.R. § 18.22(d)(1) (2022) (DOL).

60. *See, e.g.*, 8 C.F.R. § 1003.102(r) (2022) (DHS); 20 C.F.R. § 404.1740(b)(3)(v) (2022) (SSA).

61. *See, e.g.*, 12 C.F.R. §§ 109.8(a) (2022) (OCC), 263.8(a) (2022) (FRB), 308.8(a) (2022) (FDIC), 747.8(a) (2022) (NCUA), 1081.109(a) (2022) (CFPB), 1209.73 (2022) (FHFA); 31 C.F.R. §§ 8.40 (2022) (BATFE), 10.29 (2022) (IRS), 501.704(d) (2022) (Office of Foreign Assets Control); 49 C.F.R. § 1103.16(b) (2022) (STB).

62. *See, e.g.*, 12 C.F.R. § 263.94(b) (2022) (FRB); 16 C.F.R. § 4.1(e)(1)(i)(D) (2022) (FTC).

13.6 IMPLEMENTATION AND ENFORCEMENT OF THE RULES

In addition to promulgating rules specifying the appropriate conduct of representatives appearing before the agencies, agencies also address various aspects of implementation and enforcement of their rules. Agencies often have rules that specify enforcement procedures against representatives (section 13.61). A few publish disciplinary orders on their website or elsewhere (section 13.62). Agencies may also make or receive referrals to or from other disciplinary authorities (section 13.63). Finally, many agencies provide for reciprocal discipline when a representative (usually an attorney) has been disciplined by another regulatory authority (section 13.64).

13.61 Procedures for Enforcement

Agencies with rules regulating representative conduct often include procedural rules for enforcing the conduct rules, including who within the agency is responsible for initiating formal charges, who makes the initial determination, and who can hear appeals.

Some agency rules provide little procedural detail concerning how they enforce their conduct rules, other than to identify who within the agency enforces them, which is typically an ALJ. Agencies taking this minimalist approach include the Department of Agriculture,[63] the SEC,[64] and DOL.[65] Unlike these agencies, the VA puts the initial responsibility for cancelling accreditation in the hands of the general counsel, who must find a violation by "clear and convincing evidence." The general counsel's decision is a "final adjudicative determination" that may be appealed only to the Board of Veterans' Appeals.[66]

The NLRB is an example of an agency with a more detailed set of enforcement procedures. The NLRB gives an ALJ, a hearing officer, or the board authority on their own to "admonish or reprimand" a representative who engages in misconduct at a hearing. More formal proceedings can be triggered by any person, including an ALJ or the board itself, filing an allegation, which sets in motion a more elaborate set of procedures. An investigating officer, who is generally the head of the Division of Operations–Management, conducts an investigation and

63. 7 C.F.R. §§ 1.26(b)(2), 1.141(d)(1), 1.151(d), 1.328(a), 110.8(h)(3) (2022).
64. 17 C.F.R. §§ 201.102(e)(1), 205.6(a) (2022).
65. 29 C.F.R. § 18.23(a)(2) (2022).
66. 38 C.F.R. § 14.633 (2022).

makes a recommendation to the general counsel. If the general counsel decides to go forward with disciplinary proceedings, the accused representative is served with a formal complaint, given an opportunity to answer, and given a public hearing before an ALJ. Prior to the hearing, a settlement may be reached with the general counsel. The settlement must be approved by the ALJ and, if disciplinary action is included, the board. If the hearing goes forward and misconduct is found, the board may then issue a final order imposing sanctions. The sanctioned practitioner may then seek judicial review.[67]

13.62 Publication of Disciplinary Orders

Some agencies publish orders imposing discipline or sanctions on a representative, though they vary in the level of detail provided and where they publish the orders. The SEC and USPTO, for example, regularly publish on their websites disciplinary orders that include information about the grounds for discipline.[68] EOIR publishes lists on its website of currently and previously disciplined practitioners but not the grounds for discipline.[69] SSA also regularly discloses lists of sanctioned representatives in its online Freedom of Information Act Reading Room. Like the EOIR list, SSA lists do not state the grounds for discipline. Many other agencies do not publish disciplinary orders or post lists of sanctioned representatives. ACUS has recently recommended that agencies consider publishing disciplinary actions, or summaries of them, on their websites.[70]

13.63 Referrals

Some agency rules provide for referral to another disciplinary authority, either in addition to, or instead of, disciplinary action by an agency. In the case of lawyer representatives, agencies may make referrals to state disciplinary authorities in jurisdictions where the lawyer is licensed to practice. Agencies sometimes also receive referrals concerning lawyer misconduct *from* state disciplinary authorities.

---

67. 29 C.F.R. § 102.177 (2022).

68. *Administrative Proceedings*, SEC, https://www.sec.gov/litigation/admin.htm (last modified June 27, 2023) (search "Respondents" for "Esq."); *Decisions of the Office of Enrollment and Discipline*, USPTO, https://foiadocuments.uspto.gov/oed/ (last visited June 27, 2023).

69. *Attorney Discipline Program*, DOJ, EOIR, https://www.justice.gov/eoir/attorney-discipline-program (last updated June 12, 2019).

70. Administrative Conference Recommendation 2021-9, *supra* note 4, ¶ 14.

Agencies take different approaches to the question of referral. For example, DOL has a mandatory referral rule that applies whenever it disqualifies an attorney representative. The rule requires the chief judge to provide a copy of the decision and order not only to the jurisdictions in which the attorney is licensed to practice but also to the National Lawyer Regulatory Data Bank maintained by the ABA Standing Committee on Professional Discipline.[71] The VA has a permissive referral rule, which states: "In cases where the accreditation of an agent or attorney is cancelled, the Office of the General Counsel may notify all agencies, courts, and bars to which the agent or attorney is admitted to practice."[72] DHS and EOIR have a more complicated referral rule that mandates reporting of a final administrative decision imposing sanctions against a practitioner but merely permits the referral of a complaint filed against a practitioner.[73] (Both agencies also have rules requiring referral to each other.[74]) The NLRB has a policy of notifying the appropriate state bar of disciplinary sanctions it imposes on attorneys but has chosen not to formalize the policy in a rule.[75] Still other agencies have neither a rule nor a practice of making referrals.

13.64 Reciprocal Discipline

Reciprocal discipline takes place when an agency imposes discipline on a representative based on prior discipline imposed on the representative by another disciplinary authority. An attorney disciplined in another jurisdiction would not be "in good standing" in that jurisdiction and therefore would not be entitled to practice before an agency under 5 U.S.C. § 500(b), unless, perhaps, the lawyer remains in good standing in another jurisdiction.[76]

Although most agencies with rules regulating representative conduct do not have reciprocal discipline rules, a significant number do.[77] Indeed, reciprocal discipline may be the most common form of agency

71. 29 C.F.R. § 18.23(b) (2022).

72. 38 C.F.R. § 14.633(i) (2022).

73. 8 C.F.R. §§ 292.3(g) (2022) (DHS), 1003.106(d) (2022) (EOIR).

74. *Id.* §§ 292.3(d)(1), (e)(3) (DHS), 1003.105(b) (EOIR).

75. 61 Fed. Reg. 65,323, 65,330–31 (Dec. 12, 1996).

76. *See* Chaganti v. Lee, 187 F. Supp. 3d 682, 693 (E.D. Va. 2016) (finding that "the decisions of other state bars are irrelevant to the PTO's decision whether to impose reciprocal discipline in accordance with its own standards").

77. 12 C.F.R. §§ 263.94(d), (g) (2022) (FRB), 308.109(b)(1) (2022) (FDIC); 17 C.F.R. §§ 14.6 (2022) (CFTC), 201.102(e)(2) (2022) (SEC); 29 C.F.R. §§ 18.22(b)(1), 18.23(a)(1) (2022) (DOL); 31 C.F.R. § 8.52(h) (2022) (BATFE); 37 C.F.R.

discipline.[78] Significant variation exists among these rules. Some expressly require attorney representatives to self-report disciplinary actions imposed on them elsewhere.[79] Some reciprocal discipline rules are mandatory[80]—meaning that the agency must disbar or suspend an attorney who has been disbarred or suspended elsewhere—whereas others are discretionary.[81] One agency, SSA, provides detailed guidance on how an ALJ should exercise that discretion.[82]

One important issue raised by reciprocal discipline is due process. An important precedent within DHS requires the agency, before imposing reciprocal discipline, to "include the opportunity [for the practitioner] to show that the [previous] state order was based on an invalid procedure or patently inadequate evidence."[83] In addition, the USPTO has a rule allowing a representative to challenge reciprocal discipline based on due process or related concerns with the prior discipline.[84]

---

§ 11.804(h) (2022) (USPTO); 38 C.F.R. §§ 14.629(b)(5), 14.633(c)(5) (2022) (VA); 43 C.F.R. § 1.6(a) (2022) (DOI); 47 C.F.R. § 1.24(c) (2022) (FCC).

78. Jon J. Lee, *Double Standards: An Empirical Study of Patent and Trademark Discipline*, 61 B.C. L. Rev. 1613, 1659 (2020).

79. *See, e.g.*, 8 C.F.R. §§ 292.3(c)(4) (2022) (DHS), 1003.103(c) (2022) (EOIR); 20 C.F.R. § 404.1740(b)(7)–(9) (2022) (SSA); 29 C.F.R. § 18.22(b)(1)(iii) (2022) (DOL); 37 C.F.R. § 11.24 (2022) (USPTO).

80. *See, e.g.*, 17 C.F.R. § 201.102(e)(2) (2022) (SEC); 38 C.F.R. § 14.633(c)(5) (2022) (VA).

81. *See, e.g.*, 29 C.F.R. § 18.22(b)(1)(ii) (2022) (DOL).

82. 20 C.F.R. § 404.1770(a)(2) (2022).

83. *In re* Bogart, 15 I. & N. Dec. 552 (1976).

84. 37 C.F.R. § 11.24(d)(1)(i)–(iv) (2022).

Chapter 14
Access to Justice

Stefanie K. Davis

14.1 CHAPTER OVERVIEW

Bar associations, court organizations, and national and international bodies have all attempted to define "access to justice." The American Bar Association views "access to justice" as "[the] ability to access the courts and legal representation, [as well as] to engage effectively with law enforcement officials and [] make use of informal, non-state justice mechanisms."[1] The Texas Access to Justice Commission defines "access to justice" as "the ability of any person, regardless of income, to advocate for themselves and their interests."[2] The United Nations General Assembly describes "access to justice" as a right that can be exercised through "fair, transparent, effective, non-discriminatory and accountable services," including informal justice mechanisms conducted in accordance with international human rights law.[3] Although each of these organizations views "access to justice" in somewhat different terms, they all emphasize the importance of fair processes in which every individual can meaningfully participate to protect their rights.

Although the justice gap is often discussed in the context of judicial processes, it is equally important in the context of federal agency

1. *Human Rights and Access to Justice*, AM. BAR ASS'N, https://www.americanbar.org/advocacy/rule_of_law/what-we-do/human-rights-access-to-justice/ (last visited June 27, 2023).

2. *What Is Access to Justice?*, TEX. ACCESS TO JUST. COMM'N, https://www.texasatj.org/what-access-justice (last visited June 27, 2023).

3. G.A. Res. 67/1, ¶¶ 14–16 (Sept. 24, 2012).

adjudication. Because federal administrative agencies decide many questions regarding income support, health care, educational support, and other basic building blocks of life, they play a significant role in maintaining individuals' physical, emotional, and economic well-being. Each administrative agency decision—at the initial application stage and throughout the appeals process—has the potential to either improve or, unfortunately, materially damage an individual's physical and mental well-being and financial stability.

Just as in the courts, individuals often face complex processes and highly technical standards when they seek to access benefits, services, and other programs administered by federal agencies. The adjudicative processes they must navigate involve procedural and substantive issues that are unfamiliar to many individuals who are not attorneys, such as the timing and format for filing appeals, the standards they must satisfy to qualify for benefits, and the kinds of evidence needed to meet those standards. Fairness dictates that all parties to a case can proceed to reach resolution rather than be excluded from the adjudicative process for technical errors. Because the stakes are so high, it is critical that individuals have access to people and materials that can help them navigate the adjudicatory process in a way that ensures a fair outcome. This is the essence of access to justice in federal agency adjudication.

Some access-to-justice principles are embedded in constitutional due process, federal statutes, and presidential directives (section 14.2). But agencies can also take voluntary steps to make adjudicatory proceedings more accessible to and equitable for all. To the extent that agencies do not focus on ensuring procedural and substantive justice throughout adjudicative processes, they fail to provide the access to justice that vulnerable parties need and deserve. More to the point, they fail to ensure a fair consideration of parties' eligibility for the benefits they need to survive. Agency decision-makers should review their adjudication policies and procedures, as well as their external-facing materials, to ensure that all potential parties can meaningfully participate in adjudicative processes and obtain a fair result. And advocates should engage with parties and agency decision-makers to promote and design procedures that ensure meaningful access to agency programs and processes.

There are many strategies for improving access to justice in federal agency adjudication. One strategy is to take steps to expand access to legal representation. Research has shown that legal representation results in faster, more efficient processes and improved outcomes for parties.[4] More lawyers, however, are not the only solution to increasing access to justice. Other strategies include:

- Ensuring that agency materials are accessible, such as by drafting them using plain language at a base literacy level and providing them in as many languages and access modalities as possible
- Engaging beneficiaries to redesign application forms and website materials ("participatory design") and using "design sprints" to incrementally identify and eliminate obstacles to fair and efficient adjudication
- Enhancing personal assistance available to parties, such as by encouraging lay representation, or providing navigators at early stages of application and adjudication processes, and offering self-help materials

Participatory design, design sprints, and personal assistance are discussed in greater detail in sections 14.3 and 14.4. This chapter concludes with a case study of how one agency—the Department of Veterans Affairs (VA)—has put these strategies into practice (section 14.5).

The goal of these strategies is to ensure meaningful, informed participation by parties and efficient processes that lead to fair outcomes. Adoption of these strategies can improve not only the efficiency of agency processes but also the public's perception of their fairness and trustworthiness, which is critical to maintaining the rule of law and the faith of individuals in the government that serves them.

Although this chapter focuses primarily on access to justice for applicants for benefits, the principles it discusses may apply to other contexts in which individuals appear before federal adjudicatory bodies. For example, it may be appropriate for the Department of Justice (DOJ) to consider providing self-help resources to individuals who file qui tam cases under the False Claims Act. Through its Office of Legal

---

4. *See, e.g.*, JUST. IN GOV'T PROJECT, AM. UNIV., KEY STUDIES AND DATA ABOUT HOW LEGAL AID IMPROVES HOUSING OUTCOMES 1–2 (2021), https://legalaidresourcesdotorg.files.wordpress.com/2021/04/housing.pdf; LAURA K. ABEL, ECONOMIC BENEFITS OF CIVIL LEGAL AID 1 (2012), https://ncforaj.files.wordpress.com/2012/09/final-economic-benefits-of-legal-aid-9-5-2012.pdf; Rebecca L. Sandefur, *The Impact of Counsel: An Analysis of Empirical Evidence*, 9 SEATTLE J. FOR SOC. JUST. 51 (2010) [hereinafter Sandefur, *The Impact of Counsel*]. *But see* Rebecca L. Sandefur, *Access to What?*, DÆDALUS, Winter 2019, at 49, 52 [hereinafter Sandefur, *Access to What?*].

Access Programs, DOJ already works to "improve the efficiency of immigration court hearings by increasing access to information and raising the level of representation for individuals appearing before the immigration courts and the Board of Immigration Appeals (BIA)."[5] DOJ could further supplement these efforts by seeking feedback from attorneys, accredited representatives, and self-represented individuals on the fairness of the proceedings and the quality of assistance provided, if they do not already do so.

14.2 LEGAL FOUNDATIONS

Two seminal Court cases, *Goldberg v. Kelly* and *Mathews v. Eldridge*, stand for the proposition that access to justice is a necessary component of many administrative adjudications. The U.S. Supreme Court held in both cases that due process requires that, before making a final decision to deprive an individual of the economic support necessary to survive, an agency must provide the individual notice, a fair hearing before an impartial adjudicator, and the opportunity to present evidence and examine witnesses.[6] In *Mathews*, the Supreme Court succinctly stated the baseline level of process required by the Constitution in administrative agency adjudications: "[T]he procedures [must] be tailored, in light of the decision to be made, to 'the capacities and circumstances of those who are to be heard,' . . . to insure that they are given a meaningful opportunity to present their case."[7] The central principle of that case remains: Congress and agencies should develop a range of tools to enable the greatest number of parties to meaningfully participate in the adjudicative process through procedural mechanisms including notice, a fair hearing, and the opportunity to present and rebut evidence.

Some researchers and legal organizations have suggested that procedural justice, in contrast to mere procedural due process, requires agencies to provide parties with a regular, clearly defined process for seeking relief.[8] Such a process may include agency support to obtain

---

5. *Office of Legal Access Programs*, DOJ, Exec. Off. for Immigr. Rev., https://www.justice.gov/eoir/office-of-legal-access-programs (last updated Apr. 24, 2023).

6. Goldberg v. Kelly, 397 U.S. 254, 266–71 (1970); Mathews v. Eldridge, 424 U.S. 319 (1976).

7. *Mathews*, 424 U.S. at 349 (internal citation omitted).

8. *See, e.g.*, Hague Inst. for Innovation of L. & Inst. for the Advancement of the Am. Legal Sys., Justice Needs and Satisfaction in the United States of America: Legal Problems in Daily Life 132–33 (2021), https://iaals

legal representation or lay navigators to help parties understand and move through the steps of the appeals process. It may also include developing websites, self-help resources, and forms in language that can be understood by individuals at basic literacy levels and formats that make information available to individuals with visual or auditory disabilities.

Numerous statutes incorporate these principles. The Rehabilitation Act requires agencies to accommodate individuals with disabilities.[9] The Plain Writing Act of 2010 requires federal agencies to use clear language that the public can understand.[10] In response, many agencies have created their own guidance for internal drafters to use when writing regulatory or policy documents. The National Archives, for example, has developed a plain-writing checklist, style guide, principles of plain language, and other tools for drafting new forms, web pages, and policies that can be understood easily by any reader.[11]

Several executive orders also require agencies to create more equitable adjudicative processes. For example, Executive Order No. 12,988, Civil Justice Reform, directed agencies to review their internal adjudication procedures and identify areas for improvement. The order required agencies to improve their procedures to reduce delay, increase access to counsel and nonlawyer assistance, facilitate self-help options, and authorize decision-makers to exercise discretion to encourage settlement of disputes at the earliest available opportunity.[12] Executive Order No. 13,166 required agencies to accommodate individuals with limited English proficiency.[13] Most recently, Executive Order No. 14,058, Transforming Federal Customer Experience and Service Delivery to Rebuild Trust in Government, directed agencies

---

.du.edu/sites/default/files/documents/publications/justice-needs-and-satisfaction-us.pdf; AGE PLATFORM EUROPE ET AL., ACCESS TO JUSTICE: A DISCUSSION PAPER FOR THE 11TH SESSION OF THE UNITED NATIONS GENERAL ASSEMBLY OPEN-ENDED WORKING GROUP OF AGEING 10, 12 (2020), https://social.un.org/ageing-working-group/documents/eleventh/Discussion%20paper%20on%20access%20to%20justice%20January%202020.pdf; Sandefur, *Access to What?*, *supra* note 4, at 50.

9. 29 U.S.C. § 794d.

10. 5 U.S.C. § 301 note.

11. *Plain Writing at the National Archives*, U.S. NAT'L ARCHIVES & RECS. ADMIN., https://www.archives.gov/open/plain-writing (last reviewed Apr. 21, 2023).

12. 61 Fed. Reg. 4,729 (Feb. 5, 1996).

13. 65 Fed. Reg. 50,121 (Aug. 16, 2000); *see also* Exec. Order No. 13,985, 86 Fed. Reg. 7,009 (Jan. 25, 2021).

to "understand[] their customers, reduce administrative hurdles and paperwork burdens to minimize 'time taxes,' enhance transparency, [and] redesign compliance-oriented processes to improve customer experience and more directly meet the needs of the people of the United States." In that executive order, the president directed agencies that provide benefits and services to large numbers of individuals to evaluate their customer service using multiple strategies, including public engagement and human-centered design methodologies.[14]

Of course, agencies have discretion to take steps to make adjudicatory proceedings more accessible to and equitable for all. Strategies agencies can adopt include participatory design and design sprints (section 14.3) and enhancing personal assistance (section 14.4). The efforts of one agency, the VA, are discussed in section 14.5.

14.3 PARTICIPATORY DESIGN AND DESIGN SPRINTS

One strategy for improving access to justice in federal agency adjudication is participatory design, or intentionally engaging users of a process or system to identify and resolve inefficiencies in an existing system or to develop a user-driven process when a new process is needed to address an issue. Participatory design "asks people who are meant to use a system's services to help identify where it needs to be reformed, define what 'better' operation would look like, and design new interventions to reform it."[15] This type of process includes consumers—in this context, parties—as members of the team designing a new or redesigning an existing process to better serve the goals of procedural and substantive due process. Benefits of participatory design include identifying obstacles users encountered throughout a process and obtaining their suggestions for eliminating the obstacles; identifying the modalities, such as remote hearings, that users reported being most beneficial to their participation in the appeals process; and improving user perception of the accessibility and fairness of the process.[16]

A second, related strategy is adapting the software development concept of design sprints—short, intensely focused problem-solving sessions—to identify and eliminate obstacles to efficient and fair resolution of parties' cases. Adapted from the software development

14. 86 Fed. Reg. 71,357 (Dec. 13, 2021).

15. Margaret Hagan, *Participatory Design for Innovations in Access to Justice*, DÆDALUS, Winter 2019, at 122.

16. *Id.* at 120, 122.

field, design sprints are short bursts of development, design, creation, and testing.[17] By their nature, design sprints are brief and intended to address discrete aspects of a process, rather than to build or overhaul an entire process. An advantage of design sprints is that they result in incremental change, thus taking small, manageable steps to improve a process and generate increased user trust in the process. This style of process improvement may work well for agencies, which have many competing priorities and responsibilities in addition to administering fair, efficient adjudicative processes.

With both participatory design and design sprints, a thoughtful, consumer-focused approach is likely to improve not only substantive access to justice, but also parties' perceptions of agency fairness and trustworthiness.

Some researchers are applying participatory design and design sprint principles to improve court processes. For example, the Stanford Legal Design Lab and the Institute for the Advancement of the American Legal System at the University of Denver collaborated on a project to redesign the judicial divorce process. Participants included former litigants in divorce cases, court staff, and attorneys. The project consisted of "workshops in which participants reflected on the processes and experiences they went through, and then generated new concepts" for court rules and service changes. The design team will use the feedback in the project's next phase to design court interventions based on the priorities identified by the former litigants.[18]

A similar project is currently underway in New Mexico. Faculty and students in the Community Lawyering Clinic at the University of New Mexico School of Law have adapted the design sprint model to identify and develop solutions to problems experienced by litigants. The goal of the project is to develop a solution to one barrier to participating in the judicial process faced by litigants. Clinic personnel engaged attendees at the State Bar of New Mexico Annual Meeting to identify barriers to participation in court processes. Attendees identified a range of barriers, including a lack of access to transportation and child care, before collectively selecting child care as the barrier to

17. Inst. for the Advancement of the Am. Legal Sys., Listen > Learn > Lead: A Guide to Improving Court Services through User-Centered Design 1 (2019), https://iaals.du.edu/sites/default/files/documents/publications/listen-learn-lead_improving_court_services.pdf; U.S. Digit. Serv., Digital Services Playbook, https://playbook.cio.gov/ (last visited June 27, 2023).

18. Hagan, *supra* note 15, at 148.

address. Clinic personnel are identifying stakeholders to participate in the next round of the sprint, which will focus on brainstorming solutions for ensuring that litigants have access to child care at critical points in their cases before narrowing the options down to one solution to develop into a prototype.[19] This project is a practical example of engaging stakeholders to identify and make discrete changes to an existing process, which may be of interest to agencies considering ways to simplify their adjudication proceedings for the benefit of the user.

Participatory design is not foreign to the federal government. The U.S. Digital Service (USDS) published a "playbook" for creating digital services that includes many principles of participatory design. In Play 1, "Understand What People Need," the USDS instructs agencies to spend time with current and prospective users of the service as early as possible in the design process. In Play 3, "Make It Simple and Intuitive," the USDS includes several points directed at enhancing the user experience. These points include using simplified design styles and best practices in accessibility; making clear to users what step of the process they are in while working through the test; and providing users with a way to exit the process and return without losing their progress.[20] Alternatively, agencies can develop approaches that work well for their unique adjudicative bodies and the populations they serve.

14.4 PERSONAL ASSISTANCE

Access to personal assistance as early as possible in the adjudication process may increase both fairness and efficiency. Individual help may come in the form of legal representation, assistance from a family member or nonattorney experienced in the administrative adjudication process, agency-provided navigators, and self-help materials. Research has demonstrated improved outcomes for parties who have representation or personal assistance as they proceed through the adjudicatory process.[21]

---

19. Interview with Prof. Verónica Gonzales-Zamora and Eve Wakeland, U.N.M. School of Law (Oct. 27, 2021). Author note: I participated in the initial session of this project.

20. U.S. Digit. Serv., *supra* note 17. Notably, the USDS highlighted the VA Digital Service's work to create a plain-language, online tool for veterans with less-than-honorable discharges to apply for discharge upgrades. *See Helping Veterans Upgrade Their Discharge Status*, USDS, https://www.usds.gov/projects/discharge-upgrade-tool (last visited June 27, 2023).

21. *See supra* note 4.

Individual representation is often the primary way people think of ensuring access to justice. Many people understand the Sixth Amendment right to counsel as a fundamental right of Americans, but the right extends only to defendants in criminal cases. Most civil defendants and parties in administrative proceedings are not entitled to counsel.[22] The lack of a right to counsel means that many individuals seeking to obtain or maintain desperately needed financial support in the form of government programs for low-income individuals or benefits that they have earned through military service do not have the support they need to ensure financial security.[23]

Lawyers are valuable advocates, to be sure. As professionals trained in the law, attorneys are particularly well suited to helping parties understand complex adjudicative processes. In fact, research suggests that lawyers add value in two principal ways: their ability to navigate complex processes and their presence, which prompts the government fact finder to follow its own rules more closely.[24]

But in some instances, nonattorneys may also play critical roles in helping parties proceed through the adjudicative process. Research suggests that, in certain circumstances, parties who are represented or assisted by a nonlawyer have an equal or better chance of succeeding than either unrepresented parties or even parties assisted by an attorney.[25] For example, studies conducted in the United States and the United Kingdom concluded that lay advocates who had developed practical expertise in unemployment compensation appeals, social security disability compensation appeals, immigration proceedings, and mental health review tribunals represented appellants more effectively than attorneys lacking similar expertise.[26] Anecdotally, attorneys who have worked with limited license legal technicians—nonlawyer professionals who have received highly specialized training in one area of law, such as family law—reported that the technicians' training "allow[s

---

22. Legal Servs. Corp., The Justice Gap: The Unmet Civil Legal Needs of Low-Income Americans 14 (2022), https://lsc-live.app.box.com/s/xl2v2uraiotbbzrhuwtjlgi0emp3myz1 (prepared by Mary C. Slosar, Slosar Research, LLC).

23. *Id.* at 38 (finding that 50 percent of respondents reported that legal issues related to income maintenance impacted their lives "very much" or "severely").

24. Sandefur, *The Impact of Counsel*, *supra* note 4, at 73.

25. *Id.*

26. Rebecca L. Sandefur, *Legal Advice from Nonlawyers: Consumer Demand, Provider Quality, and Public Harms*, 16 Stan. J. C.R. & C.L. 283, 304 (2020).

them] to provide competent representation from day one."[27] As discussed in Chapter 13, agencies often have broad discretion to permit nonlawyers to practice before them, which can help expand the pool of qualified professionals available to represent or assist parties.

The onus of finding assistance need not fall on the parties seeking government benefits. In some jurisdictions, navigator programs exist to help unrepresented litigants negotiate their way through the proceedings to which they are parties. Navigators are generally defined as individuals who

- do not have formal legal credentials and training, but who are specially trained to help self-represented litigants with basic civil legal problems;
- do not establish an attorney-client relationship with the litigants they assist; and
- operate through a formal program under institutional auspices, which may be the state access to justice commission, a nonprofit organization, or the court itself.[28]

Navigators do not represent individuals or provide them with legal advice. Rather, their role is to guide litigants as they complete forms necessary to proceed with their case, help them to understand the court process, and provide support throughout the court process. Research has shown that, as with lawyers and nonlawyer advocates, having access to a navigator is likely to improve self-represented individuals' case outcomes and perceptions of fairness in court proceedings.[29]

---

27. Jason Solomon & Noelle Smith, Stan. Ctr. on the Legal Pro., The Surprising Success of Washington State's Limited License Legal Technician Program 12 (2021), https://law.stanford.edu/wp-content/uploads/2021/04/LLLT-White-Paper-Final-5-4-21.pdf.

28. *See, e.g.*, Mary E. McClymont, Just. Lab at Geo. L., Nonlawyer Navigators in State Courts: An Emerging Consensus 11–12 (2019), https://cdm16501.contentdm.oclc.org/digital/collection/accessfair/id/861; Administrative Order of the Chief Administrative Judge of the Courts, AO/42/14 (Feb. 10, 2014), https://www.nycourts.gov/courts/nyc/SSI/pdfs/AO-42-14.pdf; *see also* Supreme Court of the State of Alaska Order No. 1994 (adopted Nov. 29, 2022) (creating waiver to state unauthorized practice rules for community justice workers trained and supervised by attorneys employed by the Alaska Legal Services Corporation).

29. *See, e.g.* McClymont *supra* note 28, at 34–35; Rebecca L. Sandefur & Thomas Clarke, Roles beyond Lawyers: Summary, Recommendations, and Research Report of an Evaluation of the New York City Court Navigators Program and Its Three Pilot Projects 32–33, 36–39 (2016), https://www.americanbarfoundation.org/wp-content/uploads/2023/05/new

Taken together, this evidence suggests that some level of assistance to parties creates a more equitable, efficient process for agency adjudication. Although agencies may not have the funding or personnel to provide this type of assistance themselves, they can provide parties with online or other resources to obtain representation.

A final approach to providing personal assistance to parties in administrative proceedings is making self-help materials available. Self-help materials can come in a variety of forms ranging from printed or printable step-by-step guides to filling out forms and submitting them to the agency, to websites containing information about the administrative process, to videos and interactive games showing the steps of the administrative process.[30] Several state courts have created websites with plain-language information about procedures in some of the most common types of cases in which litigants represent themselves—including housing, child custody and support, and debt collection cases—that may serve as models for agencies wishing to develop similar resources.[31] In the federal agency context, the Executive Office for Immigration Review has adapted self-help guidance documents produced by nonprofit organizations to help individuals in immigration proceedings understand the steps and forms used in the removal process, as well as potential avenues for immigration relief.[32]

For self-help materials to have the greatest chance of increasing efficiency and procedural fairness in agency proceedings, they should be designed with the consumer in mind and with the input of the consumer community. As described in the following section, the VA's efforts to improve its application and adjudication processes substantially incorporate this principle.

_york_city_court_navigators_report_final_with_final_links_december_2016.pdf.

30. *See, e.g.*, Self-Represented Litig. Network, Best Practices in Court-Based Programs for the Self-Represented: Concepts, Attributes, Issues for Exploration, Examples, Contacts, and Resources (2008 ed.), https://www.srln.org/system/files/attachments/SRLN%20Best%20Practices%20Guide%20%282008%29.pdf/.

31. *See, e.g.*, *Self-Represented Litigants*, Tex. Just. Ct. Training Ctr., https://www.tjctc.org/SRL (last visited June 27, 2023); *Self-Help Guide to the California Courts*, Jud. Branch of Cal., https://selfhelp.courts.ca.gov/ (last visited June 27, 2023); *Self-Help: Represent Yourself*, Alaska Ct. Sys., https://courts.alaska.gov/shc/index.htm (last visited June 27, 2023).

32. *Self-Help Materials*, DOJ, Exec. Off. for Immigr. Rev., https://www.justice.gov/eoir/self-help-materials (last updated July 18, 2022).

14.5 CASE STUDY: THE DEPARTMENT OF VETERANS AFFAIRS

The VA has made significant efforts to improve its adjudicatory and other public-facing processes. The agency has undertaken several initiatives in recent years to improve veterans' experiences when engaging with the VA. One of these initiatives is surveying veterans who interacted with the VA about their experiences. The VA surveys veterans about 85 different areas of engagement with the agency, ranging from their experience going to a VA health center in person, to whether the veteran understood the information presented to them by a physician, to whether the veteran was satisfied with their hearing in front of the Board of Veterans' Appeals (BVA).[33]

Another strategy is reading comments about veterans' experiences with the VA posted on various social media sites. The VA gleans comments and forwards them to the relevant agency components to identify where veterans are facing obstacles to obtaining care or benefits and to develop solutions to eliminate those barriers.[34] The VA has used this feedback to improve the readability of its documents and its methods of engaging parties. These informal strategies allow the VA to get beneficiaries' perspectives and quickly put those perspectives to use improving access to information and processes.

The VA has put the information gained through their efforts to work in several concrete ways. The first was to redesign VA Form 10182, the form veterans use to appeal adverse decisions with which they disagree. The second was to develop easy-to-understand materials to file and track BVA appeals. The redesigned Form 10182 is one page and uses first-person language to guide appellants to answer the questions in the form in the way that is most accurate to them: "Hearing with a Veterans Law Judge: I want a Board hearing and the opportunity to submit additional evidence in support of my appeal that I will provide within 90 days after my hearing."

The VA also created a YouTube video featuring a veterans law judge explaining how appellants should prepare for a fair hearing.[35]

---

33. Nicole Ogrysko, *VA Sees Trust Improve by 24% in Five Years, Thanks to Veterans Experience Effort*, Fed. News Network (June 4, 2021, 11:49 AM), https://federalnewsnetwork.com/veterans-affairs/2021/06/va-sees-trust-improve-by-24-in-five-years-thanks-to-veterans-experience-effort/.

34. Interview with Cheryl Mason, Chair, BVA, VA (Sept. 6, 2021).

35. VA, *Board of Veterans Appeals Board Hearing Overview*, YouTube (Dec. 21, 2020), https://www.youtube.com/watch?app=desktop&v=UDI3C_ytJt8.

The VA sends all appellants a link to the video and follows up with appellants by text and email to remind them of their upcoming hearings. Finally, BVA has also established both a plain-language home page and a claims/appeals tracker that appellants can use to determine where in the appeals process their application is. In all instances, the VA strives to ensure that their written materials can be understood by applicants at an average reading level.

Part V
Procedures

Chapter 15
Constitutional and Statutory Foundations

Jeffrey S. Lubbers

15.1 CHAPTER OVERVIEW

Elsewhere in this guide, constitutional issues concerning the appointment and removal of officers, the right to a jury trial, and limits on agency investigatory powers are discussed. This chapter will explain the importance of the Due Process Clause of the Fifth Amendment to federal agency adjudication (section 15.21) and how the basic standard for procedural due process propounded by the U.S. Supreme Court in in *Mathews v. Eldridge* has provided the measuring stick for agency informal adjudication (sections 15.22, 15.23, 15.24). It will also address certain procedural requirements, set forth in the Administrative Procedure Act (APA), that are applicable to all proceedings (5 U.S.C. § 555), to license revocation proceedings (5 U.S.C. § 558), and to those proceedings subject to the APA's formal-adjudication provisions (5 U.S.C. §§ 554, 556–557). It will also explain how the provisions covering formal adjudication are considered to meet due process standards, but that, on the contrary, due to the paucity of APA-mandated procedures for informal adjudication, it is the *Mathews* balancing test that, for the most part, governs the procedures for informal adjudication.

15.2 PROCEDURAL DUE PROCESS UNDER THE FIFTH AMENDMENT

The Fifth Amendment provides that the federal government may not deprive any person "of life, liberty, or property, without due process of law." The 14th Amendment has a similar provision applicable to state (and local) governments. In an early case involving the city of Denver, the Supreme Court held that a landowner who disputed the amount of a tax assessed against him for paving a highway in front of his property had a due process right to a hearing before he had to pay (see Chapter 1).[1] As federal agencies were given more enforcement authority, the Supreme Court began to apply principles of due process to them. In 1952, Justice Frankfurter gave voice to this imperative in his famous concurrence in *Joint Anti-Fascist Refugee Committee v. McGrath*:

> This Court is not alone in recognizing that the right to be heard before being condemned to suffer grievous loss of any kind, even though it may not involve the stigma and hardships of a criminal conviction, is a principle basic to our society. Regard for this principle has guided Congress and the Executive. Congress has often entrusted, as it may, protection of interests which it has created to administrative agencies rather than to the courts. But rarely has it authorized such agencies to act without those essential safeguards for fair judgment which in the course of centuries have come to be associated with due process.[2]

15.21 The "Due Process Revolution" in the Supreme Court

In 1970, the Supreme Court began its "due process revolution" by deciding *Goldberg v. Kelly*,[3] which held that due process required

1. Londoner v. Denver, 210 U.S. 373 (1908).
2. Joint Anti-Fascist Refugee Comm. v. McGrath, 341 U.S. 123, 168 (1951) (Frankfurter, J., concurring).
3. 397 U.S. 254 (1970).

what amounted to a trial-type hearing—including notice and the opportunity to confront and cross-examine adverse witnesses, to present oral arguments, and to obtain counsel—before welfare benefits could be terminated. *Perry v. Sinderman*, decided two years later, expanded the notion of property deprivation to include termination of government employment.[4] At the same time, the Court was also recognizing a broader conception of liberty deprivation to include government stigmatic actions in *Wisconsin v. Constantineau*[5] and *Board of Regents v. Roth*,[6] and prison discipline in *Wolff v. McDonnell.*[7] *Goldberg* not only expanded the notion of property to include welfare benefits, it also required a pretermination hearing and then spelled out a set of required procedures that amounted to a trial-type hearing. In so doing, the Court stressed the welfare recipients' "brutal need" for the benefits—that "termination of aid pending resolution of a controversy over eligibility may deprive an eligible recipient of the very means by which to live while he waits."[8]

Given the ongoing expansion of notions of liberty and property, it seemed impossible to apply the *Goldberg* trial-type, formal-hearing process to every situation where a liberty or property deprivation was found. A shift away from *Goldberg* became apparent in the 1975 decision in *Goss v. Lopez*,[9] where the Court expanded notions of liberty and property deprivations to encompass a ten-day suspension of a public high school student. This expansion was closely contested, as a four-member minority decried the "judicial intervention in the operation of our public schools," and found the ten-day suspension to be de minimis.[10] While the majority required a "hearing," the hearing it required was decidedly informal and tailored to the educational context, requiring only "that the student be given oral or written notice of the charges against him and, if he denies them, an explanation of the evidence the authorities have and an opportunity to present his side of the story."[11]

---

4. 408 U.S. 593 (1972).
5. 400 U.S. 433 (1971).
6. 408 U.S. 564 (1972). The Court later made clear that injury to reputation was not enough; it had to be accompanied by some change in the plaintiff's legal status. *See* Paul v. Davis, 424 U.S. 693 (1976).
7. 418 U.S. 539 (1974).
8. *Goldberg*, 397 U.S. at 264.
9. 419 U.S. 565 (1975).
10. *Id.* at 585, 586 (Powell, J., dissenting).
11. *Id.* at 581.

After *Goss* was decided, Judge Henry J. Friendly of the U.S. Court of Appeals for the Second Circuit wrote his influential 1975 article, "Some Kind of Hearing," in which he described the 11 elements of what he considered to be a "fair hearing," including the rights to (1) an unbiased tribunal; (2) notice of the proposed action and the grounds asserted for it; (3) an opportunity to present reasons why the proposed action should not be taken; (4) call witnesses; (5) know the evidence against one; (6) have the decision based only on the evidence presented; (7) be represented by counsel; (8) have a record or transcript of the proceedings; (9) a statement of reasons; (10) public attendance (in some situations); and (11) judicial review. But he also recognized that the Court was at the same time recognizing more and more government actions that could trigger due process, and that the seriousness of the action should have some bearing on the procedural rights to be afforded. As he concluded: "As we go down the . . . list from the more severe actions to the less, the needle would point to fewer and fewer requirements on the list of required safeguards."[12]

15.22 The Mathews v. Eldridge Balancing Test for Determining What Process Is Due

Judge Friendly's insights proved prophetic. A year later, the Supreme Court adopted his approach in *Mathews v. Eldridge*,[13] involving the process that was due before the Social Security Administration (SSA) could terminate a beneficiary's benefits. In *Mathews*, the Court established the three-part balancing test, described in this section, for determining what process is due when there has been a finding that the federal or state government has deprived a person of life, liberty, or property under the Fifth or 14th Amendment to the Constitution. As such, it is one of the most influential and important cases in constitutional and administrative law. With respect to federal administrative agency adjudication, it forms the applicable standard for determining whether nonformal adjudications (i.e., hearings not subject to the formal-adjudication provisions of the APA) are constitutionally adequate.

In *Mathews*, both parties agreed that "[t]he dispute centers upon what process is due prior to the initial termination of benefits, pending review." After carefully reviewing SSA's procedures in benefits revocations cases, the Court began its legal analysis by putting *Goldberg* in

12. Henry J. Friendly, "*Some Kind of Hearing*," 123 U. Pa. L. Rev. 1267, 1278–79 (1975).
13. 424 U.S. 319 (1976).

its place: "In only one case, *Goldberg v. Kelly*, has the Court held that a hearing closely approximating a judicial trial is necessary. In other cases requiring some type of pretermination hearing as a matter of constitutional right the Court has spoken sparingly about the requisite procedures." Then the Court announced the test that would be used henceforth and that became known as the *Mathews* balancing test:

> [I]identification of the specific dictates of due process generally requires consideration of three distinct factors: First, the private interest that will be affected by the official action; second, the risk of an erroneous deprivation of such interest through the procedures used, and the probable value, if any, of additional or substitute procedural safeguards; and finally, the Government's interest, including the function involved and the fiscal and administrative burdens that the additional or substitute procedural requirement would entail.[14]

15.23 Application of the Balancing Test in Mathews Itself

In applying its new test, Justice Powell took pains to distinguish the social security context from the welfare context in *Goldberg*.

Factor 1: The private interest that will be affected by the official action. It is clear that the private interest affected has to be carefully analyzed and that it is not necessarily the importance of the entitlement per se. As Justice Powell stated in *Mathews*, in both that case and *Goldberg*, because the recipients would be awarded back benefits if they prevailed, their sole interest at the stage of their due process challenge "is in the uninterrupted receipt of this source of income pending final administrative decision on [their] claim."[15]

But Justice Powell distinguished the facts in *Goldberg*, pointing out that "[i]t was emphasized there that welfare assistance is given to persons on the very margin of subsistence." The Court conceded that, due to the "typically modest resources of the family unit of the physically disabled worker," the disruption of benefits may cause significant hardship. In contrast to welfare benefits, however, "[e]ligibility for disability benefits . . . is not based upon financial need," suggesting that disabled workers could still obtain other income (from welfare or other sources) while they litigated their eligibility before SSA.[16]

14. *Id.* at 335.
15. *Id.* at 340.
16. *Id.* at 340, 342.

These distinctions are at best debatable. The Court acknowledged that the delay between the interruption of benefits could be lengthy, approximately a full year. Moreover, people with a disability, as that term is used in the Social Security Act, by definition are not working and have (or at least had) a very serious long-term health problem, and in that sense may be even worse off than welfare recipients. Indeed, they may not qualify for welfare or for SSA's own needs-based program, the Supplemental Security Income (SSI) program, which also uses the same definition of "disability" as a qualification requirement for people under age 65.[17]

Factor 2: The risk of an erroneous deprivation of such interest through the procedures used, and the probable value, if any, of additional or substitute procedural safeguards. Here, the Court focused on "the fairness and reliability of the existing SSA pretermination procedures, and the probable value, if any, of additional procedural safeguards." It began with a very managerial focus: "To be sure, credibility and veracity may be a factor in the ultimate disability assessment in some cases. But procedural due process rules are shaped by the risk of error inherent in the truthfinding process as applied to the generality of cases, not the rare exceptions."[18]

Again, compared to *Goldberg*, it concluded that "[t]he potential value of an evidentiary hearing, or even oral presentation to the decisionmaker, is substantially less in this context than in *Goldberg*." It found that the required medical assessment of the worker's condition is "a more sharply focused and easily documented decision than the typical determination of welfare entitlement" where "issues of witness credibility and veracity often are critical to the decisionmaking process."[19]

But, again, this is quite debatable. Welfare cases can turn on many noncredibility issues like income stream and legal issues. And disability cases can raise many credibility issues: Does the recipient have real back pain, or is he faking? What kind of work can she actually do?

The Court conceded that there was a significant reversal rate for revocation cases appealed to administrative law judges (ALJs) but discounted that factor because of the open-file system used in the

---

17. A disabled beneficiary who was already receiving SSI benefits would be eligible for a pretermination hearing under *Goldberg* regarding those benefits because SSI is a needs-based entitlement program.

18. *Mathews*, 424 U.S. at 343–44.

19. *Id.* at 343–45.

administrative review process, which allowed recipients to submit new evidence throughout the appeal. And, notably in its discussion of this prong of the test, the Court concentrated solely on the value of accuracy (i.e., risk of error). It omitted discussion of other process values—acceptability, dignity, and the right to be heard—that suffused the *Goldberg* opinion.

Factor 3: The government's interest, including the function involved and the fiscal and administrative burdens that the additional or substitute procedural requirement would entail. Finally, the Court considered "the administrative burden and other societal costs that would be associated with requiring, as a matter of constitutional right, an evidentiary hearing upon demand in all cases prior to the termination of disability benefits."[20]

The Court's analysis of these considerations in *Mathews* is 179 degrees different from that in *Goldberg*. The Court in *Mathews* was heavily influenced by the cost of inevitably having more hearings and of continuing to pay benefits to recipients who later turn out to be ineligible after their hearing. It also refers to the incentive that pretermination hearings would give for appellants to prolong their appeals. That this had occurred in New York after the *Goldberg* case was doubtless not lost on the majority.[21] In the end, the Court deferred to the agency on its judgment that the procedure it used was sufficient. This is all very different from *Goldberg*, which also factored in the social value of continuing payments until after an oral hearing for persons previously determined to be eligible. Indeed, this social value proved to be so politically important that Congress and SSA later mandated pretermination ALJ hearings in these cases notwithstanding that *Mathews* held they were not constitutionally mandated.[22]

In the end, *Goldberg* was not overruled, but it was essentially limited to needs-based welfare cases, which themselves largely disappeared with "welfare reform" in the 1990s. One could argue that the recitation of the various grounds on which social security is supposedly different from welfare represented a polite way of breaking away from it without conspicuously overruling it only six years later.

---

20. *Id.* at 347.

21. Jason Parkin, *Adaptable Due Process*, 160 U. PA. L. REV. 1309 (2012).

22. In 1983, Congress added section 223(g) of the Social Security Act, 42 U.S.C. § 423(g), allowing recipients to elect "in such manner and form and within such time as the Commissioner of Social Security shall by regulations prescribe" to have the payment of such benefits continue until a negative decision was made after a hearing.

15.24 Mathews's Legacy—Two Views

Since *Mathews* was decided, the Supreme Court and the lower courts have applied it to a multitude of different procedural due process claims.[23] On the one hand, it has been criticized as allowing judges to make decisions based on their "subjective value choices" and for "containing a utilitarian bias that denigrates the intrinsic worth of constitutional rights."[24] On the other hand, as Cynthia Farina concludes at the end of her *Rashomon*-like "stories of the *Mathews* case," it "has given lawyers a structure for telling the story of their clients (and the people like them) in a way that judges can locate, and assess, within the constitutional framework."[25]

15.3 THE ADMINISTRATIVE PROCEDURE ACT'S PROCEDURAL REQUIREMENTS

15.31 Sections 554 and 556–557's Requirements for Formal Adjudication Meet Due Process

Section 554(a) of the APA provides that, with some enumerated exceptions, "every case of adjudication required by statute to be determined on the record after opportunity for an agency hearing" is governed by that section. Section 554(c)(2) then provides that "to the extent that the parties are unable to determine a controversy by consent, [they have an opportunity for] hearing and decision on notice and in accordance with sections 556 and 557 of this title." In other words, sections 554 and 556–557 govern formal adjudications—those where a statute provides for a hearing "on the record." As described in Chapter 18, these procedures amount to a trial-type hearing, and thereby satisfy

23. *See, e.g.*, Hamdi v. Rumsfeld, 542 U.S. 507 (2004) (applying *Mathews* test to determine hearing rights of persons detained as "enemy combatants"); City of Los Angeles v. David, 538 U.S. 715 (2003) (upholding a 27-day wait before plaintiff could be heard on his claim for a refund of a state fee for towing his illegally parked car); Brock v. Roadway Express, Inc., 481 U.S. 252 (1987) (applying *Mathews* test to decide rights of employer who was ordered to reinstate an employee while his allegations of retaliatory discharge were pending); Ingraham v. Wright, 430 U.S. 651 (1977) (applying *Mathews* test to whether advance procedural safeguards are due to students before corporal punishment is administered to them by public school officials).

24. Jerome A. Barron & C. Thomas Dienes, Constitutional Law in a Nutshell 294 (8th ed. 2013).

25. Cynthia R. Farina, *Due Process at Rashomon Gate: The Stories of* Mathews v. Eldridge, *in* Administrative Law Stories 257 (Peter L. Strauss ed., 2006).

due process. Accordingly, if an agency follows those procedures, it should generally be safe from any significant due process challenges.

15.32 Section 558 Adds Some Special Consideration for License Revocation Cases

One other oft-ignored section of the APA, section 558, applies to a certain type of case that would ordinarily require a trial-type hearing—a license revocation case. When the federal government issues licenses (e.g., for pilots), it can normally suspend or revoke such licenses as a sanction for a violation of the terms of the license. Section 558, however, provides:

> Except in cases of willfulness or those in which public health, interest, or safety requires otherwise, the withdrawal, suspension, revocation, or annulment of a license is lawful only if, before the institution of agency proceedings therefor, the licensee has been given—
>
> (1) notice by the agency in writing of the facts or conduct which may warrant the action; and
> (2) opportunity to demonstrate or achieve compliance with all lawful requirements.

15.33 Section 555's Minimal Requirements for Informal Adjudication—Mathews Applies

The definition of "adjudication" in the APA is very broad—it includes the formulation of an agency "order," which in turn is defined to mean any disposition of "a matter other than rule making but including licensing."[26] Courts have interpreted statutory "hearing" requirements lacking the accompanying "magic words" of "on the record" as not requiring the agency to necessarily be bound by the procedures in sections 554 and 556–557.[27] This type of adjudication is often referred to as "informal" adjudication, but more recently a more refined description of it divides it into cases where an evidentiary hearing is held ("Type B" adjudication) and cases where there is no evidentiary

---

26. 5 U.S.C. § 551(6)–(7).

27. *See, e.g.*, Dominion Energy Brayton Point, LLC v. Johnson, 443 F.3d 12 (1st Cir. 2006); Chem. Waste Mgmt., Inc. v. U.S. Env't Prot. Agency, 873 F.2d 1477 (D.C. Cir. 1989); City of W. Chicago v. Nuclear Regul. Comm'n, 701 F.2d 632 (7th Cir. 1983).

hearing ("Type C" adjudication). (See Chapters 17 and 18 for more on these categories.)

But despite the APA's detailed procedures for formal adjudications ("Type A" adjudication), the act conspicuously lacks a section on informal adjudication. Section 555 ("Ancillary matters") does contain some provisions applicable to all agency proceedings, so these are also applicable to informal adjudications (whether Type B or Type C). As Chapter 17 relates:

> Section 555 of the APA provides modest protections for private parties involved in adjudicatory disputes with federal government agencies, including the right to counsel (section 17.2) and the right to appear (section 17.3), requirements that agencies conclude matters in a reasonable time (section 17.4) and provide copies of transcripts on request (section 17.5), provisions governing investigations and subpoenas (section 17.6), and the requirement that agencies provide reasons for denying applications (section 17.7).

But given the wide variety of Type B adjudications—those not covered by sections 554 and 556–557, but providing for an evidentiary hearing—agencies conducting them need to decide what procedures to offer. This is nicely illustrated by Paul Verkuil's classic article, "A Study of Informal Adjudication Procedures," in which he examined the procedures used in 42 informal adjudicative programs conducted by four Cabinet departments and compared the procedures in each to the ten procedural ingredients of a trial-type hearing identified in *Goldberg v. Kelly*.[28] He found a wide variation of formality across the various programs, thus illustrating how agencies have used a sort of cost-benefit analysis in determining what level of formality would be required by a *Mathews*-type balancing test. As he concluded, "Unless a case can be made for inquisitorial-type informal procedures, the choice of procedures in the particular case falls within a range from those employed in the usual informal adjudication (the minimum) to those employed by *Goldberg* itself (the maximum)."[29]

As pointed out in Chapter 18: "Procedurally, there is often little distinction between Type A and Type B adjudications. Rather, as

---

28. Paul R. Verkuil, *A Study of Informal Adjudication Procedures*, 43 U. Chi. L. Rev. 739, 757–71 (1976). These ten procedures are similar but not identical to those recognized by Judge Friendly, *supra* note 12.

29. Verkuil, *supra* note 28, at 781.

discussed in Chapter 9, it is the regulation of the adjudicator that principally distinguishes them." On the other hand, as the Verkuil study demonstrates, some Type B adjudications are truly less formal—lacking an opportunity for cross-examination, for example. But for the purposes of this chapter, the importance of the Due Process Clause of the Fifth Amendment, and the *Mathews* case's exposition of it, serves as the essential backdrop to agency informal adjudication.

Chapter 16
Frontline Decision-Making

Matthew A. Gluth

16.1 CHAPTER OVERVIEW

As discussed in Chapter 1, the Administrative Procedure Act (APA) provides two procedural modes—formal and informal—of agency adjudication. Formal adjudication is conducted according to the APA's adjudication provisions and typically takes the form of a trial-like proceeding (see Chapter 18). Informal adjudication is a catch-all category under the APA that includes any agency action that is neither rulemaking nor formal adjudication.

As discussed in Chapter 18, some informal adjudication looks a lot like formal adjudication. But informal adjudication also includes a vast and varied category of agency actions that rely on procedures that are more bureaucratic than judicial in nature and have almost nothing procedurally in common except that they produce binding adjudicatory decisions involving disputes between government and private parties.[1] This category, referred to here as "frontline adjudication," constitutes the vast majority of administrative decisions and represents the primary way in which the public interacts directly with the government.

The range of this category extends broadly, incorporating much of what people generally consider the basic functions of government. For example, it includes everyday activities with which most people have experience, such as an individual requesting second "book" rate pricing when mailing a package with the Postal Service. It includes frequent and routine regulation of the national economy, such as an employee of the Department of Agriculture determining the quality of a cut of meat or a noncitizen applying for a work visa for employment with a U.S. corporation. And it even includes initial determinations in complex legal decisions that may later shift to more trial-like adjudication, such as an application for benefits before the Department of Veterans Affairs (VA) or Social Security Administration (SSA).

In most programs of administrative adjudication, an informal process that prioritizes efficiency and accuracy over formal procedure is sufficient to apply generally applicable law to case-specific facts and reach a final decision that satisfies all parties.[2] Few postal customers will demand formal procedures in seeking the appropriate rate for their packages, nor are meat-packers likely to wait the time required for a formal procedure to take place while their meat degrades in the factory. Even in complex cases before the VA and SSA, the sheer number of cases requires the agency to create a system by which easily resolvable cases are handled informally and quickly, assisting those most in need as efficiently as possible, while retaining a more formal procedure for cases that cannot be satisfactorily resolved through informal processes.

This chapter focuses on the wide range of frontline adjudicative processes that, in most programs, supplant or precede the sorts of trial-like processes with which administrative lawyers are most familiar. The following sections examine the characteristics of frontline adjudication (section 16.2), the categories of frontline adjudication (section 16.3), the classes of agency employees involved in frontline

---

1. MICHAEL ASIMOW, ADMIN. CONF. OF THE U.S., FEDERAL ADMINISTRATIVE ADJUDICATION OUTSIDE THE ADMINISTRATIVE PROCEDURE ACT 6, 98 (2019).

2. Emily S. Bremer, *The Rediscovered Stages of Agency Adjudication*, 99 WASH. U. L. REV. 377, 403 (2021).

adjudication (section 16.4), and a high-level overview of the typical stages of frontline adjudication (section 16.5). It concludes with a discussion of other considerations, including the role of representatives, quality assurance mechanisms, and the availability of appeal (section 16.6).

16.2 CHARACTERISTICS OF FRONTLINE ADJUDICATION

One of the principal reasons for delegating authority to federal agencies is their ability to respond more efficiently than the executive or legislative bodies to specific conditions.[3] Significant procedural requirements, such as those employed in formal adjudication, inhibit this advantage and slow the adjudicatory process.[4] Frontline adjudication, therefore, seeks to tip the balance toward flexibility and speed,[5] reserving more formal processes for those cases that cannot be satisfactorily resolved through informal methods. It has long been the case that even where formal proceedings are available, frontline processes constitute the vast bulk of administrative adjudication.[6]

In frontline adjudication, decisions are made by agency employees (see section 16.4) following review of an administrative record, which could consist solely of an application but may also require inspections, conferences, and negotiations.[7] An investigation and preliminary decision (or settlement) concludes all but a small percentage of cases (see section 16.5). In this way, frontline processes are an essential device for efficiently handling high volumes of cases, for example at agencies that administer benefits, licenses, and visas.

Agencies typically have an exceptionally broad zone of discretion to design the procedures used in frontline adjudication. Congress has sometimes created agency- or program-specific procedures, but agencies also have developed procedures over the life span of their programs, often as a way of processing cases more efficiently in response to large backlogs of cases.[8] Frontline decision-makers typically have

---

3. *Id.* at 389.
4. *Cf.* Aaron L. Nielson, *Sticky Regulations*, 85 U. Chi. L. Rev. 85 (2018).
5. Bremer, *supra* note 2, at 389.
6. Final Report of the Attorney General's Committee on Administrative Procedure 35 (1941) [hereinafter Attorney General's Committee Report].
7. *Id.* at 5.
8. Bremer, *supra* note 2, at 392.

very high caseloads, limited resources to obtain necessary information, and limited time in which to decide cases.[9] This combination results in the particular challenges that characterize frontline adjudication.

16.3 CATEGORIES OF FRONTLINE ADJUDICATION

There are many categories of frontline adjudicative processes. This section provides an overview of three broad, representative categories: licensing and grading, regulatory enforcement, and initial determinations in applications for benefits.

16.31 Licensing and Grading

Licensing arises under statutes that, broadly speaking, require public citizens to obtain government approval to engage in specified activities. Grading arises under statutes that, broadly speaking, require public entities to submit to government inspection to ensure suitability for sale or other public availability. Examples of licensing and grading include fish inspections by the Department of Commerce, tariff classifications made by Customs and Border Protection, adjudication of applications to use national forest land by the Forest Service, and, in one of the highest volume examples, visa applications by the U.S. Citizenship and Immigration Services.[10]

In both circumstances, the process works broadly as follows. The agency accepts applications for licenses or requests for grading and processes them. Applications generally would be (1) complete, meritorious, and quickly approved or granted; (2) incomplete or problematic, and thus subject to an informal development process, such as an in-person inspection, before approval or grant; or (3) unmeritorious and necessitating denial of the application or request, often after failed attempts at perfection via the informal process.[11]

There are two crucial elements to this category of informal adjudications. First, all parties have a decisive interest in a quick decision. The quality of meat and fish will soon degrade, so rapid certification of suitability for sale is essential. Employers and employees both seek quick resolution of applications for visas for foreign workers. Second, the most important element in the decision is the judgment of the

---

9. Michael Lipsky, Street-Level Bureaucracy 29 (2010).

10. Ben Harrington & Daniel J. Sheffner, Cong. Rsch. Serv., R46930, Informal Administrative Adjudication: An Overview 20–21 (2021).

11. Bremer, *supra* note 2, at 406.

person who saw and tested the product or examined the applicant. Often, the quality of the product or the skill of the applicant cannot be measured except on-site by trained experts.[12]

Formal procedures would not generally increase the likelihood of a correct decision; the knowledge and skill of the inspectors, not the elements of formal procedure, are often the crucial element in determining quality decisions.[13]

16.32 Enforcement of Regulatory Requirements

A second common instance in which agencies have the authority to make quick, informal decisions arises during emergencies or other situations that affect public safety or security.[14] Examples include grounding a plane or pilot pending an examination or disciplinary proceedings, or shutting down a factory or power plant that threatens safe work conditions or adversely affects the environment.

The process generally works as follows. The agency receives a complaint of a potential violation (or one is uncovered during an inspection or audit), investigates the potential violation, issues an interlocutory order, informally negotiates with the party, and, if no resolution is reached, proceeds to formal adjudication.[15]

In these cases, the government has a significant interest in quick resolution, due to safety or other issues affecting the common good.[16]

Although the public party retains the right to future full formal proceedings, the cost of an interlocutory order upon the recipient is often of a much greater magnitude than under applications for licenses or grades, and thus there is an increased demand for accuracy of the determination in these kinds of frontline decisions.

16.33 Claims for Benefits

A third instance in which informal, frontline adjudication commonly resolves a vast number of issues are claims for benefits before SSA, the VA, and other agencies. Applicants naturally desire a quick response to their claim of benefits, often due to dire need. Likewise,

---

12. Attorney General's Committee Report, *supra* note 6, at 36–37.
13. *Id.* at 37.
14. *Id.* at 39.
15. Bremer, *supra* note 2, at 407.
16. Attorney General's Committee Report, *supra* note 6, at 36–37.

the government, due to the large number of claims, desires a process for expediting as many claims as possible.[17]

Informal frontline adjudication in these kinds of cases often contain a shell of the procedures that would be invoked in full formal adjudication. This may be in part because these programs often include a stage for formal adjudication, but the initial frontline determination is made in an informal fashion by agency staff who also serve a secondary role of developing the evidentiary record in case more formal adjudication is needed.[18]

The process generally works as follows. An agency administering a benefits program accepts, processes, and evaluates submitted applications. The application might be complete and demonstrate without doubt that the applicant is entitled to payment. In many of these cases, the applicant would request and receive advice from an agency employee about how to prepare a successful application, thus ensuring near-immediate approval upon submission. Second, it might be obvious that information or supporting documentation necessary to determine whether the claimant is entitled to payment is missing from the application. In these cases, an employee of the administering agency informs the applicant, orally or by letter, of the deficiency and advises the applicant how the issue can be resolved. In response, many applicants remedy the deficiency, and payment is approved and made, or they might withdraw the application. If these efforts do not resolve the claim, the application is denied, and the applicant may request a hearing.[19]

16.4 EMPLOYEES INVOLVED IN FRONTLINE ADJUDICATION

Employees in frontline processes have three primary responsibilities: initiate the case (either by receiving the application or complaint or opening an audit or inspection), develop the administrative record (often through informal interactions with parties, witnesses, and others), and make an initial determination. Different employees might be responsible for performing different tasks. In programs involving less complex factual situations or simpler processes, nonlawyers are often

17. *Id.* at 38.

18. Paul R. Verkuil, *A Study of Informal Adjudication Procedures*, 43 U. Chi. L. Rev. 739, 761–62 (1976).

19. Bremer, *supra* note 2, at 405.

responsible for these tasks. In programs where legal skill sets are valued, staff attorneys perform these functions.

Where technical knowledge is necessary for the decision of cases, agencies have developed special administrative units. In the cases of licensing or grading, these may be subject-matter experts either in the area being regulated (such as meat graders) whose expertise serves as the primary evidentiary record as well as the final decision. In other cases, such as applications for benefits, these may instead be consultants who provide valuable evidence (such as a medical examination) to an agency employee who makes the final determination.[20]

In all these tasks, these employees generally have a great deal of autonomy and discretion. There are a few key reasons for this: the situations may be too complex to support full regimentation or supervision, the case volumes may be too high for supervisors to fully review all decisions, or the decisions themselves may rely upon a human element that cannot be reviewed.[21]

16.5 STAGES OF FRONTLINE ADJUDICATION

Informal, frontline adjudication includes a variety of activities: routine processing of requests for agency action, advice-giving, inspections, investigations, examinations, correspondence, conferences, mediation, negotiation, and settlements.[22] These can be grouped into broad categories: case initiation, informal consultation, investigation, settlement, and a final informal determination.

16.51 Case Initiation

The first step in any informal, frontline decision is the case initiation and contact between the public party and the agency. If initiated by the public party, this likely takes the form of an application for license or benefits, or a complaint of violation by another party. If initiated by the agency, it likely takes the form of notice of investigation or audit prepared by agency employees.

16.52 Informal Consultation

In cases for which the initial documentation is not sufficient to resolve the issue, agency employees will work informally with the public party

20. Attorney General's Committee Report, *supra* note 6, at 37–38.
21. Lipsky, *supra* note 9, at 14–15.
22. Bremer, *supra* note 2, at 402.

to obtain the proper information or status of the issue. Employees will also guide the public party in their next steps, perhaps advising them of representatives or other groups who may be able to assist them in the process or other sources of information.

16.53 Investigation and Development of the Record

This stage makes up the bulk of the process in frontline adjudications. In applications for licenses, the staff member or consultant may provide a test or other examination.[23] In grading, the staff member or consultant may evaluate in person the item under consideration. In applications for benefits, the staff member will obtain evidence to develop the record, including potentially medical or other examinations. In these cases, despite the informality of the initial determinations, the staff member must keep the record sufficiently organized for potential future formal adjudication.

This stage and the surrounding two stages often interrelate, with staff informally updating the public party as to development in the case and requesting additional information, or proposing potential mediation and settlement.

16.54 Settlement

In many circumstances, particularly in the enforcement context, the public party and the agency will informally negotiate a settlement rather than proceed to a determination.[24] Administrative employees (possibly staff attorneys in more complex scenarios) will engage in the negotiation and prepare any required documentation for the agreed settlement.

16.55 Determination

If no settlement is reached, or none is applicable to the issue, staff will make a final determination. Because of the high volume of frontline adjudications, and the desire by both parties for a quick response, agencies often invest in automation and other technological processes to issue determinations, which prevent individualized responses.

---

23. Verkuil, *supra* note 18, at 781.
24. *Id.* at 762; ATTORNEY GENERAL'S COMMITTEE REPORT, *supra* note 6, at 41.

16.6 OTHER CONSIDERATIONS

The issues discussed here are not exclusive to frontline adjudication but apply to most if not all areas of agency adjudication. However, each contains factors that specifically affect frontline adjudication.

16.61 The Role of Representatives

In many programs, parties are less commonly represented in frontline processes than they are in more formal processes. In many programs, neither the public party nor the government agency is particularly aided by representation, due to the relatively direct and simple determinations being made and the interest in speed by both parties. In such cases, agency staff will serve as de facto representatives in simple adjudications or in the early stages of potentially complex adjudications, providing guidance on completing forms and obtaining necessary documentation, and any other procedural elements necessary for the determination.

In the frontline stage of applications for benefits, where the determination is conceived of as a potential first step and not necessarily a final adjudicative decision, representation remains rare. But in cases where benefits claimants have representation at these stages, the representatives often take primary responsibility to develop the evidentiary record and provide proper compliance with procedural mechanisms.

16.62 Quality Assurance Mechanisms

Due to high volume, frontline adjudication systems do not share the robust procedural protections of formal adjudication. Instead, their focus is on accuracy and timeliness.

As such, agencies have developed metrics to measure quality, in terms of accuracy and efficiency, of their decision-making components (see Chapter 24). They often set standards in terms of performance and measure frontline workers' performance against those standards.[25] But recruitment and training also are core components of assuring quality.[26]

Certain agencies with particularly high volumes have gone further. By developing caseload management systems, they have developed the

---

25. Lipsky, *supra* note 9, at 50.

26. Attorney General's Committee Report, *supra* note 6, at 37.

ability to measure quality elements such as timeliness and accuracy.[27] By employing sampling techniques, they allow teams of reviewers to evaluate and assess frontline decisions, and to identify common errors or sectors of employees prone to error, which allows for policy changes or training measures.[28]

16.63 Availability of Appeal

If a frontline determination does not resolve the dispute between the private parties and the government, in many cases additional procedural protections are available, either in the form of a second-tier informal adjudication by a more experienced or higher level staff member[29] or in the form of a formal hearing.[30] In the alternative, private parties almost invariably retain the right to seek judicial review (see Chapter 27).

27. Jerry L. Mashaw, *Quality Assurance Systems in the Adjudication of Claims of Entitlement to Benefits or Compensation*, 1973 ACUS 160, 166–70 (1973).

28. Daniel E. Ho et al., Quality Assurance Systems in Agency Adjudication: Emerging Practices and Insights 14, 19–21 (2021) (report to the Admin. Conf. of the U.S.).

29. Attorney General's Committee Report, *supra* note 6, at 38.

30. Bremer, *supra* note 2, at 382; Attorney General's Committee Report, *supra* note 6, at 35.

Chapter 17

Proceedings Not Involving a Legally Required Evidentiary Hearing

Michael Asimow

17.1 CHAPTER OVERVIEW

In many adjudications, a decision-maker resolves a dispute between a private party and the federal government without being legally required to conduct an evidentiary hearing. Such adjudications are properly described as "informal." This contrasts with more formal proceedings (i.e., those regulated by the formal-hearing provisions of the Administrative Procedure Act (APA) and those in which another statute or executive branch policy requires an evidentiary hearing). As described in Chapter 1, such proceedings are referred to as "Type A" and "Type B," respectively. True informal adjudications, the subject of this chapter, are referred to as "Type C."

Type C adjudications are extremely common, particularly in these areas:

- Grants, benefits, loans, and subsidies
- Licensing and accrediting
- Foreign policy and national security determinations
- Inspections, tests, and safety
- Orders subject to de novo judicial review
- Orders relating to tax and tariff collection
- Indian affairs[1]

A typical example of Type C adjudication is the process for licensing national banks. The statute and regulations describe an inquisitorial notice-and-comment-type process for determining whether the Office of the Comptroller of the Currency should grant an application for a banking license. The decision is based on whatever information the office discovers in its investigation, public comments, a hearing held if the comptroller determines there is a need for one, or any other source of information, including that supplied in meetings with interested parties.[2]

This chapter describes the procedural requirements for Type C adjudications. It focuses on sections 555 and 558 of the APA. Although these sections also apply to Types A and B adjudications, the statutory and regulatory protections for litigants in such proceedings are more extensive than those set out in sections 555 and 558. As a result, these sections are most important in Type C adjudication. Even in Type C adjudication, of course, other statutes and agency rules might require additional or alternative procedures, and due process requirements sometimes apply.

Section 555 of the APA provides modest protections for private parties involved in adjudicatory disputes with federal government agencies, including the right to counsel (section 17.2) and the right to appear (section 17.3), requirements that agencies conclude matters in a reasonable time (section 17.4) and provide copies of transcripts on request (section 17.5), provisions governing investigations and subpoenas (section 17.6), and the requirement that agencies provide reasons for denying applications (section 17.7). Section 558(c) provides procedural protections for private parties engaged in licensing disputes with federal agencies (section 17.8).

---

1. For numerous additional examples of Type C adjudication, see MICHAEL ASIMOW, ADMIN. CONF. OF THE U.S., FEDERAL ADMINISTRATIVE ADJUDICATION OUTSIDE THE ADMINISTRATIVE PROCEDURE ACT 89–98 (2019).

2. 12 U.S.C. §§ 26, 27; 12 C.F.R. §§ 5.7–.13 (2022); *see also* Camp v. Pitts, 411 U.S. 138 (1973).

17.2 RIGHT TO COUNSEL

Under section 555(b), "[a] person compelled to appear in person before an agency or representative thereof is entitled to be accompanied, represented, and advised by counsel or, if permitted by the agency, by other qualified representative." According to the *Attorney General's Manual on the Administrative Procedure Act*, this provision does not apply to persons who appear voluntarily or in response to a request—only to those persons whose appearance is compelled or commanded.[3] The most obvious application of this provision is to provide a right to counsel for persons compelled by subpoena to appear and testify before agency investigators. However, the meaning of the term "represented" in section 555(b) can vary according to context. For example, the Ninth Circuit held that while counsel may have a right to raise objections in trial-like proceedings on the record, the term "represented" does not empower counsel to object to questions in a Federal Communications Commission (FCC) fact-finding investigation.[4]

Case law under section 555(b) stresses that agencies need a concrete and particularized reason to deny a person's choice of counsel. Thus, a court invalidated a Nuclear Regulatory Commission (NRC) regulation providing that if "a reasonable basis exists to believe that the investigation or inspection will be obstructed, impeded or impaired, either directly or indirectly, by an attorney's representation of multiple interests, the agency official may prohibit that attorney from being present during the interview."[5] The NRC's rationale was that employees who chose to be represented by the employer's lawyer might be intimidated from giving candid testimony against the employer. The court held that counsel of the witness's choice cannot be excluded absent "concrete evidence that his presence would obstruct and impede the investigation." In addition, section 555(b) requires an agency to allow an attorney to be accompanied by an expert to assist counsel, such as an accounting expert in a complex Securities and Exchange Commission investigatory proceeding involving accountant misconduct.[6]

---

3. Attorney General's Manual on the Administrative Procedure Act 61 (1947); *see also* Suess v. Pugh, 245 F. Supp. 661 (N.D. W. Va. 1965).

4. Fed. Commc'ns Comm'n v. Schreiber, 329 F.2d 517, 526 (9th Cir. 1964).

5. Pro. Reactor Operator Soc'y v. Nuclear Regul. Comm'n, 939 F.2d 1047, 1051–52 (D.C. Cir. 1991); *see also* Sec. & Exch. Comm'n v. Csapo, 533 F.2d 7 (D.C. Cir. 1976).

6. Laccetti v. Sec. & Exch. Comm'n, 885 F.3d 724 (D.C. Cir. 2018); Whitman v. Sec. & Exch. Comm'n, 613 F. Supp. 48 (D.D.C. 1985).

The provision permitting persons to be represented by counsel "does not grant or deny a person who is not a lawyer the right to appear for or represent others before an agency or in an agency proceeding."[7] The *Attorney General's Manual* states that it is up to agencies whether to allow nonlawyers to practice before them. The same is true of the required qualifications of lawyers. During consideration of the APA in the 1940s, the House rejected an amendment providing that any member of the bar in good standing shall be eligible to practice before any agency. Instead, according to the *Attorney General's Manual*, agencies would continue to have power to control the qualifications of lawyers who practice before them. Congress later enacted the Agency Practice Act, which provides that an attorney in good standing in any state may represent persons before federal agencies.[8] Even under the Agency Practice Act, however, agencies can exclude persons of improper character from practice or exclude parties or counsel from participation in proceedings by reason of unruly conduct. Agencies also can impose reasonable time limits during which former employees may not practice before the agency.[9] See Chapter 13 for more information on representatives in agency adjudicative proceedings.

17.3 RIGHT TO APPEAR

17.31 Parties to Agency Proceedings

Under section 555(b), a party is "entitled to appear in person or by or with counsel or other duly qualified representative in an agency proceeding" (i.e., any agency process for adjudication, rulemaking, or licensing). As discussed in Chapter 11, a "party" includes "a person or agency named or admitted as a party, or properly seeking and entitled as of right to be admitted as a party, in an agency proceeding, and a person admitted by an agency as a party for limited purposes."[10]

It is unclear whether this right to "appear" allows an agency to conduct informal adjudication exclusively through written submissions without opportunity for oral argument or other oral presentation. Such all-written procedures, described in greater detail in Chapter 22, are not uncommon in the world of informal adjudication.

---

7. 5 U.S.C. § 555(b); *see also id.* § 500(d)(1).

8. *Id.* § 500.

9. Attorney General's Manual on the Administrative Procedure Act, *supra* note 3, at 65–66; *see also* Herman v. Dulles, 205 F.2d 715, 717 (D.C. Cir. 1953).

10. 5 U.S.C. § 551(3).

Nevertheless, the *Attorney General's Manual* at least suggests that section 555(b) entitles a party to informal adjudication to make an oral presentation.[11]

17.32 Interested Persons

The APA confers a second and broader right to appear, stating: "So far as the orderly conduct of public business permits, an interested person may appear before an agency or its responsible employees for the presentation, adjustment, or determination of an issue, request, or controversy in a proceeding, whether interlocutory, summary, or otherwise in connection with an agency function."[12] An "interested person" is one whose interests are or will be affected by the agency action that may result from the proceeding.[13]

Notice that, unlike the right of "parties" to appear, this provision is not limited to "parties" nor to "agency proceedings" (that is, adjudication, rulemaking, or licensing). Instead, it applies to all "agency functions," such as grantmaking or settlement negotiations.[14] But note also that the APA appears to give greater appearance rights to a party than an interested person, who "may appear" only "so far as the orderly conduct of public business permits."

This reference to a right to "appear before an agency or its responsible employees" would seem to entitle members of the public whose interests would be affected by an agency action to compel relatively high-level agency employees to meet with them.[15] Case law has not clarified what constitutes an appearance. Under one approach, the right to appear in section 555(b) might extend the due process right to notice and a nonadversarial hearing to informal adjudication contexts in which due process does not apply.[16] Case law has also not clarified which agency personnel are "responsible employees."

---

11. Attorney General's Manual on the Administrative Procedure Act, *supra* note 3, at 62.

12. 5 U.S.C. § 555(b).

13. Attorney General's Manual on the Administrative Procedure Act, *supra* note 3, at 70.

14. *Id.* at 63–64.

15. *See* SourceAmerica v. U.S. Dep't of Educ., 368 F. Supp. 3d 974 (E.D. Va. 2019).

16. Miles Constr., LLC v. United States, 108 Fed. Cl. 792, 805 (2013). *But see* Attorney General's Manual on the Administrative Procedure Act, *supra* note 3, at 63.

The *Attorney General's Manual* broadly construed the statutory right to appear. It stated that "any person should be given an opportunity to confer or discuss with responsible officers or employees of the agency matters in which he is properly interested." A responsible officer or employee is "one who can decide the matter or whose function is to make recommendations on such matters—rather than officers or employees whose duties are merely mechanical or formal." On the other hand, the act "does not require that every interested person be permitted to follow the chain of command to the head of the agency. It was not intended to require the directors of the Reconstruction Finance Corporation, for example, to confer personally with every applicant for a loan."[17]

The *Manual* cautions that the right of interested persons to meet with agency officials is limited by the language "so far as the orderly conduct of public business permits." Although the right to confer and the limitation to orderly conduct of public business "should be construed to achieve practical and fair results,"[18] section 555 does not create a right for an interested person to compel the agency to institute a hearing or take other action that it does not wish to take.[19]

The opportunity to appear refers to situations in which "an agency takes significant action without prior formal proceedings," including "interlocutory" and "summary" proceedings. The persons affected by such actions should, if feasible, be allowed to appear and present their views on the proposed action. However, this right to confer is not intended to interfere with important public functions such as assuring air safety.[20]

17.4 CONCLUSION OF MATTER IN A REASONABLE TIME

Section 555(b) requires that, "[w]ith due regard for the convenience and necessity of the parties or their representatives and within a reasonable time, each agency shall proceed to conclude a matter presented

17. Attorney General's Manual on the Administrative Procedure Act, *supra* note 3, at 63.

18. *Id.*; *see also H. Rep. 1980, 79th Cong. 2d Sess.*, *in* Administrative Procedure Act: Legislative History 264 (1946) [hereinafter *H. Rep. 1980*]; deVyver v. Warden, 388 F. Supp. 1213, 1222 (M.D. Pa. 1974).

19. Block v. Sec. & Exch. Comm'n, 50 F.3d 1078, 1085 (D.C. Cir. 1995).

20. *See* Attorney General's Manual on the Administrative Procedure Act, *supra* note 3, at 64.

to it." According to the *Attorney General's Manual*, this provision "merely restates a principle of good administration,"[21] but it must be construed with another APA provision that authorizes a reviewing court to "compel agency action unlawfully withheld or unreasonably delayed."[22] The problem of how and when courts should remedy unreasonable agency delay is discussed in Chapter 27.

17.5 COPY OF TRANSCRIPT

Under section 555(c), "[a] person compelled to submit data or evidence is entitled to retain or, on payment of lawfully prescribed costs, procure a copy or transcript thereof, except that in a nonpublic investigatory proceeding the witness may for good cause be limited to inspection of the official transcript of his testimony." The *Attorney General's Manual* observes that this provision is limited to data or evidence submitted by a particular witness. It does not entitle the submitter to copies or transcripts of data or evidence submitted by other persons. And it extends only to persons compelled to testify or submit data, not to those who were merely requested to do so or who did so voluntarily.[23]

The "except" clause, referring to "non-public investigatory proceedings," means that agencies need not disclose transcripts in cases in which prosecutions may be brought later, and it is "obviously detrimental to the due execution of the laws to permit copies to be circulated."[24] The phrase "non-public investigatory proceedings" covers "all confidential phases of investigations, formal or informal, conducted by agencies to determine whether there have been violations of law."[25] Section 555 does not require agencies to state reasons for denying requests to procure transcripts.[26]

Section 555 should be read today in conjunction with section 11 of the Federal Advisory Committee Act, which generally requires that agencies make copies of transcripts of agency proceedings available to persons on request.[27]

---

21. *See id.* at 65.
22. 5 U.S.C. § 706(1).
23. Attorney General's Manual on the Administrative Procedure Act, *supra* note 3, at 66; *see also* United States v. Murray, 297 F.2d 812 (2d Cir. 1962).
24. Attorney General's Manual on the Administrative Procedure Act, *supra* note 3, at 66–67.
25. *Id.* at 67.
26. *See* Com. Cap. Corp. v. Sec. & Exch. Comm'n, 360 F.2d 866 (7th Cir. 1968).
27. 5 U.S.C. app. § 11.

17.6 INVESTIGATIONS AND SUBPOENAS

Under section 555(c), "[p]rocess, requirement of a report, inspection, or other investigative act or demand may not be issued, made, or enforced except as authorized by law." This provision requires that investigatory actions taken by agencies, such as required reports or physical investigations, must be authorized by statute. The provision seems to add nothing to existing law.[28]

Under section 555(d), "[a]gency subpenas [sic] authorized by law shall be issued to a party on request and, when required by rules of procedure, on a statement or showing of general relevance and reasonable scope of the evidence sought." This provision makes agency subpoenas available to private parties to the same extent as they are available to agencies. It covers both subpoenas to testify and to produce documents and is limited to "parties" to agency proceedings.

According to the *Attorney General's Manual*, section 555(d) means that agency subpoenas must be issued on request of private parties; subpoenas can be limited by standards of relevance and reasonable scope only if agency procedural rules so provide. But the *Manual* also states that agencies can refuse to issue subpoenas that appear to be so irrelevant or unreasonable that a court would refuse to enforce them.[29] An agency can also refuse to issue a subpoena to an expert witness without arrangements for compensating the expert.[30] An agency's refusal to issue a subpoena to a private party is not judicially reviewable at the time of the refusal but only in conjunction with review of a final order.[31]

Section 555(d) continues:

> On contest, the court shall sustain the subpoena or similar process or demand to the extent that it is found to be in accordance with law. In a proceeding for enforcement, the court shall issue an order requiring the appearance of the witness or the production of the evidence or data within a reasonable time

---

28. *See* ATTORNEY GENERAL'S MANUAL ON THE ADMINISTRATIVE PROCEDURE ACT, *supra* note 3, at 66; Serr v. Sullivan, 270 F. Supp. 544 (E.D. Pa. 1967).

29. *See* Greene Cnty. Plan. Bd. v. Fed. Power Comm'n, 559 F.2d 1227, 1233 (2d Cir. 1976).

30. ATTORNEY GENERAL'S MANUAL ON THE ADMINISTRATIVE PROCEDURE ACT, *supra* note 3, at 68; Va. Petroleum Jobbers Ass'n v. Fed. Power Comm'n, 293 F.2d 527 (D.C. Cir. 1961).

31. Bristol-Myers Co. v. Fed. Trade Comm'n, 469 F.2d 1116, 1118–19 (2d Cir. 1972).

under penalty of punishment for contempt in case of contumacious failure to comply.

The *Attorney General's Manual* states that this provision restates existing law and does not narrow the broad standards for enforcement of agency subpoenas that had been articulated by courts prior to 1946.[32]

17.7 REASONS FOR DENIAL OF APPLICATIONS

Under section 555(e),

> [p]rompt notice shall be given of the denial in whole or in part of a written application, petition, or other request of an interested person made in connection with any agency proceeding. Except in affirming a prior denial or when the denial is self-explanatory, the notice shall be accompanied by a brief statement of the grounds for denial.

This provision imposes a general requirement that an agency explain its reasons for a denial of a written application, petition, or other request. The statement of grounds for denial, "while simple in nature, must be sufficient to advise the party of the general basis of the denial."[33] This reason-giving requirement has broad application and may be the most significant portion of section 555. It is less demanding than the reason-giving requirements imposed by the APA in Type A adjudication[34] and seems similar to the requirement of reason-giving imposed by due process.[35]

A good illustration of the significance of the reason-giving requirement is the D.C. Circuit's decision in *Roelofs*. There, the court held that the Discharge Review Board and the Board for Correction of Military Records must state reasons for rejecting an application to upgrade a military discharge from general to honorable. It linked this requirement to fundamental rights of procedural justice. Quoting an earlier case, the *Roelofs* court stated that section 555(e) embodies

---

32. Attorney General's Manual on the Administrative Procedure Act, *supra* note 3, at 68–69 (citing Endicott Johnson Corp. v. Perkins, 317 U.S. 501 (1943), and Okla. Press Publ'g Co. v. Walling, 327 U.S. 186 (1946)).

33. Attorney General's Manual on the Administrative Procedure Act, *supra* note 3, at 70.

34. *Cf.* 5 U.S.C. § 557(c)(3)(A); *see also* Geo. Transfer & Rigging Co. v. United States, 380 F. Supp. 179, 186 (D. Md. 1974).

35. *Cf.* Goldberg v. Kelly, 397 U.S. 254, 271 (1970).

> the simple but fundamental requirement that an agency or official set forth its reasons, a requirement that is essential to the integrity of the administrative process, for it tends to require the agency to focus on the values served by its decision, hence releasing the clutch of unconscious preference and irrelevant prejudice.[36]

Numerous other cases have applied the reason-giving requirements of section 555(e). The Parole Board must state its reasons for denying an application for parole.[37] The Comptroller of the Currency must state its reasons for rejecting a request for a public hearing on a bank merger.[38] An Interior Department official must explain why he summarily rejected a county's objection to the official's earlier conclusion (still under review in the department) that an Indian tribe had a historical connection to land on which the tribe proposed to build a casino.[39] The Drug Enforcement Administration must explain why it rejected an application to proceed in forma pauperis in order to avoid the $5,000 bond-posting requirement to challenge a forfeiture.[40] The Transportation Security Administration must give reasons for rejecting an air carrier's request to use alternative procedures to those in an air safety directive and explain why it rejected requests that it modify its bin advertising program.[41]

Section 555(e) contains a narrow exception to the reason-giving requirements for instances when an agency affirms a prior denial or when a denial is self-explanatory. But according to the APA's legislative history:

> Prior denial would satisfy this requirement only where the ground previously stated remain the actual grounds and sufficiently notify the party. Self-explanatory denial must meet the same test; that is, the request must be in such form that its

36. Roelofs v. Sec'y of the Air Force, 628 F.2d 594, 599–600 (D.C. Cir. 1980); *see also* Matlovich v. Sec'y of the Air Force, 591 F.2d 852, 857–61 (D.C. Cir. 1978); Remmie v. Mabus, 898 F. Supp. 108, 119–21 (E.D.N.Y. 1995).

37. King v. United States, 492 F.2d 1337, 1343 (7th Cir. 1974).

38. Washington v. Off. of the Comptroller of the Currency, 856 F.2d 1507, 1513 (11th Cir. 1988).

39. Butte Cnty. v. Hogen, 613 F.3d 190, 193–95 (D.C. Cir. 2010).

40. Tourus Recs., Inc. v. Drug Enf't Admin., 259 F.3d 731, 737 (D.C. Cir. 2001).

41. SecurityPoint Holdings v. Transp. Sec. Admin., 769 F.3d 1184, 1187–88 (D.C. Cir. 2014); Amerijet Int'l, Inc. v. Pistole, 753 F.3d 1343, 1349–50 (D.C. Cir. 2014).

> mere denial fully informs the party of all he would otherwise be entitled to have stated.[42]

The connection between the reason-giving requirement of section 555(e) and the reason-giving requirement for judicial review is not entirely clear. For judicial review purposes, an agency's statement of reasons must be sufficient to determine whether the decision was rational, meaning that it is supported by the administrative record, was based on consideration of correct factors, and was not a clear error of judgment.[43] An unexplained agency action violates both section 555(e) and the APA's arbitrary-and-capricious test. In such cases, the matter should be remanded to the agency to state its reasons.[44] Several cases appear to equate the reason-giving requirement of section 555(e) with the judicial review reason-giving requirement,[45] but it is unlikely that the two requirements are identical.[46] Section 555(e) requires only a "brief statement of the grounds for denial," a requirement less onerous than the explanation requirements imposed by the arbitrary-and-capricious test.

Other cases link the reason-giving requirement in section 555(e) to judicial review in a different way. If the merits of the agency action in question are not subject to judicial review (because review is precluded by statute or the action is committed to agency discretion),[47] the reason-giving provision of section 555(e) does not apply to those decisions.[48]

Several cases arising under section 555(e) consider whether undisclosed reasons stated in pre-decisional agency documents satisfy section 555(e). Courts have upheld unexplained agency decisions under these circumstances, on the theory that remand for further explanation would be wasteful. The agency would simply rewrite its decision to incorporate the reasoning contained in the pre-decisional documents.[49] It is unclear whether a post-decisional explanatory memorandum

42. *H. Rep. 1980*, *supra* note 18, at 268.

43. Citizens to Pres. Overton Park v. Volpe, 401 U.S. 402, 416 (1971).

44. Fla. Power & Light Co. v. Lorion, 470 U.S. 729, 744 (1985).

45. *See* Gillette v. Fed. Energy Regul. Comm'n, 737 F.2d 883, 886–87 (10th Cir. 1984); Friends of the Bow v. Thompson, 124 F.3d 1210, 1219–20 (10th Cir. 1997).

46. *See* Dunlop v. Bachowski, 421 U.S. 560, 573–74 (1975).

47. *See* 5 U.S.C. § 701(a).

48. *See* Bollow v. Fed. Rsrv. Bank of S.F., 650 F.2d 1093, 1101–02 (9th Cir. 1981); High Country Citizens All. v. Clarke, 454 F.2d 1177, 1192 (10th Cir. 2006).

49. *See* Olivares v. Transp. Sec. Admin., 819 F.3d 454, 462–65 (D.C. Cir. 2016).

could satisfy section 555(e), since such memoranda are ordinarily not considered by courts in reviewing the merits of the decision.[50]

17.8 PROCEDURAL PROTECTIONS IN AGENCY LICENSING

Section 558(c) provides procedural protections for private parties engaged in licensing disputes with federal agencies, whether such disputes are Type A, B, or C adjudication. This section has three distinct components, involving license applications, withdrawals, and renewals.

The APA defines the term "license" broadly to include "the whole or a part of an agency permit, certificate, approval, registration, charter, membership, statutory exemption or other form of permission."[51] Thus, the provisions of section 558(c) apply to any form of legally required federal permission. However, section 558(c) does not apply to denial of a federal subsidy because an applicant failed to satisfy the conditions of the subsidy program.[52] It is unclear whether the procedural protections provided in section 558(c) apply to a plaintiff who is *indirectly* harmed by the denial of a federal license to another person.[53]

17.81 License Applications

Section 558(c) provides:

> When application is made for a license required by law, the agency, with due regard for the rights and privileges of all the interested parties or adversely affected persons and within a reasonable time, shall set and complete proceedings required to be conducted in accordance with sections 556 and 557 of this title or other proceedings required by law and shall make its decision.

This provision appears to have little practical importance. As discussed, section 555(b) requires agencies to conclude matters presented

50. *See* Aguayo v. Harvey, 476 F.3d 971, 976–77 (D.C. Cir. 2007). This decision may be limited to habeas corpus cases reviewing claims of conscientious objection to military service.

51. 5 U.S.C. § 551(8).

52. *See* Horn Farms v. Johanns, 397 F.3d 472, 478–79 (7th Cir. 2005).

53. *See* Ursack, Inc. v. Sierra Interagency Black Bear Grp., 639 F.3d 949, 961–63 (9th Cir. 2011). *But see N.Y. Pathological & X-ray Lab'ys, Inc. v. Immigr. & Naturalization Serv.*, 523 F.2d 79 (2d Cir. 1975).

to it within a reasonable time. Courts seldom require agencies to act before they are ready to do so. This sentence in section 558(c) refers to proceedings required to be conducted in accordance with sections 556 and 557, which are provisions relating to Type A adjudication. However, this sentence has no effect on licensing disputes that are treated as Type B or Type C adjudication.[54]

17.82 License Withdrawals

Section 558(c) contains protections for licensees when an agency seeks to withdraw, suspend, revoke, or annul a license. Section 558(c) does not apply if the dispute between a licensee and the government concerns the validity of the licensing criteria (as opposed to whether the licensee failed to satisfy those criteria).[55] This makes sense since a warning letter would be useless in cases in which the dispute turns on the criteria for revoking a license. While section 558(c) applies to a temporary as well as a permanent permit, it does not apply to a permit that expires by its own terms, again because a warning letter would be useless.[56]

Section 558(c) does not provide a right to a hearing (formal or informal) in the case of a license withdrawal.[57] It merely requires two things: written notice of the problem and an opportunity to demonstrate or achieve compliance.

Written notice to the licensee must list the facts or conduct that may warrant the action, as opposed to a bland statement that "permit action is warranted."[58] The provision does not make clear whether that notice needs to be given close in time to the agency's decision to withdraw the license. In one case, an agency provided an air carrier with a written notice that its certificate of authority to provide air transportation would be cancelled if it remained dormant for more than one year. That notice was sufficient to justify revocation of the certificate

---

54. *See* Marathon Oil Co. v. Env't Prot. Agency, 564 F.2d 1253, 1260 (9th Cir. 1977).

55. *Ursack*, 639 F.3d at 963; *see also* Mako Commc'ns, LLC v. Fed. Commc'ns Comm'n, 835 F.3d 146, 152 (D.C. Cir. 2016).

56. Atl. Richfield Co. v. United States, 774 F.2d 1193, 1200–01 (D.C. Cir. 1985).

57. *See* Empresa Cubana Exportadora de Alimentos y Productos Varios v. Dep't of Treasury, 638 F.3d 794, 802 (D.C. Cir. 2011).

58. Anchustegui v. U.S. Dep't of Agric., 257 F.3d 1124, 1129 (9th Cir. 2001); Blackwell Coll. of Bus. v. Att'y Gen., 454 F.2d 928, 936 (D.C. Cir. 1971); Lawrence v. Commodity Futures Trading Comm'n, 759 F.2d 767, 773 n.13 (9th Cir. 1985).

18 months later because the revocation was not an "unfair surprise."[59] The court distinguished an earlier case in which warnings were given 18 years before revocation, a time gap that violated section 558(c).[60]

Section 558(c) requires that the licensee have an opportunity to demonstrate or achieve compliance with the defects identified in the warning letter. This generally requires a second chance but does not require a third or fourth chance; repeated similar violations of the permit can trigger revocation without sending additional warning letters.[61] Section 558(c) does not require a second chance in cases of "willfulness." To rely on this exception, an agency must make a finding of willfulness that is supported by substantial evidence.[62] Case law contains numerous definitions of the term "willful." One line of cases defines "willfulness" "by repeated violations, intentional wrongdoing, or gross neglect of a known duty, but not by simple negligence."[63] Another line states that a party acted willfully if it intentionally does an act that is prohibited, irrespective of evil motive or reliance on erroneous advice, or acts with careless disregard of statutory requirements.[64] A third group defines the term as "an intentional disregard of or plain indifference to the statutory requirements."[65]

Further, the second-chance provision of section 558(c) does not apply if public health, interest, or safety requires otherwise. This phrase refers to a situation in which immediate cancellation of a license is necessary to protect the public interest, without regard to the equities or injuries to the licensee, as in the case of immediate suspension of a pilot's license after an accident.[66]

---

59. Air N. Am. v. Dep't of Transp., 937 F.2d 1427, 1437–38 (9th Cir. 1991).

60. Hutto Stockyard, Inc. v. U.S. Dep't of Agric., 903 F.2d 299, 304 (4th Cir. 1990).

61. Buckingham v. U.S. Dep't of Agric., 603 F.3d 1073, 1084–87 (9th Cir. 2010).

62. *Hutto Stockyard*, 903 F.2d at 304–05; *Lawrence*, 759 F.2d at 772; Halvonik v. Dudas, 398 F. Supp. 2d 115, 125 (D.D.C. 2005).

63. *Hutto Stockyard*, 903 F.2d at 304; Cap. Produce Co. v. United States, 930 F.2d 1077, 1079 (10th Cir. 1991).

64. Kleiman & Hochberg, Inc. v. U.S. Dep't of Agric., 497 F.3d 681, 691 (D.C. Cir. 2007).

65. Luna Tech, Inc. v. Bureau of Alcohol, Tobacco & Firearms, 183 F. App'x 863, 866 (11th Cir. 2006).

66. Attorney General's Manual on the Administrative Procedure Act, *supra* note 3, at 91; *see also* Tucson Rod & Gun Club v. McGee, 25 F. Supp. 1025, 1030 (D. Ariz. 1998).

17.83 License Renewals

When a licensee has made timely and sufficient application for a renewal or for a new license in accordance with agency rules, a license permitting an activity of a continuing nature does not expire until the application has been finally determined by the agency.[67] The *Attorney General's Manual* states that this provision reflects existing law and practice:

> It is only fair where a licensee has filed his application for a renewal or a new license in ample time prior to the expiration of his license, and where the application itself is sufficient, that his license should not expire until his application shall have been determined by the agency. In such a case, the licensee has done everything that is within his power to do and he should not suffer if the agency has failed, for one reason or another, to consider his application prior to the lapse of his license. Agencies, of course, may make reasonable rules requiring sufficient advance application.[68]

The leading case on the license renewal provision is *Pan-Atlantic Steamship Corp. v. Atlantic Coast Line Railroad*.[69] That case involved a provision in the Interstate Commerce Act (enacted before the APA) providing that the Interstate Commerce Commission (ICC) could issue a temporary license to permit water carriers to provide service in emergency situations. Such temporary licenses "shall be valid for such time as the Commission shall specify, but not for more than an aggregate of one hundred and eighty days." Pan-Atlantic received a temporary license and applied for a permanent license, but the ICC had not completed processing of the latter application when the 180-day period expired. The ICC granted a temporary extension of the temporary license until it decided the application for a permanent license. Competing railroads challenged this decision. The U.S. Supreme Court held that the later-enacted APA provision enabled the ICC's action, stating:

We see no reason why the provisions of this later Act may not be invoked to protect a person with a license from the damage he would suffer by being compelled to discontinue a business of a

---

67. 5 U.S.C. § 558(c).

68. Attorney General's Manual on the Administrative Procedure Act, *supra* note 3, at 91–92.

69. 353 U.S. 436 (1957).

continuing nature, only to start it anew after the administrative hearing is concluded.[70]

The provision against expiration of a license while a renewal application is pending applies only to "a license with reference to an activity of a continuing nature." Therefore, the section does not require the extension of the expiration date of a construction permit because construction is not an activity of a continuing nature.[71] And it does not apply to the expiration of a license occurring after the license has been assigned and the assignor failed to apply for a renewal of the license.[72]

---

70. *Id.* at 439. The decision in *Pan-Atlantic* was 6–3. The dissenters argued that the APA provision should not apply to a temporary, emergency license issued without the normal elaborate hearing requirements for granting such licenses.

71. Miami MDS Co. v. Fed. Commcn's Comm'n, 14 F.3d 658, 659–60 (D.C. Cir. 1994); *see also* Bankers Life & Cas. Co. v. Callaway, 530 F.2d 625, 634 (5th Cir. 1976).

72. Kay v. Fed. Commcn's Comm'n, 525 F.3d 1277, 1278 (D.C. Cir. 2008).

Chapter 18

Proceedings Involving a Legally Required Evidentiary Hearing

Jeremy S. Graboyes

18.1 CHAPTER OVERVIEW

An "evidentiary hearing," as used in this guide, means an adjudicative proceeding in which all parties have an opportunity to submit and rebut arguments and evidence and the adjudicator renders a decision based solely on an "exclusive record" (i.e., information provided by the parties and matters officially noticed).[1] Evidentiary hearings can take different forms in different federal programs. Most are structured as adversarial proceedings, but some are explicitly nonadversarial (see Chapter 8). Some rely on formal procedural and evidentiary rules like those used in the federal courts; others are relatively informal. Evidentiary hearings can be conducted in person, or they can be conducted remotely by videoconference or teleconference (Chapter 21) or through the exchange of written materials (Chapter 22).

Not all "hearings" are evidentiary hearings. Hearings held to receive input from members of the public, for example, are not considered evidentiary hearings because they do not provide the exclusive source of information for the adjudicator. Oral arguments before an agency appellate body are not considered evidentiary hearings if they do not include an opportunity for submission of new evidence.

As discussed in Chapter 15, constitutional due process requires "some kind of hearing" whenever the government intends to deprive a private party of life, liberty, or property.[2] That hearing often takes the form of an evidentiary hearing. A statute, executive order, or agency rule can also require an opportunity for an evidentiary hearing even when due process requires none, but mere reference to a "hearing" or "notice and hearing" is usually insufficient to require an evidentiary hearing.[3]

The formal-adjudication provisions of the Administrative Procedure Act (APA)—5 U.S.C. §§ 554, 556–557—outline basic parameters for an evidentiary hearing. Therefore, any statute that includes the APA's magic words ("on the record after opportunity for an agency hearing") or otherwise invokes its formal-adjudication provisions requires an opportunity for an evidentiary hearing. Hearings conducted according to these provisions are sometimes called "Type A"

---

1. Michael Asimow, Admin. Conf. of the U.S., Federal Administrative Adjudication outside the Administrative Procedure Act (2019).

2. *See* Goldberg v. Kelly, 397 U.S. 254, 269–71 (1970); Henry J. Friendly, *"Some Kind of Hearing,"* 123 U. Pa. L. Rev. 1267 (1975).

3. *See* Pension Benefit Guarantee Corp. v. LTV Corp., 496 U.S. 633, 653–56 (1990).

adjudications (see Chapter 1). Type A adjudications are conducted by many regulatory agencies and in some public benefits programs, including ones administered by the Department of Labor (DOL) and Department of Health and Human Services (HHS).

Many agencies conduct evidentiary hearings that are not governed by the APA's formal-adjudication provisions. These "informal" evidentiary hearings are sometimes called "Type B" adjudications (see Chapter 1). Procedurally, there is often little distinction between Type A and Type B adjudications. Rather, as discussed in Chapter 9, it is the regulation of the adjudicator that principally distinguishes them. Type B adjudications are conducted by agencies and subagencies including the Executive Office for Immigration Review (EOIR), U.S. Patent and Trademark Office (USPTO), Board of Veterans' Appeals (BVA), Merit Systems Protection Board (MSPB), and Civilian Board of Contract Appeals.[4]

This chapter provides a basic overview of the procedures used in proceedings that involve a legally required opportunity for an evidentiary hearing. Building on Chapter 10, it begins with a discussion of integrity in Type A and Type B adjudications (section 18.2). It turns next to timing and notice of the hearing (sections 18.3 and 18.4). The next sections address prehearing procedures (section 18.5), hearing conduct (section 18.6), and post-hearing development (section 18.7). The chapter concludes by discussing how decisions are rendered following an evidentiary hearing (section 18.8) and opportunities for reconsideration, reopening, and review (section 18.9).

18.2 INTEGRITY

Although many adjudicative procedures include a legally required opportunity for an evidentiary hearing, most cases never advance to one. Most can be resolved satisfactorily through frontline processes (see Chapter 16). These methods are, as a rule, faster, less costly, and more efficient than evidentiary hearings. If a proceeding can be resolved using such methods, it is typically beneficial to all parties involved to avoid the time and expense of an evidentiary hearing.

But frontline processes are not sufficient to satisfactorily resolve all cases. Some cases are of "such far-reaching importance to so many interests that sound and wise government is thought to require that proceedings be conducted publicly and formally so that the information

---

4. Asimow, *supra* note 1.

on which action is to be based may be tested, answered if necessary, and recorded." In other cases, the parties' conflicting interests are simply not "capable of solution by informal methods." Judicialized procedures—characterized by clear rules, formal opportunities to present and rebut evidence and arguments, and an emphasis on authority and impartiality—are especially important in both scenarios.[5]

Impartiality, along with the public appearance of impartiality, is pursued through several procedural requirements. In Type A adjudications, adjudicators must use an exclusive record to render decisions and are barred from engaging in ex parte communications. These requirements ensure that all parties have a fair opportunity to review and respond to all informational inputs.[6] The Administrative Conference of the United States (ACUS) recommends similar requirements for Type B adjudications.[7] Consistent with ACUS recommendations, many agencies have issued rules requiring decision-makers to recuse themselves in cases of actual and apparent bias.[8]

Impartiality is also pursued through transparency, which, as discussed in Chapter 28, facilitates external oversight and helps promote public confidence.[9] With relatively few exceptions, evidentiary hearings in both Type A and Type B adjudications are, and have long been, open to the public.[10] Hearing-level adjudicators are generally required to explain their decisions, and many agencies make those explanations publicly available.[11]

---

5. Final Report of the Attorney General's Committee on Administrative Procedure, S. Doc. No. 8, at 43 (1941) [hereinafter Attorney General's Committee Report].

6. 5 U.S.C. §§ 554(d), 556(e), 557(d).

7. Administrative Conference Recommendation 2016-4, Evidentiary Hearings Not Required by the Administrative Procedure Act, ¶¶ 1–2, 81 Fed. Reg. 94,314, 94,315 (Dec. 23, 2016).

8. Administrative Conference Recommendation 2018-4, Recusal Rules for Administrative Adjudicators, 84 Fed. Reg. 2,139 (Feb. 6, 2019); *see also* Louis J. Virelli III, ACUS, Administrative Recusal Rules: A Taxonomy and Study of Existing Recusal Standards for Agency Adjudicators (2020).

9. Attorney General's Committee Report, *supra* note 5, at 68; *see also* Administrative Conference Recommendation 2021-6, Public Access to Agency Adjudicative Proceedings, ¶ 5, 87 Fed. Reg. 1,715, 1,716–17 (Jan. 12, 2022).

10. *See* Administrative Conference Recommendation 2021-6, *supra* note 9, ¶ 5; Attorney General's Committee, *supra* note 5, at 68.

11. *See* Administrative Conference Recommendation 2017-1, Adjudication Materials on Agency Websites, 82 Fed. Reg. 31,039 (July 5, 2017).

Finally, impartiality is pursued through structural means. One option is for agency heads to conduct evidentiary hearings. Agency heads are vetted through presidential appointment and Senate confirmation, and, as political appointees, may be more responsive to presidential and congressional oversight than career officials. As a practical matter, however, agency heads typically lack the time to preside over trial-like hearings.[12] And their status as political appointees has historically raised questions about their ability to render decisions apolitically.[13]

Evidentiary hearings are more commonly conducted by career officials whose primary responsibility is conducting hearings and rendering decisions. The nearly 2,000 administrative law judges (ALJs) employed by federal agencies form the most recognizable category of such officials. The vast majority of ALJs conduct hearings under benefits programs administered by the Social Security Administration (SSA), HHS, and DOL; most of the rest work at regulatory agencies like the National Labor Relations Board (NLRB). As described in Chapters 8–10, the APA regulates how agencies select, manage, compensate, and discipline ALJs.[14] These mechanisms are intended to insulate ALJs from undue interference from or influence by officials with interests or functions thought to be in tension with impartial decision-making, such as political appointees, prosecutors, and investigators.[15]

In addition to ALJs, there are thousands of other career officials whose primary responsibility is conducting evidentiary hearings and rendering decisions. These officials go by many titles (e.g., veterans law judges, administrative patent judges) but are often referred to collectively as "administrative judges" (AJs). Although the APA's protections do not apply to AJs, other statutes and executive branch policies regulate how agencies select, manage, compensate, and discipline them.[16] ACUS has recommended that agencies design and administer hiring processes for AJs to ensure they "will act impartially and maintain

12. Attorney General's Committee Report, *supra* note 5, at 43.

13. Ramspeck v. Fed. Trial Exam'rs Conf., 345 U.S. 128, 131–32 (1953).

14. *But see* Lucia v. Sec. & Exch. Comm'n, 138 S. Ct. 2044 (2018); Exec. Order No. 13,843, 83 Fed. Reg. 32,755 (July 13, 2018); *see also* Administrative Conference Recommendation 2019-2, Agency Recruitment and Selection of Administrative Law Judges, 84 Fed. Reg. 38,930 (Aug. 8, 2019).

15. Butz v. Economou, 438 U.S. 478, 513–14 (1978).

16. Kent H. Barnett, *Some Kind of Hearing Officer*, 94 Wash. L. Rev. 515 (2019); Kent Barnett & Russell Wheeler, *Non-ALJ Adjudicators in Federal Agencies: Status, Selection, Oversight, and Removal*, 53 Ga. L. Rev. 1 (2018).

the appearance of impartiality" and separate AJs and their staff from enforcement staff.[17]

18.3 TIMING OF THE HEARING

An opportunity for an evidentiary hearing ordinarily must precede a government action that deprives a person of a protected interest in life, liberty, or property.[18] Due process permits a post-deprivation hearing only in limited circumstances, for example when an agency must act quickly to protect the public interest or a predeprivation hearing is impractical or impossible.[19]

The APA says little about when hearings must take place. For Type A adjudications, timing must be fixed with "due regard . . . for the convenience and necessity of the parties."[20] For Type A and Type B adjudications, agencies must conclude matters presented to them with "due regard for the convenience and necessity of the parties or their representatives and within a reasonable time."[21] Program-specific statutes and rules sometimes provide greater specificity regarding the timing of hearings. HHS, for example, is statutorily required to provide a hearing on Medicare appeals within 90 days after a party requests one.[22]

18.4 NOTICE OF THE HEARING

Where it applies, due process requires "timely and adequate" notice of a hearing.[23] Statutes and agency rules often also impose specific notice requirements. There are five key questions when it comes to giving notice:

1. To whom should notice be given?
2. When should notice be given?
3. How should notice be given?
4. Who should give notice?
5. What information should notice contain?

---

17. Administrative Conference Recommendation 2019-9, Recruiting and Hiring Agency Attorneys, 84 Fed. Reg. 71,355, 71,358 (Dec. 27, 2019); Administrative Conference Recommendation 2016-4, *supra* note 7, ¶¶ 3–4.

18. Goldberg v. Kelly, 397 U.S. 254 (1970).

19. Fed. Deposit Ins. Corp. v. Mallen, 486 U.S. 230, 246–47 (1988); Hodel v. Va. Surface Mining & Reclamation Ass'n, 452 U.S. 264, 299–303 (1981).

20. 5 U.S.C. § 554(b).

21. *Id.* § 555(b).

22. 42 U.S.C. § 1395ff(d)(1)(A).

23. *Goldberg*, 397 U.S. at 267.

This section takes each question in turn.

First, to whom should notice be given? In Type A adjudications, the APA requires, unhelpfully, that agencies provide notice to "[p]ersons entitled to notice."[24] Parties to a proceeding and intervenors are clearly entitled to notice, but others might also be entitled to notice by statute, rule, or general norms of due process. Occupational Safety and Health Review Commission (OSHRC) rules, for example, require that notice be given to employees affected by alleged workplace health and safety violations.[25] Depending on the nature or purpose of a proceeding, policy considerations may weigh in favor of providing notice to persons beyond parties and intervenors, or even the public generally.

Second, when should notice be given? Where it applies, constitutional due process requires that notice be "timely."[26] As with most due process matters, what constitutes "timely" notice will depend on the circumstances. The APA does not specify how far in advance of a hearing notice must be given. In practice, "[w]hether a given period of time constitutes timely notice will depend upon the circumstances, including the urgency of the situation and the complexity of the issues involved in the proceeding."[27] For Type B adjudications, ACUS has recommended that agencies adopt rules requiring notice be given "sufficiently far in advance so that [parties] may prepare for hearings."[28] Some statutes specify how far in advance of a hearing notice must be given. The Federal Trade Commission Act, for example, requires 30 days' notice of a hearing.[29] Many agencies have also adopted their own rules regarding the timing of notice. An SSA rule, for example, requires at least 75 days' notice of a hearing.[30]

Third, how should notice be given? Where it applies, due process requires that notice be "reasonably calculated under all the circumstances to apprise" a person of the proceeding.[31] The APA does not provide how agencies must provide notice.[32] For Type B proceedings, ACUS has recommended only that agencies give notice "by appropriate

---

24. 5 U.S.C. § 554(b).
25. 29 C.F.R. § 2200.7(i), (j) (2022).
26. *Goldberg*, 397 U.S. at 267.
27. Attorney General's Manual on the Administrative Procedure Act 46 (1947) [hereinafter Attorney General's Manual].
28. Administrative Conference Recommendation 2016-4, *supra* note 7, ¶ 6.
29. 15 U.S.C. § 45(b).
30. 20 C.F.R. § 404.938(a) (2022).
31. *Cf.* Mullane v. Cent. Hanover Bank & Tr. Co., 339 U.S. 306, 314–15 (1950).
32. Olin Indus. v. Nat'l Lab. Rels. Bd., 192 F.2d 799 (5th Cir. 1951).

means."[33] As with timing, the appropriate means for giving notice will depend on the circumstances. Mail is perhaps the obvious choice for giving notice, but notice by electronic means is increasingly common. Where nonparties might have an interest in a hearing, it may be sufficient to publish notice in the *Federal Register.*[34] In other cases, it may be necessary to post notice in a conspicuous location, publish notice in a local newspaper, or give notice by some other means to informal specially interested persons.[35] Agencies can also use their own websites to provide general notice of upcoming hearings.[36]

Fourth, who should give notice? Responsibility for giving notice can vary depending on whether the government or a private party initiates the proceeding.[37] Specific statutes or agency rules typically specify who is responsible for notifying whom.[38]

Finally, what information should a hearing notice contain? Where it applies, constitutional due process requires that notice be "adequate."[39] For Type A adjudications, the APA requires, at a minimum, that notice include (1) "the time, place, and nature of the hearing"; (2) "the legal authority and jurisdiction under which the hearing is to be held"; and (3) "the matters of fact and law asserted."[40] The statement of the matters of fact and law asserted need not be detailed so long as they "advise the parties of the legal and factual issues involved."[41] Notices of hearing frequently include other important information as well.[42] For Type B adjudications, ACUS has recommended that agencies consider including additional information about topics such as discovery and subpoena procedures, information about representation, availability of video or telephone hearings, opportunities for alternative dispute resolution (ADR), and filing deadlines.[43]

---

33. Administrative Conference Recommendation 2016-4, *supra* note 7, ¶ 6.

34. 44 U.S.C. § 1508; *see also* N. Ala. Express, Inc. v. United States, 585 F.2d 783, 786 (5th Cir. 1978); Administrative Conference Recommendation 76-2, Strengthening the Information and Notice-Giving Functions of the Federal Register, 41 Fed. Reg. 29,653 (July 19, 1976).

35. 29 C.F.R. § 2200.7(i) (2022).

36. Administrative Conference Recommendation 2021-6, *supra* note 9, ¶ 12.

37. *See* 5 U.S.C. § 554(b).

38. 29 C.F.R. § 2200.7(i) (2022).

39. Goldberg v. Kelly, 397 U.S. 254, 267 (1970).

40. 5 U.S.C. § 554(b).

41. Attorney General's Manual, *supra* note 27, at 47.

42. Administrative Conference Recommendation 2016-4, *supra* note 7, ¶ 6; *see also* Model Adjudication Rules § 300(A) (ACUS 2018).

43. Administrative Conference Recommendation 2016-4, *supra* note 7, ¶ 6.

18.5 PREHEARING DEVELOPMENT

The purpose of an evidentiary hearing is to gather the evidence and arguments needed to render a fair and accurate decision. But an evidentiary hearing alone, without preparation, is unlikely to be the fairest or most accurate way to develop a record and elicit views; it is certainly not the most efficient way. Agencies, like courts, have developed a range of prehearing procedures intended to help collect and exchange evidence and arguments, identify and clarify contested issues, expedite and simplify proceedings, and resolve issues (e.g., stipulations) or even entire cases without the need for a hearing.

Prehearing procedures vary considerably across federal agencies according to the needs and circumstances of specific programs and proceedings. This section focuses on nine types of prehearing procedures: submission of facts and written arguments (section 18.51); discovery (section 18.52); subpoenas (section 18.53); use of federal transparency laws (section 18.54); agency-assisted evidentiary development (section 18.55); prehearing conferences (section 18.56); ADR (section 18.57); withdrawal, dismissal, and summary judgment (section 18.58); and waiver of oral hearing (section 18.59).

18.51 Submission of Facts and Written Arguments

Agencies must give all interested parties an opportunity to submit facts and arguments "when time, the nature of the proceeding, and the public interest permit."[44] Pleading and responsive pleading are common practice at some agencies and can be a useful way to identify and clarify contested issues. Indeed, the APA specifically contemplates that agencies will require responsive pleading by rule in appropriate contexts,[45] and many agencies have adopted rules that require or authorize adjudicators to require parties to submit a prehearing statement.[46] In other contexts, particularly where parties are commonly unrepresented, it may be less helpful or unfair to expect parties to submit written arguments before a hearing.[47]

---

44. 5 U.S.C. § 554(b)–(c).
45. *Id.* § 554(b).
46. *Cf.* Model Adjudication Rules § 245 (ACUS 2018).
47. *Cf.* Goldberg v. Kelly, 397 U.S. 254, 269 (1970); *see also* Administrative Conference Recommendation 2016-6, Self-Represented Parties in Administrative Proceedings, 81 Fed. Reg. 94,319 (Dec. 23, 2016).

18.52 Discovery

Discovery refers to a collection of procedures by which parties to a proceeding can obtain evidence from each other. Due process does not necessarily require prehearing discovery,[48] nor does the APA expressly provide for it.[49] Nonetheless, discovery has long been considered a best practice given its potential to promote "more expeditious conduct of the hearing itself, the encouragement of settlement between the parties, and greater fairness in adjudication."[50]

Many programs include opportunities for discovery, either by statute or agency rule. Indeed, discovery provides the primary means for developing the evidentiary record in some contexts, most notably in proceedings before the Patent Trial and Appeal Board and the Trademark Trial and Appeal Board.[51] Elsewhere, discovery is circumscribed or unavailable, for example in the immigration courts.[52] Although discovery is generally considered a best practice, there can be good policy reasons for limiting it in specific contexts. The NLRB, for example, limits discovery given the strong potential for witness intimidation in labor litigation.[53]

Although the Federal Rules of Civil Procedure are inapplicable to agency proceedings unless adopted by statute or rule,[54] agency discovery practices often mirror discovery in federal civil litigation.[55] As in the courts, common discovery methods include requests for

---

48. Kelly v. Env't Prot. Agency, 203 F.3d 519 (7th Cir. 2000).

49. *See* Pac. Gas & Elec. Co. v. Fed. Energy Regul. Comm'n, 746 F.2d 1383, 1387 (9th Cir. 1984); Kenrich Petrochems., Inc. v. Nat'l Lab. Rels. Bd., 893 F.2d 1468, 1484 (3d Cir. 1990); Nat'l Lab. Rels. Bd. v. Valley Mold Co., 530 F.2d 693, 695 (6th Cir. 1976); Frilette v. Kimberlin, 508 F.2d 205, 208 (3d Cir. 1974); Nat'l Lab. Rels. Bd. v. Interboro Contractors, 432 F.2d 854 (2d Cir. 1970).

50. Administrative Conference Recommendation 70-4, Discovery in Agency Adjudication, 38 Fed. Reg. 19,786 (July 23, 1973); *see also* Administrative Conference Recommendation 2016-4, *supra* note 7, ¶ 10.

51. Michael Asimow, *Best Practices for Evidentiary Hearings outside the Administrative Procedure Act*, 26 Geo. Mason L. Rev. 923, 955 (2019).

52. Margaret B. Kwoka, *First-Person FOIA*, 127 Yale L.J. 2204, 2257–61 (2018); Geoffrey Heeren, *Shattering the One-Way Mirror: Discovery in Immigration Court*, 79 Brook. L. Rev. 1569 (2014).

53. Roger J. Au & Son, Inc. v. Nat'l Lab. Rels. Bd., 538 F.2d 80, 83 (3d Cir. 1976); Title Guarantee Co. v. Nat'l Lab. Rels. Bd., 534 F.2d 484, 491 (2d Cir. 1976).

54. Pac. Gas & Elec. Co. v. Fed. Energy Regul. Comm'n, 746 F.2d 1383, 1387 (9th Cir. 1984).

55. Fed. Mar. Comm'n v. S.C. State Ports Auth., 535 U.S. 743, 758 (2002).

production of records or objects, requests for admission, depositions, and interrogatories. While procedures vary across agencies, the ACUS Model Adjudication Rules set forth representative rules.[56] Other topics rules might address include who manages discovery (i.e., the adjudicator or the parties), procedures for handling privileged or confidential information (see section 18.65), and sanctions for a party's failure to comply with a valid discovery request.

18.53 Subpoenas

Agencies typically have broad statutory authority to issue subpoenas to compel testimony or the production of documents. The APA permits agencies, including ALJs, to issue subpoenas "authorized by law" on a party's request.[57] Although parties typically request a subpoena to obtain testimony or records from a third party, subpoenas might also provide a means in some circumstances to obtain testimony or records from another party when discovery is limited or unavailable.

There is no absolute right to issuance of a subpoena. For both Type A and Type B adjudications, the APA permits agencies to issue procedural rules that require parties to provide "a statement or showing of general relevance and reasonable scope of the evidence sought."[58] ACUS has recommended that agencies "explain their subpoena practice in detail."[59]

Agencies typically lack independent authority to enforce their subpoenas.[60] Instead, a party seeking to enforce a subpoena must ask a federal district court to sustain it. If the court finds that the subpoena is "in accordance with law," it will issue an order to enforce it "under penalty of punishment for contempt in case of contumacious failure to comply."[61] Courts typically require a showing that (1) the proceeding

---

56. Model Adjudication Rules §§ 230–239 (ACUS 2018).

57. 5 U.S.C. §§ 555(d), 556(c)(2).

58. *Id.* § 555(d).

59. Administrative Conference Recommendation 2016-4, *supra* note 7, ¶ 11; *see also* Administrative Conference Recommendation 74-1, Subpena Power in Formal Rulemaking and Formal Adjudication, 39 Fed. Reg. 23,041 (June 26, 1974).

60. Interstate Com. Comm'n v. Brimson, 154 U.S. 447 (1894); Nat'l Lab. Rels. Bd. v. Interbake Foods, LLC, 637 F.3d 492, 497–500 (4th Cir. 2011); Atl. Richfield Co. v. U.S. Dep't of Energy, 769 F.2d 771, 793 (D.C. Cir. 1984); Sec. & Exch. Comm'n v. Wheeling-Pittsburgh Steel Corp., 548 F.2d 118, 123–24 (3d Cir. 1981); Nat'l Lab. Rels. Bd. v. Int'l Med. Sys., Ltd., 640 F.2d 1110, 1115–16 (9th Cir. 1981).

61. 5 U.S.C. § 555(d).

is conducted pursuant to a legitimate purpose; (2) the information sought is relevant to the inquiry; (3) the information sought is not already within the agency's possession; and (4) the required administrative steps have been followed.[62]

18.54 Use of Federal Transparency Laws

Parties sometimes rely on the Freedom of Information Act (FOIA) and Privacy Act to obtain agency records for purposes of an adjudication. These statutes were not enacted for this purpose,[63] nor do they provide a particularly effective vehicle for obtaining records in time for a scheduled hearing. Nonetheless, private parties may turn to these statutes to obtain records in contexts where discovery is limited or unavailable.[64] This has contributed to mounting FOIA backlogs at some agencies.[65] ACUS, for its part, has recommended that, aside from discovery, "[p]rocedural regulations should permit parties to inspect unprivileged materials in agency files that are not otherwise protected."[66]

Program-specific statutes and rules may also provide a vehicle for accessing records for purposes of an adjudication. The Immigration and Nationality Act, for example, provides that in removal proceedings, "the alien shall have access to the alien's visa or other entry document, if any, and any other records and documents, not considered by the Attorney General to be confidential, pertaining to the alien's admission or presence in the United States."[67]

---

62. United States v. Powell, 379 U.S. 48, 57–58 (1964); United States v. Morton Salt Co., 338 U.S. 632, 652 (1950); Penfield Co. of Cal. v. Sec. & Exch. Comm'n, 330 U.S. 585, 605 (1947).

63. Nat'l Lab. Rels. Bd. v. Sears, Roebuck & Co., 421 U.S. 132, 143 n.10 (1975).

64. Administrative Conference Recommendation 83-4, The Use of the Freedom of Information Act for Discovery Purposes, 48 Fed. Reg. 57,463 (Dec. 30, 1983); Kwoka, *supra* note 52, at 2257–61; Edward A. Tomlinson, *Use of the Freedom of Information Act for Discovery Purposes*, 43 Md. L. Rev. 119, 155 n.182 (1984); Appleseed Network Immigr. Collective, Getting Off the Assembly Line: Overcoming Immigration Court Obstacles in Individual Cases 19–25 (2016). *But see* Roger J. Au & Son, Inc. v. Nat'l Lab. Rels. Bd., 538 F.2d 80 (3d Cir. 1976).

65. Kwoka, *supra* note 52, at 2256–57; Regina Germain, *Putting the Form in Immigration Court Reform*, 84 Denver L. Rev. 1145, 1146–47 (2007).

66. Administrative Conference Recommendation 2016-4, *supra* note 7, ¶ 10.

67. 8 U.S.C. § 1229a(c)(2).

18.55 Agency-Assisted Evidentiary Development

Although the proponent of an order typically has the burden of producing evidence (see section 18.62), some agencies have processes designed to help private parties, especially unrepresented parties, obtain relevant evidence. This is more common in benefits adjudication, which is often nonadversarial. While assistance often occurs prior to the hearing stage of an adjudicative process,[68] there may be opportunities for assistance at the hearing stage as well.[69]

18.56 Prehearing Conferences

Agencies convene comparatively informal, prehearing conferences at different stages of a proceeding and for many different purposes.[70] They go by many names, depending on the program and purpose, including prehearing conference, settlement conference, discovery conference, informal conference, and scheduling conference. But they are all, at their core, "primarily a way to organize the proceedings to achieve optimum productivity and avoid wasting time and effort." As described in the ACUS *Manual for Administrative Law Judges*: "An effective prehearing conference can be useful in identifying areas of disagreement (and agreement), setting a schedule or agenda for any pretrial discovery, and taking other steps to lay the groundwork for either: (a) settlement, or (2) an efficient, orderly, and fair hearing."[71] Prehearing conferences can be an important tool for case and docket management.[72]

The APA explicitly authorizes, even encourages, presiding officials in Type A adjudications to hold conferences for the settlement or simplification of the issues.[73] Adjudicators can require the attendance at such meetings "of at least one representative of each party who has authority to negotiate concerning resolution of issues in controversy."[74]

ACUS has recommended that agencies adopt similar procedural rules for Type B adjudications giving adjudicators discretion to convene

---

68. *See, e.g.*, 38 U.S.C. § 5103A.

69. *See, e.g.*, Social Security Ruling, SSR 17-4p, 82 Fed. Reg. 46,339 (Oct. 4, 2017).

70. *See* Model Adjudication Rules § 220 (ACUS 2018).

71. Morell E. Mullins, ACUS, Manual for Administrative Law Judges 18 (3d ed. 1993).

72. Administrative Conference Recommendation 86-7, Case Management as a Tool for Improving Agency Adjudication, 51 Fed. Reg. 46,989 (Dec. 30, 1986).

73. 5 U.S.C. § 556(c)(6).

74. *Id.* § 556(c)(6), (8).

prehearing conferences, adding that parties should be required to "exchange witness lists and expert reports" beforehand.[75]

18.57 Alternative Dispute Resolution

ADR, discussed in Chapter 20, plays a prominent role at the hearing stage of many agency adjudicative processes. The APA authorizes presiding officials in Type A adjudications to hold conferences for the settlement of the issues by the use of ADR, to inform the parties as to the availability of ADR, and even to encourage their use.[76] ACUS has made similar recommendations for Type B adjudications, recommending that agencies "encourage and facilitate ADR."[77]

18.58 Withdrawal, Dismissal, and Summary Judgment

Agency rules often set forth procedures for parties to withdraw an adjudication.[78] Many agencies have also adopted rules that permit adjudicators, on a party's motion or on their own motion, to dismiss an adjudication or to summarily decide it without an evidentiary hearing. Grounds justifying dismissal vary across programs. Examples include failure to appear at a hearing[79] or failure to comply with an adjudicator's order.[80]

Summary judgment allows an agency, like a court, to decide a case or issue without an evidentiary hearing when there is no genuine issue of material fact. Although the APA contains no provision that explicitly provides for summary judgment, ACUS recommended as early as 1970 that "[e]ach agency having a substantial caseload of formal adjudications" should adopt summary judgment procedures. ACUS stated that the elimination of "unnecessary evidentiary hearings" in such cases can eliminate delays, particularly at agencies with substantial caseloads.[81] ACUS later recommended that agencies should consider

75. Administrative Conference Recommendation 2016-4, *supra* note 7, ¶ 8.
76. 5 U.S.C. § 556(c)(6), (7).
77. Administrative Conference Recommendation 2016-4, *supra* note 7, ¶ 12.
78. *See* Model Adjudication Rules § 180(A) (ACUS 2018).
79. *See, e.g.*, 20 C.F.R. § 404.957(b)(1) (2022) (SSA).
80. *See, e.g.*, Model Adjudication Rules § 180(B) (ACUS 2018).
81. Administrative Conference Recommendation 70-3, Summary Decision in Agency Adjudication, 38 Fed. Reg. 19,785 (July 23, 1973); *see also* Ernest Gellhorn & William F. Robinson, Jr., *Summary Judgment in Administrative Adjudication*, 84 Harv. L. Rev. 612 (1971). *But see* Alexander I. Platt, *Is Administrative Summary Judgment Unlawful?*, 44 Harv. J. L. & Pub. Pol'y 239 (2021).

adopting similar procedures for Type B adjudications.[82] Many agencies that conduct evidentiary hearings have adopted such processes. Although their specifics vary, representative procedures can be found in ACUS's Model Adjudication Rules.[83] While summary judgment is broadly permitted, it cannot be used to shift the burden of proof from the party who bears it.[84]

An analog to summary judgment exists in SSA's nonadversarial process for deciding applications for disability benefits. ALJs and staff attorneys are authorized to issue decisions without a hearing when the evidence in the record for a case supports a finding in favor of all parties on all issues. Parties retain their right to a hearing if they are dissatisfied with the decision.[85]

18.59 Waiver of Oral Hearing

Rather than requiring an oral hearing, statutes and agency rules more often provide an opportunity for an oral hearing. Many agencies have adopted rules providing that an adjudicator need not conduct an oral hearing if all parties waive their right to one. In such cases, the adjudicator typically prepares a record of the filings and evidence submitted by the parties, which forms the exclusive record for decision-making.[86]

18.6 THE HEARING

18.61 Regulating the Conduct of the Hearing

The APA grants presiding officials in Type A adjudications broad authority to regulate the conduct of hearings "[s]ubject to published rules of the agency and within its powers,"[87] and AJs may be given similarly broad authority.[88] The primary way in which agencies regulate the conduct of hearings is through generally applicable rules of practice. Some proceedings follow rules that emulate those codified in the Federal Rules of Civil Procedure;[89] others are fairly informal or more distinctly administrative in nature. Some allow individual adju-

---

82. Administrative Conference Recommendation 2016-4, *supra* note 7, ¶¶ 8, 21.
83. Model Adjudication Rules §§ 230–239 (ACUS 2018).
84. United States v. Menendez, 48 F.3d 1401, 1413–14 (5th Cir. 1995).
85. 20 C.F.R. §§ 404.942, 404.948 (2022).
86. *See, e.g.*, 24 C.F.R. § 180.610 (2022) (Department of Housing and Urban Development).
87. 5 U.S.C. § 556(c)(5).
88. *See, e.g.*, 8 C.F.R. § 1240.1(c) (2022) (EOIR).
89. *See, e.g.*, 29 U.S.C. § 661(g) (OSHRC).

dicators greater discretion to regulate the hearing as they see fit; others structure the hearing process with greater specificity.

One way in which adjudicators can impose order on a proceeding is through the availability of sanctions. For Type B adjudications, ACUS has recommended that agencies, if permitted, "authorize decisionmakers to sanction attorneys and parties for misconduct." Sanctions can include "admonitions, monetary fines, and preclusion from appearing before the agency."[90]

But there are other ways adjudicators can regulate the conduct of a hearing. An important consideration is the extent to which an adjudicator participates in the presentation of evidence and development of the record. Depending on the program and the specific proceeding, it may promote accuracy and efficiency for an adjudicator to play a more active role in questioning and seeking information from parties and their representatives than is common in judicial trials.[91]

18.62 Burden and Standard of Proof

The proponent of an order has the burden of proof in a Type A adjudication unless a statute provides otherwise.[92] The APA does not define the term "burden of proof." It has been variably used over the years to refer to both the burden of production and the burden of persuasion. A party with the burden of production is responsible for submitting evidence in support of a proposition. A party with the burden of persuasion is responsible for persuading the adjudicator of the truth of the proposition. Although people still sometimes use the term "burden of proof" to encompass both concepts, the U.S. Supreme Court has interpreted "burden of proof" as used in the APA to mean burden of persuasion, not burden of production.[93]

Depending on the context, the proponent of an order can be a private party (e.g., an individual who applies for a government benefit or license) or the government (e.g., an agency that seeks to impose

---

90. Administrative Conference Recommendation 2016-4, *supra* note 7, ¶ 17.
91. Administrative Conference Recommendation 86-7, *supra* note 72, ¶ 7.
92. 5 U.S.C. § 556(d).
93. Dir., Off. of Workers' Comp. Programs v. Greenwich Collieries, 512 U.S. 267, 276 (1994); *see also* Worlds Inc. v. Bungie, Inc., 903 F.3d 1237, 1242–43 (Fed. Cir. 2018); Nat'l Mining Ass'n v. U.S. Dep't of the Interior, 251 F.3d 1007, 1013–14 (D.C. Cir. 2001); Garvey v. Nat'l Transp. Safety Bd., 190 F.3d 571, 579–80 (D.C. Cir. 1999); Nat'l Lab. Rels. Bd. v. Louis A. Weiss Mem'l Hosp., 172 F.3d 432, 442 (7th Cir. 1999); Nat'l Mining Ass'n v. Babbitt, 172 F.3d 906, 910 (1999); Lovilia Coal Co. v. Harvey, 109 F.3d 445, 452–53 (8th Cir. 1997).

a sanction on a private party for violating the law). Agencies generally can, consistent with statutory allocations of the burden of proof, establish rational presumptions and reasonable burden-shifting frameworks.[94]

As in civil litigation, the standard of proof in an administrative proceeding is typically the preponderance of the evidence.[95] A statute or agency rule may impose a more demanding standard of proof in specific programs, particularly where liberty interests are at stake.[96]

18.63 Submission and Admissibility of Evidence

An adjudicator is authorized to "rule on offers of proof and receive relevant evidence," but the APA directs agencies to provide "as a matter of policy . . . for the exclusion of irrelevant, immaterial, or unduly repetitious evidence."[97] These minimal evidentiary requirements suggest that the APA's drafters believed "the technical rules of evidence [should] not be applicable to administrative hearings."[98] They certainly give agencies broad discretion to adopt evidentiary practices suitable for the hearings they conduct. In practice, evidentiary rules range from the informal to the elaborate. At one end of the spectrum, the Social Security Act allows presiding officers to receive evidence "even though inadmissible under rules of evidence applicable to court procedure."[99] At the other end, some statutes and agency rules direct adjudicators to use the Federal Rules of Evidence (FRE), at least as guidance.[100]

ACUS has recommended against importing the FRE wholesale into administrative practice because many of the FRE's exclusionary provisions (e.g., the hearsay rule) were designed to control fact-finding by jurors.[101] Uncritical reliance on such rules can be "unnecessary, inappropriate, and counterproductive" in agency adjudications, where no jury is present and fact-finding is always the province of a

---

94. Nat'l Lab. Rels. Bd. v. Baptist Hosp., Inc., 442 U.S. 773, 787 (1979); Roach v. Nat'l Transp. Safety Bd., 804 F.2d 1147, 1159 n.11 (10th Cir. 1986).

95. *See, e.g.*, *Greenwich Collieries*, 512 U.S. at 276; Steadman v. Sec. & Exch. Comm'n, 450 U.S. 91, 95–104 (1981).

96. Woodby v. Immigr. & Naturalization Serv., 385 U.S. 276, 286 (1966).

97. 5 U.S.C. § 556(c)(3), (d).

98. Attorney General's Manual, *supra* note 27, at 76.

99. 42 U.S.C. § 405(b)(1).

100. *See, e.g.*, 37 C.F.R. §§ 41.152, 42.62 (2022) (USPTO).

101. Administrative Conference Recommendation 86-2, Use of Federal Rules of Evidence in Federal Agency Adjudications, ¶ 1, 51 Fed. Reg. 25,642 (July 16, 1986).

professional adjudicator.[102] Indeed, hearsay is broadly admissible in administrative proceedings, at least as a constitutional matter, so long as it bears adequate indicia of reliability.[103]

ACUS has instead recommended that agencies adopt rules that give presiding officials discretion to "exclude unreliable evidence" and "use the weighted balancing test in Rule 403 of the Federal Rules of Evidence."[104] Under Rule 403, a decision-maker "may exclude relevant evidence if its probative value is substantially outweighed by a danger of one or more of the following: unfair prejudice, confusing the issues, . . . undue delay, wasting time, or needlessly presenting cumulative evidence."[105] In practice, adjudicators often admit evidence into the record without closely assessing its reliability, saving evaluation of its reliability for the decision-making process. As a general rule, administrative practice is more concerned with how evidence is used in decision-making and less concerned with its admissibility.[106]

Neither the due process principle that parties may submit evidence nor the APA's statement that an adjudicator may "receive relevant evidence" forecloses Congress by statute or an agency by rule from requiring parties to establish certain facts in a particular way. Specific documentation may be required, for example, to prove a party's age, education, or citizenship;[107] prior military service;[108] the existence and severity of a medical impairment;[109] or prior criminal conviction.[110]

18.64 Presentation of Evidence

Evidence can take a number of forms, including documentary evidence, live testimony at the hearing, and affidavits and depositions. Parties in Type A adjudications are entitled to "present [their] case or defense by oral or documentary evidence."[111] This includes a general right to call

102. Richard J. Pierce, *Use of the Federal Rules of Evidence in Federal Agency Adjudications*, 39 ADMIN. L. REV. 1, 1–2 (1987).

103. *See* Richardson v. Perales, 402 U.S. 389 (1971); Hoska v. U.S. Dep't of the Army, 677 F.2d 131, 138–39 (D.C. Cir. 1982); Calhoun v. Bailar, 626 F.2d 145, 148–50 (9th Cir. 1980).

104. Administrative Conference Recommendation 86-2, *supra* note 101, ¶ 2.

105. FED. R. EVID. 403.

106. U.S. Steel Mining Co., Inc. v. Dir., Off. of Workers' Comp. Programs, 187 F.3d 384 (4th Cir. 1999).

107. ATTORNEY GENERAL'S MANUAL, *supra* note 27, at 76–77.

108. *See, e.g.*, 38 C.F.R. § 3.203 (2022) (Department of Veterans Affairs).

109. *See, e.g.*, 20 C.F.R. pt. 404, subpt. P, app. 1 (2022) (SSA).

110. *See, e.g.*, 8 C.F.R. § 1003.41 (2022) (EOIR).

111. 5 U.S.C. § 556(d).

witnesses at a hearing. However, a determination whether the testimony of a particular witness should be permitted is generally within the sound discretion of the adjudicator subject to due process and other legal requirements.[112] An adjudicator may, for example, reasonably exclude witness testimony that would be irrelevant or cumulative.[113] Special procedures for handling witnesses, such as sequestration, may be advisable in some circumstances.[114]

Expert testimony can be critically important in administrative adjudications that involve scientific or technical matters. The requirements for qualifying an expert witness under the FRE (i.e., *Daubert v. Merrell Dow Pharmaceuticals*[115]) are inapplicable in administrative proceeding unless adopted by statute or agency rule. Agencies instead typically have wide discretion to determine expert witness qualifications.[116]

An opportunity for rebuttal is also foundational to a fair hearing under the Due Process Clause.[117] The APA entitles parties in Type A adjudications to "submit rebuttal evidence, and to conduct such cross-examination *as may be required for a full and true disclosure of the facts*."[118] The italicized clause in the preceding sentence makes clear, however, that parties do not have an absolute right to cross-examine all witnesses in all cases. Whether cross-examination is "required for a full and true disclosure of the facts" will depend on the nature of particular testimony and the purpose and usefulness of the intended cross-examination.[119]

For Type B adjudications, ACUS has similarly recommended that agencies "should allow an opportunity for rebuttal, which can take the form of cross-examination of an adverse witness as well as additional written or oral evidence." ACUS recommended that agencies "should have discretion to limit or preclude cross-examination or have

---

112. *See, e.g.*, Davis v. Off. of Pers. Mgmt., 918 F.2d 944 (Fed. Cir. 1990).

113. *See, e.g.*, Lowder v. Dep't of Homeland Sec., 504 F.3d 1378 (Fed. Cir. 2007).

114. *See, e.g.*, Nat'l Lab. Rels. Bd. v. Stark, 525 F.2d 422 (2d Cir. 1975).

115. 509 U.S. 579 (1993).

116. *See* Biestek v. Berryhill, 139 S. Ct. 1148 (2019); Consolidation Coal Co. v. Dir., Off. of Workers' Comp. Programs, 294 F.3d 885 (7th Cir. 2002).

117. Morgan v. United States, 304 U.S. 1, 18 (1938); N. Am. Coal Co. v. Miller, 870 F.2d 948, 950 (3d Cir. 1989).

118. 5 U.S.C. § 556(d) (emphasis added).

119. *See, e.g.*, Demenech v. Sec'y of Dep't of Health & Hum. Servs., 913 F.2d 882, 884 (11th Cir. 1990); Butera v. Apfel, 173 F.3d 1049, 1057–59 (7th Cir. 1999); Cent. Freight Lines, Inc. v. United States, 669 F.2d 1063, 1068 (5th Cir. 1982).

it be conducted in camera in appropriate cases," for example when (1) "[t]he dispute concerns a question of legislative fact where the evidence consists of expert testimony"; (2) "[c]redibility is not an issue"; (3) "[t]he only issue is how a decisionmaker should exercise discretion"; (4) "[n]ational security could be jeopardized"; or (5) "[t]he identity of confidential informants might be revealed."[120]

18.65 Protecting Sensitive Information and Records

Agency adjudications often involve the exchange of sensitive information or records, some of which may be protected from disclosure by law. Depending on the context, examples may include personal medical information, personal financial information, confidential business information, trade secrets, national security information, law enforcement information, or privileged communications (e.g., attorney-client communications, attorney work product, agency predecisional materials).

Agencies have devised a range of practices to protect sensitive information and records, such as closing a proceeding or part of a proceeding to public observation, redaction of sensitive information, use of protective orders, and filing sensitive records under seal. Similar rules may apply at the prehearing stage, especially during discovery.[121]

18.66 Official Notice

Official notice, sometimes called "administrative notice," is the administrative corollary of judicial notice in the courts. Both permit an adjudicator, on a party's request or sua sponte, to accept a fact as true without requiring proof. But while judicial notice in the federal courts is limited to facts that are "not subject to reasonable dispute,"[122] agencies are generally free to officially notice technical and scientific facts within their area of specialized expertise.[123]

---

120. Administrative Conference Recommendation 2016-4, *supra* note 7, ¶ 24.

121. *See* Model Adjudication Rules §§ 150, 237, 322 (ACUS 2018); *see also* Ernest Gellhorn, *The Treatment of Confidential Information by the Federal Trade Commission*, 116 U. Pa. L. Rev. 401 (1968).

122. Fed. R. Evid. 201(b).

123. Kapcia v. Immigr. & Naturalization Serv., 944 F.2d 702, 705 (10th Cir. 1991); Union Elec. Co. v. Fed. Energy Regul. Comm'n, 890 F.2d 1193, 1202–03 (D.C. Cir. 1989); McLeod v. Immigr. & Naturalization Serv., 802 F.2d 89, 93 n.4 (3d Cir. 1986); *see also* Ernest Gellhorn, *Rules of Evidence and Official Notice in Formal Administrative Hearings*, 1971 Duke L.J. 1 (1971); Attorney General's Manual, *supra* note 27, at 79–80; Kenneth Culp Davis, *An Approach to Problems*

As a due process matter, agencies can only take official notice of a contested material fact if a party can reasonably request an opportunity to rebut it.[124] The opportunity to show the contrary includes not only the opportunity to rebut a fact but also the opportunity to challenge the inferences that an adjudicator draws from it, even if the fact itself is undisputed.[125] The APA's formal-adjudication provisions explicitly state that "[w]hen an agency decision rests on official notice of a material fact not appearing in the evidence in the record, a party is entitled, on timely request, to an opportunity to show the contrary."[126] As a textual matter, the APA's rule does not distinguish between adjudicative and legislative facts. Some have argued that the APA's rule applies to all contested material facts,[127] but that view is not universally held.[128]

Agency procedures for official notice vary.[129] Substantively, agencies often grant adjudicators broad discretion to take official notice of facts within the agency's specialized knowledge.[130] Official notice can be more routinized in high-volume programs, such as the immigration courts and SSA, where factual questions recur frequently across cases.[131] Official notice of frequently recurring facts can promote efficiency, accuracy, and inter-decisional consistency.[132] ACUS has recommended that agencies issue rules on official notice.[133]

---

of Evidence in the Administrative Process, 55 HARV. L. REV. 364, 383 (1942); Walter Gellhorn, *Official Notice in Administrative Adjudication*, 20 TEX. L. REV. 131 (1941); ATTORNEY GENERAL'S COMMITTEE, *supra* note 5, at 71–78, 398–403.

124. *See* Ohio Bell Tel. Co. v. Pub. Utils. Comm'n, 301 U.S. 292, 300–06 (1937).

125. Chhetry v. U.S. Dep't of Just., 490 F.3d 196, 200 (2d Cir. 2007); Rogue v. Immigr. & Naturalization Serv., 954 F.2d 769, 773 (D.C. Cir. 1992); S. Cal. Edison Co. v. Fed. Energy Regul. Comm'n, 717 F.3d 177, 187 (D.C. Cir. 2013); de la Llana-Castellon v. Immigr. & Naturalization Serv., 16 F.3d 1093, 1099 (10th Cir. 1994); *Union Elec. Co.*, 890 F.2d at 1202; *Kapcia*, 944 F.2d at 705–06.

126. 5 U.S.C. § 556(e).

127. 2 KRISTIN E. HICKMAN & RICHARD J. PIERCE, JR., ADMINISTRATIVE LAW TREATISE § 9.6.1 (6th ed. 2019).

128. 2 CHARLES H. KOCH, JR., ADMINISTRATIVE LAW AND PRACTICE § 5:55[2](a) (3d ed. 2010).

129. JEREMY S. GRABOYES, ACUS, INDEPENDENT RESEARCH BY AGENCY ADJUDICATORS IN THE INTERNET AGE 21–27 (2019).

130. *See* MODEL ADJUDICATION RULES § 323 (ACUS 2018).

131. *See* 8 C.F.R. § 1003.1(d)(3)(iv) (2022); 20 C.F.R. § 404.1566(d) (2022).

132. *See* GRABOYES, *supra* note 129, at 21–27; *see also* ATTORNEY GENERAL'S COMMITTEE, *supra* note 5, at 71.

133. Administrative Conference Recommendation 2019-6, Independent Research by Agency Adjudicators in the Internet Age, ¶ 4, 84 Fed. Reg. 71,350,

18.7 POST-HEARING DEVELOPMENT

The evidentiary hearing does not necessarily conclude development of the record in a proceeding. The APA, for example, entitles parties in Type A adjudications to a "reasonable opportunity" to submit proposed findings and conclusions and supporting reasons.[134] That reasonable opportunity might take place after the hearing has occurred. Program-specific statutes or agency rules, or adjudicators in specific proceedings, may also permit parties to submit additional evidence after the hearing has ended. For example, the record for decision-making by the BVA includes any evidence submitted within 90 days following the hearing.[135] Other parties may, of course, be entitled to a reasonable opportunity to rebut post-hearing evidence.

In most proceedings involving an evidentiary hearing, the record closes at some point at or after the hearing. The adjudicator will not accept additional evidence once the record is closed or will only consider additional evidence under limited circumstances. Closure practices can be less stringent in programs where parties are more frequently self-represented.[136]

18.8 THE DECISION

The hearing stage of an adjudicative process culminates with an order that is typically accompanied by a statement including factual findings, legal conclusions, and accompanying rationale. For convenience's sake, this chapter refers to the order and statement collectively as the "decision," though terminology may vary across programs. There are seven key questions when it comes to the decision:

1. Who renders the decision?
2. What is the record for decision-making?
3. How is the record evaluated?
4. What is the form of the decision?
5. What is the effect of the decision?
6. How is the decision prepared?
7. How is the decision noticed and disseminated?

71,352 (Dec. 27, 2019).

134. 5 U.S.C. § 557(c)(1)–(2).

135. 38 U.S.C. § 7113(b)(2)(B).

136. *See* Model Adjudication Rules § 370 (ACUS 2018).

First, who renders the decision? Unless the agency presided at the hearing, the presiding official in a Type A adjudication, typically an ALJ, renders the decision "unless he [or she] becomes unavailable to the agency."[137] Some agencies have adopted rules or policies describing what it means for an ALJ to be "unavailable" and what happens in such circumstances.[138] The same is generally true in Type B adjudications.

Second, what is the record for decision-making? As described in the overview for this chapter, a defining attribute of proceedings involving an evidentiary hearing is decision-making based on an "exclusive record" that consists solely of information provided by the parties and matters officially noticed. In Type A adjudications, the APA mandates that "[t]he transcript of testimony and exhibits, together with all papers and requests filed in the proceeding, constitutes the exclusive record of decision."[139] The same principle applies in Type B adjudications, either by statute or rule. ACUS has recommended that agencies that conduct Type B adjudications adopt rules that "require a decision to be based on an exclusive record."[140]

Third, how is the record evaluated?[141] The APA says little about how evidence should be evaluated except that, unless another statute provides otherwise, a decision rendered in a Type A adjudication must be supported by "substantial evidence."[142] Under the APA, a reviewing court will only set aside a decision made in a Type B adjudication if it is found to be "arbitrary, capricious, an abuse of discretion, or otherwise not in accordance with law."[143] In practice, many program-specific

---

137. 5 U.S.C. § 554(d).

138. *See, e.g.*, 10 C.F.R. § 2.313 (2022) (Nuclear Regulatory Commission); 22 C.F.R. § 1423.20 (2022) (Federal Labor Relations Authority); 27 C.F.R. §§ 71.100, 771.100 (2022) (Bureau of Alcohol, Tobacco, Firearms, and Explosives); 28 C.F.R. § 68.29 (2022) (EOIR); 29 C.F.R. § 102.36 (2022) (NLRB); 29 C.F.R. § 1603.203 (2022) (Equal Employment Opportunity Commission).

139. 5 U.S.C. § 556(e).

140. Administrative Conference Recommendation 2016-4, *supra* note 7, ¶ 1.

141. *See, e.g.*, Russell L. Weaver, *ALJ Support Systems: Staff Attorneys and Decision Writers*, 16 J. NAT'L ASS'N ADMIN. L. JUDGES 89 (1996); John J. Mathias, *The Use of Legal and Technical Assistants by Administrative Law Judges in Administrative Proceedings*, 1 ADMIN. L.J. 107 (1987).

142. *See, e.g.*, Black Beauty Coal Co. v. Fed. Mine Safety & Health Rev., 703 F.3d 553 (D.C. Cir. 2012); Jenkins v. Immigr. & Naturalization Serv., 108 F.3d 195 (9th Cir. 1997).

143. Fla. Power & Light Co. v. Lorion, 470 U.S. 729, 744 (1985); Camp v. Pitts, 411 U.S. 138, 142–43 (1973); Citizens to Preserve Overton Park v. Volpe, 401 U.S. 402, 416 (1971).

statutes specify a less deferential standard. Standards of review used by agency appellate reviewers (see Chapter 19) will also affect how hearing-level adjudicators evaluate the record.

Some agencies have adopted rules governing how adjudicators should weigh evidence;[144] adjudicators in other programs have more discretion to evaluate the record as they see fit. Though beyond the scope of this chapter, there have been attempts to study how ALJs, in particular, assess evidentiary records and reach decisions.[145]

Fourth, what is the form of the decision? Decisions can look very different across agencies. Some resemble judicial opinions in form and style. Others are compiled using templates and boilerplate language and are more characteristically bureaucratic.[146] Decisions are typically written, but in some circumstances, agency rules may permit oral decisions, which are transcribed or recorded and made part of the record.[147] No matter their form or medium, decisions nearly always contain the same basic elements. In Type A adjudications, the APA requires that decisions include a statement of "findings and conclusions, and the reasons or basis therefor, on all the material issues of fact, law, or discretion presented on the record," and "the appropriate rule, order, sanction, relief, or denial thereof." The record—if not the decision itself—must also "show the ruling on each finding [and] conclusion presented [by the parties]."[148] For Type B adjudications, the APA requires only that a notice denying a written application, petition, or other request must "be accompanied by a brief statement of the grounds for denial" except when the notice affirms a prior denial or the denial is self-explanatory.[149] In practice, however, decisions in Type A and Type B adjudications are indistinguishable.[150]

Fifth, what is the effect of the decision? The APA defines three types of decisions issued by presiding officials (as opposed to agency

---

144. *See, e.g.*, 20 C.F.R. § 404.1520c (2022) (SSA).

145. Chris Guthrie et al., *The Hidden "Judiciary": An Empirical Examination of Executive Branch Justice*, 58 DUKE L.J. 1477 (2009).

146. *See* Daniel J. Sheffner, *Access to Adjudication Materials on Federal Agency Websites*, 51 AKRON L. REV. 447, 497 (2017); *see also* Bjornson v. Astrue, 671 F.3d 640, 644–46 (7th Cir. 2012) (Posner, J.).

147. *See* Administrative Conference Recommendation 2016-4, *supra* note 7, ¶ 25.

148. 5 U.S.C. § 557(c).

149. *Id.* § 555(e).

150. *Cf.* Administrative Conference Recommendation 2016-4, *supra* note 7, ¶ 25.

heads). An *initial decision* "becomes the decision of the agency without further proceedings unless there is an appeal to, or review on motion of, the agency within time provided by rule." The agency can, by general rule or in specific cases, reserve to itself the duty to render a decision even when it did not preside over the hearing. In such circumstances, the presiding official renders a *recommended decision*, which becomes part of the record before the agency. Recommended decisions are common at some agencies but rare at others. A fourth type—the *tentative decision*—is available in determining applications for initial licenses.[151] In practice, terminology can vary considerably across agencies. It is typically better to consult the applicable statute or rule for the terminology used in a particular program.

Sixth, how is the decision prepared? Decisions can be prepared through different processes. In lower volume programs, an adjudicator might draft a decision or work closely with an assigned law clerk to draft it. In higher volume adjudication programs, an adjudicator might draft decision-writing instructions and review and sign the completed decision, but initial drafting may be delegated to an assigned clerk or a shared pool of decision-writers.[152] Various studies have addressed how legal and administrative staff support decision-making by ALJs.

Finally, how is the decision noticed and disseminated? The APA specifies only that "[p]rompt notice shall be given of the denial in whole or in part of a written application, petition, or other request of an interested person made in connection with any agency proceeding."[153] In practice, due process, statutes, and other sources of law will determine who is entitled, as a matter of law, to notice of a decision and how notice is given. FOIA also requires that agencies post on their websites all "final opinions, including concurring and dissenting opinions, as well as orders, made in the adjudication of cases."[154] As discussed in Chapter 28, the application of that requirement to nonprecedential decisions is disputed.

18.9 RECONSIDERATION, REOPENING, AND REVIEW

As discussed in greater detail in Chapter 19, agency rules typically provide parties with an opportunity to seek review of a decision issued

151. 5 U.S.C. § 557(b).

152. *See, e.g.*, SSA, Hearings, Appeals, and Litigation Law (HALLEX) Manual § I-2-8-20.

153. 5 U.S.C. § 555(e).

154. *Id.* § 552(a)(2)(A).

following an evidentiary hearing. Agency rules might also provide for interlocutory review, permitting parties in limited circumstances to appeal a ruling—typically one involving an important question of law or policy—before the adjudicator issues his or her final decision.[155] Review is, in most cases, the responsibility of the agency head or an appellate body staffed by career officials.

Aside from appellate review, agency rules might give parties the right to request that a presiding official reconsider or reopen his or her decision.[156] Agencies have inherent authority to reconsider or reopen their prior decisions, so long as reconsideration or reopening occurs within a reasonable time after the first decision.[157]

---

155. *See, e.g.*, 5 C.F.R. § 1201.92 (2022) (MSPB); 12 C.F.R. § 1081.211 (2022) (Consumer Financial Protection Bureau); 13 C.F.R. § 134.215 (2022) (Small Business Administration); 16 C.F.R. § 3.23 (2022) (Federal Trade Commission); 16 C.F.R. § 1025.24 (2022) (Consumer Product Safety Commission); 29 C.F.R. § 2200.73 (2022) (OSHRC); 29 C.F.R. § 2700.76 (2022) (Federal Mine Safety and Health Review Commission).

156. *See* Model Adjudication Rules § 370 (ACUS 2018).

157. Macktal v. Chao, 286 F.3d 822 (5th Cir. 2002); Saqr v. Holder, 580 F.3d 414 (6th Cir. 2009); Tokyo Kikai Seisakusho v. United States, 529 F.3d 1352 (Fed. Cir. 2008); Sierra Club v. Van Antwerp, 560 F. Supp. 2d 21 (D.D.C. 2008); Consol. Rail Corp. v. Surface Transp. Bd., 93 F.3d 793 (D.C. Cir. 1996).

Chapter 19

Agency Appellate Review

Christopher J. Walker and Matthew L. Wiener

19.1 CHAPTER OVERVIEW[1]

Final adjudicatory authority of an agency resides in the head of the agency unless it has been assigned by statute or delegated by the agency head to another reviewing authority such as a multimember review board. Courts generally review the final decision of the agency head (or the reviewing authority), not the decision of an administrative law judge (ALJ) or other hearing-level adjudicator (see Chapter 27).[2] Almost all federal agency adjudication systems have adopted some sort of internal agency review—sometimes called "administrative review"[3] or, as this chapter calls it, "agency appellate review"—of hearing-level adjudicators' decisions. (For more information on hearing-level decision-making, see Chapter 18.)

19.2 DEFINING AGENCY APPELLATE REVIEW

Defining agency appellate review can be problematic, especially outside the context of review of ALJ decisions. The term does not have a single accepted meaning in agency adjudication, as appellate review does in the federal courts. Numerous adjudication programs hear "appeals"—and may even have "appeal" in their names—but they would not normally be thought of as undertaking an appellate function. While these programs provide for review of a frontline official's

---

1. This chapter incorporates material from the second edition of this guide and reproduces substantial portions of the authors' report on agency appellate systems, Christopher J. Walker & Matthew Lee Wiener, Admin. Conf. of the U.S., Agency Appellate Systems 5–20 (2020). The report underlies Administrative Conference Recommendation 2020-3, Agency Appellate Systems, 86 Fed. Reg. 6,618 (Jan. 22, 2021). See also Christopher J. Walker et al., Admin. Conf. of the U.S., Precedential Decision Making in Agency Adjudication (2022), which underlies Administrative Conference Recommendation 2022-4, Precedential Decision Making in Agency Adjudication, 88 Fed. Reg. 2,312 (Jan. 13, 2023).

2. Note, however, that under the Administrative Procedure Act (APA), a decision of a hearing-level adjudicator that has become final, by operation of statute or rule, is subject to judicial review even if the party seeking review forewent an available administrative appeal, unless agency rule made the filing of the appeal a prerequisite to judicial review. *See* 5 U.S.C. § 704. While Congress may change this default rule, as § 704 provides, the courts may not impose appellate exhaustion requirements where the agency has failed to do so by rule. *See* Darby v. Cisneros, 509 U.S. 137 (1993). That said, the generalization in the text holds true: in most cases, judicial review is of the agency head's decision.

3. *E.g.*, Model Adjudication Rules §§ 400–450 (Admin. Conf. of the U.S., rev. 2018).

adjudication decision rendered after an informal decision-making process (see Chapter 16),[4] they usually do so through a de novo evidentiary proceeding that results in a "new" decision, which itself is then subject to higher level agency review. (The evidentiary record before the frontline official may still play an important role in the proceedings.) The proceedings are more trial-like than appellate. Examples include adjudication proceedings conducted by the Department of Health and Human Services' Office of Medicare Hearings and Appeals and the Merit Systems Protection Board's administrative judges in the exercise of the board's so-called "appellate jurisdiction."

At the same time, the term "appellate review" cannot be reserved exclusively for agency programs (of which there are many) that review adjudication decisions resulting from a full evidentiary hearing on the basis of a closed and exclusive record of documentary evidence, transcripts, and case filings of the sort familiar in federal courts.[5] One reason why is that any number of adjudicative offices that otherwise perform only traditional appellate functions sometimes hear new evidence on appeal in a way unknown to federal court appellate practice. The Appeals Council at the Social Security Administration is but one example.

Another reason is that some adjudicative offices that perform mostly trial-like functions also perform appellate functions. The trial and appellate functions can even be commingled. A notable example (though an outlier, to be sure) is offered by the Patent Trial and Appeal Board (PTAB) at the U.S. Patent and Trademark Office (USPTO). It has both hearing-level and appellate jurisdiction. Even its original-jurisdiction adjudications have an appellate character. Its judges sit in three-member panels and issue final agency decisions, reviewing decisions by patent examiners. The decisions are subject to reconsideration, sometimes with additional judges added to the panel, by order of the USPTO director. The director, through a precedential opinion panel, may designate panel decisions as precedential and hence binding

---

4. As distinct from, say, a prosecutorial-type decision to issue a complaint. *See* Michael Asimow, Admin. Conf. of the U.S., Federal Administrative Adjudication outside the Administrative Procedure Act 8–9 (2019).

5. *See* Fed. R. App. P. 10.

on the program's several hundred judges in all future cases.[6] Any number of other adjudication programs likewise defy easy categorization.[7]

19.3 STRUCTURES OF AGENCY APPELLATE REVIEW

Agency appellate review can be structured in a myriad of ways.[8] In his 1983 study for the Administrative Conference of the United States, Professor Ron Cass used a typology under which he identified 22 possible appellate structures, 14 of which were then in use in programs of formal adjudication alone.[9] He identified which structure each program employed, either by statutory requirement or administrative discretion.[10] Such a cataloguing exercise that covered both formal and informal adjudications would be near impossible.

Most agency appellate programs, though, can comfortably fit within one of the four broad categories that follow, allowing for minor qualifications.[11] As our classification system reflects, an important feature of appellate review programs is whether they provide for some form of agency-head review. Agency-head review is a standard feature of most agency adjudication systems, and it may be constitutionally required (see section 19.33). As the U.S. Supreme Court recently emphasized, the Administrative Procedure Act (APA) "from its inception, authorized agency heads to review" hearing-level decisions (see section 19.5, which discusses 5 U.S.C. § 557), "[a]nd 'higher-level agency reconsideration' by the agency head is the standard way to

---

6. *See* Christopher J. Walker & Melissa F. Wasserman, *The New World of Agency Adjudication*, 107 CAL. L. REV. 141, 157–60, 178–80, 194–96 (2019); ASIMOW, *supra* note 4, at 163–71.

7. Compare the Civilian Board of Contract Appeals, discussed in ASIMOW, *supra* note 4, at 115.

8. *See* ASIMOW, *supra* note 4, at 84; *see also* KENNETH CULP DAVIS, DISCRETIONARY JUSTICE: A PRELIMINARY INQUIRY 145 (1969) (emphasizing "divers[ity]" of appellate agencies).

9. *See* RONALD CASS, ADMIN. CONF. OF THE U.S., AGENCY REVIEW OF ADMINISTRATIVE LAW JUDGES' DECISIONS 157–59 (1983); *cf.* Russell L. Weaver, *Appellate Structures in Executive Departments and Agencies*, 48 ADMIN. L. REV. 251, 253–270 (1996) (placing "review structures" into one of four categories).

10. *See* CASS, *supra* note 9, at 201–17. A summary table appears on page 217.

11. *See* WALKER & WIENER, *supra* note 1, at 7–9; WALKER ET AL., *supra* note 1, at 11–16.

maintain political accountability and effective oversight for adjudication that takes place outside the confines of" of the APA.[12]

19.31 Direct Review of Hearing-Level Adjudicator's Decision by Agency Head

In this category, the agency head directly reviews the decision of a hearing-level adjudicator. No agency-head delegate or intermediate review body is interposed between the adjudicator and the agency head. Review is usually either as of right at the request of a party (mandatory review) or at the discretion of the agency head (either on the application of a party or, less commonly, its own initiative). Even when review is discretionary, a statute or, more commonly, a procedural rule often sets forth a standard or criteria to guide or circumscribe the discretion. Many agencies that fall into this first category are traditional independent regulatory boards and commissions. They include the National Labor Relations Board (review as of right in unfair labor practice cases), the Securities and Exchange Commission (review at the discretion of the agency head, but granted as a matter of course), and the Merit Systems Protection Board (review at the discretion of the agency head).

19.32 Review by an Agency-Head Delegate—Often a Multimember Appellate Body—Resulting in a Final Decision Unreviewable by the Agency Head

In this category, the agency head delegates his or her authority to review the lower level adjudicator's decision to a subordinate official(s), often a multimember appellate body, who issues a final decision on the agency head's behalf. (The agency could be an administration within an agency.[13]) The delegation is sometimes, though not usually, made with explicit statutory authorization. The delegation is almost always on a standing, categorical basis rather than a one-time, individual-case basis. Review can be as of right or discretionary. Notable appellate

12. United States v. Arthrex, 141 S. Ct. 1970, 1984 (2021) (quoting Walker & Wasserman, *supra* note 6, at 157); *see* Walker & Wasserman, *supra* note 6, at 174–88; Harold J. Krent, *Presidential Control of Adjudication within the Executive Branch*, 65 CASE W. RSRV. L. REV. 1083 (2015); Weaver, *supra* note 9. *But cf.* Rebecca S. Eisenberg & Nina A. Mendelson, *The Not-So-Standard Model: Reconsidering Agency-Head Review of Administrative Adjudication Decisions*, 75 ADMIN. L. REV. 1, 20–32 (2023).

13. *See* Weaver, *supra* note 9, at 265; *see also* 5 U.S.C. § 551(1) (referring to agencies "within" agencies).

bodies in this category include the Social Security Administration's Appeals Council and, subject to narrow exceptions and with allowances for minor qualifications, the Environmental Appeals Board at the Environmental Protection Agency.

19.33 Review by a Statutorily Authorized Appellate Decision-Maker—Often a Multimember Body—Resulting in a Final Decision Unreviewable by the Agency Head

Unlike the previous category, in which the agency creates an appellate body, this category involves a statutorily created appellate body. A statute vests authority in an agency official(s) (often a multimember board) to issue final decisions. Review by the official can be mandatory or discretionary, but is usually mandatory. The decision is unreviewable by the agency head, as a matter of either law or practice. Examples include the Department of Veterans Affairs' Board of Veterans' Appeals (BVA) and the Department of Labor's Benefits Review Board. The PTAB, noted earlier, can also be put in this category.

This structure may raise constitutional questions. In *United States v. Arthrex*, the Supreme Court held that Congress's vesting of final (i.e., unreviewable) decision-making authority in PTAB judges violated the Constitution's Appointments Clause, since those judges are appointed by a Cabinet secretary rather than the president with the Senate's consent (as required for principal officers). The Court remedied the violation by "severing" the statutory provision withholding review authority from the USPTO director, a principal officer, with the result that PTAB decisions are now subject to discretionary director review. As for other similar statutory review structures such as those previously identified, the Court noted that they were either distinguishable or "potentially" so on one ground or another. The decisions of the BVA, for instance, are subject to review by an Article I court whose members are principal officers.[14]

19.34 Review by an Intermediate Appellate Adjudicator—Often a Multimember Appellate Body—Resulting in a Decision Subject to Agency-Head Review

In this category, a statute or agency rule assigns appellate review to an intermediate adjudicator, often a multimember appellate body. That adjudicator's decision will be subject to (usually discretionary) review by the agency head. The most notable example is the Justice

14. *See Arthrex*, 141 S. Ct. at 1985.

Department's immigration adjudication program, under which decisions of the Board of Immigration Appeals are subject to discretionary review by the attorney general.[15] Another notable example is the Department of Labor's Administrative Review Board, whose decisions the Secretary of Labor has made subject to discretionary secretarial review.[16] In these programs, though, agency-head review is rarely exercised.

19.4 OBJECTIVES OF AGENCY APPELLATE REVIEW

"Modern administrative law," as Professor Thomas Merrill chronicled a decade ago, "is built on the appellate review model of the relationship between reviewing courts and agencies."[17] This appellate review model resembles judicial review of trial court civil litigation. In particular, the appellate court reviews a closed record, and the standard of review varies based on the comparative competence of the trial and appellate courts. At one extreme, appellate courts defer to trial courts as to factual findings. At the other extreme of purely legal questions, appellate courts engage in more searching review.

When we think of appellate review within an agency, we may be tempted to gravitate to this familiar appellate model of judicial review of administrative action. Put differently, we may view the objectives of agency appellate review as the same as those for judicial review. That would be a mistake. Agency appellate review may well serve distinct purposes. For example, James Freedman in 1969 identified two distinct models for agency appellate review: (1) the "judicial model," which consists of error correction and the application of law to fact without engaging in policymaking; and (2) the "administrative model," which includes "deciding appeals in adjudicating cases as well as formulating policy."[18] In assessing whether Congress should enact legislation to authorize intermediate appellate review boards at federal agencies, Professor Freedman emphasized that Congress should not mandate a

---

15. *See generally* Walker & Wasserman, *supra* note 6, at 171–73.

16. Secretary's Order No. 01-2020—Delegation of Authority and Assignment of Responsibility to the Administrative Review Board, 85 Fed. Reg. 13,186 (Dep't of Lab. Mar. 6, 2020).

17. Thomas W. Merrill, *Article III, Agency Adjudication, and the Origins of the Appellate Review Model of Administrative Law*, 111 Colum. L. Rev. 939, 940 (2011).

18. James O. Freedman, *Review Boards in the Administrative Process*, 117 U. Pa. L. Rev. 546, 558–59 (1969).

one-size-fits-all model and set of procedures. After all, "agencies that establish Review Boards will not do so for the same reasons," and the models they adopt "will reflect different estimates of different needs in different agencies."[19]

In surveying agency appellate programs and interviewing their leaders across the federal regulatory state, it becomes immediately apparent that the judicial model of appellate review is not the predominant one within agencies, although it does play an important role in many programs. Neither is there—nor should there be—one unifying model. Agencies operate appellate review programs for distinct purposes. Sometimes the agency does so because Congress has commanded a certain objective or multiple objectives in appellate review. Other times, the agency itself has exercised its discretion to focus appellate review on certain objectives, which hopefully advance the statutory purposes of the agency adjudication program as a whole.

This is not merely a point of academic interest. The purpose of appellate review will dictate—or should dictate, if the agency is functioning competently—the key procedural choices an agency must make. One helpful example is whether (when the agency has a choice) appellate review is discretionary or mandatory, and, if discretionary, what criteria are used to decide which appeals to hear. An agency cannot answer those questions without considering the agency's objectives in appellate review. Consider, for instance, the U.S. Supreme Court's approach to managing its discretionary certiorari docket. Supreme Court Rule 10 outlines the considerations for granting review. It notes that review is "granted only for compelling reasons," and then it sets forth three reasons that are "neither controlling nor fully measuring the Court's discretion." The three reasons proffered (a circuit court conflict, a state supreme court conflict, and "an important question" of federal law) all underscore that the Court's discretionary docket is not about just error correction. Indeed, Rule 10's final sentence makes that plain, providing that a petition "is rarely granted when the asserted error consists of erroneous factual findings or the misapplication of a properly stated rule of law."[20]

With the vast and varied administrative adjudications taking place in the federal administrative state today, it should surprise no one that there is not one unified model of agency appellate review. Nor should there be in light of the diverse purposes in each administrative

19. *Id.* at 575.

20. Sup. Ct. R. 10 (considerations governing review on certiorari).

adjudication program. What is surprising, however, is that the literature has not seemed to develop a taxonomy of objectives that would motivate agency appellate review models. At least seven such objectives can be identified.[21]

19.41 Error Correction

A conventional rationale for appellate review is to correct errors in the hearing-level adjudication.[22] These errors could involve articulating the legal standard, applying the law to particular facts, and perhaps even fact-finding. The correction of an error itself may be a compelling justification for appellate review. Moreover, as Steven Shavell has explained, an efficient appellate review process "may render society's investment in the appeals process economical by comparison to its improving the accuracy of the trial process—an approach that, by its nature, would require extra expenditure in every case."[23] In other words, an agency may decide that, if the goal is to minimize erroneous adjudication outcomes generally, investing in appellate review is more cost-effective than investing in further improving the hearing-level agency adjudications.[24]

19.42 Inter-Decisional Consistency

The importance of inter-decisional consistency among hearing-level adjudications is a core objective for agency appellate review.[25] As David Hausman has put it in the immigration adjudication context, "Uniformity is both a goal of appeals processes and an indication that they are functioning properly."[26] In other words, agency appellate

---

21. *See generally* Walker & Wiener, *supra* note 1.

22. *See generally* Chad M. Oldfather, *Error Correction*, 85 Ind. L.J. 49 (2010).

23. Steven Shavell, *The Appeals Process as a Means of Error Correction*, 24 J. Legal Stud. 379, 381–82 (1995).

24. A related purpose that we group with error correction is "error prevention: inducing trial court judges to make fewer errors because of their fear of reversal." *Id.* at 425–26. The threat of further review may well encourage the hearing-level adjudicators to avoid errors in the first place.

25. This focus on consistency is not new. Back in the 1980s, it was captured in Jerry Mashaw's "bureaucratic rationality" model for administrative action, which aims "to minimize the sum of error costs and administrative costs." Jerry L. Mashaw, *Conflict and Compromise among Models of Administrative Justice*, 1981 Duke L.J. 181, 185 (1981); *see also* Robert A. Kagan, *Inside Administrative Law*, 84 Colum. L. Rev. 816, 820 (1984).

26. David Hausman, *The Failure of Immigration Appeals*, 164 U. Pa. L. Rev. 1177, 1181 (2016).

review should seek to ensure that like individuals are treated the same, regardless of the identity of the hearing-level adjudicator. In the patent adjudication context, Professors Michael Frakes and Melissa Wasserman have argued that inter-decisional inconsistency can be evidence of hearing-level adjudicators committing routine errors and can erode public confidence that the adjudication system is fair and nonarbitrary.[27] Some scholars of the social security adjudication system have similarly argued that consistency can serve as a proxy for accuracy, apart from whatever due process norms the former serves.[28]

19.43 Policymaking

In the judicial appellate review context, the "creation and refinement of law" is often proffered as a core rationale.[29] In the agency appellate review context, the somewhat analogous function of policymaking may be a legitimate objective. Chapter 5 discusses the choice between rulemaking and adjudication in the formulation of policy. There is a long history of agency heads—as well as intermediate review bodies—utilizing appellate review to establish or further develop policy for the agency as a whole.[30] It is important to note that policymaking through appellate review is not just about implementing the agency's (or presidential administration's) policy preferences within the agency's statutory authority. It can also advance agency appellate review's objectives of error correction and inter-decisional consistency. As Judge Henry Friendly observed long ago, a critical problem with administrative action "is the failure to develop standards sufficiently definite to permit decisions to be fairly predictable and the reasons for them to be understood."[31] Policymaking via agency appellate review can lead to greater consistency in adjudication outcomes at both the hearing and appellate levels.

---

27. Michael D. Frakes & Melissa F. Wasserman, *Patent Trial and Appeal Board's Consistency-Enhancing Function*, 104 Iowa L. Rev. 2417, 2421–23 (2019).

28. *See, e.g.*, Richard J. Pierce, Jr., *Political Control versus Impermissible Bias in Agency Decisionmaking: Lessons from* Chevron *and* Mistretta, 58 U. Chi. L. Rev. 481, 510 (1990).

29. Oldfather, *supra* note 22, at 49.

30. *See generally* Walker et al., *supra* note 1.

31. Henry Friendly, The Federal Administrative Agencies: The Need for Better Definition of Standards 5–6 (1962).

19.44 Political Accountability

The "standard federal model" for administrative adjudication, as Professor Ronald Levin has observed, continues to vest final decision-making authority in the agency head.[32] One reason for that is political accountability. In *Lucia v. Securities & Exchange Commission*, for instance, the Court held that ALJs at the SEC are at least "inferior officers" under the Appointments Clause of the Constitution, and thus must be appointed by the agency head (or the president).[33] In a concurring opinion joined by Justice Gorsuch, Justice Thomas grounded his approach in the importance of political accountability in the administrative state: "[B]y specifying only a limited number of actors who can appoint inferior officers without Senate confirmation, the Appointments Clause maintains clear lines of accountability—encouraging good appointments and giving the public someone to blame for bad ones."[34] Agency appellate review, when designed to facilitate agency-head oversight, can similarly help advance this political accountability value by ensuring that the Senate-confirmed agency head, or the head's designee, can exercise final decision-making authority in agency adjudication.

19.45 Management of the Hearing-Level Adjudication Program

Due to concerns for decisional independence of the hearing-level agency adjudicators and for the separation of enforcement and adjudicative functions at the agency, the adjudicative functions that hearing-level officials undertake are often quite insulated from the agency head and other high-level policymakers (see Chapters 9 and 10). Yet for political accountability and other policy reasons, and in some cases because a statute mandates a particular approach, the agency head needs to ensure that hearing-level adjudications are as fair, consistent, and efficient as possible. Some agencies may also have a related objective of preventing fraud at the hearing level. Appellate review helps the agency head promote and ensure such values in the hearing-level adjudication program. It does so through the mix of values already discussed—error correction, inter-decisional consistency, and policymaking.

---

32. Ronald M. Levin, *Administrative Judges and Agency Policy Development: The Koch Way*, 22 Wm. & Mary Bill Rts. J. 407, 412 (2013).

33. 138 S. Ct. 2044, 2049 (2018).

34. *Id.* at 2056 (Thomas, J., concurring); *see also* Jennifer L. Mascott, *Who Are "Officers of the United States"?*, 70 Stan. L. Rev. 443, 564 (2018).

19.46 Organizational Effectiveness and Systemic Awareness

A related benefit of appellate review is, as Professor Russell Weaver has put it, that it "helps the agency head gain greater awareness of how a regulatory system is functioning."[35] Such awareness does not just assist the agency head and agency leadership more generally in tailoring training and instruction for the agency's adjudicators. It also helps the agency head consider whether adjustments to the regulatory scheme are necessary via rulemaking, precedential adjudication, agency guidance, legislative recourse, or other means. Such awareness is even more critical with respect to agencies that have substantial enforcement or similar regulatory responsibilities.

19.47 Reduction of Federal Court Litigation

A final objective for agency appellate review is to reduce the number of cases that get appealed to the federal courts. This is an objective that Congress cares about generally when creating administrative agencies and procedures. And it is particularly salient in the agency adjudication context, where adjudication is often perceived as a cheaper, more efficient alternative to traditional litigation in federal court. Consider, for instance, Congress's creation of the PTAB in the America Invents Act of 2011.[36] The act was enacted, in part, to respond to the growing criticism that the USPTO issues too many invalid patents, which harms consumer welfare.[37] Although federal courts can invalidate invalid patents, the cost of patent litigation had skyrocketed over the prior decade. This has hampered the ability of patent holders with meritorious claims to challenge invalid patents in federal court. The new patent adjudication proceedings were designed to create a cheaper, faster alternative to district court litigation.[38] Agency appellate review can play an important role in filtering out cases from reaching federal courts—thus reducing the use of federal court resources for administrative actions and making the administrative process cheaper and more accessible for everyday Americans.

35. Weaver, *supra* note 9, at 289.

36. Leahy-Smith America Invents Act, Pub. L. No. 112-29, 125 Stat. 284 (2011).

37. *See* Michael D. Frakes & Melissa F. Wasserman, *Does the U.S. Patent and Trademark Office Grant Too Many Bad Patents?: Evidence from a Quasi-Experiment*, 67 STAN. L. REV. 613, 621 (2015).

38. *See* Walker & Wasserman, *supra* note 6, at 157–58.

19.5 ADMINISTRATIVE REVIEW PROCEDURES

The standard or default approach in the administrative adjudication context largely tracks the federal court model by allowing an appeal of a hearing-level adjudicator's decision as of right.[39] But, unless constrained by statute, agencies may modify that approach by administrative rule, and many do. At some agencies, review is limited to specific grounds—for instance, that factual findings are unsupported by substantial evidence. At other agencies, appellate review is discretionary with the reviewing authority, although a rule might set forth the criteria according to which discretion is exercised. Some agencies allow the reviewing authority to hear an appeal sua sponte, or on its own initiative.

An agency's enabling act or its procedural rules furnish details of the administrative review process.[40] Not surprisingly, the procedures vary by agency. A few generalizations about appellate review bear noting. First, the agency must inform losing parties of the means for seeking administrative review of an initial decision.[41] Second, the party claiming that the administrative review authority has jurisdiction bears the burden of demonstrating that jurisdiction.[42] Third, the multimember agency head or other reviewing authority must have a quorum of its members in order to review an initial decision.[43]

Generally, parties seeking administrative review must satisfy requirements similar to those that apply to judicial review. They must adhere to filing deadlines and must exhaust remedies by raising issues before the presiding officer before such issues can be considered by the reviewing body.[44] However, unless prohibited by statute or agency regulation, the review authority may consider an issue sua sponte even

---

39. *See* 5 U.S.C. § 557.

40. *See, e.g.*, Bethesda Hosp. Ass'n v. Bowen, 485 U.S. 399 (1988). For examples of agency rules, see MODEL ADJUDICATION RULES §§ 400–450 (ADMIN. CONF. OF THE U.S., rev. 2018).

41. *See, e.g.*, Gonzalez v. Sullivan, 914 F.2d 1197, 1203 (9th Cir. 1990) (due process requires notice reasonably calculated to afford parties their right to present objections). Frequently, agency regulations require such notice. *See, e.g.*, Shiflett v. U.S. Postal Serv., 839 F.2d 669, 673 (Fed. Cir. 1988).

42. *See, e.g.*, Clark v. U.S. Postal Serv., 989 F.2d 1164, 1167 (Fed. Cir. 1993); Van Werry v. Merit Sys. Prot. Bd., 995 F.2d 1048, 1050–52 (Fed. Cir. 1993).

43. *See, e.g.*, New Process Steel L.P. v. Nat'l Lab. Rels. Bd., 560 U.S. 674, 687–88 (2010).

44. *See, e.g.*, *Clark*, 989 F.2d at 1167; Nat'l Lab. Rels. Bd. v. George Koch Sons, Inc., 950 F.2d 1324, 1337 (7th Cir. 1991).

though the issue had not been raised before the ALJ or even reopen the proceeding and take additional evidence.[45]

19.6 AGENCY APPELLATE DECISIONS

The initial decision is part of the record and must be disclosed to the parties prior to the agency review stage as well as for purposes of judicial review. The APA provides that the parties are entitled to a reasonable opportunity to submit for the consideration of the agency reviewers "(1) proposed findings and conclusions; or (2) exceptions to the decisions or recommended decisions of subordinate employees or to tentative agency decisions; and (3) supporting reasons for the exceptions or proposed findings and conclusions."[46] As a result of this provision, the parties are entitled to disclosure of an initial decision prior to the decision by the agency reviewers.[47]

The agency head or other reviewing authority may adopt the hearing-level adjudicator's initial decision without providing independent findings or reasons. Such adoption does not violate the agency's obligation to consider the issues in the case or to make findings or give reasons for its decisions.[48] In cases of summary adoption, the reviewing court takes the initial decision as that of the agency.[49] However, if the agency head's approval of the ALJ decision is ambiguous or incomplete, a reviewing court may insist that the agency head elaborate on the decision.[50]

Unless agency rules or decisional law provides otherwise, as they sometimes do, agency heads or other reviewing authorities owe no deference to initial decisions. The APA provides that "on appeal from or review of the initial decision, the agency has all the powers which it

45. 5 U.S.C. § 557(b) (reviewing body has all powers that it would have in making initial decision except as it may limit the issues on notice or by rule).

46. *Id.* § 557(c).

47. *See, e.g.*, Ballard v. Comm'r, 544 U.S. 40, 62 (2005).

48. *See* Chen v. Immigr. & Naturalization Serv., 87 F.3d 5, 7–8 (1st Cir. 1996) (citing many cases); Guentchev v. Immigr. & Naturalization Serv., 77 F.3d 1036, 1038 (7th Cir. 1996). *But see* Tukhowinich v. Immigr. & Naturalization Serv., 64 F.3d 460, 464 (9th Cir. 1995) (finding that reviewing authority failed to provide independent consideration since it assumed that the judge's decision considered certain relevant factors that the judge had failed to consider).

49. *See, e.g.*, Alaelua v. Immigr. & Naturalization Serv., 45 F.3d 1379, 1382 (9th Cir. 1995).

50. *See, e.g.*, Armstrong v. Commodity Futures Trading Comm'n, 12 F.3d 401, 404 (3d Cir. 1993); *Tukhowinich*, 64 F.3d at 465.

would have in making the initial decision except as it may limit the issues on notice or by rule."[51] Where the agency and the ALJ disagree on issues of law, facts, discretion, or policy, a court reviews the decision of the reviewing authority, not the ALJ's decision.[52]

At the same time, however, the initial decision is part of the record for purposes of judicial review.[53] The reviewing authority must therefore explain its rejection of the initial decision's factual findings.[54] This is especially true with respect to credibility judgments based on the demeanor of witnesses. If the reviewing authority disagrees with the initial decision, this disagreement may detract from the substantiality of the evidence supporting the agency's decision.[55] Nevertheless, the agency heads or other reviewing authority are empowered to reverse an initial decision, even, for example, on a matter of witness credibility if it finds the witness's testimony implausible and justifies its departure from the initial decision.[56]

Some agencies treat their appellate decisions as precedential—that is, binding on lower level adjudicators unless or until overruled—and others as non-precedential. This aspect of appellate review is addressed briefly in Chapter 2.

---

51. APA, 5 U.S.C. § 557(b); *see, e.g.*, Vineland Fireworks Co. v. Bureau of Alcohol, Tobacco, Firearms & Explosives, 544 F.3d 509 (3d Cir. 2008).

52. *See, e.g.*, Deere & Co. v. Int'l Trade Comm'n, 605 F.3d 1350, 1358 (Fed. Cir. 2010); Ryan v. Commodity Futures Trading Comm'n, 145 F.3d 910, 918 (7th Cir. 1998).

53. 5 U.S.C. § 557(c).

54. *See, e.g.*, Simon v. Simmons Foods, Inc., 49 F.3d 386, 389–90 (8th Cir. 1995); Dart v. United States, 848 F.2d 217, 230 (D.C. Cir. 1988); Harberson v. Nat'l Lab. Rels. Bd., 810 F.2d 977, 984 (10th Cir. 1987); Local 441, Int'l Bhd. of Elec. Workers v. Nat'l Lab. Rels. Bd., 510 F.2d 1274, 1276 (D.C. Cir. 1975).

55. The leading case is *Universal Camera Corp. v. National Labor Relations Board*, 340 U.S. 474, 496 (1951), which states:

> We intend only to recognize that evidence supporting a conclusion may be less substantial when an impartial, experienced examiner who has observed the witnesses and lived with the case has drawn conclusions different from the Board's than when he has reached the same conclusion. The findings of the examiner are to be considered along with the consistency and inherent probability of testimony. The significance of his report, of course, depends largely on the importance of credibility in the particular case.

56. *See id.* at 492; Fed. Commc'ns Comm'n v. Allentown Broad. Corp., 349 U.S. 358, 364 (1955).

Chapter 20
Alternative Dispute Resolution

Judith R. Starr

20.1 CHAPTER OVERVIEW

Alternative dispute resolution (ADR) refers to various techniques for resolving disputes other than through litigation in traditional legal forums such as courts and formal administrative tribunals. Common ADR techniques include mediation and arbitration. The use of ADR in the federal government dates back more than a century. Beginning with the creation of the Department of Labor in 1913, Congress made ADR a major tool for the federal government in resolving labor disputes. Over the past several decades, Congress has enacted generally applicable and program-specific legislation to encourage agencies to integrate ADR into all areas of administrative practice.[1]

Today, ADR is available across a wide spectrum of agency functions—from licensing, permitting, and land use proceedings, to disputes over international trade practices, employment discrimination, and drug pricing.[2] ADR programs exist in many contexts, including

1. For an in-depth review of the history and practices of agency ADR programs, see Kristen Blankley et al., Admin. Conf. of the U.S., Alternative Dispute Resolution in Agency Administrative Programs (2021).

2. *See, e.g.*, *John S. McCain III National Center for Environmental Conflict Resolution: ECR in the Federal Government*, Udall Found., https://www.udall.gov/OurPrograms/Institute/Leadership.aspx (last visited June 27, 2023) (National Environmental Policy Act); U.S. Int'l Trade Comm'n, Section 337 Mediation Program: Tenth Update 10 (2019); *Mediation*, U.S. Equal Emp. Opportunity Comm'n, https://www.eeoc.gov/mediation (last visited June 27, 2023); 340B

where an agency adjudicates a matter between private parties,[3] where an agency adjudicates a claim against it such as a contract bid protest,[4] and where an agency seeks to enforce federal law against a private party.[5] Procedurally, ADR is available in both informal and formal proceedings; some agencies offer it before any formal action, such as a complaint, is filed.[6]

20.2 LEGAL AUTHORITY FOR ALTERNATIVE DISPUTE RESOLUTION

First passed in 1990 with a sunset provision, then amended and made permanent in 1996, the Administrative Dispute Resolution Act (ADRA) amended the Administrative Procedure Act (APA) to provide agencies with general authority to use a variety of ADR processes in connection with administrative proceedings.[7] ADRA also amended the Contract Disputes Act to authorize the use of ADR in procurement disputes.[8] Congress designed ADRA not only to authorize the use of ADR for agency dispute resolution but to affirmatively encourage it, having found that traditional administrative proceedings had become "increasingly formal, costly, and lengthy." Therefore, it required all federal agencies to examine the potential for using ADR in a variety of administrative programs, including agency adjudications both formal and informal and to disputes that are external-facing (i.e., involving regulated entities and/or the public) and internal-facing (e.g., workplace disputes). ADRA also required agencies to adopt agency-specific policies addressing the use of ADR, to train ADR personnel, and to appoint senior officials as dispute resolution specialists with primary responsibility for implementing ADRA and agency ADR policies.[9]

Pricing Program; Administrative Dispute Resolution Regulation, 85 Fed. Reg. 80,632 (Dec. 14, 2020) (Affordable Care Act).

3. *See, e.g.*, 18 C.F.R. pt. 385, subpt. F (2022) (Federal Energy Regulatory Commission).

4. *See, e.g.*, 48 C.F.R. § 633.214-70 (2022) (State Department).

5. *See About NLRB: Decide Cases*, Nat'l Lab. Rels. Bd., https://www.nlrb.gov/about-nlrb/what-we-do/decide-cases (last visited June 27, 2023).

6. *See, e.g.*, 57 C.F.R. § 1.737 (2022) (Federal Communications Commission).

7. Administrative Dispute Resolution Act of 1996, Pub. L. No. 104-320, 110 Stat. 3870; Administrative Dispute Resolution Act, Pub. L. No. 101-552, 104 Stat. 2736 (1990) (codified as amended at 5 U.S.C. §§ 571–584).

8. Pub. L. No. 101-552, § 6, 104 Stat. 2736, 2745–46 (codified as amended at 41 U.S.C. § 7103(f)); *see also* 48 C.F.R. §§ 33.204, 33.214, 33.103(c) (2022).

9. Pub. L. No. 101-552, §§ 2, 3, 104 Stat. 2736, 2736–37 (1990).

Nonetheless, ADRA recognizes that ADR is not appropriate in every case. It provides a list of circumstances in which an agency should consider not using ADR:

- An authoritative resolution is required for precedential value and ADR would not produce an authoritative precedent.
- The matter involves significant policy issues and ADR would not likely serve to develop policy.
- Consistency of results is especially important and ADR proceedings might not produce consistent results.
- The matter significantly affects persons or organizations who are not parties to the proceeding.
- A full public record of the proceedings is important and ADR would not provide one.
- The agency must maintain continuing jurisdiction over the matter and ADR would interfere with fulfilling that requirement.[10]

Although ADRA encourages agencies to offer ADR, it does not require that they do so.[11] However, other laws may require agencies to offer ADR in specific circumstances. For example, agencies are required to offer ADR to equal employment opportunity claimants and when they decide grievances under federal labor contracts.[12] Further, ADRA conditions use of ADR on the consent of the parties. However, its use is mandated by statute in some contexts, primarily in the area of private labor relations.[13]

ADRA does not occupy the field of agency adjudication but coexists with more specific types of ADR legislation. One area in which the use of ADR is well established is environmental collaboration and conflict resolution (ECCR). ECCR refers to third-party-assisted environmental collaboration as well as environmental conflict resolution to resolve problems and conflicts that arise in the context of environmental, public lands, or natural resources issues, including matters related to energy, transportation, and water and land management.[14]

The Environmental Policy and Conflict Resolution Act of 1998 (EPCRA) created the National Center for Environmental Conflict Resolution to facilitate the use of ADR across agencies with environmental

10. 5 U.S.C. § 572(b).
11. *Id.* § 572(c).
12. *See* 29 C.F.R. § 1614.102(b)(2) (2022); 5 U.S.C. § 7121.
13. *See, e.g.*, 29 U.S.C. § 183; 41 U.S.C. § 151 *et seq.*
14. *See* Off. of Mgmt. and Budget & Council on Env't Quality, Memorandum on Environmental Conflict Resolution (Nov. 28, 2005).

law responsibilities.[15] EPCRA established procedures for federal agencies to access the National Center's resources and authorized funding for them. The law reflected the congressional goal to provide a neutral place inside the federal government but "outside the Beltway" where public and private interests can reach common ground.[16] The National Center's objectives include:

- Resolving federal environmental, natural resources, and public lands disputes in a timely and constructive manner rather than through litigation
- Promoting collaboration and conflict resolution activities across environmental stakeholders
- Providing education and training on collaborative problem-solving and consensus building[17]

In 2012, the chair of the Council on Environmental Quality and the director of the Office of Management and Budget jointly issued a Memorandum on Environmental Conflict Resolution directing agencies to increase the effective use of ECCR.[18]

20.3 MODALITIES OF ALTERNATIVE DISPUTE RESOLUTION

ADRA defines "ADR" as including the following processes: conciliation, facilitation, mediation, fact-finding, minitrials, arbitration, and the use of ombuds.[19] Agencies are also free to adopt additional modalities, such as restorative practice and conflict coaching.[20] There is some overlap among the terms used in ADRA as techniques have developed

---

15. Environmental Policy and Conflict Resolution Act of 1998, Pub. L. No. 105-156, 112 Stat. 8.

16. Udall Found., Udall Foundation 2021 Performance and Accountability Report 52 (2021).

17. *John S. McCain III National Center for Environmental Conflict Resolution*, Udall Found., https://udall.gov/OurPrograms/Institute/Institute.aspx (last visited June 27, 2023).

18. *See* Off. of Mgmt. and Budget & Council on Env't Quality, Memorandum on Environmental Conflict Resolution (Sept. 7, 2012).

19. 5 U.S.C. § 571(3).

20. Restorative practices seek to hold accountable an individual who caused harm, focus on the needs of the harmed party, and work to reintegrate all parties back into the community. *See Community Relations Service*, U.S. Dep't of Just., https://www.justice.gov/crs (last visited June 27, 2023). Conflict coaching is often used as a tool to address communications problems among parties. *See Frequently*

since the statute's passage. While mediation, arbitration, and ombuds are the most common ADR modalities across federal agencies, all modalities listed in ADRA are in use, although terminology may vary.[21]

In arbitration, a third-party neutral decides the submitted issue after reviewing the evidence and hearing argument from the parties. Arbitration involves the presentation of evidence and witnesses to a neutral third party. Compared to litigation, arbitration is typically a private process occurring outside of public view.[22] Decisions by arbitrators are considered binding because federal law only provides for the most limited review of arbitrator awards.[23] Modern arbitration practice tends to resemble litigation, but private and with a decision-maker of the parties' choosing.[24]

By contrast, mediation involves a neutral third party to assist the parties in negotiating an agreement. The mediator has no independent authority and does not render a decision; the parties themselves control the decision-making. Unlike some other ADR modalities, such as facilitation, mediation is usually limited to solving discrete problems. When a mediation is successful, the parties formalize their agreements into a contract. If unsuccessful, the parties proceed in litigation, adjudication, or another process. Mediators use a wide variety of strategies to solve problems, such as listening actively, managing impasses and heightened emotions, and working with parties to create and evaluate settlement proposals. While some mediators focus on enabling conversation among the parties (called facilitative mediation), other mediators may direct the process, provide advice, and give informal recommendations to resolve the dispute (called evaluative mediation). A third type of mediation, transformative mediation, focuses on repairing the relationship between the parties.[25]

Asked Questions about Ombuds, INT'L OMBUDS ASS'N, https://www.ombudsassociation.org/ombuds-faq (last visited June 27, 2023).

21. *See* BLANKLEY ET AL., *supra* note 1, at 16.

22. *See* Kristen M. Blankley, *The Ethics and Practice of Drafting Pre-Dispute Resolution Clauses*, 49 CREIGHTON L. REV. 743, 770 (2016).

23. *See, e.g.*, 9 U.S.C. § 10(a) (providing review of an arbitrator's award for ethical misconduct, arbitrator bias, serious flaws in the process, and arbitrators exceeding the powers given to them by contract).

24. *See* Thomas J. Stipanowich, *Arbitration: The "New Litigation,"* 2010 ILL. L. REV. 1, 8–9 (2010).

25. *See* ROBERT A. BARUCH BUSH & JOSEPH P. FOLGER, THE PROMISE OF MEDIATION: THE TRANSFORMATIVE APPROACH TO CONFLICT (rev. ed. 2005); Leonard Riskin, *Decisionmaking in Mediation: The New Old Grid and the New New Grid*

The meaning of conciliation has changed over time. In past decades, the term was used to depict a reconciliation process led by a third party to a dispute.[26] Today, however, conciliation is often used to refer broadly to any process involving a third-party neutral in which the role of the neutral could range from facilitating discussions to recommending how to resolve a dispute.[27] The lack of a shared understanding of conciliation reflects that it is defined differently in different areas of the law. For example, in federal labor law, Congress has defined the process as one where the neutral takes a more active role than a mediator.[28] Under civil rights law, the process is a prerequisite to further action once the Equal Employment Opportunity Commission finds discrimination has occurred.[29] Some programs use the term "conciliation" interchangeably with "mediation," while other programs distinguish between the two. When a program offers both mediation and conciliation, the conciliator often takes a more hands-on and potentially evaluative role than a mediator.[30]

Facilitation "helps parties reach a decision or a satisfactory resolution of the matter to be addressed."[31] A facilitator usually conducts meetings but may not become deeply involved in the discussion or issue. Facilitation often refers to a process during which a group engages in collaborative discussion with the help of a third party.[32] Like conciliation, some people and programs use the term interchangeably with mediation, but facilitation usually refers to a process that is more party-driven and may involve a large number (i.e., dozens)

System, 79 NOTRE DAME L. REV. 1 (2003); Leonard Riskin, *Mediator Orientations, Strategies, and Techniques*, 12 ALTS. TO HIGH COST LITIG. 111 (1994).

26. Many family courts have "conciliation" programs. *See, e.g.*, CAL. FAM. CODE § 1820 (2022).

27. *See, e.g.*, Katherine Lynch, *Private Conciliation of Discrimination Disputes: Confidentiality, Informalism, and Power*, 22 WILLAMETTE J. INT'L DISP. RESOL. 49, 66 (2014).

28. *See, e.g.*, 29 U.S.C. § 183.

29. *See* 42 U.S.C. § 2000e-5(b).

30. Thomas J. Stipanowich & Veronique Fraser, *The International Task Force on Mixed Mode Dispute Resolution: Exploring the Interplay between Mediation, Evaluation, and Arbitration in Commercial Cases*, 40 FORDHAM INT'L L.J. 839, 848 (2017).

31. *See* Administrative Conference Recommendation 86-3, Agencies' Use of Alternative Means of Dispute Resolution, 51 Fed. Reg. 25,643 (July 16, 1986).

32. SAM KANER, FACILITATOR'S GUIDE TO PARTICIPATORY DECISION-MAKING xx (2014).

of stakeholders.[33] Facilitation need not involve a concrete dispute but may address problems with communications among individuals and groups. Facilitated processes may include both large-group and small-group meetings to accomplish the goals of the project.

A fact-finding proceeding entails the "appointment of a person or group with the technical expertise in the subject matter to evaluate the matter presented and file a report establishing the facts."[34] Fact-finding is a quasi-adjudicative process during which the parties, usually through their attorneys, present evidence and arguments to a neutral party, and the neutral makes a determination of likely outcomes at trial. The evaluation can take many forms but one common form is findings of fact and conclusions of law. In this context, fact-finding is the functional equivalent of "early neutral evaluation" (often abbreviated ENE), which is defined as the use of "a neutral or impartial third party to provide an objective evaluation, sometimes in writing, of the strengths and weaknesses of the case."[35] The evaluation is made for settlement purposes only; if the parties do not settle after the determination, the dispute resolution process continues as if the fact-finding had not occurred.

A minitrial is "a structured settlement process in which each side presents a highly abbreviated summary of its case before senior officials."[36] The minitrial is structurally similar to the fact-finding proceeding, involving the presentation of evidence and argument by lawyers for the parties. A third-party neutral's role is limited to guiding the presentations because the purpose of the minitrial is not to persuade the neutral third party but rather the principal decision-makers. The principals may have the opportunity to ask questions to the lawyers presenting the cases during or after the process.[37] The purpose of the minitrial is to expose the strengths and weaknesses of each side's claims and to provide information necessary to aid in settlement discussions. Once the presentations conclude, the senior officials have the opportunity to discuss settlement options with the parties behind

---

33. *See, e.g.*, Janice M. Fletcher, *One Size Does Not Fit All: Differentiating ADR Processes*, 49 S. Tex. L. Rev. 1039, 1043–44 (2008).

34. Administrative Conference Recommendation 86-3, *supra* note 31.

35. *See Early Neutral Evaluation*, U.S. Equal Emp. Opportunity Comm'n, https://www.eeoc.gov/federal-sector/early-neutral-evaluation (last visited June 27, 2023).

36. Administrative Conference Recommendation 86-3, *supra* note 31.

37. Kristen M. Blankley & Maureen Weston, Understanding Alternative Dispute Resolution 241 (2017).

closed doors and without any attorneys or third-party assistance. As with fact-finding, if the minitrial does not result in a settlement, the parties proceed as if the minitrial had not happened.

Ombuds' offices vary in the services they provide, making this modality difficult to define with any precision. As a general matter, an ombuds is usually an employee of an organization with multiple powers of investigation and dispute resolution.[38] Despite being organizational employees, ombuds have great independence, resulting in flexibility to resolve stakeholders' issues. Ombuds usually follow standards of practice (i.e., ethical standards) focusing around four principles: (1) independence, (2) neutrality, (3) confidentiality, and (4) informality.[39] Ombuds provide many services, including, depending on the situation, listening to problems, providing information, investigating complaints, resolving conflicts, advocating for changes within the organization, and writing reports.[40] Ombuds most often work one-on-one with a stakeholder who reports a problem or frustration, but some ombuds provide mediation services to multiple parties to a dispute.

20.4 NEUTRALS AND NEUTRALITY

The involvement of a "neutral" is a key element of ADR techniques under federal law. A "neutral" is "an individual who, with respect to an issue in controversy, functions specifically to aid the parties in resolving the controversy."[41] A neutral may be a federal employee or any other individual acceptable to the parties in an ADR proceeding but must have no official, financial, or personal conflict of interest with respect to the issues in controversy, unless such interest is fully disclosed in writing to all parties and all parties agree that the neutral may serve.[42]

---

38. *See* Harold J. Krent, *Federal Agency Ombuds: The Costs, Benefits, and Countenance of Confidentiality*, 52 ADMIN. L. REV. 17, 20–21 (2000).

39. IOA STANDARDS OF PRAC. (INT'L OMBUDSMAN ASS'N 2005); *see also* CAROLE S. HOUK ET AL., ADMIN. CONF. OF THE U.S., A REAPPRAISAL—THE NATURE AND VALUE OF OMBUDSMEN IN THE FEDERAL AGENCIES, PART 1: EXECUTIVE SUMMARY 13–15 (2016).

40. *See* CAROLE S. HOUK ET AL., ADMIN. CONF. OF THE U.S., A REAPPRAISAL—THE NATURE AND VALUE OF OMBUDSMEN IN THE FEDERAL AGENCIES, PART 2: RESEARCH REPORT 286 (2016).

41. 5 U.S.C. § 571(9).

42. *Id.* § 573(a).

ADRA's definition of "neutral" is consistent with federal ethics rules regarding the avoidance of conflicts of interest and bias.[43] It also guards against the appearance of bias by requiring a neutral to disclose conflicts. This disclosure enables parties to enforce the neutrality requirement because a neutral ordinarily "serves at the will of the parties."[44] This approach—requiring neutrality and disclosure of conflicts of interest—is consistent with industry standards of ethics in mediation,[45] arbitration,[46] and ombuds practices.[47]

One additional element of neutrality is freedom from the possibility of financial gain that arises out of the dispute resolution process. Although not addressed specifically in ADRA, this is specifically addressed in the federal ethics rules applicable to all federal employees,[48] and national standards in mediation,[49] arbitration,[50] and ombuds practice[51] generally prohibit a neutral from receiving a gain or incurring a loss as a direct result of the process. Neutrals who are lawyers may have additional responsibilities to disclose conflicts of interest resulting from work arising out of a former engagement as a neutral.[52]

The Federal Mediation and Conciliation Service (FMCS), a federal agency that provides dispute resolution and conflict management services in labor and other disputes, maintains explicit rules prohibiting its neutrals from using their position for private gain.[53] This ensures that neutrals who are not federal employees and thus not subject to

---

43. *See* 5 C.F.R. § 2635.101(b) (2022).

44. 5 U.S.C. § 573(b).

45. Model Standards of Conduct for Mediators Standards II, III (Am. Bar Ass'n 2005); Uni. Mediation Act § 9 (Unif. L. Comm'n 2003).

46. *See* 9 U.S.C. § 10(a)(2); Code of Ethics for Arbs. in Com. Disputes Canon II (Am. Bar Ass'n & Am. Arb. Ass'n 2004); Revised Unif. Arbitration Act § 12 (Unif. L. Comm'n 2000).

47. IOA Standards of Prac., *supra* note 39, § 2.1.

48. 5 C.F.R. § 2635.401–.403 (2022).

49. Model Standards of Conduct for Mediators, *supra* note 45, Standard III(f).

50. Code of Ethics for Arbs. in Com. Disputes, *supra* note 46, Canon VI(D).

51. IOA Standards of Prac., *supra* note 39, § 2.1.

52. *See* Model Rules of Pro. Conduct r. 1.13 (Am. Bar Ass'n 2020).

53. FMCS Directive 8101, § 5 (2015); 29 C.F.R. pt. 1400, app. § III (2022).

federal ethics rules are subject to similar standards. Agencies also can put such requirements in their contracts with private neutrals.[54]

20.5 CONFIDENTIALITY AND PRIVILEGE

Confidentiality is a bedrock principle underlying ADR processes. Confidentiality protects against the disclosure of both oral and written communications outside an ADR proceeding (i.e., in a court or administrative tribunal) and more broadly. Confidentiality protections apply to nearly all ADR processes, whether they are based on consensual decision-making or adjudication. In consensual processes such as mediation, the guarantee of confidentiality encourages frank discussion and disclosure of information;[55] in adjudicative processes such as arbitration, confidentiality protects the parties from intrusion by the press or others.[56] Confidentiality works to protect specific disclosures while also protecting ADR processes as a whole.[57]

Privilege, by contrast, protects the disclosure of an ADR communication before a court or tribunal but does not necessarily protect against disclosures to other third parties. The Uniform Mediation Act (UMA) provides the clearest example of the distinctions between the two. Although the UMA is not federal law and only adopted in about one-quarter of U.S. states, its provisions are still instructive to this inquiry. Under UMA section 8, mediation communications are confidential only "to the extent agreed by the parties or provided by other law."[58] Unlike other common privileges, such as the attorney-client privilege, the UMA treats mediation communications as privileged even if they are not kept confidential.[59]

The ADRA provision entitled "confidentiality" covers both confidentiality and privilege. The statute provides that neutrals and parties

54. For example, applicable ethical standards are set forth in the Environmental Protection Agency's statement of work for contractor neutrals, available at https://www.epa.gov/sites/default/files/2018-06/documents/cprs_contract_statement_of_work__0.pdf.

55. Mark. H. Grunewald, *Freedom of Information and Confidentiality under the Administrative Dispute Resolution Act*, 9 ADMIN. L.J. AM. U. 985, 997 (1996).

56. *See* Richard C. Reuben, *Confidentiality in Arbitration: Beyond the Myth*, 54 U. KAN. L. REV. 1255, 1284 (2006).

57. *See* John E. Hartsell, *The Sounds of Silence: Promoting Alternative Dispute Resolution in Air Force Procurement by Putting Confidence into Confidentiality*, 53 AIR FORCE L. REV. 183, 193 (2002).

58. UNIF. MEDIATION ACT § 8 (UNIF. L. COMM'N 2003).

59. *Id.* § 4.

"shall not voluntarily disclose or through discovery or compulsory process be required to disclose any dispute resolution communication or any communication provided in confidence to the neutral."[60] ADRA generally makes any "dispute resolution communication" confidential. A "dispute resolution communication" is "any oral or written communication prepared for the purposes of a dispute resolution proceeding, including any memoranda, notes or work product of the neutral, parties, or nonparty participant."[61] Any dispute resolution communication that is disclosed in violation of these provisions is not admissible in any proceeding relating to the issues in controversy with respect to which the communication was made.[62]

Exceptions apply when the parties and the neutral agree to disclosure, when the communication is already public, and in other limited circumstances.[63] Further, written agreements arising out of dispute resolution processes are not protected.[64] The protections available under ADRA may be modified or waived by agreement of the parties and the neutral.[65] Similar to other privileges, such as the attorney-client privilege, evidence that is "otherwise discoverable" does not become inadmissible "merely because the evidence was presented in the course of a dispute resolution proceeding."[66]

In addition to ADRA, specific programs provide for confidentiality through regulations. Some agencies have promulgated regulations specifically addressing confidentiality and privilege, including the Department of Agriculture,[67] the Federal Communications Commission,[68] and the Surface Transportation Board.[69]

Confidentiality is not only a legal obligation but also an ethical obligation of neutrals. National standards in mediation,[70] arbitration,[71] and ombuds practice[72] stress the importance of maintaining confidentiality.

---

60. 5 U.S.C. § 574(a), (b).
61. *Id.* § 571(5).
62. *Id.* § 574(c).
63. *Id.* § 574(a).
64. *Id.* § 574(g).
65. *Id.* § 574(d).
66. *Id.* § 574(f).
67. *See* 7 C.F.R. § 780.9(e) (2022); *id.* § 614.11(g).
68. 47 C.F.R. § 1.244 (2022).
69. 49 C.F.R. § 1109.3(d) (2022).
70. Model Standards of Conduct for Mediators, *supra* note 45, Standard V(a).
71. Code of Ethics for Arbs. in Com. Disputes, *supra* note 46, Canon VI.
72. IOA Standards of Prac., *supra* note 39, § 3.1.

In a similar vein, FMCS Directive 8101 prohibits the misuse of non-public information in its standards of ethics and conduct.[73] The Code of Professional Conduct for Labor Mediators also includes a duty of confidentiality.[74]

20.6 RESOURCES

As agency ADR processes evolve, practitioners need to stay current with the offerings of the agencies with which their clients are involved. Resources are available at agencies and interagency bodies that promote ADR.

ADRA of 1996 authorized FMCS to assist agencies with their ADR programs, to provide neutrals and training, and to consult with the Interagency ADR Working Group on a roster of neutrals.[75] Today, FMCS provides mediation and conflict resolution services to industry, government agencies, and communities.[76] The FMCS Institute for Conflict Management provides centralized classroom training, both live and web-based, in mediation, negotiation, arbitration, workplace violence prevention, and organizational development. It is an approved recertification provider by the Society for Human Resource Management (one of the largest human resources membership associations focused on professional development and certification of competencies), and many of its courses are approved for continuing legal education for attorneys.[77] FMCS also participates in and promotes conferences and workshops and provides customized training modules.[78] Its website features multimedia presentations that highlight lessons learned from ADR successes and discussions of its potential for problem-solving.[79]

The National Center provides a broad range of dispute resolution services for any environmental conflict involving the federal

---

73. FMCS Directive 8101, § 5 (2015).

74. 29 C.F.R. pt. 1400, § V, app (2022).

75. *See* Administrative Dispute Resolution Act of 1996, Pub. L. No. 104-320, § 7, 110 Stat. 3870, 3871–72.

76. *About Us*, FMCS, https://www.fmcs.gov/aboutus (last visited June 27, 2023).

77. FMCS, Providing Practical, Customized Conflict Training (2017), https://www.fmcs.gov/wp-content/uploads/2017/03/FMCS-InstituteV3.pdf.

78. *Conferences and Workshops*, FMCS, https://www.fmcs.gov/services/education-and-outreach/conferences-and-workshops/ (last visited June 27, 2023).

79. *Documents and Data*, FMCS, https://www.fmcs.gov/resources/documents-and-data/ (last visited June 27, 2023).

government. Its website contains summaries of cases in which it successfully assisted resolving complex multiparty disputes using ECCR.[80] Parties in these cases have included federal agencies, state agencies, environmental groups, and local residents. Issues have included environmental cleanup, endangered species protection, impact on residents from federal and state development projects, and land use issues arising from tribal developments. The website contains multiple resources for persons who may be considering ECCR, such as webinars, and a glossary of ECCR and ADR terminology.[81]

Finally, the Interagency ADR Working Group, established by presidential memorandum in 1998,[82] has issued a number of useful guidance documents on topics such as the interaction between the Freedom of Information Act and ADR confidentiality requirements.[83] As many of these documents were issued early in the 21st century, they need to be read with later developments in mind. Nonetheless, they continue to be a good source for identifying and analyzing issues.

---

80. *John S. McCain III National Center for Environmental Conflict Resolution: Project Case Summaries*, UDALL FOUND., https://www.udall.gov/OurPrograms/Institute/ProjectCaseSummaries.aspx (last visited June 27, 2023).

81. *John S. McCain III National Center for Environmental Conflict Resolution: Find a Mediator or Facilitator—Choosing an ECR Professional*, UDALL FOUND., https://www.udall.gov/OurPrograms/Institute/ChoosingECRProfessional.aspx (last visited June 27, 2023).

82. Memorandum from President William J. Clinton to the Heads of Executive Departments and Agencies on Facilitating and Encouraging Agency Use of Alternative Dispute Resolution and Negotiated Rulemaking (May 1, 1998).

83. *See* INTERAGENCY ADR WORKING GRP. STEERING COMM., PROTECTING THE CONFIDENTIALITY OF DISPUTE RESOLUTION PROCEEDINGS: A GUIDE FOR FEDERAL WORKPLACE ADR PROGRAM ADMINISTRATORS (2006).

Chapter 21

Formats for Participation in Oral Proceedings

Jeremy S. Graboyes

21.1 CHAPTER OVERVIEW

Adjudication, like many processes for administrative decision-making, requires the exchange of information among agency decision-makers and agency and nonagency participants. Participants in an adjudication—adjudicators, parties, witnesses, and others—can exchange evidence, views, and other information through the exchange of records or during live, oral proceedings. Some processes rely solely on the exchange of written or other recorded materials. Indeed, as discussed in Chapter 22, there has been a trend in some programs toward the use of "written" or "paper" evidentiary hearings. But many processes, as a matter of law or practice, involve at least some opportunity for a live, oral proceeding before an adjudicator.

There are many different types of oral proceedings, and their names vary across programs. Examples include evidentiary hearings, investigatory hearings, informal hearings, prehearing conferences, scheduling conferences, settlement conferences, informal conferences, status conferences, fact-finding hearings, and oral arguments. Some, like evidentiary hearings, are held principally for the receipt of evidence. Others, like oral arguments in many appellate proceedings, might concern only the interpretation of legal principles and their application to uncontested facts. Still others, like scheduling conferences, serve a primarily procedural purpose. Some proceedings are elaborate and trial-like, while others are highly informal.

Oral proceedings were, until the 1970s, nearly always conducted in person—that is, with all participants gathered in the same physical space (e.g., a hearing room). Technological and telecommunications advances have introduced a succession of formats for remote participation: telephone, traditional video teleconferencing (VTC), and virtual (section 21.2). Each format has its potential benefits and drawbacks. This chapter focuses on these potential benefits and drawbacks in terms of efficiency (section 21.3), accessibility (section 21.4), and substantive accuracy (section 21.5). Policymakers must also be aware of each format's potential effects on other goals and values of federal agency adjudication, including procedural fairness, participant satisfaction, privacy, confidentiality, and transparency.[1]

The legal and policy question that has garnered the most attention is: Who determines the format by which a party participates in an oral proceeding—Congress, the agency, an individual adjudicator, or the party—and according to what criteria (section 21.6)? Other questions discussed in this chapter concern the format by which parties examine or confront adverse parties and witnesses (section 21.7) and the response to technical and other problems that might arise during a proceeding in which one or more individuals participate remotely (section 21.8).

21.2 PARTICIPATION FORMATS GENERALLY

There are presently four principal formats by which parties, witnesses, and others participate in oral proceedings. Individuals can participate "in person" (i.e., in the same space as the adjudicator) (section 21.21), or remotely by telephone (section 21.22), by traditional VTC (section 21.23), or virtually (section 21.24). The following table illustrates the basic features of each format:

1. *See* Jeremy Graboyes, Admin. Conf. of the U.S., Legal Considerations for Remote Hearings in Agency Adjudications 21–23 (2020).

	In Person	VTC	Virtual	Telephone
Live audio	X	X	X	X
Live video	X	X	X	
May require special room or equipment	X	X		
Same space as adjudicator	X			

It is important to note that formats for participating in oral proceedings continue to evolve as technologies develop and societal expectations change. Agencies were quick to adopt fully virtual proceedings during the COVID-19 pandemic, for example, and virtual proceedings have quickly become institutionalized across the federal government. Going forward, we are likely to see more frequent use of "hybrid" proceedings in which different people participate in different ways. In a hybrid proceeding, one party might participate in person, for example, while another party participates virtually, and a witness participates by telephone.

Given rapid and ongoing development in this area, this chapter does not attempt to catalog agency procedures for implementing different formats for remote participation. Readers should consult the various recommendations of the Administrative Conference of the United States (ACUS) for current best practices.[2]

21.21 In-Person Participation

Oral participation was long synonymous with "in person." All participants gathered in the same space. The nature of that space could vary dramatically. Proceedings before the Interstate Commerce Commission, for example, took place in a large hearing room in Washington that had all the formal majesty of a courtroom or a congressional committee room: a polished wood bench, elaborate furnishings, and room for spectators. Meanwhile, Social Security Board referees in the 1940s

---

2. *See*, *e.g.*, Administrative Conference Recommendation 2021-6, Public Access to Agency Adjudicative Proceedings, 87 Fed. Reg. 1,715 (Jan. 12, 2022); Administrative Conference Recommendation 2021-4, Virtual Hearings in Agency Adjudication, 86 Fed. Reg. 36,083 (July 8, 2021); Administrative Conference Recommendation 2014-7, Best Practices for Using Video Teleconferencing for Hearings, 79 Fed. Reg. 75,114 (Dec. 17, 2014); Administrative Conference Recommendation 2011-4, Agency Use of Video Hearings: Best Practices and Possibilities for Expansion, 76 Fed. Reg. 48,795 (Aug. 9, 2011).

rode circuit, traveling 1,500 miles per month to conduct hearings in post offices, town halls, schools, and libraries.[3]

Agencies still conduct in-person proceedings in a variety of facilities. Many conduct proceedings from a central facility, often located at their headquarters near Washington, D.C. Oral arguments before the Environmental Appeals Board take place at the Environmental Protection Agency's Washington headquarters, for example, and the Board of Veterans' Appeals (BVA) conducts in-person hearings "at its principal location" in Washington.[4] Some agencies, especially those with large caseloads, maintain networks of local offices. The Social Security Administration (SSA) has more than 160 hearing offices across the country, for example, and the Executive Office for Immigration Review (EOIR) manages more than 60 immigration courts. Some agencies conduct proceedings in public or private facilities that they do not manage. EOIR proceedings might take place in Department of Homeland Security detention centers, for example, and hearings before Occupational Safety and Health Review Commission administrative law judges (ALJs) often take place in local courthouses. Some proceedings take place in private facilities convenient to parties such as local conference centers and hotel event spaces.

The spaces in which in-person proceedings take place vary widely, ranging from employees' offices to multipurpose conference rooms to specially built hearing rooms. Each has its place and its purpose, as ACUS recognized long ago.[5] An informal meeting that involves few participants and generates no public interest need not take place in an auditorium, and a complex evidentiary hearing that generates substantial public interest should not take place in a cubicle.

Although remote participation has become increasingly common across federal programs, in-person participation often remains the standard against which other formats are compared.

21.22 Telephone Participation

The telephone was invented in the 19th century, but it was not until a century later—once telephone ownership became widespread and

3. Ernest R. Burton, *The Appeals System in Old-Age and Survivors Insurance*, Soc. Sec. Bull., July 1946, at 4, 5.

4. 38 U.S.C. § 7107(c)(1)(A).

5. *See* Administrative Conference Recommendation 68-1, Adequate Hearing Facilities (1968).

teleconferencing became feasible—that its use became common in administrative adjudication.

State agencies administering unemployment insurance programs first piloted the use of telephone hearings in unemployment compensation cases in the 1970s.[6] After studies identified efficiency and other benefits from their use, federal agencies began considering whether they too should conduct some proceedings telephonically. SSA commissioned a report on New Mexico's pilot program,[7] the Commodity Futures Trading Commission offered telephone hearings in simplified procedures for reparations cases,[8] and the Department of Health and Human Services (HHS) authorized the Departmental Grant Appeals Board to conduct prehearing and informal conferences by telephone.[9]

A 1986 study for ACUS found that teleconferencing had become the favored format among Departmental Grant Appeals Board members, even for evidentiary hearings, and its use seemed to make proceedings more efficient.[10] ACUS recommended that federal adjudicators "take full advantage of telephone conferences as a means to hear motions, to hold prehearing conferences, and even to hear the merits of administrative proceedings when appropriate."[11]

---

6. *See* Jerome R. Corsi & Thomas L. Hurley, *Attitudes toward the Use of the Telephone in Administrative Fair Hearings: The California Experience*, 31 ADMIN. L. REV. 248 (1979); Jerome R. Corsi & Thomas L. Hurley, *Pilot Study Report on the Use of the Telephone in Administrative Fair Hearings*, 31 ADMIN. L. REV. 485 (1979); *see also* Bruce Graham, *The Iowa Unemployment Appeals Telephone Process*, 12 J. NAT'L ASS'N ADMIN. L. JUDGES 153 (1992); Allan A. Toubman et al., *Due Process Implications of Telephone Hearings: The Case for an Individualized Approach to Scheduling Telephone Hearings*, 29 U. MICH. J. L. REFORM 407 (1996).

7. UNIV. OF N.M., THE USE OF TELEPHONE CONFERENCING IN ADMINISTRATIVE FAIR HEARINGS: MAJOR FINDINGS OF THE NEW MEXICO EXPERIMENT WITH WELFARE APPEALS, SSA PUB. NO. 13-11749 (1982).

8. Marianne K. Smythe, *The Reparations Program of the Commodity Futures Trading Commission: Reducing Formality in Agency Adjudication*, 2 ADMIN. L.J. 39, 63 (1988); *see also* Administrative Conference Statement #13, Dispute Resolution Procedure in Reparations and Similar Cases, 53 Fed. Reg. 26,032 (July 11, 1988).

9. 46 Fed. Reg. 43,816 (Aug. 31, 1981).

10. RICHARD B. CAPPALLI, ACUS, MODEL FOR CASE MANAGEMENT: THE GRANT APPEALS BOARD (1986).

11. Administrative Conference Recommendation 86-7, Case Management as a Tool for Improving Agency Adjudication, ¶ 10, 51 Fed. Reg. 46,989, 46,990 (Dec. 30, 1986).

Shortly thereafter, the Health Care Financing Administration—the predecessor to today's Centers for Medicare and Medicaid Services—proposed establishing a new corps of ALJs that would conduct most Medicare hearings by telephone. The public and congressional response was skeptical. Congress requested that HHS and the Government Accountability Office (GAO) conduct further analyses of the proposal.[12] GAO recommended that HHS first pilot the use of telephone hearings before implementing them systemwide.[13]

Teleconferencing is still routinely used to conduct oral proceedings. Its use for informal meetings and prehearing and scheduling conferences is fairly commonplace and uncontroversial.

Its use for evidentiary hearings varies. At some agencies, like SSA, telephone hearings are used only in extraordinary situations.[14] At the Office of Medicare Hearings and Appeals and the Internal Revenue Service, on the other hand, parties routinely participate by telephone.[15] Telephone proceedings might decline in popularity as it becomes just as easy to conduct proceedings virtually.

21.23 Traditional Video Teleconference Participation

Although attempts at videotelephony date from the early 20th century, it was not until the digital revolution of the 1980s and 1990s that the technology became good enough, the telecommunications infrastructure widespread enough, and the equipment cheap enough to make VTC a viable option for conducting oral proceedings in federal agency adjudications.

Government officials quickly realized VTC's potential to facilitate efficient management of high-volume, geographically dispersed caseloads. In 1994, Congress authorized the BVA to hold VTC hearings with claimants' consent.[16] EOIR adopted a rule the following year permitting VTC hearings even without parties' consent.[17] SSA began piloting the use of VTC to conduct hearings before an ALJ in 1996

---

12. Omnibus Budget Reconciliation Act of 1987, Pub. L. No. 100-203, § 4037, 101 Stat. 1330, 1330–80.

13. GAO, B-230538, Medicare Claims: HCFA Proposal to Establish an Administrative Law Judge Unit 41 (1988).

14. SSA, Hearings, Appeals, and Litigation Law (HALLEX) Manual § I-2-0-15C.

15. HHS, OMHA Case Processing Manual § 15.2.3.

16. Board of Veterans' Appeals Administrative Procedures Improvement Act of 1994, Pub. L. No. 103-271, § 7, 108 Stat. 740, 742–43.

17. 60 Fed. Reg. 26,351 (May 17, 1995).

and adopted a rule in 2003 that allowed ALJs to schedule hearings by VTC in certain circumstances.[18] Other agencies, such as the Merit Systems Protection Board and Railroad Retirement Board, soon followed suit.[19]

The chief benefit of VTC participation over telephone participation was that it allowed participants to see each other. The chief challenge was that VTC, as first implemented, required a system of cameras, displays, microphones, and speakers, as well as a codec to digitally transmit video and audio over a phone network or the internet. While most participants had ready access to a telephone, they typically lacked access to the technological and telecommunications infrastructure needed to participate by VTC.

Agencies dealt with this challenge in different ways. Some installed VTC systems in local offices for use in adjudications. SSA, for example, began setting up VTC systems in field offices and hearing offices. The Department of Veterans Affairs set up VTC systems at regional offices. At some agencies, parties could participate using VTC systems operated by other federal or state institutions (e.g., prisons, the Iowa Communications Network). Beginning in 2008, SSA allowed parties and representatives to participate using agency-certified VTC systems installed at representatives' offices.[20]

In 2011, ACUS identified VTC use as a potential best practice for agencies with high-volume caseloads. It recommended that agencies consider using VTC to conduct hearings and other oral proceedings when such use "would not impair the fairness of the proceedings or the participants' satisfaction with them."[21] A subsequent recommendation, in 2014, identified best practices for selecting and installing VTC hardware, training adjudicators and staff, budgeting, and assessing the impacts of VTC use on participant satisfaction and substantive outcomes.[22] ACUS published a handbook on VTC best practices the following year.[23]

---

18. 68 Fed. Reg. 69,003 (Mar. 5, 2003).

19. Nathaniel Flanders & Amber Williams, ACUS, Memorandum on the History of Agency Video Teleconferencing Adjudications (2014).

20. Off. of the Inspector Gen., SSA, A-05-09-19101, Representative Video Project (2011).

21. Administrative Conference Recommendation 2011-4, *supra* note 2.

22. Administrative Conference Recommendation 2014-7, *supra* note 2.

23. Martin E. Gruen & Christine R. Williams, ACUS, Handbook on Best Practices for Using Video Teleconferencing in Adjudicatory Hearings (2015).

Although VTC has yielded real benefits in terms of efficiency and cost-effectiveness, its use, particularly in the immigration courts and at SSA, has also met with substantial criticism. Benefits of VTC, and criticisms against its use, are discussed later in this chapter.

21.24 Virtual Participation

Traditional VTC participation and virtual participation are often lumped together as "video" participation. Although similar, there are important distinctions between them. VTC participation traditionally required participants to travel to a centralized facility or use equipment certified by an agency. Virtual participation, on the other hand, allows participants to appear from a location of their choosing, such as a home or office, using a software application run on a personal device such as a computer, tablet, or smartphone.

Developments starting in the early 2000s paved the way for virtual participation in agency adjudications. They include the launch of web conferencing programs like Skype, increased ownership of personal computers, and expanding access to high-speed internet. Although some agencies used virtual participation before 2020, its proliferation is attributable to the onset of the COVID-19 pandemic. As agencies closed their facilities to employees and the public, they turned to web conferencing programs like Zoom, Microsoft Teams, and Cisco Webex to conduct proceedings in wholly virtual spaces.[24] (At least one agency, the Department of Veterans Affairs, uses a program developed and operated by the agency.)

The chief benefit of virtual proceedings, compared with traditional VTC proceedings, is that nonagency participants can participate from a location of their choosing using personal equipment. This eliminates the need for travel in most cases, making scheduling easier, reducing costs for agencies and nonagency participants, and improving accessibility. Agencies also do not need to procure and maintain equipment and space for use by virtual participants.

But virtual participation can also present challenges, particularly for individuals who still lack access to a personal device, reliable broadband internet, or a quiet space from which to participate. Virtual participation can also be challenging for people who are not

---

24. *See generally Coronavirus (COVID-19) and Adjudication*, ACUS, https://acus.gov/coronavirus-and-adjudication (last visited June 27, 2023); Leslie Birnbaum, *Due Process and Administrative Hearings in the Time of COVID-19: Help, I Need Somebody!*, 41 J. Nat'l Ass'n Admin. L. Judiciary 140 (2021).

familiar with web conferencing platforms, have trouble using them to participate in formal legal proceedings, or are unable to independently troubleshoot technical issues when they arise. Virtual participation—which involves the use of personal devices, public networks, commercial web conferencing software, and private spaces—can also, in some contexts, raise unique concerns about privacy, confidentiality, data security, and the integrity of agency proceedings.[25]

It is clear that many agencies will continue to conduct at least some proceedings virtually after they fully reopen their facilities.[26] ACUS recommended in 2021 that agencies "offer virtual hearings consistent with their needs, in accord with principles of fairness and efficiency, and with due regard for participant satisfaction."[27]

21.3 EFFECTS ON EFFICIENCY

Agencies have embraced remote participation for several reasons, but efficiency is chief among them. It is no coincidence that ACUS first addressed telephone participation in a recommendation on case management,[28] and subsequent recommendations have also highlighted the potential for remote formats to improve efficiency.[29] Many agencies have turned to remote participation as part of efforts to reduce backlogs, address delays, and improve productivity.

There are a number of ways in which the use of remote participation formats can promote efficiency. Remote participation saves time and money and simplifies scheduling by reducing or eliminating the need for travel by adjudicators and other agency and nonagency participants. The option for remote participation also makes it easier and more cost-effective for agencies to secure interpretation and transcription services, particularly in areas where services are limited.

Expanded use of remote participation further allows agencies to centralize their operations. When parties participate remotely, agencies can assign cases to any available adjudicator, no matter where in the country they are located, rather than relying solely on local adjudicators. This can help agencies alleviate the effects of localized staff

25. *See* GRABOYES, *supra* note 1, at 21–22.

26. *See, e.g.*, Use of Videoconferencing Technology to Conduct Unfair Labor Practice and Representation Case Proceedings, 86 Fed. Reg. 61,090 (Nat'l Lab. Rels. Bd. Nov. 5, 2021).

27. Administrative Conference Recommendation 2021-4, *supra* note 2.

28. *See* Administrative Conference Recommendation 86-7, *supra* note 11.

29. *See supra* note 2.

shortages and manage localized increases in case volumes. SSA, for example, has established several National Hearing Centers to augment capacity at local hearing offices.[30]

Agencies may realize additional efficiencies when they conduct proceedings entirely by telephone or virtually, because they do not need to make equipment or facilities available to nonagency participants. In such proceedings, adjudicators can preside from private offices or while teleworking without the need for separate hearing rooms, which may be in short supply.

But remote participation is not costless. Agencies must invest in the necessary technology and telecommunications infrastructure. Experience also indicates that it may take longer to conduct some proceedings remotely than in person. It may be more difficult for adjudicators to manage large numbers of remote participants, for example, or participants may have more difficulty sharing exhibits when they participate remotely. Technical difficulties can complicate proceedings in which participants appear remotely. And inexperience with remote participation may complicate proceedings, necessitating training and support for agency and even nonagency participants.[31]

Policymakers must also balance any efficiency gains against impacts on other goals and values of federal agency adjudication, including accessibility (section 21.4) and accuracy (section 21.5).

21.4 EFFECTS ON ACCESSIBILITY

Remote participation formats have the potential to increase access for many individuals, including, as ACUS has identified, for

> individuals whose disabilities make it difficult to travel to hearing facilities or participate in public settings; individuals who live in rural areas and may need to travel great distances to hearing facilities; and low-income individuals for whom it may be difficult to secure transportation to hearing facilities or take time off work or arrange for childcare to participate in in-person or traditional video hearings.[32]

---

30. Off. of the Inspector Gen., SSA, A-12-11-11147, The Role of National Hearing Centers in Reducing the Hearings Backlog (2012).

31. Fredric I. Lederer & Ctr. for Legal and Ct. Tech., Analysis of Administrative Agency Adjudicatory Hearing Use of Remote Appearances and Virtual Hearings: Report to ACUS 10 (2021).

32. Administrative Conference Recommendation 2021-4, *supra* note 2.

The option for remote participation can make it easier and more cost-effective for agencies to secure interpretation services, particularly in areas where services are limited. It can also make it easier for private parties to secure representation, especially for low-income individuals in geographic areas where low-cost or pro bono representation is limited or unavailable.[33]

On the other hand, remote participation can be difficult for many people. Children may have difficulty participating remotely, for example. The American Bar Association (ABA) has recommended that "video teleconference should not be used in immigration proceedings involving children" except in "exigent circumstances where the child and any counsel of record have consented."[34] The limitations of remote interpretation might make it difficult for individuals with limited English proficiency to effectively participate in remote proceedings.[35] And remote participation might erect barriers to access for people with disabilities, including individuals with hearing or vision impairments; individuals who, as a result of physical or mental disorders, speak softly or have speech impairments; individuals with auditory or visual hallucinations; individuals with epilepsy or other seizure disorders; individuals who, as a result of mental impairments, do not recognize the individual with whom they are remotely interacting as the adjudicator who will decide their case, distrust technology, or fear being recorded; and individuals with intellectual disabilities, borderline intellectual functioning, brain injury, learning disabilities, and developmental disabilities such as autism.[36]

Because the government does not provide telephone or virtual participants with the equipment, telecommunications services, quiet space, and on-site technological support necessary for effective participation,

---

33. *Id.*; Fatma Marouf & Luz Herrera, *Technological Triage of Immigration Cases*, 72 Fla. L. Rev. 515, 570–73 (2020); Lenni B. Benson & Russell R. Wheeler, ACUS, Enhancing Quality and Timeliness in Immigration Removal Adjudication 93–94 (2012).

34. ABA, Achieving America's Immigration Promise: ABA Recommendations to Advance Justice, Fairness, and Efficiency 31–32 (2021).

35. Maya P. Barak, *Can You Hear Me Now? Attorney Perceptions of Interpretation, Technology, and Power in Immigration Court*, 9 J. on Migration & Human Sec. 207 (2021); Eugenio Mollo, Jr., Note, *The Expansion of Video Conferencing Technology in Immigration Proceedings and Its Impact on Venue Provisions, Interpretation Rights, and the Mexican Immigrant Community*, 9 J. Gender Race & Just. 689, 702–12 (2006).

36. Graboyes, *supra* note 1, at 15.

telephone and virtual participation can also erect barriers.[37] Many low-income individuals do not have consistent access to a high-quality personal device or private internet or telephone services. People in rural areas may lack high-speed internet access. And many individuals may "have difficulty, feel uncomfortable, or lack experience" using a personal device and web conferencing software to participate in a legal proceeding.[38] Agencies must consider the needs of the populations with whom they interact.[39]

21.5 EFFECTS ON SUBSTANTIVE ACCURACY

Agencies and outside researchers have long attempted to measure whether different participation formats produce different substantive results, and ACUS has repeatedly urged agencies to monitor the use of remote formats to ensure they are not producing different substantive outcomes.[40] Data from EOIR and SSA indicate that nonagency parties may be more likely to receive favorable outcomes when they participate in evidentiary hearings in person rather than by VTC,[41] but the conclusions to be drawn from those data are disputed.

Agencies like EOIR and SSA, and some researchers, have disputed the existence of disparities in decisional outcomes, asserted that disparities are not statistically significant, or argued that the relationship between different formats and decisional outcomes is not necessarily causal.[42] Others have suggested several reasons why remote

37. Alicia L. Bannon & Douglas Keith, *Remote Court: Principles for Virtual Proceedings during the COVID-19 Pandemic and Beyond*, 115 Nw. U. L. Rev. 1875, 1890–93 (2021).

38. Administrative Conference Recommendation 2021-4, *supra* note 2.

39. Legal Aid Interagency Roundtable, Access to Justice in the Age of COVID-19, at 18–23 (2021).

40. Administrative Conference Recommendation 2021-4, *supra* note 2, ¶ 13; Administrative Conference Recommendation 2014-7, *supra* note 2, ¶ 11; Administrative Conference Recommendation 2011-4, *supra* note 2, ¶ 3(b).

41. Dane Thorley & Joshua Mitts, *Trial by Skype: A Causality-Oriented Replication Exploring the Use of Remote Video Adjudication in Immigration Removal Proceedings*, 59 Int'l Rev. L. & Econ. 82 (2019); Ingrid V. Eagly, *Remote Adjudication*, 109 Nw. U. L. Rev. 933 (2015); *Access to Courts and Videoconferencing in Immigration Court Proceedings*, 122 Harv. L. Rev. 1181, 1181–93 (2009); Frank M. Walsh & Edward M. Walsh, *Effective Processing or Assembly-Line Justice? The Use of Teleconferencing in Asylum Removal Hearings*, 22 Geo. Immigr. L.J. 259 (2008).

42. *See, e.g.*, Setting the Manner for the Appearance of Parties and Witnesses at a Hearing, 83 Fed. Reg. 57,368, 57,371 (SSA Nov. 15, 2018); GAO, GAO-18-37,

participation formats might, in some contexts, produce different substantive outcomes. They include:

- Technical issues affecting a party's opportunity to be heard may be more likely to arise when a party participates remotely (see section 21.8).[43]
- Agencies may not be using appropriate technology or procedural practices to conduct proceedings in which participants appear remotely.[44]
- Mental or physical impairments may negatively impact participants' ability to engage effectively in a remote format.[45]
- Remote participation may complicate interpretation for participants with limited English proficiency.[46]
- Adjudicators may have greater difficulty assessing the credibility, demeanor, presentation, or symptomology of parties who participate remotely.[47]
- Parties may feel greater discomfort when they interact with an adjudicator remotely or have difficulty using the technology involved in remote participation.[48]
- Participants may become distracted or fatigued more easily when they interact remotely.[49]

Social Security Disability: Additional Measures and Evaluation Needed to Enhance Accuracy and Consistency of Hearings Decisions 76 (2017); GAO, GAO-17-438, Immigration Courts: Actions Needed to Reduce Case Backlog and Address Long-Standing Management and Operational Challenges 76, 145 (2017); Harold J. Krent & Scott Morris, ACUS, Achieving Greater Consistency in Social Security Disability Adjudication: An Empirical Study and Suggested Reforms 28–29 (2013).

43. *See* Legal Assistance Found. of Metro. Chi. & Chi. Appleseed Fund for Just., Videoconferencing in Removal Proceedings: A Case Study of the Chicago Immigration Court (2005).

44. *See* Benson & Wheeler, *supra* note 33.

45. *See supra* text accompanying note 36.

46. *See* Barak, *supra* note 35; Mollo, *supra* note 35.

47. *See* 84 Fed. Reg. 69,298, 69,300–01 (Dec. 18, 2019); *see also* Liz Bradley & Hillary Farber, *Virtually Incredible: Rethinking Deference to Demeanor When Assessing Credibility in Asylum Cases Conducted by Video Teleconference*, 36 Geo. Immigr. L.J. 515 (2022); Walsh & Walsh, *supra* note 41, at 268–69; Jeffrey Janaro & Christopher Clifton, *A Virtual Reality: Preserving the Right to Appear "In Person" before an Administrative Separation Board*, 25 Rich. Pub. Int. L. Rev. 43, 58 (2022).

48. *See* Administrative Conference Recommendation 2021-4, *supra* note 2.

49. *See* Lederer & Ctr. for Legal and Ct. Tech., *supra* note 31, at 11.

- Remote participation may not foster the same degree of engagement, interpersonal rapport, empathy, or emotional connection among participants.[50]
- Self-represented parties who participate remotely may be less likely to avail themselves of procedures that could help them.[51]
- Nonlocal adjudicators who preside over remote proceedings may have less familiarity with local conditions or lack informal but collaborative working relationships with local counsel.[52]
- Remote proceedings may be conducted in a way that is less publicly transparent, and the lack of public transparency may meaningfully impact participants' behavior.[53]
- Physical separation of parties from their representatives or representatives from adjudicators may negatively impact the quality of representation provided.[54]

Problems are more likely to exist in some contexts than in others, and policymakers, individual adjudicators, and other participants must consider what format is best suited for a particular program, a particular proceeding, and a particular participant. One factor to consider is participants' prior experience, training, and ability. Lawyers who regularly participate virtually in agency proceedings are less likely to face difficulties than self-represented parties who have not previously participated in an agency proceeding. A second factor to consider is the purpose of a proceeding. Although remote participation in an evidentiary hearing may be inadvisable in a particular case, it may be convenient for informal or procedural proceedings such as prehearing and settlement conferences.[55] A third factor to consider is the nature of the information to be exchanged at a proceeding. Although views may be shifting, at least with respect to video participants,[56] there has long been concern that adjudicators face greater difficulty

50. *See* Susan A. Bandes & Neil Feigenson, *Empathy and Remote Legal Proceedings*, 51 Sw. L. Rev. 20 (2021); Eagly, *supra* note 41, at 977–83; Walsh & Walsh, *supra* note 41, at 269–70.

51. *See* Eagly, *supra* note 41, at 933.

52. *See id.* at 988–89.

53. *See id.* at 994–1000.

54. *See* Rusu v. Immigr. & Naturalization Serv., 296 F.3d 316, 322–24 (4th Cir. 2002); Bannon & Keith, *supra* note 37, at 1887.

55. Administrative Conference Recommendation 2021-4, *supra* note 2; Bannon & Keith, *supra* note 37, at 1912; Aaron Haas, *Videoconferencing in Immigration Proceedings*, 5 Pierce L. Rev. 59, 86 (2006).

56. Lederer & Ctr. for Legal and Ct. Tech., *supra* note 31, at 9–10.

assessing the demeanor of remote participants. But remote participation may be less objectionable when demeanor evidence is not relevant or a participant's credibility is not at issue.[57]

21.6 DETERMINING HOW PARTIES PARTICIPATE

The legal and policy question that has attracted the most attention is: Who determines the format by which a party participates in an oral proceeding and according to what criteria? This question arises most prominently in high-volume adjudication programs, such as those administered by EOIR and SSA. The government, by statute or rule, has sometimes reserved to an agency or individual adjudicators the authority to determine how individual parties will participate in hearings. Many stakeholders argue that remote participation is appropriate only when a party requests to participate remotely or consents to doing so. Organizations that have taken this view include the ABA (for immigration court hearings), the American Immigration Lawyers Association, the National Organization of Social Security Claimants' Representatives, and the Association of Administrative Law Judges (which represents SSA ALJs). Some members of Congress have also voiced opposition to compelling parties to participate remotely (see Chapter 26). ACUS, for its part, has encouraged expanded use of remote participation in appropriate circumstances but recommended that agencies use VTC "on a voluntary basis," allowing parties to participate in person when that is their preference.[58]

As a legal matter, many have argued that constitutional due process guarantees parties a categorical right to an in-person hearing.[59] Some people with disabilities have also argued that agencies violate their right to due process when they deny their request to participate remotely.[60] Courts have almost universally rejected arguments that it

---

57. *Rusu*, 296 F.3d at 322–24.

58. Administrative Conference Recommendation 2011-4, *supra* note 2, ¶ 3(a).

59. *See, e.g.*, Haas, *supra* note 55, at 86; Cormac T. Connor, Note, *Human Rights Violations in the Information Age*, 16 Geo. Immigr. L.J. 207, 221–26 (2001); Neil Fox, Note, *Telephonic Hearings in Welfare Appeals: How Much Process Is Due?*, 1984 U. Ill. L. Rev. 445 (1984).

60. *See, e.g.*, Calderon v. Comm'r of Soc. Sec., No. 6:12-cv-426-Orl-18TBS, 2013 WL 3242395, at *4–6 (M.D. Fla. June 25, 2013).

is categorically unconstitutional for an agency to compel a party to participate in a particular format over the party's objection.[61]

Courts instead evaluate what due process requires on a case-by-case basis.[62] Following *Mathews v. Eldridge*, they balance the public and private interests at stake in a particular case along with the costs and benefits of the challenged procedure and reasonably available alternatives (see Chapter 15).[63] Courts typically will find a due process violation only when a party can show that they suffered harm or prejudice as a result of participating in a particular format. As a practical matter, courts have only rarely found that an agency violated due process when it compelled a party to participate in a particular manner. This is probably due to the fact that agency policies typically account for situations in which a due process violation is most likely to arise or provide individual adjudicators flexibility to handle such situations when they arise.

Parties in some programs do have a statutory right to choose how they participate. For example, while the BVA may schedule claimants to participate by traditional VTC or in person, it must grant a claimant's request to participate in an alternative manner, including virtually.[64] Immigration court officials may schedule respondents to participate in person or by VTC, but they can only schedule removal hearings by telephone with the respondent's consent.[65] As a general

61. *See, e.g.*, Mendoza Reyez v. Att'y Gen. of the U.S., 767 F. App'x 358, 362 (3d Cir. 2019); Gibbs v. United States, 517 F. App'x 664, 668 (11th Cir. 2013); Vilchez v. Holder, 682 F.3d 1195, 1199 (9th Cir. 2012); Melgar v. Att'y Gen. of the U.S., 442 F. App'x 695, 698 (6th Cir. 2011); Swidecki v. Dep't of Com., 431 F. App'x 900, 902–03 (Fed. Cir. 2011); Leiva-Molina v. Holder, 439 F. App'x 571, 573 (9th Cir. 2011); Miller v. Att'y Gen. of the U.S., 397 F. App'x 780, 793 (3d Cir. 2010); Jhin v. Off. of Pers. Mgmt., 368 F. App'x 118, 121–22 (Fed. Cir. 2010); Veliz v. Holder, 375 F. App'x 148, 149 (2d Cir. 2010); Toyama v. Leavitt, 408 F. App'x 351, 353 (Fed. Cir. 2010); Chavez-Vasquez v. Mukasey, 512 F. App'x 1115, 1118 (7th Cir. 2008); Raphael v. Mukasey, 533 F.3d 521 (7th Cir. 2008); Eke v. Mukasey, 512 F.3d 372, 382 (7th Cir. 2008); Ligoussou v. Mukasey, 297 F. App'x 11, 12 (1st Cir. 2008); Fall v. Gonzales, 218 F. App'x 385, 389 (6th Cir. 2007); Brienza-Schettino v. Att'y Gen. of the U.S., 221 F. App'x 140, 145 (3d Cir. 2007); Burroughs v. Dep't of the Army, 254 F. App'x 814, 818–19 (Fed. Cir. 2007); *Rusu*, 296 F.3d at 321–22; Butler v. Apfel, 144 F.3d 622, 627–28 (9th Cir. 1998); Casey v. O'Bannon, 536 F. Supp. 350, 352–54 (E.D. Pa. 1982).

62. *See, e.g.*, *Mendoza Reyez*, 767 F. App'x at 362; *Vilchez*, 682 F.3d at 1199; *Eke*, 512 F.3d at 383; *Rusu*, 296 F.3d at 316; *Casey*, 536 F. Supp. at 352–54.

63. 424 U.S. 139, 334–35 (1976).

64. 38 U.S.C. § 7107(c).

65. 8 U.S.C. § 1229a(b)(2).

matter, courts are unlikely to interpret a general statutory requirement for a "hearing" to grant parties a right to participate in a particular manner.[66]

Another potential statutory source of rights is section 504 of the Rehabilitation Act, which provides that "[n]o otherwise qualified individual with a disability . . . shall, solely by reason of her or his disability, be excluded from the participation in, be denied the benefits of, or be subjected to discrimination . . . under any program or activity conducted by an Executive agency . . . ."[67] Some have argued that section 504 requires agencies to provide parties a reasonable opportunity to participate in person if they have disabilities that would negatively affect their ability to participate remotely.[68] Section 504, if interpreted in this manner, would presumably also require agencies to provide parties a reasonable opportunity to participate remotely if they have disabilities that would negatively affect their ability to travel to a hearing site or participate in person. While courts have not definitively interpreted section 504 in this context, agencies should be mindful that section 504 generally requires agencies to provide reasonable accommodations to persons with disabilities.[69]

Some agencies have, by rule, granted parties a right to choose how they participate. SSA rules, for example, give parties a 30-day window to opt out of receiving a VTC hearing.[70] About 15 percent of claimants opted out of appearing by VTC in fiscal year 2022.[71] Although SSA

---

66. *See, e.g.*, Robinson v. Comm'r of Internal Revenue, 572 F. App'x 846, 847–48 (11th Cir. 2014); Murphy v. Comm'r of Internal Revenue, 469 F.3d 27, 30 (1st Cir. 2006); Kindred v. Comm'r of Internal Revenue, 454 F.3d 688, 691 n.4 (7th Cir. 2006); Bigby v. Immigr. & Naturalization Serv., 21 F.3d 1059, 1963 (11th Cir. 1994). *But see* Terrell v. United States, 564 F.3d 442, 444 (6th Cir. 2009) (holding that a statute granting prisoners a right to "appear" before the Parole Commission required an opportunity to appear in person); Purba v. Immigr. & Naturalization Serv., 884 F.2d 516, 517–18 (9th Cir. 1989) (finding that an agency violated a statute granting parties a right to be present "before" an adjudicator when it compelled a party to participate by telephone).

67. 29 U.S.C. § 794(a).

68. *See* 84 Fed. Reg. 69,298, 69,300–01 (Dec. 18, 2019); Cassandra H. Chee, Comment, *Rehabilitating Our Immigration System with the Rehabilitation Act: Rejecting Video Teleconferencing and Presumptively Requiring In-Person Court Appearances as a Reasonable Accommodation for Mentally Incompetent Detainees*, 70 Am. U. L. Rev. 665, 698–723 (2020).

69. *Cf.* Alexander v. Choate, 469 U.S. 287, 301 (1985).

70. 20 C.F.R. §§ 404.936(d), 416.1436(d) (2022).

71. *Video Hearing (VH) Opt-Out Numbers and Rates for Hearing Requests Received FY 2022*, https://www.ssa.gov/appeals/DataSets/archive/00_FY2022/A01

once proposed eliminating this opportunity, it withdrew the proposal after receiving negative public and congressional feedback.[72]

21.7 DETERMINING HOW EXAMINATION TAKES PLACE

Parties have occasionally alleged that agencies cannot, as a constitutional matter, compel them to remotely examine or confront adverse parties and witnesses. Courts have rejected challenges raised under the Sixth Amendment's Confrontation Clause,[73] which does not apply in administrative proceedings.[74] While courts have not identified a categorial due process right to examine or confront adverse parties or witnesses in person,[75] there are instances in which agencies have, as a matter of law or policy, found remote examination or confrontation to be legally inadequate. Several agencies have, for example, ruled that parties and witnesses should ordinarily not participate by telephone when their credibility is at issue. Agencies increasingly accept testimony by VTC and virtually, however.[76]

_VH_Opt-Out.html (last visited June 27, 2023).

72. 84 Fed. Reg. at 69,300.

73. *See, e.g.*, Akinwande v. Ashcroft, 380 F.3d 517, 522 (1st Cir. 2004); Gibbs v. Sec. & Exch. Comm'n, 25 F.3d 1056 (10th Cir. 1994) (Table); Peretti v. Nat'l Transp. Safety Bd. Fed. Aviation Admin., 999 F.2d 548 (10th Cir. 1993) (Table).

74. Sec. & Exch. Comm'n v. Jerry T. O'Brien, Inc., 467 U.S. 735, 742 (1984).

75. *See, e.g.*, EF Int'l Language Schs. v. Nat'l Lab. Rels. Bd., 673 F. App'x 1, 3–4 (D.C. Cir. 2017); Reyes v. U.S. Att'y Gen., 565 F. App'x 785, 787–88 (11th Cir. 2014); Aslam v. Mukasey, 537 F.3d 110, 114–15 (2d Cir. 2008); Hepp v. Astrue, 511 F.3d 798, 805–06 (8th Cir. 2008); *Akinwande*, 380 F.3d at 522; Beltran-Tirado v. Immigr. & Naturalization Serv., 213 F.3d 1179, 1185–86 (9th Cir. 2000); Alderman v. Sec. & Exch. Comm'n, 104 F.3d 285, 288 n.4 (9th Cir. 1997); *see also* Barrera-Quintero v. Holder, 699 F.3d 1239, 1247–49 (10th Cir. 2012) (upholding telephonic testimony by an Immigration and Customs Enforcement agent in an immigration court proceeding but cautioning that in other cases "the lack of in-person confrontation might so undercut the purposes of cross-examination as to deprive a lawful resident of the fundamental protections of procedural due process").

76. *See, e.g.*, William Beaumont Hosp., 370 N.L.R.B. No. 9 (2020); Morrison Healthcare, 369 N.L.R.B. No. 76 (2020); EF Int'l Language Schs., 363 N.L.R.B. No. 20 (2015); Robertson v. Dep't of Transp., 113 M.S.P.R. 16 (2009); Koehler v. Dep't of Air Force, 99 M.S.P.R. 82 (2005); Westside Painting, 328 N.L.R.B. No. 110 (1999).

Parties have also occasionally (and unsuccessfully) challenged an adjudicator's decision *not* to permit a witness to testify remotely.[77]

21.8 RESPONDING TO PROBLEMS WITH REMOTE PARTICIPATION

As noted in section 21.5, technical issues affecting a party's opportunity to be heard may be more likely to arise when a party participates remotely. There are many reasons why participants may have difficulty communicating with each other when a party participates remotely, such as a bad telephone or internet connection, poor-quality video or audio, inadequate equipment, or cumbersome procedures for sharing evidence. Parties sometimes allege that a technical problem deprived them of due process or a right guaranteed by statute, rule, or agency policy.

In general, courts will only provide relief under due process or a statutory or regulatory guarantee when a party can show that they suffered actual prejudice or harm as a result of a technical problem and that the problem is likely to have affected the substantive outcome of their case. This can be difficult to prove.[78] Courts have remanded for a new hearing where a VTC participant was unable to review important documents,[79] where an immigration court did not record a witness's telephonic testimony,[80] where an expert's telephone testimony "cut out,"[81] and where the hearing transcript indicated that telephonic testimony was frequently "indiscernible" or "inaudible."[82] Courts have declined to remand cases when they found the technical issue harmless, for example where an adjudicator was briefly unable to see a remote party,[83] where testimony was marked "indiscernible" in the transcript but the broader context suggested the participants were able

77. *See, e.g.*, Barriga v. Barr, 804 F. App'x 22, 23 (2d Cir. 2020); Zhang v. Att'y Gen. of the U.S., 632 F. App'x 680, 683 (3d Cir. 2015).

78. *See, e.g.*, Fall v. Gonzales, 218 F. App'x 385, 389 (6th Cir. 2007); Rusu v. Immigr. & Naturalization Serv., 296 F.3d 316 (4th Cir. 2002).

79. Raphael v. Mukasey, 533 F.3d 521 (7th Cir. 2008).

80. Millian-Zamora v. Ashcroft, 228 F. Supp. 2d 272, 277–80 (E.D.N.Y. 2002).

81. Edwards v. Astrue, No. 3:10cv1017, 2011 WL 3490024, at *10–11 (D. Conn. Aug. 10, 2011).

82. Semenov v. Att'y Gen. of the U.S., 346 F. App'x 783, 787–90 (3d Cir. 2009); Ainsworth v. Astrue, Civil No. 09-cv-286-SM, 2010 WL 2521432, at *2–4 (D.N.H. June 17, 2010).

83. Loya v. Colvin, Civil Action No. 13-cv-02497-KMT, 2015 WL 1384268, at *4 (D. Colo. Mar. 20, 2015).

to communicate,[84] and where only a few words were inaudible and not so significant as to create an "evidentiary gap" that could change the outcome of the proceeding.[85]

84. Vilchez v. Holder, 682 F.3d 1195, 1199 (9th Cir. 2012); Jhin v. Off. of Pers. Mgmt., 368 F. App'x 118, 121 (Fed. Cir. 2010); Garza-Moreno v. Gonzales, 489 F.3d 239, 241–42 (6th Cir. 2007); Rusu v. Immigr. & Naturalization Serv., 296 F.3d 316, 323–24 (4th Cir. 2002); Cherry v. Comm'r of Soc. Sec., No. 17-CV-7999 (VEC), 2019 WL 1305961, at *10 (S.D.N.Y. Mar. 22, 2019); Momentum EMS v. Sibelius, Civil Action No. 4:11-CV-298, 2014 WL 199061, at *10–11 (S.D. Tex. Jan. 13, 2014); Bates v. Astrue, Civil Action No. 07-074-JJF, 2008 WL 1736819, at *13 (D. Del. Apr. 11, 2008).

85. Ford v. Astrue, No. 3:07-cv-835-J-TEM, 2009 WL 789895, at *3–6 (M.D. Fla. Mar. 23, 2009).

Chapter 22
Written Hearings

Richard J. Pierce, Jr.

22.1 CHAPTER OVERVIEW

As discussed in Chapter 21, participants in an adjudication can exchange information needed for decision making orally or through written (or other recorded) materials. Although many agency processes include some opportunity for an oral evidentiary hearing, there has been a gradual trend toward the use of written hearings in adjudications. That trend is likely to continue. Agencies increasingly understand that, due to changing judicial attitudes toward the necessity or desirability of oral hearings in adjudication, they can make use of written procedures in many circumstances, even when a statute explicitly requires an opportunity for a "hearing." Agencies also recognize that they can reduce delays and manage increasing caseloads more efficiently by substituting written hearings for oral hearings. This chapter describes the dramatic change in judicial attitudes over the past 40 years (section 22.2); the current legal framework governing agency use of written hearings, especially limitations on agencies' discretion to use them (section 22.3); and policy considerations relevant to the exercise of that discretion (section 22.4).

22.2 CHANGING JUDICIAL ATTITUDES

The trend toward written hearings dates to at least 1973, when the U.S. Supreme Court decided *United States v. Florida East Coast Railway*.[1] That case concerned a rule, not an adjudication, by the Interstate

1. 410 U.S. 224 (1973).

Commerce Commission (ICC). A statute authorized the ICC to issue the rule only "after a hearing." Instead of conducting an oral hearing, the ICC issued a notice in which it stated its intention to issue the rule and provided all interested members of the public, including regulated railroads, an opportunity to explain in writing why they believed such a rule was unnecessary or inappropriate.

A railroad argued the rule was invalid because the ICC had based the rule on findings of contested issues of material fact without conducting an oral hearing to allow regulated entities to challenge the factual predicates for the rule with oral testimony and cross-examination of opposing witnesses. The Supreme Court rejected that argument. It held that the term "hearing" is ambiguous and could refer to a variety of procedures through which parties are given notice of an agency's intended action and an opportunity to contest the factual predicates for an action through some means. The nature of the hearing required to allow parties to contest the factual predicates for an action depends on the context in which the agency conducts the hearing.

The Court rejected the argument that the term "hearing" in the Interstate Commerce Act referred to the kind of hearing that the Administrative Procedure Act (APA) describes in 5 U.S.C. §§ 556 and 557. Those provisions require an agency to provide the opportunity for an oral evidentiary hearing that includes almost all of the procedural safeguards that are available when a court conducts a bench trial. Hearings of that type are traditionally referred to as "formal hearings." The Court held that a statute requires an agency to provide a formal hearing when it explicitly requires the agency to provide a formal oral evidentiary hearing or when it states that the agency can take an action only "on the record after opportunity for an agency hearing." That is the language that the APA uses to trigger application of the formal-hearing procedures for rulemakings.[2] In the absence of either, the APA only requires the written notice-and-comment procedures of 5 U.S.C. § 553.

Two justices dissented in *Florida East Coast Railway.* They blended arguments based on statutory language with due process considerations as the basis for their opinion that the ICC was required to provide an oral evidentiary hearing before it issued the rule. The majority cited *Londoner v. City & County of Denver* and *Bi-Metallic Investment Co. v. State Board of Equalization* in response (see Chapter 1). The majority reasoned that due process did not require the

2. 5 U.S.C. § 553(c).

agency to provide the regulated railroad an oral hearing because the factual findings at issue "were used in the formulation of a basically legislative-type judgment, for prospective application only, rather than in adjudicating a particular set of disputed facts."[3]

Although the APA uses the same phrase—"on the record after opportunity for an agency hearing"—to trigger application of the formal-hearing procedures for adjudications,[4] it was not at all clear that the *Florida East Coast Railway* holding had any effect on adjudications. Some courts applied the holding to adjudications where the relevant statute conditioned the agency's power to act on a "hearing" rather than an "on the record" hearing,[5] but most concluded that the holding applied only to rulemakings and that a statute that required a "hearing" in an adjudication required an oral evidentiary hearing.[6]

Three developments combined to change the ways in which courts determined the scope of the holding in *Florida East Coast Railway*. First, courts increasingly recognized that written hearings require much less time to complete than oral hearings with no apparent reduction in the accuracy of the resulting fact-finding process.[7] (The Supreme Court had repeatedly characterized agency hearings as "nigh interminable."[8])

Second, the Supreme Court's opinion in *Mathews v. Eldridge* strongly suggested that the Supreme Court considered written hearings to be sufficient to satisfy due process in at least some types of adjudications. The Court's reasoning made clear that the type of hearing required to satisfy due process in the context of an agency adjudication depends, in part, on the nature of the facts that are disputed.[9]

---

3. *Fla. E. Coast Ry.*, 410 U.S. at 245–46.
4. 5 U.S.C. § 554(a).
5. *See, e.g.*, Taylor v. Dist. Eng'r, U.S. Army Corps of Eng'rs, 567 F.2d 1332 (5th Cir. 1978).
6. *See, e.g.*, Seacoast Anti-Pollution League v. Costle, 572 F. 2d 872 (1st Cir. 1978); Marathon Oil v. Env't Prot. Agency, 564 F.2d 1253 (9th Cir. 1977); U.S. Steel Corp. v. Train, 556 F.2d 822 (7th Cir. 1977).
7. *See, e.g.*, AJA Assocs. v. Army Corps of Eng'rs, 817 F.2d 1070 (3d Cir. 1987); Cascade Nat. Gas Co. v. Fed. Energy Regul. Comm'n, 955 F.2d 1412 (10th Cir. 1992).
8. *See, e.g.*, Fed. Power Comm'n v. La. Power & Light Co., 406 U.S. 621, 643 (1972); Fed. Power Comm'n v. Hunt, 376 U.S. 515, 527 (1964); Sunray Mid-Continent Oil v. Fed. Power Comm'n, 364 U.S. 137, 144 (1960); Atl. Refin. Co. v. New York, 360 U.S. 378, 389 (1959).
9. Mathews v. Eldridge, 424 U.S. 319, 343–44 (1976).

An oral hearing might be required in a case, like *Goldberg v. Kelly*,[10] in which the most frequently contested issue of fact is resolved through the testimony of lay witnesses, and oral testimony subject to cross-examination is important for determining their relative credibility. But an oral hearing might not be required in a case, like *Mathews*, in which the most frequently contested issue of fact is a person's health state, and the primary sources of evidence are doctors who have the professional training and experience needed to evaluate claims of disability and no apparent source of bias.[11]

Finally, the Supreme Court issued its opinion in *Chevron v. Natural Resources Defense Council.* The Court held that if a statute is "silent" or "ambiguous" with respect to a specific issue, courts should defer to an agency's "permissible construction" of the statute in question rather than simply imposing its own construction on the statute.[12] Since the Court had already held that the term "hearing" is ambiguous in *Florida East Coast Railway*, the *Chevron* opinion provided agencies with the opportunity to argue that they could interpret "hearing" to require only a written hearing in an adjudication, and then defend that statutory interpretation as "permissible."

During the decades following the Court's issuance of its *Chevron* opinion, every appeals court that had previously held that *Florida East Coast Railway* applied only to rulemakings overruled its precedents and held that it also applies to many adjudications.[13] In each case, the court upheld the agency's exclusive reliance on a written exchange of data and views to satisfy the statutory requirement that the agency conduct a hearing in a class of adjudicatory proceedings. In each case, the court held that an oral evidentiary hearing is required only to resolve a contested issue of adjudicative fact—as opposed to an issue of policy or of legislative fact—and then only when credibility is an issue. And in each case, the court concluded that the agency was reasonable with respect to its belief that a class of issues could be resolved more

10. 397 U.S. 254 (1970).

11. *Mathews*, 424 U.S. at 343–44.

12. Chevron U.S.A., Inc. v. Nat. Res. Def. Council, 467 U.S. 837, 842–43 (1984).

13. *See* Ill. Com. Comm'n v. Fed. Energy Regul. Comm'n, 721 F.3d 764 (7th Cir. 2013); United Farm Workers of Am. v. Env't Prot. Agency, 592 F.3d 1080 (9th Cir. 2010); Dominion Energy Brayton Point v. Johnson, 443 F.3d 12 (1st Cir. 2006); Chem. Waste Mgmt. v. Env't Prot. Agency, 873 F.2d 1477 (D.C. Cir. 1989); Buttrey v. United States, 690 F.2d 1170 (5th Cir. 1982).

expeditiously, and at least as accurately, through use of a written hearing as through use of an oral evidentiary hearing.

In *Chemical Waste Management, Inc. v. Environmental Protection Agency*, for example, the D.C. Circuit held it was permissible for an agency to interpret the term "hearing" to mean a written exchange of views in adjudications as long as the agency provides an adequate statement of reasons in support of its interpretation. The agency had reasoned that it need not provide an oral evidentiary hearing in such proceedings because

> the factual issues that . . . arise "will relate almost entirely to technical (or policy) matters" that create "little need to establish witness veracity or credibility through observation of a witness's demeanor on cross-examination" and therefore "can just as easily (perhaps more effectively) be resolved through analysis of the administrative record and the written submissions and oral statements of the parties."[14]

In *Dominion Energy Brayton Point v. Johnson*, the First Circuit upheld an agency's interpretation of "public hearing" to refer to a written exchange of data and views as a "reasonable" and "permissible" interpretation of an ambiguous term. In the court's words, the agency's interpretation "took into account the relevant universe of factors. . . . (1) the private interests at stake, (2) the risk of erroneous decisionmaking, and (3) the nature of the government interest."[15] It is interesting to note how this approach combines the process for interpreting a statute that requires a "hearing" with the process for determining the type of hearing that due process requires. The three factors that the agency and the court considered in the process of deciding whether it was reasonable for the agency to use written procedures rather than oral procedures in hearings to resolve some types of adjudications are the same three factors that courts use, following *Mathews*, to determine whether an administrative procedure satisfies the requirements of due process.[16]

---

14. *Chem. Waste Mgmt.*, 873 F.2d 1477.
15. *Dominion Energy Brayton Point*, 443 F.3d at 18.
16. *Mathews*, 424 U.S. at 335.

22.3 CURRENT LEGAL FRAMEWORK

There are three legal limits on an agency's discretion to use written procedures rather than an oral evidentiary hearing in an adjudication: (1) agency rules, (2) statutory language, and (3) due process. First, an agency is required to comply with its own rules of procedure to the extent that those rules are designed to protect the interests of parties to agency proceedings.[17] Thus, while an agency can change its rules of procedure within the boundaries created by statutes and due process, an agency must comply with a rule that states that it will provide an opportunity for an oral evidentiary hearing in a class of adjudications.

Second, the agency does not have the discretion to use a written hearing if a statute contains language that explicitly requires the agency to provide an opportunity for an oral evidentiary hearing or renders the APA's formal-hearing procedures applicable to a class of adjudications by using the "magic" words: "on the record after opportunity for agency hearing." The APA's formal-hearing procedures do contain one exception to the general rule requiring an oral evidentiary hearing. In determining claims for money or benefits or applications for initial licenses, an agency "may, when a party will not be prejudiced thereby, adopt procedures for the submission of all or part of the evidence in written form."[18] Agencies can also adopt reasonable procedures for summary judgment (see Chapter 18).

In the absence of language that renders the formal-hearing procedures applicable to an adjudication, the only provision of the APA that applies to an adjudication is 5 U.S.C. § 555.[19] That provision is appropriately titled "ancillary matters." It provides only for the right to be represented by counsel, the right to request the agency to issue a subpoena, the right to a copy of any statement a party makes to an agency, and the right to prompt notice of a decision to deny a petition filed with an agency. It does not provide for a right to an oral evidentiary hearing.

Finally, an agency does not have the discretion to use a written hearing if due process requires it to use an oral evidentiary hearing. Courts determine the procedures required by due process through consideration of the same three factors used to determine the permissible interpretation of the statutory term "public hearing" in *Dominion*

---

17. Service v. Dulles, 354 U.S. 363 (1957); Accardi v. Shaughnessy, 344 U.S. 260 (1954).

18. 5 U.S.C. § 556(d).

19. Pension Benefit Guarantee Corp. v. LTV Corp., 496 U.S. 633, 655 (1990).

Energy Brayton Point: (1) the importance of the interests at stake; (2) the risk of erroneous decision-making through use of a written hearing and the probable value of an oral hearing; and (3) the nature of the government's interest, including the fiscal and administrative burdens that an oral hearing would entail.

As a due process matter, courts are likely to hold that agency adjudications to decide whether to impose a significant penalty on an individual or a company require an agency to provide an opportunity for an oral evidentiary hearing. The typical penalty proceeding requires an agency to resolve contested issues of fact like who did what, when, where, and why. Those are the kinds of contested issues of fact that cannot be resolved without an oral hearing, including the opportunity for cross-examination, because the agency often must determine the credibility of witnesses who provide conflicting testimony.

22.4 POLICY CONSIDERATIONS

In many circumstances, an agency can reduce the time and resources required to adjudicate a dispute and reduce the delay in obtaining a hearing with no sacrifice in the accuracy of the fact-finding process by relying entirely on a written exchange of evidence and views. When the relevant statute provides an agency with the discretion to do so, it should rely entirely on a written hearing if that choice of procedures is consistent with the balancing test that the Supreme Court has long used to determine the procedures that an agency should use to adjudicate a dispute: (1) the nature of the private interest at stake; (2) the risk of erroneous decision-making through use of a written hearing; and (3) the nature of the government's interest, including the fiscal and administrative burdens that an oral hearing would entail. As the Administrative Conference of the United States concluded, that test is likely to yield a decision to rely entirely on a written hearing in cases that solely involve disputes concerning the interpretation of statutes or regulations or legislative facts as to which experts offer conflicting views.[20]

20. Administrative Conference Recommendation 2016-4, Evidentiary Hearings Not Required by the Administrative Procedure Act, ¶ 21, 81 Fed. Reg. 94,314, 94,316 (Dec. 23, 2016).

Part VI

Management, Oversight, and Coordination

Chapter 23
Operation and Management

Gerald K. Ray

23.1 CHAPTER OVERVIEW

Management is fundamentally the organization of people to complete tasks. In federal adjudicative programs, those tasks center around the taking of claims and appeals, the gathering of evidence, and the evaluation of the evidence in accordance with applicable laws and regulations, leading to resolution of claims and appeals through issuance of agency decisions and the release of appropriate notices to the parties involved.

Operational managers in this context are responsible for maintaining efficient and accurate claims processing. That often requires attending to operational matters such as the acquisition and maintenance of workspace, acquisition and maintenance of information technology systems, budget formulation, policy formulation, human resources and labor management, training, records management, legal counsel, and congressional liaison. Although such matters might be considered ancillary to adjudication, they are, in fact, fundamental to the sound administration of adjudicative programs.[1]

Agencies have developed very different organizational structures for managing the operational functions associated with adjudication. This is to be expected. A program that requires only a small staff and a single office to process a small annual caseload will have very different needs than a program that requires thousands of employees in dozens of offices nationwide processing hundreds of thousands of cases per year. In small programs, a single office and a few managers may be responsible for case processing and most operational matters. The largest programs may have an organizational structure divided into several subcomponents, each of which has primary responsibility for a certain aspect of the work necessary to perform the organization's mission. Although operational managers within subcomponents are primarily responsible for their staff's performance of assigned tasks, successful operation of the entire system often requires that they have a working knowledge of the functions assigned to other subcomponents and must perform tasks in support of or in conjunction with those subcomponents.

Despite this variation, there are commonalities in how agencies manage the operation of adjudicative programs. This chapter examines how operational managers measure and evaluate the performance of adjudicative programs (section 23.2) and how they use that information to take actions to manage and, when necessary, improve adjudicative performance (section 23.3).

23.2 MEASURING PERFORMANCE

As discussed in Chapter 4, administrative adjudication can serve many goals, including fairness, accuracy, consistency, efficiency, and participant satisfaction. Agencies have developed methods to measure and evaluate how well adjudicative programs achieve such goals. This section begins by discussing how some agencies use workflow mapping

1. *See* Jerry L. Mashaw, *Management Side of Due Process: Some Theoretical and Litigation Notes on the Assurance of Accuracy, Fairness, and Timeliness in the Adjudication of Social Welfare Claims*, 59 CORNELL L. REV. 772 (1974); Daniel L. Skoler, *The Many Faces of High-Volume Administrative Adjudication: Structure, Organization, and Management*, 16 J. NAT'L ASS'N ADMIN. L. JUDGES 43 (1996); Russell L. Weaver, *Management of ALJ Offices in Executive Departments and Agencies*, 47 ADMIN. L. REV. 303 (1995); Russell L. Weaver, *ALJ Support Systems: Staff Attorneys and Decision Writers*, 16 J. NAT'L ASS'N ADMIN. L. JUDGES 89 (1996).

and data analytics to measure and evaluate performance more accurately (section 23.21). It then addresses how agencies determine and use three common performance metrics: productivity of adjudicative personnel (section 23.22), timeliness of agency decision-making (section 23.23), and decisional quality (section 23.24).

23.21 Workflow Mapping, Data Capture, and Analysis

Agencies have long collected information and data about the operation of their adjudicative programs in order to measure performance, identify problems, and devise solutions. A good first step is to comprehensively document the business process for adjudicating cases, identifying the different stages of processing, the staff associated with each stage of processing, all of the specific tasks the staff is expected to perform at each stage, the expected outputs or staff actions at each stage of the process, and the flow of work from one stage to the next. Flowcharting the work may highlight opportunities to improve the overall business process or case flow of the operation by highlighting choke points, gaps, and redundancies in the process and can help identify staffing misalignments that might result in bottlenecks in the case flow.

Once the workflow is detailed and analyzed, managers should consider having employees capture data about the numbers and types of actions they process. As a note of caution, data capture takes time away from other activities, so careful thought should be given to what data is captured, particularly if it is captured manually by staff engaged in case processing. Ideally, employees would utilize an electronic case management system (eCMS) designed to efficiently capture case processing data for use by operational managers. If an eCMS is available, the manager should review the information that the eCMS captures and the reporting capabilities of the eCMS. The manager can propose changes to the eCMS as necessary to ensure that the data captured is sufficiently robust to enable meaningful analysis.

Increased eCMS use has allowed agencies to collect vastly more, and more accurate, data. Although agencies primarily use such systems to manage caseloads, store case records, and move cases through their operation, a well-designed eCMS can also capture granular data on individual cases that can be useful for measuring productivity, timeliness, and decisional quality.[2] As the granularity of the data

2. Administrative Conference Recommendation 2018-3, Electronic Case Management in Federal Administrative Adjudication, 83 Fed. Reg. 30,686 (June 29, 2018).

captured increases, so too do the opportunities to use data analytics and perhaps even artificial intelligence (AI) to improve processing at each step.[3]

Data analytics involves the acquisition, cleaning, mining, and analysis of data. The results of data analysis can be either descriptive or predictive. Descriptive analysis focuses on the current functioning of the operation. It helps managers identify general trends and provide concrete answers to specific inquiries about case processing, such as the number of currently pending cases; the number of cases processed during a given time period; and the number of days it took, on average, to process them. Predictive analysis utilizes current and historical information to make assessments or predictions about the future or otherwise unknown events. It commonly relies on econometric techniques and statistical methods such as data mining, predictive modeling, and machine learning.

23.22 Productivity of Adjudicative Personnel

It is important for an operational manager to understand just how productive personnel are in performing various tasks. The manager will need data regarding each of the tasks that personnel perform. The data can be as rudimentary as the number of final work outputs (e.g., decisions) produced over a given period of time divided by the number of staff involved in processing the work. However, this simple calculation may not provide useful information in many contexts, especially in larger programs in which different categories of employees perform different functions or programs in which work outputs vary considerably across cases.

There are ways to measure productivity more accurately, for example by developing separate metrics for different categories of employees (e.g., adjudicators, staff attorneys, paralegals, clerical staff, etc.). In this way, managers can identify or create specific output measurements for all similarly situated employees, such as decisions written by decision-writers per day or hearings held by adjudicators per day. An even more accurate approach would account for time not spent on

---

3. *See* GERALD RAY & GLENN SKLAR, CTR. FOR A RESPONSIBLE FED. BUDGET, AN OPERATIONAL APPROACH TO ELIMINATING BACKLOGS IN THE SOCIAL SECURITY DISABILITY PROGRAM 16–20 (2019); Gerald K. Ray & Jeffrey S. Lubbers, *A Government Success Story: How Data Analysis by the Social Security Appeals Council (with a Push from the Administrative Conference of the United States) Is Transforming Social Security Disability Adjudication*, 83 GEO. WASH. L. REV. 1575, 1605–08 (2015).

casework, for example the use of leave or time spent engaging in non-casework activities such as meetings, trainings, details, or union activities. A manager can capture and review this information by asking employees to complete a weekly activity sheet showing various periods of management-approved non-casework activities.[4]

Different time values can also be assigned to subsets or categories of work, based on the complexity of the work. For example, agency regulations may require more robust rationale in support of a decision denying benefits than required in support of a dismissal for untimely filing of an appeal. Setting upper and lower bounds for these time values (e.g., no completed work in any category is valued at less than 30 minutes and no completed work in any category is valued at more than eight hours of expected processing time) can facilitate a calculation of realistic time values based on the total hours in casework and the numbers of cases processed within each defined category of work (as further described in section 23.23).

23.23 Timeliness of Agency Decision-Making

An agency decision can have a profound impact on the parties affected by that decision. So can a delay in providing that decision. It is incumbent upon operational managers to take steps to promote timely decision-making by the agency. Managers frequently promote timeliness by setting goals for timely case processing. This requires measuring processing times for individual cases and determining an appropriate case processing goal for the entire operation.

There are several ways to measure a case's processing time. A very broad measure of timeliness might consider the elapsed time from the date a claim was filed or complaint was issued to the date of final resolution after exhaustion of all appeals within the agency. Agencies that have adopted a multistage process for adjudication (see Chapter 7) might also measure processing times at each stage of the adjudicative process, such as from the date a hearing-level component receives a case through the date that same component issues a decision. Regardless of the method chosen, it is critical for agencies to be internally and publicly transparent about how they measure processing time (see Chapter 28).

It is not uncommon for agencies to set case processing goals based on average processing time across all cases, which can be easily calculated. For example, an agency might strive for average processing time not to exceed a set number of days. But average processing time

4. Ray & Sklar, *supra* note 3, at 4–5.

can obscure how long individual cases have been pending. Another approach is to focus on the most aged cases, for example by setting goals to have no cases remaining unprocessed at the end of the fiscal year that have been pending beyond a targeted length of time. To be effective, goals should be challenging but obtainable.

Effective data capture enables operational managers to track case processing and set effective goals. By evaluating data on the time it takes personnel to complete actions throughout the adjudicative process, managers can also determine where bottlenecks are arising. This knowledge may enable the manager to make staffing adjustments to improve timeliness, for example by temporarily detailing staff to the steps in the process where bottlenecks are forming, to ensure that cases continue to flow smoothly through the operation.

It is important to remember that case processing times may not be entirely within the control of operational managers. It is possible to develop a timeliness measure that accounts for delays attributable to nonagency parties. But sometimes exigent circumstances, such as workload surges in response to exogenous factors, can cause backlogs to develop quickly.[5] Although there are operational measures agencies can take to address backlogs, such as obtaining additional staffing or implementing streamlined processes, agencies may have to wait for budgetary approval, comply with personnel practices, cope with hiring freezes, or seek input and obtain approval to revise procedures. When setting timeliness goals, agencies should be aware of exogenous factors that might affect case processing times and limitations on their ability to respond quickly and effectively to emerging operational challenges.

23.24 Decisional Quality

Of all the actions an operational manager can take to improve the quality of work produced, perhaps the most important is to develop and communicate to the staff a clear definition of quality (see Chapter 24). A good definition should be readily understandable and measurable and should address decisional accuracy in a meaningful way. Although all administrative decisions need to be "legally sufficient," that term is not well defined and is open to interpretation. Thus, it is best to refine the definition to include more measurable concepts. For

5. *See generally* Adam S. Zimmerman, *Surges and Delays in Mass Adjudication*, 53 GA. L. REV. 1336 (2019).

example, a quality decision might be described as one that is factually accurate, procedurally adequate, policy compliant, supported by the record, timely issued, as well as legally sufficient.

Once a clear definition is established, it is important to capture information about the quality of the work performed, particularly information that might help identify and redress the most common errors. As a first step, knowledgeable employees can be tasked with identifying and categorizing what they believe to be the most common types of errors so structured data can be captured about those errors. Mentors and other quality assurance reviewers (see Chapter 24) can then produce a quality checklist for use by case reviewers.

An electronic case analysis tool can greatly aid in ensuring employees follow the appropriate decisional structure and capture relevant data at all steps in the case review process. Ideally employees will use the tool to capture structured data from each reviewed case on a broad range of issues, including data about the most common errors. The quality effort will improve if the agency can deploy a standardized decisional format to guide decision-makers through the key steps that lead to an accurate decision.

Especially for high-volume adjudication programs, once enough data is captured, it is relatively easy to track variances in decision patterns and to determine which issues yield the most errors. If errors are made at a relatively high frequency across many offices, the manager should consider assigning some staff to conduct more focused reviews of error-prone cases to gain further insight into why the errors are being made. Managers can use the information gleaned from such reviews to improve staff training or the clarity of policies and procedures.

23.3 MANAGING PERFORMANCE

Agencies rely on the metrics and tools described in the previous section to maintain or, if necessary, improve an adjudicative system's performance. Depending on the context, agencies have a number of different managerial controls at their disposal. This section focuses on six common managerial controls: staffing (section 23.31), training (section 23.32), performance management (section 23.33), case management (section 23.34), process and policy improvement (section 23.35), and operational leadership (section 23.36). Other potential managerial controls include appellate review (Chapter 19) and a suite of techniques referred to as "quality assurance" (Chapter 24).

23.31 Staffing

One managerial control is staffing. Adjudication requires personnel—adjudicators, of course, but often also staff attorneys, paralegals, and clerical staff according to the needs of particular programs. The performance of an adjudicative program is, in large part, a function of staffing. One important step operational managers should undertake is to periodically review the position descriptions of all staff members and update them to reflect changes in business processes and the effects of automation improvements. Position descriptions should address the specific duties required of employees in each position but retain sufficient flexibility to enable assignment of other duties as business exigencies may require. Additionally, managers should periodically analyze the numbers of cases that flow through each stage of the business process to identify necessary adjustments in the type of staff that need to be hired. To maintain efficiency, an operational manager must keep abreast of current staff capacity and accurately project future staffing needs.

Staffing is typically driven by the amount of work an agency or agency subcomponent expects to receive and process over the course of a fiscal year. Projections of work receipts can be as simple as calculating average receipts for a period of time, perhaps five or ten years, or can account for anticipated increases or decreases in case receipts in response to legislative or regulatory developments, economic or demographic trends, or other factors.

Staffing is also a function of attrition (e.g., separation, retirement). Agencies typically have data related to staff attrition, and average separation from service by age and years of service can be calculated for most staff positions. Managers can compare this information to the age and years of service of existing staff to plan for expected attrition and future staffing needs.

Finally, staffing is a function of the expected future productivity of current staff. Managers can develop training curves to reflect the diminished productivity of newly trained employees and expected increases in productivity as they gain experience. Managers would be wise to account for time that staff spend on tasks ancillary to adjudication, such as mentoring or training new hires; expected leave usage; and reduced productivity for people on performance improvement plans.

Staffing requires a working knowledge of federal personnel law. Although a full discussion of federal personnel law is beyond the scope of this guide, operational managers in adjudicative systems may find two recommendations of the Administrative Conference of the United States (ACUS) particularly helpful: Recommendation 2019-9, Recruiting and Hiring Agency Attorneys,[6] and Recommendation 2019-2, Agency Recruitment and Selection of Administrative Law Judges.[7]

23.32 Training

Operational performance is not a function of staffing alone but also the knowledge and expertise that staff acquire. New staff are often unfamiliar with the laws, policies, and procedures used to adjudicate cases in a particular program. It is quite common for administrative agencies to provide some training to newly hired adjudicators, staff attorneys, paralegals, and others about the general subject matter of the work being processed, as well as about the law, regulations, and procedures that are to be applied in their adjudicative actions. It is also common for agencies to use mentors to round out training and assist new employees in accurately applying the applicable laws and policies to the subject matter under review. This approach can produce acceptable results and has been used for many years by many agencies. At a minimum, this approach requires that agencies develop accurate and effective training programs and ensure mentors provide complete and accurate information to trainees.

Operational effectiveness may benefit if managers use modern adult-learning methods and principles to develop training programs. Adult-learning techniques are premised on the notion that most adults learn better by being taught not only what to do but also how to do whatever they are being taught. Many agencies provide training on applicable laws and policies and rely on mentors or peer reviewers to assist new employees in accurately applying them to real-world cases. However, agencies can also design training programs to include many examples of how to apply applicable laws, policies, and procedures in real-world cases. This may help employees understand and retain information faster, improve decisional quality, and enhance productivity.

Another approach is to assign several trainees to work on the same case and then have them discuss their approach together before producing a single, final product to send to a mentor. This type of experiential learning, which requires trainees to reflect on the work they

---

6. 84 Fed. Reg. 71,355 (Dec. 27, 2019).
7. 84 Fed. Reg. 38,930 (Aug. 8, 2019).

produce and actively participate in group discussions about the key issues involved in the work process, helps them improve their overall understanding of the subject matter and solidifies their understanding of how to process their work quickly and accurately.

Training opportunities are not limited to new employees. Agencies can develop training modules to provide information to staff about recent legal or other important developments. Managers can also use data captured in case management systems to identify common case-processing issues and develop training modules that provide links to applicable laws and policies and explain how to successfully apply them. If the agency captures data on the performance of individual personnel, managers may be able to provide individualized recommendations about specific training opportunities to adjudicative personnel. This promotes continuous learning and improvement. For more seasoned employees, self-directed learning can be effective.[8]

23.33 Employee Performance Management

An important part of the administration of federal programs is performance management. Administrative law judges (ALJs) are, of course, a notable exception. As discussed in Chapter 9, agencies may not rate ALJs' job performance or grant them awards or performance incentives, and agencies can only take disciplinary action against an ALJ for good cause established and determined by the Merit Systems Protection Board on the record after an opportunity for a hearing. The intent of these prohibitions is to insulate ALJs' decision-making from undue influence or interference by others.

There has been litigation regarding agencies' ability to manage ALJs in other ways, in particular through the imposition of production goals. The Seventh Circuit, at least, has held that production goals do not offend the Administrative Procedure Act if they have only an "incidental and unintentional effect" on decision-making.[9]

For most other employees, federal law and Office of Personnel Management (OPM) rules require that employees be given an annual performance appraisal. Federal law and OPM rules also specify how agencies can reward employees for good performance and take disciplinary actions based on unacceptable performance.[10] Negotiated

8. *See* Ray & Lubbers, *supra* note 3, at 1599–601.
9. Ass'n of Admin. L. Judges v. Colvin, 777 F.3d 402, 405 (7th Cir. 2015).
10. 5 U.S.C. § 4301 *et seq.*; 5 C.F.R. § 430.101 *et seq.* 2022.

bargaining unit agreements can also affect how agencies manage employees' performance.

Performance ratings typically rate employees on several dimensions, often including timeliness, productivity, decisional quality, and interpersonal skills. It can be difficult for managers to assess the quality of employees' work product if they only see a small sample of the work produced by each employee. As a result, effective measures of employee productivity, timeliness, and quality can be essential to fair and accurate performance appraisal.

It is important that any numeric-based performance expectation not be arbitrarily developed but instead be based on a reasonable calculation of acceptable performance and account for different workloads. Some agencies, particularly those that manage high-volume adjudication programs, have developed elaborate systems to determine performance expectations for adjudicative staff. But the calculations involved in establishing reasonable productivity expectations need not be particularly complex.

In programs involving a high volume of relatively fungible cases, calculating average productivity may be as simple as having one year's worth of information about how many hours employees spent on casework and the number of cases of each category that they processed in those hours. A range around the average could be established as a performance expectation representative of successful performance, and employees outside that range might be considered to have outstanding or less than successful productivity.[11]

Adding some complexity to the performance calculations, to take into account the varying degrees of complexity of the work performed, will not only improve the accuracy of the performance expectations, but also likely lead to greater employee satisfaction and acceptance of the performance expectations. This can be done by categorizing the various work products employees produce, and developing a multivariable equation to ascribe weight to those work products based on the perceived complexity or difficulty of each category.

23.34 Case Management

Agencies have adopted procedures and technologies over the years to manage caseloads more efficiently and accurately.[12] One of the most

11. Ray & Sklar, *supra* note 3, at 6–10.

12. *See* Administrative Conference Recommendation 86-7, Case Management as a Tool for Improving Agency Adjudication, 51 Fed. Reg. 46,989 (Dec. 30, 1986).

significant developments has been the shift away from paper-based files and case management systems toward electronic recordkeeping and electronic case management. ACUS has recommended that federal adjudicative agencies consider implementing an eCMS in order to, among other things, "reduce costs" and "increase both efficiency and accuracy in the processing of cases."[13]

23.35 Policy Clarification and Improvement

One common issue that makes it difficult to address quality issues is a potential lack of clarity or specificity in agency policies. When policies are too open to interpretation, personnel may develop incorrect or inconsistent personal heuristics for decision-making. Especially in high-volume adjudicative programs, where cases may be factually and legally similar, operational managers may be able to improve decisional accuracy and inter-decisional consistency by working with policymakers to clarify or improve existing policies, either by providing interpretive guidance or by revising underlying policy documents.

The data potentially available from a robust eCMS can be leveraged to improve staffing allocations, budget estimates, and employee training. It also can create opportunities to introduce natural language processing (NLP) and machine-learning algorithms that can speed case processing while improving accuracy. At least one federal agency, the Social Security Administration, has built an NLP and machine-learning quality assurance tool capable of identifying and highlighting several dozen types of decisional errors, providing adjudicators an opportunity to correct such errors before their decisions are issued.[14]

23.36 Operational Leadership

The operational manager is responsible for setting the tone for the organization, establishing operational goals, facilitating resolution of problems that may arise, and communicating operational needs and performance to executives and interested external parties. There are many theories of personnel management, but the most effective methods tap into the intrinsic motivation of subordinates. Many people appreciate working for knowledgeable managers who understand the work they perform, expect managers to address unforeseen problems

13. Administrative Conference Recommendation 2018-3, *supra* note 2.

14. Kurt Glaze et al., *Artificial Intelligence for Adjudication: The Social Security Administration and AI Governance*, *in* OXFORD HANDBOOK ON AI GOVERNANCE (Justin Bullock et al. eds., forthcoming 2023).

as they arise, and like the opportunity to exercise some autonomy in their work.

Federal adjudication programs often rely on autonomous decision-making by adjudicators, so it makes sense for operational managers to foster autonomy. One successful approach, used by some military leaders, is known as *auftragstaktik*, or mission-type orders. Rather than use a command-and-control approach by which subordinate leaders wait for instruction from people above them, auftragstaktik relies on the judgment of subordinate leaders to make decisions to progress the overall goals that have been set by the operational manager.

For this to work, the operational leader must communicate clear goals and expectations but leave most of the details of how to accomplish those goals to subordinate managers. The operational leader must monitor the progress toward those goals and should be in close communication with subordinate leaders to assist them when necessary in problem-solving to achieve the goals. Goals should be challenging but achievable, with transparent methodology about how the goals were derived shared with subordinate managers and staff. Progress toward goals should be broadly shared as well. Subordinate managers should be provided increasing levels of responsibility, with opportunities to build self-confidence and to use independent thinking in problem-solving. This can be an especially effective technique in larger adjudicative programs that are often hierarchically organized.

Allowing subordinates to make operational decisions increases creativity and development of new approaches that can be shared as best practices to foster operational improvement. Ideally, subordinate managers will open opportunities for staff to share ideas as well, so that the people directly involved in performing the work can offer ideas to improve operation. Many process improvements in agency adjudicative systems have originated with subordinate managers or staff who were given autonomy to innovate. One caution is that some may use their autonomy to pursue inefficient ideas, so it is important for all operational managers to interact regularly to maintain focus on the achievement of operational goals.

Chapter 24
Quality Assurance

Austin Peters, Gerald K. Ray, David Marcus, and Daniel E. Ho

24.1 CHAPTER OVERVIEW

Administrative law demands rational and consistent agency decision-making. Faced with high volumes of cases, complex records, and strained resources, agency adjudication systems have long struggled to meet the demands of "bureaucratic justice."[1] Many agencies have sought to meet these demands through quality assurance programs. The term "quality assurance" describes the internal processes agencies use to monitor, assess, and improve the quality of adjudicatory decisions.[2] Agencies can use these processes to a variety of ends, but chief among them is to identify and correct inaccuracies in decision-making.

This chapter reviews the role of "quality assurance" programs to improve the decisional quality of agency decisions. Section 24.2 describes the purpose of such programs. Sections 24.3–24.9 outline the key institutional design decisions in creating and operating a quality assurance program and discuss major design trade-offs.

---

1. Jerry L. Mashaw, Bureaucratic Justice: Managing Social Security Disability Claims (1983).
2. Daniel E. Ho et al., Admin. Conf. of the U.S., Quality Assurance Systems in Agency Adjudication 2 (2021).

24.2 PURPOSE OF QUALITY ASSURANCE SYSTEMS

Why should agencies care about quality? In several respects, the justification for an agency's commitment to quality decision-making is self-evident. Adjudication often involves matters, such as entitlement to disability benefits or defenses to deportation, where outcomes are of supreme importance to the individuals engaging with the agency. An agency's obligation to quality decision-making also emanates from due process principles.[3] If some base level of accuracy—ensuring that those entitled to prevail do so, and that those not entitled do not—cannot be guaranteed, procedural due process may demand more.

Under *Mathews v. Eldridge*'s well-known balancing framework, due process requires weighing the individual's interest in the sought-after benefit or relief, the government's interest, and "the risk of an erroneous deprivation of [the individual's] interest through the procedures used."[4] Moreover, the *Mathews* calculus is best conceived of in terms of *systemic accuracy*, not accuracy in each individual case. Procedural due process protects the accuracy of the system as a whole, and thus agencies have a constitutional obligation to systemic quality.[5]

Agencies have long battled challenges managing adjudication systems, notably inconsistent decisional outcomes that seem to defy notions of rationality.[6] The reasons for such inconsistencies are varied. Because cases often involve voluminous, complex factual records, including technical or scientific considerations, as well as complex and evolving legal frameworks, a rise in caseloads may increase pressure to meet production goals, which in turn may raise the risk of adjudicator

---

3. *See* David Ames et al., *Due Process and Mass Adjudication: Crisis and Reform*, 72 STAN. L. REV. 1, 20–25 (2020).

4. 424 U.S. 319, 335 (1976).

5. *See* Richard H. Fallon, Jr., *Some Confusions about Due Process, Judicial Review, and Constitutional Remedies*, 93 COLUM. L. REV. 309, 336–37 (1993) (describing *Mathews* as requiring procedures that achieve a "tolerable average level of accuracy"); Jerry L. Mashaw, *The Supreme Court's Due Process Calculus for Administrative Adjudication in* Mathews v. Eldridge*: Three Factors in Search of a Theory of Value*, 44 U. CHI. L. REV. 28, 48 (1976); Gillian E. Metzger, *The Constitutional Duty to Supervise*, 124 YALE L.J. 1836, 1865 (2015) (describing *Mathews*'s "decidedly systemic and managerial cast"); Robert L. Rabin, *Federal Regulation in Historical Perspective*, 38 STAN. L. REV. 1189, 1314 (1986) (describing *Mathews* as concerned with "potential error costs" to the group of potential recipients).

6. *See, e.g.*, Harold J. Krent & Scott Morris, *Inconsistency and Angst in District Court Resolution of Social Security Disability Appeals*, 67 HASTINGS L.J. 367, 378 (2016); Jaya Ramji-Nogales et al., *Refugee Roulette: Disparities in Asylum Adjudication*, 60 STAN. L. REV. 295, 325 (2007).

error.[7] Mandatory performance measures, particularly those developed to keep backlogs at bay, may pressure adjudicators to focus more on quantity and timeliness than accuracy.[8] Decisional inconsistency may also stem from adjudicators' misunderstanding of policy or indicate policy is vague.[9]

Appellate review of individual decisions, the classic mechanism for correcting errors, suffers from several limitations as a response to agency struggles with quality. As the Administrative Conference of the United States (ACUS) recognized in a 1973 recommendation, and as subsequent research has confirmed, institutional factors may blunt the appellate review's efficacy to ensure systemic accuracy.[10] For example, institutional determinants unrelated to decisional quality may affect the composition of appellate dockets and produce a misleading sample of decisions for reviewing courts and tribunals to evaluate. Individuals may lack the resources or wherewithal to avail themselves of the opportunity for appellate review.

The "system-based" understanding of due process's commitment to accuracy underscores the relative advantage of quality assurance compared to these other forms of quality review. Whereas other forms of review focus on individual decisions (e.g., judicial review), quality assurance emphasizes the improvement of aggregate accuracy.

---

7. *See*, *e.g.*, Heckler v. Day, 467 U.S. 104, 113–15 (1984) (summarizing congressional concerns about the effect of caseloads on decisional quality in Social Security Administration (SSA) adjudication); U.S. Gov't Accountability Off., GAO-21-242, Meaningful Performance Measures Could Help Improve Case Quality, Organizational Excellence, and Resource Management 28 (2021) (noting that some National Labor Relations Board stakeholders believe an emphasis on timeliness led staff to "cut corners"); Lewin Grp., Inc. et al., Evaluation of SSA's Disability Quality Assurance (QA) Processes and Development of QA Options That Will Support the Long-Term Management of the Disability Program 17 (2001) (noting "a widespread belief in a trade-off between accuracy and productivity" among SSA adjudicators); Stuart L. Lustig et al., *Inside the Judges' Chambers: Narrative Responses from the National Association of Immigration Judges Stress and Burnout Survey*, 23 Geo. Immigr. L.J. 57, 65–66 (2008) (reporting perceptions about quantity-quality trade-off among immigration judges).

8. *See* U.S. Gov't Accountability Off., GAO-21-341, Social Security Disability: Process Needed to Review Productivity Expectations for Administrative Law Judges 42 (2021); *see also* Ass'n of Admin. L. Judges v. Colvin, 777 F.3d 402, 405 (7th Cir. 2015).

9. Ho et al., *supra* note 2, at 17.

10. *See* David Hausman, *The Failure of Immigration Appeals*, 164 U. Pa. L. Rev. 1177, 1193 (2016).

Reflecting this insight, and based on research by Professor Jerry Mashaw, ACUS recommended in 1973 that agencies utilize "positive caseload management systems," including "statistical quality assurance reporting systems," to ensure accurate, timely, and fair adjudication.[11]

Our understanding has made significant progress in recent decades as more agencies have implemented quality assurance programs. As described throughout this chapter, the implementation of quality assurance varies significantly from agency to agency. For instance, the Social Security Administration (SSA) runs a large, independent team of quality assurance personnel. This team reviews a large set of cases, is guided by formalized procedures, and produces highly detailed statistical reports.[12] By contrast, peer review at some Merit Systems Protection Board (MSPB) offices is much more informal and deliberately not part of a more extensive data-gathering operation.[13] Regardless of their institutional particulars, quality assurance efforts aim to improve the overall success of decision-making systemically.

Variation is natural given different programs' needs and available resources. Many agencies—particularly small agencies with low case volumes—often have insufficient resources to devote to an independent quality assurance team staffed with full-time personnel. The perception that quality review infringes upon adjudicators' qualified decisional independence can also influence institutional design. For instance, as discussed in Chapter 9, administrative law judges (ALJs) are afforded a high degree of decisional independence. Quality assurance programs perceived to erode decisional independence and push outcomes in political directions have attracted significant legislative and judicial pushback.[14] Quality assurance programs should not be used as a tool of political control to drive specific adjudicatory outcomes; but they *should* be employed to assess whether outcomes align with agency policy, guidance, and regulations, as well as inform areas

---

11. Administrative Conference Recommendation 73-3, Quality Assurance Systems in the Adjudication of Claims of Entitlement to Benefits or Compensation, 38 Fed. Reg. 16,840 (June 27, 1973).

12. *See* Felix F. Bajandas & Gerald K. Ray, ACUS, Implementation and Use of Electronic Case Management Systems in Federal Agency Adjudication 44–52 (2018).

13. Interview with Agency Official(s), MSPB (Aug. 18, 2021) [hereinafter MSPB Interview].

14. Nash v. Bowen, 869 F.2d 675, 680–81 (2d Cir. 1989).

for policy development.[15] Caseload pressures can disincentivize agencies from devoting staff resources to quality assurance.[16] Finally, forging consensus on the meaning of "quality" remains hard. For instance, some will disagree over whether quality review should focus solely on decisional accuracy, or whether it should encompass timeliness and demeanor.

ACUS revisited the subject of quality assurance systems in 2021, adopting a new recommendation based on the past 50 years of agency practices and academic research. That recommendation reaffirmed that agencies should consider implementing quality assurance systems to promote decisional accuracy and other objectives.[17] Still, we have much to learn. Most importantly, we have little insight into how agencies have designed quality assurance efforts. Accordingly, the 2021 report to ACUS by the authors of this chapter describes several reforms that agencies could implement to improve our understanding of current quality assurance methods.[18] Improved information infrastructure and data reporting would enable more rigorous inquiry as to what works when it comes to quality assurance, facilitate cross-agency learning, and ultimately improve oversight and accountability of high-volume claims adjudication.

24.3 HOW DO AGENCIES DEFINE AND ASSESS QUALITY?

"Quality" can be hard to define, and agencies have employed a range of approaches. Most focus on decisional accuracy. SSA, for instance, defines a high-quality decision as one that is "factually accurate, procedurally adequate, supported by the record, and policy compliant."[19] The Board of Veterans' Appeals (BVA) defines "accuracy" as an

---

15. The MSPB, for example, formally includes decisional quality as an element in administrative judge performance evaluation. MSPB, Performance Elements and Standards, Attorney Examiner (Administrative Judges), GS-905-13/14/15 (2021).

16. *See* U.S. Gov't Accountability Off., GAO-18-37, Social Security Disability: Additional Measures and Evaluation Needed to Enhance Accuracy and Consistency of Hearings Decisions 40 (2017).

17. Administrative Conference Recommendation 2021-10, Quality Assurance Systems in Agency Adjudication, 87 Fed. Reg. 1,722 (Jan. 12, 2022).

18. Ho et al., *supra* note 2, at 28.

19. Kurt Glaze et al., *Artificial Intelligence for Adjudication: The Social Security Administration and AI Governance*, *in* Oxford Handbook on AI Governance 7 (Justin Bullock et al. eds., 2022).

opinion that is "deficiency free."[20] The MSPB considers the "quality of decision" based on "proper identification of all material legal and factual issues," "[a]ppropriate . . . consideration of relevant facts, evidence, and authority," "[p]roper and thorough analysis of the issues," style, and citation formatting.[21]

Other agencies define "quality" more broadly. The Equal Employment Opportunity Commission (EEOC), for instance, specifies an extensive set of determinants, including timeliness and hearing fairness, in its *Federal Sector Quality Practices for Effective Hearings, Appeals, and Oversight.*[22] Various agencies' complaint procedures recognize adjudicator comportment as crucial to their mission and to claimants' experiences.[23]

Agencies have deployed a range of ways to measure quality. One quality measure is decisional inconsistency. Broadly speaking, this measure evaluates whether adjudicators with similar dockets generate significantly different results. One ALJ deciding disability benefits appeals, for instance, granted claims 89 percent of the time, while another ALJ in the same hearing office, dealing with the same claimant population, granted claims 19 percent of the time.[24] Notably, decisional inconsistency is not an indicator of poor-quality decisionmaking per se. Adjudicator independence and the discretion that fact-intensive adjudication requires make variation an unavoidable reality. But significant disparities could indicate a cohort of adjudicators with fundamentally mistaken understandings of agency policy, or they could indicate policy ambiguity causing widespread confusion.

Another quality measure is the rate at which an adjudicator's decisions are overturned on administrative appeal or judicial review. For example, the MSPB analyzes how often an internal appeals body

---

20. U.S. GEN. ACCT. OFF., GAO-02-806, VETERANS' BENEFITS: QUALITY ASSURANCE FOR DISABILITY CLAIMS AND APPEALS PROCESSING CAN BE FURTHER IMPROVED 7 (2002).

21. MSPB, *supra* note 15.

22. EEOC, FEDERAL SECTOR QUALITY PRACTICES FOR EFFECTIVE HEARINGS, APPEALS, AND OVERSIGHT (2017), https://www.eeoc.gov/federal-sector/federal-sector-quality-practices-effective-hearings-appeals-and-oversight.

23. *See Complaints regarding EOIR Judges*, U.S. DEP'T OF JUST., EXEC. OFF. FOR IMMIGR. REV., https://www.justice.gov/eoir/complaints-regarding-eoir-judges (last updated Feb. 23, 2023); SSA, HOW TO FILE AN UNFAIR TREATMENT COMPLAINT CONCERNING AN ADMINISTRATIVE LAW JUDGE (2017), https://www.ssa.gov/pubs/EN-05-10071.pdf.

24. Krent & Morris, *supra* note 6, at 378.

overturns decisions, or how often cases are reversed by courts.[25] Some question whether appellate outcomes are a useful measure of quality because appealed cases are likely unrepresentative of the larger case pool.[26] Litigants choose which cases to appeal and strategically select cases that are more likely to succeed.[27] Parties often have asymmetric appeal rights, such as laws or regulations that only allow those denied benefits to appeal their claim.[28] In addition, many individuals lack sufficient representation or find appeals to be too costly and therefore may not bring forward meritorious claims.[29] For instance, one study of quality assurance found the prevalence of errors in all cases was indistinguishable from nonappealed cases, suggesting nonappealed cases can have a significant rate of error.[30]

A much less widely used quality measure consists of survey evidence. The BVA, for instance, surveys veterans about the quality of their adjudication process, including whether they received a timely hearing and if their adjudicator explained issues clearly.[31] One downside to using surveys is that they may tilt adjudicators toward outcomes favorable to claimants and be uncorrelated with decisional accuracy.

At some agencies, an important benchmark for making a quality determination is the standard of review employed by an agency appellate body or a reviewing court. Some agencies expressly indicate that quality review should anticipate whether an appellate reviewer would reverse or remand the decision. For instance, the BVA's quality review

---

25. *See, e.g.*, MSPB, ANNUAL PERFORMANCE REPORT FOR FY 2020 AND ANNUAL PERFORMANCE PLAN FOR FY 2021 (FINAL) & FY 2022 (PROPOSED) 7 (2020).

26. *See* HO ET AL., *supra* note 2, at 13–14.

27. Steven Shavell, *The Appeals Process as a Means of Error Correction*, 24 J. LEGAL STUD. 379 (1995).

28. Jonah B. Gelbach & David Marcus, *Rethinking Judicial Review of High Volume Agency Adjudication*, 96 TEX. L. REV. 1097, 1109 (2018); *see also Social Security Disability Benefits: Did a Group of Judges, Doctors, and Lawyers Abuse Programs for the Country's Most Vulnerable?: Hearing before the S. Comm. on Homeland Sec. & Governmental Affs.*, 113th Cong. 129 (2013) (statement of Debra Bice, Chief ALJ, SSA) [hereinafter Bice Statement] (discussing how SSA ALJ decisions granting disability benefits are not subject to appeal by the agency).

29. Hausman, *supra* note 10, at 1193 (analyzing connection between immigrants' decision to appeal and whether they have a lawyer).

30. Daniel E. Ho et al., *Quality Review of Mass Adjudication: A Randomized Natural Experiment at the Board of Veterans Appeals*, 2003–16, 35 J. L. ECON. & ORG. 239, 261 (2019).

31. BVA, DEP'T OF VETERANS AFFS., ANNUAL REPORT FISCAL YEAR (FY) 2019, at 15 (2019).

program assessed accuracy based on whether an error would be "outcome determinative" on review by the Court of Appeals for Veterans Claims.[32] In some instances, quality reviewers at the hearing level of the SSA adjudication system triage errors based on whether they are likely to cause a remand from the agency's Appeals Council.[33]

That said, an agency's articulated standard of review may not always reflect reality. Although quality assessment may have one de facto standard, pressure from internal or external stakeholders to boost accuracy measures may cause reviewers to relax their evaluation. For instance, reviewers might adopt a predictive standard based on appellate outcome but, in reality, evaluate decisions on a much more lenient curve.[34] Agencies might also resist a predictive standard out of concern that reviewing courts have flawed or unrealistic expectations about the adjudicatory responsibilities agencies shoulder.

24.4 WHOSE WORK GETS REVIEWED FOR QUALITY?

In theory, quality assurance systems can review the work of all personnel who have roles in the adjudication of cases or matters. But quality assurance systems have traditionally focused on the work of frontline and hearing-level adjudicators. For decades, SSA has run some form of quality review to analyze the disability determinations of frontline examiners and the agency's ALJ corps.[35] MSPB administrative judges (AJs) often review each other's decisions before decisions are issued, building on the review that MSPB supervisors conduct during an AJ's first year on the job.[36] The Office of Patent Quality Assurance (OPQA) randomly selects patent applications to review the work of their patent examiners.[37] The BVA's quality assurance program randomly sampled 5 percent of original decisions by the BVA.[38]

---

32. *See* BVA, U.S. Dep't of Veterans Affs., Annual Report Fiscal Year (FY) 2002, at 7 (2002).

33. Interview with Agency Official(s), SSA (Oct. 22, 2021) [hereinafter SSA Interview].

34. Ames et al., *supra* note 3, at 52–53 (explaining how one agency's standard of review for QA weakened without being formally changed).

35. *Id.* at 31–40 (describing SSA's QA efforts).

36. MSPB Interview, *supra* note 13.

37. *Promoting the Useful Arts: How Can Congress Prevent the Issuance of Poor Quality Patents?: Hearing before the Subcomm. on Intell. Prop. of the S. Comm. on the Judiciary*, 116th Cong. (2019) (responses to questions for the record of Andrew Hirshfeld, Commissioner for Patents, U.S. Patent and Trademark Office).

38. Ho et al., *supra* note 30, at 240–41.

Quality assurance can also focus on appellate reviewers. For example, SSA recently launched a program for ALJs to provide feedback to the SSA Appeal Council.[39] This initiative provides an opportunity for ALJs to raise concerns about cases remanded back to them and incentivizes ALJs to participate because raised concerns that are upheld are reflected in dispositional quality statistics maintained for each ALJ.

Quality review can also be expanded to include staff who support adjudicators. SSA's quality review program, for instance, evaluates the extent to which decision-writers prepare decisions according to agency policies.[40] A quality assurance program that only reviews adjudicator work product may fail to identify where in a decision-making process errors are made and by whom. By contrast, one that also evaluates work done by support staff may better focus attention on the source of error and identify more efficient, effective interventions.

Outlier analysis can also be used to gauge the performance of the quality review team itself. The OPQA uses their information technology (IT) system to identify whether quality reviewers are calling certain errors at an abnormally high rate.[41]

24.5 WHEN DOES QUALITY REVIEW TAKE PLACE?

Quality review can take place before or after a decision is issued or takes effect. SSA runs two well-established quality review programs that analyze disability decisions before dispensing benefits. "In-line quality review" occurs before an adjudicator finalizes his or her initial decision. Staff in SSA's regional offices randomly sample cases at various stages before completion. They review these cases for compliance with policy and whether the evidence supports the adjudicator's drafted decision.[42] Since this quality review process occurs before the adjudicator's decision is finalized, the "in-line" review helps SSA analyze instances when support staff, such as decision-writers, may struggle with correct policy application. (Supervisors at the EEOC also perform a similar form of ongoing review by reviewing draft decisions prepared by their appellate attorneys.[43]) SSA's other ongoing

39. SSA Interview, *supra* note 33.

40. Ames et al., *supra* note 3, at 40.

41. Interview with Agency Official(s), U.S. Patent and Trademark Office (Nov. 4, 2021) [hereinafter USPTO Interview].

42. SSA, Program Operations Manual System § GN 04440.008.

43. Interview with Agency Official(s), EEOC (Oct. 25, 2021) [hereinafter EEOC Interview].

assessment program is called "pre-effectuation" review. This program analyzes ALJ decisions after they are finalized but before the agency "effectuates" them by beginning payment of disability benefits to claimants. If the agency concludes the adjudicator made an error, it retains the power to change the initial decision. In addition to analyzing a disability decision "in-line," SSA also analyzes decisions after the agency begins paying disability benefits.[44]

"In-line" quality review has several advantages.[45] Deficiencies can be corrected before the agency awards or pays benefits. Less time passes between the adjudicator's work on the case and quality review, and thus the adjudicator is more likely to understand and respond to feedback. Quality review feedback that comes months or even years after an adjudicator's initial decision risks being ignored, especially if an adjudicator with a large docket has rendered numerous decisions in the interim. But agencies must avoid interfering with any decisional independence granted to adjudicators by law or agency policy.

Compared to pre-decisional review, post-decisional review is less likely to infringe on an adjudicator's pace of decision-making, as it does not require further adjudicator attention. In general, however, evidence from performance-management literature suggests that "in-line" assessment (i.e., assessment that occurs while the decision process is still underway or before benefits are issued) is more likely to be effective. By providing feedback closer in time to when an adjudicator decides a matter, such review is more likely to reflect agency-wide commitment to quality, thereby cultivating a culture of learning and improvement.[46] Experimental evidence corroborates that ongoing quality initiatives may promote real-time learning.[47] Still, some forms of "in-line" review—for instance, SSA's "pre-effectuation" assessments—can take place long after an adjudicator's initial decision.

24.6 WHO CONDUCTS QUALITY REVIEW?

In general, there are three approaches agencies take to staffing quality assurance programs. First, supervisors can review subordinates' work for quality. As discussed earlier, supervisors at the EEOC review

44. Ames et al., *supra* note 3, at 19, 38.

45. Ho et al., *supra* note 2, at 18.

46. Daniel E. Ho & Sam Sherman, *Managing Street-Level Arbitrariness: The Evidence Base for Public Sector Quality Improvement*, 13 Ann. Rev. L. & Soc. Sci. 251, 265 (2017).

47. Ho et al., *supra* note 2, at 25–26.

every decision drafted by attorneys working on appeals, and a significant component of this review involves quality assessment.[48] Likewise, MSPB supervisors conduct formal quality assessment for new AJs.[49]

Second, peers can review work, an approach that can be institutionalized or run on a more informal basis. Several MSPB regions rely extensively on a peer review system where judges review each other's draft decisions.[50] This approach generally involves assigning peers to shadow adjudicators on the same case to offer peer feedback, potentially before the final decision is issued.

Third, agencies can form independent quality review teams, which can be made up of adjudicators or other agency personnel, such as staff lawyers. ACUS's 1973 recommendation envisioned this approach.[51] Currently, SSA operates a quality assurance program that is modeled roughly along these lines.[52]

Cost and capacity might substantially impact an agency's preferred choice of personnel model. Smaller agencies or those with low case volumes may have fewer resources they can devote to an independent quality assurance team staffed with full-time personnel. For these agencies, institutional forms that draw on existing staff and involve less oversight, such as peer review, may be easier to implement. Still, informal review like peer review is not costless. To be successful, peers must dedicate time to reviewing their colleagues' work, which naturally gives them less time to decide cases.

An agency that decides to construct an independent quality review team must decide whom to hire, a question that involves trade-offs. On the one hand, quality reviewers may be appointed from outside the division of the agency handling adjudication, ensuring greater independence at the cost of less expertise. On the other hand, appointing quality reviewers from inside the division of the agency handling adjudication prioritizes expertise but poses potential conflicts of interest.

A related design problem lies in the relationship between reviewers and adjudicators. Quality reviewers who are subordinates to adjudicators may not be able to exhibit the desired independence for fear of

---

48. EEOC Interview, *supra* note 43.

49. MSPB Interview, *supra* note 13.

50. *Id.*

51. Administrative Conference Recommendation 73-3, *supra* note 11 (recommending agencies adopt a positive caseload management system and statistical QA reporting system).

52. BAJANDAS & RAY, *supra* note 12, at 44–52 (describing how the SSA Appeals Council and Division of Quality conduct quality review).

subsequent employment consequences.[53] A more benign version of this problem involves existing social relationships. Reviewers may also not be able to independently assess colleagues' work product,[54] although a recusal policy can safeguard against such potential conflicts.

Conversely, an institutional gap between reviewers and those whose work they review can breed distrust and diminish adjudicators' receptivity to feedback.[55] Quality assurance schemes centered on appellate review can illustrate these dynamics. Tension between frontline adjudicators and appellate tribunals is not uncommon. An ALJ or AJ may believe that appellate adjudicators lack sufficient understanding of the conditions they labor under, have a skewed understanding of their docket, or have unreasonable expectations for appropriate decision-making.[56] Adjudicators may also perceive appellate bodies as adopting an insufficiently deferential standard of review.

A related institutional design choice, relevant to all three approaches for staffing quality assurance programs, involves the length of time reviewers spend engaged in quality assurance efforts. Some agencies have term-limited appointments for quality assurance; others appoint quality personnel indefinitely. Short-term positions have the advantage of providing fresh perspectives and a potential infusion of quality perspectives into the front lines as reviewers return to the ranks of adjudicators.[57] Longer term positions, on the other hand, can enable reviewers to gain experience and institutional knowledge over time, reduce challenges from turnover, and ensure longer term investments in quality initiatives. Such long-term positions, however, also run the risk of groupthink, and they may produce in reviewers a sense of distance from the operational constraints of frontline work.

---

53. U.S. Gen. Acct. Off., *supra* note 20, at 7 n.7.

54. Vanessa Urch Druskat & Steven B. Wolff, *Effects and Timing of Developmental Peer Appraisals in Self-Managing Groups*, 84 J. Applied Psych. 58, 58 (1999) (describing potential for "popularity contents" in peer appraisals); Maury A. Peiperl, *Conditions for the Success of Peer Evaluation*, 10 J. Int'l Hum. Res. 429, 431 (1999) (describing potential for bias in peer evaluation).

55. Greg L. Stewart, *A Meta-Analytic Review of Relationships between Team Design Features and Team Performance*, 32 J. Mgmt. 29, 33 (2006).

56. Ames et al., *supra* note 3, at 61 (reporting results from interviews with adjudicators).

57. Such trade-off between experience and new perspectives has long been studied in the management literature. *See, e.g.*, Susan Cohen & Diane E. Bailey, *What Makes Teams Work*, 23 J. Mgmt. 239, 273 (1997); Dawn Harris & Constance Helfat, *Specificity of CEO Human Capital and Compensation*, 18 Strategic Mgmt. J. 895, 897–99 (1998).

24.7 WHICH CASES GET REVIEWED FOR QUALITY?

When caseloads and available resources permit, agencies can review every decision for accuracy. At the EEOC, for example, supervisors review every decision drafted by their attorneys working on appeals.[58] In the past, a supervisor at U.S. Citizenship and Immigration Services (USCIS) reviewed all decisions made by the Administrative Appeals Office. But the office has now transitioned to a model where they review decisions by new hires.[59] Similarly, MSPB supervisors review every decision drafted by new AJs.[60]

The sheer volume of decisions will make it infeasible for some agencies to review all decisions they issue. In such contexts, agencies must selectively choose which cases to review. Agencies have adopted several approaches to "sampling" cases. For instance, some quality review programs perform simple random sampling from the entire decision pool. OPQA randomly selects different agency actions for review.[61] For more than 15 years, the BVA's quality assurance program randomly sampled 5 percent of decisions.[62] When performed properly, simple random sampling can provide a representative perspective on quality issues.

Another case selection approach embraced by agencies—which can be used in tandem with simple random sampling—is a strategy that enables focused inquiry into distinct sources of errors. Stratified random sampling allows agencies to sample cases in a way that is representative but oversamples cases based on chosen characteristics (e.g., claim type, issue). Such an approach can focus on specific legal issues or factual circumstances that are more likely to generate errors. For instance, the SSA Appeals Council randomly samples ALJ decisions but also samples by stratifying on issues and facts. To preserve decisional independence, however, the Appeals Council does not sample cases based on the identity of the decision-maker or office that issued the decision.[63]

Sometimes, an agency's sampling strategy is not explicitly stated but rather implied by their choice of quality measure. Several agencies,

58. EEOC Interview, *supra* note 43.
59. Interview with Agency Official(s), USCIS (Oct. 12, 2021) [hereinafter USCIS Interview].
60. MSPB Interview, *supra* note 13.
61. USPTO Interview, *supra* note 41.
62. Ho et al., *supra* note 30, at 240–41.
63. 20 C.F.R. § 404.969(b)(1) (2020).

for instance, analyze appellate remands as part of their quality assessment program. The MSPB's quality measure is the percentage of AJ decisions upheld by their internal board and the federal circuit.[64] Although appellate outcomes may provide useful information, there are well-documented reasons why agencies should be cautious about relying solely on appeals for quality review.[65] Most importantly, the pool of appealed cases will not necessarily be representative of all decisions.[66]

24.8 WHAT INFORMATION DO QUALITY REVIEWERS COLLECT?

To collect information about decisions in a systematic fashion, some agencies capture quality assurance data through their case management systems. These systems vary in complexity and sophistication. At the MSPB, for instance, the regional director and paralegals manually code issues based on decisions.[67] SSA, by contrast, has implemented an electronic case management system.[68] The system stores records and documents related to each claim electronically, captures metadata about case processing, and identifies information about the witnesses, representatives, and adjudicators involved.[69]

The effective use of case management systems for quality assurance remains an open issue for many agencies. Historically, adjudicatory agencies have kept only minimal information about cases, largely for case-handling and reporting purposes. As Professor Mashaw's 1973 report to ACUS notes, capturing salient information about decisions is critical to enabling analysis and actionable insights.[70] In many instances, agencies can make simple changes to existing systems to better capture quality assurance information.[71]

Agencies with robust data infrastructures have leveraged electronic case management systems to develop innovative quality assessment

---

64. MSPB Interview, *supra* note 13.

65. JERRY L. MASHAW, ACUS, REPORT IN SUPPORT OF RECOMMENDATION 73-3, at 165 (1974) (describing the "mysteriously selective" nature of appeals).

66. HO ET AL., *supra* note 2, at 13–14.

67. MSPB Interview, *supra* note 13.

68. Bice Statement, *supra* note 28 (detailing SSA's approach to case management and QA).

69. *See* Glaze et al., *supra* note 19, at 7.

70. MASHAW, *supra* note 65, at 170–71.

71. HO ET AL., *supra* note 2, at 22.

measures and analyses. For example, agencies have conducted forms of anomaly detection (i.e., identifying unexplained discrepancies in cases) using quality review outputs or remand orders to look for certain issues, jurisdictions, or adjudicators that exhibit high propensity for errors. Such analyses might be particularly helpful in identifying areas of law where a precedent has shifted, but adjudicators have not fully adjusted, or where policy ambiguity, inconsistency, or gaps lead to recurring problems. SSA, for instance, developed a series of "heat maps" to understand which issues and field offices were subject to high error or remand rates. The agency then responded with targeted interventions, including focused trainings.[72] SSA heat maps also helped the agency prioritize areas for regulatory change, informing a series of proposals for policy clarification.[73] The BVA similarly conducted an in-depth analysis of one precedent, whose citation was associated with very high remand rates, and issued training materials for how to handle that precedent appropriately.[74]

24.9 HOW IS QUALITY REVIEW INFORMATION USED?

Once an agency has reviewed decisions for quality, it must decide how it will utilize that information to facilitate improvement in decision-making. One way agencies use quality assurance information is to provide feedback. The most obvious audience for feedback is the decision-maker responsible for issuing the order. The BVA, for example, issues memoranda to adjudicators in reviewed cases when the quality assurance team identifies a deficiency. Such feedback is likely most effective when it is issued expeditiously. For instance, SSA's How MI Doing tool is a web-based program that provides individualized information to ALJs on a continuous basis about their decision-making, including the number of decisions they have rendered and whether any of their decisions have been remanded. It also uses information

---

72. U.S. GOV'T ACCOUNTABILITY OFF., *supra* note 16, at 31.

73. Gerald K. Ray & Jeffrey S. Lubbers, *A Government Success Story: How Data Analysis by the Social Security Appeals Council (with a Push from the Administrative Conference of the United States) Is Transforming Social Security Disability Adjudication*, 83 GEO. WASH. L. REV. 1575, 1607 (2015).

74. BVA, TARGETED QUALITY ANALYSIS: APPEALS OF EXTRASCHEDULAR RATINGS UNDER 38 C.F.R. § 3.321(B)(1), at 2 (2002) (analyzing application of *Thun v. Peake*, 22 Vet. App. 111 (2008)).

from the ALJ's prior decisions and automatically flags relevant training modules.[75]

Agencies also deliver quality feedback to individual adjudicators during annual performance reviews. During their first two years at the MSPB, AJs receive a quality assessment as part of their annual performance evaluation.[76] The EEOC similarly incorporates quality review into their evaluation of attorneys' drafting appeals decisions.[77] Because there may be a significant time delay between an adjudicator's decision and the performance review, performance reviews should be one of several mechanisms for delivering quality-related feedback.[78]

Notably, legal constraints may limit an agency's ability to incorporate feedback into performance evaluation. ALJs, for instance, are exempt from performance appraisal requirements that apply to most other agency employees (see Chapter 9). The possibility of annual performance reviews may make quality feedback easier to implement for agencies with non-ALJ adjudicators. Still, agencies with such adjudicators have an obligation to conduct these reviews in a manner sensitive to principles of adjudicator independence.[79]

Some agencies also use quality assurance insights to trigger more in-depth reviews. At SSA, remand patterns or other data anomalies trigger an "early monitoring system" to identify an ALJ who may be struggling with the correct application of some policies.[80] A team of Appeals Council personnel then conducts an in-depth examination of that ALJ's decisions to identify areas of concern and develop an appropriate intervention. This "focused quality review" has also helped SSA to identify areas where policy ambiguity creates challenges for consistent, correct decision-making and thus to help guide policy clarification.[81] Outlier analysis can also be used to gauge the performance of the quality review team itself. The OPQA uses their IT system to

---

75. U.S. Gov't Accountability Off., *supra* note 16, at 33.

76. MSPB Interview, *supra* note 13.

77. EEOC Interview, *supra* note 43.

78. *See* Pierre J. Richard, *Measuring Organizational Performance: Towards Methodological Best Practice*, 35 J. Mgmt. 718, 722 (2009) (recommending firms avoid relying on a single performance measure since performance is a multidimensional construct).

79. Kent Barnett et al., ACUS, Non-ALJ Adjudicators in Federal Agencies: Status, Selection, Oversight, and Removal (2018).

80. Ames et al., *supra* note 3, at 39.

81. *See generally* Nicole Maestas et al., *The Effect of Economic Conditions on the Disability Insurance Program: Evidence from the Great Recession*, 199 J. Pub. Econ. 104410 (2021).

identify whether quality reviewers are calling certain errors at an abnormally high rate.[82]

While case-level feedback is often helpful, agencies can also deliver aggregate feedback to groups of adjudicators. The BVA tabulates aggregate performance measures, indicating the overall accuracy rate for the adjudicator corps.[83] Agencies can synthesize information from a group of decisions and identify commonly occurring errors.[84] At least one SSA hearing office issues a report along these lines summarizing district court decisions in social security cases.[85] Internal surveys of ALJs at the office suggest many support the practice. Numerous staff members indicated that the reports improved the quality of their decisions.

Quality feedback can also inform training. In a nonadjudicatory context, for instance, one agency tracked which specific issues were generating high variances between decision-makers to develop training materials, when it was not clear which direction was objectively correct.[86] Such feedback loops can help agencies function as a learning organization, enabling them to reap the benefits of continuous improvement.[87]

Adjudicators are not the only audience for quality feedback; the quality assurance team can also share insights with agency leadership and recommend how the agency might change policy and procedure to improve decisional quality. For example, the results of quality review led SSA to determine that certain issues that produced persistent adjudicator error revealed ambiguity in agency policy. These findings prompted SSA to provide policy clarification and guidance that enabled adjudicators to decide cases more consistently and accurately.[88] On occasion, USCIS working groups use information about trends in decisional quality to recommend changes to agency policy and rules.[89]

---

82. USPTO Interview, *supra* note 41.

83. BVA, *supra* note 32, at 15.

84. Ho et al., *supra* note 2, at 15.

85. David Marcus & Jonah Gelbach, ACUS, A Study of Social Security Litigation in the Federal Courts 119–20 (2016) (describing practice adopted by SSA hearing office).

86. Daniel E. Ho, *Does Peer Review Work? An Experiment of Experimentalism*, 69 Stan. L. Rev. 1, 56–57 (2017).

87. David A. Garvin, *Building a Learning Organization*, 71 Harv. Bus. Rev. 78 (1993).

88. Ray & Lubbers, *supra* note 73, at 1601.

89. USCIS Interview, *supra* note 59.

Chapter 25

Executive Influence on Federal Administrative Adjudication

Bijal Shah

25.1 CHAPTER OVERVIEW

Presidential control over agency adjudications has been widely viewed as more restrained, particularly compared to such influence over the executive or legislative-type functions of administrative agencies.[1] Still, the White House has various means to influence formal and informal agency adjudication. Indeed, recent presidents have exercised more direct, politicized power over adjudication at several agencies, for instance, on matters of immigration.[2] In addition, the White House can play a role in coordinating how agencies share overlapping[3] or

---

1. Bijal Shah, *Uncovering Coordinated Interagency Adjudication*, 128 Harv. L. Rev. 805, 856–60 (2015).

2. *See* Bijal Shah, *Civil Servant Alarm*, 94 Chi.-Kent L. Rev. 627, 643–45 (2019); Shah, *supra* note 1, at 814–20.

3. Bijal Shah, *Interagency Transfers of Adjudication Authority*, 34 Yale J. on Regul. 279, 338–39 (2017).

conflicting[4] adjudicatory power. This chapter considers some ways in which the executive directs, oversees, and controls federal agency adjudication—for instance, via executive orders (section 25.2) and the appointment and removal of agency officials (section 25.3). It also offers some best practices for limiting the politicization of administrative adjudication (section 25.4).

When discussing presidential oversight of federal agency adjudication, it is worth acknowledging the Administrative Conference of the United States (ACUS). Congress established ACUS as an independent agency in the mid-1960s to make recommendations to agencies, the president, Congress, and the Judicial Conference on matters related to administrative procedure.[5] Since then, ACUS has issued dozens of recommendations and developed model rules intended to improve adjudication across the executive branch.[6]

25.2 DIRECT PRESIDENTIAL INVOLVEMENT

As discussed in Chapter 1, federal administrative adjudication is generally divided into two categories. The first is formal adjudication, which is regulated by the Administrative Procedure Act (APA).[7] Administrative law judges (ALJs), governed by the APA, usually preside over trial-like hearings in formal adjudications.[8] The second is informal adjudication, which makes up the "vast majority of federal agency adjudications,"[9] including in the immigration context. The APA does not set out detailed requirements for informal adjudications, and these proceedings may be delineated by a statute other than the APA, agency regulations, or some other form of agency policy.[10] Non-ALJ adjudicators typically preside over informal adjudications, and their

4. Bijal Shah, *Executive (Agency) Administration*, 72 STAN. L. REV. 641, 661–62 (2020).

5. *See* Administrative Conference Act, Pub. L. No. 88-499, 78 Stat. 615 (1964) (codified at 5 U.S.C. §§ 591–596).

6. *Adjudication*, ACUS, https://acus.gov/adjudication (last visited June 27, 2023).

7. 5 U.S.C. §§ 554, 556–557.

8. *Id.* § 3105.

9. BEN HARRINGTON & DANIEL J. SHEFFNER, CONG. RSCH. SERV., R46930, INFORMAL ADMINISTRATIVE ADJUDICATION: AN OVERVIEW (2021).

10. Administrative Conference Recommendation 2016-4, Evidentiary Hearings Not Required by the Administrative Procedure Act, 81 Fed. Reg. 94,312, 94,314 (Dec. 23, 2016).

appointment and removal are not uniformly governed by statute.[11] In either formal or informal administrative adjudication, the head of an agency may also become involved in adjudicating a case.[12]

Presidential involvement in adjudication is conventionally limited. As Adrian Vermeule writes, there is "a network of tacit unwritten conventions that protect the independence of even executive agencies [as opposed to independent agencies] when engaged in adjudication." Direct presidential involvement in agency adjudication offends these conventions. Vermeule suggests that presidential involvement in adjudication "would be seen as an unprecedented exertion of power, violating longstanding unwritten traditions, and would for that reason provoke a storm of protest."[13] However, executive orders and personal involvement in adjudication may allow for some presidential control over the scope or outcomes of adjudication.

25.21 Executive Orders

An executive order is a "directive from the President of the United States that manages the operations of the federal government." Executive orders do not require approval from Congress. A "sitting U.S. President may overturn an existing executive order by issuing another executive order to that effect."[14]

Presidents have extended control over agency rulemaking and policymaking through executive orders. One area of frequent presidential action is immigration. Executive orders and presidential proclamations have been designed to increase executive influence on the scope and transparency of immigration decision-making.[15]

---

11. *Guidance on Administrative Law Judges after* Lucia v. SEC *(S. Ct.), July 2018*, 132 HARV. L. REV. 1120, 1120 (2019); Kent H. Barnett & Russell Wheeler, *Non-ALJ Adjudicators in Federal Agencies: Status, Selection, Oversight, and Removal*, 53 GA. L. REV. 1 (2018).

12. *See, e.g.*, Bijal Shah, *The Attorney General's Disruptive Immigration Power*, 102 IOWA L. REV. 129 (2017) (arguing that the attorney general's "referral and review" mechanism is a form of immigration adjudication).

13. Adrian Vermeule, *Conventions of Agency Independence*, 113 COLUM. L. REV. 1163, 1211–13 (2013).

14. *Executive Orders*, AM. BAR ASS'N (Nov. 28, 2021), https://www.americanbar.org/groups/public_education/resources/teacher_portal/educational_resources/executive_orders/.

15. *See, e.g.*, Exec. Order No. 14,010, Creating a Comprehensive Regional Framework to Address the Causes of Migration, to Manage Migration throughout North and Central America, and to Provide Safe and Orderly Processing of Asylum Seekers at the United States Border, 86 Fed. Reg. 8,267, 8,269–71 (Feb. 2, 2021)

The extent to which the president can influence adjudication directly via executive order is unclear,[16] and, historically, presidents have often shied away from doing so. For instance, as then-Professor Elena Kagan wrote, "[t]he only mode of administrative action from which Clinton shrank was adjudication. At no time in his tenure did he attempt publicly to exercise the powers that a department head possesses over an agency's on-the-record determinations."[17]

However, presidents have made efforts to use executive orders to influence adjudication indirectly. President Clinton issued at least one executive order directing agencies to improve public access to and the quality of adjudicatory processes.[18] In an executive order designed to aid the national recovery from the COVID-19 pandemic, President Trump laid out "principles of fairness in administrative enforcement and adjudication" and instructed all agency heads to modify procedures and practices accordingly.[19] The Office of Management and

(impacting how asylum applications are processed); Exec. Order No. 14,012, Restoring Faith in Our Legal Immigration Systems and Strengthening Integration and Inclusion Efforts for New Americans, 86 Fed. Reg. 8,277, 8,277–79 (Feb. 2, 2021) (harnessing interagency collaboration to strengthen access and inclusion within various immigration processes and identifying issues such as the need for efficient decision-making and barriers to accessing eligible benefits); Presidential Memorandum on Additional Measures to Enhance Border Security and Restore Integrity to Our Immigration System for the Attorney General and the Secretary of Homeland Security 1–2 (Apr. 29, 2019) (modifying the asylum system by calling for a variety of proposed regulations); Proclamation No. 10,141, Ending Discriminatory Bans on Entry to the United States, 86 Fed. Reg. 7,005, 7,005–06 (Jan. 20, 2021) (addressing policies and practices from the Trump Administration that created "discriminatory bans"); Presidential Memorandum on Implementing Immediate Heightened Screening and Vetting of Applications for Visas and Other Immigration Benefits, Ensuring Enforcement of All Laws for Entry into the United States, and Increasing Transparency among Departments and Agencies of the Federal Government and for the American People for the Secretary of State[,] the Attorney General[, and] the Secretary of Homeland Security, 82 Fed. Reg. 16,279, 16,280 (Mar. 6, 2017) (calling for a stricter screening process for visas and other immigrant applications to prevent foreign nationals from entering the United States).

16. Harold J. Krent, *Presidential Control of Adjudication within the Executive Branch*, 65 Case W. Rsrv. L. Rev. 1083, 1103 (2015) (noting this in contrast to the way presidents influence rulemaking via executive order).

17. *See, e.g.*, Elena Kagan, *Presidential Administration*, 114 Harv. L. Rev. 2245, 2306 (2001).

18. *See, e.g.*, Exec. Order No. 12,988, 61 Fed. Reg. 4,729 (Feb. 5, 1996) (suggesting, in part, the incorporation of ACUS recommendations).

19. Exec. Order No. 13,924, 85 Fed. Reg. 31,353 (May 22, 2020).

Budget (OMB) issued a memorandum implementing this executive order, which included several criteria to reduce the consequences of investigations, enforcement actions, and adjudications on the regulated public.[20]

President Trump also produced an unusual executive order that sought to constrain the scope of discretionary adjudication practices. More specifically, this executive order eliminated the Office of Personnel Management's role in selecting ALJs and removed ALJs from the competitive service.[21] In doing so, President Trump sought "to place them more squarely within the constitutional appointments framework," which would have increased political appointees' and presidential influence over agency adjudication.[22]

Although President Biden rescinded many of his predecessor's executive orders shortly after taking office,[23] he also issued an executive order outlining policy, objectives, and strategies for furthering equity for underserved and marginalized communities in the United States.[24] More specifically, this executive order acknowledges that because progress in equity "requires a systematic approach to embedding fairness in decision-making processes, executive departments and agencies . . . must recognize and work to redress inequities in their policies

---

20. OMB Memorandum for the Heads of Executive Departments and Agencies, M-20-25, Implementation of Executive Order 13924 (June 9, 2020); *see also* Anand S. Raman & Darren M. Welch, *The Impact of Executive Order 13924 and Its Implementing OMB Memorandum on Administrative Enforcement*, SKADDEN (Dec. 1, 2020), https://www.skadden.com/insights/publications/2020/12/the-impact-of-executive-order-13924.

21. Exec. Order No. 13,843, 83 Fed. Reg. 32,755 (July 10, 2018) (exempting all ALJs appointed under 5 U.S.C. § 3105 from competitive civil selection); Memorandum from Dr. Jeff T.H. Pon, Dir., Off. of Pers. Mgmt., to Heads of Exec. Dep'ts and Agencies, Executive Order—Excepting Administrative Law Judges from the Competitive Service (July 10, 2018); Memorandum from the Solicitor Gen., U.S. Dep't of Just., to Agency Gen. Counsels, Guidance on Administrative Law Judges after *Lucia v. SEC* (S. Ct.) (July 2018) (instructing that all the ALJs and "similarly situated administrative judges" should be appointed under the Appointments Clause).

22. Bijal Shah, *The President's Fourth Branch?*, FORDHAM L. REV. (forthcoming).

23. *See* Exec. Order No. 14,018, 86 Fed. Reg. 11,855 (Mar. 1, 2021); Exec. Order No. 13,992, 86 Fed. Reg. 7,049 (Jan. 25, 2021).

24. *See* Bijal Shah, *Administrative Subordination*, U. CHI. L. REV. (forthcoming) [hereinafter Shah, *Administrative Subordination*]; Bijal Shah, *Deploying the Internal Separation of Powers against Racial Tyranny*, 116 NW. L. REV. ONLINE 244, 268 (2021).

and programs that serve as barriers to equal opportunity."[25] To better implement this order, OMB requested information seeking "input, information, and recommendations from a broad array of stakeholders in the public, private, advocacy, not-for-profit, and philanthropic sectors, including State, local, Tribal, and territorial areas."[26]

President Biden has also sought to strengthen the democratic process by designing and delivering "services in a manner that people of all abilities can navigate." More specifically, he issued an order calling for agencies to "continually improve their understanding of their customers, reduce administrative hurdles and paperwork burdens to minimize 'time taxes,' enhance transparency, create greater efficiencies across Government, and redesign compliance-oriented processes to improve customer experience and more directly meet the needs of the people of the United States."[27] Pursuant to these orders, several agencies have taken steps to reduce unnecessary burdens in adjudicative and other administrative processes.

25.22 Ex Parte Communications

The White House may seek to influence an individual agency adjudication through ex parte communications. An ex parte influence happens via oral or written communication made without proper notice to all parties and not on the public record, from an "interested person outside the agency" to a member of the agency, an ALJ, or an employee involved in the decision-making process.[28]

The president may not engage in ex parte communication with an ALJ presiding over a formal adjudication.[29] In addition, norms have developed limiting presidential involvement in informal adjudication in order to preserve the "integrity of government decision making." A 2021 memorandum to White House staff imposed explicit restrictions on contact by White House personnel with agencies regarding "adjudications, benefit determinations, investigations, litigation matters, and enforcement actions involving specific parties."[30] However, there is no per se prohibition on ex parte communications in informal

25. Exec. Order No. 13,985, 86 Fed. Reg. 7,009 (Jan. 25, 2021).
26. 86 Fed. Reg. 24,029 (May 5, 2021).
27. Exec. Order No. 14,058, 86 Fed. Reg. 71,357 (Dec. 16, 2021).
28. 5 U.S.C. §§ 551(14), 557(d)(1)(A).
29. Portland Audubon Soc'y v. Endangered Species Comm., 984 F.2d 1534, 1536 (9th Cir. 1993).
30. Memorandum from Dana Remus, Counsel to the President, on Prohibited Contacts with Agencies and Departments to White House Staff (July 21, 2021).

adjudication. As a result, presidential engagement in ex parte communication with an administrative adjudicator could negatively impact due process.[31]

25.3 INDIRECT EXECUTIVE OVERSIGHT AND CONTROL

"[T]he Supreme Court has limited the President's removal and (to some extent) appointment authority over" ALJs.[32] However, the president may nonetheless indirectly shape administrative adjudication via the appointment and removal of agency officials.

25.31 Appointment

The U.S. Supreme Court has begun to enable the president to exert growing influence over administrative adjudicators by expanding the category of adjudicators subject to political appointment and oversight.[33] More specifically, the Supreme Court declared in *Lucia v. Securities & Exchange Commission* that certain ALJs are "inferior officers"[34] subject to the Appointments Clause of the Constitution and implied in *United States v. Arthrex* that administrative adjudicators could even be characterized as principal officers under certain circumstances.[35] "*Lucia* and *Arthrex* together strengthen political power over adjudicators: *Lucia*, by necessitating the hiring of certain ALJs by the President or agency head [and] *Arthrex*, by expanding direct control over technical adjudications by an agency head."[36] This increase in the category of adjudicators subject to constitutional appointments has encouraged executive efforts to intensify presidential control over the selection and appointment of adjudicators, as noted earlier,[37] and

31. *Cf.* Pension Benefit Guarantee Corp. v. LTV Corp., 496 U.S. 633, 656 (1990).

32. Krent, *supra* note 16, at 1083.

33. Bijal Shah, *Expanding Presidential Influence on Agency Adjudication*, Regul. Rev. (July 23, 2021), https://www.theregreview.org/2021/07/23/shah-agency-adjudication/.

34. 138 S. Ct. 2044, 2055 (2018).

35. 141 S. Ct. 1970 (2021).

36. Shah, *supra* note 22.

37. See discussion of Trump executive order and related guidance, *supra* notes 21–25 and accompanying text; *see also* Alison Frankel, *In Confidential Memo to Agency GCs, DOJ Signals "Aggressive" Stand on Firing ALJs*, Reuters (July 23, 2018), https://www.reuters.com/article/us-otc-dojmemo/in-confidential-memo-to-agency-gcs-doj-signals-aggressive-stand-on-firing-aljs-idUSKBN1KD2BB. The

spurred opinions by appellate judges that signal that tenure protections for ALJs may be in jeopardy.[38]

As a result, the Supreme Court has allowed the president and his or her appointees to impose additional pressure on adjudicators to "make decisions according to the interests and views of political leadership."[39] Expanding political influence over the selection of agency adjudicators,[40] including preferences regarding the background of such adjudicators,[41] may allow for greater presidential impact on the outcomes of administrative adjudication, or at least for the "easier selection of ideologically-aligned appointees."[42] As a result, increasingly unconstrained political pressure may "imperil the impartiality that due process requires."[43]

25.32 Removal

Prior to the turn of the 21st century, the Court held that quasi-judicial officers could be insulated from the president by for-cause removal protections[44] and other structural protections.[45] This framework reflects

---

executive "order reasoned that, as 'illustrated by *Lucia*, at least some—and perhaps all—ALJs are "Officers of the United States" . . . subject to the Constitution's Appointments Clause.'" *Guidance on Administrative Law Judges after* Lucia v. SEC *(S. Ct.), July 2018*, *supra* note 11, at 1122.

38. Jarkesy v. Sec. & Exch. Comm'n, 34 F.4th 446 (5th Cir. 2022) (building on *Lucia* and *Free Enterprise Fund v. Public Co. Accounting Oversight Board*, 561 U.S. 477 (2010), to hold that for-cause removal protections for Securities and Exchange Commission ALJs are unconstitutional); Fleming v. U.S. Dep't of Agric., 987 F.3d 1093 (D.C. Cir. 2021) (Rao, J., concurring in part and dissenting in part) (finding that U.S. Department of Agriculture ALJs were invalidly appointed); Axon Enter., Inc. v. Fed Trade Comm'n, 986 F.3d 1173 (9th Cir. 2021) (cert. granted) (challenging for-cause removal protections for Federal Trade Commission ALJs).

39. Shah, *supra* note 22.

40. *See* David Hausman et al., *Executive Control of Agency Adjudication: Capacity, Selection, and Precedential Rulemaking*, 40 J. L. Econ. & Org. (forthcoming).

41. *See* Catherine Kim & Amy Semet, *An Empirical Study of Political Control over Immigration Adjudication*, 108 Geo. L.J. 579 (2020).

42. Hausman et al., *supra* note 40, at 29.

43. Kent Barnett, *Regulating Impartiality in Agency Adjudication*, 69 Duke L.J. 1695, 1695 (2020).

44. Humphrey's Ex'r v. United States., 295 U.S. 602, 632 (1935).

45. ALJs also have "impartiality protections, including separation of functions requirements, ex parte practice restrictions, and tenure status. These protections were upheld by the Supreme Court shortly after the APA was enacted." Paul R. Verkuil, *Presidential Administration, the Appointment of ALJs, and the Future of For Cause Protection*, 72 Admin. L. Rev. 461, 462 (2020) (citations omitted).

the view that the president has no direct constitutional authority or implied statutory authority to remove a "member of an adjudicatory body" at will.[46]

In many cases, "ALJs may be removed only for 'good cause,' and their removal must be reviewed by the independent Merit Systems Protection Board."[47] Even though ALJs lack lifetime tenure, they have only rarely been removed from office. As Paul Verkuil writes: "Indeed, it is not much more likely that a federal judge would be removed through impeachment than that an ALJ would be removed through statutory processes."[48]

However, some believe that "Article II [of the Constitution] limits Congress's ability to cocoon executive officers, including potentially agency adjudicators, from at-will removal."[49] Accordingly, the Supreme Court is poised to hear *Jarkesy v. Securities & Exchange Commission.*[50] In this case, the Fifth Circuit evaluated provisions governing the removal of administrative adjudicators. More specifically, the court held that certain ALJs must be removable without cause because they are sufficiently important to executing the laws that the Constitution requires that the president be able to exercise authority over their functions. If the Supreme Court allows the lower court's decision in *Jarkesy* to stand, "the threat of at-will termination would reduce ALJ adherence to due process and impartial decisionmaking that eschews political considerations."[51]

---

46. Wiener v. United States, 357 U.S. 349, 356 (1958). "[T]he authority of the President to direct the discretionary powers delegated to officials" is an "open question." Kevin M. Stack, *The President's Statutory Powers to Administer the Laws*, 106 COLUM. L. REV. 263, 274 (2006). The idea that the president may exercise "agency policymaking authority despite the delegation of that authority by Congress to agencies themselves" is "controversial." Bijal Shah, *Judicial Administration*, 11 U.C. IRVINE L. REV. 1119, 1128 (2021). Arguably, "[e]ven if the President has unfettered removal authority over the heads of non-independent agencies, it matters that this removal power does not imply the power to control decision making entrusted by law to agency heads." Robert V. Percival, *Who's in Charge? Does the President Have Directive Authority over Agency Regulatory Decisions?*, 79 FORDHAM L. REV. 2487, 2488 (2011).

47. *Guidance on Administrative Law Judges after* Lucia v. SEC *(S. Ct.), July 2018*, *supra* note 11, at 1120 (citing 5 U.S.C. § 7521(a)).

48. Verkuil, *supra* note 45, at 462.

49. Barnett, *supra* note 43, at 1695.

50. 34 F.4th 446 (5th Cir. 2022).

51. Shah, *supra* note 22.

25.4 POTENTIAL BEST PRACTICES

Experts have offered suggestions to temper presidential influence over agency adjudication. The president, charged with taking care that the laws be faithfully executed, should be permitted some control of the executive branch. However, as noted earlier, one of the perils of presidential influence on administrative adjudication is the potential loss of adjudicator independence, which can lead to compromises in impartiality and due process. Another concern is transparency in agency adjudication, which could be impacted by behind-the-scenes political influence. Congress, the courts, and the president himself or herself could play a role in limiting the impact of political pressure on administrative adjudication.

25.41 Congressional Actions

One way to manage these issues is for Congress to alter the placement of adjudicative authority within the executive branch in order to protect agency adjudication from presidential influence.[52] With respect to ALJs, "an independent corps of federal ALJs, who would no longer be officers of the agencies that employ them," might better ensure ALJ neutrality in the face of political pressure.[53] Congress might also strengthen civil service protections to ensure that ALJs are not "subject to adverse employment actions on the basis of their lawful exercise of discretion."[54] With respect to immigration removal adjudication, for example, "[o]ne possibility for recalibrating the balance between the competing goals of adjudicative independence and democratic accountability is to transfer all removal proceedings into a new Article I court, as many scholars and advocates have proposed."[55] Alternatively, Congress might reconsider limits to judicial review of agency adjudication.[56]

---

52. Bijal Shah, *Congress's Agency Coordination*, 103 MINN. L. REV. 1961, 2034 (2019).

53. Richard E. Levy & Robert L. Glicksman, *Restoring ALJ Independence*, 105 MINN. L. REV. 39, 40–41 (2020).

54. *See* Kim & Semet, *supra* note 41, at 636 (discussing non-ALJ immigration judges).

55. *Id.* at 631–32.

56. Bijal Shah, *A Critical Case against Administrative Functionalism*, OHIO STATE L.J. (forthcoming).

25.42 Judicial Actions

In addition, the judiciary can help ensure that presidential interests do not overwhelm administrative adjudication. For instance, the Supreme Court could specify criteria for determining the extent to which adjudicators are subject to political and presidential appointment. As to which criteria should render an adjudicator an officer, Justice Sotomayor offers a suggestion in her *Lucia* dissent: "To provide guidance to Congress and the Executive Branch, [the Court sh]ould hold that one requisite component is the ability to make final, binding decisions on behalf of the Government."[57] Without this authority, an ALJ would remain an employee that is not subject to the appointment by an agency head, per the requirements of the Appointments Clause of the Constitution. As to which criteria might render an officer principal, the Court should reinvigorate important precedent, *Edmond v. United States*, which dictates that an ALJ that has a supervisor is an inferior officer, at most.[58] If an ALJ is an inferior officer, then he or she is not subject to appointment by the president under the Appointments Clause. "[C]larifying these terms of political appointment could stave off some undesirable consequences of political influence on administrative adjudication. In addition, more precise guidance from the Supreme Court would assist the legislature in creating statutes establishing ALJ independence that the Court would be more likely to preserve."[59]

Finally, courts might also reevaluate the scope of *Chevron* deference to adjudicative decisions, which might discourage executive branch policymaking outside the more transparent and participatory notice-and-comment process.[60]

25.43 Executive Branch Actions

Finally, the president and senior agency officials can also take actions to depoliticize administrative adjudication. They could commit the executive branch to ALJ-corps standards that prioritize impartiality; this could be accomplished by promulgating executive orders and agency rules, which Kent Barnett calls "impartiality regulations," that

---

57. Lucia v. Sec. & Exch. Comm'n, 138 S. Ct. 2044, 2065 (2018) (Sotomayor, J., dissenting).

58. 520 U.S. 651 (1997).

59. Shah, *supra* note 22.

60. *See* Bijal Shah, *Statute-Focused Presidential Administration*, 90 Geo. Wash. L. Rev. 1165, 1244–48 (2022); Shoba Sivaprasad Wadhia & Christopher J. Walker, *The Case against* Chevron *Deference in Immigration Adjudication*, 70 Duke L.J. 1197 (2021) (making this argument regarding non-ALJ immigration judges).

concretize a merit-based appointment process, good-cause removal standards, and accompanying procedural protections from removal. Even if the Supreme Court ultimately finds that the separation of powers prevents Congress from requiring the executive branch to abide by such protections, agencies may adopt them on their own initiative.[61]

Scholarly recommendations on this topic were highlighted in a recent report to ACUS. These include the suggestion that "agencies employing ALJs should seek legal advice concerning . . . whether their ALJs have been appointed in a manner consistent with the Appointments Clause," select ALJs "'who are impartial and committed to the rule of law,'" establish "a screening panel and a separate interview panel to evaluate ALJ candidates," and "consider whether it would be beneficial to enhance transparency by publicly posting details of the procedures they will use to evaluate ALJ candidates."[62] More generally, the president should encourage adjudicators to employ processes that value fairness and equity as means to bolster due process, particularly in the areas of immigration and national security.[63] At the very least, White House involvement in policymaking by adjudication should remain more limited than White House involvement in agency rulemaking,[64] which would allow administrative adjudication to be relatively impartial and nonpartisan.

---

61. Barnett, *supra* note 43.

62. Jack M. Beermann & Jennifer L. Mascott, ACUS, Research Report on Federal Agency ALJ Hiring after Lucia and Executive Order 13843 (2019); *see also* Administrative Conference Recommendation 2019-2, Agency Recruitment and Selection of Administrative Law Judges, 84 Fed. Reg. 38,930 (Aug. 8, 2019).

63. *See* Shah, *Administrative Subordination*, *supra* note 24.

64. *See* Percival, *supra* note 46, at 2538; Jennifer Nou, *Agency Self-Insulation under Presidential Review*, 126 Harv. L. Rev. 1755, 1783 (2013); Nina A. Mendelson & Jonathan B. Wiener, *Responding to Agency Avoidance of OIRA*, 37 Harv. J. L. & Pub. Pol'y 447, 509 (2014).

Chapter 26
Congressional Oversight

Jeremy S. Graboyes

26.1 CHAPTER OVERVIEW

While there is frequently congressional interest in the activities of agency adjudicative programs, the reasons for and level of interest can vary considerably. Members of Congress—or their staffs—may take a significant interest in the operation or performance of high-volume programs that affect large numbers of constituents, such as the Internal Revenue Service (IRS) and benefits programs administered by the Social Security Administration (SSA) and Department of Veterans Affairs (VA). Members may take an interest in the substantive outcomes reached by regulatory agencies in cases that disproportionately affect their constituencies. Members of Congress also have their own policy and political interests, of course, and may take an interest in programs that implement related statutes or individual cases decided under them. Aside from their statutory origins, other programs encounter little ongoing congressional interest.

Congressional oversight is the "review, monitoring, and supervision of the executive and the implementation of public policy."[1] Oversight is often said to take two forms: "police-patrol" and "fire-alarm" oversight. Police-patrol oversight involves continuous monitoring of agency actions. But police patrol is costly and time-consuming. It also requires access to reliable information about agency actions and the capacity to evaluate it.[2] Although Congress can take action when problems "emerge out of the mist," as Professor Jeff Lubbers put it, the problem with many adjudicative programs is that there is often "too much mist."[3] Compared with other agency decision-making like notice-and-comment rulemaking, adjudication often involves large numbers of decisions each year made in a fashion that can be highly decentralized and, to the outsider, haphazard.

Often more practicable, especially when it comes to larger programs, is fire-alarm oversight. Through fire-alarm oversight, Congress establishes "a system of rules, procedures, and informal practices that enable individual citizens and organized interest groups to examine administrative decisions . . . , to charge executive agencies with violating congressional goals, and to seek remedies from agencies, courts, and Congress itself."[4] Fire-alarm oversight, unlike police-patrol oversight, is reactive. But it is a rational response to the institutional constraints that congressional actors face and can be marshalled to oversee the largest adjudicative programs.[5]

Congressional actors—including Congress as a body, committees, individual members, congressional staff, and legislative branch agencies like the Government Accountability Office (GAO)—have many hard and soft powers at their disposal that can be used to oversee executive

---

1. Ben Wilhelm et al., Cong. Rsch. Serv., RL30240, Congressional Oversight Manual (2022).

2. Matthew McCubbins & Thomas Schwartz, *Congressional Oversight Overlooked: Police Patrols versus Fire Alarms*, 28 Am. J. Pol. Sci. 165, 165–66 (1984).

3. Jeffrey S. Lubbers, *Management of Federal Agency Adjudication*, 12 J. Nat'l Ass'n Admin. L. Judges 112, 142 (1992).

4. McCubbins & Schwartz, *supra* note 2, at 166.

5. Jonah B. Gelbach & David Marcus, *Rethinking Judicial Review of High Volume Agency Adjudication*, 96 Tex. L. Rev. 1097, 1131–32 (2018).

branch decision-making.[6] Each has its benefits and challenges in terms of reviewing, monitoring, and supervising administrative adjudication, and some are more prevalent than others. This chapter examines their application to federal adjudicative programs, focusing on legislation (section 26.2), actions regarding executive branch personnel (section 26.3), committee activities (section 26.4), actions by individual members or their staffs (section 26.5), and audits (section 26.6).

But Congress's oversight authority is not unlimited. Under the U.S. Supreme Court's separation-of-powers jurisprudence, for example, Congress may not reserve for itself a role in the removal of executive branch officials who perform adjudicative functions.[7] Nor can Congress establish a process to legislatively veto a decision made by an agency in the adjudication of a case.[8]

26.2 LEGISLATION

Congress can use statutes in different ways to oversee the executive branch. Through organic and enabling statutes (section 26.21), Congress sets substantive policy, organizes and reorganizes the executive establishment, and establishes procedures. Through authorizations and appropriations statutes (section 26.22), Congress can specify what agencies do, how much funding they will receive, and how funds will be spent. Congress also imposes reporting or publication requirements on agencies (section 26.23), which provides congressional and nongovernmental actors easier access to information about agencies' actions, operation, and performance. And using the process set forth in the Congressional Review Act (CRA), Congress can evaluate and quickly disapprove agency rules (section 26.24).

26.21 Organic and Enabling Statutes

Agencies, and the adjudicative programs they administer, are creatures of statute, and the statutes that create them establish their basic institutional and procedural characteristics. Consciously or not, Congress makes several decisions when it establishes a program

6. Christopher M. Davis et al., Cong. Rsch. Serv., RL30240, Congressional Oversight Manual (2021); Todd Garvey & Daniel J. Sheffner, Cong. Rsch. Serv., R45442, Congress's Authority to Influence and Control Executive Branch Agencies (2021); Jack M. Beermann, *Congressional Administration*, 43 San Diego L. Rev. 61 (2006).

7. *Cf.* Bowsher v. Synar, 478 U.S. 714 (1986).

8. Immigr. & Naturalization Serv. v. Chadha, 462 U.S. 919 (1983).

involving adjudication. Most notably to administrative lawyers, Congress decides whether to subject decision-making to the formal-adjudication provisions of the Administrative Procedure Act (APA). More fundamentally, Congress determines the specificity with which to prescribe institutional and procedural requirements. Some statutes include detailed requirements governing procedure and evidence, management of adjudicators, representation of parties, and other matters. Others give executive branch officials significant leeway to craft policies they deem suitable. Compare the laws governing benefits adjudication by the VA, which set forth detailed procedural requirements, and those governing adjudication by SSA, which are far less constraining. Statutes also structure judicial review of agency orders, inviting courts to take part in overseeing adjudication (see Chapter 27).

Legislation is, in many ways, an ongoing discourse. Bills are regularly introduced that would alter or supplement the institutional and procedural contours for a particular adjudicative program. Hearings may be held and reports prepared (section 26.4), and, in some cases, a bill becomes law. The procedural requirements for adjudication by the VA and SSA, for example, have been amended many times. The reasons offered for legislative changes are varied and reflect the range of values and goals described in Chapter 4, such as promoting fairness and due process, accuracy, consistency, timeliness, efficiency, accessibility, and program integrity.

26.22 Authorization and Appropriations

Adjudication costs money. All those values and goals described in Chapter 4—fairness, accuracy, efficiency, and so on—are, in large measure, dependent upon the availability of sufficient resources. Money can come from sources including tax revenue, user fees, or some combination thereof. The Constitution provides that "[n]o Money shall be drawn from the Treasury, but in Consequence of Appropriations made by Law."[9] Through its power of the purse, Congress manages and can, if it chooses, exercise considerable oversight over adjudicative programs.

As a general matter, Congress determines the level of funding available to agencies and agency subcomponents, including those that administer adjudicative programs. Because the decision to appropriate a particular sum of money can be one of great consequence for a program's operation and performance, agencies—some more than

9. U.S. CONST. art. I, § 9, cl. 7.

others—expend time and effort preparing detailed budget requests covering costs associated with administering and managing adjudicative programs (e.g., staffing, technology, office space). Agency officials may participate in appropriations hearings and lobby members of Congress and their staffs to secure adequate funding. Especially when it comes to high-volume programs, outside organizations may also lobby Congress to provide additional funding.

Congress sometimes specifies how an agency must spend appropriated funds—or, more controversially, how it may not.[10] Some statutes require that funds be used for a particular adjudication-related purpose. The 2017 Consolidated Appropriations Act, for example, specified that a certain portion of funds should "be used for activities to address the hearing backlog" at SSA.[11] And recent appropriations laws have required that the Executive Office for Immigration Review (EOIR) make certain funds "available for services and activities provided by the Legal Orientation Program."[12]

Alternatively, a provision might prohibit an agency from using appropriated funds for a particular adjudication-related purpose. Legislators have proposed riders, for example, that would prevent EOIR from using funds "to implement case performance numeric metrics that are linked to performance evaluations for individual immigration judges" and prevent SSA from finalizing a then-proposed rule entitled "Hearings Held by Administrative Appeals Judges of the Appeals Council."[13]

26.23 Reporting and Publication Requirements

Agencies are subject to many generally applicable reporting and publication requirements that can, in addition to promoting transparency, support ongoing police-patrol oversight by Congress and provide outside groups information needed to identify problems. As discussed in Chapter 28, a lot of information about adjudicative programs has been made publicly available under such requirements, for example through rules and orders disclosed under the Freedom of Information Act and system of records notices published under the Privacy Act.

---

10. *Cf.* Sean M. Stiff, Cong. Rsch. Serv., R46417, Congress's Power over Appropriations: Constitutional and Statutory Provisions 57–61 (2020).

11. Pub. L. No. 115-31, 131 Stat. 135, 559 (2017).

12. Pub. L. No. 177-164 (2022).

13. H.R. 8256, 117th Cong. (2022).

Congress can also direct specific agencies to submit reports or provide information related to the operation or performance of specific adjudicative programs. Reporting requirements can take a number of forms, including "notifications of actions or decisions," "descriptive reports that summarize actions taken or provide other factual information," "plans to accomplish particular goals," and "studies or evaluations relating to a specific problem or concern."[14] Reporting requirements occasionally relate to administrative adjudication, such as the backlog in adjudicating security clearance applications or permitting procedures.

26.24 Congressional Review Act

The CRA establishes an expedited legislative process for disapproving agency rules. A rule that is disapproved may not take effect or continue in effect, and no rule that is "substantially the same" as a disapproved rule may be issued thereafter absent statutory authorization. Bills are periodically introduced to disapprove a rule setting forth procedures for adjudication. A bill was introduced in 2021, for example, to disapprove the SSA rule regarding hearings held by the agency's Appeals Council discussed in section 26.22.[15] But Congress has so far voted to disapprove only one related to adjudicative procedures.[16]

The CRA applies only to "rules" and requires that an agency submit a "rule" to Congress and GAO before it can take effect.[17] Recall from Chapter 1 that the APA defines a "rule" broadly as any "agency statement of general or particular applicability."[18] Adjudicative procedures affecting the public are typically outlined in legislative rules, which are subject to the CRA. But adjudicative policies can appear elsewhere, including in guidance documents, administrative manuals, and precedents. In 2018, a congressperson requested GAO's opinion on whether two sections of SSA's *Hearings, Appeals, and Litigation Law (HALLEX) Manual* were rules for CRA purposes. The sections concerned adjudicators' use of information from social media networks and other online sources when adjudicating claims for disability benefits. GAO concluded that these sections were not subject to review

---

14. William T. Egar, Cong. Rsch. Serv., R46357, Congressionally Mandated Reports: Overview and Considerations for Congress 1–2 (2020).
15. *See, e.g.*, H.R.J. Res. 38, 117th Cong. (2021).
16. Pub. L. No. 117-22, 135 Stat. 294 (2021) (disapproving an Equal Employment Opportunity Commission rule on conciliation).
17. 5 U.S.C. § 801(a)(1)(A).
18. *Id.* § 551(4).

under the CRA "because they are rules of agency procedure or practice that do not substantially affect claimants' rights or obligations."[19]

26.3 APPOINTMENT AND REMOVAL

26.31 Appointment

The Constitution's Appointments Clause has been interpreted to distinguish between three kinds of executive branch personnel besides the president: principal officers, inferior officers, and employees. Some officials involved in agency adjudication—either as managers (e.g., agency heads) or as decision-makers in individual cases (e.g., members of several independent regulatory agencies)—are clearly principal officers. The president must appoint nominees to those positions and the Senate must advise on and consent to their appointment.

As Supreme Court opinions indicate, many agency officials involved in adjudication are inferior officers, including administrative law judges (ALJs) and some other administrative judges (see Chapter 9). Congress can require that the president appoint and the Senate confirm these officials. Alternatively, Congress can, by law, delegate their appointment to the president, an agency head, or the courts. Employees can be appointed in any manner that the political branches see fit, from Senate confirmation (rare) to civil service hiring (common).

Senate confirmation offers senators an opportunity to take steps to ensure that a nominee to a position will responsibly carry out any assigned adjudicative functions. The extent to which Senate vetting focuses on adjudication will, of course, depend on the position. Adjudication figures more prominently in the duties of some Senate-confirmed officials, such as the chair of the Board of Veterans' Appeals (BVA), than others. Also relevant is the degree to which there are ongoing questions or concerns about a particular adjudicative program. Backlogs due to a lack of a quorum at the Merit Systems Protection Board (MSPB) dominated discussions about the agency between 2017 and 2022, for example, and backlog-reduction strategies featured in the confirmation of nominated agency members. Similarly, the nominee for director of the U.S. Patent and Trademark Office was questioned

19. GAO, B-329926, Social Security Administration: Applicability of the Congressional Review Act to Sections of the Hearings, Appeals, and Litigation Law (HALLEX) Manual (2018).

about the system for adjudicating patentability following the Supreme Court's decision in *United States v. Arthrex*.[20]

But there are also downsides to requiring presidential appointment and Senate advice and consent for too many positions. These processes take scarce time and resources, and a process requiring extensive vetting for too many nominees has been blamed for delays and resulting widespread vacancies in high-level agency positions.[21] It would be impractical for the Senate to reliably vet and confirm thousands of adjudicators across the government and other high-level officials involved in adjudication.[22]

An alternative, at least for nonprincipal officers, is for Congress to set forth a process or criteria for selecting and appointing adjudicative personnel. That is what Congress did in the APA by establishing a competitive, merit-based process for selecting ALJs,[23] but the constitutionality of that process is in question and has been abandoned in practice.[24] Another example is the requirement that administrative patent judges "be persons of competent legal knowledge and scientific ability."[25] Congress might also delegate responsibility for appointing adjudicative personnel to a Senate-confirmed position or an independent body that the Senate could more closely vet and monitor.

26.32 Removal

Congress can remove executive branch officials from office through impeachment and conviction, though that is highly improbable. Aside from four presidential impeachments, the only executive branch officials who have ever been seriously investigated for impeachment were the vice president in 1826 and the Secretary of War in 1876. Where there are concerns about an official's performance of adjudicative functions, soft power methods (e.g., questioning at a public hearing, publication of audit reports, budget threats) are infinitely likelier.

Congress has historically been more interested in preventing the removal of adjudicative personnel for political reasons, reasons of policy disagreement, or other reasons that might cast into question

20. 141 S. Ct. 1970 (2021).

21. Administrative Conference Recommendation 2019-7, Acting Agency Officials and Delegations of Authority, 84 Fed. Reg. 71,352 (Dec. 27, 2019).

22. Anne Joseph O'Connell, *Actings*, 120 Colum. L. Rev. 613, 726–27 (2020).

23. 5 U.S.C. § 5372.

24. Lucia v. Sec. & Exch. Comm'n, 138 S. Ct. 2044 (2018); Exec. Order No. 13,843, 83 Fed. Reg. 32,755 (July 13, 2018).

25. 35 U.S.C. § 6(a).

the fairness and integrity of agency adjudication. Congress cannot, as a constitutional matter, reserve to itself any role in the process for removing adjudicative personnel.[26] As an alternative, Congress has imposed requirements on the process for removing some adjudicative personnel. For example, members of most independent regulatory agencies, who often participate in deciding appeals in individual cases and may craft policy through case-by-case adjudication, can only be removed for cause. And the APA establishes an elaborate process for removing ALJs from office,[27] though that process has been called into constitutional question.[28] Reason-giving and other procedural requirements may provide other options to disincentivize executive branch officials from improperly removing adjudicative personnel.[29]

26.4 COMMITTEE TOOLS

26.41 Hearings

Congressional committees—some more than others—periodically hold hearings related to agency adjudication. Hearings regarding the ongoing operation and performance of high-volume programs are particularly common, as are hearings associated with funding and bills that would govern such programs. By way of example, committee hearings since 2012 have included:

- *Examining Due Process in [SSA] Administrative Hearings*
- *VA Appeals Program: Examining the State of Modernization Efforts*
- *Strengthening and Reforming America's Immigration Court System*
- *Safeguarding the Integrity of the Immigration Benefits Adjudication Process*
- *Creating a More Efficient and Level Playing Field: Audit and Appeals Issues in Medicare*
- *The Patent Trial and Appeal Board and the Appointments Clause: Implications of Recent Court Decisions*

---

26. *Cf.* Bowsher v. Synar, 478 U.S. 714 (1986).

27. 5 U.S.C. § 7521.

28. *See* Fleming v. U.S. Dep't of Agric., 987 F.3d 1093, 1106–24 (D.C. Cir. 2021) (Rao, J., dissenting).

29. *See* Aaron L. Nielson & Christopher J. Walker, *Congress's Anti-Removal Power*, 76 VAND. L. REV. 1 (2023).

26.42 Committee Reports

Congressional committees produce reports accompanying proposed legislation, including appropriations bills. Committees frequently insert language into these reports to communicate expectations for agency decision-making, influence agency action, or request an update on agency operations. Although agencies are not legally bound to comply with statements in committee reports, they are generally incentivized to do so to maintain good congressional relations and avoid political consequences.[30] Consider a few examples from the House Appropriations Committee's report for the Consolidated Appropriations Act, 2021:

- "Within the amount provided, the agreement expects EOIR to expedite efforts to implement its new electronic case management system . . . ."
- "EOIR is directed to update its policy memorandum on the use of [video teleconferencing], so as to ensure clear and consistent guidelines are followed in all adjudication settings."
- "[U.S. Citizenship and Immigration Services (USCIS)] is expected to adjudicate citizenship and other applications in a timely manner. Not later than 90 days after the date of enactment of this Act, USCIS shall provide to the Committees a report on measures implemented to promptly reduce processing delays."
- "The Committee consider the Notice of Proposed Rulemaking (NPRM) 'Hearings Held by Administrative Appeals Judges of the Appeals Council' [discussed in sections 26.22 and 26.24] . . . to be an unjustified erosion of due process . . . [and] strongly urges SSA to immediately withdraw this proposed rule."
- "The Committee directs the Administration to develop and submit . . . a report on hiring processes, to include an explanation of the process, qualification standards, and criteria used to recruit, evaluate and hire ALJs."[31]

Committees also produce reports as part of oversight or investigative activities. These reports may lay the groundwork for future legislation or other actions discussed throughout this chapter. Committees have prepared many studies over the years related to specific administrative

30. Garvey & Sheffner, *supra* note 6, at 36–38.
31. Pub. L. No. 116-260 (2019).

adjudication programs, the management of administrative adjudicators, and other topics discussed throughout this guide.

26.5 ACTIONS BY INDIVIDUAL MEMBERS

26.51 Involvement in Individual Cases

The APA provides that an "interested person" may participate in an agency proceeding "[s]o far as the orderly conduct of public business permits."[32] The term "interested person" has been defined broadly and almost certainly includes at least those members of Congress who have "a special interest in the matter regulated."[33] Like other interested persons, members of Congress may be subject to legal requirements such as prohibitions on ex parte communications.

But members of Congress are different from other interested persons given their participation in legislative activities affecting agencies. The involvement of legislative branch actors in an individual case may raise concerns that an adjudicator will be influenced or pressured to decide a case in a particular way.

It is established that legislative pressure can violate the due process rights of aggrieved parties.[34] Courts generally consider whether due process was denied in the circumstances of the particular case.[35] In doing so, they might apply the three-factor balancing test of *Mathews v. Eldridge* (Chapter 15). Where the Due Process Clause does not apply, it is less clear whether legislative pressure requires a reviewing

32. 5 U.S.C. § 555(b).

33. H.R. Rep. No. 94-880, pt. 1, at 19–20 (1976), *reprinted in* 1976 U.S.C.C.A.N. 2183.

34. Pillsbury Co. v. Fed. Trade Comm'n, 354 F.2d 952, 964 (5th Cir. 1966); Koniag, Inc. v. Andrus, 580 F.2d 601, 610–11 (D.C. Cir. 1978); *see also* Garvey & Sheffner, *supra* note 6; Morton Rosenberg & Jack H. Maskell, Cong. Rsch. Serv., RL32113, Congressional Intervention in the Administrative Process: Legal and Ethical Considerations 3–22 (2003); Jamelle C. Sharpe, *Judging Congressional Oversight*, 65 Admin. L. Rev. 183, 197–02 (2013).

35. *See* Aera Energy, LLC v. Salazar, 642 F.3d 212 (D.C. Cir. 2011); Lichoulas v. Fed. Energy Regul. Comm'n, 606 F.3d 769, 779–80 (D.C. Cir. 2010); Esso Standard Oil Co. v. Lopez-Feytes, 522 F.3d 136, 148 (1st Cir. 2009); ATX, Inc. v. U.S. Dep't of Transp., 41 F.3d 1522, 1529–30 (D.C. Cir. 1994); Monieson v. Commodity Futures Trading Comm'n, 996 F.2d 852, 865 (7th Cir. 1993); DCP Farms v. Yeutter, 957 F.2d 1183, 1187–88 (5th Cir. 1992); Power Auth. of N.Y. v. Fed. Energy Regul. Comm'n, 743 F.2d 93, 109–10 (2d Cir. 1984); Am. Pub. Gas Ass'n v. Fed. Power Comm'n, 567 F.2d 1016, 1067–71 (D.C. Cir. 1977); Gulf Oil Corp. v. Fed. Power Comm'n, 563 F.2d 588, 610–12 (3d Cir. 1977); *Koniag*, 580 F.2d at 610.

court to reverse agency action. Courts tread lightly in this area because congressional interference may be a form of legislative oversight.

Congressional pressure might also cause an agency to consider an irrelevant factor, which could render its decision arbitrary and capricious.[36] However, courts appear cautious in applying this standard. They are concerned that a rigid application of the standard would interfere with legitimate congressional oversight or impair agency flexibility in dealing with Congress.[37]

26.52 Inquiries about Individual Cases

Members of Congress frequently send letters to agencies inquiring about the status of individual cases, typically in response to a constituent's request.[38] Such inquiries rarely pose serious legal questions because "requests for status reports" are not typically considered ex parte communications.[39] But these inquiries do impose practical costs on agencies, and agencies have occasionally been called to task for failing to respond to them in a timely manner.[40]

Some agencies that receive a high volume of congressional inquiries, such as SSA and the IRS, have developed specific policies for handling them.[41] Some agencies even prioritize processing cases in which there is congressional interest, though that raises questions of fairness and efficiency. Should some cases be prioritized over others based on whether a party took the time to contact his or her congressperson? And what are the effects of such prioritization on efficient case management?[42]

---

36. D.C. Fed'n of Civic Ass'ns v. Volpe, 459 F.2d 1231, 1245–49 (D.C. Cir. 197).

37. *ATX, Inc.*, 41 F.3d at 1528; *DCP Farms*, 957 F.2d at 1188; Chemung Cnty. v. Dole, 804 F.2d 216, 222 (2d Cir. 1986); Peter Kiewit Sons' Co. v. U.S. Army Corps of Eng'rs, 714 F.2d 163 (D.C. Cir. 1983); Sokaogon Chippewa Cmty. v. Babbitt, 929 F. Supp. 1165, 1173–81 (W.D. Wis. 1996).

38. Sarah J. Eckman, Cong. Rsch. Serv., R44726, Constituent Services: Overview and Resources 1–3 (2017).

39. *See* 5 U.S.C. § 551(14).

40. *Trials in Transparency: An Analysis of VA Cooperation with Congress in Meetings Its Oversight Responsibilities on Behalf of Veterans: Hearing before the H. Comm. on Veterans' Affs.*, 113th Cong. (2013).

41. *See, e.g.*, SSA, Hearings, Appeals, and Litigation Law (HALLEX) Manual ch. I-1-6; IRS, Internal Revenue Manual § 11.3.4.

42. *Cf.* Andy Grewal, *Lobbying the Tax Court*, Yale J. on Regul.: Notice & Comment (Dec. 31, 2021), https://www.yalejreg.com/nc/lobbying-the-tax-court/.

26.53 General Communications with Agencies

There are many ways in which members of Congress can provide input to agencies on matters of adjudicative policy and the operation and performance of adjudicative programs. Input can take place publicly when, for example, members of Congress issue press releases, make statements during committee meetings or floor sessions, or send letters to agency officials (which are often publicized). Members can also submit comments in response to NPRMs. For example, the chairs and ranking members of several Senate committees and subcommittees submitted comments in response to the SSA NPRM regarding hearings held by the agency's Appeals Council. Input can also take place privately. Congressional staff frequently correspond and meet with agency congressional liaisons.

Input need not be a one-way street. To more effectively oversee federal agency adjudication, members of Congress or their staffs request input from executive branch officials and members of the public to learn more about problems and potential solutions related to the operation or performance of adjudicative programs. It is well documented, for example, that agencies can be heavily involved in legislative drafting. Indeed, the Administrative Conference of the United States (ACUS) has recommended that congressional committees and members "aim to reach out to agencies for technical assistance early in the legislative drafting process."[43]

26.54 Study or Audit Requests

Congressional committees, subcommittees, and members of Congress can request that GAO prepare an audit report.[44] Members of Congress have sometimes requested reports on the operation or performance of particular adjudicative programs (section 26.6). Members of Congress may also request that an agency or inspector general undertake, or contract with an independent entity such as ACUS or the National Academy of Public Administration to undertake, a study related to the operation or performance of a particular adjudicative program. After Congress transferred responsibility for conducting Medicare hearings from SSA to the Office of Medicare Hearings and Appeals (OMHA)

---

43. Administrative Conference Recommendation 2015-2, Technical Assistance by Federal Agencies in the Legislative Process, 80 Fed. Reg. 78,161 (Dec. 16, 2015); *see also* Christopher J. Walker, *Legislating in the Shadows*, 165 U. Pa. L. Rev. 1377, 1382–96 (2017).

44. GAO, GAO-17-767G, GAO's Congressional Protocols (2017).

in the Department of Health and Human Services (HHS), for example, members requested that HHS's inspector general evaluate OMHA's use of telephone and video hearings and case processing times.[45] Although individual members of Congress cannot legally require an agency to undertake such action, agencies may decide to undertake the study to maintain good congressional relations.

26.6 AUDITS

Recognizing its limited institutional capacity to oversee large government bureaucracies, Congress has established "audit bureaucracies," most notably GAO within the legislative branch and inspector general offices attached to executive branch agencies. Committees and members often ask GAO to investigate matters of interest, and GAO and inspectors general are empowered to audit how agencies implement and administer federal programs.[46]

Many GAO reports have, over the years, addressed federal adjudicative programs, especially high-volume programs such as those administered by SSA, EOIR, and BVA. Topics they addressed include backlogs, timeliness, decisional quality, case management, and technology use. Reports typically conclude with recommendations for agency or congressional action, and agencies are typically offered an opportunity to respond publicly.

Inspectors general also regularly audit and publish reports related to the operation and performance of adjudicative programs.

---

45. Off. of Inspector Gen., HHS, OEI-02-06-00110, Medicare Administrative Law Judge Hearings: Early Implementation, 2005–2006 (2008).

46. Mariano-Florentino Cuéllar, *Auditing Executive Discretion*, 82 Notre Dame L. Rev. 227, 256, 290–98 (2006).

Chapter 27
Judicial Review and Oversight

Jeremy S. Graboyes

27.1 CHAPTER OVERVIEW

Like actors in other branches of government, the courts play a unique and critical role in federal administrative adjudication, reviewing individual agency decisions and, in so doing, overseeing aspects of the structure, function, and performance of whole adjudicative systems. The role played by courts in administrative adjudication is, by now, so entrenched that most people take it for granted; the absence of an opportunity for judicial review is now seen as the rare exception to a general rule of reviewability. That has not always been the case, however, and that history can be instructive.

This chapter begins by tracing the historical development of the primary model of judicial review—the appellate review model (section 27.2)—before examining the institutional characteristics of courts that determine their effectiveness in reviewing agency adjudicative orders and overseeing agency adjudicative systems (section 27.3). The final two sections address the practice and effects of judicial review. Section 27.4 provides an overview of how courts review decisions rendered in individual adjudications. Section 27.5 examines the role courts play in overseeing the structure, quality, timeliness, and procedures of agency adjudicative systems.

27.2 HISTORICAL DEVELOPMENT OF THE APPELLATE REVIEW MODEL

Nowhere does the Constitution provide for judicial review of executive branch action. The province of the courts is the "judicial power of the United States," which extends to certain enumerated categories of cases and controversies. Although that list includes "controversies to which the United States shall be a party," the courts have long interpreted the Constitution to retain the English common-law doctrine of sovereign immunity, under which a government may not be sued in its own courts without its consent.[1]

Judicial review of executive branch action has existed in some form since at least *Marbury v. Madison*,[2] but it has not always looked the same. It was not until the 20th century that the phenomenon of "judicial review" emerged as a cohesive concept. Before then, courts relied on a range of legal and later equitable grounds to justify review of administrative actions. The result was that judicial review was less pervasive and more haphazard. The nature and form of judicial review was often specific to particular actions. Private parties might bring a tort action against executive branch officers for acting outside their authority or violating a nondiscretionary legal duty, for example, or they might petition a court for a writ of mandamus or habeas corpus. Review could be robust. In cases where courts found they had jurisdiction to review executive branch actions, they often held trials, took evidence, and reached their own independent factual findings and legal conclusions—what today we would call de novo review.[3]

The modern concept of judicial review developed alongside the development of the modern administrative state in the late 19th and early 20th centuries. The cause of the shift, according to Thomas Merrill, was political wrangling over the era's most significant regulatory

---

1. *See, e.g.*, United States v. Lee, 106 U.S. 196, 226–28 (1882); *see generally* Vicki C. Jackson, *Suing the Federal Government: Sovereignty, Immunity, and Judicial Independence*, 35 GEO. WASH. INT'L L. REV. 521 (2003).

2. 5 U.S. 137 (1803); *see also* Thomas W. Merrill, Marbury v. Madison *as the First Great Administrative Law Decision*, 37 J. MARSHALL L. REV. 481 (2004).

3. Thomas W. Merrill, *Article III, Agency Adjudication, and the Origins of the Appellate Review Model of Administrative Law*, 111 COLUM. L. REV. 939 (2011); Jerry L. Mashaw, *Recovering American Administrative Law: Federalism Foundations, 1787–1801*, 115 YALE L.J. 1256 (2006); Jerry L. Mashaw, *Rethinking Judicial Review of Administrative Action: A Nineteenth-Century Perspective*, 32 CARDOZO L. REV. 2241 (2011).

agency: the Interstate Commerce Commission (ICC). Congress created the ICC in 1887 to regulate the railroads, primarily to ensure fair rates and eliminate rate discrimination. The new ICC set out to tame shipping rates, and the railroads promptly filed suit challenging its authority. In reviewing ICC actions, courts conducted trials, gathered new evidence, and exercised independent judgment on questions of fact and law. The U.S. Supreme Court upheld this approach.[4] (Justice Harlan, dissenting, proclaimed that the Court had gone "far to make [the] commission a useless body for all practical purposes.")

By the early 20th century, "the federal system of regulation of railroads centered on the ICC was widely perceived to be broken, and the U.S. Supreme Court was widely identified as the culprit which had brought it down." ICC proceedings took a long time, and the need to relitigate them caused proceedings to drag on longer. On judicial review, courts might substitute their judgment for the ICC's. The judicial branch "had become the archenemy of the forces of populism," and members of Congress and President Theodore Roosevelt sought to expand the ICC's ratemaking power and curtail the courts' authority to review ICC decisions.[5]

The result, in 1906, was the Hepburn Act. The Hepburn Act made several big changes. ICC decisions would henceforth be self-executing, taking effect 30 days after they were issued unless a railroad could persuade a court to enter a preliminary injunction before it took effect. Members of Congress spent months debating whether the standard of review should be "narrow" or "broad," but, unable to reach a consensus, they ultimately left the standard unaddressed.[6]

Facing political blowback, the Court beat a hasty retreat. It began deferring to agency findings on factual questions. It emphasized that agency decisions should be reversed only for clear and unmistakable error or manifest unreasonableness. The Court still claimed constitutional power to review the legality of executive branch actions, but it emphasized that courts may not "under the guise of exerting judicial power, usurp merely administrative functions by setting aside a lawful administrative order upon our conception as to whether the administrative order has been wisely exercised."[7] In Professor Merrill's telling, "the Court, facing a political crisis to its own authority, looked into

4. Interstate Com. Comm'n v. Ala. Midland Ry. Co., 168 U.S. 144 (1897).
5. Merrill, *supra* note 3.
6. *Id.*
7. Interstate Com. Comm'n v. Ill. Cent. R.R. Co., 215 U.S. 452, 470 (1910).

the doctrinal tool bag for something that would permit it to back off without losing face."[8]

The result was a model that, given its resemblance to the relationship between trial and appellate courts, became known as the "appellate review model." It grew entrenched through the 1910s and 1920s, becoming the predominant model by 1932, when the Supreme Court decided *Crowell v. Benson* (see Chapters 3 and 6).[9] *Crowell* solidified the appellate review model. In 1946, the Administrative Procedure Act (APA) codified the appellate review model as the default rule for judicial review of agency action.[10]

27.3 THE ROLE OF JUDICIAL REVIEW IN AGENCY ADJUDICATION

In determining what role the courts should play in overseeing agency adjudication, it is important to start by considering the judiciary's function in the constitutional system of checks and balances.[11] It is equally important to consider normative questions about the comparative advantages and disadvantages of judicial review as a means of supervising the executive branch and practical questions about courts' capacity to do so. Many scholars have addressed these questions, and there is an extensive literature analyzing the costs and benefits of external (often court-focused) administrative law versus internal (agency-driven) administrative law.[12] For present purposes, a few observations will suffice.

---

8. Merrill, *supra* note 3, at 963.
9. 285 U.S. 22 (1932).
10. 5 U.S.C. §§ 701–706.
11. U.S. CONST. art. III.
12. *See, e.g.*, JERRY L. MASHAW, BUREAUCRATIC JUSTICE (1983); Harold H. Bruff, *Coordinating Judicial Review in Administrative Law*, 39 UCLA L. REV. 1193 (1992); David Ames et al., *Due Process and Mass Adjudication: Crisis and Reform*, 72 STAN. L. REV. 1, 20–27 (2020); Jonah B. Gelbach & David Marcus, *Rethinking Judicial Review of High Volume Agency Adjudication*, 96 TEX. L. REV. 1097, 1145–47 (2018); R. Shep Melnick, *Administrative Law and Bureaucratic Reality*, 44 ADMIN. L. REV. 245 (1992); Bijal Shah, *Judicial Administration*, 11 U.C. IRVINE L. REV. 1119, 1142 (2021); Peter L. Strauss, *Revisiting* Overton Park*: Political and Judicial Controls over Administrative Actions Affecting the Community*, 39 UCLA L. REV. 1251 (1992); Christopher J. Walker, *Administrative Law without Courts*, 65 UCLA L. REV. 1621 (2018); Christopher J. Walker & Rebecca Turnbull, *Operationalizing Internal Administrative Law*, 71 HASTINGS L.J. 1225 (2020).

First, compared with the legislative and executive branches, the judiciary is passive. Where legislative and executive branch actors have significant leeway to proactively identify and remedy problems, courts rely on third parties to bring issues before them. Courts are also limited to considering those specific cases before them, which has several consequences. The ability to forum shop provides clear opportunities for gamesmanship. Additionally, attempting to address broad questions through individual questions can engender myopia. It is a practical reality of administrative adjudication that most cases will never be reviewed by a court, either because disputes are satisfactorily resolved by the agency or no party seeks judicial review. Consider the Social Security Administration (SSA), which receives millions of applications each year for retirement, disability, and other types of benefits. Administrative law judges (ALJs) decide hundreds of thousands of cases annually, the vast majority involving applications for disability benefits, and the Appeals Council reviews more than 100,000 ALJ decisions each year. District courts, in contrast, receive only about 20,000 appeals annually. A similar dynamic exists in the immigration system.[13] Even at lower volume regulatory agencies, most cases settle before reaching a court (or even an ALJ).[14] The few cases that reach courts may not be representative of the mass of cases that never reach them and may be inappropriate vehicles for addressing broader issues.

Second, courts have limited remedies available to them. The most pressing problems of agency adjudication concern access to resources and management of large, bureaucratic systems.[15] Courts cannot appropriate funds, nor do they have the capacity to manage the day-to-day business of running administrative agencies. Additionally, while courts have some flexibility to oversee the structure and procedures of agency adjudicative systems (see section 27.5) through legal interpretation, they lack the authority to engage in the sort of explicit lawmaking that Congress and agencies regularly undertake.

---

13. Lenni B. Benson, *You Can't Get There from Here: Managing Judicial Review of Immigration Cases*, 2007 U. Chi. Legal. F. 405, 408 (2007).

14. Michael Asimow, Admin. Conf. of the U.S., Greenlighting Administrative Prosecution: Checks and Balances on Charging Decisions 1 (2022).

15. *See* Richard J. Pierce, Jr., *Judicial Review of Agency Actions in a Period of Diminishing Agency Resources*, 49 Admin. L. Rev. 61, 72–77 (1997); Nicholas R. Bednar, *The Public Administration of Justice*, 44 Cardozo L. Rev. (forthcoming 2023).

Courts are not entirely powerless to address problems, however. One important article offers a few options for judges: (1) "criticize agency adjudicators in terms calculated to cause consternation or shame"; (2) "exploit bureaucratic fault lines to force an agency to respond"; (3) "adopt doctrines that raise the costs for agencies if they do not correct a problem"; (4) "draw media attention to what are otherwise obscure and ignored parts of the federal courts' docket with scathing commentary or by otherwise publicizing what can easily pass under the media's radar"; and (5) "use their considerable prestige to pursue reform while off the bench."[16]

Third, courts are lawyerly institutions that privilege uniquely legal methods of gathering information and making decisions. There are benefits to this approach, but there are drawbacks as well. Adversarial, highly proceduralized methods can promote impartiality and judicial economy, but they can also be slow and inflexible. Unlike methods of information-gathering available to Congress and agencies, judicial methods also rely primarily on third parties to educate decision-makers.[17] Indeed, it is for these very reasons that Congress often has delegated adjudicative authority to an agency rather than a court. Layering a judicialized process atop a system of less formal adjudication can have unintended consequences for the effectiveness of administrative decision-making, for example by making an explicitly nonadversarial process more adversarial in practice.[18]

Fourth, courts are only indirectly susceptible to political pressures—for example, through Congress's power of the purse and statutory changes affecting the courts' structure, composition, jurisdiction, and procedures. Still, it is clear that courts are not wholly unresponsive to political preferences, as demonstrated by the historical development of the appellate review model.

Fifth, relative to Congress and agencies, the courts are decentralized. Although a few trial and appeals courts have nationwide jurisdiction over certain types of cases, judicial review in most programs takes

16. Gelbach & Marcus, *supra* note 12, at 1145–47.

17. Allison Orr Larsen, *Confronting Supreme Court Fact Finding*, 98 VA. L. REV. 1255, 1310–12 (2012).

18. *See, e.g.*, Michael Asimow, *Inquisitorial Adjudication and Mass Justice in American Administrative Law*, *in* THE NATURE OF INQUISITORIAL PROCESSES IN ADMINISTRATIVE REGIMES 93, 107–108 (Laverne Jacobs & Sasha Baglay eds., 2013); Rory E. Riley, *Simplify, Simplify, Simplify—An Analysis of Two Decades of Judicial Review in the Veterans' Benefits Adjudication System*, 113 W. VA. L. REV. 67 (2010).

place in institutions with limited geographical jurisdiction. This can have consequences for the effectiveness of courts to supervise adjudication and promote consistency and accuracy in agency decision-making (see section 27.5). As noted earlier, the ability to forum shop also provides opportunities for gamesmanship.

Determining the proper role of the courts in reviewing agency adjudicative decisions requires consideration of these and other factors. Two important studies of SSA adjudication identified several possible functions that judicial review might perform, including:

- **A "corrective function."** Courts can correct erroneous agency decisions.
- **A "regulative function."** Courts can induce agency adjudicators to decide cases more accurately, either through fear of judicial reversal ("the in terrorem effect") or by forcing them to abide by court-fashioned rules ("the precedential effect").
- **A "legitimizing function."** Review of an agency's decision by an independent judiciary can increase public confidence in the legitimacy of outcomes.
- **A "critical function."** Courts offer agencies a "steady stream" of feedback that they can use to improve, and that is valuable for its own sake.
- **A "public information function."** Court decisions "serve as a window on an agency whose operations would otherwise be largely invisible."

How well judicial review serves these functions—and whether the costs of judicial review outweigh the benefits—varies according to different programs' specific attributes.[19]

If the APA is the result of a "fierce compromise" among competing visions for the administrative state, then the appellate review model, codified as the default rule by the APA, may represent a sort of consensus regarding the appropriate role for courts in reviewing agency adjudicative orders and overseeing agency adjudicative systems. Opinions differ, of course. As a general matter, and with respect to specific programs of agency adjudication, scholars have proposed more or less

19. Gelbach & Marcus, *supra* note 12, at 1120–21 (summarizing and quoting Jerry L. Mashaw et al., Social Security Hearings and Appeals 136–37 (1978)).

obtrusive roles for the courts.[20] Regardless, the appellate review model is an integral part of administrative law and continues to define the relationship between courts and agencies in many programs of agency adjudication.

27.4 JUDICIAL REVIEW OF AGENCY ADJUDICATIVE ORDERS

The APA contains a sweeping waiver of sovereign immunity, providing as a default rule that any "person suffering legal wrong because of agency action, or adversely affected or aggrieved by agency action within the meaning of a relevant statute, is entitled to judicial review thereof."[21] To be sure, some decisions that agencies make in the course of adjudicating cases are "committed to agency discretion by law," and, in some programs, judicial review is precluded by statute.[22] (Courts generally lack jurisdiction to review visa decisions by consular officers, for instance.) While the APA provides a general, default rule governing judicial review of agency orders, specific review statutes often supplement or supplant it in specific programs.[23] Still, there is a strong presumption in favor of reviewability. Indeed, "only upon a showing of 'clear and convincing evidence' of a contrary legislative intent" will courts generally find that they lack jurisdiction to review a final agency action.[24]

Only "final" agency actions are typically subject to judicial review. An adjudication is final when the agency has completed its decision-making process. Courts ordinarily will not review preliminary, procedural, or intermediate agency actions. Some statutes require parties to exhaust administrative remedies before a court will intervene. The APA also permits agencies by rule to require "appeal to superior

---

20. *Compare* Richard H. Fallon, Jr., *The Core of an Uneasy Case for Judicial Review*, 121 Harv. L. Rev. 1693 (2008), *with* Jeremy Waldron, *The Core of the Case against Judicial Review*, 115 Yale L.J. 1346 (2006).

21. 5 U.S.C. § 702; *see also* Administrative Conference Recommendation 69-1, Statutory Reform of the Sovereign Immunity Doctrine (implemented by Pub. L. No. 94-574, 90 Stat. 2721 (1976)).

22. 5 U.S.C. § 701(a).

23. *See generally* Jonathan R. Siegel, Admin. Conf. of the U.S., The ACUS Sourcebook of Federal Judicial Review Statutes (2022).

24. Abbot Lab'ys v. Gardner, 387 U.S. 136, 141 (1967) (quoting Rusk v. Cort, 369 U.S. 367, 379–80 (1962)); *see also* Nicholas Bagley, *The Puzzling Presumption of Reviewability*, 127 Harv. L. Rev. 1287, 1288 (2014).

agency authority," so long as an action remains inoperative pending the appeal.[25]

Instead of first exhausting administrative remedies and awaiting a final agency order, private parties sometimes initiate separate actions in district courts challenging an agency's authority to adjudicate a matter or the adequacy of its procedures. Whether collateral attacks are permitted typically turns on the language of the governing statute. Collateral suits challenging the structure of agency adjudicative systems on separation-of-powers grounds have become increasingly common (see section 27.51).[26]

In adversarial adjudications, courts also will often decline to consider issues not previously raised during administrative proceedings, either by operation of a statute or rule or by "analogy to the rule that appellate courts will not consider arguments not raised before trial courts."[27] (There is currently some debate regarding the application of the issue-exhaustion principle to structural constitutional questions.[28])

Judicial review takes place, in the first instance, either in a district court (the default for judicial actions) or an appeals court. Although rhyme and reason are sometimes lacking in congressional choices regarding the forum for judicial review of agency adjudication, the Administrative Conference of the United States (ACUS) has recommended general principles. Specifically, adjudications "based on trial-type hearings . . . should generally be made directly reviewable by courts of appeals," except in programs where cases "rarely involve[] issues of law or of broad social or economic impact warranting routine review by a multimember court" or of such high volume, and are so rarely appealed, that "district court review would significantly reduce the workload of the appellate courts."[29] Programs also vary in terms of

---

25. 5 U.S.C. § 704; *see also* Darby v. Cisneros, 509 U.S. 137 (1993).

26. *Cf.* Axon Enter., Inc. v. Fed. Trade Comm'n, 598 U.S. __ (2023); *see also* Linda D. Jellum, *The SEC's Fight to Stop District Courts from Declaring Its Hearings Unconstitutional*, 101 Tex. L. Rev. 339 (2022).

27. Carr v. Saul, 141 S. Ct. 1352, 1358 (2021) (quoting Sims v. Apel, 530 U.S. 103, 109 (2000)).

28. *See, e.g.*, Fleming v. U.S. Dep't of Agric., 987 F.3d 1093 (D.C. Cir. 2021).

29. Administrative Conference Recommendation 75-3, The Choice of Forum for Judicial Review of Administrative Action, 40 Fed. Reg. 27,926 (July 2, 1975); *see also* David P. Currie & Frank I. Goodman, *Judicial Review of Federal Administrative Action: Quest for the Optimum Forum*, 75 Colum. L. Rev. 1, 5–62 (1975).

whether judicial review takes place in a generalist court (e.g., district courts) or a specialist court (e.g., Federal Circuit).[30]

The record for review is, in most cases, the "whole record" that the agency considered in making its final decision.[31] In trial-like proceedings, the record will typically be the exclusive record for decision-making before hearing-level and any appellate-level adjudicators (see Chapters 18 and 19) and the orders and opinions those officials render.[32] The contents of the record in less formal adjudications may be set forth in a statute or rule, or it may be a matter of practice or a more ad hoc compilation.[33]

The APA's judicial review provisions distinguish between legal and factual questions. Courts are directed to "decide all relevant questions of law, interpret constitutional and statutory provisions, and determine the meaning or applicability of the terms of an agency action."[34] In so doing, they may employ deference doctrines when interpreting a statute or agency rule.[35] Many scholars have considered the extent to which courts should defer to interpretations announced in adjudications of varying formality.[36]

---

30. *See, e.g.*, Lawrence Baum, *Judicial Specialization and the Adjudication of Immigration Cases*, 59 Duke L.J. 1501 (2010); Harold H. Bruff, *Specialized Courts in Administrative Law*, 43 Admin. L. Rev. 329 (1991); Rochelle Cooper Dreyfuss, *Specialized Adjudication*, 1990 BYU L. Rev. 377 (1990); Currie & Goodman, *supra* note 29, at 62–75; Richard L. Revesz, *Specialized Courts and the Administrative Lawmaking System*, 138 U. Pa. L. Rev. 1111 (1990); Paul R. Verkuil & Jeffrey S. Lubbers, *Alternative Approaches to Judicial Review of Social Security Disability Cases*, 55 Admin. L. Rev. 731 (2003).

31. 5 U.S.C. § 706.

32. *See id.* §§ 556(e), 557(c).

33. *See* Camp v. Pitts, 411 U.S. 138 (1973); Citizens to Pres. Overton Park v. Volpe, 401 U.S. 402 (1971).

34. 5 U.S.C. § 706.

35. *See, e.g.*, Kisor v. Wilkie, 139 S. Ct. 2400 (2019) (rule); United States v. Mead Corp., 533 U.S. 218 (2001) (statute); Auer v. Robbins, 519 U.S. 452 (1997) (rule); Chevron U.S.A., Inc. v. Nat. Res. Def. Council, 467 U.S. 837 (1984) (statute); Bowles v. Seminole Rock & Sand Co., 325 U.S. 410 (1945) (rule); Skidmore v. Swift, 323 U.S. 134 (1944) (statute).

36. *See, e.g.*, Kristin E. Hickman & Aaron L. Nielson, *Narrowing* Chevron's *Domain*, 70 Duke L.J. 931 (2021); Patrick J. Glen, *The Case for* Chevron *Deference to Immigration Adjudications*, 71 Duke L.J. Online 18 (2021); Todd Phillips, *A Change of Policy: Promoting Agency Policymaking by Adjudication*, 73 Admin. L. Rev. 495 (2021); Shoba Sivaprasad Wadhia & Christopher Walker, *The Case against* Chevron *Deference in Immigration Adjudication*, 70 Duke L.J. 1197 (2021).

The APA sets forth several standards for reviewing factual questions. As a default rule, courts must hold unlawful and set aside and vacate actions, findings, and conclusions that are "arbitrary, capricious, an abuse of discretion, or otherwise not in accordance with law."[37] Except when a specific statute provides otherwise, this is the standard courts typically employ when reviewing orders made through informal adjudication.[38]

For cases subject to the APA's formal-adjudication provisions, courts generally will hold unlawful and set aside and vacate actions, findings, and conclusions that are "unsupported by substantial evidence."[39] The Supreme Court elaborated on the nature of substantial-evidence review in *Universal Camera v. National Labor Relations Board*, holding that, in determining whether an agency's findings are reasonably supported, reviewing courts must consider the record as a whole, including any evidence that might detract from the agency's findings.[40] (In *Universal Camera*, the Court held that the "whole record" included the findings of a hearing examiner, which the agency had rejected on appeal.)

Rarely, a statute will provide for de novo review, in which case courts will set aside and vacate actions, findings, and conclusions found to be "unwarranted by the facts."[41] The Freedom of Information Act is the most notable statute that provides for de novo review of agency orders.

To learn more about how courts review adjudicative orders, readers should consult the American Bar Association's companion *A Guide to Judicial and Political Review of Federal Agencies* and ACUS's *Sourcebook of Federal Judicial Review Statutes.*

27.5 JUDICIAL OVERSIGHT OF AGENCY ADJUDICATIVE SYSTEMS

The courts review tens of thousands of agency adjudicative orders each year but, as noted earlier, most agency adjudications will never be reviewed by a court, either because disputes are satisfactorily resolved

---

37. 5 U.S.C. § 706(2)(A); *see also Citizens to Pres. Overton Park*, 401 U.S. at 413–14.

38. *See, e.g.*, Phx. Herpetological Soc'y v. U.S. Fish & Wildlife Serv., 998 F.3d 999, 1005 (2021); *Camp*, 411 U.S. at 142.

39. 5 U.S.C. § 706(2)(E).

40. 340 U.S. 474 (1951); *see also* Allentown Mack Sales & Serv. v. Nat'l Lab. Rels. Bd., 522 U.S. 359 (1998).

41. 5 U.S.C. § 706(2)(F).

by the agency or no party seeks judicial review. Nevertheless, there are at least two ways in which courts exert important systemic influences.

First, the possibility or expectation of judicial review in any individual case may affect the behavior of agency officials systemically. At a basic level, agency adjudicators often follow procedures that are intended, at least in part, to facilitate judicial review. In many proceedings, adjudicators must compile an evidentiary record and prepare an opinion adequate to demonstrate to a reviewing court that the order is reasonable.[42] More broadly, research suggests that increased exposure to the courts may lead agencies to employ court-like procedures that they believe are likelier to pass muster on judicial review.[43] This makes intuitive sense. Litigation is expensive and time-consuming, forcing agencies to divert resources from other activities. Adverse judicial decisions can impose additional costs on agencies, requiring them to reprocess cases, update rules and policies to implement judicial interpretations, and train adjudicative personnel.[44] For these reasons, agencies might adopt practices ex ante that are designed to avoid litigation in most cases and to satisfy courts in the few cases where litigation does occur. This "in terrorem" effect of judicial review may be less pronounced in higher volume programs, however, where a smaller percentage of cases will ever reach the courts.[45]

Second, courts' holdings in individual cases can affect agency decision-making more broadly. Courts' acceptance or rejection of agencies' legal interpretations, factual findings, and procedural practices can have significant effects on how agency adjudicators decide whole categories of cases. Scholars have noted this "precedential effect," but they have also noted its limited impact, particularly in high-volume programs in which relatively few cases ever reach the courts, and in contexts where agencies decline to implement judicial interpretations beyond a single circuit ("intercircuit nonacquiescence")

---

42. *See* 5 U.S.C. § 557; Sec. & Exch. Comm'n v. Chenery Corp., 318 U.S. 80 (1943).

43. Scott Limbocker et al., *Anticipated Adjudication: An Analysis of the Judicialization of the U.S. Administrative State*, 32 J. PUB. ADMIN. RSCH. & THEORY 610 (2022).

44. *See* Jeffrey S. Lubbers, *Management of Federal Agency Adjudication*, 12 J. NAT'L ASS'N ADMIN. L. JUDGES 112, 116 (1992).

45. *See* MASHAW ET AL., *supra* note 19, at 139–40; Gelbach & Marcus, *supra* note 12, at 1120–21.

or in all unrelated cases ("intracircuit nonacquiescence").[46] Even in high-volume programs, however, courts have opportunities to provide feedback to and engage in dialogue with agencies through remands.[47]

This section examines the systemic effects of judicial review. It focuses on four key objects of judicial oversight: (1) the structure of adjudicative systems (section 27.51); (2) the quality of agency adjudication (section 27.52); (3) the timeliness of agency adjudication (section 27.53); and (4) the procedures used to adjudicate cases (section 27.54). This treatment is not comprehensive, and courts can play important roles in overseeing other aspects of agency adjudicative systems. Courts help ensure compliance with transparency laws, for example, which is essential to congressional and public oversight (see Chapters 26 and 28). Additionally, courts may—or, if differently structured, might—play an important role in guarding against discrimination based on race, gender, and other social identities in the administration of federal programs.[48]

27.51 Judicial Oversight of Structure

Since *Marbury*, courts have claimed broad authority to strike down statutes and rules they deem unconstitutional and executive actions taken without legal authority. As discussed in Chapter 3, courts have interpreted various constitutional provisions—including the Judicial Vesting Clause, the Appointments Clause, the Take Care Clause, the

---

46. *See, e.g.*, MASHAW ET AL., *supra* note 19, at 140–46; Matthew Diller & Nancy Morawetz, *Intracircuit Nonacquiescence and the Breakdown of the Rule of Law: A Response to Estreicher & Revesz*, 99 YALE L.J. 801 (1990); Samuel Estreicher & Richard L. Revesz, *Nonacquiescence by Federal Administrative Agencies*, 98 YALE L.J. 679 (1989); Samuel Estreicher & Richard L. Revesz, *The Uneasy Case against Intracircuit Nonacquiescence: A Reply*, 99 YALE L.J. 831 (1990); Joshua I. Schwartz, *Nonacquiescence,* Crowell v. Benson*, and Administrative Adjudication*, 77 GEO. L.J. 1815 (1989).

47. Gelbach & Marcus, *supra* note 12, at 1125–28; Christopher J. Walker & James R. Saywell, *Remand and Dialogue in Administrative Law*, 89 GEO. WASH. L. REV. 1198 (2021).

48. *See, e.g.*, Raoul Berger, *Administrative Arbitrariness and Judicial Review*, 65 COLUM. L. REV. 55 (1965); Cristina Isabel Ceballos et al., *Disparate Limbo: How Administrative Law Erased Antidiscrimination*, 131 YALE L.J. 370 (2021); Elaine Golin, Note, *Solving the Problem of Gender and Racial Bias in Administrative Adjudication*, 95 COLUM. L. REV. 1532 (1995); Steph Tai, *Racism and Informal Agency Adjudicatory Decisions, or, Is Racism Arbitrary and Capricious?*, YALE J. ON REGUL.: NOTICE & COMMENT (Aug. 5, 2020), https://www.yalejreg.com/nc/racism-and-informal-agency-adjudicatory-decisions-or-is-racism-arbitrary-and-capricious-by-steph-tai/.

Due Process Clause, and the Seventh Amendment—to regulate aspects of agency adjudicative systems.

In many cases, courts have upheld institutional design choices made by Congress or an agency. Here are a few examples: As Jeff Lubbers discusses in Chapter 6, courts have affirmed congressional choices to delegate to an administrative agency the power to decide some category of cases. In *Withrow v. Larkin*, the Supreme Court found that it did not necessarily violate the Constitution to combine adjudicative and investigative functions in a single agency.[49] In *Richardson v. Perales*, the Court found that it did not violate due process for an SSA adjudicator to also be charged with developing the factual record.[50] In *Mobility Workx v. Unified Patents*, the Federal Circuit found that the payment of bonuses to administrative patent judges based on a performance evaluation did not deprive parties of due process.[51]

In many other cases, however, the courts have found some facet of an institutional design unconstitutional, and the effects have been far-reaching. In *Lucia v. Securities & Exchange Commission*, for example, the Supreme Court found that a Securities and Exchange Commission ALJ was an "Officer of the United States" who must be appointed in accordance with the Appointments Clause.[52] Following the decision, dozens of agencies across the government rushed to ratify the appointment of thousands of adjudicators appointed by lower level officials. (President Trump also issued Executive Order No. 13,843, excepting ALJs from the competitive service,[53] though that result was not expressly required by the Court's opinion.) A question already addressed by some lower courts and likely to come before the Supreme Court in the near future is whether statutory removal protections for ALJs are consistent with the separation of powers.[54] And in *United States v. Arthrex*, the Court purported to remedy an Appointments

49. 421 U.S. 35 (1975).
50. 402 U.S. 389 (1971).
51. 15 F.4th 1146 (Fed. Cir. 2021).
52. 138 S. Ct. 2044 (2018).
53. 83 Fed. Reg. 32,755 (July 13, 2018).
54. *See* Axon Enter., Inc. v. Fed. Trade Comm'n, No. 21-86 (U.S. argued Nov. 7, 2022); Sec. & Exch. Comm'n v. Cochran, No. 21-1239 (U.S. argued Nov. 7, 2022); Decker Coal Co. v. Pehringer, 8 F.4th 1123 (9th Cir. 2021); Calcutt v. Fed. Deposit Ins. Corp., 37 F.4th 293 (6th Cir. 2022); Jarkesy v. Sec. & Exch. Comm'n, 34 F.4th 446, *reh'g denied en banc*, 51 F.4th 644 (5th Cir. 2022); Fleming v. U.S. Dep't of Agric., 987 F.3d 1093 (D.C. Cir. 2021) (Rao, J., concurring in part and dissenting in part).

Clause violation by requiring that decisions by the Patent Trial and Appeal Board be made reviewable by the director of the U.S. Patent and Trademark Office.[55] The result has been a yearslong administrative and legislative process to develop and operationalize a satisfactory process for director review.[56]

As discussed throughout this guide, the institutional design of adjudicative systems has important consequences for the fairness, accuracy, and efficiency of decision-making in individual cases. The constitutionalization of key institutional design choices provides the courts substantial authority to shape and determine the form and operation of agency adjudication.[57]

Another category of structural questions on which the courts have been asked to intervene involves the decisional independence of agency adjudicators. These disputes may be grounded in due process concerns,[58] but they are often premised on agencies' alleged noncompliance with statutory provisions regarding the relationship between them and the adjudicators they employ. Questions arise in private parties' appeals from agency adjudicative decisions,[59] but many decisional independence suits are brought by adjudicators, or professional associations on their behalf, against the agencies that employ them. Such suits have involved matters as diverse as the operation of SSA's quality assurance program,[60] the job classification and compensation of ALJs,[61] the binding effect of agency rules and directives on adjudicators,[62] the assignment of cases,[63] the provision of resources,[64] domestic violence

---

55. 141 S. Ct. 1970 (2021).

56. *See* 87 Fed. Reg. 43,249 (July 20, 2022); Patent Trial and Appeal Board Reform Act of 2022, S. 4417, 117th Cong. (2022).

57. *Cf.* Nikolas Bowie & Daphna Renan, *The Separation-of-Powers Counter-revolution*, 131 YALE L.J. 2020 (2022); Aziz Huq, *Separation of Powers Metatheory*, 118 COLUM. L. REV. 1517 (2018).

58. *See, e.g.*, Mobility Workx, LLC v. Unified Pats., LLC, 15 F.4th 1146 (Fed. Cir. 2021).

59. *See generally* Kent Barnett, *Why Bias Challenges to Administrative Adjudication Should Succeed*, 81 MO. L. REV. 1023 (2016).

60. *See, e.g.*, Nash v. Bowen, 869 F.2d 675 (2d Cir. 1989); Ass'n of Admin. L. Judges v. Heckler, 594 F. Supp. 1132 (D.D.C. 1984).

61. *See, e.g.*, Ramspeck v. Fed. Trial Exam'rs Conf., 345 U.S. 128 (1953).

62. *See, e.g.*, D'Amico v. Schweiker, 698 F.2d 903 (7th Cir. 1983).

63. *See, e.g.*, Tunik v. Merit Sys. Prot. Bd., 407 F.3d 1326 (2005); Sannier v. Merit Sys. Prot. Bd., 931 F.2d 856 (Fed. Cir. 1991).

64. *See, e.g.*, Mahoney v. Donovan, 721 F.3d 633 (D.C. Cir. 2013).

as proper grounds for removing an ALJ,[65] and performance goals for adjudicators.[66]

Adjudicators have occasionally prevailed in their lawsuits, particularly where it was clear that agency managers intended to interfere with adjudicators' decision-making. Adjudicators have been less successful in other cases, especially where courts found that any effects on adjudicators' decision-making were incidental to ordinary managerial controls. Some courts have also concluded that the decisional independence protections embedded in the APA and other statutes do not give courts jurisdiction to decide adjudicators' claims.[67]

27.52 Judicial Oversight of Quality

As discussed in Chapter 24, many agencies have implemented managerial controls to promote accurate and consistent decision-making by adjudicators. But what role should the courts play in ensuring the quality of agency decision-making? In reviewing individual orders, courts clearly play some role in ensuring that agency adjudicators comply with applicable statutes and rules[68] and have adequate evidentiary support for their decisions.

A broader definition of "quality" considers the uniformity or consistency of agency decision-making. That is, how often do different adjudicators, presented with the same law and similar fact patterns, reach similar results. As discussed in Chapter 24, significant concerns have been raised regarding the consistency of agency adjudicative systems, particularly systems that decide a large number of cases. Some scholars have suggested that systemic inconsistency offends due process and is "arbitrary and capricious" under the APA. Parties have successfully employed these arguments in some programs, particularly where there are strong norms of precedential decision-making.[69]

---

65. *See, e.g.*, Long v. Soc. Sec. Admin., 635 F.3d 526 (Fed. Cir. 2011).

66. *See, e.g.*, Ass'n of Admin. L. Judges v. Colvin, 777 F.3d 402 (7th Cir. 2015).

67. Jennifer Nou, *Dismissing Decisional Independence Suits*, 86 U. Chi. L. Rev. 1187 (2019).

68. *See* Accardi v. Shaughnessy, 347 U.S. 260 (1954).

69. *See, e.g.*, Shaw's Supermarkets, Inc. v. Nat'l Lab. Rels. Bd., 884 F.2d 34, 36–37 (1st Cir. 1989) (Breyer, J.) (holding that an agency cannot significantly depart from its own prior precedent "without explicitly recognizing that it is doing so and explaining why"); *see also* Allentown Mack Sales & Serv. v. Nat'l Lab. Rels. Bd., 522 U.S. 359, 374–77 (1998); Christopher J. Walker et al., ACUS, Precedential Decision Making in Agency Adjudication 44–46 (2022).

Courts may not be as well equipped to address concerns about inconsistent decision-making in high-volume programs, however.[70] One article offers a few options for judges: (1) "criticize agency adjudicators in terms calculated to cause consternation or shame"; (2) "exploit bureaucratic fault lines to force an agency to respond"; (3) "adopt doctrines that raise the costs for agencies if they do not correct a problem"; (4) "draw media attention to what are otherwise obscure and ignored parts of the federal courts' docket with scathing commentary or by otherwise publicizing what can easily pass under the media's radar"; and (5) "use their considerable prestige to pursue reform while off the bench."[71]

27.53 Judicial Oversight of Timeliness

Many adjudication programs, particularly high-volume programs, routinely face delays and backlogs.[72] Parties tired of awaiting long-delayed decisions on veterans' benefits, asylum and visas, and other matters have sought relief in the courts. Parties have had some success in programs in which Congress has imposed a statutory time limit on agency decision-making. Statutory time limits are relatively rare, though, and ACUS has recommended that "Congress ordinarily should not impose statutory time limits on an agency's adjudicator proceedings."[73]

In programs where Congress has not imposed a time limit on an agency, parties have relied on due process; the APA, which directs agencies to conclude matters "within a reasonable time" and grants courts' authority to "compel agency action . . . unreasonably delayed";[74] and the Mandamus Act, which authorizes courts "to compel an officer or employee of the United States or any agency thereof to perform a duty owed to the plaintiff."[75]

Courts have dismissed many such suits, finding that they lack jurisdiction to decide them or that the parties failed to state a claim

---

70. *See, e.g.*, Mashaw, *supra* note 12; Mashaw et al., *supra* note 19, at 136–37; Ames et al., *supra* note 12, at 20–27.

71. Gelbach & Marcus, *supra* note 12, at 1145–47.

72. *See generally* Adam S. Zimmerman, *Surges and Delays in Mass Adjudication*, 53 Ga. L. Rev. 1335 (2019).

73. Administrative Conference Recommendation 78-3, Time Limits on Agency Actions, ¶ 4, 43 Fed. Reg. 27,509 (June 26, 1978).

74. 5 U.S.C. § 706.

75. 28 U.S.C. § 1361.

for which relief can be granted.[76] In considering whether an adjudication is unreasonably delayed, courts often consider whether the agency has taken a patently unreasonable amount of time to make a decision, whether Congress has provided a timetable for agency decision-making, whether delay is more tolerable (e.g., "in the sphere of economic regulation") or less tolerable (e.g., "when human health and welfare are at stake"), the likely effects of expediting delayed action on other agency activities, and "the nature and extent of the interests prejudiced by delay." To hold that agency action is unreasonably delayed, a court "need not find any impropriety lurking behind agency lassitude."[77]

Medicare appeals provide one context in which parties successfully have convinced courts to intervene. In 2014, the American Hospital Association and other entities sued the Department of Health and Human Services, requesting that a district court issue a writ of mandamus compelling the agency to work through the backlog of several hundred thousand appeals. Although the district court initially dismissed the case, the D.C. Circuit directed the district court to consider whether "compelling equitable grounds" existed to issue a writ of mandamus.[78] After additional litigation, the district court ultimately entered orders directing the agency to meet court-supervised deadlines for backlog reduction. The Office of Medicare Hearings and Appeals had reduced more than 98 percent of its backlog by April 2023.[79]

Parties have also succeeded in settling unreasonable-delay claims after suing agencies. In early 2023, for example, the Department of

---

76. *See, e.g.*, Veterans for Common Sense v. Shinseki, 678 F.3d 1013 (9th Cir. 2012). *But see* Garcia v. Dep't of Homeland Sec., 25 F.4th 430 (6th Cir. 2022); *see also* Am. Immigr. Council & Am. Immigr. Laws. Ass'n, Delay Actions in the Asylum Context: Avoiding Dismissal and Proving the Case (2022); Am. Immigr. Council, Agency Delay Litigation: Opposing a Government Motion to Dismiss (2019).

77. Telecomm. Rsch. & Action Ctr. v. Fed. Commc'ns Comm'n, 750 F.2d 70, 80 (D.C. Cir. 1984); *see also* Daniel T. Shedd, Cong. Rsch. Serv., R43013, Administrative Agencies and Claims of Unreasonable Delay: Analysis of Court Treatment 4–6 (2013).

78. Am. Hosp. Ass'n v. Burwell, 812 F.3d 183, 192 (D.C. Cir. 2016).

79. Joint Status Report, Am. Hosp. Ass'n v. Becerra, No. 1:14-cv-00851-JEB (D.D.C. filed Apr. 7, 2023), https://www.aha.org/system/files/media/file/2023/04/alj-delay-april-2023-status-report-filed-4-7-23-re-aha-hospitals-sue-to-require-hhs-to-meet-deadlines-for-deciding-appeals.pdf.

Homeland Security agreed to expedite processing of certain dependent visa petitions by bundling them with adjudication of principals' petitions.[80]

27.54 Judicial Oversight of Procedures

Parties sometimes challenge the procedures used to adjudicate cases, arguing that they are unlawful. Parties may allege that procedures fail to satisfy the requirements of due process. In the mid-20th century, courts claimed significant authority to decide which procedures provided due process and which deprived parties of their constitutional rights. In cases like *Goldberg v. Kelly*,[81] the Court repeatedly found a right to "some kind of hearing" in program after program and set forth a "fixed list of procedural protections required by due process."[82] More often than not, these procedures resembled a trial-like proceeding.

Constitutionalizing adjudicative procedure in this manner gave courts substantial control over the design of agency adjudicative programs. This approach was criticized as judicial activism. Dissenting in *Goldberg*, for example, Justice Black wrote that by imposing significant procedural requirements on agencies without a clear constitutional or statutory basis for doing so, courts "wander[ed] out of their field of vested powers and transgress[ed] into the area constitutionally assigned to the Congress and the people."[83] The *Goldberg* line of cases was also criticized for judicializing agency adjudication and ignoring efficiency values of administrative decision-making. As criticism mounted and the number of government programs continued to expand, the rigid rule-based approach to interpreting due process quickly became untenable.[84]

Within a few years, the *Goldberg* approach gave way to the flexible balancing test of *Mathews v. Eldridge*,[85] discussed in Chapter 15. Although the courts still play some role in ensuring that agency adju-

80. Rae Ann Varona, *DHS Reaches Permit, Visa Deal with Foreign Worker Spouses*, Law360 (Jan. 23, 2023), https://www.law360.com/articles/1568247/dhs-reaches-permit-visa-deal-with-foreign-worker-spouses.

81. 397 U.S. 254 (1970).

82. Michael Asimow, ACUS, Federal Administrative Adjudication outside the Administrative Procedure Act 32 (2019).

83. *Goldberg*, 397 U.S. at 274.

84. *See* Henry J. Friendly, *"Some Kind of Hearing,"* 123 U. Pa. L. Rev. 1267, 1268–70 (1975).

85. 424 U.S. 319 (1976).

dicative procedures comply with the requirements of due process, their "approach today is far from the interventionist days of *Goldberg.*"[86] Under *Mathews*, Congress and agencies have significant leeway to craft different procedures for different contexts.

In addition to due process challenges, parties may allege that agency procedures are inconsistent with statutory requirements. Although courts were once comfortable grafting additional procedural requirements onto vaguely written statutes, since *Vermont Yankee Nuclear Power Corp. v. Natural Resources Defense Council*, they have hesitated to "stray beyond the judicial province to explore the procedural format or to impose upon [an] agency its own notion of which procedures are 'best' or most likely to further some vague, undefined public good."[87] While courts will consider whether agencies' procedures comply with applicable statutory and regulatory requirements, they generally will not require agencies to adopt procedures not explicitly set forth by law.

86. Shah, *supra* note 12, at 1142.

87. 435 U.S. 519, 549 (1978); *see also* Pension Benefit Guarantee Corp. v. LTV Corp., 496 U.S. 633 (1990) (extending *Vermont Yankee* to informal adjudication).

Chapter 28
Transparency

Jeremy S. Graboyes

28.1 CHAPTER OVERVIEW

Transparency serves many of the same objectives in federal agency adjudication as it does in other areas of government activity: ensuring that members of the public are aware of government policies and actions that affect them, facilitating public awareness of the nature of government activities and the performance of government decision-makers, enabling public participation, enabling external oversight of government programs, and promoting public accountability and public confidence in government decision-making.[1] At the same time, limits on transparency may be necessary to protect sensitive information, such as medical and financial records, trade secrets, and national security information, and too much transparency might chill deliberation by agency officials.

1. *See generally* Elizabeth Figueroa, *Transparency in Administrative Courts: From the Outside Looking in*, 35 J. NAT'L ASS'N ADMIN. L. JUDICIARY 1 (2015).

Many statutes, rules, and policies govern public access to federal agency records, information, meetings, and proceedings. Notable examples include the Freedom of Information Act (FOIA),[2] E-Government Act,[3] Government in the Sunshine Act,[4] Federal Register Act,[5] and Privacy Act.[6] At a high level, federal law requires agencies to proactively disclose certain records and information and open certain meetings and proceedings to the public. Certain other records and information must be disclosed and other meetings and proceedings opened on request. Then there are categories of records, information, meetings, and proceedings that agencies may, but are not required to, disclose or make publicly accessible. Finally, there are records, information, meetings, and proceedings that agencies must safeguard from disclosure or public access. Laws sometimes also specify how agencies should facilitate public access, such as by using plain language,[7] ensuring websites are accessible to people with disabilities,[8] and ensuring data is machine readable.[9] Agencies are subject to the requirements of these and other laws and policies when they perform adjudicative functions, just as they are when they perform other functions.

This chapter is not meant to provide a comprehensive overview of the laws and policies governing public access to federal agency records, information, meetings, and proceedings.[10] Instead, it focuses on public access to several important categories of adjudication-related records, information, meetings, and proceedings, specifically information about adjudicative procedures (e.g., regulations, guidance documents, forms) (section 28.2), adjudicative decisions and other case-specific records (section 28.3), adjudicative proceedings (section 28.4), and information about the management, operation, and performance of adjudicative programs (section 28.5).

2. 5 U.S.C. § 552.
3. 44 U.S.C. § 3501 note.
4. 5 U.S.C. § 552b.
5. 44 U.S.C. § 1501 *et seq.*
6. 5 U.S.C. § 552a.
7. *Id.* § 301 note.
8. 29 U.S.C. § 794d.
9. 44 U.S.C. § 3502 note.
10. For more detailed information, consult the Department of Justice's *Guide to the Freedom of Information Act* and *Overview of the Privacy Act of 1974*, and the *Federal Administrative Procedure Sourcebook*, published jointly by the Administrative Conference of the United States and the American Bar Association's Section of Administrative Law and Regulatory Practice.

28.2 INFORMATION ABOUT ADJUDICATIVE PROCEDURES

Many sources set forth or describe procedures for federal agency adjudications, including statutes, codified rules, precedential decisions, policy statements and interpretative rules, administrative manuals, staff instructions and memoranda, standing orders, practice manuals, benchbooks, internal training manuals, and other explanatory materials. Members of the public need access to at least the most significant of these materials to meaningfully participate in adjudications and understand adjudicative systems more broadly.

Federal statutes require agencies to proactively disclose many of these materials and sometimes also specify where and how agencies should proactively disclose them. The following table illustrates the most significant statutory requirements.

	Code of Federal Regulations	Federal Register	Online
Rules of procedure[11]	X	X	X
Descriptions of how to obtain, submit, and request information[12]		X	X
Statements of functions, including the nature and requirements of all formal and informal procedures[13]		X	X
General policy statements and generally applicable interpretations[14]		X	X
Other policy statements and interpretations[15]			X
Final opinions and orders[16]			X
Administrative staff manuals and staff instructions that affect the public[17]			X

11. 5 U.S.C. § 552(a)(1)(C); 44 U.S.C. § 3501 note.
12. 5 U.S.C. § 552(a)(1)(A); 44 U.S.C. § 3501 note.
13. 5 U.S.C. § 552(a)(1)(B); 44 U.S.C. § 3501 note.
14. 5 U.S.C. § 552(a)(1)(D); 44 U.S.C. § 3501 note.
15. 5 U.S.C. § 552(a)(2)(B); 44 U.S.C. § 3501 note.
16. *See* 5 U.S.C. § 552(a)(2)(A); 44 U.S.C. § 3501 note.
17. 5 U.S.C. § 552(a)(2)(C); 44 U.S.C. § 3501 note.

Agencies may also proactively disclose additional materials that set forth or describe adjudicative procedures. The Social Security Administration (SSA) has proactively disclosed agency materials used to train administrative law judges (ALJs),[18] for example, and the Executive Office for Immigration Review (EOIR) has proactively disclosed immigration court video advisals.[19] The Administrative Conference of the United States (ACUS) has recommended that agencies "provide updated access on their websites to all sources of procedural rules and related guidance documents and explanatory materials that apply to agency adjudications."[20]

People participating in adjudications may be required to use agency-specific forms. FOIA and the E-Government Act require agencies to publish "descriptions of forms available or the places at which forms may be obtained" in the *Federal Register* and online,[21] and the 21st Century Integrated Digital Experience Act directs agencies to make forms available "in a digital format."[22] Many agencies have web pages that provide access to forms used in adjudications.[23]

Although the internet now offers the most practical channel for making procedural information publicly available, statutory requirements for online posting are typically vague. FOIA requires agencies to make materials available in "an electronic format,"[24] and the E-Government Act requires agencies to make materials available on "a publicly accessible Federal Government website."[25] Although agencies can satisfy these requirements by posting proactive disclosures in a "FOIA Library" or "electronic reading room," ACUS has recommended that agencies publish adjudication-related rules, guidance documents, explanatory materials, and forms in a "logical" location on their websites and present them "in a clear, logical, and comprehensive fashion."[26]

---

18. *FOIA Reading Room*, SSA, https://www.ssa.gov/foia/readingroom.html (last visited June 27, 2023).

19. *Proactive Disclosures*, DEP'T OF JUSTICE, EOIR, https://www.justice.gov/eoir/proactive-disclosures (last updated Mar. 31, 2023).

20. *See* Administrative Conference Recommendation 2018-5, Public Availability of Adjudication Rules, ¶ 1, 84 Fed. Reg. 2,142, 2,142 (Feb. 6, 2019).

21. 5 U.S.C. § 552a(a)(1)(C); 44 U.S.C. § 3501 note.

22. 44 U.S.C. § 3501 note.

23. Links to these web pages are available at https://www.usa.gov/forms (last visited June 27, 2023).

24. 5 U.S.C. § 552(a)(2).

25. 44 U.S.C. § 3501 note.

26. Administrative Conference Recommendation 2018-5, *supra* note 20; *see also* Administrative Conference Recommendation 2016-4, Evidentiary Hearings

28.3 CASE-SPECIFIC RECORDS

28.31 Orders and Opinions

FOIA requires agencies to proactively disclose "final opinions, including concurring and dissenting opinions, as well as orders, made in the adjudication of cases." Although this formulation has existed in some form since 1946, its scope has never been clear. Read literally using the Administrative Procedure Act's (APA's) broad definitions of "order" and "adjudication" (Chapter 1), this provision would sweep in a huge number of government actions, ranging from precedential decisions of the National Labor Relations Board to "Park Police traffic tickets, and the millions of ministerial IRS [Internal Revenue Service] grants of refunds or withheld taxes each year."[27]

Kenneth Culp Davis once argued that FOIA *should* be interpreted so broadly.[28] Relying on FOIA, private parties have filed suits asking courts to compel agencies to proactively disclose or index records including U.S. Parole Board decisions denying inmate parole applications;[29] unpublished manuscript decisions of the Patent Office;[30] decisions on procedural requests regarding patent applications;[31] decisions of a Department of Health and Human Services tribunal regarding block grants under the Temporary Assistance for Needy Families program;[32] immigration judges' decisions;[33] unpublished decisions of the Board of Immigration Appeals;[34] decisions regarding complaints

---

Not Required by the Administrative Procedure Act, ¶¶ 28–29, 81 Fed. Reg. 94,314, 94,316 (Dec. 23, 2016).

27. Attorney General Edward H. Levi's Memorandum on the 1974 Amendments to the Freedom of Information Act (Feb. 1975) [hereinafter Levi Memorandum].

28. Kenneth Culp Davis, *The Information Act: A Preliminary Analysis*, 34 U. Chi. L. Rev. 761, 771–72 (1967). *But see* Peter L. Strauss, *Rules, Adjudications, and Other Sources of Law in an Executive Department: Reflections on the Interior Department's Administration of the Mining Law*, 74 Colum. L. Rev. 1231, 1241 n.37 (1974).

29. Nat'l Prison Project of Am. Civ. Liberty Union Found. v. Sigler, 390 F. Supp. 789 (1975).

30. Irons v. Diamond, 670 F.2d 265 (D.C. Cir. 1981); Irons v. Schuyler, 465 F.2d 608 (D.C. Cir. 1972).

31. Irons & Sears v. Dann, 606 F.2d 1215 (D.C. Cir. 1979); Leeds v. Quigg, 745 F. Supp. 1 (D.D.C. 1990).

32. Pa. Dep't of Pub. Welfare v. Sebelius, Civil Action No. 09-808, 2010 WL 4053848 (W.D. Pa. Oct. 14, 2010).

33. Cooper v. Exec. Off. for Immigr. Rev., 694 F. Supp. 1278 (S.D. Tex. 1988).

34. N.Y. Legal Assistance Grp. v. Bd. of Immigr. Appeals, 987 F.3d 207 (2021).

against individual immigration judges;[35] decisions by and settlements involving Bureau of Prisons personnel;[36] Animal and Plant Health Inspection Service inspection reports, official warning letters, and pre-litigation settlement agreements;[37] Office of Legal Counsel opinions;[38] Fish and Wildlife Service trophy import permits;[39] and the final report of the Watergate Special Prosecution Force.[40]

The Department of Justice (DOJ), other agencies, and the courts have almost always interpreted the statute more narrowly. DOJ, in particular, has relied on three statutory provisions over the years to limit FOIA's scope. First, FOIA specifies that an agency may only rely on, use, or cite a final order or opinion as precedent against a private party if it has been indexed and proactively disclosed or the party has "actual and timely notice of the terms thereof."[41] Relying on this provision and a congressional committee report, DOJ long asserted that FOIA only requires agencies to proactively disclose orders and opinions that have "precedential significance."[42] Although DOJ's *Guide to the Freedom of Information Act* is less definitive on this point today, it still cites sources that stand for that proposition.[43]

35. Am. Immigr. Laws. Ass'n v. Exec. Off. for Immigr. Rev., 830 F.3d 667 (D.C. Cir. 2016).

36. Prisology v. Fed. Bureau of Prisons, 852 F.3d 1114 (D.C. Cir. 2017); Tereshchuk v. Bureau of Prisons, 67 F. Supp. 3d 441 (D.D.C. 2014).

37. Animal Legal Def. Fund v. U.S. Dep't of Agric., 935 F.3d 858 (9th Cir. 2019); People for the Ethical Treatment of Animals v. U.S. Dep't of Agric., 285 F. Supp. 3d 307 (D.C. Cir. 2018).

38. Citizens for Responsibility & Ethics in Wash. v. Dep't of Just., 846 F.3d 1235 (2017); Campaign for Accountability v. Dept' of Just., 278 F. Supp. 3d 303 (D.D.C. 2017).

39. Humane Soc'y of the U.S. v. U.S. Fish & Wildlife Serv., 838 F. App'x 721 (4th Cir. 2020).

40. Niemeier v. Watergate Special Prosecution Force, 565 F.2d 967 (7th Cir. 1977).

41. 5 U.S.C. § 552(a)(2).

42. Levi Memorandum, *supra* note 27; Attorney General Ramsey Clark's Memorandum on the Public Information Section of the Administrative Procedure Act (June 1967) [hereinafter Clark Memorandum].

43. *Proactive Disclosures*, *in* DOJ, GUIDE TO THE FREEDOM OF INFORMATION ACT 4 (2020).

Some agencies, like SSA, have relied on DOJ's interpretation.[44] The Government Accountability Office explicitly rejected it,[45] however, and ACUS once recommended that FOIA should be interpreted more broadly, focusing "less on the binding nature of precedent and more on the value that decisions can have to inform and assist the public."[46] To that end, ACUS has urged agencies to proactively disclose indexes of "all significant decisions, whether or not the decisions are designated as precedential"[47] and to provide online access to decisions "in excess of" FOIA's proactive disclosure requirement after considering the benefits and costs of doing so.[48]

There are few definitive judicial statements because courts have long held they lacked legal authority to compel agencies to proactively disclose or index opinions and orders. Some courts have found, like DOJ, that FOIA only requires agencies to disclose orders and opinions that they designate or treat as precedent.[49] Other courts have explicitly rejected that interpretation.[50] Following litigation in the Second Circuit regarding the scope of FOIA's proactive disclosure requirement,[51] EOIR agreed in a 2022 settlement to make all "final" orders and opinions of the Board of Immigration Appeals (BIA), including nonprecedential decisions, available online.[52]

---

44. *See* U.S. Gen. Acct. Off., GAO/GGD-86-68, Freedom of Information Act: Noncompliance with Affirmative Disclosure Provisions 27–28 (1986).

45. *Id.*; *see also* Nat'l Prison Project of Am. Civ. Liberty Union Found. v. Sigler, 390 F. Supp. 789 (D.D.C. 1975).

46. Administrative Conference Recommendation 89-8, Agency Practices and Procedures for the Indexing and Public Availability of Adjudicatory Decisions, 59 Fed. Reg. 53,495 (Dec. 29, 1989); *see also* Margaret Gilhooley, *The Availability of Decisions and Precedents in Agency Adjudications: The Impact of the Freedom of Information Act Publication Requirements*, 3 Admin. L.J. 53, 90–91 (1989).

47. Administrative Conference Recommendation 89-8, *supra* note 46, ¶ 1.

48. Administrative Conference Recommendation 2017-1, Adjudication Materials on Agency Websites, ¶ 1, 82 Fed. Reg. 31,039, 31,040 (July 5, 2017).

49. Am. Immigr. Laws. Ass'n v. Exec. Off. for Immigr. Rev., 830 F.3d 667, 679–80 (D.C. Cir. 2016); Skelton v. U.S. Postal Serv., 678 F.2d 35, 40–41 (5th Cir. 1982); Tereshchuk v. Bureau of Prisons, 67 F. Supp. 3d 441 (D.D.C. 2014); *cf.* Tax Analysts & Advocs. v. Internal Revenue Serv., 362 F. Supp. 1298, 1303 (D.D.C. 1973).

50. *See, e.g., Nat'l Prison Project of Am. Civ. Liberty Union Found.*, 390 F. Supp. 789.

51. *See* N.Y. Legal Assistance Grp. v. Bd. of Immigr. Appeals, 987 F.3d 207 (2021).

52. Stipulation of Settlement at 3, N.Y. Legal Assistance Grp. v. Bd. of Immigr. Appeals, No. 18 Civ. 9495 (PAC) (S.D.N.Y. Feb. 9, 2022).

Second, FOIA requires that agencies proactively disclose "final" orders and opinions. The 1947 *Attorney General's Manual on the Administrative Procedure Act* distinguished "final" from "intermediate" dispositions (without explanation),[53] and, in 1967, the attorney general interpreted the provision to apply only to orders issued as part of the final disposition of an adjudicative proceeding—excluding, for example, orders and opinions issued in response to procedural motions and interlocutory appeals during a proceeding.[54] As a general matter, the courts have found that an order is "final" if it has, absent appeal, the force and effect of law, regardless of whether there exists any further opportunity for administrative review.[55] Recommended decisions, investigative reports, and initial assessments are not "final,"[56] nor are orders issued in response to procedural motions.[57] The BIA settlement described earlier similarly excludes decisions on interlocutory appeal from the universe of "final" orders and opinions.[58]

Third, FOIA requires that agencies proactively disclose final orders and opinions "made in the adjudication of cases." In 1975, the attorney general argued that "cases" referred only to "structured, relatively formal proceedings, in which the agency is functioning in a quasi-judicial capacity, and in which its decision is rendered upon a consideration of statutorily or administratively defined standards."[59] That interpretation is difficult to square with the U.S. Supreme Court's opinion in *National Labor Relations Board v. Sears, Roebuck & Co.*, in which a memorandum by the general counsel of the National Labor Relations Board explaining why he decided not to pursue an enforcement action was found to be a final opinion made in the adjudication of a case.[60]

Two courts of appeals have further interpreted "adjudication" to refer only to proceedings that "reflect a final decision as to the rights of

53. Attorney General's Manual on the Administrative Procedure Act 23 (1947).

54. Clark Memorandum, *supra* note 42.

55. Nat'l Lab. Rels. Bd. v. Sears, Roebuck & Co., 421 U.S. 132, 153 (1975).

56. Renegotiation Bd. v. Grumman Aircraft Eng'g Corp., 421 U.S. 168, 186–87 (1975); Leeds v. Comm'r of Pats. & Trademarks, 955 F.2d 757 (D.C. Cir. 1992); Kent Corp. v. Nat'l Lab. Rels. Bd., 530 F.2d 612 (5th Cir. 1976); Abtew v. U.S. Dep't of Homeland Sec., 47 F. Supp. 3d 98 (D.D.C. 2014).

57. Irons & Sears v. Dann, 606 F.2d 1215 (D.C. Cir. 1979); Leeds v. Quigg, 745 F. Supp. 1 (D.D.C. 1990).

58. Stipulation of Settlement at 2, N.Y. Legal Assistance Grp. v. Bd. of Immigr. Appeals, No. 18 Civ. 9495 (PAC) (S.D.N.Y. Feb. 9, 2022).

59. Levi Memorandum, *supra* note 27.

60. 421 U.S. 132.

outside parties" or otherwise provide relief to some party outside the agency.[61] Both cases involved requests to access decisions that agencies rendered following misconduct complaints filed by private parties against agency officials.

Agencies provide public access to adjudicative decisions in different ways. Some, like the Drug Enforcement Administration, publish opinions and orders in the *Federal Register*.[62] This may be useful in programs where cases typically include opportunities for public participation or generate significant public interest.[63] Some agencies have traditionally prepared print compendia of decisions.[64] Decisions are also frequently available through commercial databases like Westlaw and LexisNexis. But agency websites increasingly offer the most practical, accessible, and cost-effective option for publishing adjudicative orders and opinions. Agencies must index and provide online access to opinions and orders covered under FOIA's proactive disclosure provisions. More generally, President Obama's Memorandum on Transparency and Open Government directed agencies to "harness new technologies to put . . . decisions online,"[65] and ACUS has recommended that agencies consider providing online access to decisions "in excess of FOIA's requirements" after weighing the benefits and costs of doing so.[66]

Although agencies can provide access to orders and opinions in an electronic reading room, many agencies also post decisions on dedicated web pages or in online docket systems. ACUS has suggested several techniques for improving public accessibility to and understanding of decisions, for example by clearly distinguishing between precedential and non-precedential decisions, providing brief summaries for precedential decisions, preparing indexes and digests, and preparing explanatory materials that synthesize agency precedents.[67]

---

61. Am. Immigr. Laws. Ass'n v. Exec. Off. for Immigr. Rev., 830 F.3d 667 (D.C. Cir. 2016); Skelton v. U.S. Postal Serv., 678 F.2d 35 (5th Cir. 1982).

62. 21 C.F.R. § 1316.67 (2022).

63. *See* Administrative Conference Recommendation 76-2, Strengthening the Information and Notice-Giving Functions of the Federal Register, 41 Fed. Reg. 29,653 (July 19, 1976).

64. Attorney General's Manual on the Administrative Procedure Act, *supra* note 53.

65. 74 Fed. Reg. 4,685, 4,685 (2009).

66. Administrative Conference Recommendation 2017-1, *supra* note 48, ¶ 1.

67. *See* Administrative Conference Recommendation 2022-4, Precedential Decision Making in Agency Adjudication, 88 Fed. Reg. 2,312 (Jan. 13, 2023); Administrative Conference Recommendation 2020-3, Agency Appellate Systems,

When agencies do provide public access to adjudicative orders and opinions, under FOIA's proactive disclosure provisions or otherwise, they must be mindful of any legally protected information that they contain.[68] Some statutes, like the Privacy Act and Trade Secrets Act, require agencies to safeguard certain sensitive information. Additionally, FOIA explicitly authorizes agencies to redact "identifying details" when they publicly disclose orders and opinions "[t]o the extent required to prevent a clearly unwarranted invasion of personal privacy" and specifies requirements for doing so. When the Board of Veterans' Appeals (BVA) makes its decisions publicly available, for example, it redacts personally identifiable information.[69]

28.32 Filings, Notices, and Transcripts

Aside from opinions and orders, agencies maintain lots of records associated with specific cases, including applications, completed forms, pleadings, motions, briefs, petitions, evidence, transcripts, audio and video recordings, and notices. Although FOIA requires agencies to provide access to many of these materials on request, statutes typically do not require agencies to proactively disclose them. Transcripts are a notable exception. The Federal Advisory Committee Act requires agencies to make copies of transcripts of agency adjudicative proceedings "available to any person, at actual cost of duplication,"[70] and the Government in the Sunshine Act requires covered agencies to make transcripts, electronic recordings, or minutes of covered meetings "promptly available to the public."[71] Some agencies must also provide public notice of adjudicative proceedings, which may be more useful in contexts where adjudications include opportunities for public participation or generate significant public interest.[72]

Although agencies are typically not required by statute to proactively disclose filings, some have developed online docket systems, similar to the Public Access to Court Electronic Records (PACER) service in the federal courts, that provide easy public access to case-specific

---

¶¶ 22–24, 86 Fed. Reg. 6,618, 6,620 (Jan. 22, 2021); Administrative Conference Recommendation 2018-5, *supra* note 20.

68. *See* Kahn v. Fed. Motor Carrier Safety Admin., 648 F. Supp. 2d 31, 35 (D.D.C. 2009); Doe v. Dep't of Lab., 451 F. Supp. 2d 156, 175 (D.D.C. 2006).

69. Daniel J. Sheffner, *Access to Adjudication Materials on Federal Agency Websites*, 51 Akron L. Rev. 447, 474–75, 495 (2017).

70. 5 U.S.C. app. 2, § 11.

71. *Id.* § 552b(f)(2).

72. *Cf.* Administrative Conference Recommendation 76-2, *supra* note 63.

materials.[73] ACUS has recommended that agencies consider providing online access to case records "in excess of FOIA's requirements."[74] At the same time, proactive online disclosure of case-specific records may not be appropriate in all contexts. Although online disclosure promotes accessibility, easy accessibility can also implicate privacy interests by reducing "practical obscurity."[75] Online publication can also be resource intensive, especially in programs that decide a high volume of cases. Records associated with appellate proceedings "that present significant legal and policy issues likely to be of interest to regulated parties and other members of the public" might be ripe for online publication.[76] Proactive disclosure may be less appropriate for routine benefits cases that involve sensitive medical information and generate no significant public interest.

When agencies do provide public access to filings, notices, and transcripts, they must be mindful of any sensitive information that they contain. Before providing public access to case records, agencies may need to redact information that is protected by law or exempted from disclosure under FOIA.[77] Federal law also restricts disclosure of certain adjudication-related records, notably alternative dispute resolution communications (see Chapter 20).[78]

28.33 Internal Agency Communications

In the course of adjudicating cases, adjudicators may generate notes and drafts and exchange written communications with other adjudicators and adjudicative staff. Such records are generally exempted from public disclosure under Exemption 5 of FOIA and the Privacy Act.[79]

---

73. Sheffner, *supra* note 69, at 453.

74. Administrative Conference Recommendation 2017-1, *supra* note 48, ¶ 1.

75. *See generally* Patrick C. File, *A History of Practical Obscurity: Clarifying and Contemplating the Twentieth Century Roots of a Digital Age Concept of Privacy*, 6 U. Balt. J. Media L. & Ethics 4 (2017); David S. Ardia, *Privacy and Court Records: Online Access and the Loss of Practical Obscurity*, 2017 U. Ill. L. Rev. 1385, 1447–52 (2017).

76. *Cf.* Administrative Conference Recommendation 2020-3, *supra* note 67, ¶ 20.

77. *See* Kahn v. Fed. Motor Carrier Safety Admin., 648 F. Supp. 2d 31, 35 (D.D.C. 2009); Doe v. Dep't of Lab., 451 F. Supp. 2d 156, 175 (D.D.C. 2006); *see also* Ernest Gellhorn, *Business Secrets in Administrative Adjudication*, 22 Admin. L. Rev. 515 (1970).

78. 5 U.S.C. § 574.

79. *Id.* §§ 552(b)(5), 552b(d)(5); *see also* Social Security Ruling SSR 92-1p, 57 Fed. Reg. 8,131 (Mar. 6, 1992).

However, an agency may be required to disclose an internal document if it is incorporated in an order or opinion or cited as the basis for the agency's action.[80]

28.4 PROCEEDINGS

Agencies conduct millions of oral proceedings each year in the course of adjudicating cases. These proceedings can be trial-like and informal, adversarial and nonadversarial, and go by many names: investigatory hearings, prehearing and scheduling conferences, settlement conferences, evidentiary hearings, oral arguments, and so on. Some are open to public observation; many are not. Litigants and some scholars have asserted a First Amendment right of public access to agency adjudicative proceedings, particularly adversarial hearings that resemble judicial bench trials.[81] Although the Supreme Court has not decided the question, some lower courts have applied the Court's First Amendment case law to administrative proceedings.[82]

As a statutory matter, Congress has occasionally established a presumption that certain proceedings should be open to public observation. Oral appellate arguments before multimember agencies subject to the Government in the Sunshine Act, for example, are presumptively open to public observation.[83] Hearings in some programs must,

80. Nat'l Lab. Rels. Bd. v. Sears, Roebuck & Co., 421 U.S. 132 (1975); Bristol-Myers Co. v. Fed. Trade Comm'n, 424 F.2d 935, 939 (D.C. Cir. 1971); Am. Mail Line, Ltd. v. Gulick, 411 F.2d 696 (D.C. Cir. 1969); Exxon Corp. v. Fed. Trade Comm'n, 466 F. Supp. 1088, 1098 (D.D.C. 1978).

81. *See, e.g.*, Soc'y of Pro. Journalists v. Sec'y of Lab., 832 F.2d 1180 (10th Cir. 1987); Salt Lake Trib. v. Chao, No. 2:07-CV-739, 2007 WL 2963269 (D. Utah Oct. 9, 2007); Christopher B. McNeil, *The Public's Right of Access to "Some Kind of Hearing": Creating Policies That Protect the Right to Observe Agency Hearings*, 68 LA. L. REV. 1121 (2008); Comm. on Commc'ns and Media L. of the Ass'n of the Bar of the City of N.Y., *"If It Walks, Talks, and Squawks . . ." The First Amendment Right of Access to Administrative Adjudications: A Position Paper*, 23 CARDOZO ARTS & ENT. L.J. 21 (2005); Heidi Kitrosser, *Secrecy in the Immigration Courts and Beyond: Considering the Right to Know in the Administrative State*, 39 HARV. C.R.-C.L. L. REV. 95 (2004).

82. *Compare* N. Jersey Media Grp., Inc. v. Ashcroft, 308 F.3d 198, 212–13 (3d Cir. 2002), *with* Detroit Free Press, 303 F.3d 681, 700 (6th Cir. 2002); *see also* N.Y. C.L. Union v. N.Y. City Transit Auth., 684 F.3d 286, 305 (2d Cir. 2012); Whiteland Woods, L.P. v. Twp. of W. Whiteland, 193 F.3d 177, 181 (3d Cir. 1999).

83. 5 U.S.C. § 552b(b).

by statute, be "public" or "open to the public."[84] Although the APA's formal-hearing provisions do not address openness, it has been suggested that "the very concept of a hearing comparable to a judicial proceeding entails norms of openness."[85] The Attorney General's Committee on Administrative Procedure likewise concluded that, with "few exceptions," hearings in formal adjudications "should be, and almost invariably are, public."[86]

Many agencies have adopted their own rules establishing that certain proceedings, especially evidentiary hearings and appellate proceedings, are presumptively open to the public. (Other types of proceedings—investigatory hearings, prehearing conferences, settlement conferences—are often closed.) At other agencies, proceedings are always or presumptively closed. This includes benefits hearings before SSA and BVA.[87]

ACUS has recommended that agencies should "ordinarily presume that evidentiary hearings and appellate proceedings (including oral arguments) are open to public observation" but that they "may choose to close such proceedings, in whole or in part, to the extent consistent with applicable law and if there is substantial justification to do so." Substantial justification may exist when the need to protect national security, law enforcement interests, confidentiality of business information, or personal privacy interests "can reasonably be considered to outweigh the public interest in openness." For proceedings other than evidentiary hearings and appellate proceedings, policymakers will need to consider applicable legal requirements and weigh the benefits and costs of openness.[88]

Agencies must consider practical aspects of facilitating public access to adjudicative proceedings, such as providing advance public notice of open proceedings, regulating the public observers' behavior,

---

84. *See, e.g.*, 8 U.S.C. § 1534(a)(2) (deportation hearings); 29 U.S.C. § 661(g) (Occupational Safety and Health Review Commission hearings); 33 U.S.C. § 923(b) (longshore and harbor workers' compensation hearings).

85. Am. Bar Ass'n Section of Admin. L. and Regul. Practice, *A Blackletter Statement of Federal Administrative Law*, 54 Admin. L. Rev. 1, 20 (2002).

86. Final Report of the Attorney General's Committee on Administrative Procedure, S. Doc. No. 8, at 68–69 (1941).

87. Jeremy Graboyes & Mark Thomson, ACUS, Public Access to Agency Adjudicative Proceedings 17–29 (2021).

88. Administrative Conference Recommendation 2021-6, Public Access to Agency Adjudicative Proceedings, ¶ 5, 87 Fed. Reg. 1,715, 1,716–17 (Jan. 12, 2022).

and managing media and public access to high-profile proceedings.[89] Agencies must also consider how public observation takes place (i.e., in person, by telephone, online). While the internet presents new opportunities for expanding public access, it also raises privacy and security concerns in some contexts. It may be appropriate, for example, to broadcast live on YouTube a hearing that involves the regulation of a large public corporation, includes opportunities for public participation, and generates significant public interest.[90] A similar approach may be inappropriate in proceedings to determine eligibility for asylum status, which, although often open to in-person observation, can involve sensitive personal information and typically do not attract significant public interest.[91] Agencies must tailor how they provide public access to account for the unique circumstances of the programs they administer.

28.5 MANAGEMENT, OPERATIONAL, AND PERFORMANCE INFORMATION

There is significant interest in how agencies manage adjudicative systems, perform adjudicative functions, and supervise adjudicators. This section focuses on public access to six key categories of management, operational, and performance information: delegations of authority (section 28.51), policies for appointing and overseeing adjudicators (section 28.52), information about adjudicators (section 28.53), information about case management systems (section 28.54), programmatic data and statistics (section 28.55), and algorithmic tools (section 28.56). This treatment is by no means exhaustive. There can be significant external interest in other types of information, for example information about budgets and contracts.[92]

28.51 Delegations of Authority

Although federal statutes often assign adjudicative authority to agency heads, in practice agency heads rarely render initial decisions or conduct hearings. Instead, they typically delegate decision-making

89. *Id.* ¶¶ 8–14.
90. *See, e.g.*, 87 Fed. Reg. 6,644 (Feb. 4, 2022).
91. *See* GRABOYES & THOMSON, *supra* note 87, at 39–44.
92. *See* Figueroa, *supra* note 1, at 49.

authority to lower level officials. Agency heads might also delegate appellate authority to lower level officials (see Chapter 19).[93]

There is no general requirement that agencies publish internal delegations of authority.[94] As a practical matter, however, significant delegations of authority can be gleaned from a number of sources. Delegations might be reflected in procedural rules, generally applicable guidance documents, agency organizational descriptions, and statements of the general course and method by which agency functions are performed, all of which must be published in the *Federal Register*.[95] Manuals and staff instructions that agencies post online under FOIA's proactive disclosure provisions may shine light on relevant delegations.[96] Most agencies also publish organizational charts online. ACUS recommends that agencies proactively disclose delegations of adjudicative authority on their websites.[97]

28.52 Policies for Appointing and Overseeing Adjudicators

Adjudicators, like other government officials, are subject to policies governing their selection and appointment, assigning of job duties, supervision and oversight, and discipline and removal (see Chapter 9). Policies may be set forth in a mix of public and nonpublic sources, including statutes like the APA, codified regulations, formal guidance documents, organizational charts, administrative and personnel manuals, memoranda, staff instructions, position descriptions, performance plans, and labor agreements.[98]

There is heightened public interest in how agencies appoint and oversee agency adjudicators because such practices bear heavily on their actual and perceived impartiality. Many of these policies have also been the subject of constitutional challenges in recent years.[99]

93. *See* Administrative Conference Recommendation 2020-3, *supra* note 67; Administrative Conference Recommendation 68-6, Delegation of Final Decisional Authority Subject to Discretionary Review by the Agency, 38 Fed. Reg. 19,783 (July 23, 1973).

94. *See* Lonsdale v. United States, 919 F.2d 1440, 1444–47 (10th Cir. 1990).

95. 5 U.S.C. § 552(a)(1).

96. *See id.* § 552(a)(1)–(2).

97. Administrative Conference Recommendation 2020-5, Publication of Policies Governing Agency Adjudicators, ¶ 2, 86 Fed. Reg. 6,622, 6,623 (Jan. 22, 2021); Administrative Conference Recommendation 2020-3, *supra* note 67, ¶ 19.

98. Leigh Anne Schriever, ACUS, Public Availability of Information about Adjudicators 10 (2020).

99. Administrative Conference Recommendation 2020-5, *supra* note 97.

Some agencies have proactively disclosed significant materials—such as adjudicator performance plans, adjudicator performance expectations, and overviews of adjudicator hiring processes—often in electronic reading rooms.[100] Kent Barnett has recommended that agencies publish "impartiality disclosures" that clearly and concisely describe agency policies and processes on matters such as adjudicator hiring and discipline, separation of adjudicative and adversarial functions, supervision of adjudicators, and performance management.[101] ACUS has similarly recommended that agencies prominently display on their websites "a short, straightforward description of all generally applicable policies and practices, along with the legal authority, governing the appointment and oversight of [ALJs and administrative judges]."[102]

28.53 Information about Adjudicators

In addition to policies governing adjudicators, there can be public interest in information about adjudicators themselves. Financial disclosures,[103] case processing statistics,[104] and information about disciplinary actions,[105] for example, may shed light on potential conflicts of interest and adjudication-related performance issues. Some information, such as financial disclosures for ALJs, must be proactively disclosed.[106] Agencies may make other information, such as information about misconduct complaints, available on request.[107] EOIR, for example, maintains annual summaries of "Immigration Judge Complaint Statistics" on its website.[108] Other information may be protected or exempted from disclosure, including personnel and similar files "the disclosure of which would constitute a clearly unwarranted invasion of personal privacy."[109]

---

100. *See, e.g., Proactive Disclosures, supra* note 19.

101. Kent H. Barnett, *Some Kind of Hearing Officer*, 94 Wash. L. Rev. 515, 563–80 (2019).

102. Administrative Conference Recommendation 2020-5, *supra* note 97, ¶ 1.

103. *See* 5 C.F.R. § 2634.202(d) (2022).

104. SSA, Frequently Requested Social Security Administration Statistics, https://www.ssa.gov/foia/List%20of%20Frequently%20Requested%20SSA%20Statistics.pdf.

105. Am. Immigr. Laws. Ass'n v. Exec. Off. for Immigr. Rev., 830 F.3d 667 (D.C. Cir. 2016).

106. 5 C.F.R. § 2634.202(d) (2022).

107. *Am. Immigr. Laws. Ass'n*, 830 F.3d at 679–80.

108. *Proactive Disclosures, supra* note 19.

109. 5 U.S.C. § 552(b)(6); *see Am. Immigr. Laws. Ass'n*, 830 F.3d at 673–76.

28.54 Information about Case Management Systems

Federal agencies maintain paper and electronic case files and increasingly use electronic systems to manage their caseloads (see Chapter 23). When systems contain personally identifiable information, they are "systems of records" (SORs) under the Privacy Act.[110] The Privacy Act generally prohibits agencies from disclosing records contained in an SOR without the written consent of the individual to whom the record pertains. But to promote "accountability, responsibility, legislative oversight, and open government" with respect to how agencies maintain, use, and store records on individuals, the statute requires agencies to publicly disclose certain information about SORs they maintain.[111] Agencies must publish notices, called system of records notices, whenever they establish or revise an SOR. These notices, published in the *Federal Register*, include information about the types of records the agency maintains in an SOR and how the agency uses, stores, and controls access to them.

28.55 Programmatic Data and Statistics

Adjudicative systems generate a lot of data. Even before adoption of electronic case management systems, agencies could capture data on the number of cases they decided and how long it took them to do so. With the adoption of electronic case management, digitization of forms and services, and establishment of quality assurance systems (see Chapter 24), agencies increasingly have the capacity to collect and analyze vast quantities of extraordinarily granular data about case adjudication and program management.[112] Agencies use this data to manage their operations, identify issues of systemic inaccuracy and inconsistency, measure the impact of policy changes, and detect decisional anomalies. For many of these same reasons, there has long been public interest in such information.[113]

---

110. *See* Administrative Conference Recommendation 2018-3, Electronic Case Management in Federal Administrative Adjudication, ¶ 5, 83 Fed. Reg. 30,686, 30,687 (June 29, 2018).

111. S. Rep. No. 93-1183, at 1–2 (1974).

112. *See* Administrative Conference Recommendation 2021-10, Quality Assurance Systems in Agency Adjudication, 87 Fed. Reg. 1,722 (Jan. 12, 2022); Administrative Conference Recommendation 2018-3, *supra* note 110.

113. *See* Administrative Conference Recommendation 69-6, Compilation of Statistics on Administrative Proceedings by Federal Departments and Agencies, 38 Fed. Reg. 19,784 (July 23, 1973).

Many agencies proactively disclose basic statistics or key performance indicators about their adjudicative programs on their websites and in publications like annual reports. Some agencies maintain dedicated web pages that facilitate public access to more detailed reports, studies, and datasets. SSA, for example, provides public access to a large number of datasets related to the operation of its hearing-level and appellate review programs.[114] The Veterans Benefits Administration releases weekly reports from each of its 56 regional offices.[115] EOIR publishes annual statistical yearbooks and maintains a web page for "Workload and Adjudication Statistics."[116] The U.S. Citizenship and Immigration Services publishes data, reports, and studies on processing times, backlog elimination efforts, and other topics.[117] The Patent Trial and Appeal Board maintains an online library providing access to key performance measures and reports.[118]

Proactive disclosure of at least some adjudication-related statistics has long been considered a best practice. President Obama's Memorandum on Transparency and Open Government directed agencies to "harness new technologies to put information about their operations" online.[119] During the Trump Administration, the administrator of the Office of Information and Regulatory Affairs recommended public disclosure of "decisional quality and efficiency metrics regarding adjudication" to promote public accountability in enforcement decisions.[120] More recently, ACUS recommended that agencies consider "whether to publicly disclose data in case management systems in a de-identified form (i.e., with all personally identifiable information removed) to

---

114. *Public Data Files*, SSA, https://www.ssa.gov/appeals/publicusefiles.html (last visited June 27, 2023).

115. *Veterans Benefits Administration Reports*, U.S. Dep't of Veterans Affs., https://www.benefits.va.gov/reports/detailed_claims_data.asp (last visited June 27, 2023).

116. *Workload and Adjudication Statistics*, DOJ, EOIR, https://www.justice.gov/eoir/workload-and-adjudication-statistics (last updated Mar. 14, 2023).

117. *Immigration and Citizenship Data*, U.S. Citizenship & Immigr. Servs., https://www.uscis.gov/tools/reports-and-studies/immigration-and-citizenship-data (last visited June 27, 2023).

118. *Statistics*, U.S. Pat. & Trademark Off., https://www.uspto.gov/patents/ptab/statistics (last modified June 14, 2023).

119. 74 Fed. Reg. 4,685, 4,685 (2009).

120. Memorandum for the Deputy Secretaries of Executive Departments and Agencies from Paul J. Ray, Adm'r, OIRA, M-20-31, Implementation of Section 6 of Executive Order 13924 (Aug. 31, 2020).

enable continued research by individuals outside of the agency."[121] Indeed, as agencies have captured more data and made more information publicly available, proactively or on request, a robust literature has developed that uses publicly disclosed data and statistics to empirically study the performance of agency adjudicative systems.[122]

28.56 Algorithmic Tools

Agencies are increasingly deploying artificial intelligence and other algorithmic tools to promote accuracy and efficiency in adjudicative programs. Though these tools currently are used primarily to assist adjudicators and staff in the performance of adjudicative functions, they might one day be used to automate decision-making.[123] There are serious concerns about the use of algorithmic tools, and many scholars, advocates, and policymakers have called for more transparency to better enable external oversight.[124]

For simple tools, disclosure of the source code may be sufficient. But transparency is trickier when it comes to machine-learning tools.

---

121. Administrative Conference Recommendation 2021-10, *supra* note 112, ¶ 22.

122. David K. Hausman, *Reviewing Administrative Review*, 38 YALE J. ON REGUL. 1059 (2021); Ingrid Eagly & Steven Shafer, *Measuring* In Absentia *Removal in Immigration Court*, 168 U. PA. L. REV. 817 (2020); Catherine Y. Kim & Amy Semet, *An Empirical Study of Political Control over Immigration Adjudication*, 108 GEO. L.J. 579 (2020); David Ames et al., *Due Process and Mass Adjudication: Crisis and Reform*, 72 STAN. L. REV. 1 (2020); Michael D. Frakes & Melissa F. Wasserman, *Are There as Many Trademark Offices as Trademark Examiners?*, 69 DUKE L.J. 1807 (2020); Urska Velikonja, *Are the SEC's Administrative Law Judges Biased? An Empirical Investigation*, 92 WASH. L. REV. 315 (2017); Ingrid V. Eagly, *Remote Adjudication in Immigration*, 109 NW. U. L. REV. 933 (2015); Ingrid V. Eagly & Steven Shafer, *A National Study of Access to Counsel in Immigration Court*, 164 U. PA. L. REV. 1 (2015); Jaya Ramji-Nogales et al., *Refugee Roulette: Disparities in Asylum Adjudication*, 60 STAN. L. REV. 295 (2007).

123. *See, e.g.*, Cary Coglianese & David Lehr, *Regulating by Robot: Administrative Decision Making in the Machine-Learning Era*, 105 GEO. L.J. 1147, 1184–85 (2017); Kurt Glaze et al., *Artificial Intelligence for Adjudication: The Social Security Administration and AI Governance*, *in* THE OXFORD HANDBOOK OF AI GOVERNANCE (Justin Bullock et al. eds., forthcoming 2023).

124. *See, e.g.*, VIRGINIA EUBANKS, AUTOMATING INEQUALITY (2018); Bernard W. Bell, *Replacing Bureaucrats with Automated Sorcerers?*, DÆDALUS, Summer 2021, at 90; Hannah Bloch-Wehba, *Access to Algorithms*, 88 FORDHAM L. REV. 1265, 1274 (2020); Cary Coglianese & David Lehr, *AI in Adjudication and Administration*, 86 BROOK. L. REV. 791 (2021); DAVID FREEMAN ENGSTROM ET AL., ACUS, GOVERNMENT BY ALGORITHM: ARTIFICIAL INTELLIGENCE IN FEDERAL ADMINISTRATIVE AGENCIES (2020).

Machine-learning tools work by finding patterns and making predictions based on past data. End-users in agency adjudicative programs, and even tools' developers, may not fully understand how they reach decisions. As a result, disclosure of a tool's source code is less useful. Scholars have highlighted these challenges and proposed several ways in which agencies can at least be transparent about how they develop, procure, and use algorithmic tools in administrative adjudication. Although that literature is too extensive to detail here, agencies must be attentive to calls for transparency when they adopt algorithmic tools to perform adjudication-related tasks.[125]

125. Administrative Conference Statement #20, Agency Use of Artificial Intelligence, 86 Fed. Reg. 6,616 (Jan. 22, 2021).

TABLE OF CASES

B

C

D

G

H

Humphrey's Ex'r v. United States., 295 U.S. 602 (1935), 408 n.44
Hutto Stockyard, Inc. v. U.S. Dep't of Agric., 903 F.2d 299 (4th Cir. 1990), 280 n.60

I

Ill. Com. Comm'n v. Fed. Energy Regul. Comm'n, 721 F.3d 764 (7th Cir. 2013), 362 n.13
Immigr. & Naturalization Serv. v. Yang, 519 U.S. 26 (1996), 30, 415 n.8
Interstate Com. Comm'n v. Ala. Midland Ry. Co., 168 U.S. 144 (1897), 429, 429 n.4
Interstate Com. Comm'n v. Brimson, 154 U.S. 447 (1894), 293 n.60
Interstate Com. Comm'n v. Ill. Cent. R.R. Co., 215 U.S. 452 (1910), 429 n.7
Int'l Tel. & Tel. Corp. v. Loc. 134, Int'l Bhd. of Elec. Workers, 419 U.S. 428 (1975), 7 n.9
Int'l Union of Operating Eng'rs Loc. 150, 371 N.L.R.B. No. 8 (2021), 19 n.3
Irons & Sears v. Dann, 606 F.2d 1215 (D.C. Cir. 1979), 451 n.31, 454 n.57
Irons v. Diamond, 670 F.2d 265 (D.C. Cir. 1981), 451 n.30
Irons v. Schuyler, 465 F.2d 608 (D.C. Cir. 1972), 451 n.30
Izaak Walton League of Am. v. Marsh, 655 F.2d 346 (D.C. Cir. 1981), 102 n.2, 116 n.13

J

Jarkesy v. Sec. & Exch. Comm'n, 34 F.4th 446 (5th Cir. 2022), 97 n.35, 154 n.110, 408 n.38, 409, 440 n.54
Jenkins v. Immigr. & Naturalization Serv., 108 F.3d 195 (9th Cir. 1997), 305 n.142
Jhin v. Off. of Pers. Mgmt., 368 F. App'x 118 (Fed. Cir. 2010), 354 n.61, 358 n.84
Johnson v. Zerbst, 304 U.S. 458 (1938), 200 n.19
Joint Anti-Fascist Refugee Comm. v. McGrath, 341 U.S. 123 (1951), 246

K

Kahn v. Fed. Motor Carrier Safety Admin., 648 F. Supp. 2d 31 (D.D.C. 2009), 457 n.77
Kalaris v. Donovan, 697 F.2d 376 (D.C. Cir. 1983), 155 n.117
Kapcia v. Immigr. & Naturalization Serv., 944 F.2d 702 (10th Cir. 1991), 302 n.123, 303 n.125
Kay v. Fed. Commcn's Comm'n, 525 F.3d 1277 (D.C. Cir. 2008), 282 n.72
Keating v. Off. of Thrift Supervision, 45 F.3d 322 (9th Cir. 1995), 168 n.57

L

M

N

O

P

R

S

T

U

V

W

Z

INDEX

F

J

L

M

N

O